From Viking Stronghold
to Christian Kingdom

For Matilde

From Viking Stronghold
to Christian Kingdom

State Formation in Norway, c. 900–1350

Sverre Bagge

Museum Tusculanum Press
University of Copenhagen
2010

From Viking Stronghold to Christian Kingdom:
State Formation in Norway, c. 900-1350

© Museum Tusculanum Press and Sverre Bagge, 2010
Consultant: Niels Lund
Copy editor: Jordy Findanis
Cover design: Erling Lynder
Set and printed by AKA-PRINT A/S
ISBN 978 87 635 0791 2

Cover illustrations:
Upper register of the frontal from the church at Nedstryn, Western Norway, ca. 1315. It depicts the Persian king Chosroes capturing the Holy Cross and his defeat by the Byzantine emperor Heraclius. The narrative sequence shows: 1) Heraclius decapitating Chosroes, 2) Heraclius triumphantly riding with the Cross to Jerusalem, 3) Heraclius, barefoot and humble, carrying the Cross through the gates, 4) The elevation of the Cross on the altar. Photo: Svein Skare, Bergen Museum.

Viking Age animal head post from the Oseberg burial, Tønsberg, Vestfold, Museum of Cultural History, University of Oslo, Norway. Photo: Ove Holst.

Viking Age sword from Steinsvik, Hol, Nordland, Museum of Cultural History, University of Oslo, Norway. Photo: Eirik Irgens Johnsen.

This book is published with financial support from
Centre for Medieval Studies, University of Bergen
The Research Council of Norway

Museum Tusculanum Press
126 Njalsgade
DK-2300 Copenhagen S
Denmark

www.mtp.dk

Contents

Preface 9

Introduction 11

The Formation of the Kingdom of Norway 21
- The Rise of the Scandinavian Kingdoms 23
- From Harald Finehair to Harald Hardrada 25
- Unification and Division – the Moving Forces 33
- External and Internal Factors 39
- The "Civil Wars" 40
- Pretenders and Factions 42
- The Basic Factors 47
- The Consequences of the Civil Wars 53
- From the Civil Wars to the Age of Greatness 66

War, Military Organisation and Social Change 69
- From Plunder to Internal Exploitation 69
- The Origin and Development of the *leidang* 72
- *Leidang* and Elite Forces 79
- The Norwegian Empire and its Foreign Policy until 1319 85
- War Made the State, but Did the State Make War?
  – The Military Challenges 1240-1319 101
- The Social and Economic Basis of the Norwegian Military System 110
- The Towns – Centres of the Monarchy and the Church 121
- The King's Revenues 126
- Conclusion 133

Religion, Monarchy, and the Right Order of the World 137
- Old Norse Religion 137
- The Conversion to Christianity 148
- The Right Order of the World and the Christian Monarchy 157
- The Emergence of the Dynasty and Hereditary Monarchy 165
- The Courtly Culture 170

    Patriotism and Secular Legitimation of Monarchy   *174*
    Conclusion   *177*

JUSTICE, LAW AND POWER   **179**
    The Regional Laws   *179*
    What Was Law?   *182*
    Law and Society   *190*
    God's Law: The Rise of Royal and Ecclesiastical Jurisdiction   *195*
    Royal and Ecclesiastical Legislation: A New Concept of Law   *201*
    The Emergence of Public Justice: Intent and Evidence   *206*
    Justice in Practice   *215*
    A Legal Revolution?   *220*
    Conclusion   *226*

ROYAL AND ECCLESIASTICAL ADMINISTRATION – A STEP TOWARDS A REAL BUREAUCRACY?   **229**
    The Ecclesiastical Administration   *229*
    The Royal Administration   *233*
    A New Bureaucracy?   *238*
    From Oral to Written Administration   *243*
    Writing in the Royal Administration: The Quantitative Evidence   *250*
    Writing in the Royal Administration: The Qualitative Evidence   *256*
    Predictability and Distance   *267*
    The Leaders: King and Bishop   *272*
    Did Norway Become a State? Government, Obedience and Clientelism   *282*
    Conclusion   *291*

THE DIVISION OF POWER AND ITS SOCIAL FOUNDATION   **293**
    The King and the Church: From the Foundation of the
        Church Province to the Death of Håkon Håkonsson   *294*
    The Conflict about Jurisdiction and the Concordat of Tønsberg   *297*
    The Conflict in the 1280s   *303*
    The Results of the Struggle – Monarchy and Church
        in the Fourteenth Century and Later   *312*
    The Ideological Aspect: A Brain Trust in the Service of the Monarchy   *316*
    Regnum and *Sacerdotium* in Norway   *319*
    The Secular Aristocracy   *324*

The King and the Aristocracy: Ideology   *329*
  From Assemblies of the Best Men to the King's Council   *335*
  Who Were "The Best Men"?   *340*
  The Decision-Making Process   *342*
  The Problem of Regencies   *356*
  Monarchy, Aristocracy and Union during the Reign of Magnus Eriksson   *360*
  A Strong Monarchy   *365*
  The King and the People   *371*
  Conclusion   *375*

How, Why, When and How Much? The Extent and Character of Norwegian State Formation in the Middle Ages   **379**

The Kings of Norway, c. 900-1380   **389**

Literature, Sources and Abbreviations   **391**

Index   **431**

Preface

This book forms part of the projects *Periphery and Centre in Medieval Europe* and *The Nordic Countries and the Medieval Expansion of Europe. New Interpretations of a Common Past*, which are carried out currently by the Centre for Medieval Studies at the University of Bergen and the Nordic Centre for Medieval Studies at the Universities of Bergen, Gothenburg, Odense and Helsinki and funded respectively by The Research Council of Norway and NOS-HS.

Although mainly focused on Norway, the book is also intended as a contribution to the general discussion of medieval state formation and the importance of Scandinavia in this context. During the period of writing, I have profited greatly from the stimulating atmosphere of these two research centres and from discussion with and advice from colleagues in Bergen and within the Nordic network. In particular, I want to thank the members of the State Team within the Nordic Centre: Thomas Lindkvist, Leidulf Melve, Lars Hermanson, Erik Opsahl, Auður Magnúsdóttir, Antoaneta Granberg, Geir Atle Ersland, Frode Hervik, Ildar Garipzanov, Thomas Foerster and John Lind, who have read and commented on the manuscript or parts of it. I am also grateful to Niels Lund and Jørn Øyrehagen Sunde for useful comments and to Jena Habegger-Conti for correcting my English.

Sverre Bagge

Bergen, October 2009

Introduction

State formation has occupied a place of particular importance in Norwegian historiography. The reason for this is not difficult to explain: Norway has been completely independent for only a short period of its history, from the emergence of the kingdom in the period between the late ninth and the early eleventh century and 1319, and again after 1905, while it was in union with one or sometimes both of the neighbouring countries in the intervening period. Admittedly, the unions between 1319 and 1537 and between 1814 and 1905 were in principle based on equality or near equality but have often been regarded by later historians and to some extent by contemporaries as marked by some kind of subordination. The "real" Norway was the kingdom that existed before 1319 and after 1905. Thus, the history of Norway in the Middle Ages holds a particular fascination, containing, in Jens Arup Seip's words, the origin as well as the end of a kingdom.[1] This serves to explain the great importance of the Middle Ages to Norwegian historians, particularly in the nineteenth and early twentieth century, although it is not only a question of an intriguing intellectual problem but of a deep involvement in a national tragedy that at the same time served as a challenge in the contemporary struggle for independence and democracy.[2] The following account of Norwegian state formation has another aim and intellectual background. My intention is to examine Norway as a case that may serve to illuminate some general problems of European state formation in the Middle Ages, problems related both to the formation of the European system of independent kingdoms within a common cultural framework and to the inner development of these kingdoms.

Can we talk about state and state formation in the Middle Ages? The term "state" is used in a different sense in different disciplines. While social scientists, particularly social anthropologists, are inclined to use the term about any kind of lordship over larger areas or numbers of people, in some cases qualified by the term "early state",[3] historians often have stricter criteria. One of these has been the word itself: Latin *status* = condition, state, which from the late sixteenth and early seventeenth century developed into a technical term, meaning "state" in the modern sense, through the combination *status rei publicae*.

---

1 Seip, "Problemer og metode", p. 78.
2 On the Norwegian historiographical tradition, see Dahl, *Norsk historieforskning*; Hubbard et al. (eds.), *Making a Historical Culture*; Bagge, "Udsigt og innhogg".
3 Keesing, *Cultural Anthropology*, pp. 49 f.; Lewis, "Warfare"; Claessen and Skalník, *The Early State* and "*Ubi sumus?*"; Diamond, *Guns, Germs and Steel*, pp. 278-84.

This terminological change is then regarded as an expression of a new understanding of the state as an institution, existing independently of the person or persons governing it,[4] an understanding that is combined with the classical definitions of the state as a monopoly of violence or impersonal and bureaucratic government. Although the importance of such a terminological change should not be underestimated, it can hardly be regarded as decisive. Our terminology need not correspond to the contemporary one, and a new name does not mean that the phenomenon in question cannot have existed before. Among medievalists, the terminological discussion goes far back in historiography and has been revived several times in recent years, as in the discussions between Johannes Fried and Hans-Werner Goetz about the Carolingian state and between Susan Reynolds and Rees Davies about the use of the term for the Middle Ages as a whole.[5] Whereas the former discussion seems to be about the character of the Carolingian Empire, the latter is mainly about terminology, without any profound difference of opinion about the historical reality.

In the present context, I regard the terminological question mainly as a practical one. The great divide in Scandinavian history was the formation of the three kingdoms, two of which have continued to exist until the present while the third, Norway, preserved enough of its identity under Danish dominance to reemerge as an independent unit in 1814. It would then seem natural to use the term state for them from this time on, despite the rudimentary character of their political institutions. The most important concept in the following, however, is "state formation", which is a relative concept, implying centralisation, bureaucratisation, development of jurisdiction, monopoly or near monopoly of violence and so forth, and where it is more important to decide whether a process is going on in this direction than exactly how much of these criteria is necessary to use the word "state". The problem that will be discussed in the following is the changes that took place in Norway in this respect in the period until the mid-fourteenth century and how the country compared with other countries at the time in terms of "stateness".

Evidently, there has been a general agreement that whatever may be called the medieval state differed from the modern one; the question is whether it was qualitatively different or can be regarded as a stage in the development of the modern state. There has been a strong tendency among historical sociologists and early modern historians to regard the Early Modern Period as the origin of the modern state rather than the Middle Ages. This in turn is connected to the importance attached to the military element in state formation, combined with the negative view of the state as mainly an instrument

---

4 Skinner, *The Foundations* II, pp. 352-58; "Staat", pp. 1-17.
5 Fried, "Der karolingische Herrschaftsverband" and "*Gens* und *regnum*"; Goetz, "Zum politischen Denken", pp. 113-16, 170-73 and 183-89; Reynolds, "The Historiography" and "There Were States"; Davies, "The Medieval State".

of oppression; in Charles Tilly's words: "War made the state and the state made war".[6] Real states were created in the period of standing armies, guns and cannons, elaborate fortifications and heavily armed warships, which were costlier and necessitated a larger and more complex administration than the simpler military equipment of the Middle Ages. Among medievalists, different answers to the question of the existence of a state in the Middle Ages were given as early as in the nineteenth century and, at least in the second half of the century, with a certain bias for an affirmative answer. The idea of the medieval state was further developed in the English-speaking world in the twentieth century by scholars like F.W. Maitland, Charles Homer Haskins, Joseph Strayer and R. W. Southern.[7] In contrast to much of the nineteenth-century scholarship which regarded the Middle Ages as dominated by Church and Empire, and by ideas of hierarchy and the supernatural rather than rational thought, this tradition – with some exception for Southern – emphasised the rational and secular aspect of the period and regarded the development of law and administration as an attempt to solve the practical problems of government and the distribution of power. Thus the Middle Ages laid the foundation for the modern state, far more than Classical Antiquity or even the Renaissance had, as is expressed most succinctly in Strayer's short but important book on the medieval origins of the state.[8] This view can to some extent be understood against the background of English history. England was "a much governed country" in the Middle Ages – probably the "most governed" in Europe – and several of the medieval institutions, like Parliament, still exist in the twenty-first century.

By contrast, Germany moved in the opposite direction during the first half of the twentieth century, notably in the inter-war period. Percy Ernst Schramm's studies of the rituals of rulership focus on the difference rather than the similarity between medieval and modern conditions and on ideology and religion rather than practical matters.[9] Similarly, Theodor Mayer's "Personenverbandstaat" and Otto Brunner's "Herrschaft"[10] were not only different from but directly opposed to Maitland's and Haskins's anticipation of the modern, liberal and democratic state. Not only were the Middle Ages different, but this period served as a model for the new kind of state, run from Germanic roots,

---

6   Tilly, *Coercion, Capital*, p. 67; cf. also "Reflections", pp. 73-76; Reinhard, *Power Elites*, pp. 5-7. Mann, *A History of Power* I, pp. 433-37, attaches somewhat less importance to war.
7   Cantor, *Inventing the Middle Ages*, pp. 48-78, 245-86, 337-70.
8   Strayer, *The Medieval Origins*.
9   E.g. Schramm, "Die Krönung in Deutschland"; *Der König von Frankreich*; *Geschichte des englischen Königtums*.
10 Mayer, "Die Ausbildung", and Brunner, *Land und Herrschaft*.

which, according to the dominating ideology in Nazi Germany, was to replace the modern state.[11]

As might be expected, the post-war period saw a reaction to this view. Nevertheless, the Maitland tradition has increasingly come under attack since around 1970. As the earlier German tradition, but according to different criteria, the French Annales school emphasised the difference between medieval and modern conditions, and although it was originally not particularly interested in the state, it eventually came to apply these ideas to the study of it.[12] Additionally, there was a revival of the German tradition from the first half of the century in a modified form and of course without the nationalistic and Germanistic ideas emphasising personal rather than institutional relationships and lordship rather than royal government.[13] Both traditions have been influenced by social anthropology and have in turn influenced international scholarship, including in the English-speaking world.[14] However, there have also been reactions against these impulses, notably Susan Reynolds's rejection of the concept of feudalism which she replaces with a concept of society not very different in kind from the modern one in place already in the Early Middle Ages,[15] and R.I. Moore's "First European Revolution" which attributes a crucial significance to the period 975-1215 in the evolution of European society as well as in global history, when new and more intensive forms of government were established by the Church as well as the state. An ecclesiastical bureaucracy and intellectual elite developed an increasingly systematic and intolerant doctrine that was impressed on the population, and a distinctive royal bureaucracy resulted in a more effective and oppressive government in Europe than in most other civilisations.[16] The gradual formation of the nation state in the Middle Ages is also a central theme in Michael Mann's analysis of social power.[17]

The "state tradition" has had an unusually strong position in Norwegian historiography, which is perhaps not surprising given the absence of an independent Norwegian state for such a long period. Nineteenth-century scholarship largely explained the ups and downs

---

11 von See, *Königtum und Staat*, pp. 11-14; Althoff, "Die Beurteilung".
12 E.g. Duby, *Les trois ordres* on the fundamental ideas of society in the Middle Ages and Le Goff, *St Louis*, a biography of a king and a saint against the background of political practice and the ideas of kingship in the period.
13 Althoff, *Freunde, Verwandte und Getreue*; *Kaiser Otto III*; *Spielregeln*; Keller, *Zwischen Regionaler Begrenzung*; Reuter, *Germany*.
14 E.g. Geary, "Living with Conflicts", and Koziol, "Begging Pardon and Favor". Bartlett, *England 1075-1225*, pays considerably more attention to factions, personal alliances and political culture than does traditional constitutional historiography.
15 Reynolds, *Fiefs and Vassals*, but see also *Kingdoms and Communities*, where she replaces the feudal institutions with groups and collective entities.
16 Moore, *The First European Revolution* and "The Transformation of Europe".
17 Mann, *The Sources of Social Power*, pp. 416-49.

of the country's history by different institutional arrangements. The historians belonging to the school of agrarian history which developed from the 1920s onwards and in some respects represents a parallel to the Annales school[18] were in no doubt that Norway was a state in the Middle Ages – even an advanced and efficient one – although they regarded it as an instrument by which the landowners could oppress the rest of the population.[19] The focus on the state was even stronger in what may be called the institutional school which, largely along the lines of the Maitland school, saw state formation as the main trend in Norwegian history from the twelfth to the early fourteenth century, succinctly expressed in the title of Knut Helle's influential book *Norge blir en stat, 1130-1319* ("Norway Becomes a State 1130-1319").[20] For a long time, there has been a general agreement about this picture, although opinions have been divided regarding the social basis of the regime; that is, whether it worked mainly according to the interests of the landowning aristocracy or whether a strong personal monarchy was able to balance between the interests of various classes. More recently, the whole notion of "Norway becomes a State" has come under closer scrutiny, partly through studies of the saga literature as an expression of pre-state conditions against the background of social anthropology and studies of early medieval society in the rest of Europe and partly through local studies.[21] This forms a challenge for the present discussion.

A discussion of Norwegian state formation is not only about more or less "stateness" in a comparative perspective, but about the changing map of Western Christendom in the High Middle Ages.[22] From the tenth century onwards, the European state – whatever it was at that time – was exported to new areas, notably to the north and east. Western Christendom was greatly extended from the tenth century onwards in the Mediterranean, Scandinavia, and East Central Europe, an expansion that marks the beginning of the European conquest of the rest of the world. The expansion partly took the form of conquest and even colonisation, parallel to what happened during the Great Discoveries from the sixteenth century onwards, but it also led to the formation of independent kingdoms and principalities, which is its most interesting feature from our point of view. Whereas the southeastern shore of the Baltic Sea was for the most part the object of conquest and colonisation, independent kingdoms were established on both sides, namely the

---

18 On this school, see Salvesen, "The Strength of Tradition". Its relationship with the Annales school is discussed in Sandnes, "Totalhistorie og mentalitetshistorie".
19 Holmsen, *Norges historie*, pp. 251-61.
20 Helle, *Norge blir en stat*; cf. also "Tendenser", pp. 349-61.
21 Lunden, *Økonomi og samfunn*; Bagge, *Society and Politics* and *From Gang Leader*; Orning, *Uforutsigbarhet* and Njåstad, *Grenser for makt*.
22 For the following, see particularly Bartlett, *The Making of Europe*.

three Scandinavian kingdoms in the north and west and Poland, Bohemia and Hungary in the south. The different fate of these areas deserves to be an object of study in itself, but cannot be dealt with in any detail here. I shall instead confine myself to pointing out the time difference between their integration in Western Christendom: early, ninth to eleventh centuries in the case of the kingdoms, and late, from around 1150 onwards in the regions that were conquered. Early and voluntary Christianisation was thus an important asset for the six kingdoms, which in turn points to the importance of Christianity for state formation. Moreover, all six kingdoms had backgrounds as aggressors against Western Christendom. If we regard a multiplicity of centres of political power as an essential feature of Europe, in contrast for instance to China and the Islamic world,[23] as is commonly done, the expansion becomes equally important as the internal changes. Whereas most of Western Christendom had been united under one ruler in the Carolingian period and a substantial part of it under the Ottonian and Salian emperors, the expansion, combined with the weakening of central power in Germany, made the territorial principality the normal political organisation of Western Christendom. In addition to the three kingdoms of East Central Europe and Denmark on Germany's border, territorial principalities like Brandenburg, Mecklenburg and Pomerania made themselves independent of the emperor in most respects. The expansion thus established the combination of cultural unity and political division that has characterised Europe until the formation of the European Union in the second half of the twentieth century.

The following discussion will of course not present a complete comparison with the other kingdoms of the area, but it is my hope that a study of one of these kingdoms may contribute to the understanding of the export of state formation from the old to the new areas of Western Christendom, of the relationship between the imported and indigenous elements of this process and of the general relationship between the old and the new regions and in this way to stimulate further research regarding these questions. This means that the external aspect of the formation of the Norwegian state will be more prominent than usual in such accounts.[24] What happened in Norway is to some extent the result of interaction with, or influences from, other parts of Europe and, if specific to this country,

---

[23] E.g. McNeill, *The Pursuit of Power*, pp. 79-143, on the steady improvement of military technology, strategy and organisation as the result of constant competition, and Mann, *The Sources of Social Power*, pp. 430-43, on the political division within a common cultural framework as part of the European dynamic. Recently, however, several scholars have denied the importance of this feature; see Goldstone, "Efflorescences", pp. 334-39.

[24] General surveys in English of Norwegian history in the period are: Sawyer and Sawyer, *Medieval Scandinavia*; Helle, "Down to 1500"; Bagge, "The Scandinavian Kingdoms"; Helle (ed.), *The Cambridge History of Scandinavia*. The standard accounts in Norwegian are Andersen, *Samlingen*, and Helle, *Norge blir en stat*. As all these works contain references to earlier literature, I will not routinely give precise references for factual information contained in them.

can serve as one example of indigenous response to external impulses. External influences have of course been acknowledged in earlier Norwegian historiography but have largely been regarded as of secondary importance. In the words of the greatest Norwegian historian of the twentieth century, Jens Arup Seip:

> To me, the most important aspect of the historical process is not the loan in itself, but the need that made it take place and, second, the conditions that enabled the forms that had to be borrowed to be used. To use an image that may seem paradoxical: the most important thing for the historian is not the seed but the soil.[25]

Seip's functionalist approach has much to commend it and has often produced good results. He is also right in rejecting explanations of social change based exclusively on external impulses; the interaction between such impulses and the local environment always has to be taken into account.[26] In some cases it may also be difficult to distinguish between external and internal impulses. Even if Norway shows parallels with other countries, this may be the result of similar factors working independently in the same direction. Nevertheless, in some cases, notably with the introduction of Christianity and the development of the Church, there can be no doubt that the explanation is to be sought in external factors. There is no reason to think that the same social and cultural changes would have taken place if Christianity had not been brought to Norway from other countries, and there are limits as to how far its reception can be explained by needs in Norwegian society. Christianity was not only a belief system but a whole package of intellectual, social and economic changes and in addition an important factor in state formation.

In the following, I shall examine the changes that took place in the military, social-economical, ideological, legal and administrative fields between the first formation of the kingdom and the early fourteenth century which, according to common opinion, represents a peak in the development of a Norwegian state, and then compare Norway to other countries at the time. At present, this would seem a promising enterprise within the context of Norwegian as well as European historiography. The new ideas about personal relationships, rituals, feuds and mediation have mainly been applied to the Early Middle Ages and have been based on the study of narrative sources. It is now time to apply

---

[25] "... for mig står det allikevel slik at det vesentlige i den historiske prosess ikke er selve lånet, men det behov som gjorde at lånet kom i stand, og dernest de forutsetninger som gjorde det mulig at de former som måtte lånes, kunde bli brukt. For å anvende et billede som kan synes paradoksalt: det vesentlige for historikeren er ikke frøet, men jordsmonnet (Seip, "Problemer og metode", p. 78).

[26] Cf. here Seip's review of Johnsen, *Fra ættesamfunn*, and the following discussion between the two in *Historisk tidsskrift* 35.

them to the following period and re-examine the question of change or continuity against this background. In many ways Norway is different from the rest of Europe: it is a small country – in terms of population, not size – with limited sources. This may have its disadvantages but it also means that the general problems can be posed clearly and that a large number of aspects can be brought into the discussion relatively easily.

Living in a secularised society, we tend to identify the state with the monarchy, particularly in the Scandinavian countries with their long Protestant tradition. If we are interested in government, however, there is no reason to focus exclusively on the monarchy. The later state was the descendant not only of the monarchy but also of the Church, a point that is particularly obvious in Denmark-Norway, where the king at the Reformation took over most of the Church's lands and administration. From the point of view of the common people, it hardly mattered very much whether they were subject to the king, the Church, or a local lord, and the administrative and judicial systems employed by these powerholders were not necessarily very different. Admittedly, rivalry within the governing elite might have serious consequences and might even lead to the dissolution of the country in question, or to its conquest by stronger and more centralised neighbours.

In discussing Norwegian state formation, the source material available is far less than in the best-documented countries of medieval Europe, like England and Italy. There is a fair amount of narrative sources, mostly written in the late twelfth or the first half of the thirteenth century,[27] and their value for the early period is therefore doubtful and has been the subject of much discussion. Nineteenth-century scholars regarded them as largely trustworthy, although with an increasingly more sceptical attitude towards the end of the century.[28] In the early twentieth century, Lauritz Weibull in Sweden and Halvdan Koht in Norway broke with this attitude, although in widely different ways. Weibull represented a radically critical attitude, combined with systematic studies of the formation of tradition and the relationship between its various branches as a means of reconstructing the original version, and was probably influenced by Joseph Bédier's studies of French epic poetry.[29] By contrast, Koht was not particularly critical of the factual information in the sagas but claimed that they contained an overall interpretation of the past which the modern

---

27 For a survey of these sources and the relationship between them, see Andersson, "Kings' Sagas". Later studies include Lange, *Die Anfänge*, and Bagge, *Society and Politics*, pp. 14-63 and *passim*, and *From Gang Leader*, pp. 15-19 and 91-93.
28 Dahl, *Norsk historieforskning*, pp. 65-69, 195-230.
29 Weibull, *Kritiska undersökningar* (originally published in 1911). See the different interpretations by Torstendahl, *Källkritik och vetenskapssyn*, pp. 335-66; Odén, *Lauritz Weibull*; Arvidsson and Aarsleff, *Kritiska undersökningar*, and most recently Krag, "Lauritz Weibull".

historian had to take into account when using them as sources.[30] Koht's aim in this revision was to prepare the way for a new interpretation of early Norwegian history based on Marxist theory. Both the Weibulls and Koht had a great impact on later historiography, but, corresponding to the difference between them, Danish and Swedish historians were more critical of the factual information in the sagas than their Norwegian counterparts. At present, Claus Krag is the main representative of the Weibull tradition in Norway,[31] whereas there has recently been a revival of the use of the sagas as historical evidence, not primarily for factual information about the earliest period, but for norms, attitudes and rules of the game in contemporary society.[32]

From the second half of the thirteenth century, the narrative sources are replaced by an increasing number of royal and other charters, in addition to laws and other normative sources, although the vast majority of what once existed has probably been lost. This change is an advantage in one sense; documentary sources are generally considered more trustworthy than narrative ones. On the other hand, it is difficult to know to what degree the extant documentary sources are representative; in particular, they tend to give an exaggerated picture of bureaucratisation, whereas the narrative sources present the opposite. We therefore run the risk of underestimating the degree of state formation before the mid-thirteenth century and exaggerating it afterwards. Similarly, most of the documentary sources were issued by the monarchy and the Church and may consequently lead us to exaggerate the importance of these institutions. There is no easy solution to these problems; the best we can do is to keep them in mind and try to consider them when drawing our conclusions.

---

30   Koht, *Innhogg og utsyn*, pp. 96-123. Koht presented his new ideas in a lecture in 1913 which led to a heated discussion. See Dahl, *Norsk historieforskning*, pp. 239-43, and Bagge, "The Middle Ages", pp. 117 f., and "Udsigt", pp. 46 f. Koht was probably influenced by Ernst Bernheim whose lecture on medieval interpretations of history he had heard some years before, although Bernheim's *Mittelalterliche Zeitanschauungen* did not appear until 1918.
31   E.g. Krag, *Ynglingatal* and *Vikingtid og rikssamling*.
32   Lunden, *Økonomi og samfunn*; Meulengracht Sørensen, *Saga og samfund* and *Fortælling og ære*; Miller, *Bloodtaking*; Bagge, *Society and Politics*, *From Gang Leader* and "Mellom kildekritikk"; Orning, *Uforutsigbarhet*.

The Formation of the Kingdom of Norway

The origin of a country is an important problem in historiography, and much time and effort have been spent in describing how and why the various present-day national states of Europe came into being. This is also the case in Scandinavian scholarship, where the "unification" of each kingdom has had a prominent place. There is a certain national teleology behind this thinking. The country has been there from the beginning; unification is an inevitable process, ending with approximately the present-day borders.[1] In fact, the formation of the Scandinavian kingdoms is as much about division as about unification: the area was divided between three centres of power which eventually developed stable borders between them. How did this come about? Scandinavia was culturally and linguistically homogeneous. Even in the thirteenth century the term "Danish tongue" was used for the language of the entire region. There were different dialects, but the lines of division between them did not correspond to the later national borders. Religion and customs were also similar, both during the pagan and the Christian periods. Thus, no cultural or linguistic distinctions prevented the unification of each country. On the other hand, nor did such distinctions give rise to natural borders between the kingdoms that eventually emerged. It is hardly possible to present a general theory of state formation covering all known cases; nor can state formation be described as a continued process. There may be trends in this direction that are broken off, permanently or for some time, and there are dissolution of states as well as formation of them.[2] We can nevertheless point to some necessary conditions. A certain density of population and an economic surplus is necessary for the existence of a ruling elite, and the larger the population, the greater the likelihood of conflicts, which necessitates stronger government.[3]

Agriculture in Scandinavia dates back to around 4000 BC, and large parts of what later became the three kingdoms were settled already by the beginning of the Viking Age. Evidence from place names suggests population increase and expansion of agriculture during this period which have been considered an important factor in state formation. Although there is little evidence and much discussion about social structure in the pre-state period, there is now a tendency to regard the Scandinavian countries as relatively aristocratic as early as the Roman and Merovingian period and to assume the existence of large estates

---

1 This is even more prominent in the Norwegian term "rikssamling", implying that the different parts of the realm ("rike") were brought together at a certain time.
2 Mann, *The Sources og Social Power*, pp. 49-72.
3 Sahlins, "Poor Man"; Claessen and Skalník; Diamond, *Guns, Germs and Steel*, pp. 276-79.

run by great lords and with ordinary people as clients or even tenants.[4] Place names as well as archaeological evidence suggest the existence of lordship and government within lesser areas than the later kingdoms, although it is difficult to know the exact location and extent of these units. Large chiefdoms may have existed in Denmark and adjacent regions from the first centuries of the Christian era.[5] Regarding Norway, there is archaeological evidence of larger political units in the Oslofjord region, along the coast of Western Norway from Agder to Hordaland, in parts of Møre and Trøndelag and in Northern Norway around Lofoten. The recent excavations in Skiringssal in Tjølling in Vestfold have given a clearer picture of one such principality which included a town of some importance with permanent settlement, probably ruled by a lord whose residence is likely to have been the Huseby farm nearby. There may even have been some connection between this dynasty and the one celebrated in the ancient poem *Ynglingatal*, which contains several references to places in the region.[6]

"Unification" clearly means the rise of larger political units, but does it also signify qualitative change, like a more complex organisation or – perhaps most importantly – greater stability? Size is an important factor in discussions of the rise of kingdoms, in the Middle Ages as well as in other periods. Thus, France was created when Clovis conquered various smaller lordships and kingdoms around 500, England when Alfred and his successors united the various Anglo-Saxon principalities against the Vikings in the late ninth century, and the kingdoms of Scandinavia and East Central Europe when smaller principalities were merged into larger ones, normally by military conquest. There would seem to be a general tendency in the direction of larger and possibly more permanent political units in the whole area in the tenth and eleventh centuries.

This development is difficult to explain in terms of general social needs. In dry and densely settled river areas like in Egypt, China, Mesopotamia, and the Ganges region of India, state formation has been explained by the need to control and maintain irrigation systems in these "hydraulic societies", although even here, some scholars have objected that the actual political organisation by far exceeds what is necessary to maintain the irrigation systems.[7] Northern and East Central Europe offer no parallel to these systems,

---

4   Myhre, "The Iron Age", pp. 69-72. For local studies suggesting the same picture, see Skre, *Herredømmet*, pp. 128-250, on Romerike; Stylegar, "Hovedgårder", on Agder; and Iversen, *Eiendom*, pp. 118-390, summary 380-90, on Hordaland. By contrast, Dørum, *Romerike*, pp. 199-236, rejects Skre's interpretation of the conditions in this region and supports the older view of a largely independent peasant population here.
5   Bregnsbo and Jensen, *Det danske imperium*, pp. 14-39.
6   Brink, "Skiringssal" and Skre, "The Dating", "The Emergence" and "Towns and Markets", pp. 463-69.
7   Wittfogel, *Oriental Despotism*; see the criticism by Leach, "Talking about Talking about Feudalism". However, dissenting from Wittfogel, Gunawardana, "Social function", points to the importance of irrigation for state formation. See also Diamond, *Guns, Germs and Steel*, pp. 276-79.

with the possible exception of the dikes of Holland, which, however, only formed the basis of a very small political unit. Trade might be a factor, but the main centres of trade in medieval Europe, Northern Italy and the Netherlands, were also the most divided politically, and the most important transport artery, the Rhine, passed through an area of extreme political division notorious for its many toll stations.[8] Thus, the optimal size of a political unit is not determined by social and economic factors or the needs of its inhabitants, but by the size of other, competing political entities, a fact that once more points to the importance of division rather than unification. But Scandinavia should not be isolated from the rest of Northern Europe; it is hardly a coincidence that the formation of kingdoms took place at about the same time in both Scandinavia and East Central Europe.

The Rise of the Scandinavian Kingdoms

The common factor uniting the whole of Northern and East Central Europe is the rising power of Germany, the neighbour of Denmark, Poland, Bohemia, and Hungary. It seems a likely assumption that unification in all four countries was connected to pressure from this powerful neighbour. This pressure was political, military and religious; thus, there was a temporal as well as causal connection between Christianisation and state formation. Norway and Sweden, which did not border Germany, were affected indirectly by Denmark. From this point of view, political unification becomes a defensive measure. It can also, however, be understood against the background of an offensive from the peoples in the periphery against the settled areas of Western Christendom, namely the Slav and Magyar invasions in Germany and the Scandinavian Viking expeditions.

Denmark is the earliest of the Scandinavian kingdoms, which seems likely enough, for internal as well as external reasons. Denmark was actually the leading country in Scandinavia until the ascendance of Sweden in the seventeenth century, because of its wealth in agricultural land and its large and densely settled population. There is evidence of powerful Danish chieftains from the first centuries AD onwards but we do not know to what extent their realms corresponded to the later borders of Denmark. It is also uncertain whether the Danish kings mentioned in Carolingian sources from the early ninth century imply the existence of a kingdom of Denmark or whether the kings in question were simply chieftains with whom the Carolingians came in contact.[9] It is possible to follow a series of rulers until the middle of the century when there seems to be an eclipse for about a hundred years, either because the kingdom dissolved or because the decline

---

8   Postan and Miller, *The Cambridge Economic History* II, p. 184.
9   Bregnsbo and Jensen, *Det danske imperium*, pp. 8-39; Garipzanov, "Frontier Identities", pp. 113-25.

of the Carolingian Empire put an end to the attempts to Christianise and subordinate the Danish rulers, and thus to information about Denmark in Carolingian sources.[10] A revival seems to have occurred in the mid-tenth century with Harald Bluetooth who in the inscription on the Jelling stone boasts of having conquered the whole of Denmark and Norway and making the Danes Christian.

The rise of the Danish kingdom in the early ninth century may well have its background in German pressure. The conquest of Saxony by Charlemagne made the Carolingian Empire Denmark's neighbour to the south and opened it up for Carolingian conquest or penetration, while at the same time presenting a model for an ambitious conquering king. In a similar way, the final conversion of the country to Christianity around 965 is clearly connected to the rise of Ottonian power to the south, coming just after Otto I's victory over the Hungarians at Lech in 955 and his invasion of Italy and imperial coronation in 962. It also coincides with the conversion of Poland, traditionally dated to 966, and is preceded by the conversion of Bohemia some decades earlier and followed by that of Hungary some decades later. Later, war broke out between Harald and Otto II. After Otto I's death in 973, Harald attacked Saxony. Otto made a counterattack the following year, conquered Haithabu and Dannevirke and possibly larger parts of Jutland, which, however, Harald was able to regain after Otto's defeat against the Saracens in 983.[11] The Christianisation of Germany's neighbours, about which we have very little information, may alternatively be regarded as the result of increasing German influence or as a countermeasure to avoid being absorbed by German power, thus in both cases as provoked by increasing German strength.[12] The unification may be regarded in a similar way. Germany may have served as a model for the conquering king who then could use German pressure to gain support for himself – the magnates and petty kings being forced to choose between submitting to the Germans or to a national conqueror. However, the rise of the Danish kingdom under Harald and his successors is not only a defensive but also an offensive measure. The Vikings gradually operated on a larger scale and under Harald's son and successor Sven Forkbeard, the raids on England developed into systematic conquest,

---

10   For the following, see Sawyer, *Da Danmark blev Danmark*, pp. 105-29; Lund, "Scandinavia", and Skovgaard-Petersen, "The Making".
11   Lund, "Scandinavia", p. 218; cf. somewhat differently in Skovgaard-Petersen, "The Making", pp. 175 f.
12   Třeštik, "Von Svatopluk zu Boleslaw Chrobry", regards missionary activity as an integrated part of a German imperial project: first conquest, then Christianisation. Consequently, the conversion of the neighbouring countries becomes a response to German policy. Strzelzcyk, "The Church", pp. 51 f. and *passim*, cf. also "Bohemia and Poland", pp. 533-35, also points to other factors and is less certain about Germany's role in the conversion of Poland. Although the Ottonian and Salian Empire was hardly as monolithic as Třeštik seems to imply and diplomacy should be added to military conquest, there can be no doubt about the strength of the German Empire as a factor in the conversion of its neighbouring countries.

which was completed by Svein's son, Cnut the Great, who for a short time (1028-35) ruled a North Sea empire comprising England, Denmark and Norway.

From Harald Finehair to Harald Hardrada

The kingdom of Norway is the next in the series.[13] The sagas depict Harald Finehair as its founder and either state or imply that he conquered various smaller principalities until he had made himself lord of the whole country. The most widespread opinion today is that Harald's kingdom was confined to Western Norway, with suzerainty over or possibly in alliance with Trøndelag and Northern Norway, whereas the southeastern part of the country belonged to the Danish sphere of influence and the inner parts were ruled by local magnates. Very little is known about Harald; most of the details in the later sagas are unreliable. According to the Icelander Ari the Wise in the first half of the twelfth century, Harald ruled from 870 until 931/32. We do not know the evidence for this and consequently cannot trust it, but no better alternative has arisen,[14] so the current opinion is that Harald's unification must have taken place by the end of the ninth century. The main evidence for his actual conquest is a skaldic poem, *Haraldskvæði*, on the battle of Hafrsfjord, just south of present-day Stavanger, which the later saga tradition interprets as evidence of the final battle that made Harald lord of the whole country. Snorri, who gives the most detailed and systematic account, tells how Harald started in Vestfold, went north through Gudbrandsdalen, allied himself with the earl of Lade and gradually moved southwards along the coast until he defeated the last of his enemies at Hafrsfjord. Recent interpretations of the poem, however, suggest that Harald was attacked by enemies coming from the southeast, meaning that his basis of power was in Western Norway, to where most of the reliable evidence links him.[15] Although nothing much is known about Danish power at the time, Harald's unification may possibly have been a reaction against Danish dominance during the previous period and his victory at Hafrsfjord his turning back an attempt at Danish revival, although without being able to conquer the areas more firmly under Danish control or suzerainty.

The second main fact about Harald adds another important feature to this picture. Harald sent his son Håkon to King Athalstan of England to be fostered there. The cir-

---

13 For the following, see Krag, "The Early Unification of Norway" with references.
14 Koht, *Innhogg og utsyn*, pp. 34-51, tried to establish an alternative chronology by reckoning generations back from the earliest dated event, the Battle of Svolder in 1000, but this is a very uncertain method. See Einarsdóttir, *Studier*, pp. 16 ff.; Krag, "Perspektiver", pp. 19 f., and Bagge, "A Hero", pp. 195 f. A more sceptical view is represented by Jakobsson, "Erindringen", who even doubts Harald's existence.
15 von See, "Studien"; Krag, "The Early Unification of Norway", p. 187.

cumstances around this decision, as reported in the sagas, are clearly fictional, but there is some evidence in English sources of the young Håkon as well as of his English upbringing in skaldic poems. In light of later events, it seems reasonable to regard this alliance between Harald and Athalstan as directed against Denmark. Although the connection between the Viking raids on England and the Danish king is unclear, and we cannot operate with clear-cut conflicts or alliances between organised kingdoms in contemporary Scandinavia, it would certainly make sense for an English king to establish contacts with a Scandinavian ruler. Similarly, if the Danish king still had a foothold in southeastern Norway or had designs upon the country, an alliance with England would make sense from Harald's point of view.

The saga writers regard the kingdom Harald created as permanent. The main theme in the history of the country after his death therefore becomes the struggle between various pretenders over Harald's legacy. The sagas distinguish between three kinds of pretenders: Harald's many descendants who often fought amongst themselves; their rivals, the earls of Lade in Trøndelag; and the king of Denmark. Modern historians regard the foundation of the kingdom as a process lasting over several generations and are therefore less convinced of both the ambitions and the achievement of Harald's successors. Moreover, there is little evidence of continuity from Harald to the later dynasty; most probably, the line from Harald ended with his grandsons, the Eirikssons, in the 970s.[16] The competition was therefore considerably more open than it appears from the sagas.

Harald was succeeded by his eldest son, Eirik, nicknamed Blood-Axe, who after a year or two was deposed by his younger brother, Håkon, who returned from England. Håkon ruled for around thirty years (931/32–c. 960) over the same region as his father – Western Norway – and like his father also in alliance with the earl of Lade. During the second half of his reign, he had to defend himself against his nephews, the sons of Eirik Blood-Axe, who had the support of the Danish king Harald Bluetooth. Having killed Håkon in battle, the Eirikssons took over his kingdom. The sagas describe the Eirikssons as cruel and aggressive and they seem to have run into considerable problems. They ended the alliance with the earls of Lade by killing Earl Sigurd and came into conflict with the most powerful kindred in Western Norway, that of Horda-Kåre, which resulted in the death of one of the brothers. Most seriously, they lost the friendship of the king of Denmark, who instead supported Earl Håkon, son of Sigurd. Håkon defeated and killed Harald Greycloak, the leader of the Eirikssons, and took the power in Norway. Håkon later broke with the Danes, according to the sagas because he refused to accept Christianity but instead staged

---

16   Krag, "Norge som odel".

a pagan revival. This made the Danish king send the Jomsvikings to attack Norway, but Håkon defeated them in the battle of Hjørungavåg, probably in 986.

Håkon's ascent to power also meant that the centre of the kingdom was moved north to Trøndelag. His influence over the rest of the country is more uncertain. The battle of Hjørungavåg took place at Sunnmøre in the northwest, not far from Håkon's core area in Trøndelag. If the sagas were correct that Håkon ruled most of Norway when attacked by the king of Denmark, we would have expected the battle to have taken place much further south, as was the case with Håkon the Good's final battle against the Eirikssons which took place at Fitjar, between present-day Bergen and Stavanger. The actual site of the battle therefore indicates that most of Western Norway was either under Danish influence or was some kind of "no man's land" between Håkon's core area in the north and that of the Danes in the southeast. Horda-Kåre's kindred, which is mentioned again during the next reign, may have played an important part in this.

Håkon was killed in a local rebellion in 995 and replaced by Olav Tryggvason, who according to the sagas was the son of the local ruler of Viken. The sagas call him a descendant of Harald Finehair but this is probably fictional, as is also the statement that his father, Tryggve Olavsson, was killed by the Eirikssons.[17] Olav must be considered a self-made man who attempted to gain control over larger parts of the country with his base in an entirely new area. However, his main asset in the struggle for power was his Viking background, which must have brought him considerable wealth. He had raided various parts of the Baltic and North Sea areas and had participated in the Danish attacks on England in the early 990s. There he was baptised and confirmed with the English king Ethelred as his godfather. His return to Norway probably took place against the will of the Danish king Sven and may possibly be regarded as a parallel to the English alliance of his predecessor, Harald Finehair. As in the case of Harald Finehair and Håkon the Good, England would be an obvious ally for any rival of the Danes who wanted to gain power in Norway, while from an English point of view, such an alliance would be a means to counteract the threat from the Danes.[18] According to all the sources, Olav landed at Moster in the southwest, and conquered Trøndelag immediately afterwards. Most of the sources link Håkon's fall to his arrival, but this is probably a later fabrication – there are

---

17 Although most sagas state this, one of the oldest narrative sources, *Historia Norwegie*, adds an alternative explanation, namely that Tryggve was killed as the result of a local rebellion. Given the sagas' tendency to explain the history of the period as a series of dynastic struggles, this piece of information is likely to be authentic and to have been changed in the later tradition.

18 This English connection is emphasised particularly by Tøtlandsmo, *Før Norge*, pp. 40-51. See also Lund, "Scandinavia", p. 220.

traces of an older version that lacks this connection[19] – which in turn means that there is no particular reason to believe that Olav started his conquest in Trøndelag. His natural power base was Viken, where he had relatives and where he strengthened his position by marrying two of his sisters to prominent men there.[20] According to the sagas he also started his campaign to convert the country there.[21]

In Western Norway, Olav formed an alliance with the mightiest kindred in the region, that of Horda-Kåre, and gave his sister in marriage to Erling Skjalgsson, who according to the sagas was its most promising young man. Snorri also tells how Erling received the lordship over most of Western Norway (that is the area from Sognesjøen and south to Lindesnes, comprising most of the Gulatingslag) according to the same conditions as Harald Finehair had given his sons.[22] In Snorri's view, Erling thus becomes a kind of under-king to the ruler of the whole country. Snorri of course had no exact knowledge about the agreement between Olav and Erling, nor of what Harald Finehair had given to his sons. However, he must have had some information about the power and importance of Horda-Kåre's kindred[23] and of Erling's position in the following period until his death in 1028. The episode – which is also to be found in earlier sources – gives an impression of the vague line of division between the king, who in the saga writers' opinion was at least nominally the ruler of the whole country, and the various local chieftains, whether or not they are referred to as kings in the sagas. What remains an open question is whether Olav concluded an alliance with the actual power holder in the region or whether he built him up to be its ruler on his own behalf. Most likely, he did something in the middle of the two extremes. The later conflict between Erling and his second cousin indicates that Erling had been elected by the king to be his man in a special sense. On the other hand, given the fact that Olav was hardly a descendant of Harald Finehair and that we do not know if there were any royal estates or specifically royal privileges in the region to be taken over by a new king, it seems likely that Olav must have allied himself with the most powerful kindred in the region. Finally, the fall of the Eirikssons as well as Earl Håkon's limited control over Western Norway suggest that Horda-Kåre's descendants had already

---

19   Bagge, "The Making", p. 497.
20   Theodoricus Monachus ch. 13.
21   The oldest sources give little information about this campaign. By contrast, Snorri gives a detailed itinerary with exact chronology, basically in the form of a movement from Viken to the west and north along the coast. This seems reasonable enough, but is produced from his rearrangement of Odd Monk's account, which is neither logical nor probable and likely to be pure fiction. See Andersson, "The Conversion", and Bagge, "The Making", pp. 477-79, 506.
22   *HkrOT* ch. 58.
23   On a possible alliance between this kindred and Harald Finehair and in particular his son Håkon the Good, see Tøtlandsmo, *Før Norge ble Norge*, pp. 70-78; Bagge, "Håkon the Good", pp. 191-93, and Helle, "Den opphavlige vestlandsregionen", p. 18.

taken control of at least a considerable part of the Finehair dynasty's resources in the region south of Sogn.

In contrast to the southern part of the country, Olav seems to have gained Trøndelag through regular conquest, whether this happened shortly after Earl Håkon's fall or later, in connection with Christianisation. The sources depict Trøndelag as the core area of paganism and give many examples of resistance to the new religion. Olav used drastic means to suppress paganism and founded Trondheim as a stronghold to control the region. Olav also introduced Christianity in Northern Norway and formed friendships with various chieftains in the area. Against this background, Olav might compete with his successor and namesake for the rank as the first ruler of the whole country. It may be objected that his system of government resembles more closely a loose assembly of provinces connected with personal links between the king and his clients, but this is likely to be the case at later stages of the kingdom as well. Olav succumbed to an alliance between the kings of Denmark and Sweden, in which Håkon Ladejarl's son Eirik also participated, and was defeated and killed in a battle in Øresund, conventionally referred to as the Battle of Svolder.[24] Norway was now divided between the victorious kings of Denmark and Sweden with the two earls of Lade as King Sven of Denmark's representatives in Trøndelag and Western Norway. The new regime seems mostly to have kept Olav's arrangements, binding most of his clients, notably Erling Skjalgsson, to its service.

This situation was changed by another Viking chieftain, Olav Haraldsson, who conquered the country in 1015-16 and kept it until he was exiled by an alliance of Cnut the Great and Norwegian magnates in 1028 and then killed in the battle of Stiklestad on his return two years later.[25] Like Olav Tryggvason, this Olav arrived from England, most probably after breaking with his former ally, King Cnut, who was fighting for the lordship of the country, and possibly after some understanding with the English king Ethelred. Olav managed to conquer the country surprisingly quickly. A stroke of luck was probably an important factor: he managed to capture the young Earl Håkon Eiriksson, whose father had just left the country for England, forcing him to give up his claim for Norway in return for his life. In addition, Olav seems to have had relatives and connections in the eastern part of the country, and finally, he brought with him a large amount of gold and silver from his Viking and mercenary career in England which he clearly used to gain followers. His government shows considerable similarity to that of Olav Tryggvason. He

---

24   The battle has been the subject of much discussion among historians. See Weibull, *Kritiska undersökningar*, pp. 111-43; Ellehøj, "Olaf Tryggvasons fald"; and Bagge, "The Making", pp. 499 f. The oldest sources, notably Adam of Bremen, place it in Øresund, whereas a later tradition claims that it took place near an otherwise unknown island of Svolder, off the coast of Northern Germany near Rügen.
25   On the following, see Bagge, "Mellom kildekritikk og historisk antropologi".

seems to have been active in most of the country but had his main base in the east, where, according to the saga tradition, his father had been a petty king in the coastal region southwest of the Oslofjord (Grenland, now part of Telemark fylke).

Snorri gives a clear picture of how Olav established a network of clients in this part of the country, first as an addition to the petty kings, and then by replacing them. These men seem to have had their base in the region. They also remained loyal to Olav during the rebellion against him. Nor is there, curiously enough, any evidence that Cnut tried to attack Eastern Norway during his expedition in 1027/28. Outside this region Olav allied himself with the Arnesons in Møre, a region between Trøndelag and the central parts of Western Norway of which little is known in the previous period. In this way Olav may have planned to gain a foothold in the two important regions to the north and the south. He seems to have conquered Trøndelag in a similar manner as his predecessor Olav Tryggvason. He may also have made use of Trondheim as a base. His zeal for Christianity, perhaps combined with personal ambitions, caused him to use harsh measures against those suspected of participating in pagan cult. Olav also seems to have made connections to some local people, probably men of second rank, whom he promoted. By contrast, he had a poor relationship to Einar Tambarskjelve, the leading magnate in the region who had possibly been Olav Tryggvason's client and certainly a close ally of the earls. Unlike in Eastern Norway, Olav's dealings with Trøndelag largely had the character of an occupational regime, and this region also formed the centre of opposition against him. The Battle of Stiklestad took place there, and the army fighting against Olav seems to have been recruited mainly from Trøndelag. Olav also developed a bad relationship with Olav Tryggvason's old clients in Northern Norway while forming links with "new men" in the region.

Western Norway was the region where Olav had least control, a place he rarely visited and where, according to Snorri, he never spent a winter. According to Snorri, the relationship between Olav and Erling Skjalgsson was bad from the beginning and Erling was in the end killed by Olav, just before Olav's exile. The last conflict between the two is attested to by a skaldic stanza, but only the prose sources deal with its background. According to Snorri, who gives the most detailed account, Olav refused to renew the grants Olav Tryggvason – and later the earls – had given Erling. The conflict between them was exacerbated by Erling's relative Asbjørn from Northern Norway who ran into conflict with Olav's local representative (*årmann*, ON *ármaðr*) and killed him but was then saved from Olav's revenge by Erling's intervention. The story probably has a kernel of truth but neither the chronology nor its relevance for the conflict between Olav and Erling is clear. Nevertheless, the story shows that Olav had sufficient influence over Western Norway to have a local representative there and, furthermore, that he used other means to counteract

Erling's influence, namely by allying himself with one of Erling's relatives, Asbjørn, the man who eventually killed Erling.

Olav's conflicts with Erling as well as with some other magnates, such as Einar Tambarskjelve in Trøndelag and Hårek of Tjøtta and Tore Hund of Northern Norway, have been regarded as a policy directed specifically against the magnates. In the case of Erling, Olav may have objected to the size of the region under his control, but otherwise, it is difficult to find any radical difference between the magnates on Olav's side and those who were against him. The main difference between the two categories – apart from chance events leading either to friendship or enmity – is the difference between the magnates Olav chose himself and those who had already been promoted by his predecessors. In a society based on gift exchange and personal ties, there are good reasons for a ruler to prefer men whom he has promoted himself to those promoted by his predecessors. The logic is the same as in the parable in the New Testament, in which the one who has received most, will also love most (Luke 7,41-43). A man who receives confirmation of the privileges he already has, will feel less gratitude and consequently be less loyal than one who receives them for the first time. Furthermore, it is impossible for a ruler to satisfy all of the magnates; he has to promote some at the cost of others. In Olav's case, rewarding his friends and clients probably became an increasing problem during his reign. He started with great generosity based on booty from England, but he had few chances of filling up his purse as long as Cnut controlled both Denmark and England. He had to economise, possibly to the extent that he was regarded as mean, and he certainly had little chance of competing with Cnut when challenged by him for control over the country. Olav therefore differs less from his predecessors than earlier scholars have often thought. He seems largely to have followed in the footsteps of earlier Viking kings, the Eirikssons and Olav Tryggvason, but a relatively long reign and lucky circumstances in its beginning allowed him to carry out this policy with greater success than they did. However, when Cnut the Great had gained full control over England and Denmark, he turned against Norway and defeated Olav in alliance with a number of Norwegian magnates. The saga writers, notably Snorri, tend to attach more importance to the magnates than to Cnut in explaining Olav's fall, but this may be due to nationalistic considerations: the brave Norwegians could not be defeated by Danes, only by other Norwegians. Cnut's strength may well have been decisive, particularly when combined with his wealth and generosity, which made the Norwegian magnates prefer him to Olav. From this point of view, Cnut acted in the same manner as Olav himself when conquering Norway in 1015-16.

Olav's fall brought the Danes into power once more, this time with more direct control than any time previously, which led to strong reactions by the local magnates and people.

Olav was soon regarded as a saint and was canonised by a local synod by 1031. Two of his former enemies, Einar Tambarskjelve and Kalv Arnesson, who were disappointed when King Cnut had not rewarded them according to their deserts, brought his son Magnus back from exile in Russia. The Danes were quickly expelled and Magnus became king with the two magnates as his main counsellors. Kalv, however, soon had to leave the country, as he had fought against Olav at Stiklestad and was even said to have dealt him one of the fatal wounds. Magnus also managed to become king of Denmark, which according to the sagas resulted from an agreement between Magnus and Cnut's son Harthacnut that whoever lived longer would inherit the other's kingdom. Towards the end of his reign (1045) he had to share the power with his uncle Harald, Olav's half-brother, who returned with considerable wealth after several years of service as a mercenary in Byzantium and shortly afterwards succeeded him as sole ruler.

Harald has been regarded as the ruler who managed to defeat the opposition with which Olav had struggled. According to the sagas, he was on bad terms with Einar Tambarskjelve from the very beginning of his reign, and he soon got rid of him and his son by inviting them to a meeting and killing them. He also got rid of Kalv Arnesson which made Kalv's brother Finn – Olav's closest friend and formerly Harald's own friend and counsellor – leave him to join his enemy King Sven in Denmark. Finally, a long and dramatic conflict occurred between Harald and Håkon Ivarsson, a relative of the Ladejarls as well as Einar Tambarskjelve, interrupted by brief periods of truce and friendship. Harald also seems to have enjoyed stricter control over the country than his predecessors. He is depicted negatively in the clerical sources, whereas the secular sagas paint a more complex picture of him as a ruthless and treacherous but extremely clever ruler, and a man of many talents and considerable charm. He seems to be the first king to have established some control over the inner parts of Eastern Norway, where skaldic poems celebrate his sacking and burning, and he was also able to mobilise considerable resources for the long war against Denmark and for his final expedition against England. He effectively managed to replace his predecessors' clients with his own, including a foreigner, Ulv Uspaksson, an Icelander who had been his comrade in arms in Byzantium, but also some men who had served his predecessors, like his brother-in-law Torberg Arnesson (brother of Finn and Kalv) and his descendants, and Halldor Brynjolvsson, who, like his father, had served King Olav. Harald did not consistently replace the old aristocracy with foreigners or men of low origin; he mostly recruited his friends and clients from the same social class as his predecessors, but he no doubt saw to it that they were more strictly subordinated to him than his predecessors had managed to make them.

Unification and Division – the Moving Forces

The preceding brief summary of a long series of events, based on meagre and often unreliable and contradictory evidence in the later narrative sources, gives a good idea of the difficulties in grasping the main factors in the formation of the Norwegian kingdom. In contrast to the picture represented by the saga tradition and to some extent also by modern historiography, there was no potential kingdom of Norway waiting to be united, nor any conqueror who had decided to carry out the unification. Instead, we are dealing with a number of individuals attempting to gain as much wealth and power as possible and fighting one another to achieve these aims. Is it nevertheless possible to find a pattern in these events?

In modern times, when land communication is most important, the Norwegian landscape presents formidable obstacles to communication; in the Middle Ages, however, Norway had the advantage of excellent sea communications, with a long, protected coast that could be used throughout the year, as the sea in this area rarely freezes in winter. Under such conditions, Norway was one of the easiest countries of Europe to unite. A further advantage was that no single part of the country could be easily defended against the rest. Once united, it might be made to remain so relatively easily. On the other hand, if all powers along the coast were equally strong, what were the odds of one of them conquering the others? Normally, unification would seem to have its origin in one centre of particular strength, either economic or military, or to be imposed from abroad. In the case of Norway, the western coast would seem the most likely starting-point, both because it was the part of the country that could most easily be controlled by a fleet and because it was well located for conquests to the east and north. The first stage of the unification conforms to this reasoning but not the following ones. Actually, all the main regions of the country except Northern Norway were at some point the stronghold of the central power, and during the last and decisive phase, Western Norway apparently played a subordinate role. Thus, external factors would seem to have been particularly important in the case of Norway. This is also supported by the previous account which confirms the general rule that control of Norway had to be based either on Danish support or on wealth and military experience from Viking expeditions or mercenary service abroad, or both. Denmark was the great power throughout the period, and according to some recent scholars more or less completely controlled Norway during most of it.[26] By contrast, the sagas may be suspected of having exaggerated the importance of the inner Norwegian struggles and toned down the Danish intervention.

---

26 Krag, "The Early Unification", pp. 189-91; Skre, "Towns and Markets", pp. 466-68.

In the tenth century, Danish support largely seems to have decided the struggle for power in Norway. The Danish king may also have controlled the southeastern part of the country, although the relationship between his overlordship and the regional magnates is unclear. The fall of Olav Tryggvason and to an even greater extent that of St Olav led to more intense control which in the end backfired. The break-up of Cnut's empire after his death in 1035 must certainly have contributed to this, but the more fundamental fact was that lordship over the country was based on a combination of military pressure and alliances with local chieftains. The period 1030-35 would then seem to illustrate the problems in establishing direct rule. Its introduction might easily have united the local aristocracy in opposition against the intruder, as well as assured that this opposition rallied around an alternative ruler over the whole country, which was actually what happened when Olav's friends and enemies joined together in an alliance against the Danish rulers. Thus, first Danish support and then reaction against Danish dominance were important factors in the creation of the kingdom of Norway.

From early on the Danish king had a firm base in cultivated land, and probably also in the trading centre of Haithabu, and was able to combine these resources with surplus from Viking expeditions to embark on ambitious projects of foreign conquest from the late tenth century. Viking surplus probably also played a role in the rise of the kingdom of Sweden, although, given the inland character of this country, the degree of its importance is more doubtful. Norway on the other hand is the Viking kingdom *par excellence*, as all of its rulers between around 930 and 1066 had a Viking or mercenary background and most of them came directly from abroad to take power in the country. Norway had less agricultural land than its two neighbours, but the Norwegians had access to highly valuable merchandise – the furs of Northern Norway and the Kola Peninsula – and were also well placed, together with the rest of Scandinavia, to act as intermediaries on the trade routes between Russia and Byzantium and Western Europe, a trade that apparently gave a substantial surplus. The Swedish historian Sture Bolin claimed that the trade route via Russia and the Baltic replaced the Mediterranean as the main connection between Western Europe and the Arab and Byzantine world.[27] Although this is an exaggeration, the northern trade route must still be regarded as important.[28] The first Norwegian mentioned by name in history was actually engaged in the fur trade. This was Ottar of Hålogaland whose narrative of his journey from Northern Norway to King Alfred's court in Wessex was written down in Anglo-Saxon as a preface to a translation of Orosius.

---

27   Bolin, "Muhammed, Karl den store och Rurik".
28   See most recently Blomkvist, *The Discovery of the Baltic*, pp. 36-44.

The Viking expeditions contributed to military specialisation as well as to the creation of an economic basis for stronger principalities by giving chieftains the gold, silver, and luxury items that could be used for gaining followers. Gift exchange was an important political and economic factor in the Viking age and beyond, and both royal generosity and the valuable objects that were given are celebrated in the skaldic poetry.[29] The wealth from the Viking expeditions made it possible for chieftains to attach more men to their service than earlier, who could then be used to gain further wealth. The two Olavs as well as Harald Hardrada serve as examples of this, at least in the beginning of their careers. Earlier, Håkon the Good, who was not a Viking chieftain but who probably brought with him wealth from his foster father King Athelstan, also illustrates this. However, this wealth was likely to increase the number of chieftains as well as that of their followers and consequently did not necessarily lead to larger political units. Nor did the surplus necessarily have to be spent on creating national kingdoms. Many chieftains preferred to establish themselves abroad in the British Isles, Normandy, or Russia. Moreover, as long as it was easy to gain wealth from Viking expeditions, the principalities that emerged were likely to be unstable: new chieftains with fresh resources might easily expel the old ones. This happened repeatedly in Norway in the tenth and early eleventh century. Thus Håkon the Good was defeated and killed by his nephews the Eirikssons, who in turn were replaced by Håkon Ladejarl.

Consequently, the Viking expeditions appear to have made a greater surplus available to be invested in lordship, created greater ambitions among the chieftains, and led to more intense struggles between them, but did not directly lead to consolidated kingdoms, at least not in the case of Norway. This instead seems to have resulted from the *end* of the Viking expeditions. When the strengthening of feudal Europe in the eleventh century had put an end to the Viking expeditions, the only way for ambitious chieftains to gain wealth and power was within Scandinavia. In the case of Norway, this period coincided with large parts of the aristocracy and the people rallying around indigenous kings who resisted Danish dominance. In this respect, Norway is similar to the kingdoms of East Central Europe whose emergence also coincides with the end of the raiding expeditions against Germany and other parts of Western Christendom: the Slavs were defeated by Henry I in 929 and 933, and a Polish duchy emerged a few decades later. The Hungarians were defeated by Otto I in 955, and the principality (kingdom from AD 1000) of Hungary was established towards the end of the century.

---

29   Fidjestøl, *Selected Papers*, pp. 117-32.

There is also a correspondence between the Viking kings and the new religion, Christianity.[30] As far as we know, religion and political power were closely connected in the pagan period. There was apparently no professional priesthood; the chieftains acted as cultic and religious leaders (below pp. 146 f.). We can assume that the position of chieftain was not particularly stable; there was probably competition between several leading men for local power. Nor would it have been impossible for a newcomer, returning from abroad with booty and armed men from Viking expeditions, to establish himself as the leader of some area. It would probably also have been possible, although more difficult, for him to become the overlord of a larger number of such chieftains, as apparently Harald Finehair did when, according to the sagas, he "united the whole of Norway", or, more probably, made himself the lord over the western coast.

On the other hand, nothing in the pagan religion gave any support to this kind of lordship, and to a newcomer from abroad, the lack of firmly rooted political and religious leadership over one area was clearly a handicap. By contrast, Christianity was a unitary religion, with one cult, one God and a professional cult organisation which immediately abolished the religious importance of local chieftains. The sources occasionally draw the parallel between the rule of one king and the belief in one God, thus indicating the logical connection between the new religion and larger political entities.[31] Furthermore, although the king was not necessarily the head of this organisation, he had considerable control over it in the Early Middle Ages, notably in a country where Christianity was a new religion. Admittedly, the ecclesiastical organisation must have been too weak in the beginning to add very much to the king's power. Nevertheless, Christianity had a centralising effect by virtue of being a new religion. The struggle for this religion gave the king the opportunity to replace a number of powerful chieftains with men loyal to him who, as protagonists of the new religion, needed his support. In other words, the change of religion made it possible for the king to emerge as the leader of a "party" with a relatively strong loyalty to him, just as King Sverre had by the end of the twelfth century. This did not necessarily weaken the aristocracy as such; the magnates maintained their strong position in local society by

---

30 For the following, see Bagge, "Christianisation", pp. 114-16, and "The Kingdom of Norway". For the other Scandinavian countries, see most recently Gelting, "The Kingdom of Denmark", and Blomkvist, Brink and Lindkvist,"The Kingdom of Sweden".

31 In an addition to *Fagrskinna*, Harald explicitly points to this parallel (*Fsk.* p. 386), whereas in *Heimskringla*, he swears by the Almighty God that he will conquer Norway (*HkrHH* ch. 4). According to the latter source, Harald also disliked the pagan magic, *seiðr* (ibid., ch. 35).

building churches and appointing priests to them,[32] but at least in the beginning it made them more closely attached to the king. Finally, Christianity also gave the king an incentive to conquer new areas in order to propagate the new religion. Despite the problem of the reliability of the sagas, it is hardly a coincidence that they contain more information about the movements of the two missionary kings Olav Tryggvason and St Olav than they do about their predecessors.

It may be objected, firstly, that this explanation completely ignores religious and cultural factors and regards people at that time as acting solely out of rational self-interest and secondly, that it exaggerates the importance of the kings for the conversion. The answer to the first objection is that such considerations are fully compatible with a religious attitude. There was hardly a sharp distinction between the religious and the secular sphere in the early Middle Ages, certainly not in paganism and considerably less in Christianity than in later ages. Consequently, success in the secular field might easily be transferred to the religious one. Nor was contemporary religion an objective system of dogma, but rather intensely personal, so that there was a strong connection between allegiance to a leader and allegiance to his gods. Concerning the second objection, recent scholarship, particularly within archaeology, has mostly regarded the Christianisation as a gradual process and been critical of the emphasis on the missionary kings in the sagas. East-west orientation of burials, Christian objects in the graves and various other features have often been regarded as evidence of the gradual penetration of Christianity. Having examined a considerable amount of archaeological material from various parts of the country, however, Sæbjørg Nordeide concludes that there is little evidence of this.[33] Although the importance of contacts with Christian Europe through Viking and trading expeditions and in other ways should not be neglected, it therefore seems that the importance of the kings was crucial, notably in establishing an organised church and in banning pagan cult. On these matters, the sagas are probably right, although they exaggerate the importance of the two main missionary kings, Olav Tryggvason (995-1000) and St Olav Haraldsson (1015-30). Actually, after the death of Harald Finehair in the 930s all rulers of Norway except one were Christian and probably contributed in various ways to the final result.

---

32 In accordance with the account in the sagas, Norwegian historians have usually attributed greater importance to the kings in the conversion of their country than their counterparts in Denmark and Sweden have. Nineteenth-century scholarship also regarded the conversion as a victory for the king over the aristocracy, an interpretation that was challenged by Koht, *Innhogg og utsyn*, pp. 142-55. Later historians have expressed differing opinions on the matter. Skre, "Missionary Activity", supports Koht, whereas I have earlier pointed to the centralising effect of Christianity which must have strengthened the king's power. See Bagge, "Kristendom og kongemakt", pp. 19-23, and "Christianization and State Formation", pp. 124-27.

33 Nordeide, *The Viking Age*.

Finally, why just Norway? Or more specifically, why was Scandinavia divided into three kingdoms and with the borders that emerged during the eleventh century? Although the contemporary kings hardly considered these borders as final or "natural", their basic outlines actually remained until the great changes in the mid-seventeenth century. In explaining this result, the alternative to national teleology is not chance events, but geopolitical factors, above all the importance of sea power. The elegant, well-built Viking ships could move quickly over great distances. Moreover, they could carry provisions for considerably longer periods than an army moving over land, which was usually limited to three days.[34] The Scandinavians could therefore plunder as well as build principalities over the whole area around the North and the Baltic Seas and were in frequent contact with its kings and princes. It is uncertain whether Denmark was united from Jutland or from the islands, but the Bluetooth dynasty is most likely to have had its base in Jutland. A power controlling Jutland could of course easily have conquered the surrounding islands as well as the coast on the other side of Øresund, Scania. This area was separated from the core areas of the Swedish kingdom by forests and thinly populated land. As we have seen, the Danes could also have expanded further north along the coast and were as likely to get hold of the Oslofjord area as the Norwegians were. Controlling the whole of the Norwegian coast would have meant long lines of communication. This would in turn necessitate that this aim was given high priority, which does not seem to have been the case during the period in question. Moreover, attempts at conquest might also lead to reactions from the Norwegians and to the emergence of a power that could more easily control the area. This may actually be what happened in the case of Harald Finehair. Once such a kingdom was established, it was able to compete with the Danes for control of the Oslofjord area. The outcome was uncertain for a long time, and the Danes were still trying to gain the region as late as the mid-twelfth century (below p. 49). There is hardly any geopolitical inevitability in the Norwegian victory in this case, but it may be explained by the fact that the king of Norway was likely to give higher priority to this problem than the king of Denmark who had other fields of expansion, notably Northern Germany and the southern shore of the Baltic Sea. This was particularly the case under Olav Tryggvason and his successors whose rule was centred in the Oslofjord area.

An important factor in these considerations is the late unification of Sweden which also has a geopolitical explanation. Admittedly, Rimbert does mention a Swedish king in the mid-ninth century, but he was probably a local ruler in the area near Birka in the Mälar region.[35] Sea power was important in Sweden as well, but the political unification seems

---

34   Mann, *The Sources of Social Power*, pp. 9 f., 137-39.
35   Rimbert, *Vita Ansgari* chs. 11, 19.

to have centred around the great lakes rather than the coast. Sweden naturally falls into two parts: Götaland in the west around the lakes of Vänern and Vättern, and Svealand in the east, around Lake Mälaren. The two regions were divided by dense forests and few kings were able to exert control over both of them before the mid-thirteenth century.[36] By that time the coastal region of Götaland had already been divided between Norway and Denmark. Only in the mid-thirteenth century was the king of Sweden able to gain a tiny corridor out to the sea at the mouth of Göta Älv, near present-day Gothenburg. Dense forests also separated both regions from Scania, which therefore came to belong to Denmark. By contrast, there was less foreign competition in the east, so that the principality of Svealand was not only able to reach the coast but also to expand on the other side of the Baltic Sea, in the southern and western part of present-day Finland. In the inter-Nordic struggles, however, for a long time the Swedish king had to confine himself to supporting the weaker power in the Danish-Norwegian struggles in order to prevent the unification of both countries under one king. Thus, Swedish intervention may have been of some importance both in separating Norway from Denmark and in securing Norwegian control of Viken, which was an advantage from a Swedish point of view because it prevented the same power from controlling both sides of the Göta Älv.[37]

External and Internal Factors

The main emphasis in the previous account of the first phase of Norwegian state formation has been on external factors. European models have not been discussed, as their importance is difficult to assess. The main factors are the Viking and trading expeditions, the surplus from which was invested in clients and political power at home, the pressure from Germany which contributed to the unification of Denmark and thus indirectly influenced the two other kingdoms, the competition between the centres of power in Scandinavia which eventually led to its division into three kingdoms, and finally the importance of Christianity as an incentive for conquest and as an instrument in the monopolisation of power. The conversion to Christianity took place at about the same time as the formation of the kingdom in each of the six "new countries" of Western Christendom, but the causal relationship between the two phenomena is not easy to ascertain. Most likely there is a

---

36   There is less evidence for the early history of Sweden than there is for the two other countries, and opinions about the process have been widely divided. It is clear that there was a strong division between Svealand and Götaland and that few kings controlled both regions until the second half of the twelfth century, and probably not really until Earl Birger, around 1250. See Sawyer, *När Sverige*; Lindkvist, "Kings and Provinces", and Blomkvist, *The Discovery of the Baltic*, pp. 579-623.
37   Krag, "The Early Unification", pp. 200 f.

coalescence between the two factors rather than a strict division into cause and effect. In Norway, however, the importance of the Viking kings coming from abroad points to Christianity as more likely to be the cause of the unification than vice versa. Whatever the answer to this question, the greatest impact of Christianity probably lies in the following period, partly in its contribution to the continued existence of the kingdoms, partly in its role in their further development.

The most important internal factors – population increase and the expansion of agriculture – contributed to the Viking expeditions, not because the lack of arable land forced the Scandinavians to establish themselves abroad, but because it created the necessary man-power for the foreign expeditions. Population density is also a factor in state formation and may in the case of Scandinavia be regarded as a necessary condition, although hardly sufficient to explain the rise of the three Scandinavian kingdoms and the division between them at this particular time.

The "Civil Wars"

After a period of internal peace for nearly a hundred years, conflicts over the succession broke out in the 1130s and lasted, with interludes, until 1240, which marked the beginning of a new period of internal peace usually considered to be Norway's period of greatness. The inner conflicts, conventionally although somewhat anachronistically referred to as "the civil wars", have been subject to considerable discussion, and various explanations for their outbreak and character have been suggested. Many of these explanations seem to exaggerate the importance of the problem, implicitly regarding peace as the normal condition and war as needing a special explanation. In reality, however, armed conflicts between powerful men were normal in the Middle Ages, and similar conflicts occurred in the other "new" countries of Western Christendom as well as in the old ones. Institutional arrangements as well as social structures may make such conflicts more or less likely or more or less serious. In the case of Norway, the rules of succession – or perhaps the lack of such rules – have often been regarded as a serious problem. All male descendants of a king, at least the agnatic descendants, whether they were born in wedlock or not, had an equal right to claim the throne and could in principle be recognised by any local assembly, although Øreting in Trondheim apparently had a particular status in royal elections. If two or more kings were recognised at the same time, they had to make an arrangement between them or fight over the throne.

If a peaceful arrangement was made, as happened several times in the period 1045-1157, no territorial division took place. The king had no fixed residence in this period, but travelled around the country, largely receiving his incomes in the form of *veizla*, i.e.

provisions for himself and his men in the local region. When there were several kings, they usually travelled in different parts of the country, probably according to some pre-arranged pattern, occasionally meeting for eating, drinking, and discussion. It is clear that this arrangement implied great risks for conflict. No rule forced the pretenders to agree to divide the throne between them; a stronger candidate, or a candidate believing himself to be the stronger, might easily try to fight his rival. Once an agreement was made, plenty of situations might lead to conflicts between the co-rulers, such as the sharing of common incomes, who was to preside over the common meetings, and quarrels between their adherents. The sagas give many examples of such conflicts. Division between the kings meant a division of wealth and power but not necessarily of ambition.[38] From one point of view, the Law of Succession of 1163/64, which introduced individual succession and clear rules for election (below pp. 166 f.), represents an attempt to solve this problem, but was more probably intended to secure the throne for Magnus Erlingsson, the candidate of the victorious faction at the time. The law actually introduced the most intense phase of the struggles.

Although the traditional rule of succession was likely to lead to conflict, the contrast between the prolonged period of struggles from 1130-1240 and the peaceful periods before and after has made many historians regard the problem of succession as a symptom rather than a cause of the conflicts. In the Marxist interpretation of Norwegian history, developed most systematically by Andreas Holmsen, competition between the pretenders formed the "sparks" which set fire to the material for conflict that had built up during the preceding period.[39] In the previous period, population growth close to the limit of the existing resources had strengthened the aristocracy and created a proletariat of poor peasants. The former class was now ready to take over the political power, while those belonging to the latter were willing to follow leaders who could give them better living conditions. At the same time, the polarisation between the classes had not reached the same level all over the country, which contributed to regional differences corresponding to the social ones. There was a conflict between the "aristocratic" regions, Western Norway and Viken, and the more "democratic" ones, Trøndelag and the inner part of Eastern Norway. Thus, in Holmsen's view the civil wars have a crucial importance as the breakthrough of a new society, based on a strong clerical and secular aristocracy with the king as their instrument. The civil wars have also been explained by long-term divisions between family clans, going back to the struggles in the tenth and eleventh centuries,[40] and by ideological

---

38 See the discussion between Bjørgo and me about the importance of the rule of succession for the outbreak of conflicts: Bjørgo, "Samkongedøme", and Bagge, "Samkongedømme".
39 Holmsen, *Norges historie*, pp. 225-27.
40 Koht, *Innhogg og utsyn*, pp. 111-23, and "Norsk historie i lys frå ættehistoria".

divisions, notably those between the prelates fighting for *libertas ecclesiae* and the adherents of the traditional ideal of a Church dominated by the king and the laity. Finally, some scholars, including myself, distinguish between deeper changes leading to the prolonged conflicts and the divisions between factions, regarding the latter as purely random – as conflicts between groups of magnates linked together with personal ties without any significant social, geographic or ideological difference between them.[41]

Pretenders and Factions

In order to choose between these alternatives, let us examine the conflicts in somewhat greater detail. They started within the royal family. In the late 1120s, a man named Gilchrist (commonly called Harald Gille) came from Ireland to Norway, claiming to be a son of the late king Magnus Barelegs and proving it by undergoing an ordeal. The ruling king, Sigurd, accepted him as his half-brother, but forced him to swear not to claim the throne as long as Sigurd himself and his son Magnus were alive. After Sigurd's death in 1130, Harald broke the oath and forced Magnus to share the kingdom with him. In 1134, Magnus attacked Harald and defeated him in the Battle of Färlev in Bohuslän. Harald fled to Denmark and returned shortly afterwards with Danish aid to defeat Magnus in Bergen in January 1135. He took him captive, mutilated him and placed him in a monastery. The sagas attribute Harald's success to his friendliness and generosity and Magnus's meanness and unpopularity. Normally, one would believe that the son of a late king who had grown up in the country could easily have defeated a rival who had arrived in the country only some years before and who was not even able to speak the language correctly.[42] Thus, the magnates' support must have been decisive in Harald's victory. Moreover, Harald did not arrive in Norway on his own initiative but was brought there by the magnate Hallkjell Huk from Blindheim in Sunnmøre, whose descendants were to play an important part in the later struggles in the country. We know nothing of Hallkjell's motives, but he probably had a connection to the British Isles and may even have been a relative of Harald's mother.[43] He of course also profited from Harald succeeding in being recognised as heir to the throne. There seems to be no continuity between this conflict and the next one which broke out in the 1150s. The circle around Harald Gille apparently stuck together during his short reign as sole king and, after his murder in 1136, they defended his sons, Sigurd (aged five) and Inge (aged three), against the new pretender, Sigurd Slembe, who sought

---

41 Lunden, *Norge under Sverreætten*, pp. 39-56; Bagge, "Borgerkrig og statsutvikling", pp. 151-56, and "The Structure", pp. 302-17.
42 Bagge, *Society and Politics*, pp. 156-57.
43 Tjersland, "Sagaætter", pp. 130-33.

to mobilise Magnus's old adherents by taking the blinded and mutilated king out of the monastery. After Sigurd's and Magnus's defeat and death in 1139, Sigurd and Inge ruled together until they reached majority around 1150. They must also have agreed in accepting a third, elder son, Øystein, born before Harald's arrival in Norway, who was acclaimed king in 1142. The new conflict broke out between the adult kings in 1155.

The earliest sources, *Ágrip* (c. 1190) and *Morkinskinna* (c. 1220), describe its background as follows.[44] Geirstein, father of King Sigurd's mistress, who was an aggressive and overbearing man, proposed to Gyda, a rich widow in the neighbourhood, but was rejected. He then started to bully her by driving his cattle into her fields, after which he was killed by one of Gyda's servants. Gyda, who was now in a desperate situation, risking revenge from Geistein's sons in addition to the king's wrath, turned to her relative Gregorius Dagsson. He was willing to protect her and killed both of Geirstein's sons when they came to capture her. After this, Gregorius understood that he had become King Sigurd's enemy and turned to Sigurd's brother Inge for protection. Gregorius then became Inge's most trusted friend and the leader of his army. This story is not included in *Fagrskinna* (c. 1220) and *Heimskringla* (c. 1230), both of which turn directly to the clash between the kings in 1155, although they clearly imply a bad relationship between King Sigurd and Gregorius. According to this later version, Sigurd and Øystein, meeting to solve a conflict between them, had agreed to depose Inge, regarding him as unfit to be king because he was crippled as a result of an accident in his childhood when being carried by one of his men in a battle. The plan was to be carried out during a meeting between all three kings in Bergen. Sigurd and Inge arrived first for this meeting and a quarrel broke out between their men, resulting in the death of one of Inge's men. During a meeting of Inge's adherents, Gregorius and Inge's mother, Queen Ingrid, urged the king to take revenge immediately rather than wait for an offer of compensation. This line of action was taken and resulted in Sigurd being killed. When Øystein arrived shortly afterwards, according to *Heimskringla* Gregorius wanted to attack him as well, but negotiations were opened and ended in some kind of peace, after which Øystein left the town and went to the east. The bad relationship between the two kings continued, and two years later war broke out again and Øystein was killed.

The sagas are clearly biased against Sigurd and Øystein and favourable towards Inge. The two former are described as haughty, violent, and aggressive and Øystein also as being mean, whereas Inge is said to have been mild, friendly, generous, and popular with the people. Inge's success, despite his physical handicap, is explained by his popularity which caused the majority of the magnates to join him. This becomes particularly clear in the

---

44 *Ágrip* ch. 60, pp. 78 f. (the manuscript breaks off before the end of the story); *Msk.* ch. 398.

account of the conflict between Øystein and him, according to which a number of prominent men left Øystein to join Inge.[45] Øystein was even killed by one of his former adherents, Simon Skalp, son of Hallkjell Huk, who brought Harald Gille to Norway. Thus, the sagas indicate a similar pattern to the one in the conflict between Harald and Magnus: a king has to share his wealth and power with his adherents in order to be able to rule.

Concerning the explanation for the conflict between the kings, there are good reasons to accept the story of Gregorius and the Geirsteinsons. Although the version in the sagas may have been arranged to make Gregorius appear in a more favourable light, there is no reason to doubt the story as such. The distance between the time it happened and the earliest sources is not great by saga standards,[46] and it is psychologically and sociologically reasonable. A host of similar stories occur in the saga literature, and although not every one of them needs to be true, they illustrate the normal development of conflicts in contemporary society. The same applies to the clash in Bergen between Sigurd and Inge's adherents. The presence in one town of a large number of armed young men in the service of different lords, combined with heavy drinking, would be likely to lead to conflicts and violence. There are numerous other examples in the saga literature, including the contemporary sagas. In this case, the man who was killed was apparently of some standing. He – as well as his killers – are mentioned by name, and he is said to be an old retainer (*hirðmaðr*) who had served many kings. However, in such cases the normal procedure would be to demand compensation, or alternatively to demand that the killers be punished, not to turn directly against the killers' patron. The line of action taken clearly indicates a wish on Gregorius's part and possibly also on Inge's part to get rid of Sigurd.

Gregorius's and Inge's excuse for this in the saga tradition is the alleged conspiracy between Sigurd and Øystein against Inge. In the meeting in Bergen between Inge and Sigurd and their adherents, Inge declares that he has been informed about the plan and accuses Sigurd. Sigurd denies the accusation, claiming it to be Gregorius's invention. Modern historians tend to agree with Sigurd. The story of the conspiracy is likely to have been invented as an excuse for Inge's aggressive behaviour. Moreover, if Sigurd and Øystein had really planned to depose Inge, one might have expected them to coordinate their movements better. Instead, Sigurd arrived in Bergen well before Øystein and was numerically far inferior to Inge. Under such circumstances, he ought to have taken great care to avoid any conflict until Øystein arrived. These events have therefore been taken as

---

45   According to Heimskringla, after the break with Inge in 1157 Øystein encouraged his men to fight for him but received the following reply: "Let your gold chests follow you and defend the country for you" ("Fylgi gullkistur þinar þér nú ok veri land þitt", *HkrIngi* ch. 31).
46   The source may have been Eirik Oddsson's Ryggjarstykki, written around 1160, which the later sagas have used.

evidence of the formation of an aristocratic party, based in Viken and Western Norway and aiming at taking full control of the government of the country. Although this is clearly taking things too far, Inge's faction included some able and ambitious magnates, the most prominent of which were Gregorius and Erling Ormsson, nicknamed Skakke (the Wry-necked). Gregorius is portrayed as the chivalrous hero – brave, generous, strong, and handsome – whereas Erling is the cool, cynical and clever general and political leader.

The hypothesis about there being a clearer division between two factions is confirmed by the subsequent events. The death of Øystein ought to have led to both factions gathering around the last of the three brothers, Inge, as apparently happened after Harald Gille's victory. However, Øystein's remaining adherents elected a son of Sigurd, Håkon, nicknamed the Broadshouldered, who was then ten years old and thus hardly the one who took the initiative. The actual leader of the faction was his foster-father, Sigurd of Røyr. From a dynastic point of view, it would seem to have been fairly easy to reach a compromise in such a situation, either by including Håkon as a co-ruler beside Inge, but with the older Inge as the leader, or by appointing Håkon as Inge's successor, similar to the compromise reached in the English Civil War when Stephen accepted his adversary Mathilda's son, Henry II, as his successor. Inge apparently had no son at the time. However, the bitterness or rivalry or ambition on both sides was apparently too great for this to happen. Instead, war broke out and lasted for several years. For the most part Inge's adherents had the upper hand, but in January 1161 Gregorius was suddenly killed and Inge shortly afterwards. Once more, the faction that had lost its leader refused to accept their adversaries' candidate who was now, according to traditional opinion, the nearest heir to the throne. They had to pick their candidate among the various cognates of the royal family and finally decided in favour of Erling's son Magnus, whose mother Kristin was King Sigurd Magnusson's daughter.

Erling then became the undisputed leader of the faction and defeated and killed Håkon the following year. A series of other pretenders were raised against him, usually alleged sons of Sigurd and Øystein, mostly of Sigurd who was known for his affairs with a number of women. They were all defeated, with the exception of the last one, led by Sverre Sigurdsson. Claiming to be another son of Sigurd Haraldsson, Sverre gathered around him the remains of a faction called the Birchlegs[47] early in 1177 and through a series of brilliant campaigns managed to fight his way to the throne, killing Erling in battle in 1179 and Magnus in 1184. The rest of his reign until his death – peacefully, not in battle – in 1202 in many ways forms a parallel to Erling's reign, with a series of new pretend-

---

47   The name was originally derogatory: the men were too poor to have shoes, so they had to use birch around their legs instead.

ers rising against him, most of whom claimed descent from Magnus, who had the same reputation as a womaniser as Sverre's alleged father Sigurd. As in the case of Erling, the last of these rebellions, by the so-called Croziers (*baglar*),[48] who formed in 1196, proved the most serious. The division between the two factions continued until 1217, although with long periods of peace. With the death of the Crozier king in that year, a settlement between the two factions was reached and the leaders agreed to divide Eastern Norway – the core area of the Croziers – between them. The losers in this agreement formed new factions and fought on until 1227, when the last of their leaders surrendered. A split within the Birchlegs in 1239-40, between Sverre's grandson Håkon and Skule Bårdsson of the Rein kindred, half-brother of the earlier Birchleg king Inge (1204-17), marked the end of the civil wars. After Skule's defeat and death in 1240, no pretender challenged Sverre's descendants.

The divisions during the civil wars thus show a remarkable continuity. The factions formed in the 1150s continued for a long time under different names until 1217. They were preceded by an earlier division in the 1130s with which they apparently had no connection, and were succeeded by a split in the Croziers, following the reconciliation with the Birchlegs in 1217, and by a split in the Birchlegs in 1239-40. From 1161 they represented clearly distinct dynasties, the descendants of Sigurd Magnusson, on the one hand, against those of Harald Gille on the other, but this is a secondary development. By 1157, the division was strong enough for the adherents of Sigurd and Øystein to oppose Sigurd's son to their former leaders' half-brother Inge and for the latter's adherents to reject him. The later factions distinguished themselves by their leaders' real or alleged descent and by their composition; after a pretender's death, his adherents or their descendants rallied around another pretender of the same label. To a great extent, the pretenders seem to have been mere puppets – boys or very young and inexperienced men – which indicates, first, that the idea of a dynasty had become sufficiently important for real or alleged royal descent to be compulsory for any pretender to the throne, and, second, that the moving forces were the magnates rather than the kings themselves. This may indicate the existence of a strong aristocracy that preferred "mild" and "generous" kings that could easily be led, as in the case of Harald Gille and Inge. Although this applies to the majority of pretenders, it does not apply to the most important ones. Sverre was a very strong leader who succeeded largely because of his personal qualities, and in the previous period Erling Skakke represented a similar kind of leadership. Thus, most of the period was actually comprised of strong leaders, which is logical enough in a period of intense struggles.

---

48   The name is derived from *bagall* = staff, usually the bishop's staff (Lat. *baculum*), a reference to the alliance of this faction with the prelates during their struggle against Sverre.

The Basic Factors

The existence of two strongly opposed factions over a period of around sixty years would seem to support the "deeper" explanations of the division between them that have been suggested by earlier historians: that they represented different social strata, regions, or ideologies. None of these divisions can be detected, however, during the crucial period when the factions were actually formed, between 1155 and 1161.[49] Attempts to characterise the adherents of Håkon Sigurdsson as having been mainly recruited from the lower classes find no support in the sources. Håkon led an "ordinary" faction, including prominent men and having considerable support in various parts of the country.[50] The only evidence for the existence of an opposition between Viken and Western Norway and the rest of the country is the fact that the two leaders of the Inge faction, Gregorius and Erling, were based in the lower Telemark and the Sunnhordland area respectively. The kings' movements in the period give no support to the theory of whole regions in permanent opposition to one another. The statement in the sagas that Cardinal Nicholas Brekespeare, who organised the Church province in 1152/53, criticised Sigurd and Øystein while calling Inge his son, has led some historians to assume that Sigurd and Øystein represented a National Church attitude in contrast to the latter's Gregorianism, and even that the papal schism that broke out in 1159 was reflected in the Norwegian civil wars: the Håkon faction supporting the schismatic Victor IV and the Inge faction Alexander III. Although there is some evidence that the Håkon faction supported Victor IV,[51] this cannot have been the result of any long-term ideological division, but must rather be explained as the result of an actual or attempted alliance with King Valdemar of Denmark, who supported Victor IV. The Cardinal's attitude towards the kings can easily be explained by their different personal lives and by the fact that Inge was legitimately born and his brothers were not. No doubt, as we shall see, all three factors played a role in the internal conflicts, but they do not explain why they broke out or how the factions were divided.

On the contrary, the division between the factions was essentially random, based on personal loyalty and including friendship, kinship and marriage or other links based on the exchange of women. Serious objections have been raised against the earlier theory of

---

49 Bagge, "Borgerkrig", pp. 166-68, and "The Structure", p. 305.
50 Koht, *Innhogg og utsyn*, pp. 117-18; Bagge, "Samkongedømme og enekongedømme", pp. 253-54; Bagge, "Borgerkrig", p. 166, and *Society and Politics*, p. 216, n. 46. For a more thorough examination of the problem, arriving at basically the same conclusion, see Arstad, *Kongsemner*, pp. 15-19, on Håkon and "Ribbungopprør", pp. 63-90.
51 Otto Morena states in his chronicle of Frederick Barbarossa that a number of kings, including the king of Norway, sent envoys to excuse themselves from meeting at the council of Lodi in June 1161 but recognised Victor as pope (RN I no. 106). If the information is true, the king in question must have been Håkon, as Inge had been killed on 1 February and there is evidence that the Inge faction supported Alexander III. See the note in RN; see also Johnsen, *Studier*, p. 381, who rejects this information, and Arstad, *Kongsemner*, pp. 20 f.

a development from a "society of kindred" to a "society of state,[52] in particular the argument that the Norwegian kinship system was bilateral and consequently did not lead to the formation of great clans.[53] Nor is there any evidence that the factions formed in the 1150s were generally based on pre-existing divisions between magnate families.[54] They are more likely to have been based on individual magnates' personal relationships to individual kings, such as Gregorius's conflict with Sigurd which caused him to join Inge's faction. Once a choice had been made, however, it typically became permanent and was passed over to the magnate's descendants. Admittedly, there are many exceptions to this, but not so many as to form an argument against the importance of family ties. Friendship should be added to kinship as a basis for faction formation, although there is a sliding transition between the two. Despite the fact that there was no automatic solidarity within the kindred, friends were often chosen among relatives. Additionally, personal relationships were deliberately used to link prominent adherents more closely to their leaders. As in earlier times, the kings gave daughters and other female relatives in marriage to their most trusted adherents. Thus, Erling Skakke, as we have seen, was married to King Sigurd Magnusson's daughter – a result of his close friendship with Inge – while the two Hallkjellsons, Simon and Jon, were married to two daughters of Harald Gille. The kings themselves normally married foreign princesses, if they married at all, but they had mistresses from prominent Norwegian families who served to form alliances, in addition to fulfilling the sexual and emotional needs of such relationships.[55]

The kings' personal links also reached outside the country, which poses the question of the Nordic aspect of the civil wars.[56] To some extent the factional divisions in the 1130s corresponded to similar ones in Denmark. Magnus Sigurdsson was originally married to a daughter of the Danish prince Knud Lavard but repudiated her in 1133, two years after her father had been murdered, probably because he now considered her part of the losing faction in Denmark. There is also a story about him trying to betray Knud's brother Erik Emune during the latter's visit in Norway.[57] However, it turned out that Magnus had backed the wrong horse, as Erik defeated and killed his adversaries, King Niels and his son Magnus, in the Battle of Fodevig in June 1134. This event may have

---

52   E.g. Johnsen, *Fra ættesamfunn*, pp. 57-67 and *passim*; Andersen, *Samlingen av Norge*, pp. 185-201.
53   Sørensen, *Saga og samfund*; Sawyer, *Kings and Vikings*; Gaunt, *Familjeliv i Norden*; Vestergaard, "The System of Kinship", pp. 160-93; Sjöholm, *Sveriges medeltidslagar*; Bagge, *Society and Politics*, pp. 112-17; Hansen, "Slektskap, eiendom og sosiale strategier" and "The Concept of Kinship".
54   Thus Halvdan Koht, *Innhogg og utsyn*, pp. 115-21, and "Norsk historie i lys frå ættehistoria", pp. 89-104.
55   Bagge, *Society and Politics*, pp. 117-21.
56   Sawyer, "The 'Civil Wars' revisited", pp. 44-53, 63-69, underlines the importance of this, but confines herself to listing the genealogies of the various Nordic dynasties.
57   Saxo, *Gesta Danorum*, XIII.11.4-7.

led to Magnus's own attack on Harald two months later, which may thus be regarded as a preemptive measure, aimed at getting rid of his rival before the latter could exploit his alliance with the victorious faction in Denmark. After his victory over Magnus, Harald married Ingrid Ragnvaldsdatter, the daughter of a Swedish prince previously married to the Danish prince Henrik Skadelår, a cousin of Knud, Erik and Magnus. Henrik had been a close friend of Magnus Nielsen and had taken part in the murder of Knud Lavard. He was killed in the Battle of Fodevig. Ingrid's marriage to Harald may thus be regarded as an example of the not unusual practice in the Middle Ages of the victors marrying their fallen enemies' wives. From Harald's point of view, she was a valuable asset, linking him to the royal houses of both neighbouring countries. Ingrid herself is unlikely to have mourned her late husband; according to the sources, her marriage to Henrik was not happy, and at one point she tried to leave him. She defended her son Inge's interests in the later conflicts and formed connections to the leading circles in the country by twice marrying a Norwegian magnate.

However, the alliance between Harald and Erik did not last, as the deposed and mutilated King Magnus managed to persuade Erik to invade Norway in 1137 to aid him in the struggle against Harald's sons. We do not know whether the motive for this was some conflict with Harald[58] or simply a wish to exploit the troubled situation in Norway in order to conquer the country. The invasion failed and Erik was killed shortly afterwards. In the following decades there is little evidence of connections across the borders; the first struggles between Harald's sons were confined to Norway. In 1157, Knud Lavard's son Valdemar defeated his rivals and made himself the sole king of Denmark. Although his position was not uncontested, the victory increased his opportunities to interfere in the neighbouring regions, including Norway. The relationship between the two countries in the 1160s is difficult to untangle; the accounts in the sagas and in Saxo are widely different, but there is some evidence that Valdemar mainly supported Erling's and Magnus's adversaries.[59] This changed in 1170 when Erling became Valdemar's earl and held Viken – which Valdemar claimed as Danish territory – as a fief from him. In the following period there was a firm alliance between the Magnus faction and Denmark; Magnus himself received considerable aid from Denmark as did also the various pretenders claiming to be his descendants. Archbishop Eirik spent his exile there, and the most important of the factions fighting Sverre, the Croziers, was formed on Danish soil. By contrast, the Birch-

---

58 Munch, NFH II, pp. 762 f., 783 f., hints at a deterioration after Harald's victory, possibly because of Harald's marriage to Ingrid. Although she had hardly any reason to hate Erik because of her husband's death, she had two sons with him who might have wanted to avenge their father and who had reasons to fear Erik who ruthlessly exterminated all descendants of his rivals, even his brother and his offspring.
59 Helle, *Norge blir en stat*, pp. 69-73; Arstad, *Kongsemner*, pp. 20 f., 29 f.

legs received support from Sweden. Characteristically, Sverre married a Swedish princess after his victory. The value of Swedish aid, however, is more doubtful. Sweden was weaker than Denmark, and there was almost constant rivalry between two dynasties, that of Erik and that of Sverker. There is therefore little evidence of any substantial Swedish forces intervening in Norway. The greatest value of Sweden was probably that the country served as a place of refuge for Norwegian rebels, although the wilderness and thinly inhabited land in the border regions of the two countries may have served this purpose regardless of the Swedish ruler's consent. This may to some extent explain the fact that the last opposing force against the Birchlegs, the Ribbungs, found refuge in Sweden, although the reason for this could also have been the kinship between the last Ribbung leader, Knut Håkonsson, and some of the leading men in Sweden.[60] As a counterweight against Denmark during the critical phase around 1200, Sverre concluded an alliance with King John of England which in turn formed part of the latter's anti-French network.[61]

The relationships across the borders were important during the civil wars and may even have been more important than the sagas indicate because of their tendency to focus on internal matters. Thus, *Sverris saga* repeatedly states that Magnus received ships and men in Denmark without giving any information of how it happened or the Danish kings' motives in giving this support. Nevertheless, there is little to suggest that the struggles had a general inter-Nordic character with factions based in several countries fighting for power all over the area. Moreover, the sagas give the impression that foreign influence was resented. Massive Danish invasions in Norway were mostly unsuccessful, and pretenders with strong ties to another country had difficulties in being accepted (below, pp. 174-77). So far, the traditional picture of the struggles in each country as internal seems to be correct.

The gradual consolidation of the factions may to some extent serve to explain the length and bitterness of the conflicts. Family loyalty normally led sons to follow their fathers' example and thus to carry the division on from one generation to the other. The urge for revenge for fallen relatives had the same effect. Concerning the continued conflict in the 1160s and 1170s, Snorri points to Erling's strict attitude towards his enemies, which gave them no incentive to seek reconciliation but made them continue their struggle to the bitter end.[62] Although according to his saga Sverre was willing to forgive his enemies and made several attempts to reconcile prominent men from Magnus's faction, he seems to have had much the same effect on his enemies as Erling, possibly in part because of the

---

60   Arstad, *Kongsemner*, pp. 124-28.
61   Benham, "Philip Augustus", pp. 45-49.
62   *HkrME* ch. 37; Bagge, *Society and Politics*, pp. 93-94, 197.

number of enemies killed during his numerous and bloody battles, and partly because of the suspicions about his origin and his lack of connections to the traditional elite. He may also have resembled Erling more than the saga is willing to admit.

Despite these reasons for continued factional division, we still need a structural explanation for the long duration of the conflicts and, above all, for a clear distinction between the period of the civil wars and the periods before and after. Holmsen's demographic-economic explanation may therefore still be valid, even if it fails to explain the division between the factions. However, his idea of a drastic polarisation of society over a relatively short period of time is not easy to reconcile with the recent interpretation of early Norwegian society as fairly aristocratic. Furthermore, although there is some evidence of overpopulation and strain on the resources in Norway as well as in the rest of Europe in the early fourteenth century, it is hardly possible to conclude from this that the situation was the same nearly 200 years earlier. Admittedly, social tension may result from demographic strain long before a population maximum is reached, depending on the existing social structure,[63] but such a crisis does not explain the greater tendency among the magnates to fight one another. Holmsen's resource crisis is likely to have led to greater wealth among the magnates. Although increased wealth may also lead to increased rivalry,[64] there is more to suggest that the problem for the Norwegian aristocracy was poverty rather than wealth.

The end of the Viking expeditions in the first half of the eleventh century would seem to have been the first step in this direction. Although the possibility of gaining wealth by plundering abroad did not completely disappear – it was to some extent replaced by crusades and foreign conquest – it was greatly reduced after the end of the Viking Age. From now on, royal and aristocratic wealth had to be based mainly on the country's own resources, namely on land, as Holmsen points out. There is therefore every reason to expect a development towards greater exploitation of the peasant population, although it is doubtful whether this was sufficient to compensate for the loss of Viking wealth. The question then is: Why did the crisis not come much earlier? Maybe it did, resulting in the violent struggles during the first half of the eleventh century from the reign of the last real Viking king, St Olav, until the death of his half-brother Harald, i.e. in the period 1015-66. Particularly during the latter's reign, a number of prominent magnates were killed. This period can therefore be regarded as an anticipation of the inner struggles of the

---

63 Goldstone, *Revolution*, pp. 31-37, with examples from the English and French Revolution.
64 Cf. the example of Hungary where increased wealth apparently had the same consequences; see Engel, *The Kingdom of St Stephen*, pp. 91-98.

twelfth century, or more likely as a period of such a great reduction in the old aristocracy that it postponed the resource crisis for nearly a hundred years.

Thus, Harald's ruthless policy towards the old aristocracy laid the foundation for a period of stability and an aristocracy loyal to the king. It probably also increased the king's wealth which enabled Harald's successors to attract magnates to their service and reward them. As far as we can see from our meagre sources, there was considerable continuity in the aristocracy in the following period, which is likely to have created a resource crisis. Periods of joint rule, notably the longest (1103-23), may have produced the same effect, as competition between the kings led to increased generosity towards the aristocracy. The king's resources were not endless, and with no inner conflicts and extermination of losers taking place, his possibility of rewarding his followers must have diminished from generation to generation. In addition, new demands on the king's resources, as well as those of the aristocracy, were now being made as a consequence of the introduction of a new religion. The ecclesiastical organisation was built up from a few poor priests in the king's direct service in the 1020s and 1030s to a powerful, aristocratic organisation at the time of the foundation of the Church province in 1152/53.

We have of course no way of calculating the resources available to the king and the aristocracy at any time during the eleventh and twelfth century, nor is there any direct statement in the sources – mainly narratives – about a resource crisis. Generally, any theory about social structure in this period has to be based on assumptions or highly circumstantial evidence. However, we do know that the Church must have increased its wealth considerably, and the absence of inner conflicts makes it likely to assume that an increase in the number of magnates and consequently a reduction in the king's and the individual magnates' resources occurred. Furthermore, in the same way as before, meanness or generosity in kings was important in deciding how much support they received. A decline in the kings' and the magnates' incomes may thus explain the ease with which generous kings could attract clients to their service, the clients' willingness to join them in struggles for the throne, and, above all, the crucial decision that was made in the 1150s and 1160s not to seek reconciliation despite the fact that the rules of succession would seem to indicate that both factions ought to be able to accept the same ruler.

Why, then, did the wars eventually end? The resource crisis would appear to have been solved by the end of the twelfth century through the extermination of a large part of the old aristocracy in a series of battles from the 1170s onwards, plus the confiscation of the losers' estates. Additionally, a psychological explanation seems to be indicated by the agreement between the Birchlegs and the Croziers in 1208. The older and leading men on both sides wanted peace, whereas the younger men who had not yet had the opportunity to gain wealth by plundering wanted the war to continue. A compromise was reached, however; the younger generations in both factions went on a joint raiding expedition to the Orkneys. In 1208, a large number of magnates belonging to the Magnus faction had been killed, whereas many young and ambitious Birchlegs had gained sufficient wealth to prefer keeping what they already had rather than risking everything in continued war. Furthermore, new opportunities for gaining wealth were probably opened up through the expansion of the royal administration. Thus, the resource crisis had solved itself through around half a century of warfare. However, the end of the conflicts did not mean a return to the situation before they started, but considerable social change. This means that we have to re-examine the factors that were previously used to explain the outbreak of the civil wars as consequences rather than causes.

The Consequences of the Civil Wars

Socially, there was a change from an aristocracy of local leaders to an aristocracy of the realm which has often been dated to the reign of Sverre. *Sverris saga* states that many men who had formerly been paupers and robbers were promoted to high rank under Sverre but gives no examples of this actually happening.[65] The saga rarely gives information about the ancestral background and relationship of the leading men of Sverre's faction who are mentioned by name, a fact that does not necessarily indicate that these men were of low origin.[66] Furthermore, membership of the aristocracy is not easily identified. The only criterion in the sources is whether the person in question holds the office of *lendmann* (pl. *lendmenn*; ON *lendr maðr*, pl. *lendir menn*). This office was not hereditary, although there was a certain tendency for men of the same families to be appointed, and the king normally chose wealthy and powerful men (cf. below p. 119). Consequently, Sverre's faction may have included many men of equal wealth and power as those who were known as *lendmenn* but who had not been appointed, perhaps because they had chosen the wrong side at an earlier stage of the internal struggles. Sverre himself seems deliberately to have avoided appointing *lendmenn*, except the very prominent men who belonged to families who had customarily held this office. Instead he used a new kind of royal official, the *sysselmann* (pl. *sysselmenn*, ON *sýslumaðr*, pl. *sýslumenn*), who was more directly subordinated to the king. This policy may, to some extent, explain the imbalance between the number

---

65 *Sverris saga* ch. 40. The only possible example is the *lendr maðr* Ulv of Lauvnes, who is called *þorparasonr* (=son of a cottar) by one of Magnus's men (*Sverris saga* ch. 90), but such abuse need not imply more than that he lacked a social background that suited his rank of *lendr maðr*. See Bagge, "Borgerkrig", p. 169.

66 We know, for example, from *Heimskringla* that Sverre's *lendr maðr* Ulv Fly was the son of one of King Sigurd Haraldsson's leading men, and could trace his ancestry back to a prominent court offical from the mid-eleventh century (*HkrHHard* ch. 37). These facts are not mentioned in *Sverris saga* (Bagge, "Borgerkrig", p. 168).

of *lendmenn* among Sverre's adherents and among the adherents of his adversaries.[67] On the other hand, the fact that Sverre did appoint some *lendmenn* indicates that he might have appointed more if his adherents had included a high number of men belonging to families whose members were accustomed to being promoted in this way.

Thus, although the saga's statement about paupers and robbers rising to the top of society is hardly representative of Sverre's faction, his faction did have a different social composition than that of his adversaries. An examination of the various factions struggling against Erling's regime suggests a gradual deterioration in social status. Håkon Sigurdsson's adherents included a large number of prominent men. At least fourteen of the twenty-five mentioned by name belonged to the social elite, and several of them were descendants of the greatest magnate families in the country.[68] The rest are likely to have been fairly prominent as well; usually only men of some standing are mentioned by name in the sagas. The faction continued to exist after Håkon's death with another son of Sigurd as its king and with largely the same members, although its aristocratic character seems to have been somewhat weakened.[69] The next faction, under Olav Ugjæva ("The Unlucky"), who descended through his mother from King Øystein Magnusson (d. 1123), apparently had no connection to Sigurd and Øystein and is more likely to have been the result of a split in Erling's faction. This faction seems to have had considerable support from wealthy commoners in the inner parts of Eastern Norway.[70] By contrast, the name of the last faction, the Birchlegs, clearly suggests the proletarian background of the majority of its members. The sagas also characterise the original Birchlegs as robbers and poor men. After their conquest of Trondheim in 1176, however, and again after Sverre's victory over Erling in 1179, they are said to have been able to recruit more prominent men.

The general picture emerging from these observations seems reasonable enough. Wealthy and prominent men were less likely to risk everything by taking part in a rebellion, and the repeated failure of Erling's opponents meant that it was mainly those who had nothing to lose who would try again. Characteristically, the most proletarian of the factions resisting Erling was the last one which took up arms at a time when he was in a very strong position, eight years after the previous pretender Olav Ugjæva's defeat and four years after peace was made with Denmark. Only some initial success would have led old sympathisers and ambitious or discontented elements to join them. With the possible exception of the episode of Olav Ugjæva, we can also eliminate a common explanation

---

67 Only eleven *lendmenn* are mentioned on Sverre's side, compared to forty on that of Magnus's; see Storm, "Om Lendermandsklassens Tallrighed", pp. 152 ff., and Bagge, "Borgerkrig", pp. 167, 169.
68 Arstad, *Kongsemner*, pp. 15-17.
69 Ibid., pp. 15-17.
70 Ibid., pp. 27-31.

for the outbreak of new struggles, namely divisions within the victorious faction. Erling and later his son Magnus seem to have been able to hold their faction together; there are only a few examples of defections. Thus, although social division and class struggle were not the origin of the conflicts, there was an increasing difference in the social composition of the factions in the 1160s and 1170s. The importance of the proletarian element during this period may to some extent support Holmsen's idea of the suppression of and increased poverty among the lower classes during the previous period, but can hardly be interpreted as evidence of a class struggle. The proletarians joining the rebellions should not be identified with the people. They were first and foremost warriors, fighting for themselves and their leader and not in any way identifying with the social stratum to which they had originally belonged. Furthermore, the existence of such a proletarian element may to some extent be the result of the wars themselves.

The fact that the faction uniting the majority of the old aristocracy was eventually defeated by a faction largely recruited from lower levels of society leads to two important conclusions. First, this could only happen as the result of better organisation and leadership in Sverre's faction, or in other words, through Sverre's military and organisational genius. *Sverris saga* presents a fascinating picture of a great man and leader, which at least gives some clues to his success and that of his men. In addition to his men's better training and his own tactical and strategic abilities, Sverre shows great skill in leading his men and in obtaining the best possible performance from them. In his battle speeches, as rendered in the saga, Sverre appeals to his men's desire for gain, both of material and immaterial kind. But the saga also gives an impressive portrait of Sverre the man, which suggests the emotional ties between him and his men; Sverre's extraordinary ability as a leader and his appeal to other men, his sensitivity to his men's reactions, his courage, tactical skill, endurance in difficulties and sense of humour, explains why he was able to gather his faction around him, hold it together and lead it from victory to victory.[71]

Second, Sverre's leadership as well as his victory were likely to lead to a different relationship between the king, the aristocracy, and the people. The new elite's attitude to the common people is well illustrated in *Sverris saga*, which shows greater contempt for and hostility towards the peasants than any other of the Old Norse sagas. The bias against the peasants in *Sverris saga* should not, however, be understood as the aristocrats' contempt for the common people but rather as the "professional" warriors' contempt for the non-professionals. In a similar way, the social distance between the leader and his followers would have likely led to a stronger leadership than in the more traditional factions. Admittedly, the saga continually insists on the importance of Sverre having his men's volun-

---

71 Bagge, *From Gang Leader*, pp. 11-26.

tary support. He was not a military commander according to the model of later eras; his leadership was based on his men's trust in him. In practice, however, this gave him a very strong authority, based on a long and impressive record of success. Although this trust was of course personal and would not automatically be transferred to Sverre's successors, it might have been exploited by another strong leader as a basis for a stronger monarchy.

This finally leads us into the much discussed question of Sverre's historical importance. To many nineteenth-century historians, Sverre was the great, towering figure, determining the course of Norwegian history for the following centuries, either directly, or, to Ernst Sars,[72] as a symptom of the evolutionary forces changing Norway from the most aristocratic to the most democratic of the Nordic countries. Twentieth-century scholarship has generally attributed less importance to him, regarding the consolidation of the aristocracy under Erling and Magnus as the foundation of the new society of the subsequent period, the emergence of which Sverre temporarily managed to halt.[73] By contrast, the conclusion from the preceding observations may instead be seen as pointing in the direction of Sverre's crucial importance as the founder of a more strictly hierarchical society than would have been possible if the alternative faction had won. However, we should not underestimate the effect of the conflicts themselves on both factions. The initial formation of factions favoured weak and generous kings and gave the magnates considerable power collectively, whereas the prolonged struggles necessitated discipline and strong leadership, whether from the king himself or from one or a small group of leading magnates. They were also likely to lead to stronger links between the members of the factions and thus within the aristocracy as well. Thus Erling Skakke in many ways seems to form a parallel to Sverre. Erling is not depicted as a traditional hero but as an extremely clever politician and general. According to *Heimskringla*, he was a strict but just and efficient ruler and therefore popular with the people.[74] Snorri gives no detailed description of how he held his faction together, but he implies that trust in Erling's skill and a fear of having him as an enemy were important factors. Although the sagas are vague on this point, Erling probably showed considerable diplomatic skill in uniting the aristocracy under his own leadership as the ruling elite. Additionally, the question of Sverre's long-term importance also depends on how far-reaching the changes were that took place in the following period.

---

72   Sars, *Udsigt* II, pp. 119-78.
73   This applies above all to Schreiner, "Kong Sverre"; Holmsen, *Norges historie*, 227-38, and Lunden, *Norge under Sverreætten*, pp. 129-38, whereas the older generation of Marxist historians, above all Koht, *Kong Sverre*, pp. 62-76, but also to some extent Bull, *Det norske folks* II, pp. 216-31, attribute greater importance to him.
74   *HkrME* ch. 37.

With the reconciliation between the Birchlegs and the Croziers from 1208, and permanently from 1217, a new elite was formed which continued to hold power during the following generations, a situation parallel to the one between 1066 and 1130. This elite was more closely linked to the king and apparently more distant from the common people than the one during the previous period, particularly by being royal office-holders with well-defined rights and duties. The formation of this united elite and the administrative reforms from the late twelfth century onwards represented the first step towards the formation of the aristocracy as an estate that gradually came into being beginning in the late thirteenth century (below pp. 324-29). There are thus two trends in the social composition of the elite: stronger subordination to the king and closer links between the members of the aristocracy; which means that there are trends in the direction of monarchic as well as aristocratic rule.

As we have seen, we can fairly safely rule out the possibility of antagonism between regions as the *origin* of the civil wars. Consistent regional divisions only occurred at a relatively late stage, beginning in the 1160s and then more permanently during Sverre's first years as a pretender. Regional divisions are an almost inevitable consequence of any prolonged war, the warring parties consolidating their hold on particular areas. Warfare during the Norwegian civil wars was very mobile. The towns were few and small, and the first castles were not built until the 1180s. Particularly during the first phase of the wars but also to some extent later, the opposing armies moved around, trying to challenge the enemy and win a decisive victory. As a consequence of these movements, they frequently changed the areas under their control. When, during the more intense struggles from Sverre's uprising and onwards, the factions became more closely attached to particular regions, these divisions could easily be explained by strategical considerations.[75]

Western Norway was always held by the stronger faction or "the established king", by Erling and Magnus during most of the time until 1184 and by Sverre afterwards. This region could only be controlled from the sea, which necessitated a large fleet. A fleet was costly to build and maintain and needed a large crew, in practice drawn from the peasant levy, the *leidang* (ON *leiðangr*). Tactical skill and a better quality of men could largely compensate for a numerical inferiority in land battles. At sea, however, a large number of men were needed to manoeuvre the ships. In addition, it was more difficult to catch the enemy by surprise. While in a land battle, a small but well-trained army could easily cause a numerically superior but qualitatively inferior enemy to flee, in a similar situation at sea such an enemy would have no other alternative than to fight. Finally, it was more difficult

---

[75] See Bagge, "Borgerkrig", pp. 162, 184-188.

to avoid battles against superior enemies at sea than on land, and consequently more difficult to conduct guerrilla warfare.

A fleet was important in Trøndelag and the region around the Oslofjord as well, but both these regions could also be attacked from land. By contrast, the inner parts of Eastern Norway had to be conquered by land warfare, although ships could be used in the great lakes. The difficult terrain of this region, with its large forests and mountainous areas, was ideally suited for guerrilla warfare. In addition, the border regions towards Sweden offered the possibility of retreating into another country. Consequently, rebellions would normally start in the inner parts of Eastern Norway. After some successful fighting, the rebels would then try to gain a foothold in one of the wealthier and more central regions, either Trøndelag or the Oslofjord area, but would find it difficult to control both of them at the same time. These regions would therefore normally be controlled by different factions. Having gained control of one of these regions, the faction in question would then try to assemble a fleet and conquer Western Norway. This pattern is confirmed by a number of examples during the civil wars, particularly from the rebellion of Sverre onwards. Thus it is significant that the Birchlegs started their rebellion in the inner parts of Eastern Norway,[76] while the last rebellion *against* the Birchlegs took place in the same region.

While the regional divisions can explain neither the outbreak of the civil wars nor the faction formation, they point to a significant change in the power basis and the political importance of the factions. The conflicts clearly originated within the elite, and for a long time, the fighting mainly took place between the members of the elite and their retainers and "volunteers". However, the sagas also give a glimpse of the magnates as local leaders who were able to mobilise the people of their districts. During the more intense and prolonged wars from Sverre's period onwards, such mobilisation became a normal phenomenon and larger regions were involved on different sides. The kings and pretenders were not only faction leaders, they became dependent on popular support, which again gave the people more influence on "matters of state", as shown in the royal elections among the two warring factions in 1204 and 1207 respectively when the "people's candidate" won against the "warriors' candidate" on both occasions (below p. 373). Characteristically, as a result of this development the country was divided between the two factions by a formal

---

[76] According to *HkrME* chs. 36-41, the Birchlegs were confined to the inner parts of Eastern Norway and the Oslofjord region during the first two years after taking up arms. Then they obtained ships in the Oslofjord region, went north along the coast and conquered Trondheim. Although they received many new followers in the Trøndelag region, these facts clearly show that they had no original connection with Trøndelag. Sverre differed from the original Birchlegs in moving north instead of south from the inner regions of Eastern Norway, eventually establishing himself in Trøndelag.

settlement in 1208. Earlier, and fairly frequent, periods of co-rule had not led to territorial divisions. Thus, such divisions are a significant phenomenon during the second and third phases of the civil wars, but they are the consequence rather than the cause of the wars.

The regional aspect of the civil wars can also be regarded from another point of view, as consolidation rather than division. With the possible exception of Trøndelag, the regions, namely the four legal areas in which the country was divided, were hardly consolidated mini-kingdoms with a strong feeling among their population that they belonged to a community. They received fairly regular but short visits from the king and had no common organisation apart from the regional assemblies which met once a year and the fact that their areas to some extent corresponded with the ecclesiastical division into dioceses. The later phase of the civil wars must have meant a considerable change in this respect. For around five years, Trøndelag was the permanent residence of a king, Sverre, whose area of power was confined to this region during most of the period. He must have mobilised considerable resources and manpower from the region and thus been a burden to its inhabitants, but, as the saga indicates, must also have taken care not to demand too much to avoid the people turning against him. Western Norway, the region of the established king, changed sides during the period from staunchly supporting King Magnus to being a Birchleg stronghold. Some of the leading families in the region, the kindreds of Blindheim (Møre), Ståreim (Nordfjord), and Gjerde (Sunnhordland), wholly or mostly continued to support the Croziers, which meant that they had to spend most of Sverre's reign in exile in the east. In the west, Sverre was clearly able to recruit others to replace them, and he and his successors seem to have been able to mobilise a considerable loyalty there, as is shown particularly clearly in the election of his grandson, Håkon Håkonsson, in 1217. On this occasion, support from Western Norway proved decisive, whereas Trøndelag tended to support the most prominent local Birchleg family, represented by Skule Bårdsson, half-brother of the late King Inge. By contrast, Sverre never managed to control Eastern Norway, which now became the stronghold of the Croziers who in the period after Sverre's death were confined to this area just as Sverre had been in Trøndelag during his first years.

During the period of Erling Skakke and Sverre the war was also waged in the *ideological* field. The ideological differences concerned three main issues, the first of which was the attitude towards the Church.[77] Magnus's faction concluded an agreement with the Church in the 1160s, granting it privileges, while Magnus received unction and coronation, the first occurrence of this ceremony in Norwegian – and even Scandinavian – his-

---

77   Helle, *Norge blir en stat*, pp. 57-69, 85-90; Gunnes, *Kongens ære*, pp. 269-83.

tory. The Church also supported Magnus's faction against rebels, including Sverre. This alliance marked a new epoch in Norwegian history. After a gradual growth in wealth and importance, the Church now for the first time came forward as a major political factor. The sagas, probably based on Sverre's propaganda, represent the agreement with Erling in 1163/64 as a *quid pro quo*, the Church bolstering Magnus's weak claims on the crown against increased privileges, whereas in reality, Archbishop Øystein Erlendsson was probably already a member of Erling's faction as King Inge's former treasurer.[78] In addition to the coronation, the Church gave strong ideological support to Erling and Magnus, using the Crusading ideology to support his fight against "rebels and criminals". In this respect, Øystein acted as a "party member" as well as a prelate.

As we have seen (p. 47), there is little to suggest a pro-Gregorian or pro-Church ideology as the basis for the formation of the Inge-Erling-Magnus faction. There are even hints in the saga of the Icelandic bishop Torlak that Erling was not particularly well disposed towards the Church.[79] The alliance in 1163/64 must therefore mainly be considered as tactical. Although the sagas' account of the horse trading between Erling and Øystein is a later invention, there is no doubt that the Church had a lot to offer in the situation in which Erling found himself. Admittedly, Magnus's election as king was hardly illegal, as Sverre maintained, but his problem was that his relationship to the dynasty was so distant that many other pretenders had equally strong claims. The ecclesiastical idea of one king ruling the country on God's behalf, and the special protection and dignity granted this king through unction and coronation, formed a strong argument against potential pretenders. These advantages might well justify the concessions to the Church, which, moreover, did not necessarily weaken Erling's faction. The mid-twelfth century seems to have represented the great breakthrough of Norwegian aristocrats entering the Church. Øystein himself is a prominent example. Increased wealth for the Church might serve as a means to promote the interests of cherished members of the ruling faction. Although the ideal of *libertas ecclesiae* might limit the possibility of the ruling elite to reward particular people, the problem was apparently not too big as long as there were close links between the prelates and Erling's faction.

From the prelates' point of view, the privileges were of course a great advantage. As long as they maintained strong personal ties with Erling's faction and kept their identity as members of the aristocracy, they must have considered the support of the faction an acceptable price to pay, especially as the faction in question was also successful. How-

---

[78] Gunnes, *Erkebiskop Øystein*, pp. 89–95; Sandaaker, "Magnus Erlingssons kroning"; Bagge, "Den heroiske tid", pp. 68 f.
[79] Gunnes, *Erkebiskop Øystein*, pp. 240–43.

ever, the prelates should not be regarded solely as aristocrats and faction members; both ideologically and materially they identified themselves with the Church and eventually changed from active participation in the struggles to neutrality and mediation. Sverre's success in the 1180s led to the first reconciliation with Øystein in 1183. When the conflict began again in the 1190s, ecclesiastical principles were apparently more important than factional loyalty, although the two can hardly be completely distinguished from one another. Shortly after Sverre's death in 1202, his son made his peace with the Church, and in the following period the Church took a neutral attitude, with the exception of Bishop Nikolas of Oslo, who had strong family links to the Crozier leaders, but who apparently did not use the ecclesiastical ideology against his adversaries in the same way as Øystein had.

Sverre's answer to his adversaries' ideological mobilisation was both to develop an alternative ideology and to imitate that of his adversaries. In purely ecclesiastical matters, he stood for a traditional "national" Church, headed by the king and in opposition to the Gregorian ideas of the prelates. In *A Speech against the Bishops* from the end of Sverre's reign, an anonymous adherent of his very ingeniously uses Gratian to argue for this point of view.[80] A certain anticlericalism, or at least anti-Gregorianism, continued to exist among Sverre's successors and adherents during the following period.[81] Sverre's anticlericalism in the 1190s may have had something to do with his local attachment to Trøndelag. For a long time the conflict did not concern the Church as a whole, but only Archbishop Eirik (1189-1205) who resided in this region. The issues included lay control over local churches, fines to the Church and the number of men in the archbishop's service. On all these issues Sverre was likely to have the support of the local population and might appear as their champion against the encroachments of the archbishop.

The second ideological issue concerns the opposition between a "traditional" monarchy or monarchy "of the people", and the new, authoritarian and ecclesiastical ideas of kingship by the grace of God. The latter ideology is clearly expressed in Magnus's unction and coronation and the alliance between his faction and the Church in the 1160s, and additionally in the speeches *Sverris saga* attributes to Magnus to defend his right to the throne against Sverre's attacks. Logically, Sverre ought to have embraced more traditional ideas, of which there are also traces in his propaganda, notably his defence of the traditional principle of succession, allowing all sons of a king, whether or not they were legitimate, to ascend to the throne. This idea also accords with the more general attitude in *Sverris saga*, that of the king as the "best man", meaning that the reason for choosing a king from the

---

80 Gunnes, *Kongens ære*; Bagge, "Oratio contra clerum", p. 455.
81 Bagge, *The Political Thought*, pp. 113-54.

royal line was that this line was likely to produce the men with the best qualifications, and thus that Sverre's victories become evidence of his royal descent.[82] However, Sverre also takes over the authoritarian and monarchical ideology, applying it far more consistently than his adversaries in the form of explicit propaganda in *A Speech against the Bishops* and in actual practice in his new organisation of local government. In this context, we are dealing with an "ideological escalation" rather than with two factions fighting one another with different ideological weapons.[83] Sverre also attached great importance to the legitimation the Church was able to give him through unction and coronation. According to the saga, he dreamt that Samuel gave him the royal unction in the same way that he had given it to David, and one of the issues between Archbishop Eirik and him was Sverre's wish to be crowned, which was eventually fulfilled, although without the archbishop's approval, in 1194. Afterwards, he seems to have used his coronation as an argument for his right to the throne. Both he and his grandson and successor, Håkon Håkonsson, made great efforts to obtain divine support in this way.[84] Sverre's ideology thus shows considerable inconcistency, which is probably the result of his pragmatism; he sought ideological support where he could get it.[85]

The third issue may be regarded as a subdivision of the other two: Sverre defending the principle of agnatic succession, and Magnus that of legitimate birth and coronation. The former principle corresponded – more or less exactly – to traditional ideas, the latter to the new ideas introduced by the Church and expressed in the documents issued in connection with the alliance between Magnus's faction and the Church in the 1160s. The opposition between the two principles is brought forward very clearly in *Sverris saga*. However, even this ideological division proved temporary. Magnus's faction later acclaimed a number of alleged illegitimate sons of Magnus as kings, while Sverre's faction chose a son of Sverre's alleged sister Caecilia as its king in 1204 (above p. 46).

Although none of these ideological oppositions can be regarded as the origin of the conflicts, they all contributed to greater cohesiveness within the factions. It may be significant that the use of permanent names corresponded to some extent with the occurrence of ideological divisions.[86] Admittedly, the name "Birchleg" has nothing to do with ideology, and its permanence is due to Sverre's importance and success rather than to ide-

---

82 Bagge, *Society and Politics*, p. 130, and *From Gang Leader*, p. 57. See below pp. 148, 162.
83 Bagge, "Kingship in Medieval Norway", pp. 41-52.
84 Bagge, "Herrens Salvede", pp. 29-34, and *The Political Thought*, pp. 43-49.
85 Bagge, "'Gang leader' eller 'the Lord's anointed'", pp. 114-16.
86 Names of the factions are a novelty in this period. The first faction to have a name were the adherents of Olav Ugjæva who were called *hettusveinar*, i.e. "hat men", possibly after Olav's foster-father, Sigurd Agnhatt (Munch, NFH III, p. 19).

ology. By contrast, after Magnus's death, the Magnus faction repeatedly rebelled against Sverre under different names until the Croziers came forward in 1196 and formed a continuous opposition against the Birchlegs under different kings. Most importantly, the ideological escalation during the civil wars contributed to important changes in government and politics. Dynastic continuity was more strongly emphasised and was eventually formalised in the laws of succession of 1260 and 1273, replacing the mixture of heritage and election with heritage as the sole criterion. The ecclesiastical idea of *rex iustus* was combined with elements of traditional National Church ideas in a powerful ideology of the king as God's representative on earth who was responsible for governing the Church as well as the people. Although Sverre's successors to some extent continued the anticlerical tradition of the Birchlegs, they had to buy their acceptance from the Church with concessions, and in general, the Church strengthened its position in Norwegian society during the following period.

The civil wars led to stronger social, geographical, and ideological divisions, which, however, made a more intense concentration of political power possible, eventually leading to greater unity. Taken together, all three factors examined above contributed to the formation of a more hierarchic and authoritarian society in the following period. The "party discipline" created a more homogenous elite, the regional divisions intensified local government, and the ideological divisions created stronger loyalty between the faction members as well as between their leader and them. Thus the outcome of the civil wars was a strong, stable and centralised government, which permanently brought an end to the internal struggles – clear evidence that the system had changed. In contrast to Holmsen, I believe that this change should not only be explained by long-term social development, but also by the conflicts and the factions themselves. The crisis for the aristocracy was apparently solved both by the elimination of a considerable part of the elite during the struggles and by extending the financial basis of the state through the introduction of fines and regular taxes – the latter clearly as a result of the wars. The new administrative system with *sysselmenn* seems to have been introduced nationwide because of the need to gain firm control of recently conquered areas. And so, the greater cohesiveness and permanence of the factions – notably the Birchlegs – from Sverre's time onwards, together with the "ideological escalation", contributed to the formation of a new elite that was more directly attached to the king's service than the old one. This elite showed greater loyalty to the king while at the same time formed a more homogenous "aristocracy of the realm" which might eventually turn into an estate.

The stages in the formation of a homogenous aristocracy can be followed in *Hákonar saga*. The first step was taken upon the death of the kings on both sides in 1217. Although the Birchlegs had not consulted the Croziers when their king died in the beginning of the year, the latter agreed to recognise Håkon as king. The saga reports that Håkon and Skule hastened to Viken with forty ships, most of them large, and met the leading Croziers in Tønsberg. The negotiations were hard. The Croziers initially demanded to keep all their districts, but in the end had to give up half of them.[87] The Birchlegs' speed and their great force were apparently decisive in achieving this result. During the temporary truce in 1208, the Birchlegs already appeared as the stronger party and the Croziers' will to fight was clearly reduced. On the other hand, the Croziers were not without an alternative; they were looking for a new pretender in Denmark who was actually found somewhat later. There was thus the same difference between those who stood to lose through continued war and those who stood to gain. To this was added the problem of those who directly lost because of the peace, the Croziers who lost their *sysler* to the Birchlegs and their clients. The Crozier leaders who negotiated in Tønsberg probably kept theirs, but many others had good reasons for discontent. This discontent is also largely the explanation for the new rebellions that broke out shortly afterwards, first the Slittungs (1217-18) and then the Ribbungs (1219-27) – both derogatory names like that of the Birchlegs. Like the original Birchlegs, they included some proletarians, but the Ribbungs in particular got considerable support from prominent men.[88] The following conflict cemented the union between the Birchlegs and the Crozier elite, as did probably also the conflict between Håkon and Skule in 1239-40.

In the latter of these conflicts, Håkon seems to have gained the support of the majority of the magnates, including the old Crozier leaders (below pp. 81-85). However, his effort to keep their loyalty during the ensuing war with Skule shows that he could not take their support for granted. Correspondingly, Skule's strategy was to win the majority of the magnates over to his side by some early spectacular victory. In his account of these events, Sturla tries to depict Håkon's victory as evidence of God's intervention and a victory for justice, but the pragmatic considerations referred to above are nevertheless fairly prominent in his text. The king's authority seems to still have been largely based on his success and personal popularity. The monopoly situation after 1240 might work both ways. On the one hand, the lack of alternative candidates might lead the magnates to close ranks around the ruling king; on the other, the party loyalty created during the civil wars was likely to dissolve. Thus, the name "Birchleg" disappeared after Håkon's victory over Skule, except in reference to the past.

---

87   *HH* chs. 27-28.
88   Arstad, "Ribbungopprør".

The Norwegian civil wars appear to have been an important factor in state formation.[89] Denmark's civil wars seem to have been an example of the same, although without the social change within the elite that took place in Norway. The Danish "civil wars" (1134-57) were essentially struggles between factions based on family or other personal relationships ending in a power monopoly for one of them.[90] Although the contrast between the period of struggles and the Valdemarian age of greatness in the following period may have been exaggerated in earlier scholarship, the Valdemar faction had managed to suppress its rivals and was able to consolidate its position by building up a royal administration and by gaining considerable control of the ecclesiastical one. Parallels to Sweden may also be drawn, although internal struggles were more or less continuous in this country. Nevertheless, the victory of the Erik dynasty represented by Birger Jarl in the mid-thirteenth century led to centralisation and the development of a stronger royal government.

However, centralisation is by no means a universal result of internal struggles. Germany is usually regarded as the primary example of the opposite; the collapse of the royal government has often been understood as the result of the two long periods of internal struggles: the Investiture Contest 1075-1125 and the struggle for the succession between Henry VI's death in 1198 and the victory of his son Frederick II in 1215. Both periods strengthened the magnates who were able to force the rival kings to buy their support through privileges and concessions and who consolidated their hold over local territories.[91] The same forces were at work during the English Civil War 1138-52 when the magnates frequently changed sides if it could serve their interests. Although this conflict led to no long-term disaster, possibly because of its relative brevity and the fact that it was followed by Henry II's strong government, it can hardly be said to have led to a consolidation of the central government. Nor can we say this about the two periods of internal struggles in Germany, despite the fact that more recent scholarship tends to regard them as less disastrous than scholars in the nineteenth and early twentieth century did.[92]

It seems that both these examples differ from the Scandinavian ones in the composition and permanence of the factions. This may seem more surprising in the case of Germany than in England, as the strong ideological divisions in the former were absent in the latter. Nor, as we have seen, were the ideological divisions particularly strong in Scandinavia. Two, probably interrelated, factors may be able to explain the difference. The

---

89   Cf. Gluckman, *Politics*, pp. 123-68, with various examples from Africa which point to rebellions consolidating existing regimes, whereas in Norway they led to important changes.
90   Hermanson, *Släkt, vänner och makt*, pp. 209-50.
91   Barraclough, *Medieval Germany*, pp. 135-64, 219-46.
92   Keller, *Zwischen regionaler Begrenzung*, pp. 164-216, and Althoff, *Kaiser Heinrich IV*, pp. 86-115.

first is military technology and organisation. In this early period of Scandinavian internal struggles, there were few castles and their military importance was limited. Consequently, victory depended on the strength of a mobile army or, particularly in Norway, fleet. As long as he had no castle, the military strength of the individual magnate was limited, as was his possibility of demanding favours in return for participation. Victory depended on unity; consequently, the logical division was into two factions of approximately equal size fighting one another.[93] The second factor is the less gentlemanly way of waging war in Scandinavia. A struggle normally ended in the death of one of the pretenders, and many prominent men were killed on both sides. As we have seen, this tended to keep the factions together, probably also prolonging the struggles. By contrast, pretenders, magnates and other prominent men were rarely killed in English and Continental struggles, and if they were taken captive, they were normally released against ransom. Revenge was therefore rarely a motive for keeping the factions together. This may be due to the existence of castles which were difficult to conquer and which usually changed hands as the result of negotiated surrender,[94] and to the greater difference between the elite and the common people, which created solidarity within this group across the struggling factions.

From the Civil Wars to the Age of Greatness

The consolidation resulting from the civil wars led to a military organisation and to a technology more similar to the European one, first and foremost in Denmark, to a lesser extent in Sweden and only to a very limited extent in Norway. The two former countries experienced a new series of internal struggles, Denmark during most of the period from 1241-1340 and Sweden in the early fourteenth century, and then again from around 1360, and at frequent intervals during the entire period until 1523. These conflicts were mainly about succession, but they may have been aggravated by the new military technology which strengthened the power of the aristocracy compared to that of the king and may thus partly be understood as conflicts between monarchy and aristocracy. By contrast, Norway entered what is commonly regarded as its period of greatness after the end of the civil wars in 1240. This was the era when the realm governed by the Norwegian king reached its greatest extension; the political organisation, as well as literature, learning, and the arts, were most fully developed and the king of Norway was able to conduct an active foreign policy towards the neighbouring countries as well as within the traditional sphere of interest to the north and across the North Sea. This period will form the main topic in

---

[93] Bagge, "Borgerkrig og statsutvikling", pp. 158 f. with reference to Barth, "Segmentary Opposition", pp. 72 ff.
[94] Cf. Gillingham, "Conquering the Barbarians" and "1066 and the Introduction of Chivalry".

the following discussion about the degree and kind of state formation in Norway in the Middle Ages. The end of this period is usually placed either in 1319, when the last agnatic descendant of Sverre, Håkon V, died and Norway entered the union with Sweden, the first in a series of Nordic unions, or in 1349, when the Black Death struck the country. It seems clear, however, that the Black Death was a more important factor in Norway's later decline than the union with Sweden. In principle, the union of 1319 should be regarded as a victory rather than a defeat for Norwegian foreign policy. In the first phase, during Magnus Eriksson's minority from 1319-31, the two countries were ruled independently of each other. Magnus's coming of age in 1331 meant a closer relationship between the two countries and a greater emphasis on Swedish affairs by the king, which is likely to have led to the decision to end the union in 1343-44. From an administrative point of view, however, things continued largely as they had in the previous period, and the first half of the fourteenth century contains the richest source material for studying the government in practice during Norway's period of greatness. By contrast, although the Black Death did not immediately lead to great changes in government and administration, the sources from the following period are more meagre and show a reduced activity in the central government. At the end of the century, the union of Kalmar in 1397 led to a radical change, the introduction of a central government for all three Nordic countries in Denmark. In the following discussion, the main emphasis will be on the period 1240-1350 and on the issue of break or continuity in comparison to the previous period. However, the focus will be on the period as a whole, which means that less attention will be paid to the Nordic unions and the changes that took place in the period from 1319-50.

War, Military Organisation and Social Change

"War made the state, and the state made war". Charles Tilly's famous dictum about the early modern state applies to Norway in the Middle Ages as well, at least to the extent that the early formation of the Norwegian kingdom was largely the result of successful warfare. War was also decisive for the continued existence of kingdoms and for their internal development. One of the most distinctive features of the exports from the centre to the periphery of medieval Europe is in the field of military technology. People in the northern and western periphery, the British Isles and Scandinavia, fought on foot, or, in the latter case, largely on ships, whereas light cavalry dominated in the east. The military technology of the centre, with heavy cavalry supplemented by crossbow-men and castles, was to a greater or lesser extent introduced to both areas, through either conquest or imitation.[1] This in turn had social consequences. The new military technology was more costly than the old and led to greater professionalisation, which in turn meant a greater distinction between the aristocracy and the common people. According to common opinion, Norway was less affected by the military changes than its neighbouring countries while similar changes took place in the social and economic field. The following chapter will therefore discuss the degree of military professionalisation after the end of the civil wars, foreign policy and the use of military forces during this period, the changes in social structure and the distribution of wealth from the Viking Age until the early fourteenth century and, finally, the relationship between military and social change.

From Plunder to Internal Exploitation

The formation of the agrarian or feudal state in Western Europe in the Middle Ages is often explained by the transition from an economy of plunder to an economy of agrarian exploitation, or, perhaps more adequately, by an increasing reliance on the latter rather than on the former.[2] Thus, the Carolingian Empire, and to some extent also its Ottonian successor, are considered to have received a large part of their surplus from great, annual campaigns against various neighbouring peoples in which a considerable part of the

---

1   Bartlett, *The Making*, pp. 60-84.
2   Duby, *Guerriers et paysans*; Reuter, *Germany*, pp. 174-80.

population took part. In the following period, a military specialisation took place, leading to a clearer division between an aristocratic elite and the great mass of the population who were reduced to being peasants, spending most of their time producing the surplus necessary to support the military and clerical elite. Wars were of course still fought, but were increasingly about gaining control over land. A shift in this direction seems to have taken place over large parts of Western Europe in the post-Carolingian period, although with great variations in the tempo as well as in the extent of the process. Nor was the Carolingian Empire solely based on plunder, as great estates, worked by slaves or unfree peasants, clearly existed in some regions, as, for instance, in the area around Paris.[3]

If we turn to Scandinavia, we find evidence of an economy of plunder in the period immediately before the formation of kingdoms, namely in the Viking Age. The Viking expeditions created a substantial surplus and a considerable amount of manpower, in the form of combined rowers and warriors, was needed to gain this surplus. The relationship between the surplus gained from the Viking expeditions and the corresponding surplus gained later from agrarian exploitation can be illustrated by the fact that the annual tax income of the king of Norway in the High Middle Ages, 3000 marks, was between two and fifteen percent of each of the payments the Vikings received from the king of England in the late tenth and early eleventh centuries for ending their attacks.[4] Admittedly, Norway was the poorest of the three Scandinavian kingdoms and probably particularly poor in terms of ready money, and the payments were received at a time when the Vikings were at the peak of their power. There is nevertheless much to indicate that the Viking expeditions created a great surplus and even from an economic point of view, that the Viking Age was the golden age of Scandinavia, while the inclusion of the region into Christian Europe represented a decline. The end of the Viking Age meant an end to, or at least a strong reduction of, the opportunity for obtaining wealth from plundering expeditions abroad as well as a reduced importance of the trade route between east and west over Scandinavia. Ordinary warfare plus crusades against the pagans might to some extent compensate for this loss, notably in Denmark, as might trade in commodities that were abundant in the north (furs and later also fish), but the only really substantial way of compensating would be to increase internal exploitation.

A development in this direction seems to have taken place in all three Nordic kingdoms, but more so in Denmark and Sweden than in Norway. As in the rest of Europe, this at least partly coincided with a change in military technology, from mass mobilisation to elite

---

[3] Wickham, "Rural Society".
[4] Steinnes, *Gamal skatteskipnad* I, pp.169 f. The Vikings received £10,000 in 991, £16,000 in 994 and £36,000 in 1006. Finally, Cnut the Great imposed a tax of £72,000 in 1018; see Sawyer, "The Viking Expansion", p. 118. One mark *brend* (burnt) is c. 50 g. silver, whereas one pound sterling is 320 g.

forces and from sea warfare to land warfare. Heavy cavalry was used from the first half of the twelfth century in Denmark and somewhat later in Sweden. From the late twelfth century onwards, the Danish peasant levy was gradually replaced by full-time warriors, who were exempt from taxes in return for their service while the tax burden on the rest of the population increased.[5] The formal expression of the new order in Sweden came in *Alsnö stadga* (the Statute of Alsnö), probably in 1280, which is usually regarded as a kind of "constitution" for the Swedish aristocracy, confirming the principle of specialised military service on horseback in return for privileges.[6] The last step in the transition was the introduction of castles, the first of which were built in the twelfth century. In the 1240s, the king of Denmark had twenty of them, while ten belonged to the duke of Southern Jutland.

The great expansion took place in the following period as the consequence of the more intense internal struggles from 1286 and also during Erik Menved's wars in the early fourteenth century. After a rebellion in Jutland, which was put down in 1313, the king built a number of castles in this region, while up to then most of the castles had been in the border regions and along strategic sea passages. In Sweden, small and simple castles were built in the twelfth century, while the really large and elaborate constructions date from the thirteenth century, particularly from its second half, and the following centuries. These new castles could serve as residences for the king and his representatives and as fortifications. Similar changes took place in East Central Europe. Western military technology was adapted, partly through imitation, partly as the result of defeats against Western – notably German – armies and partly as result of the Mongols' attacks in 1241-42 and later. The result was a strengthening of the top aristocracy who resided in stone castles and shared the king's governing power.[7]

The new military technology not only improved the king's military capacity, it also led to far-reaching administrative and social changes. The castles were expensive both to build and maintain but enabled the king to exploit the people more efficiently. Roughly speaking, under favourable circumstances an elite force of heavy cavalry could defeat an ordinary levy on foot that was ten times as large. In a similar way, the modern castles that became common in this period covered only a fragment of the ground of earlier fortifications, but were far taller.[8] Thus the castles gave their small number of defenders an even greater advantage against attackers than the armour and other equipment of a knight. However, the reduced number of warriors did not lead to any reduction in the

---

5   Löfqvist, *Riddarväsen*, pp. 24-66; Bagge, "The Scandinavian Kingdoms", pp. 730 f.
6   Löfqvist, *Riddarväsen*, pp. 89-97; Rosén, *Svensk historia* I, pp. 162 f.
7   Bartlett, *The Making*, pp. 70-76; Engel, *The Realm of St Stephen*, pp. 104 f., 125-28, 147-51, 183-86; Rowell, "The Central European Kingdoms", pp. 754-68.
8   Bartlett, *The Making*, pp. 65-70.

costs of warfare, probably rather the contrary. Thus, in reducing the number of armed men the king needed, and increasing the cost of keeping them, the castles furthered the transition from the populary levy to a limited number of royal retainers, financed by taxes from the majority of the population. Both for strategic reasons and because of the cost and labour necessary to build and keep the castles, they were also used as administrative centres. The older royal administration consisted of a combination of stewards of the king's estates, who fulfilled various functions on behalf of their master, and allies among the local magnates. Basically, this system was retained in Denmark and Sweden, but was transformed by the development of castles, their commanders becoming the governors of the surrounding area.

The Origin and Development of the leidang

This sketch of the Danish and Swedish development corresponds to the opinion of the majority of scholars, and it is also widely accepted that Norway differed from its neighbouring countries by only partially developing a military elite. Recently, however, the startingpoint for this development – the existence of a popular levy – has been questioned. The traditional opinion among historians has been that the military system in the Scandinavian countries from the Viking Age onwards was based on the popular levy (No. *leidang*, ON *leiðangr*, Da. *leding*, Sw. *ledung*), which was primarily intended for sea warfare. Thus warfare was probably the origin of the earliest political organisation of the country and the earliest tax. This organisation is only to be found in the eastern part of Sweden and only in the coastal regions of Norway. According to the sagas, the *leidang* was introduced by King Håkon the Good to replace the hated tax imposed upon the people by his father, Harald Finehair, after his conquest of the country.[9] Like in other Germanic societies, taxes were a sign of submission and therefore considered degrading. The change to the *leidang* meant that the people became free once more and that their financial and military contribution was in their own interest. There is little to suggest that this information is based on any authentic tradition; it most likely expresses thirteenth-century ideas about the origin of a central political authority in the country and of the people's duties towards the contemporary ruler.[10] It does, however, indicate a close connection between military service and the payment of taxes. The main evidence for the *leidang* organisation in Norway are the laws of Gulating and Frostating, probably dating from the late elev-

9   The tax is mentioned in *Fsk.* p. 19. *Egils saga* ch. 4 and *HkrHH* ch. 6 mention in addition that Harald appropriated all land (*óðall*) in the country, a statement that has led to an extensive scholarly discussion. See a summary with references in Andersen, *Samlingen*, pp. 87-91.
10 Bagge, *The Political Thought*, pp. 34-38.

enth or early twelfth centuries. This organisation has been considered an important point in favour of the widespread idea in nineteenth- and early twentieth-century Scandinavian scholarship of a relatively democratic society in the early Middle Ages, in which the common people (ON *bændr*) had a decisive influence on political decisions.

The revision of this view is based on the recent tendency to regard early medieval society as highly aristocratic. In the case of Denmark, Niels Lund has revived Erik Arup's interpretation, maintaining that no real *leding* existed until around 1170, when the *leding* obligations were specified in the extant laws of Scania and Jutland. Lund rejects the earlier interpretation that these provisions reduced the number of men mobilised for the *leding* and that they formed the first step towards the replacement of the popular levy with an elite force.[11] Lund also discusses the Norwegian and Swedish organisation, concluding that there is little evidence that these existed very much earlier. Lund's scepticism here accords well with the recent tendency to reject the idea of an oral law existing for a century or more until it was written down. Although Scandinavian kings must already have had considerable forces at their disposal in the Viking period, as indicated above all by the Danish conquest of England in the early eleventh century, according to Lund these forces consisted of magnates and their clients who joined the king on their own accord. Such mobilisations are mentioned repeatedly in the narrative sources.

However, Lund's thesis is not entirely convincing. In the case of Denmark, one problem is that the *leding* is actually mentioned as a duty incumbent on the peasants in King Cnut's privilege for the cathedral chapter of Lund of 1085, nearly hundred years earlier than its alleged introduction.[12] Lund explains this reference as an attempt to introduce a new burden on the population, making a connection with the notorious tax that provoked the rebellion leading to the king's death. In a similar way, he interprets the occasional references to the *leding* in the following period as pertaining to a tax.[13] Although Lund is probably right in emphasising the importance of the magnates, we cannot exclude the possibility that their mobilisations were based on a system similar to the *leding* as described in the later laws. It is difficult to imagine a popular levy entirely outside the control of the magnates (below p. 80). Moreover, the considerable archaeological evidence of military mobilisation in Denmark in the tenth century, including the large camps which have now

---

11 Lund, *Lid, leding og landeværn*, pp. 246-74 and *passim*; see also "Is leidang a Nordic or European phenomenon?".
12 Here the chapter is given jurisdiction over the land donated by the king with three exceptions, including failure to participate in the *leding*: "Si expedicionem neglexerit. erga regem emendet" (*Gåvobrevet 1085*, p. 15). See also Albrectsen's and Gelting's reviews, Malmros, "Kongemagt og leding" and "Fyrstedigtningens kildeværdi" and Lund, "Leding, bønder og inerti" and "Leding, skjaldekvad og bønder".
13 Lund, *Lid, leding og landeværn*, pp. 164-86.

been dated by dendrochronology to the reign of Harald Bluetooth (c. 960-85), points in the direction of a stronger monarchy than Lund, and before him Arup, have been willing to admit to. Would not this monarchy have been able to create a military organisation, even if in practice it was largely controlled by the magnates? The contemporary military forces, based on sea power, also necessitated a large number of men as rowers, making a good argument for introducing an organisation like the *leding*.

In the case of Norway, Lund fails to discuss the admittedly limited evidence that does exist for the *leidang* before the extant laws, namely some refences in the skaldic poetry. The word *leidang* is used in a contemporary skaldic poem on the battle of Hjørungavåg in the 980s, and Øyvind Finnsson's memorial poem on King Håkon the Good (*Hákonarmál*) mentions mobilisation of the people from Rogaland to Hålogaland before the king's last battle at Fitjar around 960.[14] Finally, there are some striking similarities between the Norwegian *leidang* organisation and the contemporary Anglo-Saxon *fyrd* which may support the sagas' claim that it was introduced by Håkon the Good who had been brought up in England.[15]

None of these statements forms incontrovertible evidence of the early age of the *leidang* organisation. The word *leidang* need not be a technical term in this early period, and we have no guarantee that skaldic poems were actually contemporary. However, in a situation where the evidence is extremely scanty, it seems a better method to use what little there is in order to arrive at the most likely conclusion than to believe that everything begins at the time when we happen to have reasonably good sources. At least in the case of Norway, two *a priori* arguments may give further support to this conclusion. First, sea warfare necessitated greater forces than land warfare. A large number of rowers were needed to move the ships, and at least in some cases the ships had to be moved during battle, so fighters were needed in addition to the rowers. Whatever form of military organisation existed at the time must have included a large part of the ordinary population. This organisation may well have differed from the *leidang* we meet in the regional laws, and the men may have been commanded by local leaders rather than the king, although we should not underestimate the power and importance of the king in at least parts of the country. There is an impressive series of royal estates along the western coast, particularly in Hordaland.[16] Second, if the Norwegian *leidang* was organised at the time when the laws were written down, in the late eleventh or early twelfth century, we have to explain why this happened just then, in a period when there were apparently no threats

---

14 See discussion of these poems in Ersland, "Kongshird", pp. 30 f.
15 Helle, *Gulatingslova* p. 35; Williams, "Hákon *Aðalsteins fóstri*", pp. 119-23.
16 Iversen, *Eiendom,* pp. 380-90.

from external enemies. From this point of view, the troubled period in the tenth or early eleventh century would seem much more likely. An actual danger is more likely to make people accept new burdens than an imagined one. The reign of Håkon the Good, who only ruled Western Norway and repeatedly had to defend himself against his cousins' attacks, would therefore seem the ideal period, as the oldest *leidang* organisation apparently only comprised this region.

Håkon's *leidang* may even have been anticipated by earlier, more local organisations as a system of boathouses built for large ships but according to a different pattern than the medieval organisation identified in the Roman and Migration period. Instead of the even distribution found in the *skipreide* system, these boathouses are concentrated in certain areas: Lista, the central area of Hordaland, and, above all, the area around present-day Stavanger.[17] There is also evidence of the ship as an important element in the social organisation of the Viking period and earlier. There was a strong solidarity between the members of the crew, united under the leadership of one lord, a unit that might also have played a political role. The fact that ships were used for burials is significant in this context. A possible Christian parallel is the storing of mast, sails and other *leidang* equipment in the church, a practice that may have a symbolic and not only a practical explanation.[18] Although this function of the ship is not necessarily evidence of the early origin of the *leidang*, it does suggest a social organisation that could be adapted to the military needs of the early rulers of larger regions.

The laws of Frostating and Gulating describe in detail the organisation of the *leidang* and the peasants' duty to contribute to it.[19] The coastal regions in the north and west were divided into districts called *skipreidar* which had to build and man one ship and provision the crew for a period of two months. Viken, the area around the Oslofjord, probably also had a *leidang* organisation from early on, but here the *skipreide* organisation was not introduced until the late thirteenth century. Instead, the *leidang* was based on the *lide*, the number of farms which were to muster one man for the mobilisation.[20] The inland regions had no *leidang* organisation. Most scholars have also maintained that taxes were not introduced there until the late thirteenth century. Dørum, however, argues that the inland taxes were considerably older as well as higher than usually believed, although lower than in the coastal regions.[21] According to the laws the total number of ships for the

---

17 Myhre, "Boathouses". Stylegard and Grimm, "Boathouses", question some of Myhre's conclusions, pointing to uncertainties in the dating of many of the finds.
18 Varenius, "Maritime Warfare"; Larsson, *Ships and Society*; Garipzanov, "Ships" with references.
19 F VII and G 295-315.
20 Bjørkvik, *"Leidang"*, cols. 432-42.
21 Dørum, *Romerike*, pp. 237-68 with references to earlier scholars.

whole country is 308, most of which had twenty seats, whereas those of the Gulatingslag (the Law District of Gulating), which had the heaviest burden, had twenty-five seats. This increase was most probably introduced in the late twelfth century, possibly by King Sverre. The laws do not state how many men there were per seat; the minimum of two, one rower on each side, will give a total of around 14,000, but most probably there were more; it might have been necessary to fight and to row at the same time, and it would be necessary to change rowers when moving fast over long distances. An addition to a law manuscript from around 1400 lists 100 men per ship, which would mean four or five per seat, depending on the size of the ship. Based on this information, most historians have calculated the total number to be 26,000-33,000.[22]

Although the *leidang* could also be used for land warfare, sea warfare was the most important, at least until the thirteenth century. Most decisive battles during the civil wars took place at sea, and in addition, sea transport gave extra mobility. Sea battles were fought in a similar manner as land battles. The ships were placed alongside one another; the fighting took place on the deck and could move from ship to ship.[23] However, manoeuvring before joining the ships might give advantages or disantvantages that could prove decisive for the outcome.[24] Large and tall ships posed a tactical advantage, similar to walls in land warfare. On the other hand, smaller and lower ships were faster and easier to manoeuvre. A way of combining the two advantages was to use removable towers and castles during battle.

The link between military service and taxation is formed by the contributions to the provisioning of the *leidang* force. The king had an obvious interest in getting hold of these contributions, and the peasants might also have been willing to give them in return for not having to serve in person. The Law of Gulating implies that the *leidang* should be paid yearly and gives rules for the payment in the case of people moving from one district to another, whereas the Law of Frostating only mentions the military service.[25] The first explicit mention of the *leidang* as a tax in this region is in *Sverris saga*, when Magnus Erlingsson returns to Trøndelag in 1182 after three years' absence, during which the region had been

22 Hertzberg, "Ledingsmandskabets", Bull, *Leding*, p. 42, and Ersland, "Kongshird", pp. 85 f. By contrast, Helle, *Norge blir en stat*, p. 191, and *Gulatingslova*, pp. 165-67, arrives at the minimum of 14,000 by reckoning only one man per oar.
23 Wamers, "The 9th Century Danish-Norwegian Conflict".
24 E.g. in the Battle of Fimreite in 1184, where Magnus Erlingsson conducted a "siege" of Sverre's largest ship, the enormous Mariasuden, while Sverre's men attacked Magnus's fleet from the opposite end and conquered one ship after another until the remainder of Magnus's ship sunk under the weight of all the men who had fled from the conquered ones. If Magnus, whose men were numerically superior, had followed the advice of one of his most experienced men and attacked Sverre's smaller ships first, the battle may have had a different outcome. See *Ss.* chs. 88-93 and Bagge, *From Gang Leader*, pp. 42-48, and "Sårt biter sulten lus", pp. 19-22.
25 G 298; cf. Bull, *Leding*, p. 38.

under Sverre's rule. Magnus then directs severe accusations against the peasants and demands *leidang* and other dues for the last three years.[26] As stated in the saga, this implies that the *leidang* was now well established as a regular tax. We cannot therefore exclude the possibility that the tax in the Frostatingslag may be as old as the one in Gulatingslag. However, the king's words in the saga are not an exact rendering of what was actually said and may reflect a more established practice at the time the saga was written in the early thirteenth century, possibly as late as around 1220 (below p. 162 n. 75). *A priori* it would also seem a likely hypothesis that the civil wars contributed to this result. Although the fact that it was a duty for the peasants to contribute provisions implied a close connection between military service and taxation,[27] the increasing use of elite forces during this period and the presence of such forces in "negotiations" with the peasants may easily explain why such a tax was increased or introduced in new regions.[28] During the civil wars, the amount that had to be paid probably depended on the particular king's strength and the forces he brought with him to the meeting with the peasants.[29] The relevant passage in the National Law a hundred years later clearly gives the impression of a compromise: the king should not demand more *leidang* in peacetime than half of the amount due in war, unless the peasants were willing to grant him more out of love and with the consent of good men. In return, the king promised not to demand any other taxes, except free transport and the rent of his farms as due according to the laws.[30] Thus, the National Law still seems to regard the regular *leidang* as a favour granted to the king and in principle open to negotiations which may in turn suggest that the compromise was fairly recent, perhaps from some time near the end of the civil wars or even later. It has been suggested that the *leidang* was not established as a regular tax until the late thirteenth or early fourteenth century.[31]

The examples we have of the actual use of the *leidang* give a similar picture. Generally, the sagas indicate a flexible use of the *leidang* from both parties in the conflict. The *leidang* was mobilised in selected parts of the country and parts of the force were probably persuaded to fight longer than the norm through some kind of compensation, thus turning it into a kind of semiprofessional force. Various combinations of contributions in kind and in men seem to have been devised in particular cases. However, there are also some indications that rules existed for how much the king might use the *leidang*. Early in 1197 Sverre held meetings with the people in Hålogaland, Trøndelag and Møre and demanded

---

26   *Ss.* ch. 69; Orning, *Uforutsigbarhet* pp. 208 f.
27   Ersland, "Kongshird", p. 55.
28   Bull, *Leding*, pp. 43-45.
29   Orning, *Uforutsigbarhet*, pp. 206-38.
30   L III.1.
31   Lunden, *Sverreættens*, p. 298; Dørum, "Materiell basis", pp. 90 f.

leidang. Somewhat later the same year, he apparently also mobilised other parts of Western Norway. With this force he went eastwards and defeated the Croziers in Oslo.[32] The next year, however, he seems to have been helpless against the Croziers who were able to conquer most of the country. It apparently did not occur to Sverre to mobilise the *leidang* once more. He did, however, go to Trondheim which he managed to hold against the Croziers, and early in 1199 he succeeded in persuading the people of Trøndelag to build ships for him, which he used to defeat the Croziers at Strindsjøen, a battle that became the turningpoint in the war.[33] It is clear from the description in the saga, however, that this was a voluntary contribution. The saga does not directly mention a military *leidang* in Trøndelag, although the fact that the next year Sverre dismissed the force from Trøndelag from his great mobilisation against the Croziers in Eastern Norway points in this direction. With the exception of the people of Trøndelag, this latter mobilisation looks similar to the one in 1197, and it also reached a climax in a battle in Oslo. In a similar way, in 1181 and 1184 Sverre was able to fight sea battles with large fleets which are likely to have been manned by *leidang* forces, although the saga does not directly say so, while his forces were apparently smaller in the meantime. This may be related to the strategic situation but may also suggest, as the examples from 1197 and 1200,[34] that the *leidang* could not be mobilised every year. A possible exception, however, might be Magnus Erlingsson's mobilisations in 1180 and 1181. Magnus mobilised the whole of Western Norway before the Battle of Ilevollene (1180), but left for Denmark after his defeat.[35] He returned from there the next spring and had a considerably larger fleet than Sverre in the Battle of Nordnes in 1181. Despite his defeat there, he was also able to pursue Sverre to Trondheim.[36] The saga does not directly state where Magnus recruited his men on this occasion, but Eastern Norway is an obvious possibility. He probably also had some men from Denmark, and, given his popularity, he may also have been able to recruit volunteers from parts of Western Norway. On his return from Denmark in 1184, he stopped several places along the coast on his way to Fimreite and was able to recruit men there. The saga explicitly mentions that people from Sogn came out in boats and entered Magnus's ship to join him. Magnus's eloquence in the meetings he held is also mentioned as a reason why people joined him.[37]

The same pattern seems to be repeated after the civil wars. Håkon Håkonsson mobilised the *leidang* against Denmark in 1253 and then again in 1256. After his enormous

---

32   *Ss*. chs. 133-36.
33   *Ss*. chs. 154; cf. 158-59.
34   *Ss*. chs. 162-65.
35   *Ss*. chs. 44, 48.
36   *Ss*. chs. 52-58.
37   *Ss*. chs. 83-85, 87.

mobilisation in his failed attempt to defend the Hebrides and Man in 1263, there was no question of another mobilisation the next year. However, peace was not achieved until 1266. Did King Magnus – Håkon's successor – wait for three years until it was possible to mobilise the *leidang* once more, but then decided for a peace settlement instead? And did a realistic threat of a new expedition contribute to the relatively favourable conditions (from a Norwegian point of view) in the Treaty of Perth in 1266? Later, during the war with Denmark, the *leidang* was mobilised both in 1289 and 1290, but we do not know whether the forces came from the same part of the country. After the latter of these expeditions, there was a hiatus until 1293. A major mobilisation was then planned for 1295 in alliance with Duke Valdemar of Southern Jutland which led to the treaty of Hindsgavl before any fighting took place.[38]

There is thus no direct example of a full *leidang* being mobilised from the same region in two successive years. Together with some later examples, this may even suggest that the late medieval development of a new tax every three years, called *utfareleidang*, which amounted to the full contribution of an actual mobilisation but without the participation of armed men, may have some basis in an implicit rule that the king was only entitled to mobilise the *leidang* every three years.[39] In any case, there were certainly limits to how much the king could demand. This not only depended on custom but also on the king's personal popularity, and here Magnus was more successful than Sverre. Magnus's mobilisation before Fimreite may also illustrate the sliding transition between the popular levy and the elite forces. Neither equipment nor training meant any absolute barrier between the popular levy and the elite forces, unlike the heavy cavalry in countries like England, France, and Germany.

Leidang *and Elite Forces*

The *leidang* was probably never the only military force. There is archaeological evidence of elite forces from the first centuries AD,[40] and the opposition between the popular levy and the elite warriors attached to the service of kings and magnates occurs in the skaldic poetry. It is also difficult to imagine the Viking expeditions without a certain professional element, although there may well have been a sliding transition between the professional

---

[38] Fagerland, *Krigføring og politisk kultur*, pp. 98-108.
[39] *Utfareleidang* as a tax is mentioned in the regency government's ordinance of 1280 (below p. 304) as a duty incumbent on the Church which was exempt from active participation in war. Thus, the tax may only have been intended at this time as a financial contribution to war from non-participants. According to Bjørkvik, "Leidang", cols. 439 f., the authorities only managed to levy it in some districts. Cf. also the rule in the Law of Scania that *udgærdsleding* should only be ordered every four years (Lund, *Lið, leding og landeværn*, pp. 247-49).
[40] Skre, *Herredømmet*, pp. 251-66.

and the "popular" element during this period as well as during the civil wars. In practice, the two seem to have been mixed in various ways. *Lendmenn* and local magnates appear in practice to have mobilised and commanded the *leidang* often, usually supplemented by their own trusted men.[41] However, the arrival of Sverre on the stage increased the importance of the elite forces. The Birchlegs who accepted Sverre as their leader early in 1177 were, according to the saga, poor men without proper dress or arms who had suffered a severe defeat and who were only willing to continue the war because they had no other option. Sverre's military genius consisted in making these men into a formidable elite force and leading them to a series of victories which made him the lord of the country. Although Sverre was an excellent tactician, his various tricks were not in themselves particularly advanced, but they needed loyal, motivated, and disciplined men in order to be carried out successfully.[42] In addition, Sverre also introduced another novelty, namely castles. He built Sion in Trondheim in 1180 as well as a castle in Bergen in the 1190s. The castles were apparently intended to secure some kind of permanent foothold in the towns, as they could be held by a small number of men against superior forces. By contrast, the only means of holding a town earlier had been to tie down a large number of men who could then not be used elsewhere. Consequently, control over towns had frequently changed between the factions. Although it could not prevent the enemy from capturing the town, it could prevent him from gaining permanent control over it and force him to detach a large part of his army in besieging the castle. The castles and the elite force thus served the same purpose, to enable a smaller force to defeat or equal with a larger one. Both kinds of forces would have to be supported by contributions from the common people and were also eminently able to enforce such contributions. It would therefore seem that Sverre's reign became a step in the development from a military force based on broad participation by the common people to one based on a military elite financed by the surplus of the peasants' production. The attitude to the common people in *Sverris saga* also supports this. The saga normally gives a very negative description of the performance of the peasant levy and openly admits that Sverre's Birchlegs were unpopular with the people.[43] Nevertheless,

---

[41] See Snorri's references to mobilisation of the *leidang* in the saga of St Olav: Erling Skjalgsson's ship when participating in a *stefnoleiðangr* (=*leidang* in connection with negotiations, *HkrOH* ch. 22); Finn Arnesson mobilising the *leidang* in Hålogaland, including the forces mustered by Tore Hund (*HkrOH* ch. 139), and Gregorius Dagsson mobilising men from the region to defend himself against the Geirstenssons (*Msk.* p. 452; transl. p. 397). See also Ersland, "Kongshird", pp. 50 f. *Sverris saga* contains several references to local magnates mobilising the people against Sverre, which should probably be understood as *leidang* (e.g. *Ss.* chs. 16, 21, 23).

[42] Bagge, *From Gang Leader*, pp. 20-51, and "Sårt biter sulten lus", pp. 12-18.

[43] Lunden, *Norge under Sverreætten*, pp. 65 ff.; Bagge, *From Gang Leader*, pp. 65-71.

the castles do not seem to have played a decisive role during the civil wars; mobile forces, at sea or on land, were still more important.[44]

The last phase of the civil wars, Skule's rebellion in 1239-40, can be understood to some extent as an encounter between the *leidang* and the professional forces.[45] Skule, who had less support than Håkon and thus had to rely on quality rather than quantity, had a numerically inferior but well trained and equipped force. He planned the rebellion well in advance by seeking information about the enemy's movements and preventing Håkon and his men from doing the same. He started the rebellion by proclaiming himself king on 6 November 1239, at an apparently unsuitable time of the year to start a war, as is illustrated by the fact that his attempt to catch Håkon by surprise by sending a fleet to Bergen failed because of bad weather. However, a winter expedition favoured numerical inferiority because of the difficulties in obtaining provisions. Skule was therefore able to consolidate his position by killing Håkon's men in Trøndelag and the adjacent area, taking over their districts and receiving provisions for an expedition southwards.

According to the saga, Håkon, having learned of Skule's rebellion, immediately announced the news to his men and the townspeople, ordered a general mobilisation, and assembled his forces in Bergen where he remained until he moved to Trondheim in the beginning of February. This apparent passivity earned him the nickname "Sleep" from his enemies. Some modern historians regard this as one of Sturla's rare admissions of Håkon's dullness and mediocrity.[46] Given the situation surrounding the composition of the saga, this is a very unlikely assumption.[47] Furthermore, the nickname contrasts markedly with Håkon's energy and determination later in the war, and with the war's favourable outcome from Håkon's point of view, which is probably Sturla's reason for mentioning this criticism of Håkon. There would actually seem to be very good reasons for Håkon to postpone his attack on Skule during the winter of 1239-40. He could not expect to catch Skule by surprise. Consequently, if Skule did not want a battle in Trondheim – which he had every reason to avoid, given Håkon's numerical superiority – he would certainly leave for Eastern Norway before Håkon's arrival. From Håkon's point of view, the later he did so, the better, as this delay would give Håkon's men in the region more time to prepare the defence. If Skule would have attacked Eastern Norway immediately after Christmas, without waiting for Håkon to move, then Håkon would have been in a better position to reinforce his men in Eastern Norway if he remained in Bergen than if he was on his

---

44   Arstad, "… underlig forgjaget", pp. 48-51, and "Castle Warfare", pp. 163-67.
45   The following account of Skule's strategy is based on Arstad, "Strategi". For the account of Håkon's movements, see also Bagge, *Gang Leader*, pp. 133-39.
46   Koht, "Skule jarl", p. 429; Holmsen, *Norges historie*, p. 253.
47   Bagge, *From Gang Leader*, pp. 91-93.

way to Trondheim. In connection with Håkon's journey to Trondheim, Sturla actually mentions that the king, shortly after having learned about Skule's rebellion, had sent a letter to Knut Håkonsson (the former Ribbung leader) in Viken, who was one of Skule's rivals, giving him the rank of earl and asking him to prepare for the defence of Eastern Norway.[48] Finally, Sturla describes in some detail Håkon's Christmas celebrations and the great expenses he incurred. Because he had to provide for such a great number of men and the revenues from Viken were not forthcoming, he had his silver plate broken up and distributed.[49] A modern minister of war might think that Håkon's silver plate could have been spent for a more useful purpose in such a situation, but showing generosity was probably the most profitable behaviour in which Håkon could have engaged. As the stronger party, Håkon's main aim was to preserve his men's loyalty and force Skule to attack with largely inferior forces.

It appears from Sturla's account that Håkon, having arrived in Trondheim, was not too anxious about Skule's movement southwards. During his stay in the town he received a message that Knut and the *lendmenn* had around 3000 men with them and expected to be able to defeat Skule should he attack them.[50] Consequently, Håkon preferred to wait in Trondheim, apparently to prevent Skule from returning to the town after a defeat, while at the same time keeping watch on his adherents in Trøndelag. He abstained from plundering their farms, giving them until 14 April (the beginning of summer) to make a settlement with him.[51] He probably expected to receive news of Skule's defeat before that date, which would have made these men submit.

However, Håkon's calculation failed. Despite great numerical inferiority – 1200 against nearly 3000 men, Skule defeated Håkon's men in the Battle of Låka (9 March) near Eidsvoll. Skule managed to entice the Birchlegs, who trusted in their great numerical superiority, to attack uphill and in deep snow, whereas Skule's men had trampled the snow under them so that it was hard and they could move more easily. After this victory, the way to Oslo was open for Skule and he entered the town. Håkon's strategic situation was suddenly changed after this defeat. He could no longer trust in his numerical superiority and wait for Skule to attack; he would himself have to attack by reaching Oslo as soon as possible to prevent Skule from gaining the whole of Eastern Norway, including the loyalty of Håkon's former adherents in the region. He made settlements with some of Skule's men in Trondheim – the saga does not mention what happened to the farms of those who did not settle with Håkon – and captured those of Skule's ships that he found

[48] *HH* ch. 212.
[49] *HH* ch. 210.
[50] *HH* ch. 216.
[51] *HH* ch. 214.

useful, destroying the rest. Thus, for a time at least, he had secured his own superiority at sea while bringing Skule into a difficult situation similar to that of Sverre during his setbacks of 1181-83 and 1197-99 when he was confined to waging war on land. Having had his son Håkon acclaimed king at Øreting – clearly in order to settle the succession in case he was himself killed in battle – Håkon took his fleet southwards along the coast to attack Skule in Oslo. He had luck with the wind, arrived early in Oslo and managed to catch Skule by surprise and defeat him, a defeat that proved decisive. Skule then retreated to Trondheim where he was deserted by most of his adherents and finally attacked and killed by his relative, Åsolv of Austrått, who had earlier defected to Håkon because of a conflict over some land.

Most historians have regarded Skule's rebellion as doomed at the outset.[52] This is probably not correct. Knut Arstad has recently given good arguments for the contrary point of view and put Skule's strategy and reliance on elite forces in a broader perspective: the exclusive reliance on elite forces was not confined to Sverre's early years but was repeated by the Croziers under Erling Stonewall (1204-07) and the Ribbungs under Sigurd (1218-26) and with great success. Both these leaders won spectacular victories over far more numerous *leidang* forces and may have served as Skule's models.[53] Arstad is probably right on both these points. Skule's strategy may well have been based on lessons from these leaders – against whom he had actually fought – and the importance of having the numerical superiority might have seemed less obvious at the time than to modern historians. All these examples, however, including that of Sverre, show the ability of the elite forces to win battles but not to win the war. The Croziers, the Ribbungs and Skule were all defeated; the first two admittedly only after the death of their great leaders, and Sverre did not become sole king until he had mobilised a sufficient force of the *leidang* to win sea battles.

In Skule's case, even the battle of Låka shows his precarious position. To win he had to combine offensive strategy with defensive tactics. He moved with great speed against the enemy, but having encountered him, he had to entice him to attack as the defender had a clear advantage in a pitched battle, particularly under the conditions prevailing at Låka, but also in summer. To achieve this, he had to leave a very advantageous position in favour of a less advantageous one where the enemy, trusting in his numerical superiority, decided to attack. After such a defeat, however, how likely would the enemy be to repeat this decision? Through his numerical advantage, Håkon would have been able to force Skule not only to choose an offensive strategy but also offensive tactics in which he had less chances

---

52 Holmsen, *Norges historie*, pp. 252-55; Lunden, *Norge under Sverreætten*, pp. 203-8; Helle, *Under kirke og kongemakt*, p. 77.
53 Arstad, "Strategi", pp. 51-54.

of success. Skule could thus hardly win the war with the help of elite forces alone; the danger from Håkon's point of view was that his impressive victory at Låka might lead to a shift of loyalty in Eastern Norway in Skule's favour which would enable him to gain the larger number of men. This was what Håkon rushed to Oslo to prevent.

It is not impossible that Skule could have succeeded if he had won the battle in Oslo or, alternatively, if Håkon had been delayed so much that Skule had gained control over Eastern Norway. He might at least have achieved a favourable arrangement with Håkon. Although Håkon could expect some loyalty by virtue of having been the recognised king for more than twenty years as well as, most probably, because of greater personal popularity, neither advantage was so great that it would have been impossible for Skule to make a sufficient number of men change sides if he improved his position radically.[54] The aftermath of the Battle of Oslo nevertheless shows the difference between the two antagonists' position. While Håkon reacted to the defeat at Låka with great energy and the mobilisation of a large force, Skule's forces dwindled away after the defeat in Oslo, despite the fact that he was able to withraw from the battle with a substantial part of them intact.[55] Skule was now in a similar situation as Sverre during his early years. He still had an army and he might still be able to fight in Trøndelag and Eastern Norway. The saga reports a discussion among Skule's men about what to do. The men from Eastern Norway advised Skule to keep to the border regions and gather men from there to renew the attack, while those from Trøndelag wanted to return to Trondheim and get ships there, "for Norwegians are used to moving by ships if they are waging war."[56] This was the advice taken, but no ships were manned. Most of Skule's men left him and fairly easily came to terms with Håkon, while Skule himself remained in Trondheim, waiting for the inevitable. Whether or not Skule's men knew about Håkon's destruction of Skule's fleet is of little importance; Skule would in any case be largely numerically inferior at sea and would hardly have any chance of success. His only chance was guerrilla warfare of the kind Sverre had conducted during his first years. However, neither Skule's character nor the situation made it very likely that he could repeat Sverre's success. There is little to suggest that the kind of men Skule relied on were willing to risk everything to follow him around in forests and mountains when they could keep what they had by making their peace with Håkon. After many years of warfare, the willingness to risk everything in a rebellion was probably less than in 1177 and, moreover, Sverre's success was an exception and not easily repeated. From this point of view, Skule's rebellion represents a return to normality. Support from the leading men

---

54 Arstad, "Strategi", pp. 42-45.
55 *HH* ch. 235.
56 "ok sogdu þat Nordmanna hatt at fara aa skipum, ef þeir skulu ofrid hallda" (*HH* ch. 232).

in the country, and for them by the people, was decisive; the *leidang*, supplemented by a limited number of elite forces in the service of magnates, would normally, at least in the long run, defeat a numerically inferior force even if the latter was of better quality and was better led. At least this was the conclusion likely to have been drawn from the civil wars. To what extent did the following period, with internal peace and stronger involvement with other countries demand changes in the military means and organisation?

The Norwegian Empire and its Foreign Policy until 1319

As we have seen, the distinction between internal and foreign policy only emerged gradually with a clearer division between the three Nordic kingdoms. The external and internal struggles in the tenth and eleventh centuries eventually resulted in a division of land between the three centres of power in Scandinavia which was mostly respected until the mid-thirteenth century. Although the internal struggles often involved more than one country, there were apparently no systematic attempts at conquest at the cost of the neighbouring countries. Moreover, all three countries had their natural field of expansion outside Scandinavia: Denmark in Northern Germany and along the southern and eastern shore of the Baltic Sea, Sweden further north and east in the same area, and Norway in Finnmark and towards the Kola peninsula and in the islands north and west of the North Sea. In the case of Norway, alternative routes of expansion were blocked until the mid-thirteenth century. The long Swedish-Norwegian border area mainly consisted of mountains, forest and thinly inhabited land which served as protection for both countries, and Denmark to the south, as the strongest of the Scandinavian countries, was more likely to expand at the cost of Norway than vice versa. The west and north were also natural directions of expansion in a period when the main military power was sea power and the majority of the kings had their background as Viking chieftains. Some of the sagas state that Harald Finehair made an expedition to the Orkneys, but this may well have been a later invention.[57] Olav Tryggvason and St Olav, who both had backgrounds

---

57 Sawyer, "Harald Fairhair and the British Isles", and *Kings and Vikings*, pp. 13, 111, rejects this information, as does Wærdahl, *Norges konges rike*, pp. 49-51, while Bjørgo, "Makt og avmakt", pp. 23-32, and Helle, "Den opphavlige Vestlandsregionen", pp. 16 f., accept it. Sawyer is clearly right when pointing to the lack of independent evidence for the saga tradition. The saga writers may well have invented Harald's conquest to bolster later Norwegian claims on the islands. Less convincing is his argument from the explanation in the saga of the immigration to Iceland as a reaction to Harald's tyranny: as the immigrants had also come from the British Isles, Harald's conquest must have reached even them. First, it is doubtful whether we can attribute such a degree of consistency to the saga writers. Second, and most important, the tradition of Harald causing the emigration to Iceland was rejected by Halvdan Koht because it was incompatible with his chronology for the oldest history of Norway which he posed as an alternative to the chronology of sagas. However, Koht's chronology rests on weak foundations. See above p. 25 n. 14.

as Vikings and mercenaries in the British Isles, also sought influence in this area. In 1066, St Olav's half-brother and successor Harald Hardrada invaded England in order to claim the throne in his capacity as Cnut the Great's successor after Edward Confessor had died without issue. Harald was defeated and killed in the Battle of Stamford Bridge, and none of his successors tried to follow his example. However, the western isles, largely inhabited by people of Scandinvian descent, still belonged to the Norwegian sphere of interest. Around the turn of the next century Magnus Barelegs (1093-1103) spent most of his reign on conquests in the west, gained control over the Orkneys, the Hebrides and Man, and fought to establish a foothold in Ireland, where he was killed. His successors gave up Ireland, but upheld the claim on the islands. The rulers there had to recognise the king of Norway as their overlord, and in certain periods the king of Norway was also able to assert some control over them. This claim was strengthened through the foundation of the Norwegian archdiocese in 1152/53, in which all these islands were included. They also played some part in the Norwegian civil wars; one of the rebellions against Sverre started in the Orkneys. After it was put down, the earl Harald Maddadson had to accept Sverre as his direct overlord, and, at least for some time, the islands became more strongly linked to the king of Norway.[58]

Having quelled Skule's rebellion, Håkon Håkonsson spent the last twenty-three years of his long reign on various foreign enterprises, partly offensive, partly defensive. He sought to strengthen Norwegian control over the islands in the west and was partially successful. However, the Norwegian revival in this area coincided with a similar one in Scotland, directed at the Hebrides and Man which were just off the western coast of Scotland and of course much closer to this country than to Norway. Alexander II was on the brink of attacking the islands when he suddenly died in 1249, leaving a son, Alexander III, who was a minor. When he came of age, Alexander continued his father's policy, first trying to buy the islands and then, when King Håkon refused, attacking them. Håkon responded by launching an expedition against Scotland, arriving with a fleet of 120-200 ships in July 1263. His strategy was the same as during his earlier expeditions to Denmark (below pp. 89-91): to force the enemy to concessions through a demonstration of power and, if necessary, to enforce the message by plundering the coast. The Scots, however, started negotiations which they managed to drag out until the autumn when they knew that the Norwegians would have to withdraw. Some plundering expeditions were carried out but with little effect, as the Scots' army followed on land and prevented the Norwegians from going ashore. Håkon also had difficulties with the *leidang* men, many of whom deserted, and finally he had to withdraw to the Orkneys where he died on 13 December. His son

---

58   Imsen, "Earldom and Kingdom", pp. 164-69.

and successor Magnus took up negotiations with the Scots and ceded the islands in return for an annual sum in the Peace of Perth on 2 July 1266.

Given the position of the islands, just off the coast of Scotland and very distant from Norway, as well as Scotland's strength at the time, this result would seem almost inevitable. In addition, diplomatic reasons made it next to impossible to continue the war in the 1260s.[59] The key factor here was England. King Alexander of Scotland was married to a daughter of King Henry III of England who had also been King Håkon's friend for a long time, a friendship that was expressed in frequent diplomatic missions and exchange of gifts and in regular trading connections. For Henry III, it would therefore be natural to mediate between the two enemies, the more so as English interests were best served by status quo. If the king of England could not have the islands himself, it was clearly better that they be controlled by a distant power like Norway than by a close one like Scotland. King Henry therefore sought to prevent the war in a letter to King Håkon late in 1262. His possibility for intervening, however, was limited because of the conflict with the barons. The period of Scottish-Norwegian negotiations in 1264-66 coincided with the most dramatic phase of this conflict, King Henry's defeat and captivity in the Battle of Lewes on 14 May 1264 and his victory and Simon of Montfort's death in the Battle of Evesham on 4 August 1265. In this period, King Henry depended on Scottish support and thus had to throw his full weight behind the Scottish cause in the negotiations. Thus, King Magnus risked having both kingdoms on the British Isles as his enemies if he continued the war. Against this background, peace was the only realistic alternative. Given the situation, the conditions were also fairly favourable. Apart from the annual sum, which came to be paid irregularly or not at all, he received a guarantee for his possession of the Orkneys and Shetland. The Scots also admitted that the islands had belonged to Norway, which provided the reason for the payments.

The loss of the Hebrides and Man was to some extent compensated by Greenland and Iceland submitting to the Norwegian king, the former in 1261 and the latter in 1262-64.[60] Greenland was very distant and hardly of great importance as a possession. Although the trading of valuable commodities like furs and walrus teeth was of some importance, the connection to Norway was probably more important for the Greenlanders than for the Norwegians. Iceland was also distant but closer and more accessible than Greenland. Iceland was not a very rich country but did possess some valuable commodities, the most important of which was wool cloth (*vadmål*), but also luxury items like hunting birds; Icelandic falcons were, according to Emperor Frederick II, the best. From the thirteenth

---

59 For the following, see Bjørgo, "Makt og avmakt", pp. 70-81.
60 Bjørgo, *Makt og avmakt*, pp. 68-70.

century onwards, the Icelandic fisheries became more important and some fish was exported. In return for these products, Iceland imported grain – which they could grow only in very small quantities – and various luxury products for the elite.[61] Most of the traded goods went on Norwegian ships, as the Icelanders were not able to build ships because of their lack of wood. The Icelanders thus had similar interests as the Greenlanders in the relationship with Norway. The attempts to make the Icelanders submit to the Norwegian king started in the beginning of Håkon's reign and did not succeed until its very end. There was no question of a Norwegian conquest; the country was probably too distant as well as too poor to feed an army for any length of time. Instead, King Håkon engaged various Icelandic chieftains to work for his cause in return for power and privileges. For a long time, these attempts met with little success, as the chieftains usually forgot their promises when they returned from Norway. From 1237 onwards, however, King Håkon, in cooperation with the archbishop, managed to impose Norwegian bishops on the Icelandic sees. After Duke Skule's fall in 1240 he was also able to work more systematically on his Icelandic project and managed to play the various conflicting chieftains off against one another. In the 1250s, he controlled most of the Icelandic chieftaincies and was able to distribute them to his favourites. Given this, the final submission in the beginning of the next decade was only a formal expression of what had already been the political reality. However, the Icelanders did not surrender unconditionally, but agreed with the king on certain conditions.[62] The main political institutions, like the Allthing, continued to exist, although in a different form, and in the first period after the submission, the country was governed by an Icelandic chieftain as the king's representative. In the following period, Norwegian influence increased, reaching its peak during Håkon V's reign.[63]

Perhaps the most important initiative King Håkon undertook in the north was his involvement in Northern Norway. As we have seen, there is evidence that strong chieftains existed in Helgeland and the Lofoten area from far back in history, and these areas were also included in the Norwegian kingdom that was formed in the tenth and eleventh centuries. The region further north, however, was a kind of no man's land, mainly inhabited by Sami people, where Norwegians, Swedes, Russians and others sought to get hold of the wealth of the area – furs, walrus teeth and falcons – by trade, plundering or taxation.[64]

61   Torsteinsson, *Island*, pp. 31, 75 f., 105-7.
62   The basis for the union between Norway and Iceland was, according to Icelandic historians, two treaties from 1262-64 and 1302 respectively, preserved in manuscripts from the sixteenth century. Recently, Patricia Bulhosa, *Icelanders and the Kings of Norway*, has maintained that the treaties are forgeries from the early fifteenth century. See also Helgi Þorlaksson's review which defends the traditional point of view.
63   Wærdahl, *Norges konges rike*, pp. 167-90.
64   For this and the following, see Opsahl, *I kongenes tid*, pp. 211-16, and Hansen and Olsen, *Samenes historie*, pp. 150-61.

The sagas regard the "Finn tax" (the tax from the Sami which was apparently farmed out), which apparently became a royal monopoly during the reign of St Olav, as one of the greatest privileges granted to the king's favourites (below p. 185). In the thirteenth century, Norwegian involvement in the far north became stronger. Population growth and a lack of agricultural land in the south made Norwegians take up land as far north as Troms, and the king and the Church began missionary activity among the Sami. Håkon Håkonsson built a church in Troms in what is now the town of Tromsø, and sought to protect Norwegian interests in the north by negotiating a treaty with Novgorod, a rival power in this area. Although the peace between the two countries did not last, King Håkon had taken an important step in moving the Norwegian border further into the no man's land in the north. The time for reaching an agreement was a favourable one, as the prince of Novgorod was involved in the struggle against the Mongols. The saga mentions this struggle as a reason for Håkon declining a proposal to his daughter.[65] Finding the conditions in Novgorod too insecure, he married her off in Castile instead. Håkon also allowed some refugees from the Mongols to settle in Northern Norway. Håkon Håkonsson's expansion to the north was continued by his grandson and successor Håkon V, who built a castle in Vardø, not far from the present Russian border.

From the mid-thirteenth century, Norwegian foreign policy became increasingly oriented towards the neighbouring countries to the east and south, Sweden and Denmark. After nearly a hundred years of relative peace, stability and an active foreign policy in Denmark, struggles for the throne broke out between the sons of Valdemar II the Victorious after his death in 1241, which gave King Håkon an opportunity to intervene.[66] He started by approaching Sweden whose ruler, Earl Birger, had complained about Håkon's expedition across the border to fight the Ribbungs in 1225. This matter was settled at a meeting in 1249 which also led to the marriage between Håkon's eldest son, also named Håkon, and Birger's daughter Rikitza. In the following years, Håkon tried to intervene in Denmark several times, partly with and partly without Swedish aid. Whereas the saga explains Håkon's attacks against Denmark as a reaction to the Danes plundering Norwegian ships, modern historians have regarded this as a pretext for attempting to annex the wealthy region of Halland, just across the Norwegian border.[67] However, it is difficult to regard Håkon's actions in the 1250s as particularly aggressive, considering the opportunity the turmoil in Denmark at that time offered for foreign intervention. Only once did Håkon actually go to war in Denmark, during a brief period in 1256, after which peace

---

65   *HH* ch. 271.
66   For the following, see *HH* chs. 276-86; Helle, *Norge blir en stat*, pp. 128-30; and Bjørgo, "Makt og avmakt", pp. 65-70.
67   Helle, *Norge blir en stat*, pp. 128-30; Bjørgo, "Makt og avmakt", pp. 65-69.

was achieved without territorial gain. A joint expedition with the Swedes in 1252 was cancelled when the Swedes did not turn up, and an expedition in 1253 ended in negotiations without any fighting. On both occasions, Håkon received less support from the Swedes than expected, probably because they did not want Norwegian expansion across the Göta Älv, their only channel to the sea on the western coast. Håkon may well have wanted a slice of Danish territory, but was very reluctant to use military means to obtain this end.

This becomes particularly clear in 1259, when Håkon arrived in Denmark to aid King Christoffer whom he had recently befriended but who, he learned, had just died. The country was in a desperate situation. Just before his death, Christoffer suffered a crushing defeat against his nephew Erik, son of the late King Abel, and his ally Jaromir who had invaded Denmark on behalf of the Church after Christoffer was excommunicated. At the same time, the Holsteiners attacked from the south. Instead of exploiting the situation, however, Håkon returned to Norway. Two years later, when the regency for Christoffer's son Erik Klipping (led by his mother, Margrete Sambiria) was still facing serious problems, Håkon took advantage of the crisis by marrying his son Magnus to Ingeborg, a daughter of the late King Erik Plovpenning who had been murdered by his brother Abel in 1250. The year before, Birger's son Valdemar had married Ingeborg's sister Sofia, which linked the rulers of both Nordic kingdoms to the same Danish sideline.[68]

The late King Erik had left four daughters who, according to normal custom, were entitled to an inheritance or a dowry, which the regency government, in order to avoid further divisions of the royal lands, sought to deny them by placing them in convents. Thus, the marriage gave Håkon and his descendants a legitimate claim in Denmark. Under favourable circumstance it might also lead to a dynastic alliance. Sons from the marriage – of which there were actually two, Eirik and Håkon – would be high on the list of heirs to the Danish throne, competing with the Abel line for the succession if King Erik died without sons. Sofia's Swedish marriage may also have been of some importance; Håkon hardly wanted the Swedes to have a better claim in Denmark than himself. Thus, Håkon clearly felt that he needed a legitimate claim on Danish land. The reason for this is not necessarily that Håkon was always scrupulously just, as the saga will have it, but that he was a cautious strategist who did not regard his military resources as sufficient to wage a war of conquest against Denmark, despite the situation there. Although the *leidang* was a considerable force, it in principle could only be used to defend the country itself or its possessions. Exceptions were later made to this rule, but Håkon either did not succeed in persuading the magnates and the people to agree to them or he did not try. Another

---

68 Paludan, "Tiden 1241-1340", p. 499; Rasmussen, "Kong Eriks døtre".

weakness of the *leidang* was that it could only be used for a limited period, although such restrictions were normal in the Middle Ages. Thus earlier historians are probably correct in attributing a wish for territorial gain in Denmark to Håkon but not in regarding his actions in the 1250s as a war of conquest. Håkon sought to achieve his aims through diplomacy and a marriage alliance, using his armed forces primarily to stage power demonstrations and only turning to military action as a last resort.

A comparison between Håkon's two military interventions raises the question: Why did he not simply give up the Hebrides and concentrate on Denmark instead? His lordship over the Hebrides was hardly very profitable; whatever the wealth of the islands themselves, the profit the king of Norway gained from them was small, as his control of them was far less than of Shetland and the Orkneys.[69] They were too distant and too close to Scotland, which had now become strong enough to compete for control over them. By contrast, Halland was a wealthy region because of its rich fisheries, and situated just across the border from Norway, while the ruling Danish dynasty was in a desperate situation around 1260. Thus, gaining Halland would seem to be easier as well as more profitable than defending the Hebrides. Nevertheless, Håkon spent more energy on the latter than on the former. The reason for this cannot be *Realpolitik*, at least not directly. Håkon had a well-established claim to the former territory but not to the latter. The saga may therefore be right in depicting him as the just king who defended his own rights while respecting those of others. Generally, medieval rulers would normally seem to have appealed to some kind of legal claim when starting a war against their Christian counterparts, although the justice of such claims may of course have been open to discussion. This was not only a question of the king's conscience but of the possibility for obtaining support from his men or from potential allies. In Håkon's case, his decision to defend the Hebrides concerned his honour, which is also implied in the saga. When the Scottish king offered to buy the islands from Håkon – which in hindsight would seem to have been an attractive offer – Håkon, according to the saga, replied that he was not so poor that he needed to sell his land to others. In the case of Denmark, the lack of a claim might mean difficulties in finding allies in the country, maybe even sufficient support from his own men, and the danger of a counterattack in the case of a Danish revival. Thus, Håkon must have regarded the marriage between Magnus and Ingebjørg as essential for continuing his Danish policy.

Håkon's successor Magnus largely took over his father's foreign policy but did not attempt any further expansion. Having made peace with Scotland in 1266, he managed

---

69   Sawyer, *Kings and Vikings*, pp. 110-12; Wærdahl, *Norges konges rike*, pp. 166-70; Bjørkvik, "Grenselandproblem".

to normalise the relationship with England and Scotland in the following years. On 21 August 1269, he concluded the Treaty of Winchester with England which granted free trade between the two countries. He developed a good relationship with King Edward I of England and also approached King Alexander III of Scotland. Within Scandinavia, he did raise the claim for his wife's inheritance but was not willing to go to war against Denmark. However, Magnus's peaceful policy might also have included some dangers. In 1275, the king of Sweden, Valdemar, was deposed by his brother Magnus with Danish aid, but received support from Norway. The new Swedish king eventually concluded an alliance with Denmark which was later sealed by a double marriage and which brought Sweden on the side of the ruling Danish dynasty. Thus, the deposed Swedish king enjoyed the Norwegian king's support without ever regaining his kingdom, whereas the ruling kings of the two neighbouring countries – both stronger and more populous – became united in a double marriage alliance.

After Magnus's death in 1280, the regency for his sons, probably strongly influenced by the dowager queen, intensified the attempts to claim her dowry. They started a diplomatic offensive for this purpose, probably with support from the Danish opposition. At the same time, however, they put restrictions on the German trade that provoked a conflict with the German towns which then organised a blockade of Norway in which Denmark took part. The government found it best to seek an arrangement with the Germans, but the situation became even more serious when at the same time the Earl Alv Erlingsson attacked and plundered German ships, contrary to the promises issued by the government. The result was King Magnus of Sweden's arbitration in Kalmar in 1285, according to which the king of Norway had to pay a fine of 6000 marks to the towns and revoke the restrictions on German trade. Learning from bitter experience, King Eirik, later in his reign, as well as his successor Håkon V consistently tried to avoid conflicts with Denmark and the German towns at the same time, as appears most clearly from the fact that the great offensive against Denmark in 1295 was preceded by an agreement with the German towns and the extension of their privileges.[70]

Shortly after the defeat in Kalmar, a new opportunity to interfere in Denmark presented itself. The Danish king Erik Klipping was murdered in 1286 and a number of the most prominent Danish magnates were accused of the murder. The murder remains an unsolved mystery, despite a number of hypotheses in the Middle Ages as well as in modern times. A widespread opinion that is still held today is that those convicted were actually innocent and that the accusation was a political move from the circle surrounding Queen Agnes, the widow of the late king, to get rid of their enemies. The convicted

---

70   Helle, *Norge blir en stat*, p. 257.

Danish magnates found refuge in Norway, and with their help King Eirik of Norway and his brother Duke Håkon launched a series of raids on Denmark which ended in a temporary peace in Hindsgavl in 1295 with favourable conditions from the Norwegian point of view.

The friendship with the two British kingdoms continued during a large part of Eirik's reign. Eirik himself married a daughter of his grandfather's old enemy, Alexander III, in 1281. The immediate aim of this marriage may have been to secure an ally in the coming conflict with the German towns. During this conflict, King Eirik was also able to profit from his father's friendship with King Edward I of England who refused to join the German trade boycott of Norway. The relationship with England and Scotland took a new turn at King Alexander's sudden death in 1286.[71] Queen Margaret had already died in 1283 but left a daughter with the same name who then became the nearest heir to the Scottish throne. Through King Edward's mediation the Scottish regents agreed to receive her as queen in 1289, and shortly afterwards she was betrothed to Edward's son, the future Edward II. However, the young Queen Margaret died on the Orkneys on her way to Scotland in 1290. In the following years, prolonged negotiations were conducted over the Scottish succession which ended in the parliament in Berwick-on-Tweed in 1292, presided over by Edward I. Here King Eirik also presented his claims as his daughter's heir. At the same time, he married Isabella, the granddaughter of one of the Scottish pretenders, Robert Bruce. Even if King Eirik did not seriously expect to become king of Scotland, he certainly hoped to profit from his good relationship to Edward I by gaining some financial advantages. He may also have hoped that Edward would favour Robert Bruce, which would then re-establish the close relationship with the king of Scotland from the days of Alexander III. Here, however, he was disappointed. Edward supported John Balliol whom he regarded as the most accommodating towards English interests, and Eirik was assuaged with the recognition of his right to his late wife's dowry which, as a matter of fact, was not a bad deal, as the legal foundation of the Norwegian claims was doubtful.[72] Although afterwards Edward tried to make the new Scottish king satisfy the Norwegian demands, including the payment of the annual sum according to the peace of Perth, the relationship between him and John Balliol soon deteriorated. When war broke out between England and France in 1294 and the Scots joined France early in 1295,[73]

---

71   For the following, see Helle, *Norge blir en stat*, pp. 259 f.; Bjørgo, "Makt og avmakt", pp. 70-81.
72   Brynildsrud, *Audun Hugleiksson*, pp. 39-55; Bjørgo, "Langs diplomatiets frontlinjer", p. 30.
73   An understanding between the two parties seems to have been reached in the spring, and in July, a delegation was appointed to arrange a marriage between John Balliol's son and King Philip's niece (Powicke, *The Thirteenth Century*, p. 612). See also Prestwich, *Edward I*, pp. 370-85 and 469-76, on Edward's conflict with France and Scotland.

King Eirik had the opportunity to renew the war against Scotland in an alliance with England, but instead chose an alliance with France.

On 22 October 1295, the Norwegian envoy Audun Hugleiksson concluded a treaty with King Philip IV of France against England. The king of Norway agreed to assist the king of France with a fleet of 300 ships and 50,000 men in four months per year in return for a payment of 30,000 pound sterling, 6000 marks of which were paid in advance. On the same date, a Scottish envoy promised on behalf of the king of Scotland not to go to war against Norway as long as the alliance with France lasted and to fulfil the Norwegian claims on Scotland.[74] There is also evidence of some Scottish payments to Norway,[75] but outside of this, the payment of the advance to Audun was the only part of the treaty to be fulfilled. The treaty has often been commented upon by Norwegian historians as a desperate measure in order to gain money – possibly in order to pay the debt of 1285 – and as an example of irresponsibility and foolhardiness on the part of the Norwegian government during these years.[76] The force mentioned in the treaty is of course completely unrealistic. The number of ships corresponds to the maximum mobilisation of the *leidang* which, however, was only manned by 30,000 at the most but possibly only around half of that number (above p. 76). In addition, it is difficult to imagine a total mobilisation of the *leidang* fleet for four months – one more than in the National Law – for several consecutive years, and even less likely to imagine such a mobilisation abroad. Moreover, the total payment, 30,000 pounds, was low for such a great force, and according to the treaty, the Norwegians had to mobilise the force first and receive the payment afterwards. Therefore, the only possible explanation of the treaty was that it was not intended to be fulfilled.[77] The French king paid his Norwegian counterpart 6000 marks to produce a realistic threat against England, and the king of Norway pocketed this sum without worrying about any military mobilisation.

Similar treaties were not unusual in the Middle Ages. Many promises were made without being carried out, at least not fully. The situation in the autumn of 1295 was that Philip IV had conquered most of Gascony (the fief the king of England held in the southwest), including the main city, Bordeaux, but wanted an end to the war because of the costs in keeping garrisons in the region.[78] Thus it would appear that the more prob-

---

74 DN XI no. 5, XIX nos. 398-404, 406.
75 DN XIX no. 405.
76 Munthe, "Audun Hugleiksson", pp. 13-32 ; Bjørgo, "Makt og avmakt", pp. 90 f.
77 Bjørgo, "Langs diplomatiets frontlinjer", pp. 35-38. Bjørgo suggests that the advance was intended as a loan, but the general situation makes it more likely that it was a subsidy that the French did not expect to receive back, despite the provisions about this in the treaty.
78 For this and the following, see Strayer, *The Reign of Philip the Fair*, pp. 317-24, and Carpenter, "The Plantagenet Kings", pp. 349-53, who, incidentally, do not mention the treaty with Norway.

lems he could create for Edward in other areas the better. Both parties spent money in securing allies among various other princes or in preventing the other party from doing the same. Edward managed to mobilise Flanders against Philip, with little success in the beginning, but it was probably because of this alliance that he had Gascony returned to him at the peace in 1303. For Philip, the treaty with Norway was therefore one of several means of increasing the difficulties of the English. Above all, it was intended to prevent a Norwegian attack on Scotland which would have improved King Edward's position on his northern front. The alliance was therefore in all likelihood the result of a French initiative; there is even direct evidence of this in a French annal entry.[79]

Thus, the treaty clearly made sense from a French point of view. In assessing its value from a Norwegian perspective, it must first be pointed out that King Eirik was in an excellent bargaining position, as he also had the option of making a deal with the English. The French treaty gave him a large sum of money and promises from the Scots, but no guarantees of French support in having these promises fulfilled.[80] Would he have been able to get more from the English? This is of course impossible to know, but given his difficult position in 1295, King Edward might well have been willing to grant as much as King Philip or even more. Around the turn of the year 1294-95, Edward allegedly answered King Eirik's complaints about the arrears on the payments from Scotland by encouraging him to reconquer the Hebrides.[81] Although for many years King Eirik had received little more than verbal encouragement from Edward when presenting his claims, the alliance with France could hardly have been the result of impatience with this attitude. Although the Norwegians may not have regarded it in this way, King Edward had actually been very accommodating, given the character of the Norwegian claims. Edward's reluctance to interfere more directly on behalf of Eirik was clearly the result of his need to secure his control of Scotland. By the time of the last contact between the two kings, the winter of 1294-95, Scotland was on the brink of a rebellion which broke out early in 1295. For the first time since the 1260s, Norway had the possibility to profit from enmity between England and Scotland and even received active encouragement from Edward through the suggestion to attack the Hebrides. Why did King Eirik not exploit this opportunity rather than allying himself with England's enemies? The only possible explanation is that he believed that the English would be defeated. This would also seem a reasonable conclusion in in 1295, with King Philip in possession of the English fiefs in Gascony

---

79 Johnsen, "Audun Hugleiksson", p. 761; Brynildsrud, *Audun Hugleiksson*, p. 66; Bjørgo, "Langs diplomatiets frontlinjer", p. 33.
80 The 6000 marks were apparently a substantial sum, the equivalent of around 1150 kg silver or a little less than the king of Norway's total annual incomes (below pp. 126 f.).
81 RN II no. 774-75, referred in DN XIX no. 412; Bjørgo, "Langs diplomatiets frontlinjer", p. 32.

and Scotland in alliance with France against England. Nevertheless, the conclusion was wrong. Edward invaded Scotland early in 1296 and shortly afterwards defeated John Balliol and took him captive.[82] On 8 October 1297, a truce was agreed upon between France and England which lasted until the final peace treaty in 1303. King Eirik had gained his 6000 marks, but the Scottish promises were now worthless, and the opportunity of striking a favourable bargain with the English was lost.

King Eirik's reign (1280-99) is the most eventful, dramatic and warlike in the field of foreign policy in the whole period from 1240-1319. The Norwegian policy in that period has often been regarded as adventurous and irresponsible. This characterisation seems to be justified regarding the events of 1284-85, but otherwise the policy seems to have been rational and fairly successful. The peace of Hindsgavl in 1295 represents the maximum of concessions gained from Denmark. The treaty with France from the same year is a realistic attempt to profit from the English-French conflict, although it eventually turned out that the Norwegians had backed the wrong horse.

The following reign of Eirik's brother and successor Håkon V (1299-1319) represents both a continuation and a revision of the previous period. The relationship with England improved after the truce with France in 1297. Apparently shortly after his accession to the throne in July 1299, King Håkon once more approached King Edward, asking for aid in obtaining the payments from Scotland, but we do not know the outcome of this.[83] In 1294 Håkon had sent an embassy to England with the intention of marrying an English lady, but without result. Some scholars have interpreted this as a disagreement about the alliance with France in 1295, which at least partly explains Audun Hugleiksson's fall immediately after Håkon's succession.[84] However, Håkon's marriage plans were probably intimately linked to the general foreign policy; thus, the alliance with France was accompanied by plans for the duke to marry a French lady.[85] It is also difficult to imagine that such initiatives were taken without Håkon's consent. Håkon therefore probably accepted the change of alliance in 1295, but he may nevertheless have blamed Audun afterwards for the result, as rulers often do. In any case, Håkon was on good terms with both England and France during the first decade of his reign. From around 1310, the relationship with England started to deteriorate, partly because of quarrels about compensation to merchants for damages, partly because of the new Scottish uprising from 1306 under Robert Bruce, grandson of the pretender in 1292, whose sister, King Eirik's widow, was

---

82   The English won a decisive victory at Dunbar on 27 April, and John Balliol surrendered on 2 July (Powicke, *The Thirteenth Century*, pp. 613-15).
83   DN XIX no. 412; Bjørgo, "Langs diplomatiets frontlinjer", p. 39.
84   Munch, NFH IV.2, p. 259 n. 1; Johnsen, "Audun Hugleiksson", p. 762, and below p. 340.
85   Brynildsrud, *Audun Hugleiksson*, pp. 63 f., 79-81.

still living in Norway (she died in 1358). The link to Scotland is expressed in the renewal of the treaty of Perth in 1312, which represents a return to the policy of 1295, although under somewhat different circumstances. This time, the Norwegians backed the right horse but to little avail: the Scots defeated the English in the Battle of Bannockburn two years later and regained their independence, but the annual payments did not become more regular than in the previous period.[86]

The main field of Håkon's foreign policy was Norway's relationship with the other Scandinavian countries. This is already apparent in his marriage in 1299, shortly before he succeeded his brother. He married Eufemia of Arnstein, daughter or most probably granddaughter of Prince Witzlaw of Rügen who had earlier sided with the Danish king but now became an ally of Norway. Håkon renewed the peace of Hindsgavl several times in the following period although it was interrupted by minor skirmishes and mutual accusations. Shortly after 1295, the Danish-Swedish alliance was strengthened by a double marriage. In 1296 Erik Klipping's successor, Erik Menved, who had reached majority in 1294, married Ingeborg, sister of King Birger of Sweden, in 1296, and two years later King Birger married Erik's sister Margrete. This probably forms the background for King Håkon V's betrothal in 1302 of his daughter Ingebjørg, aged one, to Duke Erik, a younger brother of the Swedish king Birger. The betrothal marked the beginning of a series of dramatic events which involved all three Nordic kingdoms but centred around the conflict between King Birger and his brothers. Throughout the period, King Birger enjoyed the support of his Danish brother-in-law Erik Menved, whereas King Håkon usually supported the Swedish dukes. Among a series of armed conflicts, negotiations and treaties, two dramatic events stand out. In 1306 the dukes launched a surprise attack on their brother and took him captive at his estate, Håtuna. Thanks to Erik Menved's intervention, they eventually had to release him but obtained a division of Sweden into three parts, all of which became hereditary and made the royal title the only distinction between Birger and his brothers. Birger got his revenge in 1317 when he invited his brothers to celebrate Christmas with him in his castle at Nyköping and then had them arrested and probably starved them to death in prison. Nevertheless, Birger's revenge brought him no tangible benefit; he was chased out of Sweden by the dukes' adherents and died in exile in Denmark in 1321, while Duke Erik's son and Håkon's grandson Magnus Eriksson, aged three, became king of both Norway and Sweden in 1319.

Norwegian historians have mostly regarded these conflicts as the first step in Norway's decline in the later Middle Ages, an interpretation that has often been supported with reference to the union. Furthermore, earlier scholarship regarded Håkon V as a peaceful and

---

86   Bjørgo, "Makt og avmakt", pp. 114 f.

decent monarch who was outwitted by more ruthless adversaries. More recent research has revised this picture under the influence of the Swedish historian Jerker Rosén's subtle and thorough examination of the whole conflict between Birger and his brothers,[87] but still maintains that Håkon was defeated. Håkon's aim was to use Duke Erik in the same way as the Danish outlaws in the previous period to gain control of the economically and strategically important coast of Halland and Scania, but the duke proved too strong and clever, using Håkon as his instrument in promoting his own interests instead of vice versa. In 1308 Håkon, disillusioned by the duke's behaviour, changed sides in return for promises from Erik Menved of control over Halland and then betrothed his daughter to King Birger's son Magnus. In the ensuing war, Håkon received little help from his Danish ally and lost most of what he had gained in Hindsgavl in the peace of Hälsingborg in 1310. Disappointed by this defeat, he withdrew from further involvement in the inter-Nordic conflicts, but approached the dukes once more and concluded a marriage alliance with them in 1312. Duke Erik married Håkon's daughter Ingebjørg and his brother married another Ingebjørg, the daughter of Håkon's late brother Eirik. After King Birger's treachery, Håkon gave military aid to the Swedish rebels but apparently without influencing the outcome very much. At his death on 8 May 1319 he was, with good reasons, worried about the future: the union with Sweden with a child on the throne.

Most of the hard facts in the summary above are correct enough, but the interpretation of Håkon's actions and motives nevertheless fails to convince.[88] First, there is little to suggest that Håkon had aggressive plans against Denmark. Most probably, his aims were to protect the gains of the peace of Hindsgavl in 1295, to end the Norwegian isolation that resulted from the Swedish-Danish alliance concluded through the double marriages of 1296 and 1298, and to derive maximum profit from his own daughter's marriage. His Danish policy was defensive rather than offensive, which is logical enough given the considerable Danish revival after Erik Menved came of age in 1294 and above all after 1302. There is no certain evidence that Håkon was ever directly involved in active warfare against Denmark, although he usually sided with the Swedish dukes against King Erik Menved. The only war of his reign of any length was the one against the Swedish dukes in 1308-10. It was no success, but the losses were compensated by the marriage alliance with the dukes in 1312. Generally, Håkon appears as a reluctant and cautious player in the political and diplomatic game, intent to avoid great risks. He was less brilliant than his Swedish son-in-law and temporary enemy Duke Erik, and has often been accused

---

87 Rosén, *Striden*.
88 For the following, see Bagge, "Aims and Means".

of being outwitted by him, but he did not strain his kingdom's resources in the way Erik Menved did in Denmark.

Secondly, Håkon's main aim was dynastic rather than territorial. This was at least the case in the later phase of his reign, after he must have understood that he would not have a male heir. The decisive year was 1312, when his wife, Queen Eufemia, died and the weddings between the Swedish dukes and the Norwegian princesses took place shortly afterwards. For some reason or other Håkon did not make a new attempt to get an heir by remarrying but apparently decided to solve the problem through the Swedish dukes. The fact that Håkon had a daughter who was likely to succeed him was of course an enormous asset for him in the political game. The difficult decision was how best to spend this asset. The alternatives were either Duke Erik or King Birgers's son Magnus; Ingebjørg had been promised to the former in 1302 but he had been replaced by the latter in 1308 when Håkon had joined Birger and Erik Menved against the Swedish dukes. The reason for this change was twofold: an attractive offer from Erik Menved, probably combined with threats in case Håkon rejected the offer, and because Håkon may have doubted whether the duke would be able to keep the gains he had obtained through his coup in Håtuna. The peace of 1310, according to which the Swedish dukes kept two thirds of Sweden with the right to pass it onto their heirs, must have convinced Håkon that he had backed the wrong side and made it clear that Erik was the better candidate. Under favourable circumstances, the marriage between Erik and Ingebjørg would lead to a formidable extension of the Norwegian king's lands to the east. By contrast, Magnus's part of Sweden was both poorer and more distant from Norway. Given this, the treaty of Hälsingborg had considerably reduced Magnus Birgersson's attractiveness as Håkon's son-in-law. Whereas in 1308 Håkon might have hoped for a son-in-law who would become the real ruler of Sweden, he was now faced with one who would be totally dependent on his Danish uncle. Moreover, Magnus (born 1300) was young and inexperienced and most probably would have to fight his formidable uncle, who, by contrast, had shown himself as a brilliant politician and military leader, despite the fact that his actions had not always conformed to Håkon's wishes.

Through the marriage alliance of 1312, Håkon V had improved his position radically, not only compared to the situation two years before, but also to the one at the time of his accession to the throne. Then he was faced with a strong alliance between the two neighbouring countries, both richer and more populous than Norway, and by the stronger of them, Denmark, on its way to overcoming the inner struggles during the previous decades. In 1312 Sweden had been divided into three parts, two of which were Håkon's allies. Moreover, Håkon could hope to be succeeded by a son born of the marriage between Erik and Ingebjørg who could add one third of Sweden and Halland in Denmark to his Norwegian kingdom. This hope was fulfilled by the birth of Magnus Eriksson in 1316. Had Håkon lived long enough to learn about Erik Menved's death and the situation in Denmark during the following years, he would probably have felt that all his dreams had come true. His grandson had become king of Sweden; the Danish king had lost his foothold in Sweden, and at King Erik's death German magnates held most of the Danish castles which the king had mortgaged in order to finance his ambitious policy in Northern Germany. King Erik's brother Christoffer, who succeeded him, was unable to improve the situation and Denmark entered its most chaotic period in the Middle Ages, during which it was an easy prey for interventions from its neighbours. Thus, there were good opportunities for continuing the aggressive anti-Danish policy from the 1290s, and they were actually taken, first by Håkon's daughter Ingebjørg and then by his grandson Magnus after he reached majority in 1331. Admittedly, Ingebjørg's attempt was a failure; she ran into conflict with the Swedish as well as the Norwegian aristocracy and was deposed from the regency in Sweden in 1322 and in Norway in 1323. Magnus succeeded in gaining Scania in 1332 but only by contracting a heavy debt which caused him financial difficulties during most of his reign. We cannot know if Håkon himself would have been more successful, but it seems highly likely that he would have regarded the new situation as a great opportunity and conducted a similar policy as his daughter and grandson did.

Norwegian foreign policy in the period 1240-1319 shows considerable continuity with that of the previous period. It was still largely determined by an orientation towards the north and the sea; the British Isles and the islands in the north played a major part. Superficially, this policy also seems to have resulted in a defence of the status quo rather than in new expansion, the loss of the Hebrides and Man having been compensated by a gain of Iceland and Greenland. Actually, however, Norway improved its position quite considerably; the loss of the Hebrides and Man was more than made up for by stricter control over the remaining islands plus over Iceland, modelled on the centralisation of the mainland that took place in the same period.[89] The result of the involvement in the struggle for the Scottish succession and the war between England and France is more difficult to assess, as we do not know exactly what its aims were. Clearly, King Eirik's chances of becoming king of Scotland were slim, as he was most probably aware of himself, but the demands for financial compensation, notably the arrears in the payment agreed upon in the Treaty of Perth, were pursued with great energy and consistency, although with limited success; the main result was the 6000 marks received from France. It is difficult to know whether an alternative alliance with England would have been more profitable, although the actors probably thought so in 1296 and the following years.

89 Wærdahl, *"Norges konges rike"*, pp. 153-90.

The greatest novelty in the period was the stronger engagement in the south and east, towards Denmark, Sweden and the German towns. The latter became increasingly more important as trading partners from the mid-thirteenth century onwards. A restrictive policy leading to direct confrontation in the early 1280s failed, and several privileges were issued in the following years, partly because of economic needs, partly in order to secure the neutrality of the towns in the conflict with Denmark. Nevertheless, the Norwegian government managed to conduct a moderately restrictive policy in the following years without direct confrontation (below pp. 352 f.). In its relationship to the two neighbouring countries, the advantage of Norway in this period was its internal stability, whereas both Sweden and Denmark suffered from prolonged internal conflicts. This allowed a more offensive Norwegian policy than in the previous period, although its aggressive character has often been exaggerated in previous scholarship. Its aims seem to have been dynastic rather than territorial, although the prospect of territorial gain and financial profit cannot be excluded. From a dynastic point of view, this policy was also ultimately a success, making Håkon V's grandson king of both Sweden and Norway.

War Made the State, but Did the State Make War? – The Military Challenges 1240-1319

From a military point of view, the peace at home combined with a greater orientation towards other countries meant new challenges. This applies particularly to the involvement with the two other Scandinavian countries which had already adopted European military technology with castles and heavy cavalry. In two meetings between the king and his men in 1273, entered in the Hird Law shortly afterwards, the royal *sysselmenn* agreed to muster a specified number of men in the case of war, paid for by incomes from their districts.[90] Some scholars have regarded this force as a step in the direction of replacing the military *leidang* with professional forces, while others have doubted whether it ever came into existence in practice, as the king's men apparently took a heavy new burden upon themselves.[91] It has also been suggested that the decision about the elite force was based on experience from the war in Scotland where the Norwegians were unable to en-

---

90 H ch. 31, pp. 132-40.
91 For the latter point of view, see Schreiner, "Hærmakt", pp. 115 f., and Fladby, "Oppløsningen", p. 89, whereas Holmsen, *Nye studier*, p. 165, points to the heavy burden without expressing his opinion on whether the promises were carried out or not. However, in "Integreringen av innlandsdistriktene', p. 10, he regards the contingent in the king's service as men the *sysselmenn* already had around them. Cf. also Dørum, *Romerike*, p. 276.

gage the Scots on land.[92] Experience from the few military engagements in the previous period may have had some importance but it may nevetheless be doubted whether such an elite force would have led to a different outcome of the war in Scotland. The strategic plan behind this expedition was not to engage the Scots in battle but to use the fleet as a power demonstration.

Moreover, the elite force was hardly a novelty in the 1270s; most probably, such forces were a continuation of the companies (*sveit*) under the *sysselmann*'s command during the civil wars[93] and may therefore have been available to Håkon on his expedition to Scotland. A *lendmann* was allowed to have up to forty men; and it seems unlikely that the *sysselmann* had less than half this number. A source from 1331 mentions a duty incumbent on a farm at Romerike to provide for the *sysselmann* with fifteen men and five servants on a certain day of the year.[94] The duty may have been specific for this particular farm, but the number of men may at least give an indication of the number of a *sysselmann*'s retainers.[95] Admittedly, in 1308 Håkon V states that the *lagmann* and the *sysselmann* should have two retainers each when travelling around together to settle cases between people, but this passage only indicates how many men the peasants had to pay for on such journeys and says nothing of the total number of men in a *sysselmann*'s service.[96] It is inconceivable that a *sysselmann* had only two retainers in his service. The *sysselmann* would largely have replaced the *lendmann*. He was an aristocrat, governed a large district, and his duty was to keep law and order and take action against crime and violence in a society where most adult men had arms and were able to use them. Both for practical reasons, and as a sign of status, he clearly had to surround himself with a not insignificant number of armed men which he appears to have been perfectly able to finance (below p. 126). Therefore the provisions of 1273-74 most probably refer to these forces. The king demanded to have a certain number of such men at his disposal for three months in case of war. We do not know to what extent these men were already at the *sysselmenn*'s disposal. It is quite possible that the *sysselmenn* needed to hire some new men to meet the king's demands or to improve their training or equipment; the point is that the elite force of 1273-74 cannot have been a total novelty but must have been based on an already existing military elite. Nor is it necessary to imagine these men as permanent members of the

---

92 Bjørgo, "Makt og avmakt" p. 77.
93 Bagge, "Borgerkrig og statsutvikling", pp. 191-95.
94 DN I no. 213.
95 Opsahl, *Herresvein-institusjonen,* p. 103, suggests that the document here refers to a hunting party because of the duty to also provide for five greyhounds, but admits that the men were most probably retainers.
96 "ok hafue tua suæina. a þæira kost sem syslumadr" (DN XI no. 6, p. 13). "a þæira kost" most likely means "at the peasants' cost"; i.e. the king set a limit, not to the total number of men but to a number the peasants had to provide for.

sysselmenn's household; at least in the beginning, they could not have acted as a kind of bodyguard for the *sysselmenn*.[97]

However, Erik Opsahl has suggested an alternative interpretation, namely that the force in question represents the elite of the ordinary men of the *leidang*, those owning more than eighteen marks who were obliged to have almost the same equipment as the lower ranks of the *hird*, the guests and the housecarls.[98] This category is apparently new in the National Law; the two extant regional laws make no distinction between categories of *leidang* men. Opsahl supports his argument with a detailed discussion about the number of men to be mustered from the various parts of the country according to the Hird Law.[99] It may be objected that these men were part of the ordinary *leidang* mobilisation and thus supposed to live off the ordinary contribution from the peasants, whereas the men mentioned in the Hird Law were to be supported by the *sysselmenn*. Why would the king make his *sysselmenn* pay for the wealthiest men in peasant society when they were already provided for by a well-established tax? Additionally, there seems to have been a clear distinction between the ordinary *leidang* and the men in the service of *lendmenn* and other aristocrats.[100] Finally, the men mentioned in the National Law are defined according to their wealth, whereas a specific number is mentioned in the Hird Law. It is inconceivable that the two numbers can have corresponded. Even if the king and his men knew the exact number of men in this category in each district, which is highly unlikely, there cannot have been the same number of them per *skipreide* in every district of Western Norway and Trøndelag. It thus seems more likely that we are dealing with two different, but coordinated attempts by the king to improve his armed forces, one by creating an elite among the ordinary men of the *leidang* and another by using the *sysselmann*'s retainers. We may also assume that the two forces would have tended to merge in practice. The *sysselmenn* would probably have to recruit at least a part of their retainers locally, and might perhaps easily persuade the wealthiest men to become their retainers rather than serving as the elite of the *leidang*.

In addition to the elite forces, Sverre's successors continued to build castles, although fewer than in the neighbouring countries, both for defensive and offensive purposes. The

---

97 Bagge, "Borgerkrig og statsutvikling", pp. 174-76. At least they would hardly have been part of the *sysselmann*'s household around 1240, when Skule's men attacked Håkon's *sysselmenn* and killed them. The saga does not mention that any of the *sysselmenn* were able to put up a proper defence.
98 L III.12.
99 Opsahl, *Herresvein-institusjonen*, pp. 93-132; cf. also "Bastard Feudalism" p. 201. Opsahl's conclusion is accepted by Ersland, "Kongshird", pp. 78 f.
100 Cf. Håkon V's ordinance about mobilisation i Trøndelag (DN I no. 121) with the distinction between the king's men and the common people and H 32 stating that a royal retainer (*hirdmann*) should join either the king or the *sysselmann* in case of war in his district.

castles of Bergen, Tønsberg and Oslo were combined fortifications and royal residences. Most important from a military point of view, however, were the castles along the borders, erected by Håkon V. Vardøhus in the far north was built to secure that region for the Norwegian crown. Akershus in Oslo, erected as a royal residence as well as a fortress, was able to withstand Duke Erik's siege in 1308 and was apparently already a strong fortress under Håkon V. Further east, in the border region towards the two other countries, Håkon Håkonsson built Ragnhildarholm in Göta Älv which Håkon V replaced with Bohus, built as a stronghold during the inter-Nordic conflicts in a better strategic position in the early fourteenth century. Bohus eventually became the strongest fortress in Scandinavia and of crucial importance in the struggles over power in the whole of Scandinavia in the fifteenth and early sixteenth centuries.

On the other hand, neither the elite force nor the relatively few castles replaced the *leidang*, nor were they intended to do so. On the contrary, King Magnus's extension of the period of a *leidang* mobilisation from two to three months, his attempt to strengthen it by demanding better equipment from the wealthiest part of the crew and its regular use in armed conflicts in the following period all suggest that the elite force was intended as a supplement to and not a replacement of the *leidang*. The explanation for this has been sought in economic as well as geographical factors.[101] The agrarian historians have usually regarded the king of Norway in the Middle Ages as extremely poor, which consequently meant that even if the *leidang* were converted into a higher tax, the king would only have been able to afford an elite army that was too small to be competitive in a Nordic context. It has also been pointed out that Norwegian terrain was not suited for heavy cavalry, which apparently never played a significant role in Norway, or at least not until the fourteenth century. Nevertheless, fighting on horseback may have been more usual than most historians have been willing to admit.[102] Sverre sometimes directed his forces from horseback, but he and his men do not seem to have fought in this way.

There is some truth in both explanations, although heavy cavalry might well have been able to play a role along the Swedish-Norwegian border. The main factor, however, is the same as during the civil wars, namely the importance of the sea; all targets of Norwegian foreign policy except the areas south of the Göta Älv were situated across the sea.[103] Admittedly, as the fleet in the thirteenth century mainly served as a means of transport – there is no evidence of any battle at sea after the Battle of Strindsjøen in 1199 – the

---

101   Holmsen, *Norges historie*, pp. 258 f.; Benedictow, *Fra rike til provins*, pp. 450 f.; Bagge, "Borgerkrig og statsutvikling", pp. 191-95.
102   Opsahl, *Herresveinstitusjonen*, pp. 137-39.
103   I.e. the explanation lies more in the military aims than in the character of Norwegian landscape and society; see Opsahl, *Herresveinstitusjonen*, pp. 138 f.

traditional ships might have been replaced by big and heavy cogs that could transport more men and horses, as became common in other countries from the thirteenth century onwards.[104] However, these ships could only move by sails and were therefore less adapted to quick raids on enemy shores, which was the usual form of warfare in foreign countries. Therefore the Norwegian king still needed a high number of combined rowers and warriors and largely seems to have continued to use the traditional Viking ships or "long ships" (ON *langskip*) which were low and narrow and could be rowed with great speed. He also built higher and broader ships that resembled the cogs. Sverre built Mariasuden as a floating fortress which played a decisive role in the battle of Firmreite in 1184, and Håkon Håkonsson built even larger ships, the largest of which, Kristsuden, was used in the expedition against Scotland.[105] Similar ships must also have been used in the war against the German towns in 1284-85, as traditional long ships could hardly have captured German cogs. It would therefore seem that the Norwegian fleet developed in a similar direction as in other countries, where rowing ships, in the form of galleys, were still necessary because of their speed and manoeuvrability.[106] Thus, the *leidang* was still an essential element in the Norwegian military forces around 1300. If the king wanted elite forces on horse or on foot, they had to come as an addition to rather than as a replacement of the *leidang*, which set limits on how much he was able to afford. Nor could he afford to use mercenaries to any great extent, although there is some evidence that he employed them.[107]

Despite these limits to their military capacity, the Norwegians were able to defend themselves against attacks from the neighbouring countries. Contemporary military technology favoured the defenders rather than the attackers. Moreover, it was difficult to conquer Norway by land and the Norwegian fleet protected the country from sea attacks. During the war with the Swedish dukes in 1308-10, Duke Erik managed to conquer Oslo in the winter of 1308-09, but not the castle of Akershus, and sacked the region around the town. Two different accounts exist of the outcome of a battle in Oslo in 1309 against local Norwegian forces, in all likelihood the *leidang*, perhaps led by magnates with elite forces.[108] According to *Erikskrönikan*, the Norwegians, 3000 in numbers, suffered

---

104 Bill, "Castles at Sea".
105 Bjørgo, "Skipstypar", pp. 10, 13 f.; Helle, *Kongssete*, pp. 393 f.
106 Bill, "Castles at Sea", pp. 52-54.
107 Fagerland, *Krigføring*, pp. 102-5, on English mercenaries in Norwegian service in the 1280s. A brief reference to mercenaries in connection with the negotiations with the Danish and Swedish kings in 1285 (DN V no. 14, 1285, see below pp. 266 f.) may possibly refer to this force. Mercenaries are also mentioned in Sverre's service towards the end of his reign (*Ss.* ch. 174) and in the accusations against Ingebjørg in 1323 (DN VII no. 100).
108 *Erikskrönikan*, pp. 132 f.; *Isl. Ann.*, pp. 202, 341. The Icelandic Annals refer to the force as "Liðungar", i.e. people of Lier, a region just outside Oslo.

heavy losses at the hands of Erik's men – they fell like grass – but the duke withdrew from Oslo soon afterwards, allegedly because of illness. By contrast, some short notices in the Icelandic Annals state that nearly thirty Norwegians and an unknown number of Swedes were killed and that Duke Erik fled. We thus seem to have an example of the usual situation in which both parties claim to have won. *Erikskrönikan* is probably composed between fifteen and twenty years after the event, but is heavily biased in favour of Duke Erik and often inaccurate. The date of the two annals giving this information, the Skálholt and Gottskalk Annals, is unknown. The original manuscript for the part of the former dealing with this period must have ended in 1348, for the latter in 1394, but the information probably stems from an earlier written source, common to both, as the two accounts are almost identical.[109]

Modern historians have expressed different opinions on the relative trustworthiness of *Erikskrönikan* and the Annals.[110] In choosing between the two versions of the battle, it is noteworthy that the former almost exclusively consists of conventional rhetoric; the only specific detail is the statement that the Norwegian force passed a bridge, a piece of information that is also in the alternative version. By contrast, the terse statement in the Annals, containing a reasonable assessment of the Norwegian losses, gives a more convincing impression, although a lack of rhetorical embellishment does not equate with truth. The decisive piece of information, however, is the duke's retreat, on which both sources agree, but for which *Erikskrönikan* gives an entirely unconvincing reason. If Duke Erik were staying in Oslo, enjoying all the wealth of the city in the way the chronicle describes and had just inflicted a crushing defeat on his enemies, why would illness make him take on a fatiguing and dangerous journey through barren territory in mid-winter? The obvious conclusion is that the battle had made it too dangerous for him to stay where he was. The *a priori* argument, adduced by some scholars, that mercenaries would defeat a popular levy in a pitched battle, is of little weight. First, we know neither the number nor the quality of Erik's forces, and, second, this general rule is not without exception. A few years before the battle in Oslo, an army based on the popular levy from the Flemish towns had defeated a French army of about equal size but with a heavy contingent of knights at Courtrai on 11 July 1302. There are also several similar examples from the same period, such as when the Scots fought against the English at Bannockburn (1314), the Swiss against the Austrians at Morgarten (1315), and the peasants of Ditmarschen against the

---

109 Storm, "Forord", pp. xv-xviii, xxv-xxxii; Axelson, *Annalistik*, pp. 159-61.
110 Bull, *Leding*, pp. 146 f., Ersland, "Kongshird", pp. 104 f., and Opsahl, *Herresveininstitusjonen*, pp. 146 f., are inclined to accept the version of the Annals, whereas Helle, "Opptakten", pp. 27-28, and Fagerland, *Krigføring*, pp. 133 f., prefer *Erikskrönikan*.

knights of Holstein (1319),[111] in addition to the well-known examples from the Hundred Years War and the victories of the Swedish peasant levy over the Danes in the fifteenth century, for instance in the Battle of Brunkeberg (1471).

In offensive operations, the typical Norwegian strategy was to use power demonstrations by the fleet and, if this failed to have the desired effect, to raid the enemy's coast. This strategy failed in Scotland in 1263, but was reasonably successful against Denmark in the 1250s and in 1289-95. In the only prolonged war fought on land in the period, the war against the Swedish dukes in 1308-10, Håkon V had some success in offensive operations when supported by Erik Menved but lost what he had gained when the Danish king made a separate peace with the dukes early in 1310. This example shows the limits of the Norwegian military equipment in offensive operations when confronted with an enemy who commanded knights and mercenaries.

In comparing the strength of the different Nordic countries, the Danish and Swedish kings' greater surplus must be weighed against the value of Norwegian peasants' contribution by serving in person. Being less densely populated and having less agricultural land than its neighbours, Norway was also militarily the weakest of them. The changes in military technology from the twelfth century onwards partly increased and partly reduced this weakness. Castles and mounted elite forces made the neighbours superior in land warfare, whereas the decline of the Danish fleet in the thirteenth century made the Norwegians superior at sea and enabled them to raid the coasts of Denmark during the conflicts in the second half of the thirteenth century. Regardless of the relative strength of the three countries around 1300, however, there can be no doubt that the existing military system made Norway stronger than it would have been with the alternative one. By replacing the *leidang* with elite forces, Norway would have lost its speed of movement and ability to raid coastal areas without gaining any superiority in land warfare, as the king of Norway would hardly have had the financial means to create a force stronger than that of his counterparts in Sweden and Denmark.

Nevertheless, the conflicts during Håkon V's reign increased the importance of land warfare and thereby the elite forces, and this development continued in the following period. In December 1332, King Magnus Eriksson issued an ordinance forbidding the king's men and other magnates to have armed retainers in their service and let them swear an oath of fealty to their masters, with the exception of men who belonged to their masters' household.[112] In 1347, however, he summoned the king's men with their retainers

---

111   Verbruggen, *The Art of Warfare*, pp. 99 and 166-73.
112   NGL III no. 71.

in connection with the coming war against Russia,[113] and in the following period, such forces clearly formed a substantial part of the royal army. The reason for this development may possibly have been an increase in these kinds of forces during the regency in the 1320s, but we are hardly dealing with a completely new element; there must have been some connection between these men and the elite forces prescribed in the Hird Law and in the ordinance of 1308. Magnus may have reacted to others than the *sysselmenn* keeping such forces, or to the *sysselmenn* regarding them as their own rather than the king's men and demanding an oath of fealty from them. The ordinance may also have been a reaction to a temporary crisis, the rebellion of Erling Vidkunsson and his allies.[114] Thus there is not necessarily a radical change in the king's attitude to the magnates' armed retainers, although the importance of such forces clearly increased during the fourteenth century. This applies in particular to the period after 1363, when Magnus was deposed in Sweden and later spent six years in captivity (1365-71). His son Håkon spent most of his reign fighting to regain the Swedish throne, with Norway and Western Sweden as his base. The war was thus mainly fought on land and at some distance from Norway, which meant that the king relied on elite forces, plus smaller contingents of the *leidang* combined with payments from those who were excused from serving. Thus, whereas the second half of the thirteenth century meant a renaissance for the sea-based *leidang*, the importance of the elite element and thereby the aristocracy increased in the fourteenth century, and particularly in its latter half. This was largely the result of the union with Sweden and the inner conflicts in that country during the second half of the century.

Returning to the period before 1319, we must conclude that the foreign policy was reasonably successful during this period, at least if we regard it from a dynastic rather than a nationalist point of view, which most probably accords with contemporary ideas. The reason for this success should be sought in the diplomatic rather than the military field. The most striking fact about Norwegian foreign policy in the period is how few wars there were – taking place in the following years: 1256, 1263, 1284-85, 1289, 1290, 1293, 1295, 1308-10 and 1318. In most of these cases the war consisted in raids against the coast of the enemy country, most often with allies inside or outside the country in question. Håkon V's allegedly aggressive foreign policy was confined to one and a half year of war against the Swedish dukes, plus various kinds of support to King Erik Menved's enemies (cf. above pp. 97-99). In the 1250s, Håkon Håkonsson repeatedly sought aid from Sweden and was reluctant to go to war without it. In 1289-95, Eirik Magnusson was allied with the Danish

---

113   NGL III no. 81.
114   Opsahl, *Herresveininstitusjonen*, pp. 23-28, 53-63. By contrast, Schreiner, "Hærmakt og riksstyre", pp. 116-20 does not believe that the elite force of 1273-74 ever became a reality, and regards the forces in the fourteenth century as a novelty. On Erling's rebellion, see below p. 360.

outlaws and later with the duke of Southern Jutland. Finally, in what would seem to have been the most risky operation, the war against the Swedish dukes in 1308-10, Håkon V would never have gone to war if he had not received firm promises from Erik Menved.

Not only was diplomacy important the few times the king of Norway actually went to war, but his main hope of territorial gain was linked to diplomacy rather than war, namely to marriage alliances. The marriage between Magnus and Ingeborg in 1261 formed the basis for Norwegian claims on Denmark in the following period, the marriage between Eirik and Margaret in 1281 might have led to a union between Norway and Scotland, and the marriage between Princess Ingebjørg and Duke Erik in 1312 was intended to unite the western part of Sweden with Norway but actually led to a union between both countries under Håkon V's grandson. The importance of marriage alliances was a general European phenomenon, enhanced by the changes in military technology, particularly the increasing use of castles, which favoured the defenders over the attackers. This increased the possibility for a smaller unit or fief to remain independent of the central power, while at the same time reduced the possibility of a military conquest of large territories. Here marriage was a better strategy, as expressed in the Habsburgs' famous adage: "Bella gerunt alii, tu felix Austria, nube". A similar slogan might also have been appropriate for the Norwegian kings, although they were less lucky than the Habsburgs. The Norwegian dynasty depended even more on marriage alliances and diplomacy than other dynasties at the time, as Norway was the poorest and militarily weakest of the three Nordic countries and could not hope to expand at the cost of its neighbours by purely military means. However, the cautious Norwegian policy can hardly be the result of poverty alone, as the difference between the Norwegian and the Danish king in the early fourteenth century was that the Norwegian king adapted his ambitions to his financial means, whereas his Danish counterpart did not. Erik Menved's almost continuous warfare in Northern Germany had exhausted the Danish monarchy's resources at his death in 1319 and contributed to the situation during the interregnum (1332-40) when the country was controlled by the king's German creditors.

In accordance with these realities, Norway had a well-developed diplomatic service by contemporary standards. *Hákonar saga* lists a long series of diplomatic missions, mainly from 1240 onwards, to various countries, including one to the sultan of Morocco, and describes in some detail the embassy to Castile with Håkon's daughter Kristina who was to marry a Castilian prince. Some of these embassies may have had more a ceremonial than a political aim, but in general, there can be no doubt about the importance of diplomacy in Norwegian foreign policy in the period. For instance, Håkon Håkonsson received diplomatic support from the Emperor Frederik II in his conflict with the German towns, thanks to the good relationship between the two rulers. Altogether we know of ninety missions to other countries in the period 1240-1319, and there were probably many more. Resident ambassadors were still unusual in the thirteenth century, in Norway as well as in other countries, but there was clearly a group of men, consisting partly of clerics, partly of laymen, who were repeatedly used as envoys and who must have gained considerable experience. Often such specialists conducted the real negotiations, whereas a group of particularly high-ranking representatives returned later to conclude the formal agreement.[115] By contrast, the king himself rarely went abroad to take part in such negotiations (below pp. 267-70).

The skill and professionality of this corps is difficult to assess on the basis of the available evidence. Some blunders may be pointed out, such as the war against both the German towns and Denmark at the same time in the 1280s, or Håkon V's alliance with Erik Menved against the Swedish dukes, and possibly also the change of alliance in 1295, but in these cases the decision-makers were probably more to blame than the envoys. Moreover, diplomatic blunders were also committed by the current great powers. Thus, in Michael Prestwich's words, the English acceptance of an alleged token occupation of the fiefs in Gascony in 1294 which turned out to be an actual one "must rank with the appeasement policies before the Second World War as among the most dismal episodes of English foreign policy".[116] There is no evidence of a similar disaster for the Norwegian diplomatic service. Generally, this service seems to have had many of the same features as the services of other countries at the time.[117]

The Social and Economic Basis of the Norwegian Military System

The new military technology that was introduced in the European periphery in the twelfth and thirteenth centuries had obvious economic, social and political consequences. It was more expensive and it needed fewer men. Consequently, a larger number of peasants than before were needed to provide for the military elite by building castles, feeding their garrisons as well as the knights and their horses and producing an economic surplus to pay for the knights' costly equipment. At the same time, the greater military capacity of the elite was eminently able to force the peasant population to make these contributions.[118] A development along these lines actually seems to have taken place over most of the western

---

115 Bjørgo, "Makt og avmakt", pp. 49-60.
116 Prestwich, *Edward I*, p. 380.
117 Autrand, "The Peacemakers", pp. 254-59.
118 Cf. Finer, "State- and Nation-Building", p. 96 and *passim*, on the "extraction – coercion cycle", in his case applied to the increased taxation to finance standing armies in the Early Modern Period, but relevant in the Middle Ages as well.

and northern periphery, although we know too little about the conditions in the early period to decide how radical the change was.

According to the same logic, Norway, where no military revolution took place, at least not until well into the fourteenth century, ought to have shown greater continuity from the Viking Age to the High Middle Ages. Whether this was actually the case is open to discussion, as evidence for the social structure in the early period is as scanty as in the rest of the countries of the northern and eastern periphery. The following distribution of land, the most important source of wealth in the Middle Ages, has been suggested for the first half of the fourteenth century: 7 percent to the king, 40 percent to the Church, 20 percent to the secular aristocracy, and 33 percent to the peasants.[119] The calculation is based on the value of the land, as stated in the land rent. Equally important as the distribution of landownership, or perhaps more so, is the size of the contributions from the peasants to the elite – the land rent, taxes, and fines. Here there is a clear correspondence between the lack of military specialisation and the taxes, which were significantly lower in Norway than in the neighbouring countries.[120] By contrast, the land rent was approximately the same in all three countries, allowing for local variations, as were most of the contributions to the Church as well, with the exception that in Norway one fourth of the tithe went to the poor and was disposed by the peasants, whereas it in Denmark was divided into three, to the bishop, the priest and the church. The Swedish arrangement varied over time and between the different dioceses.[121]

It is manifestly impossible to make a similar calculation of landownership in the Viking Age, but we may nevertheless discuss to what extent the conditions in the early fourteenth century differed from those several hundred years before. For a long time the established orthodoxy among agrarian historians has been that the conditions did differ and that a radical transformation took place from the eleventh century onwards. Thus, while admitting that an aristocracy already existed in the Viking Age, Andreas Holmsen maintains that the majority of the people were freeholders in this period but became tenants under great landowners in the following one.[122] He finds evidence of this change in the detailed rules about land rent in the National Law in contrast to the brief references in the regional laws and the numerous social categories in the latter as opposed to the simple dichotomy between aristocracy and peasants in the former. Furthermore, he points to the foundation of monasteries and towns as the expression of a greater con-

119   Bjørkvik, "Nyare forskning", p. 88.
120   However, see Ulsig, "Landboer", p. 137, who suggests that the current estimate of the Danish taxes may be too high.
121   Hamre, "Tiend"; Dahlerup, "Tiend"; Schück, "Tiend".
122   Holmsen, *Norges historie,* pp. 213-23.

centration of landownership which allowed a wealthy clerical and lay elite to live off the surplus of the peasants' production and export it in return for luxury goods from abroad. He explains this by economic-demographic conditions, similar to those suggested for the rest of Europe in the period: a rising population meant an increasing pressure on the agricultural land which was scarce in Norway. This in turn made the peasants dependent on great landowners who were at that time able to increase the land rent, in contrast to what apparently happened in many other parts of Europe where the clearing of much more abundant stretches of new land made the landowners lower the rent and improve the conditions to attract workers. The place names serve as evidence of this explanation, showing that a large number of new farms were taken up during the High Middle Ages, most of them small and poor, thus indicating lack of arable land. Holmsen's explanation has been developed further by Kåre Lunden who gives an even gloomier picture of the social conditions of medieval Norway: the great majority of the people lived on existence minimum, 2000 calories a day, whereas the upper classes appropriated one third of the available resources, which must have amounted to almost all of the available surplus.[123] These calculations are based on very flimsy evidence. We do not know how many people lived in the country in the period of maximum population in the first half of the fourteenth century; the estimates vary between 300,000 and 500,000, without any compelling arguments to prefer either number, and estimates of the total agricultural production are of course even more uncertain.

Lunden largely accepts Holmsen's economic-demographic conclusions, but attaches greater importance to the political and military aspect. The aristocracy gained control not only by profiting from a demographic crisis, but by using military power to force the peasants to pay, and finally by uniting under a strong monarchy to exploit them more efficiently. In addition, fear of hell and purgatory made peasants donate their land to the Church. Most recently, Knut Dørum has accepted Holmsen's description of the transition, while seeking the explanation in more political factors – the king's confiscations of farms during the struggles in the eleventh century and later during the civil wars, and the development of the royal and ecclesiastical administration in the following period. Dørum defends his view through a detailed examination of the region of Romerike.[124]

The idea of a radical social transformation met with opposition as early as in the 1960s, notably by Knut Helle who questioned the evidence of the laws in particular.[125] The opposition has increased in recent years. Most archaeologists regard Norwegian society as

---

123 Lunden, *Norge under Sverreætten*, pp. 308-12, and "Det norske kongedømet".
124 Dørum, *Romerike*, pp. 186-236 and *passim*.
125 Helle, "Tendenser", pp. 352-54; *Norge blir en stat*, pp. 158-61, and *Under kirke og kongemakt*, pp. 119-22.

already aristocratic from the first centuries AD, thus finding considerable continuity from the Viking Age to the High Middle Ages (see above pp. 21 f.). Furthermore, the occurrence of a demographic crisis in the High Middle Ages is less certain today than it was a generation ago, in Norway as well as in the rest of Europe.[126] Whereas a demographic-economic development along the lines suggested by Holmsen and other agrarian historians probably did take place, several objections can be raised regarding specific points. It is doubtful whether Holmsen is right that a Malthusian situation had occurred by the mid-fourteenth century. According to most scholars, the Norwegian population and cultivated land had reached the same level as the medieval maximum around the middle of the seventeenth century, but new farms continued to be taken up in the following period, and the population had doubled by 1801.[127] Admittedly, a number of new industries were established during this period, but hardly enough for the conditions of the agrarian population to have changed fundamentally. As we have seen (p. 51), it is also unlikely that a crisis along the lines suggested by Holmsen had occurred by the mid-twelfth century and that it led to the centralisation of political power during the following period.

Nor is the alternative to the high medieval system necessarily a predominance of freeholders. Most probably, there were a large number of slaves in the Viking Age, possibly even earlier.[128] Furthermore, the complicated rules in the regional laws for the manumission of slaves suggest a series of stages between slavery and being fully free. A possible rise in the number of tenants in the High Middle Ages can therefore hardly have been the only result of free peasants losing their independence or lands; a substantial number of them must have been recruited from former slaves when slavery gradually disappeared, most probably during the twelfth century. Finally, the absence of the later system of tenancy does not imply full freedom for the average peasant; archaeological and place name studies have suggested the existence of peasants on small farms in various kinds of dependence on great magnates.[129] Rather than a total social revolution from the Viking Age to the High Middle Ages, we may therefore imagine a shift from a population at various levels of dependence to local magnates to one with greater centralisation and a more uniform relationship between a peasant population largely consisting of tenants and a class of great lay and ecclesiastical landowners.

Even if we reject the idea of a total revolution, however, there are still arguments for a considerable social change. A priori, the change from plundering to internal exploitation after the end of the Viking expeditions would likely have led to a change in the direction

---

126   Freedman, "Rural Society", pp. 82-95.
127   Dyrvik, "1536-1814", pp. 131-43.
128   Iversen, *Trelldommen*, pp. 141-46.
129   Iversen, *Eiendom*, pp. 186-97, 253-60, 312-24, 373-79.

suggested by Holmsen, despite the absence of a military revolution. The Viking expeditions enabled the chieftains to acquire a greater part of their economic surplus outside the country's frontiers, and parts of the population could also profit by this activity, possibly to the extent that we may speak of a kind of "military democracy".[130] In this way, we can also view the development of the state as an emergency solution for the elite when the Viking expeditions ended, and as something that brought greater burdens upon the farming population. Moreover, a clear distinction between ownership and tenancy of land is a late development, not really occurring until the relatively late Law of Frostating and, above all, with the National Law.[131] Although Holmsen may exaggerate, he is probably right that the difference between the regional laws and the National Law regarding land rent and social categories does indicate a certain amount of social change. Holmsen's arguments are further strengthened by a comparison between the Eddic poem *Rigstula*, which regards the farmer named Karl (=Man) as the normal member of society – with the earl above him and the slave below him – and the social categories presented in the thirteenth-century sources.[132] The allegory of society as a body in *The Speech against the Bishops* contains a detailed account of the various ranks of warriors and administrators in the king's service who are compared to the back, shoulders and arms of the body, but only refers briefly to "the peasants and the common people" who are compared to the legs and the feet. The author of *The King's Mirror* represents a similar attitude, referring with contempt to the *kotkarlar* (cottars) outside the royal court and urging the king's men to keep them in their place so as not to run the risk of them making any mischief. Finally, it is certain that the distribution of land suggested for the early fourteenth century cannot have been the same as in the Viking Age: the Church evidently received its share after the introduction of Christianity, most likely from the second half of the eleventh century onwards.

In a comparative perspective, the relative wealth of the Church and the peasants and the relative poverty of the lay aristocracy are the most striking features of the calculations presented above. Normally, the percentage belonging to the Church would have been around 20-30, whereas peasants owning their own land were a small minority in the more densely populated areas of Europe, including Denmark.[133] It must be pointed

---

130 Andrzejewski, *Military Organization*, pp. 60 f., 73 f.
131 Iversen, "Property and Land Tenancy".
132 Bagge, "Old Norse Theories", pp. 13-20, 27-32.
133 Orrman, "Rural Population", pp. 582-84; Ugulen, "... alle the knabe", pp. 521-77 with references. Exact calculations of the percentage of land owned by various categories are rare for this period, but the general impression is that the relatively high percentage of land owned by peasants according to Bjørkvik's calculation is an exception.

out, however, that Bjørkvik's calculations for Norway are mainly based on retrospection from the more complete sources from the mid-seventeenth century, and that in particular deductions from the situation around the Reformation to the early fourteenth century are very uncertain. By the time of the Reformation, the Church's share amounted to 47-48 percent, which is probably fairly exact, whereas the 40 percent around 1300 is based on very circumstantial evidence. Not only is there little evidence about landownership from this period, but the agrarian crisis after 1350 had considerable consequences when calculating percentages of incomes from land. The average land rent is believed to have been reduced to around 25 percent but with individual variations ranging between 5 and 50 percent, according to location and probably also according to categories of owners.[134] Moreover, aristocratic and to some extent ecclesiastical landownership have been shown to fluctuate more than has been assumed by earlier agrarian historians.[135]

Another objection to Bjørkvik's estimate is that it seems to be higher than the average for Europe as a whole and that it implies a far greater annual increase in Church property from Christianisation until around 1300 than in the following period, despite the amount of cheap land available in the Later Middle Ages as well as the inclination to donate land to the Church during the many epidemics and due to the high mortality rate in this period.[136] However, we do know of some very substantial donations from the king to the Church in the thirteenth century, probably after a great increase in the number of royal estates resulting from confiscations during the civil wars, for which there are no parallels in the Later Middle Ages. This includes the Augustinian house of Utstein, one of the wealthiest monastic institutions in the country, most probably founded by King Magnus Håkonsson[137] who in his testament also gave the largest donation known from any Norwegian king to various ecclesiastical institutions,[138] and, above all, Håkon V's foundation of the royal chapels which apparently received nearly half of the crown lands.[139] On the other hand, according to Anders Emmanuelsson, the Church's lands in the diocese of

---

134 Moseng et al., *Norsk historie*, p. 288.
135 Weidling, "Kven åtte jorda?"
136 Ugulen, "… alle the knabe", pp. 521-24.
137 The date is uncertain, but the buildings – which are the best preserved from any monastic foundation in Norway – clearly date from the mid-thirteenth century (Eide, "Om Utsteinklosterets bygningshistorie"). Nenseter, *Å lære andre*, pp. 30-41, also gives historical arguments for this date, rejecting the earlier hypothesis that Utstein was a continuation of the Olav monastery in Stavanger which he claims to have been Benedictine. Haug, "Klosteret på Utstein", pp. 122-32, accepts Nenseter's conclusion about the relationship to the Olav monastery, but maintains that Utstein was founded in the mid-twelfth century, although without presenting any substantial evidence for this conclusion. See most recently Helle, "Stavanger by".
138 DN IV no. 3, 1277.
139 Bjørkvik, "Dei kongelege kapella"; Bagge, *Den kongelige kapellgeistlighet*, pp. 89-93.

Oslo increased by 34 percent during the fourteenth century, which, if representative, suggests that Bjørkvik's estimate for around 1300 is too high.[140]

A large part of the wealth of the Church clearly came from donations, although there is also evidence of land being bought and mortgaged without being redeemed or transferred as a payment of fines. The donors were ordinary people as well as great landowners. In some cases they are identified in the sources, but we mostly have to use indirect evidence. Large farms must have been given by wealthy people, the king or wealthy aristocrats. Small parts may often have come from ordinary people, but there is no reason to think that this was always the case, as the great landowners often had very scattered lands and might have given some of it to the Church.[141] The question then is: did the donations to the Church significantly increase the percentage of land owned by great landowners and worked by tenants, or were they mainly a transfer from great secular landowners? The agrarian historians' view of a change from freeholders to tenants implies that a large part of the lands of the Church must have come from ordinary peasants. Concerning the really large donations, however, they have mostly pointed to the king. The main evidence for this is the analysis of great complexes of ecclesiastical property in good agricultural areas, particularly near the towns. This land is believed to have been confiscated by the king during the struggles either in the late tenth and early eleventh centuries or during the civil wars, and then given to the Church. The king is believed to have gathered considerable landed wealth through confiscations during the numerous conflicts, for instance in Trøndelag when St Olav suppressed the pagan chieftains and his son Magnus took revenge for his father's death, in the rich agricultural regions north of Oslo which were conquered by St Olav and again by Harald Hardrada, and around Bergen and Stavanger which were two of Harald Finehair and his successors' core areas.[142] The agrarian historians have attempted to calculate the exact amount of these confiscations through an analysis of ecclesiastical estates, based on the assumption that these estates were donations from the king.

Recently, Dagfinn Skre has suggested that much of this land may have come directly from great aristocratic landowners and thus that the unification did not lead to a substantial transfer of land from peasants or magnates to the king.[143] By contrast, Knut Dørum

---

140 Emmanuelsson, *Kyrkojorden*, p. 71. The basis for this estimate is Bishop Øystein Aslaksson's cadaster for around 1400, the most complete of its kind in the Middle Ages.
141 Emmanuelsson, *Kyrkojorden*, p. 166.
142 Holmsen, *Nye studier*, pp. 101-46, on Trøndelag and the area north of Oslo; Bjørkvik, "Eit kyrkjeleg godskompleks", pp. 57-63, who traces a core area in the lands of the monastery just north of Bergen that probably stems from a royal donation at the foundation, and *Jordeige*, pp. 74-78, on similar conditions in Ryfylke and Jæren.
143 Skre, *Herredømmet*, pp. 109-24. In addition to his analysis of the landed estates at Romerike, Skre points to an example suggesting that royal confiscations did not necessarily mean that the previous owner completely lost his land, but that he may have received it back from the king as a kind of fief (op. cit., pp. 55 f.).

has defended the traditional opinion. Both scholars draw their evidence from Romerike, north of Oslo. Dørum has given good arguments that a larger number of farms than those listed by Skre had belonged to the king at some time, although some of them may have been confiscated during the struggles in the 1220s rather than in the eleventh century.[144] In particular, it seems *a priori* likely that large donations of land to the bishops came from the king. The evidence for the king as the founder of the bishoprics is strong, and large donations such as these may well have been given in connection with the foundation. If not, they are still most likely to have come from the king. A wealthy aristocrat who had a vast amount of land to donate would have been more likely to establish a monastery with a particular link to his own family than to let his lands form part of the estates of an already wealthy bishopric, unless, of course, he was himself the bishop. We actually know of some such donations. Two of the greatest magnates during the early phases of the civil wars, Gregorius Dagsson and Erling Skakke, both founded monastic institutions: the former the nunnery of Gimsøy near Skien, the latter the Augustinian monastery of Halsnøy, the richest monastery in the country. Later the earl Skule Bårdsson founded the nunnery of Rein in Trøndelag. It seems quite clear that both the king and the lay aristocracy donated land to the Church, as did the prelates themselves, from the mid-twelfth century at the latest, once they had become part of the aristocracy. An estimate of the relative importance of the two categories of secular donors is given by Emmanuelsson who suggests that the bishop of Oslo received 40 percent of his lands from the king and 20 percent from the lay aristocracy.[145] Generally, Emmanuelsson is closer to Skre than to Dørum in his estimates, but admits that the king was a great donor until the end of the thirteenth century but not in the Later Middle Ages.

Even if the role of the king in building up the Church should be somewhat reduced compared to the traditional hypothesis, the Church must have contributed to the centralisation of landed wealth: several independent estates, owned by resident wealthy peasants or aristocrats, were turned over to a central institution which then rented them out to tenants. All bishoprics and some of the larger monasteries owned these kinds of estates, which means that at least a substantial part of the donations to the Church had this effect. Moreover, ecclesiastical estates had another centralising effect. As the Church was an institution that "never died", there was no division between heirs, whereas aristocratic estates were accumulated as well as divided according to the vicissitudes of inheritance. Canon law also forbade alienation of ecclesiastical property, and although this was not

---

144 Dørum, *Romerike*, pp. 69-188.
145 Emmanuelsson, *Kyrkojorden*, pp. 212 f. The basis for this estimate is the greater increase in the bishop's land before 1300 than after.

always respected, there is no evidence of any substantial reduction of ecclesiastical property in Norway.

This conclusion can be further substantiated by the division of ecclesiastical property between the various ecclesiastical institutions. By the end of the Middle Ages, the land belonging to the Church is estimated to have been divided in the following way: a little less than one third to local churches and priests, a little more than one sixth to the episcopal sees and about the same to the cathedral chapters, one fourth to the monasteries, and one tenth to the royal chapels.[146] The five bishops and their cathedral chapters thus had more than 30 percent of the whole. This made the archbishop the greatest landowner in the country next to the king, with 7000-8000 pails (*laupar* = 15.43 kg) of butter per year, or nearly twice as much as the greatest secular landowner (below p. 120), in addition to his other, very substantial revenues.[147] The other bishops had far less, but enough to make them the wealthiest aristocrats in the country. Furthermore, the cathedral chapters were almost as wealthy as the bishops and received portions of the tax and fine incomes of the dioceses. Both the institutions and the individual canons thus represented substantial wealth. By contrast, the monasteries had significantly less. The three wealthiest, Halsnøy in Sunnhordland, Hovedøy outside Oslo and Munkeliv in Bergen, had incomes of respectively 680, 600 and 590 pails,[148] which made the whole monastic community the equivalent of a wealthy magnate outside the top circle and placed their abbots somewhat lower on the scale. In addition, the bishops had incomes from tithes and fines, which further increased the difference between them and the monasteries, unless the latter controlled local churches and could appropriate their portion of the tithes. Incorporation of local churches of course increased the percentage of ecclesiastical wealth appropriated by the central institutions more than indicated above.

The monarchy was also a new institution, not much older than the Church, and although its basis was probably some kind of centralised authority in various parts of the country, it is likely to have contributed to further centralisation in the same way as the Church. If a substantial part of the ecclesiastical lands came from the king, he must also have played an important part in the concentration of landed wealth. Moreover, he was still by far the largest landowner in the country in the early fourteenth century, with estates calculated at the value of 21,000 pails. A considerable part of this land is likely to have come from confiscations, mainly during the periods of internal struggles in the

---

146 Helle, *Norge blir en stat*, p. 238.
147 Bjørkvik, *Folketap*, pp. 62 f.; Dybdahl, *Trondheim erkesetes økonomi*, pp. 314 f. The estimates are based on retrospection from late medieval sources and must be regarded as approximate. Bjørkvik suggests 8000 pails and Dybdahl 7000.
148 Bjørkvik, *Folketap*, p. 63.

late tenth and early eleventh centuries and from 1130-1240. The development of royal jurisdiction also resulted in land being transferred to the king as fines. Finally, the king eventually claimed ownership of land not owned by anyone else, which made people taking up new land in such areas the king's tenants.

If Bjørkvik's calculation is correct, the lay aristocracy does not seem to be an important factor in the concentration of landed wealth, except in so far as it contributed to the wealth of the Church, which is likely to have been the case. However, Bjørkvik's calculation is most probably too low. The main problem regarding lay landownership is distinguishing between the aristocracy and the peasants. The Norwegian aristocracy is conspicuous by its absence in most twelfth- and early thirteenth-century sources, not appearing as a separate category in official documents, such as the Law of Succession of 1163/64 or in accounts of assemblies convoked by the king. Powerful men who oppose the king in the sagas are normally referred to as *bœndr* (farmers/peasants). The only individuals distinct from this category were the ones who had received a title from the king, either *jarl* (earl), of which there seems to have been normally only one at a time in the twelfth and thirteenth centuries, or *lendmenn* who were more numerous but hardly numbered more than twenty or thirty at a time.[149] These titles were not hereditary, although sons of *lendmenn* were often granted the title after their father's death. There are even examples of *lendmenn* within the same family over eight (Bjarkøy) and nine (Giske) generations.[150] During the thirteenth century, a new criterion of aristocratic status developed: membership in the organisation of the king's retainers, the *hird*, which entailed some relatively modest privileges in the form of a limited tax exemption and the right to be judged by special courts (below pp. 325-27, 331).

In practice, however, aristocrats are not easily distinguished from the rest of the population. Family names were not used until the late fourteenth and fifteenth century and even then not consistently, and individual aristocrats did not necessarily use their titles in the charters.[151] It is therefore possible that the line of division between the two categories should be drawn differently than in Bjørkvik's calculation and that a larger percentage should be attributed to the aristocracy. This in turn would make Norway less of an exception than the original calculation suggests. Moreover, if we are interested in social structure, a formal definition of the aristocracy is of limited interest. From a social and

---

149 Storm, "Om Lendermandsklassens Tallrighed", pp. 129-88; the conclusion, pp. 84-88, suggests a little more than twenty in the twelfth century and less than fifteen in the thirteenth, which is significantly lower than earlier calculations. Later historians have largely followed Storm. Kleivane, *Høvding*, pp. 157-85, sets the number at 20-25 in the twelfth century with up to 30 over shorter periods, and just under 20 in the period 1240-80.
150 Kleivane, *Høvding*, p. 158.
151 Ugulen, "… alle the knaber", p. 65.

economic point of view, we can define aristocratic status as the ability to have an aristocratic lifestyle without working the land; which means, in addition to possessing one or more residential farms, having substantial incomes from possessing farms worked by tenants. We may suggest a criterion of how much land is necessary to enable a man to have an aristocratic lifestyle, but it is in most cases impossible to tell whether a particular individual fills this criterion or not. On the collective level, the question to be asked is whether the around 60 percent or more of the landed wealth owned by the laity mainly consisted of large estates where most of the land was cultivated by tenants, or whether there was still a numerous class of small landowners. This is also a difficult question to answer. Certainly, 33 percent peasant ownership does not mean that all this land was owned by small freeholders; a large percentage may well have belonged to people who had more than one farm and thus formed an elite within peasant society. Nor do we know whether there was any economic difference between the titled aristocracy we meet at court and in the king's service and this local elite, although there likely was.

A comparison between the top layers of the lay and ecclesiastical aristocracies nevertheless confirms the relatively greater wealth of the latter. Only one lay family appears in the same category regarding landed wealth as the bishops, namely that of Bjarkøy-Giske after the two estates had been joined by marriage in the early fourteenth century. By that time the owner of the estates, Erling Vidkunsson, who led the regency for Magnus Erlingsson in the 1320s, had an annual income of 4200 pails. The second wealthiest family, that of Sørum, had only around half of this income, whereas the great majority of the class – around 600 families – hardly had much more than the wealthy peasants.[152] According to Bjørkvik's calculation, between eleven and twenty of the families owned around twenty percent of the total landed incomes of the country and the three wealthiest nine percent. In principle, there is therefore no clear evidence that the lay aristocracy of the early fourteenth century was wealthier than that of the Viking Age, although we may imagine that the expansion of the monarchy led to the formation of an aristocracy more strongly linked to the king and with property spread over a larger part of the country than in the earlier period.

Although Bjørkvik's calculations are very uncertain and he may have exaggerated the percentage belonging to the Church and the peasants, there are some indications that these groups had relatively more land than those in most other countries. The reason for this may be sought in the slow development of a military elite in Norway. Because of the continued use of the *leidang*, the Norwegian king may have found it less necessary than his counterparts in other countries to strengthen the lay aristocracy with large donations

---

152   Bjørkvik, *Folketap og sammenbrudd*, pp. 73 f.; Dybdahl, "Giskeættens jordegods".

of land and may therefore have given more to the Church. If this holds true, there may be a connection between the relative strength of the Church and that of the peasants, as well as of the relative weakness of the lay aristocracy.

Despite the difficulties in estimating the landed wealth in the early fourteenth century compared to that of the Viking Age, we may conclude that there was a trend towards greater concentration of landownership in the intervening period. Thus, Norway developed in a similar way as the rest of the northern and eastern periphery, despite its lack of military specialisation. This in turn forms an argument for Holmsen's explanation, based mainly on population strain, as opposed to that of Lunden who also emphasises military power. This explanation is further strengthened by the fact that its main beneficiary seems to be the Church rather than the king and the aristocracy. The situation after the Black Death serves as further evidence for this conclusion: the land rent sunk to around 20 percent of the previous level – far more than in the neighbouring countries as well as in most others – and an enormous number of farms were deserted.[153] There is no indication that more people died from the plague in Norway than in other countries. The most likely explanation is therefore twofold: that the aristocracy lacked alternative ways of exploiting the land and that it was unable to force the peasants to pay more, both because of their scattered holdings.[154] Consequently, population pressure and scarcity of land seem a better explanation for the high land rent in the High Middle Ages than military power. However, the introduction of Christianity and the development of the royal and ecclesiastical organisations must have had similar effects as the population strain, which shall be discussed in greater detail in the following chapters.

The Towns – Centres of the Monarchy and the Church

The centralisation of landed property discussed above not only consisted in land being transferred from small individual peasants to great landowners, but also in a transfer from local to central owners. The likely confiscation and donation to the Church of large complexes of farm land are good examples of this. Instead of being the centre of a local power, these farms became parts of the large estates of owners who did not reside in the area, in most cases a bishop who resided in a town. Holmsen is therefore right in regarding the rise of towns from the eleventh and twelfth centuries onwards as an indication of a transformation in land ownership.

---

153 Salvesen, "Landskyldutviklingen", pp. 137-41; Sandnes, *Ødegårder,* "Kronologi og årsaker"; Gissel, *Desertion,* pp. 158-71.
154 Bagge and Mykland, *Norge i dansketiden*, p. 25.

There has been an extensive discussion about town origins in Norway. The two main points of view go back to P. A. Munch who regarded the towns as the result of spontaneous growth and to Gustav Storm who claimed that they were royal foundations.[155] The former view was the more widespread until around 1950, whereas the latter has gained more adherents in recent decades. Opinions are still divided, and various combinations of the two views also exist. The fact that all towns that existed in the Middle Ages were founded after the rise of the monarchy and the introduction of Christianity forms a strong argument in favour of Storm's view. Admittedly, a ninth-century town has been excavated at Skiringssal in Tjølling in present-day Vestfold fylke, but it only lasted for a hundred years and was deserted around 960.[156] Moreover, it is difficult to imagine what kind of social and economic needs would lead to the spontaneous growth of towns in a country like Norway. There has obviously been trade since far back in history, as well as larger and smaller marketplaces, and possibly also clusters of houses and farms where exchange took place. However, in a country where most of the population was spread thinly over a long coast and there were plenty of good harbours, it seems more likely that economic exchange took place in a large number of smaller places that often shifted, than in larger, permanent settlements with a special status, as the towns were both in Norway and in other countries in the Middle Ages. Long distance trade might form an exception to this, but in the Early Middle Ages it mostly seems to have consisted in Norwegians going abroad with their merchandise. Besides, long distance trade is unlikely to involve a permanent number of people sufficient for forming the basis of towns.[157] By contrast, the king and the Church had clear interests in the existence of towns, both as residences and as centres of trade, and are therefore likely to have been the main forces behind the urbanisation. For great landowners, drawing the surplus from farms spread over a wide area and wanting to exchange their surplus for imported goods, there were obvious advantages in gathering the whole to one place and in buying and selling in large quantities. Kings and great lords might also profit from trade by taxes, tolls or rights to preemption. Moreover, bishops normally resided in towns, both because it was the tradition and because they could live more comfortably and administer more efficiently from there, and the king eventually followed suit. The lay aristocrats apparently did not move to the towns to the same extent, but they often had houses there and needed to be there frequently in order to serve the king.

---

155 Munch, *Historisk-geografhisk Beskrivelse*; Storm, "De kongelige Byanlæg". On the historiography, see Helle, *Kongssete*, pp. 94-113, and "Fra opphavet", pp. 42-44, and Hansen, *Bergen*, pp. 23-30.
156 Skre et al., *Kaupang*, conclusions in Skre, "The Emergence" and "Towns and Markets".
157 Helle, "Fra opphavet", p. 33.

Although the sites chosen by kings and bishops may have had an earlier history as settlements and centres of trade, this early history is of limited importance to their eventual town status; many more such places must have existed without developing into towns. Some of them, like Skiringssal, may also have reached a size comparable to the later towns, which may in turn be evidence of local centres of power before the unification of Norway. Future excavations may well uncover parallels to Skiringssal and thus change our picture of towns as belonging mainly to the Christian era, although this does not necessarily mean that they were the result of spontaneous growth, as the recent interpretation of Skiringssal strongly suggests its dependence on a local lord.[158] Trade needed protection, while at the same time profit from trade was a strong incentive for rulers to set up towns and marketplaces. If towns are found to have been more widespread in the Viking Age or even earlier than hitherto assumed, it will increase our information about the political conditions in the period before the unification, but also, if the example of Skiringssal is representative, it will confirm the impression of less stability in the political formations at the time.

The towns founded in the Christian period need not have been larger or more numerous, but they did survive until the Reformation, most of them even to the present. From the twelfth century at the latest the medieval towns were institutions with a separate law (The Bjarkøy Law) and an administration different from that of the countryside. When the sagas state that a king founded a town, they probably mean that he conferred this particular status on it.[159] Although it is uncertain whether these statements are based on any authentic evidence, the criterion itself may make this more likely than if the saga writers simply had wanted to honour the self-growing towns with a royal founder. The towns' status as royal and ecclesisastical administrative centres also secured them a permanent population. A bishop's residence necessitated a lay population of at least several hundred, in the form of servants, merchants and artisans, people engaged in the building and maintenance of the cathedral and so forth. Moreover, the land rent from large districts outside the town was brought there and was partly consumed, partly exchanged for other commodities which in turn increased the population.[160]

Recent research suggests that the oldest of the Norwegian towns is Trondheim (usually called Nidaros in the Middle Ages), founded at the end of the tenth century (the traditional date is 997) by King Olav Tryggvason as a stronghold from which to control the important, conquered area of Trøndelag.[161] According to the sagas another early town,

---

158 Skre, "Preparing the New Campaign", pp. 44-47, "Towns and Markets".
159 Helle, *Kongssete,* pp. 86-90.
160 For examples of this, see e.g. Helle, *Kongssete,* pp. 118-20, and Nedkvitne and Norseng, *Byen under Eikaberg,* pp. 153-79.
161 For this and the following, see Andersson, "Urbanisation", pp. 325-29 with references.

Sarpsborg, was founded by St Olav, which may well be correct. Olav had his core area in the southeast and may have established Sarpsborg as a stronghold in order to control the area and as protection against his rivals in the neighbouring countries. The sagas attribute the founding of Oslo to Olav's half-brother Harald Hardrada, who probably also had his base in the east. He spent most of his reign attempting to conquer Denmark, while also launching several expeditions to the inner parts of Eastern Norway to suppress that region. Oslo would have been useful for both purposes. However, an alternative hypothesis, based on some archaeological evidence of an earlier settlement, is that Oslo was founded by the Danes to control the Oslofjord area after their victory at Svolder.[162] Further to the southeast Tønsberg was previously regarded as the oldest town in the country because of a reference to its existence before the battle of Hafrsfjord in *Heimskringla*, but so far, there is no archaeological evidence for this early date. Written evidence suggests that Tønsberg was a town from the early twelfth century at the latest.[163] Both Oslo and Tønsberg are surrounded by rich agricultural land and form natural centres of local exchange. Oslo later became the residence of a bishop, while Tønsberg had several important ecclesiastical institutions and a royal residence. Konghelle, near the Swedish border, is mentioned as a meeting place for kings in the eleventh century, but as a town only from the reign of Sigurd Magnusson (1103-30).[164]

According to the sagas, Bergen was founded by Olav Kyrre around 1070, a date that has been accepted by most scholars.[165] Recently, however, Gitte Hansen has tentatively suggested an earlier date after finding traces of settlement which she dates to around 1020/30, a date that would point in the direction of St Olav as the founder.[166] In light of the argument above (p. 122), a connection between these traces and the later town seems doubtful. Nor is St Olav a very likely candidate for the establishment of Bergen, as Western Norway was apparently the part of the country over which he had least control.[167] Generally, there is a striking lack of references to Western Norway in the sagas during the reign of Olav and his two nearest successors. It would seem more logical for Olav Kyrre, who was able to take over a pacified country after his strict father, to have formed closer links to Western Norway and to have attempted to profit from the important trade routes along the western coast. In the following period, Bergen also became an episcopal

---

162 Nedkvitne and Norseng, *Byen under Eikaberg*, pp. 14-73; Molaug, "Oslo blir by".
163 Helle, "Fra opphavet", pp. 57 f.; Ulriksen, "Tønsberg".
164 Ibid., p. 58 f.
165 Helle, *Kongssete*, pp. 86-94, 111-13 with references.
166 Hansen, *Bergen*, pp. 127-31.
167 Bagge, "Mellom kildekritikk og historisk antropologi", pp. 189 f., and above p. 30. See also Helle, "Fra opphavet", pp. 45-48.

residence. When the diocesan organisation was established, probably during Olav's reign, the official residence of the bishop of Western Norway was Selja, where the relics of the patron saint of the diocese, St Sunniva and her followers, had been found. However, the bishop soon moved to Bergen, and in 1170 the see, together with the relics, was officially moved. Finally, Stavanger and Hamar were founded in the twelfth century as residences for the bishops of the new dioceses.

There thus seems to be a strong connection between the rise of the monarchy and the rise of towns, and in some cases even strategic reasons for the founding of them. During the twelfth century, the king increasingly began to reside in towns, and in the thirteenth century the king's itinerary mainly consisted in movements between them. The Church was of even greater importance. Two of the smaller towns, Stavanger and Hamar, were almost exclusively upheld by the bishops, which became evident after the Reformation when the towns dwindled into insignificance. Trondheim also declined significantly after the abolition of the archdiocese. Only Bergen and Oslo continued to flourish, the former because of the fish trade, the latter because it became the main residence for the Danish administration in Norway.

While the towns' residential function was probably the main explanation for their origin and continued to form the basis of their existence, they also served as centres of trade. This applies above all to Bergen, the main centre of international trade in Norway and, beside Stockholm, the largest town in Scandinavia in the Middle Ages, with between 5000 and 10,000 inhabitants, making it a town of medium size by northern European standards. The growth of towns is thus evidence of the same strengthening of the landowning class as indicated by the demographic and economic development. The towns served as residences for the new royal and ecclesiastical elites and their subordinates, and their function as centres of trade was mainly based on the export of land rent in the form of fish and agricultural products which were exchanged for luxury commodities. By contrast, they were to a very limited extent centres of production, apart from what was needed for the inhabitants of the towns themselves. Nor was there, unlike most other countries in Europe, a wave of founding new towns from around 1200 onwards. Whereas around twenty percent of the population of England and ten percent of that of Scotland is believed to have lived in towns around 1300, the corresponding percentage of the Norwegian population is hardly more than five. This is also related to the fact that most of the export trade was in the hands of German merchants and that no important class of merchants developed in the Norwegian towns during the Middle Ages (below pp. 350-53).[168]

---

168 Richard Holt, "What if the Sea were Different?". Holt seeks an explanation for the lack of urbanisation and commercialisation in Norway in the weakness of the aristocracy and the absence of feudalisation.

The King's Revenues

The foreign policy and the absence of a military revolution suggest that the king's share of this concentration of wealth was relatively modest. This has also been the common opinion among agrarian historians since Asgaut Steinnes's great study of royal taxation[169] which estimated the king's total annual income – taxes, fines, land rent, etc. – to around 8000 marks or 1500 kg silver. Steinnes's calculation implies that the three main categories of royal revenues were approximately equal. Evidently, the fines are the most uncertain category, as they must have varied from year to year and between the various districts. Nor have any accounts of the fines been preserved from the period before 1350, and very few for the rest of the Middle Ages. On the basis of retrospection from scattered accounts from the Later Middle Ages, Benedictow estimates the fines to have been around 40 percent of the tax,[170] whereas Bjørkvik regards them as equal to both the tax and the land rent and thus the largest of the three categories – 32,250 pails of butter or 10,750 marks.[171] Bjørkvik's calculation is based on more complete material for the period 1548-1612, when the judicial and administrative system was still largely similar to the medieval one, and adjusted to allow for the decline in the population after 1350 and a certain weakening of the royal administration in the Later Middle Ages. The more complete material makes this calculation preferable to Benedictow's, although it is still very uncertain.[172] Even if we have to adjust Bjørkvik's numbers downwards, however, there seem to be good arguments for regarding the fines as the largest category of income.

As Norwegian society at the time was mainly agrarian, calculations of royal revenues have mostly paid little attention to incomes from towns and trade. Recently, however, Svein Gullbekk has pointed to minting as a considerable source of income.[173] Although some coins were struck in Norway as early as the late tenth century, regular minting was not introduced until the reign of Harald Hardrada in the mid-eleventh century. Harald, who had brought with him a large amount of silver and treasures from Byzantium and Russia, began

---

169 Steinnes, *Gamal skatteskipnad*.
170 Benedictow, *Fra rike til provins*, pp. 450 f.
171 Bjørkvik, *Samanbrudd*, p. 51.
172 Bjørkvik's method is explained in greater detail in Dørum, *Romerike*, p. 278, who refers to a letter from him. Bjørkvik reduces the average from the period 1548-1612 by 15 percent to get back to the period of the Reformation, apparently to adjust for the increase in population during the sixteenth century and the suppression of the ecclesiastical jurisdiction which must have increased the king's incomes from fines. Furthermore, he estimates that the fines declined more than the tax during the Later Middle Ages, 70-75 percent against 60-65 percent. Both calculations are open to discussion; the increase after the Reformation may well have been more than 15 percent and it is not obvious that the income from fines decreased more than the tax in the Later Middle Ages. See Blom, *Norge i union*, pp. 543-711, and Imsen, *Bondekommunalisme*, pp. 139-72, who conclude that the agrarian historians have exaggerated the breakdown in the royal administration in the Later Middle Ages.
173 For the following, see Gullbekk, *Pengevesenets fremvekst*, pp. 19-99, 129-78.

by issuing good quality coins which then gradually deteriorated during his reign. He seems, however, to have succeeded in having his coins accepted as the usual means of payment and in preventing the use of foreign coinage. After him there is an unbroken tradition of minting down to the collapse of Norwegian coinage in the later fourteenth century. The fact that a royal monopoly of minting existed in Norway during this period is in itself evidence of some strength in the monarchy, as it shows sufficient trust in the king for the people to have accepted his mint as a means of payment at a higher value than its content of silver, and his ability to exclude foreign coinage. Moreover, this inflated value gave the king a substantial income, in particular if he managed to have coins with a low percentage of silver accepted at full value. The king of Norway did not succeed completely in this, as there was a distinction between burnt (pure), silver and coins, and between weighed and counted coins, as well as some restrictions regarding the use of coins, but he nevertheless gained a substantial profit from minting low quality coins. Gullbekk has estimated this profit at up to 300 to 400 percent. Its size in absolute terms of course depends on the amount of coins in circulation, on which there are widely different opinions,[174] but Gullbekk suggests that it may in some years have reached 7500-10,000 marks burnt (2500-3300 kg silver) or as much or even more than the king's other estimated annual revenues.[175] However, this sum seems too large; the Danish king's income from minting is estimated at only 12 percent of the whole (or 1100-2200 kg silver) around 1230, and money is likely to have been in wider use in Denmark than in Norway, in addition to the fact that the Danish population was much larger (below pp. 128 f.). The king of Norway's income from the *Finnferd* (p. 185) and customs duties from the export of stockfish may also have been considerable; a recent calculation suggests 300-550 marks burnt for the former and 500 for the latter.[176] Although most of these sums are very uncertain, it would still seem that Steinnes's calculation is too low and that the total must have amounted to at least 10,000 marks burnt or probably more.

There has been some discussion as to whether the king actually received the taxes he was due. On the basis of examples from the civil wars Orning suggests that taxes, military service and other payments and duties were the subject of constant negotiation,[177] but

---

174 See Lunden, "Money Economy" and "Mynt, andre pengar", pp. 16-23, who argues that money was little used, even if Gullbekk's calculation of 10-20 million of the king's coins in circulation in the late thirteenth century is correct. Holt, "What if the Sea were Different" also points to the lack of commercialisation in Norwegian society and the limited use of money.
175 Gullbekk, *Pengevesenets fremvekst*, p. 175. Cf. also p. 129 on Philip IV of France who in eighteen months in 1298-99 earned 1.2 million *livres tournoises* by debasing the coins, whereas his other incomes in the same period amounted to 800.000 *livres*. In Hungary, the king's income from minting is calculated at 35 percent of the total in the twelfth century (Engel, *The Realm of St Stephen*, pp. 62 f.).
176 Moseng et al., *Norsk historie*, p. 216.
177 Orning, "Den materielle basis", pp. 457-60.

these examples are hardly representative of the following period. On the contrary, the system guaranteed the king certain contributions while at the same time it protected the peasants against extra demands. Appeals to "the good old customs" and "the old, lawful taxes" were regularly used to counteract such steps from the authorities. As Dørum convincingly shows, it must have been easy for the king to know how much he was due, and the admittedly limited evidence from the Later Middle Ages does not suggest that the peasants lagged behind with their payments. This evidence also suggests that tax incomes declined less than the land rent,[178] which in turn forms the argument that this part of the royal revenues was fairly constant. It is also doubtful how much Orning's example from England under King John can tell about Norwegian conditions.[179] To the extent that it can, it points in the opposite direction of what Orning implies, showing that the king of England was able to increase his revenues at an impressive rate when necessary – they were doubled from 1210 to 1211 and again from 1211 to 1212 – and not that he had to negotiate to get his due from year to year. If Norway had resembled England, we would have to conclude that the king's incomes were higher, the king stronger and the government more state-like than the agrarian historians maintain.

The Norwegian royal revenues were of course far lower than the English ones. They are also considered to have been lower than those of the other Scandinavian kings. Thanks to the preservation of a series of documents from around 1230 (the main part of which is dated to 1231), usually referred to as King Valdemar (the Victorious)'s cadaster, we have much information about the Danish royal revenues around this time, although there is considerable scholarly disagreement about the interpretation of the source. The income from the *leding* is estimated at 20-40,000 marks (3750-7500 kg) silver, which makes around 40 percent of the total. The other major source of income at the time was the royal domains with 32 percent, whereas town incomes made 8 percent, fines and wrecks 8 percent and mint 12 percent. With 50-100,000 marks (9375-18,750 kg) silver the Danish royal revenues are thus five to ten times higher than the Norwegian ones in the early fourteenth century.[180] The Danish population around 1230 is estimated at around 1.3 million, largely on the basis of Valdermar's cadaster. With the same increase as in England, the corresponding number for the mid-fourteenth century becomes nearly 2 million.[181]

178 Dørum, "Materiell basis", pp. 88-92, regards the decline in tax incomes as proportional to the decline in population but not more, whereas Moseng et al., p. 306, estimates the reduction of taxes at 60-65 percent and the reduction of the land rent at 80 percent.
179 Orning, "Kongemaktens", p. 681; cf. Bartlett, *England*, pp. 159-77.
180 Erslev, *Valdemarernes Storhedstid*, pp. 153-84; Poulsen, "Kingdoms on the Periphery of Europe", p. 109. However, Ulsig, "Landboer og bryder", pp. 152 f., suggests that the current calculations of the tax may be exaggerated.
181 Hybel and Poulsen, *The Danish Resources*, pp. 124-29.

Estimates for the Norwegian population in the mid-fourteenth century vary between 300,000 and 500,000, which, with the same increase as in Denmark, would correspond to between 200,000 and 334,000 around 1230 or between one sixth and one fourth of the Danish population. Most probably, however, the king of Norway's incomes were also lower around 1230 than in the mid-fourteenth century. Although the king's percentage of landed estates was higher, the land rent was probably lower, as were the fines; the great expansion of royal justice had hardly begun at this time. On the other hand, the Danish king's incomes were drastically reduced in the period after 1241, when much land was lost and a large percentage of the tax-paying peasants submitted to aristocratic landowners who were then able to appropriate the taxes.[182] A revival took place with the strengthening of the monarchy from the mid-fourteenth century, when parts of the royal lands that had been aleniated were recovered and the king succeeded in imposing extraordinary taxes on the population which became common practice.

The most relevant comparison will therefore be the two monarchies at their peak, Norway around 1350 and Denmark around 1230, when the Danish incomes were five to ten times higher and the Danish population only two and a half to four times higher. As all calculations of medieval populations are based on deductions from more or less complete estimates of numbers of farms or, in the most fortunate cases, heads of households, comparisons between countries should be based on calculations on the same end of the scale for both. In this case the Danish population could hardly have been more than three or four times larger than the Norwegian one. In comparison, the two populations were approximately equal in size, 440,000 for Norway and 450,000 for Denmark around 1660, when the demographic material is better, and continued to be so during the following period.[183] At this time, however, Denmark had lost some of its most populous provinces to Sweden in addition to the demographic crisis it suffered during the preceding period of wars, and Southern Jutland at this time formed a separate province that was not included in the reckoning. Nevertheless, the numbers from around 1660 make it difficult to believe in a Danish population six times larger than the Norwegian one in the mid-fourteenth century.

These numbers make the medieval Danish king's relative wealth several times as large as that of his Norwegian counterpart, which demonstrates the former's greater success in imposing burdens on his people. It must also be added that the reduction in income in the period 1241-1340 does not mean that the burden on the people was reduced, but that the surplus went to other parts of the elite, notably the aristocracy. In absolute terms –

---

182 Technically, land being transferred in this way was said to be exempted from taxes, which some historians have understood as meaning that the peasants did not have to pay but which in reality meant that they paid to the landowner instead of the king (Ulsig, "Landboer og bryder", pp. 154 f.).
183 Dyrvik, *Truede tvillingriker*, pp. 95 f.

which is of course the most important when comparing the military strength of the two countries – there is even less doubt about Danish superiority throughout the period. The Norwegian tax was also far lower than it became later, around one fifth of the level in the mid-seventeenth century. In total, however, the peasants paid approximately the same to the upper classes in the seventeenth century as in the High Middle Ages; the difference was that the land rent was five times higher in the early fourteenth century.[184] The Norwegian peasants were therefore not so much better off than their counterparts in Denmark and Sweden as the difference in taxes would indicate.

Even if Steinnes's estimate is too low, the recent, higher estimates hardly make the king of Norway seem particularly wealthy. However, as the example from England quoted above illustrates, the regular incomes of medieval monarchs were usually very small; many other examples show the same.[185] The crucial question is how much the king was able to mobilise in case of war. There are various hints at extra taxes but we do not know their size and there is little to suggest that they were very substantial until the early sixteenth century, with the exception of the areas around the main castles, where higher burdens were imposed on the peasants in the form of extra taxes and labour services.[186] The most important extra resource was of course the *leidang* which put quite a substantial army or fleet at the king's disposal for two months, without costs and for even longer against extra payments, which was an important asset. Nevertheless, the generally cautious and peaceful foreign policy conducted by Norwegian kings in the period 1240-1319 indicates that there were clear limits on how much they could extract from their subjects for such purposes. The neighbouring countries, notably Denmark, spent much more, although in some cases – like that of Erik Menved (1286-1319) – with disastrous results.

We do not know exactly how much of these revenues went directly to the king and how much to his officials. The land rent and tax were supposed to go directly to the king, whereas most of the fines went to the *sysselmenn* who, according to Dørum's calculation, which seems reasonable, received two thirds of them.[187] Thus, if we accept Bjørkvik's calculation, the *sysselmann*'s total income from this source amounted to 22,000 pails of

---

184 Holmsen, *Nye studier*, pp. 28-46.
185 Reinhard, *Power Elites*, p. 13; Ormrod, "The West European Monarchies", pp. 138-44, on England and France in the fourteenth century.
186 Poulsen, "Kingdoms on the Periphery of Europe", pp. 114 f.; Moseng et al., *Norsk historie*, pp. 305-7.
187 Confiscations and the special fines homicides had to pay for being allowed to stay in the country, plus fines for *brefabrot* went directly to the king. We only have information about the other fines as they concerned the towns, where they were divided into three, between the *sysselmann*, the royal representative in the town and the community of the burghers. It seems unlikely that the king received more from the countryside than the towns, whereas the burghers in the towns were more likely to have received a portion than the peasants. Consequently, the *sysselmann* may well have received the whole amount in the countryside. See Holmsen, *Nye studier*, p. 173, and Bagge, "Borgerkrig", p. 178 n. 105.

butter or 7000 old marks. Each *sysselmann* would then, on average, have had an income of 440 pails of butter, or nearly 150 old marks, which corresponds to the rent from seventy to eighty farms of normal size in Eastern Norway. Even if the correct number were considerably lower than this, the king's service must have been extremely attractive to members of the aristocracy. Nor would the *sysselmenn* have any difficulty in keeping the amount of men listed in the provisions from 1273-74 permanently in their service.[188]

Nevertheless, the king in person received a larger part of the royal revenues than his counterparts in the neighbouring countries. The Danish and Swedish system, like those of most other European countries, probably created greater gross surpluses, in the sense that the number of agricultural labourers rose and that each of them paid a larger percentage of the family's earnings to the king or the landowner. It is questionable to what extent it also created a greater net surplus. Some calculations – admittedly based on very fragmentary material from the Later Middle Ages in Sweden – indicate that most of what was paid in taxes by the peasants went to support the lord of the castle and his household and garrison.[189] The greater surplus in the neighbouring countries was thus not only invested in military efficiency or other services to the king but also in conspicuous consumption and a higher standard of living for the aristocracy. This seems largely to conform to the general pattern in Northern and East Central Europe. Whereas in the mid-twelfth century Otto of Freising describes Hungary as a country ruled by an absolute king and without aristocratic privilege,[190] a strong Western European style ecclesiastical and lay aristocracy developed in all three East Central European kingdoms during the thirteenth century through the development of the Church, population increase, including immigration, and the adaptation of Western military technology, heavy cavalry and castles. The construction of the latter increased particularly as a consequence of the Mongol attacks in 1241-42, 1259 and 1287. Politically, the consolidation of the aristocracy was demonstrated by attempts to restrict the king's power and defend the privileges of the aristocracy, as in the Golden Bull in Hungary of 1222 which forms a parallel to the Magna Carta in England.[191] In the beginning the military transformation may have favoured the king, but the surplus from the increased exploitation of the peasant population largely went to

---

188 As the fines were the *sysselmann*'s most important source of income, the amount of men to be mobilised from each district was clearly based on some idea of the size of this income from various parts of the country, although it is hardly possible to calculate the exact sums on the basis of this, as Holmsen tries to do (Holmsen, *Nye studier*, pp. 173 f.).
189 Lönnroth, *Statsmakt och statsfinans*, pp. 142-52; Hybel and Poulsen, *The Danish Resources*, pp. 320-22; Retsø, *Länsförvaltningen*.
190 Otto of Freising, *Gesta Frederici* I.33; Bagge, "Ideas and Narrative", pp. 359 f. Although exaggerated, this description is on some points confirmed by other evidence (Engel, *The Realm of St Stephen*, p. 59).
191 Engel, *The Realm of St Stephen*, pp. 93-95; Rowell, "The Central European Kingdoms", pp. 754-68.

the lay and ecclesiastical aristocracy – which might create considerable problems for the monarchy in the Later Middle Ages.

Thus, the Norwegian military organisation created a smaller surplus than its counterparts in Denmark, Sweden and East Central Europe but gave the king greater control which to some extent supports the interpretation of an alliance between the king and the peasants in Norway in the Middle Ages (see below pp. 371-75). The military organisation also made the Norwegian king come closer to the classical modern definition of the state as having a monopoly of legitimate violence. Although local officials may well have had greater control of the organisation than indicated in the largely official sources, there is no evidence from the period 1240-1319 of local magnates mobilising the *leidang* against the king. There is some evidence of magnates using armed retainers – and possibly also clients in local communities – against the king, Alv Erlingsson in 1287 and the magnates rebelling against Magnus Eriksson in the 1330s (below pp. 354, 360-64), but it would seem that control over royal castles or the position as *sysselmann* would have been necessary to mobilise any substantial forces, at least before 1319. The possibility for the aristocracy to emerge as an independent power in opposition to the king was also clearly more limited than in a system based on a military elite, the most important members of which acted as commanders of the royal castles. It was also highly unusual for members of the aristocracy to have their own castles. The only examples from before 1319 are Earl Alv Erlingsson of Isegran in the Glomma estuary, within the confines of present-day Fredrikstad in the southeast, and Baron Audun Hugleiksson of Jølster in Sunnfjord (Western Norway). The former was clearly a military stronghold, but we do not know if the latter was as well or was instead a grand residence.[192] Admittedly, during the first half of the fourteenth century, the elite force mustered by the *sysselmenn* had developed into retainers serving their patrons and swearing an oath to them. Some royal ordinances tried to stop this development, but in the end the king had to accept it and try to make use of these forces for his own needs.[193] Thus, a certain amount of feudalisation took place during the first half of the fourteenth century, but the forces under an individual magnate's command were probably too small for him to be able to resist the king. The only magnates with some kind of independent forces in their service were the bishops, notably the archbishop (below p. 231). Additionally, the archbishop and most probably the other bishops as well had stone residences which might have served as castles. There are also some examples from the

---

192 Excavations have uncovered the foundations which are large enough to suggest a heavy building, i.e. of stone (Nedrebø et al., *Audun Hugleiksson*, pp. 134-57).
193 Schreiner, "Hærmakt og riksstyre", pp. 117-20; Opsahl, "Bastard Feudalism".

Later Middle Ages that they were engaged in military actions, although their forces were always inferior to those of the king.

The apparent poverty of the Norwegian king therefore did not necessarily correspond to a military weakness. On the other hand, if the kings of more aristocratic countries managed to create good working relationships with the aristocracy (as in Denmark after 1340, Sweden under the Sture regime 1470-1520[194] and in the kingdoms of East Central Europe for long periods of the fourteenth and fifteenth centuries) such an arrangement might have strengthened their military and administrative capacities. The relative strength of these different military systems must therefore be estimated on the basis of their actual performance. The greater peace and stability in Norway in the period 1240-1319 enabled the Norwegian king to perform fairly well in the Nordic competition, but in the long run, the military power of the neighbouring countries, above all Denmark, proved superior.

Modern accounts of state formation from the Middle Ages to the Early Modern Period often focus on the change from a domain state to a tax state, from the king "living on his own" to the head of state exploiting the resources of his country. Some trends in this direction can be found in the West European monarchies by the Later Middle Ages.[195] In Denmark as well as Norway we find a relatively high percentage of "public" incomes already in the thirteenth century, although there is no clear shift towards an increase in these kinds of income in the following period, with the possible exception of the extraordinary Danish taxes. If the calculation above is correct, however, there is a characteristic difference between the size of the two kinds of public incomes: higher taxes in Denmark, 40 percent against 30 or less in Norway, and higher fines in Norway, 30-50 percent against less than 8 percent in Denmark, corresponding to the greater importance of warfare in Denmark and of justice in Norway.

Conclusion

No military revolution took place in Norway, and as far as we can see, there was considerable continuity in the military organisation from the tenth to the early fourteenth century. The king's control over the *leidang* may have increased, castles were added to the existing equipment and an elite force was built up under the control of the royal officials, a force that may nevertheless have had its parallels in the previous period. Norway thus

---

194 In his extensive study of the Swedish administration 1434-1520, Retsø accepts the traditional view of a small surplus from the *len* ("fiefs"), but explains it as a practical way of governing the realm: as long as the ruler could trust the commander of the *len*, he would receive all the services he needed without having to arrange for the transport and sale of a large amount of taxes in kind (Retsø, *Länsförvaltningen*, pp. 355-73 and *passim*).
195 Ormrod, "The Western European Monarchies", pp. 157 f.

adapted to the military technology of the centre to a lesser extent than most other countries in the northern and eastern periphery of Western Christendom. The explanation of this difference must be sought partly in limited economic resources, partly in distance from the centre which protected the country from foreign conquest and not least in the importance of the sea, not only in controlling Norway itself but also in the targets of Norwegian foreign policy which almost all needed to be approached from the sea.

Geographically, Norwegian foreign policy shows considerable continuity from the Viking Age to the fourteenth century. Whereas the borders towards the two neighbouring countries to the south and east were approximately drawn relatively early and did not change very much until the mid-seventeenth century, the situation was more open in the north and in the islands across the North Sea to the north and west. Claims in these areas were already established in the eleventh century, maybe even earlier, whose success varied according to the relative strength of the Norwegian kings and the local rulers. The consolidation of the Norwegian kingdom after the civil wars led to a more active policy over the whole region which succeeded in the cases of Iceland, Greenland and Northern Norway, while Scottish expansion in the same period led to the loss of the Hebrides and Man. The latter part of Håkon Håkonsson's reign also inaugurated a more active Nordic policy which was continued in the following period and which led to a great success from a dynastic, although not necessarily a national point of view, the union with Sweden in 1319.

An active diplomacy, directed at a wide range of countries, was used to achieve these ends. The most important military instrument was the fleet, which was mainly used for power demonstrations and only as a last resort for active fighting. On land, the Norwegian forces were sufficient for defensive, but rarely for offensive purposes. Expansion was sought through marriage alliances rather than conquest. This foreign policy was considerably more modest and peaceful than that of other kingdoms at the time and it adapted to the limited resources of the country, of which rulers in the period 1240-1319 were well aware but which they tried to exploit as much as possible without overstraining them. Nevertheless, this foreign policy showed some characteristic features of the period. There were few successful wars of conquest between the established kingdoms of Western Christendom in the High Middle Ages. Defensive weapons were stronger than offensive ones; the ability to wage war for longer periods was limited by the vassals' limited duty to serve and by the lack of cash to pay for mercenaries for any great length of time. Consequently, dynastic alliances and legal claims and the alliances needed to pursue them were often used instead of or in addition to warfare. In this respect, Norway differed in degree rather than in kind from other countries at the time.

The absence of a military revolution has its counterpart in low taxes and a relatively modest income for the king. However, the social and economic changes were greater than the military ones. A considerable concentration of landed wealth must have taken place from the Viking Age to the early fourteenth century, above all through the expansion of the Church but also through the development of the monarchy and possibly through the lay aristocracy as well. This in turn contributed to the rise of towns according to contemporary European models and to the deeper integration of Norway in the European trade network. Taken together, these differences point to explanations of social change other than the military one. Apart from demography, these include religion, law, and administration, which will be dealt with in the following.

Religion, Monarchy, and the Right Order of the World

In addition to military technology, the most obvious example of the exports from the core area of Western Christendom is the religion itself, Christianity. The importance of this factor has also been subject to discussion in Norwegian historiography, although the difference between Norway and the other "new" countries is probably less apparent with the religion than in the case of the military technology. However, as already appears from the discussion of social and economic conditions, the importance of Christianisation and the inclusion of Norway in the Catholic Church is not confined to religion in the narrow sense. The establishment of the Church on Norwegian soil led to far-reaching changes in culture as well as institutions and was of crucial importance for the monarchy as well. These changes can be traced to a greater extent in Norway than in many other countries of Western Christendom due to the survival of its relatively extensive secular, or non-Christian literature that also includes evidence of the former religion. Thus, this chapter will not only deal with the reception of Christian ideas but with their meeting with indigenous traditions and the various impulses of a religious and secular nature that laid the ideological foundations for Norwegian state formation.

Old Norse Religion

Christianity was not only a religion different from the traditional one; it was a different kind of religion, with a systematic doctrine, organisation and rituals that were performed in essentially the same way all over Western Christendom, despite some variation in details. The pagan religion lacked all this, but how should it be characterised positively? The first problem relating to this are the sources. Admittedly, we have more evidence for Old Norse paganism than for the pre-Christian religion of the South Germanic or Slavonic peoples, but still far less than for Christianity. In particular, we know little of the cult. The best evidence concerns the mythology of which we have an, admittedly late, systematic description in Snorri's *Edda* and a collection of mythological poems, the majority of which most scholars believe to have been transmitted orally from the pagan period, thus constituting authentic evidence of the pagan religion.[1] This material, however, raises a number of problems about representativeness, interpretation, the relationship to cult and religious practice, and so forth. In the present context, it nevertheless constitutes important evidence for the modes of thought about the world and society that were challenged by the new religion and the possible compromises that resulted from this conflict.

The form of the myths contained in these sources illustrates well the difference between the old and the new religion. The myths consist of stories about gods and heroes. There are often different versions of the same story, and gods or other supernatural figures may have different roles or different characters in different stories. Given this, they resemble the orginal Christian myths in the Old Testament which the Church fathers and the medieval theologians eventually managed to transform into a systematic doctrine, with considerable effort and ingenuity. It is clear that the extant myths are not simply stories but contain something resembling ethics or theology, giving examples of certain kinds of actions or containing reflections on the world, society and human life. On the other hand, we must beware of dealing with them in the same way as the Christian theologians dealt with the Old Testament myths, making them into a systematic doctrine. We find scattered comments on the extension and appearance of the natural and the supernatural world in the myths, but are these comments fragments of a systematic picture or simply various and mutually contradicting statements? We get information about various categories of supernatural beings and their marriages and kinship in a way that is likely to bear some relationship to human society, but is the picture consistent, and if so, should it be understood as a picture of classes or estates within one society or as the relationship between different tribes or something in between? Most fundamentally, the mythology is likely to reveal something about the understanding of the order of the world in Old Norse society, but how "ordered" is this order? Although it is outside the scope of the present study to deal with these problems in full, some comments on them are necessary in order to understand the transition from paganism to Christianity and its consequences.

As in most other mythologies, including the one in Genesis, the account of the creation gives an important clue to the interpretation of the world and man's place in it. The main source for this in Old Norse mythology is the most famous of the Eddic poems, *Vǫluspá*, which tells the story of the creation of the world in the distant past, its decline and future

---

1   There has been much discussion on these questions. See most recently Clunies Ross, *Prolonged Echoes*, pp. 20-33, and Fidjestøl, *The Dating*, pp. 187-203. In contrast to the skaldic poetry, however, where the complicated metre gives some guarantee for authentic transmission, the Eddic poems are metrically simpler and thus less protected. We may therefore have to distinguish between the content which is likely to reflect myths from the pagan period, and the form which may have undergone some changes during the period of transmission in a similar way as the Homeric poems and the Serbian poetry studied by Parry and Lord.

destruction and finally the new, perfect world that will replace the present one.² The often brief and cryptic allusions here can be supplemented to some extent by two other Eddic poems, *Vafnðruðnismál* and *Grímnismál*, plus, with some more caution, by Snorri's account in *The Younger Edda*.³ In the beginning, there was only empty space, *Ginnungagap*. The first living creature was the giant Yme who begat children from under his arms: the giants (ON *jǫtnar*, sg. *jǫtunn*).⁴ A primordial cow, Audhumbla, originated at the same time as Yme and produced the first creature resembling a human being, Bure, by licking salt stones. Bure in turn had a son Bor who married the giant woman Bestla. They became the parents of Odin who then became the father of the other gods, plus Vile ("will") and Ve ("sacred space"). The gods became creators in a more deliberate and systematic way. According to *Vǫluspá*, the sun, the moon and the stars appeared during this early phase of the creation, but it was the gods who gave them their right places in the universe and gave names to night and day and organised time. Having killed Yme and made the world from his body, the gods assembled on their meeting place, Idavollen (the work-plain), and decided to create the dwarves; the poem then spends several strophes listing their names. The dwarves may possibly have created the first human beings, the man Ask and the woman Embla.⁵ This is not explicitly mentioned in *Vǫluspá*, which, however, agrees with the other sources that the gods did not make the humans, but found them lying on the shore, without soul, life or thought, all of which were the gods' gift to them. After this, the poem gives a short glimpse of the peace and harmony reigning in the newly created world, before strife is introduced through a cryptic allusion to the death of Gullveig, which has given later commentators much trouble.⁶

Details in this story may point to influences from Christianity, such as the ordering of time and the distinction between creating man and woman and giving them life and thought, although some of these features may simply be common to many such myths. In any case, the differences are more significant concerning the story as a whole. First, there is neither an almighty creator, nor creation *ex nihilo*. Creation, or at least the most important aspect of it, is understood as an analogy to building and forming, not giving birth.

---

2   *Vǫluspá*, vv. 1-25, *Edda*, pp. 1-6.
3   The following is largely based on Clunies Ross, *Prolonged Echoes*, pp. 144-228, which gives a detailed analysis of the different stages in the account, with extensive references to the sources. See also De Vries, *Altgermanische Religionsgeschichte* II, pp. 359-72, and Steinsland, *Norrøn religion*, pp. 110-21.
4   This is not mentioned in *Vǫluspá*, but in *Vafnðruðnismál*, str. 21 and 33, *Edda*, pp. 48, 51. Cf. Clunies Ross, *Prolonged Echoes*, pp. 152-55.
5   The names are most probably derived from tree names. Ask is ash, whereas the etymology of Embla is more disputed. One possibility is that it is a diminutive of *alm* = elm. This naming of the first human beings has parallels in Iranian and Phrygian and probably also in Greek religion (De Vries, *Altgermanische Religionsgeschichte* II, pp. 371 f.; Hultgård, "The Ash and Embla Myth").
6   *Vǫluspá*, str. 21, *Edda*, p. 5; cf. Clunies Ross, *Prolonged Echoes*, pp. 198-211.

As emphasised particularly by Clunies Ross, this makes creation very much a masculine task – which corresponds to the Christian as well as many other creation myths – and gives the gods a crucial function, despite their late arrival. They confine themselves to the higher aspect of the creation, establishing an order in the world, and giving man life and thought. In contrast to the Christian creation myth, the Old Norse myth is thus evolutionary; the lower creatures come first – the higher, the gods and the humans – later. In particular, it is significant that the giants are older than the gods who are even descended from them. Finally, although the death of Gullveig and the problems in its wake may suggest a vague resemblance to the Christian myth of the Fall, there is no explicit reference to moral wrong, nor should this event be regarded as a sudden arrival of evil in an otherwise perfect world. As is evident from the beginning of the story, conflict and death are present from the start, and the struggles in which the gods become involved after the creation of the humans were most probably caused by the killings of the first creatures whose descendants wanted revenge. Although the gods represent a higher stage in the evolution, particularly regarding intellectual capacity, they are neither morally perfect nor almighty. In particular, their role in the work of creation seems to be based on a theory of the constancy of energy; they have to spend their resources in making something new. Thus, Høne and Lodur, who give colour and intelligence to the first human couple, are later without these qualities.[7] Odin, who also participates, is apparently more resourceful and manages to retain the qualities for himself, at least parts of them, but he also has to make heavy sacrifices to achieve what he wants; he gives away one eye in order to learn wisdom.

The rest of the poems as well as the prose stories rendered in Snorri's Edda confirm and develop this impression. These sources largely describe struggles and competition between the gods and the giants in which the gods usually win, but often only after sacrifices and humiliation. The giants are regarded as inferior to the gods in some respects but not as radically different. Some giant women can even be very attractive and desired by the gods. The fact that the giants live in a different place and apparently have their own social organisation forms an argument for regarding them as another tribe rather than as a lower class, although they need not necessarily fit into either category.[8] There are two categories of gods: the *æser* (ON *æsir* – males, sg. *áss*) and *åsynjer* (ON *ásynjar* – females, sg. *ásynja*) on the one hand and the *vaner* on the other. They had earlier been enemies – there is an allusion to this in *Vǫluspá* – but were reconciled and belong to the common pantheon. The

---

[7] Mundal, "Skaping og undergang", pp. 203-6; cf. pp. 196-98 on the creation and on the gods losing the power to make gold when they created the dwarves.

[8] This interpretation differs from that of Clunies Ross, *Prolonged Echoes*, pp. 48-50, 93-102, who regards the giants as lower class.

division between the gods and the giants corresponds to the geography of the natural and supernatural world as expressed in the three terms "Åsgard", "Midgard" and "Utgard", the sites of the gods, the humans and the giants respectively. Some scholars have attempted to draw maps of these places and compared the division between Midgard and Utgard with that between the cultivated land of the farm and the wilderness, but it is doubtful how precise these contemporary ideas were.[9] In any case, the term "Midgard" for the world of the worshippers of the Norse gods gives the Scandinavians a more central place than the Christian world picture does.

The marriage pattern of the three groups of supernatural beings points to the hierarchy between them.[10] The *æser*, who are on top of the hierarchy, are hypergamous and can take wives or mistresses from both of the other categories, whereas the goddesses are forbidden for the giants and possibly also for the *vaner* (there is at least no evidence of *vaner* marrying *åsynjer*), and several of the poems deal with the problems resulting from the giants' failure to respect this order. When, in *Þrymskviða*, the giants steal Tor's hammer and demand the goddess Frøya as their king's bride in return for giving it back,[11] the gods are in a terrible dilemma. Without his hammer, Tor is nothing, while marrying a goddess to the low-ranking giants is equally disastrous. To save the situation, Tor has to dress up in woman's clothes – which was taboo in the divine as well as the human world – pretending to be Frøya. A series of burlesque scenes follow, in which the enormous "bride" eats an ox and eight salmon and drinks three barrels of mead, until "she" receives the hammer in her lap, tears off the disguise and kills the bridegroom and the other giants gathered for the wedding. In a similar way, it is an extreme humiliation to the gods, which cannot be tolerated, when the *vane* god Frøy proposes to the giantess Gerd and is rejected. Gerd resists for a long time but a series of terrible threats forces her to submit.[12] However, in accordance with the logic that every advantage has to be bought with some sacrifice, the gods pay dearly for their victory. Frøy has to give away his sword, which is never returned to him, so that he has to manage without it in the final struggle under Ragnarok.

Within the community of the gods, Odin is the father and the leader. Odin's central position is attested in several sources but there is little mention of the power relationship between the other gods, apart from some references to deliberations among them on Idavollen. The main reason for Odin's importance and authority seems to be his personal qualities, his skill, intelligence and cleverness. The only other god who can compete with

9 Clunies Ross, *Prolonged Echoes*, p. 51; Brink, "Mytologiska rum", pp. 291-98.
10 For the following, see Clunies Ross, *Prolonged Echoes*, pp. 85-143.
11 *Þrymskviða, Edda*, pp. 111-15.
12 *Skirnismál, Edda*, pp. 69-77. On *Skirnismál* as a poem about the origin of the Ynglingar dynasty, see Steinsland, *Det hellige bryllup* and *Den hellige kongen*, pp. 53-69.

him in importance is Tor, who is usually regarded as his son, but who excels in brute force rather than intelligence. Odin's qualities are more highly regarded, as they were developed at the final stage of creation, whereas the giants had already excelled in brute force. From this point of view, Odin represents what is good, although in a very different sense than the Christian idea of good.

Nor does the relationship between the gods and the giants correspond to the opposition between good and evil. Despite their inferior rank, the giants are a normal element in the world picture. They were there before the gods; they have their own society, similar to that of the gods; and as long as they do not try to rise above their allotted status by marrying or having sexual relationships with the goddesses, there is nothing wrong with them. By contrast, Loke is a more sinister figure. He is partly the gods' enemy and partly their ally. The main example of him in the former capacity is when he stages the death of Balder, Odin's son, who is thoroughly good and noble and the perfect being, loved by everyone. Having heard a prophecy about Balder's death, the gods demand all creatures on earth to swear that they will not harm him. However, they forget the mistletoe which Loke manages to turn into the deadly weapon that kills Balder. Afterwards, the gods get another chance to save Balder, namely the promise that he will be returned to them if all creatures ask for this to happen. All actually do, except one old woman who of course is Loke in disguise. Here we meet the opposition between good and evil more explicitly than anywhere else in the mythology as well as the idea that the perfect being is bound to die, an idea that may possibly but not necessarily have been inspired by Christianity.

We are never told why Loke wants to kill Balder. One possible motive is revenge. As Loke is partly of giant origin, he may have picked the best man among the gods to avenge their killing of Yme. As Loke is only half a giant, he would not seem the obvious choice to carry out such an act of revenge. Moreover, he acts completely by himself; the other giants do not appear in the story at all. An alternative explanation may therefore be sought in the contrast between the two characters; Loke is not only morally but also genetically Balder's exact opposite. Balder is born from the marriage between Odin and his wife Frigg. He may thus be regarded as Odin's legitimate heir. He belongs entirely to the gods' world and represents the final stage in perfection in the evolution starting with the death of Yme. Loke's origin is never mentioned directly but he seems to be the result of a union between a goddess and a giant.[13] On the one hand, this gives him ties to both groups, but on the other, it represents such a taboo that it renders him unacceptable to the gods and quite possibly also to the giants. Moreover, not only is Loke's birth a break of a taboo but also his own sexual connections. He begets Odin's horse, Sleipner, by mak-

---

13   Meulengracht Sørensen, *At fortælle historien*, pp. 30 f.; Clunies Ross, *Prolonged Echoes*, pp. 64 f.

ing himself into a mare and mating with a stallion. Here he breaks a double taboo, acting sexually as a woman and overstepping the border between man and animal. He is also the father of some of the most awful creatures in the mythological world: the Fenris wolf, the Midgard worm and Hel.[14] Thus, Loke belongs nowhere; he has to make himself useful from situation to situation through his falsity and cleverness. He plots to kill Balder but also aids Tor in getting back his hammer. When breaking the taboo by becoming Sleipner's mother, he actually helps the gods in a difficult situation; thus, he does the dirty work for them.[15] Balder and Loke represent purity and pollution respectively in absolute form.

However, representing the taboo forces, Loke plays a more productive role in Old Norse religion than the devil does in Christianity; he is clever and resourceful and helps the gods in difficult situations. Some contact with the taboo forces seems to be necessary for survival, as may perhaps be illustrated by Balder's fate: he is too pure to survive. At least this conclusion seems to be supported by Odin's example. From one point of view, as the highest of the gods he is the very opposite of Loke. He represents a new and higher stage in creation, and he is the leader of the gods. On the other hand, he disregards the taboos more often than any other of the gods. He learns sorcery (*seid*) which, at least according to Snorri, is dishonourable for a man; he even dresses as a woman to learn this art. He learns the art of poetry by stealing the poetic mead from the giant Suttung who had placed his beautiful daughter deep inside a mountain to protect the treasure. By making himself into a worm, Odin enters the cave, seduces the daughter and betrays her, taking the mead with him. Considering Sleipner's origin, it would immediately seem surprising for Odin to use such a horse, but apparently this origin is exactly the reason for its magical qualities. Odin's origins may have something to do with these proclivities, as he is related to the giants, although there is nothing incestuous in his origin.

More generally, however, both he and Loke serve as perfect illustrations of Mary Douglas's analyses of purity and pollution.[16] By distinguishing between pure and impure and setting borders between them, regulating communication and above all sexual relationships, people order their universe, more or less strictly. The Jewish dietary rules and the Indian caste system are extreme examples, but the Old Norse mythology expresses the same basic idea. On the other hand, what is impure is also strong and serves as a basis

---

14   Steinsland, *Norrøn religion*, p. 230.
15   According to Snorri, the gods had promised a giant the sun, the moon and the goddess Frøya in return for building a wall around Åsgård for them in the firm belief that he would never be able to fulfil the work in the allotted time. The giant set an enormously strong horse to work on the wall and was about to finish the wall on time when Loke made himself into a mare and distracted the horse. On the story, see Steinsland, *Norrøn religion*, p. 83.
16   Douglas, *Purity and Danger*, pp. 94-113, 159-79.

for sorcery and magic. Typical material here is that which is associated with death or pollution, corpses (particularly of people who have suffered a shameful or unhappy death), blood (particularly menstrual blood), faeces and so forth.[17]

As might be expected, there is at least some correspondence between taboo and pollution among the gods and among their human worshippers. There is a strong taboo against a man assuming the role of a female or an animal; according to the laws, a man accused of such acts is allowed to kill the accuser. Thus, men were regarded as superior to women. Certain women could still achieve nearly equal status by virtue of their personal characteristics, which were not necessarily the same as men's; these included wisdom, eloquence, and ability to exploit their female beauty to acquire what they wanted.[18] Less is known about the marriage pattern and what may be considered the human equivalent to the three classes of supernatural beings. As we have seen, the gods were hypergamous, which seems to correspond to the marriage pattern described in the regional laws.[19] This must have changed later, at least within the elite, in accordance with the normal pattern in Western Christendom.[20] At this time, it must at least have been possible to marry daughters to men of slightly lower rank, although the standard in both periods seems to have been marriages between approximately equal partners. If the woman's rank was significantly lower than the man's, concubinage would be the preferred alternative. While there is thus a general resemblance between the marriage pattern among the gods and the system found in the early laws, it is more doubtful whether the categories of supernatural beings have a human equivalent. The Sami may possibly have been regarded as a parallel to the giants.[21] The sagas give examples of Norwegian men marrying or having sexual relationships with Sami women but not normally vice versa.[22] It should also be mentioned that the Eddic poem *Rigstula* describes a tripartite division of humanity into aristocrats (*jarl*= earl or nobleman), commoners (*karl*= man or commoner) and slaves, all of which

---

17   Douglas, *Purity and Danger*, p. 94, and *Natural Symbols*, p. 139.
18   Clover, "Regardless of Sex", states, in accordance with Laqueur's theory, that Old Norse society did not recognise any qualitative difference between men and women, but distinguished between "hard" and "soft", the former category consisting of most men in their prime plus some strong and heroic women, whereas most women, plus children and old men, belonged to the latter. Although this competitive rather than hierarchical attitude accords well with what is otherwise known about Old Norse society, the theory probably should be modified to the extent that women usually excel in different ways than men. They use their beauty and intelligence to make men carry out their will, as illustrated by Gudrun in *Laxdæla saga* and Hildegunn in *Njáls saga*, both of whom, particularly the former, use their charm, beauty and ingenuity to make men carry out their will (Bagge, *Mennesket*, pp. 34-36).
19   Vestergaard, pp. 188 f.
20   Bagge, *Society and Politics*, p. 120; Magnúsdóttir, *Frillor och fruar*, pp. 181-84.
21   Mundal, "The Perception of the Samis", pp. 111 f.
22   However, the introduction to *Volundarkviða, Edda*, p. 116, attributes such an origin to Volund and his brothers, who married King Lodve's daughters.

are endogamous. In the case of the top layer, we note that the young Jarl has to find his bride far away, from another aristocratic family, headed by Herse.[23] Moreover, there is a chronological division between these layers similar to the one in the myth of creation. The slave couple is called Åe and Edda (great-grandfather and -mother), the commoners Ave and Amma (grandfather and -mother) and the aristocrats Father and Mother. There is evidence that contemporary aristocrats regarded themselves as descended from the gods, and they may thus have identified themselves with the gods' restrictive marriage pattern, controlling their women and preventing them from marrying below their rank. The sagas of the Icelanders give a vivid impression of how a father's honour was threatened when a suitor approached his daughter without permission.[24] Although *Rigstula*'s division of people into aristocracy, commoners and slaves hardly corresponds to the division among the supernatural beings, a kind of social hierarchy exists in both worlds. In contrast to the later Christian doctrine, this division does not express an ordained higher order, but simply states the close correlation between status and personal characteristics. The successful always win and live a life of beauty and luxury, while the unsuccessful are ugly and dirty and have to accept the dirt floor and the cold, lumpy porridge.

The ethical doctrine, as expressed in the Eddic poem *Hávamál*, gives a similar picture of the supernatural world. The poem opens by describing a wanderer arriving at an unknown house. After a long journey over mountains and wilderness, he needs fire, food, clothes and friendly words. But he has to be careful when opening the door; he does not know if enemies are sitting inside. To obtain all this he needs wisdom, not in the sense of philosophical insight but what we would call social intelligence. He must strike the right balance between self-assertion and pride and silence and modesty; he must neither be credulous nor suspicious and reticent.[25] The poem goes on, giving practical advice on how to survive and succeed among other people. The ultimate success is measured after death in the most famous stanzas of the poem: all living creatures die but a man's memory never dies.[26] Thus, there is a judgement after death, not in an afterlife but in how the dead is regarded by other men. This ethical doctrine is at the same time social and egocentric. Its aim is to show the individual person how to succeed in life, not how he or she should serve the community or mankind or carry out some high ideal. On the other hand, success depends solely on the individual's status in the eyes of others. In a similar way, the skaldic poetry celebrates generosity, heroic deeds and victory, including the ability to feed ravens and wolves on the bodies of slain enemies, and the sagas, mostly written in the thirteenth

---

23 *Rigst.* str. 39.
24 Bandlien, *Strategies of Passion*, pp. 67-85.
25 *Hávamál*, st. 1-11; cf. Bagge, "Du savoir-vivre pratique", 116 f.
26 *Hávamál*, st. 76-77.

century, largely represent the same attitude. The relationship between the pagan gods and their worshippers seems to have been more of a mutual contract than it is in Christianity: the gods gave luck and prosperity in return for sacrifices. It was possible to favour one of several gods and to seek an alternative protector if rejected by the first.

The most important aspect of the old religion was clearly the cult, on which we have the least information. There are some descriptions of it in the sagas but their trustworthiness is doubtful.[27] In addition, place names and archaeological evidence give information of cult places and the relative importance of the various gods, but no clear picture of the religious practice. The essential rite was the sacrifice (*blót*). Here meat and drink were sacrificed to the gods but, like in many other ethnic religions, most of it was apparently consumed by their human worshippers. The place where the sacrifices occurred is called *hóf*. Earlier scholars assumed that this was a separate building, and some even imagined a kind of parish system that was later taken over by the Christian Church. After Oluf Olsen's devastating attack on this theory in 1965,[28] there has been wide agreement that no special cult building existed but that the sacrifices were celebrated in ordinary houses, which would also seem to be in accordance with the original meaning of *hóf* as farm. Nevertheless, recent excavations have uncovered some special cult buildings, although it is still likely that ordinary houses were used in most cases. Moreover, place names point to a considerable amount of organisation around the cult, with central farms being used as sites for worship and dependent ones responsible for various contributions and, in general, to a strong sense of sacrality associated with the landscape.[29] The most important sacrifices were held three times a year, in spring, in autumn and in mid-winter, around the time when the sun turns. All three were turned into Christian feasts after the conversion, celebrated in the same way with eating and drinking, but now with toasts to God and the saints. The distribution of sacrifices is thus connected to the agricultural year, as is also expressed in the formula – admittedly known only from the Christian period but likely to have originated in pagan times – of sacrificing for good harvest and peace.[30]

Like other parties, the sacrifical ones also seem to have been financed by contributions from the participants, although powerful men may have given more or even financed a whole party. The political aspect of this emerges clearly from the account in *Heimskringla*

---

27   The most detailed is Snorri's account of the sacrifices at Lade and Mære (*HkrHG* ch. 18). Of more recent contributors, Düwel, *Das Opferfest* rejects the story, whereas Steinsland, *Den hellige kongen*, pp. 111 f.; Sørensen, *At fortælle historien*, pp. 113-22, and Sundqvist, *Freyr's Offspring*, pp. 184-213, take a more positive attitude.
28   Olsen, *Horg, hof og kirke*.
29   Brink, "Mytologiska rum", pp. 298-313.
30   "Til árs ok friðar". On the pagan origin of the formula, see Hultgård, "Altskandinavische Opferrituale", pp. 242-54, and "*Ár*"; Klingenberg, *Heidnisches Altertum*, pp. 123-94, and Steinsland, *Norrøn religion*, p. 279.

of Asbjørn Selsbane who gave great annual parties – sacrificial ones in the pagan period and in honour of God and the saints in the Christian period – for his local community in order to increase his power and prestige in competition with his uncle Tore Hund. Despite bad harvests, Asbjørn finds it hard to give up these parties and in the end sets out on his fateful expedition to the south to buy grain from his other uncle, Erling Skjalgsson.[31] Thus, even if the mythology is relatively silent on larger social networks, the cultic practice points in this direction. There is even some evidence of central cult sites for larger regions, such as Lejre and Gudme in Denmark, Uppsala in Sweden, Arkona on the island of Rügen and Borg in Lofoten in Northern Norway.[32]

This leads to the much discussed problem of sacred kingship in the pagan religion, an idea that was rejected as a part of the reaction against the Germanistic school in the post-war period, but is now gaining ground once more.[33] It is clearly present in *Rigstula*, where the first king, Kon ung, is educated by his divine grandfather.[34] Furthermore, two such myths have been preserved in skaldic poetry, one about the Ynglingar, the other about the Håleygjar.[35] The former was regarded, at least in the later tradition, as the genealogy of the royal dynasty that came to power with Harald Finehair, although the poem does not mention him. The extant poem begins with Fjolne but there are allusions to descent from the god Frøy later in the poem. Frøy is said to be the progenitor in *Historia Norwegie*, whereas Snorri regards Frøy as a descendant of Odin. Admittedly, the authenticity of this poem has been disputed, most recently by Claus Krag who claims that it is a learned construction from the twelfth century, but almost all the reviews and other comments on Krag's book have rejected this hypothesis and confirmed the authenticity of the poem.[36] *Håleygjatal*, composed to honour the earls of Lade, forms further evidence of attempts to link a princely kindred to the ancient gods; the poem traces the earls' genealogy back to Odin.[37]

31 *HkrOH* ch. 117; Bagge, *Society and Politics*, p. 68. On hospitality and the political aspect of it in general, based on Icelandic material, see Monclair, *Lederskapsideologi*, pp. 143-205.
32 Steinsland, *Norrøn religion*, pp. 268-70. The reliability of Adam of Bremen's account of the sacrifices in Uppsala (*Gesta* IV.26-27, pp. 257-60) has been the subject of much discussion. For a recent, negative verdict, see Janson, *Templum nobilissimum*. However, Sundqvist, *Freyr's Offspring*, pp. 112-35, and "Uppsala och Asgård" has given good arguments that it is based on real information about the pagan cult.
33 The main attack on the theory was delivered by Baetke, "Yngvi und die Ynglingar". For recent, more positive interpretations, see Steinsland, *Den hellige kongen*, pp. 53-59; Bagge, "Christianization", pp. 119 f., and Sundqvist, *Freyr's Offspring*, pp. 18-38. For a survey of the whole discussion, with extensive bibliography, see "Sakralkönigtum", including Sundqvist, "Skandinavische Quellen" on Scandinavian conditions.
34 Bagge, "Old Norse Theories", pp. 7-45.
35 Steinsland, *Norrøn religion*, pp. 50, 406, 416.
36 Krag, *Ynglingatal*; cf. reviews by Fidjestøl and Sandnes; Sundqvist, *Freyr's Offspring*, pp. 43-54 and "Aspects of Rulership", pp. 90-97, and Skre, "The Dating".
37 *Skjalded.* A 1, pp. 68-71; B 1, pp. 60-62.

In contrast to the Christian idea of sacrality introduced later, the pagan sacrality was not derived from an idea of order and hierarchy in the world, nor was it linked to an ethical doctrine of how society should be governed. Heroic attributes followed blood, and kinship with the gods was a guarantee of such characteristics. It also seems that this idea was linked to that of "good year and peace"; there is evidence in the skaldic poetry of the king being regarded as responsible for good and bad harvests; the different evaluation in the sagas of Håkon the Good, the Eirikssons and Håkon jarl seems to be based on such a tradition.[38] The king's responsibility for "peace" may at first sight seem to contradict the mainly martial image of the king in the sagas and the skaldic poetry, but it actually confirms it. Peace is not the absence of war, but the result of successful war. The pagan concept of sacrality was compatible with *Vǫluspá*'s representation of the world as an arena of different forces in mutual competition and it did not offer the ruler any protection against rival powers. The king held his power by virtue of being "the best man". There was no monopoly of divine descent or divine protection and the ruler might therefore be deposed by another with similar qualities. The pagan sacrality was closely connected to the concept of luck which might favour a ruler for a certain time and then desert him.[39] As in Hobbes's *Leviathan*, legitimacy was based on actual power.

The Conversion to Christianity

The transition to Christianity meant qualitative changes: from myth to dogma, from oral religion to a religion of the book and from religion as ordinary social practice to rites carried out by an organised, professional hierarchy. The beginning of Genesis describes God as the sole creator who creates everything in accordance with His own will. He proceeds in an orderly and systematic way and by the end of His work of creation sees that "everything is good". There is some difference between the two accounts of the creation regarding the exact sequence and the duration of the process, but there is no real evolution and no difficulty for God in carrying out his plan.[40] Thus, Christianity introduced the idea of an ordered hierarchy in the world, instituted by God, not only in human society

---

38   Bagge, "Christianization", p. 120.
39   Like sacred kingship, some scholars have also regarded this idea as derived from Christianity, pointing to the parallel in the Latin *fortuna*. However, it took a long time for the latter concept to be integrated into Christian thought, and the well-developed Old Norse terminology, which does not seem to show any foreign influence, is also an argument in favour of the local origin of the idea. See most recently Bagge, "Christianization", p. 120 with references.
40   Cf. the comment in *Elucidarius*, pp. 48 f., the Old Norse translation of Honorius Augustodunensis, *Elucidarium*, that God created the world in an instant and then divided everything into categories during the six days.

but also in nature,[41] which replaced the pagan idea of open competition among human beings as well as among the gods and other supernatural beings. According to Christian doctrine, the injustice, violence, and conflict which were as evident in the new society as in the old did not belong to nature's order, but were a result of sin, which had entered the world through two sinful acts, first by Lucifer and then by Adam and Eve. Both sins consisted in rebellion against God through disobedience, which was consequently the fundamental sin that drove mankind out of Paradise. What happened in the original sin was that the woman allowed herself to be led by the animal and the man let himself be led by the woman, instead of following the correct order which placed the man highest, then the woman, then the animals. As the lord of creation, the man was to be superior to the woman and have exclusive rights to clerical positions. Correspondingly, it was God's will that kings and chieftains should rule over the general population. Rule by force was a consequence of original sin, and the earthly hierarchy was not the same as the heavenly. In Paradise, personal piety was decisive, and here women could rank higher than men, and the poor and the weak higher than the world's rich and powerful.

The Christian cosmology had radical ethical consequences. Not only did it emphasise the virtue of obedience and insist on a hierarchical order of the world, but in accordance with its view of the present world as basically sinful, it condemned many aspects of human behaviour which in pagan and ordinary secular thought were regarded as permissible or even virtuous. Sexual desire was basically sinful and could only be accepted as a necessary means of conceiving children. Pride was a sin and humility a virtue; violence was not a means to defending one's own interests and improving one's status but was only allowed in defending justice or Christianity. Christianity celebrated different qualities from the pagan ones – humility, suffering, abstinence, protection of the weak and the love of one's neighbour – as expressed in the Christian equivalent to *Hávamál*, Alcuin's *De virtutibus et vitiis*, translated into Old Norse some time in the twelfth century and preserved as a part of the Old Norse Book of Homilies.[42] The book lists the various virtues and vices, as the expression of what is intrinsically good and evil, urging the faithful to practice the former and shun the latter, so as to live according to God's will and receive His reward in the next life. The criterion is not "the others" and the aim is not social acceptance.

Furthermore, Christianity was a religion of the book. The liturgy as well as the doctrine were based on books which were introduced in the country in association with the Christianisation. This in turn resulted in a new relationship between the oral and the written, the transfer of narrative, poems, and laws from memory to script, accompanied

---

41 Bagge, "Nature and Society", pp. 7-25.
42 *Gamal norsk homiliebok*, pp. 1-33.

by considerable changes in their content and expression. According to *The King's Mirror*, the wisest man is the one who gains his knowledge from books,[43] a statement that demonstrates a new understanding of authority, no longer from the ancient wisdom of old and wise members of the local community, but from foreigners who might have been dead for many centuries and who wrote in the learned language Latin, comprehensible only to the ecclesiastical and intellectual elite. Thus, there is a close connection between dogma, learning, and organisation: the members of the higher clergy received their income, power and prestige because of their European learning and insight into God's mysteries, and, above all, their ability to administer them. By virtue of their consecration, the priests were the only ones who could mediate with God by administering the sacraments. This understanding of knowledge is at least partly connected to the metaphysical and ethical doctrine. Sinful human beings cannot by themselves know the transcendent God; they need His revelation which in turn is contained in the Scriptures and needs to be interpreted by the clergy who have dedicated themselves to God's service and possess the wisdom and piety necessary to understand and transmit His message. Admittedly, the Church also acknowledged the human intellect as a source of knowledge, but even here books were to be trusted more because they transmitted the internationally recognised knowledge of the great thinkers. Not only the revelation came from abroad, but also the knowledge about the world and its qualities. Whereas the Scandinavian peoples had earlier lived in Midgard where they were as close to the gods as any other people, if not more so, they were now moved to the periphery of a world whose centre was Jerusalem.[44]

Symbolic and cultural power was of course in principle nothing new. In the Eddic poems, Odin is presented as the wisest of all. He possesses secret wisdom, which helps him to triumph over his enemies. There are "cultural experts", in the form of priests and priestesses, magicians, medicine men, wise old men or women, in most societies. Writing also existed earlier, clearly also associated with expertise. The "hero" in *Rigstula*, Kon ungr, the god Rig's grandson, who becomes wiser and more powerful than his father, learns runes and magic from his divine grandfather.[45] Still, writing was less important during the age of runes, since it was most probably only used for short inscriptions. Little is known about how cultural experts were recruited during this period. Being of good extraction might have been important, but so were also personal qualities, as in the political and military arenas. In the field of magic and law, "trade secrets" may have made control difficult, while it was easier to gain control of eloquence at political and other assemblies, as

---

43   *Kgs.*, pp. 4 f.
44   Bagge, "On the Far Edge", pp. 355 f.
45   *Rigspula*, str. 43-45, *Edda*, p. 286; Bagge, "Old Norse Theories", pp. 9, 34.

well as in ordinary conversations. Here the audience decided what was good and bad. In the saga literature, eloquence stands out as a very important quality among leaders, and there is reason to believe that this was also the case earlier. Pre-Christian culture did not lack experts, but their dependence on non-experts was considerably greater than was the case later on. By contrast, monitoring Christian experts was more or less, by definition, out of the question. The congregation did not decide whether the liturgy was presented correctly or if the priests' preaching was consistent with the Bible or the Church's dogmas. As Christianity became established and people became acquainted with the mass and the basic aspects of the Church's teaching, monitoring became more of a possibility, but the actual control agencies were outside the local communities, residing with the bishop or the Pope. In early Christian times the people, or more likely the local aristocracy, elected priests, but after a while this right fell to the bishop, cathedral chapters, or the monasteries, which weakened the monitoring possibilities. The clear cultural divide which was drawn up between the clergy and lay people can also be viewed from a power perspective. By gaining acceptance of norms which to an extent ran completely contrary to those of secular society, the clergy represented a higher symbolic authority. Later on, secular, polite culture was to do the same.

It is an oft-repeated truth, which to some extent applies to all cultures, that language is power. In Norway during the Middle Ages, language created clearer distinctions between those who had power and those who did not than in the subsequent periods. In addition to the fundamental "power to define", expressed through the elite's decrees, the knowledge of Latin, the language of the Church and the educated, created a definitive gap between the clergy and most lay people. "The learned men" were at first a marginal and somewhat resented group, but eventually became an elite, as both the culture and a number of important transactions in society were based on writing. Outside the purely local communities, the majority was thus wholly dependent on the expertise of the elite. Lodin Lepp's attitude when the Icelanders refused to accept the law the king had formulated is characteristic (below p. 204): How can ordinary, uneducated people meddle with such questions? The old experts were people one knew; they risked having to defend their interpretations and decisions face-to-face, while the new experts could barricade themselves behind their books. In addition, they lived far away from most local communities.

In this way symbolic and cultural power had worked in the same direction as the demographic-economic development and strengthened the pre-eminence of the elite. Nevertheless, the expert status of the elite was not only its strength, but could also be a weakness. How could the elite legitimise its pre-eminence if there was no mutual basis of communication with the general population? How effective was script as a medium when only a few people could read? How could one make people accept Christianity if the contents of the faith were inaccessible to them? To a certain degree the method must have been to proclaim the message in such a way that the public could understand it. All through the Middle Ages, members of both the clerical and secular elite travelled around the country and held assemblies with the peasants. Letters from bishops and kings were read out from the church green, making them accessible to the general public, and Christian literature was to a considerable degree translated from Latin into the vernacular.

It can be discussed, and has been discussed, to what extent the Christian religion actually influenced the thought and behaviour of the ordinary population. A strong tradition in the nineteenth century regarded Norway as less Christian than most other countries in medieval Europe, in accordance with an understanding of the country as unique and exceptional.[46] From a nationalistic point of view, there was a tendency to identify the medieval Norwegians with the saga heroes rather than the ideals of the clergy, and to the Protestant historians there was some consolation in the thought that their ancestors had not succumbed to the more extreme expressions of medieval Catholicism. In the early twentieth century, these ideas received expression famously in Edvard Bull's account of religious life in the period.[47] Bull was a Marxist and neither a nationalist nor a believing Protestant, but nevertheless strongly influenced by his predecessors. As a materialist, he also attributed little importance to ideas compared to the basic material conditions, imagining an immovable peasant society that could only be superficially affected by any idea coming from abroad: "No gale causes a ground swell on the depth of a hundred fathoms, no new doctrine or belief leads to unrest in the enormous, conservative forces that determine men's minds."[48]

Bull was soon opposed by the literary historian Fredrik Paasche who concluded from a study of the religious poetry that the Norwegians must have been as Christian as any other people in medieval Europe.[49] Although the conclusions that can be drawn from such evidence are limited, later historians have tended to agree with Paasche rather than Bull,[50] not least because Bull's evidence hardly supports his conclusions. Furthermore, recent studies on oral societies do not confirm the picture of such societies as immobile, but rather suggest that they may have changed rapidly despite their inhabitants' belief in the contrary.[51] Despite a considerable distance between the explicit doctrine expressed in

---

[46] On the historiography, see Bagge, "Norsk kirkehistorie", pp. 30-33.
[47] Bull, *Folk og kirke*, pp. 11-14, 254 f. and *passim*.
[48] "Ingen storm reiser grundbrått på 100 favnes dyp, ingen ny lære eller ny tro bringer ulage i de vældige konservative magter som rår over menneskers sjælsliv" (Bull, *Kristendom og kvad*, p. 422).
[49] Paasche, *Kristendom og kvad*, pp. 29-35, 209-12 and *passim*.
[50] Kolsrud, "Kirke og folk"; Holmsen, *Norges historie*, pp. 217 f.
[51] E.g. Keesing, *Cultural Anthropology*, pp. 368-74, 382-86.

the extant texts and ordinary attitudes, the people's basic adherence to Christianity and the Church can hardly be doubted. The most important argument for this is the Church's wealth and consequently the burdens the people took upon themselves for the sake of religion.[52] Ferdinand Næshagen has recently objected that if the Church's share of the landed property was divided by the number of people who lived in the country during the long period when the Catholic Church dominated, individual contributions become insignificant; he thus implies that there was actually not very much religious fervour.[53] In this context, however, the point is not strong personal commitment from the majority of the population, but a general recognition of the Church and the importance of religion. The fact that the donations in many cases were small, or that the gifts to the Church could have been the result of convention, or even a means to increase the status of the giver, is from this point of view irrelevant. The fact that gifts were given to the Church to the exclusion of most other causes is a strong enough testimony to its social importance. What the individual giver thought and felt is another question, which would of course be very difficult to discern through the available source material.

Apart from this general observation, our information about religious beliefs among the common people is limited. There is little evidence of a cult of the ancient pagan gods, but more of various other supernatural beings. Various forms of magic must also have been widespread and some of the saints venerated in local society may actually have been pagan deities in disguise.[54] Concerning ethics, which played some part in the debate between Bull and Paasche, the evidence is better, as the sagas give much information about behaviour within the lay aristocracy and how it was regarded.[55] There is also evidence in charters and the laws, and additionally in a didactic source like *The King's Mirror*. Not surprisingly, the sagas, despite general acceptance of and occasional references to Christian doctrine and ethics, are closer to *Hávamál* than to Alcuin, celebrating courage, masculine virtues and worldly success, accepting revenge and struggles for power and taking a relaxed attitude to kings' and great men's sexual affairs. This is hardly different from the rest of Western Christendom. Nor did the Church really expect the laity to live according to its ideals. What it did expect was that they should recognise its norms and confess their sins. From the point of view of the laity, this seems to have amounted to two sets of norms, one to be practised in daily life and one in specifically religious contexts and particularly

---

52   Bagge, "Kirken og folket", pp. 212-15.
53   Næshagen, "Medieval Norwegian Religiosity".
54   Bull, *Folk og kirke*, pp. 190-96; Ejerfeld, "Magi", cols. 214-18; Halvorsen, "Trolldom"; Segev, *Medieval Magic*. As Segev points out, however, a considerable part of the magic known from medieval Norway has a learned origin and is not a continuation of earlier pagan practice.
55   For the following, see Bagge, *Da boken kom til Norge*, pp. 123-45, and "Du savoir-vivre pratique", pp. 121-26.

before death. However, *The King's Mirror* makes an interesting attempt to reconcile these two sets of norms by distinguishing between both different layers of society and between person and office. The virtues to be practised differ between the merchant, the royal retainer and the king, both in the sense that they have different "professions" or social roles, according to which they act on behalf of God and society, and in the sense that higher social rank implies higher demands and greater insight in the nature of virtue.

Within the framework of this basic similarity between Norway and the rest of medieval Europe, we may venture some suggestions regarding specific features. On the one hand, there is a remarkable amount of religious literature in the vernacular, mostly translations of saints' legends, which, together with the provincial statutes from the period 1280-1351, suggest an effort by the Church authorities to educate the common people. Admittedly, most of this material is preserved in Icelandic manuscripts, but as Iceland belonged to the Norwegian Church province, it is difficult to imagine that it was not also known and used in Norway. Second, Bull's conclusion that there was a general antagonism between the clergy and the laity is based on very limited evidence and has been contradicted by a recent study which concludes that the Church was less involved in conflicts with the people than the state.[56] On the other hand, there is less evidence of the new and more personal forms of devotion in the High and Later Middle Ages, associated particularly with the mendicants, as well as of advanced theology. This may partly be explained by the limited source material, largely the result of its destruction during the Reformation. Nevertheless, stronger evidence of these trends is to be found in other parts of the periphery, above all in Bohemia, where a religious revival in the High Middle Ages developed into the Hussite movement from the late fourteenth century onwards. Furthermore, Sweden witnessed the Birgittine movement in the fourteenth century. Admittedly, a saint like Birgitta is an exception anywhere, and she spent much of her life outside Sweden, but she had a great impact there and her order was an important feature in the religious life of the country and even survived for some time after the Reformation.[57] Finally, Denmark had a real Reformation movement which probably had its background in late medieval humanism and *devotio moderna* to which there seems to be no parallel in Norway. The "production" of indigenous saints is also an important criterion in this discussion. Here Norway is definitely "cold" according to Vauchez's terminology, with few indigenous saints.[58] Moreover, the most important of them, St Olav, had little in common with the type of saint cor-

---

56   Bull, *Folk og kirke*, pp. 19-86; Njåstad, *Grenser for makt*, pp. 63-96, pp. 95 f.
57   Fröjmark, *Mirakler*, pp. 102-28, 170-80.
58   Vauchez, *Sainteté*, pp. 121-29, 154-62; cf. Bagge, "Ideologies", pp. 476-85.

responding to the new trends in piety from the thirteenth century onwards of which St Francis can serve as a model.

Thus, Norway was no exception to the general penetration of Christianity in medieval Europe but had more in common with the outskirts and the countryside than the cities and the main communication routes where new forms of devotion spread more easily and people were under pressure from various impulses. The importance of this for the official Church still needs to be considered. On the one hand, there might be less opposition, on the other, less enthusiasm for reform movements, saints and devotions. Nevertheless, there is no necessary correspondence between new forms of religious life and the strength of the Church as an organisation and its social importance.

From a materialistic point of view, the conversion meant that a cheap and unbureaucratic religion was replaced by an expensive and bureaucratic one. Admittedly, finds like the Oseberg burial suggest that great resources were spent on religion in the pagan period as well, corresponding to similar expenses in the Christian period. In both cases we are dealing with resources that were spent or "buried", without any significant redistributive effect. Although any quantitative comparison between the two is hazardous, it seems unlikely that less was spent on such purposes in the Christian than in the pagan period. The difference was that the monuments were visible, not buried in the ground. They were set up in churches where they testified to the piety of the deceased and their families and their adherence to the community of the faithful, while at the same time marking their wealth and status in comparison to other benefactors of the Church. However, the main difference between the two religions from this perspective lies in the resources that did have a distributive effect – the tithes, donations of land, fines, and other incomes that went to support the clergy. Whereas the pagan religion apparently mainly gave its cult leaders a surplus of prestige, the participants in the Christian cult paid a high price for what in material terms did not amount to more than a thin wafer received once or a few times a year. Christian worshippers invested in spiritual surplus, eternal salvation and divine aid even in their earthly lives. What the believers received in return was the Church's spiritual treasures, such as supernatural help with problems on earth, and above all help to gain eternal life after death. Assuming that people believed in the Church's message, there was a give-and-take relationship between the Church's never-ending surplus of spiritual treasure, and the believers' limited surplus of material treasure. In addition, the Church profited from a number of central and prestigious undertakings and customary rituals: baptisms, weddings, burials, masses for the soul, sale of maintenance for life at monasteries and so forth.

The surplus derived from the contributions of the faithful secured the higher clergy a standard of living far above that of the average population; the bishops were the greatest magnates of the realm, and prelates, abbots, canons and even monks and nuns in the most important monasteries belonged to the aristocracy. The clergy might thus be regarded as a parasitic class, and even believers might have thought that they gave little in return for the wealth they received. However, this wealth did not exclusively benefit the clergy; parts of it were returned to broader strata of the population in the form of hospitals, alms, salaries, gifts, cultural and intellectual activities, and numerous opportunities for laymen to make a career in the service of the ecclesiastical aristocracy. Moreover, the clerics were not only parasitic, they constituted an organised bureaucracy with a well-defined purpose – admittedly only partly conforming to the Weberian ideal – in which office-holders were appointed and certain skills were necessary for appointment. The establishment and expansion of the ecclesiastical bureaucracy thus formed a major step towards an organised government, which expanded further as a consequence of Christian doctrine as well as ethics. The professional clergy not only appropriated a substantial part of the surplus of the agricultural production, but also to a great extent interfered in people's behaviour. It is doubtful whether it would have been possible to bureaucratise any other social function than religion to the same extent under contemporary conditions. As Halvdan Koht puts it, the Church gained control over fields that had not previously been under control of any public authority, such as marriage and sexuality, thus not reducing the king's power but extending the field of the central authority. Consequently, the Church could gain without the state losing.[59] A number of other examples may be added to those of Koht.

The Christian doctrine was expressed in a series of concrete rules, the adherence to which was controlled by the clergy. Every Sunday was a public holiday when the faithful had to abstain from work and, according to the decree from the Lateran Council in 1215, to attend mass in the parish church. The Council also introduced compulsory confession and communion once a year. A considerable number of holidays came in addition to the Sundays; on average around one out of four days was a holiday in the Middle Ages. Furthermore, food restrictions, either against the eating of meat or only allowing a very restricted diet, applied to all Fridays plus two long periods each year – Advent before Christmas and Lent before Easter – as well as some shorter ones. The Church also had detailed rules for legitimate marriage, including severe restrictions against marrying relatives, and very strict norms about sexual morality. The Christian cult was to take place in a special building which in principle should only be used for this purpose, although it was in practice used for other purposes as well (pp. 75, 307). The church was centrally placed in the local community, representing the only sacred point in the landscape. The "monumental religion" was expressed in buildings, from small local churches to great cathedrals, built

---

59   Koht, *Innhogg og utsyn*, p. 271.

for the glory of God and at the same time visual evidence to the people of the importance of the Church and Christianity. Pictures, in the form of paintings and sculptures, were also extensively used by the Church which was by far the most important commissioner of art. Here we are also dealing with a double function: the glory of God and the teaching of the people. Furthermore, the Church was also an important forum for kings and lay aristocrats to show their greatness and piety in the form of altars and memorials. By contrast, the landscape was full of sacred places in the pagan period, and although there is some evidence of cult buildings even then, they were hardly exclusive in the same sense. Finally, the local Christian church was subordinated to a greater organisation, the diocese, which in turn was a part of the universal Church, centred in Rome. The introduction of Christianity thus meant that a far larger sphere of people's lives came under public control. Thus, despite the doubt that may be raised concerning ordinary people's beliefs, the evidence for the political, social, and economic importance of Christianity is overwhelming.

The Right Order of the World and the Christian Monarchy

"My kingdom is not of this world", Jesus says to Pilate.[60] The distinction between politics and religion that is normally taken for granted in modern, western societies is an exception in a global context. Normally, there is a strong connection between the two, not only in Old Norse paganism but also in most other religions, even in the nearest parallel to Christianity, Islam. It then seems a paradox that this unworldly religion has been the most efficient state-builder of all. Part of the paradox is of course solved by the fact that there was a difference between theory and practice. The quotation above stems from a period when Christianity was the religion of a small, partly persecuted minority, whereas the medieval Church was a wealthy and powerful institution. In fact, however, the attitude in this quotation does serve to explain the political role of the Church in medieval and later society. Being away from the world meant that the Church had to form its own society, whereas its ethics and doctrine meant that it did not take society for granted as it actually existed, at least to a lesser extent than the traditional ethnic religion did. The Christian religion might therefore potentially become a revolutionary force, as in the Investiture Contest,[61] while its ideas as well as its organisation might be exploited by secular powers to build strong states. Despite the fact that the Christian ethics was of limited importance for how people actually conducted their lives, it was an important element in the political ideology that was developed in the service of the state.

60   John 18.36.
61   Tellenbach, *Libertas*.

The Church arrived in Norway with a well-developed, international ideology, closely linked to its own administration and functions, which it developed further during the following centuries. By contrast, the monarchy, which established its lordship over the whole country from about the same time, was a less well-defined institution, subject to various ideological impulses, one of which, from the late tenth century, was Christianity. In the following period, Christianity became increasingly important as the ideological foundation of the monarchy, although for a long time in competition with other impulses. There is a clear parallel between the change from pluralism and competition to power monopoly and hierarchy in the divine as well as in the human world. The period from around 1150 to 1300, when these doctrines were developed and set down in writing, was also a period of expansion for the Church and the monarchy and of the development of royal and ecclesiastical jurisdiction and legislation. The story of the Fall of Man is told in two important Old Norse texts, both originating in the royal court: *The King's Mirror* (c. 1255) and *Stjórn* (early fourteenth century), a translation of Genesis and the first half of Exodus with excerpts from theological commentaries,[62] but was probably used in political agitation already by Sverre. In *The King's Mirror*, the story serves as an example of a just judgement, balancing the various considerations the judge has to take into account, symbolised by the allegorical figures of the four sisters, Justice, Truth, Mercy and Peace. Thus, the royal office which exists to serve justice and give everyone his or her due is identified with God's own governance of the world. At the same time, the Fall necessitates harsh measures against sinners which the author justifies later in his work, although he does not regard the royal office as a result of the Fall but of Creation: when man is created in God's image, it is because he is intended to rule all other creatures. Therefore, the king, more than any other human being, imitates and should imitate God.[63] Finally, Adam's and Eve's sin consists in disobedience which is the gravest of sins, a doctrine that is explicitly applied to the relationship between the king and his subjects later in the work.

The introduction of royal unction and coronation, which became permanently established in 1247, the Law of Succession of 1163/64 and the following laws of 1260 and 1273 are all clear expressions of the Christian concept of order. In the arenga of Magnus Erlingsson's privilege to the Church, the young king elaborates on the king's subordination and obedience to God, on the heavy responsibility laid upon him to rule justly, and appeals for God's aid and protection, according to the example of David, whom God

---

62   *Kgs.*, pp. 75-84; cf. Bagge, *The Political Thought*, pp. 54-59, 225-33; *Stjórn*, pp. 35-41; cf. Astås, *Biblical Compilation*, and Bagge, *Da boken*, pp. 109-20.
63   Bagge, *The Political Thought*, pp. 22-25. On the development of this doctrine from Late Antiquity onwards, see Berges, *Fürstenspiegel*, pp. 26 f., and Kantorowicz, "Deus per naturam", pp. 263 ff.

took away from the herd and anointed as king.[64] Nor was this doctrine confined to the circle around the archbishop and Magnus Erlingsson's faction; it is very prominent in Sverre's anticlerical pamphlet, *A Speech against the Bishops*. In the allegory of the body politic opening this pamphlet, the king is said to be the heart of the body and thus its real ruler. In the following, the author argues in detail for the heavy responsibility God has laid upon the king for protecting and governing the people. In *The King's Mirror* (c. 1255), the king's government over the realm is compared to God's over the universe, and not only the monarchy, but also the social hierarchy, as expressed in the four estates, is regarded as instituted by God.[65] There is thus a clear difference between the idea of estates in this work and that of the Eddic poem *Rigstula*. The estates of *The King's Mirror* work together to fulfil the aim of mankind, whereas those of *Rigstula* are simply the expression of the physical and social differences that can be observed by all.[66] Thus the Christian idea of the right order of the world occurs in a series of official and normative sources from around 1150 onwards, in an ecclesiastical direction in connection with the alliance between the Church and Magnus Erlingsson and in a monarchical one by the Sverre dynasty.

In accordance with this cosmology, the medieval Church developed a doctrine of kingship as an office, modelled on the clerical office, a doctrine that is also apparent in Norwegian sources from Magnus Erlingsson's privilege (c. 1170) to *The King's Mirror* and the National Law. These sources distinguish clearly between the person and the office, regarding the latter as bestowed upon the king by God in order to promote justice on earth. In contrast to the pagan notion, the Christian idea of the king's sacrality did not include any idea of the king's divine descent. The king as a person was just an ordinary human being, whereas his office was instituted by God to represent Him on earth. Despite this more indirect concept of sacrality, its consequences were more far-reaching than those of pagan society. In particular *The King's Mirror* develops in great detail the contrast between the person as a weak and sinful human being and the office, which represents God's power and glory.[67]

The distinction between person and office, which is prominent in *The King's Mirror*, could be used both to strengthen and weaken the power of the monarchy. The idea of the king holding an office on God's behalf set him apart from other people and gave him greater authority. On the other hand, the distinction between office and person made it possible in principle to contest the person without contesting the office. There are many

---

64   *Lat. dok.* no. 9; cf. Tobiassen, *Tronfølgelov*, pp. 191-221.
65   Bagge, "Nature and Society", pp. 5-42, and "Ideologies and Mentalities", pp. 465-68 with references.
66   Bagge, "Old Norse Theories", pp. 7-45.
67   Bagge, *The Political Thought*, pp. 22-26, 61-64, 161.

examples in Europe during the Middle Ages of this argumentation against the king.[68] In Norway, however, the idea of the monarchy as an office mainly seems to have been used to strengthen the king. This is already the case in Magnus Erlingsson's privilege as well as in the documents issued in connection with his coronation, although their strong emphasis on the Church bestowing God's grace on the king through unction and coronation means that God's will is mediated to the king through the Church. By contrast, *A Speech against the Bishops* and *The King's Mirror* reject this mediation and point to the direct connection between God and the king. Both sources, in particular the latter, contain a number of assertions regarding the king's enormous power. He represents God on Earth, and disobedience to him is tantamount to disobedience towards God. God is the one who has determined how society is to be arranged. Power is no longer an expression of personal freedom, or based on respect and recognition from others. Instead, power is delegated by God as a necessary means of creating justice. The king owns the land and all its inhabitants, obliging everyone to serve him and take on the burdens he lays on them. Honour and rank are granted solely by the king. Finally, the king decides over life and death; he can kill or spare those he wishes.[69]

The statements about the king's ownership and his power over life and death seem to suggest an absolute and arbitrary power, but become somewhat less drastic when interpreted within their context. The former statement is intended as an argument for public justice, stating that this power does not belong to the offended party but only to the king as the supreme judge on God's behalf, whereas the latter opposes bureaucratic obedience to traditional ideas of friendship and patronage. Both statements therefore aim at strengthening governmental power as such, not the king's power at the expense of other "public institutions". Even so, they represent an authoritarian attitude and a strong challenge to current ideas of the relationship between the king and his subjects. The same applies to the discussion in the work about the king who is evil or unqualified. The author has quite a lot to say about this subject and is in no doubt about the heavy responsibility incumbent on the king, nor of God's punishment of him if he fails in his duties. However, the punishment is left to God, not to the king's subjects. This is the message demonstrated in the way the author renders the biblical account of David and Saul, in which David twice abstains from killing Saul, even when he had the opportunity to do so, and even though Saul was his enemy and persecuted him. Saul was an evil king, but David still did not have the right to kill him. The king is responsible only to God and can only be judged by Him. *The King's Mirror* ends with a description of the king after his death before God's

---

68 E.g. in Lampert of Hersfeld; cf. Bagge, *Kings, Politics*, pp. 274 f.
69 Bagge, *The Political Thought*, pp. 22-26, 31-39, 63 f.

judgement seat, where he has to render an account of how he has administered his high office. The threat of God's punishment, on Earth and particularly in Heaven, should keep the king on the right path, but human beings have no right to intervene.[70]

Whereas the sacrality in itself had some counterpart in the pagan period, explicit ideology as such is more likely to have been a novelty. The struggles in the second half of the twelfth century, partly the one between the Sverre and Magnus factions, but above all that between Sverre and the Church, were also fought with ideological weapons, as is evident particularly in *A Speech against the Bishops*. As demonstrated by other aspects of Sverre's propaganda, as well as by other sagas, propaganda in itself was hardly new. Eloquence was an important quality in a leader and verbal arts were highly regarded, but the speaker apparently appealed to the audience's interests as well as argued for a certain course of action. *A Speech against the Bishops* introduced ideological arguments about right and wrong as its main theme, but used some of the same rhetorical techniques, such as irony, direct appeals to the audience and striking examples, corresponding to the popular agitation known from other sources. The tradition seems to have continued in the following century. *The King's Mirror* deals extensively with difficult and controversial questions about royal government and the relationship between the king and the Church, although not in a style resembling popular agitation. By contrast, the rhetoric of some of the letters issued by the royal chancery, notably during the new conflict with the Church in the 1280s, seems to reflect this tradition.[71]

However, as in other matters, the change from one concept of sacrality to another was a gradual process, and there was a considerable amount of compromise between old and new. The crucial question is not when this ideology was introduced, but when it became dominant, suppressing the older one. The narrative sources give a better impression of this process than the documentary and didactic ones whose practical importance is difficult to assess. Although this is also a problem in the case of the narrative sources, they allow us to measure to what extent these ideas are used in sources that do not directly and explicitly proclaim a particular message. This is of course difficult to answer from the limited source material we have, but the narrative sources are nevertheless numerous and detailed enough to give some indications.[72] The two Latin chronicles from the second half of the

---

70   Bagge, *The Political Thought*, pp. 163-66.
71   Bagge, *Da boken*, pp. 416-24 and below pp. 317 f.
72   This is also my main answer to the critics who have accused me of neglecting the influence of Christian ideas of kingship in the earlier period in my studies of the sagas, most recently Dørum, *Romerike*, pp. 435-60. These studies aim at tracing the picture of society, human actions and relationships, *in these sagas*. Although I believe that the sagas are important sources for actual conditions and attitudes, they have to be supplemented by other sources to give a more complete picture of actual conditions.

twelfth century both consistently evaluate the kings according to the *rex iustus* ideology but are on the other hand so sketchy in dealing with government and politics that they can hardly tell very much about its practical importance. Moreover, their influence in secular circles is doubtful.

The greatest of the kings' sagas, Snorri's *Heimskringla*, probably from around 1230, contains clear traces of the Christian *rex iustus* ideology, mainly in the portrait of St Olav. His daily life is described as that of a good Christian king, similar to the later description in *The King's Mirror*, consisting of prayers, mass, and the distributions of justice. The account of the last part of his life is pure hagiography, but this is not representative of the work as a whole. Here the picture of the king as "the best man" dominates, whose power is based on skill, courage, eloquence and the ability to gain his men's respect and defeat his opponents. This work in several respects contains a view of monarchy and society in opposition to that of sources like *The King's Mirror* and *Hákonar saga*.[73] To what extent this represents a deliberate opposition to the official ideology and to what extent it is the expression of different attitudes coexisting within the court and the aristocracy a generation or so before these two sources remains an open question.[74] In any case, *Heimskringla*'s audience can hardly have been exclusively Icelandic, as Snorri was a close friend of Earl Skule and in all likelihood must have made his work known to him and his circle, as a gift or in other ways.

The somewhat older *Sverris saga*, part of which may have been composed already during Sverre's lifetime and the rest some time before around 1220,[75] also contains strong religious elements. There are traces of hagiography in the account of Sverre's early life, although probably less than has sometimes been thought. Sverre constantly points to his

---

73   Bagge, *Society and Politics*, pp. 68-70, 158-61.
74   The question of ideology in the sagas is a controversial one. My own point of view is that they do contain opinions on various matters but were usually not composed in order to defend a particular view on the government of society and other controversial issues. See Bagge, *Society and Politics*, pp. 100-10, 240-47, and "Ideology and Propaganda", as well as my discussion with Birgit Sawyer: Sawyer, "Samhällsbeskrivningen", and Bagge, "Samfunnsbeskrivelsen". Whereas Sawyer and I disagree on the ideological purpose of *Heimskringla*, we both regard its ideology as different from, or in opposition to, that of the contemporary Norwegian monarchy. By contrast, Nedkvitne, *The Social Consequences*, pp. 128-33, has gone to extreme lengths in a differerent ideological interpretation of the kings' sagas, regarding their authors simply as the mouthpieces of the monarchy, without any discussion of arguments to the contrary.
75   The earliest part of the saga, probably the one dealing with the beginning of Sverre's career, was according to the prologue written under Sverre's supervision, a larger part possibly during Sverre's lifetime, whereas at least the part dealing with the period after 1185 most probably dates from after 1214, because of a reference to Archbishop Guttorm who was elected this year. The author of the first part, the Icelandic abbot Karl Jonsson, was in Norway from 1185-88, so the part written under Sverre's supervision must date from this period. See most recently Bagge, *Gang Leader*, pp. 15-18; Krag, *Kong Sverre*, pp. 46-48, and Þorleifur Hauksson, *Sverris saga*, pp. LX f., all with references to earlier literature.

lawful right to the kingdom, to God's protection of him and to his consecration by God through his dreams, which forms the equivalent of Magnus Erlingsson's unction and coronation, at least until Sverre himself receives the same dignity in 1194. The dreams in the early part of the saga have been sent to him by God. Throughout the saga, Sverre is depicted as a good Christian who forgives his enemies, prays to God, respects the churches and urges his men to do the same. In the early part of the saga as well as in some of the great speeches – at the death of Erling (1179) and Magnus (1184) – he places his own struggles in a cosmic perspective. He is the rightful heir while his adversaries have no right to the throne. In rising above their status, they have made themselves guilty of haughtiness (*dramb/superbia*) – the basic sin which is the most hateful to God, as shown in the examples of the great sinners in history, Lucifer, Adam and Eve, Pharaoh and Saul.[76] By contrast, Sverre often points to his own similarity to David and his strong connection to St Olav, the national saint. Nevertheless, the saga does not develop these examples into a real *rex iustus* ideology. God's purpose in raising Sverre to the throne is never mentioned, and there are few references to Sverre's just government and duties to the people. Quite the contrary, the saga openly admits that his adversaries were popular with the people, whereas his own men were hated, and it only gives a few glimpses of Sverre as a ruler. It has little to say about his aims in fighting his opponents, except winning the throne for himself. Most of the narrative shows Sverre as a charismatic leader of his men, whereas the population in general receives little or only negative attention. Finally, open and unrestricted appeals to his men's greed are as characteristic of Sverre's battle speeches as references to God and Christianity.[77]

Thus, many of these elements must be understood as an assimilation of the traditional idea of luck to the Christian idea of God's providence, in the same way that the skald celebrates Harald Gille's victory as the expression of God's will.[78] God is first and foremost a great patron who aids Sverre in defeating his enemies. Sverre's royal blood and the qualities derived from it are already evident at his birth. When growing up, he shows a character that does not correspond to what he believes to be his descent, the son of an artisan, nor to his station in life, to be a priest. He is violent and has a hot temper and he has strange dreams which suggest something greater than his present conditions. All this is explained when his mother reveals to him that he is the son of a king. This causes him to go to Norway and finally, despite bleak prospects, to try to fight for the status to which

---

76   Ss. ch. 99; cf. Bagge, *From Gang Leader*, pp. 62-65.
77   Bagge, *From Gang Leader*, pp. 25-33. Cf. the discussion about the interpretation of *Sverris saga*: Fredrik Charpentier Ljungqvist, "Kristen kungaideologi"; Lars Lönnroth, "Sverrir's Dreams", and Sverre Bagge, "'Gang Leader' eller 'the Lord's Anointed'".
78   Antonsson, "Some Observations", p. 77.

he is born, a step that is encouraged by new dreams which confirm that he acts according to God's vocation. His victory over Erling and Magnus and his ability to defend his throne against a series of factions rising against him show him as "the best man" and give the final evidence that he is actually a king's son.[79]

The real breakthrough for the Christian *rex iustus* ideology in the narrative sources is therefore *Hákonar saga*. Here Håkon is consistently, or almost consistently, depicted as the Christian *rex iustus*. He is God's elect and the right heir to the throne, but refuses to take up arms to gain his right, trusting in God instead. He shows great concern for the people he is set to rule over, he defends the rights of the monarchy against unjust demands from the Church, he is unfaltering in his belief in God, he is scrupulously just in his decisions, and he defends his country against foreign aggressors while respecting the rights of others. Like in *The King's Mirror*, God's protection of the king has become the expression of an idea of objective justice,[80] which in turn forms the basis for a central political organisation.

The immediate conclusion from the examination of the saga literature would therefore be to place the great breakthrough in the period between the composition of *Heimskringla* and that of *Hákonar saga*, namely between around 1230 and 1265, but it is hardly possible to give an exact date. Whereas *Hákonar saga* was commissioned by the court and probably written in close contact with King Magnus and his counsellors, *Heimskringla*'s author was an Icelandic chieftain, apparently without any direct Norwegian patronage. Admittedly, the early part of *Sverris saga* was also written at the king's commission, but the milieu of the rest of the saga seems to be a warrior environment, dominated by veterans from Sverre's battles.[81] *A Speech against the Bishops* shows that there were other dimensions to Sverre's ideas of kingship than those dominating in his saga. Moreover, *Fagrskinna*, an earlier saga, covering almost the same period as *Heimskringla* and written in Norway, possibly by a Norwegian, is more concerned with the royal office and tones down the competition between various kings and magnates, thus to some extent anticipating *Hákonar saga*'s ideology. This is probably also the saga mentioned as the last work read aloud to Håkon Håkonsson at his deathbed, in a version also containing *Sverris saga*.[82] Thus, the narrative sources give an impression of the tension between two ideologies of kingship and show the gradual penetration of the Christian *rex iustus* ideology, but do not give a precise chronology. *The King's Mirror* and *Hákonar saga*, together with other sources,

---

79　Bagge, *From Gang Leader*, pp. 52-71.
80　Bagge, *From Gang Leader*, pp. 61-65, 80-88, 147-60. For a similar development in Germany from the tenth to the twelfth century, see Bagge, *Kings, Politics*, pp. 389-407 and *passim*.
81　Bagge, *From Gang Leader*, pp. 15 f.
82　*HH* ch. 329.

indicate that this ideology must have achieved a dominating position in the court circles by the middle of the thirteenth century, although with traces of the old ideas, but that its influence goes back at least a hundred years.

The Emergence of the Dynasty and Hereditary Monarchy

The tension between traditional and Christian ideas of monarchy and the transition from the former to the latter emerge most clearly from an examination of the development of the dynasty and hereditary monarchy. As we have seen (above p. 26), the formation of a dynasty took place at a considerably later date than stated in the saga tradition, which in this respect depends on twelfth- and thirteenth-century ideas about the origins of the dynasty ruling at the time. This would immediately seem to be quite logical. Harald Finehair was a conqueror whose position was built on power and personal contacts, not on any idea of kingship as an office. Harald would clearly have been interested in passing his kingdom on to his sons, but he would have been unlikely to have convinced the rest of the country and its magnates that his descendants should have a legal claim to the throne for all future. This applies even if we accept the authenticity of the *Ynglingatal*, which gives evidence that a Viking Age kindred tried to trace its ancestors back to the gods, but not that it was the only one to do so. Although the idea of dynastic continuity existed in the ninth and tenth centuries, there was no generally recognised right for one dynasty to succeed to the throne. On the contrary, the throne was the object of open competition, at least until the mid-eleventh century.

The next period, 1066-1163/64, or in reality until 1260, may be regarded as a period of limited competition. In the period after 1066 it was generally agreed upon that the throne was reserved for one kindred. During the internal conflicts from the mid-twelfth century onwards, when a large number of pretenders fought for the throne, no magnate, no matter how powerful he was, claimed the throne for himself, but only members of the dynasty. We do not know exactly when this rule was introduced. As usual, a series of kings from the same dynasty (three generations from 1066-1130) must have been an important factor. The cult of Olav Haraldsson (1015-30), who was canonised by a local assembly shortly after his death, and the skill and ruthlessness of his half-brother Harald Hardrada (1046-66) from whom the following kings traced their descent, played a role. The royal saints were characteristic of the new kingdoms which were formed from the tenth century onwards and are closely associated with the foundation of a dynasty. Does this imply a Christian version of an earlier notion of sacred kingship, or is it a genuine Christian conception which was used in a dynastic context? The latter alternative seems the more likely. The earliest royal saints, among them the Merovingian and Anglo-Saxon kings, were saints despite their royal rank rather than because of it. Only gradually was a link formed between sainthood and royalty; St Olav is actually one of the earlier examples of this combination.[83] Moreover, there was also a considerable difference between the pagan and the Christian version of sacred kingship. According to Christian thinking, holiness is a personal attribute which is not passed on through generations. However, combined with the dynastic line of thought, the existence of a royal saint could bolster the position of the heir. There is therefore no doubt that Olav's holiness was significant for the dynasty and the monarchy in the years that followed.

Earlier historians discussed whether the monarchy in this period was elective or hereditary. The answer must be that the royal succession contained elements of both.[84] The pretender had to appear at a local assembly and be elected there. In principle, any assembly could act in this way, although Øreting in Trondheim apparently had a particular status. However, we are not dealing with a well-established "constitution" but with a competitive system, not unlike that of the previous period, only that there were some limits as to who might participate in the competition. This also implies that the ideology underlying royal elections in this period was the same as in the previous one, namely that the king should be "the best man", an idea connected to the traditional one of sacred kingship. This understanding of royal succession was replaced by one based on an entirely different ideology in the Law of Succession of 1163/64[85] which stated that there should only be one king at the time. Only legitimate sons of the previous king were recognised, with preference for the eldest, and, most importantly, the king was to be elected by a national assembly, meeting in Trondheim after the previous king's death. Attempts to ascend to the throne in any other way were to be punished by outlawry and excommunication. Dynastic succession was in one way strengthened, in that the eldest son of the previous king became the preferred candidate. However, the election prescribed in the law was no blank slate. The king was to be elected by an assembly defined in detail in the law, in which the bishops would have a decisive vote. This assembly had the right to reject the eldest son if they found that he lacked the moral qualifications for this high office. If so, they might choose freely among his other sons. If there were no son, they would have relatively great

---

83   Hoffmann, *Die heiligen Könige*, pp. 58-89; Klaniczay, *Holy Rulers*, pp. 62-113; Antonsson, "Some Observations" and *St Magnus*, pp. 103-45, 221-25.
84   The importance of election in the early period was pointed out by Taranger, "Om kongevalg"; see also Seip, "Problemer og metode", pp. 57-63.
85   The law has been subject to much discussion. See Tobiassen, "Tronfølgelov", pp. 221-73, and a summary of the earlier discussion in Helle, *Norge blir en stat*, pp. 60-62. The most recent contribution is Bagge, "Motstandsretten", pp. 391-96.

liberty in choosing between various candidates, according to their descent as well as their qualifications.

The ideological basis of this law was the Christian doctrine of the *rex iustus*. Whether the king should be elected or inherit his office was a practical matter, although the Church tended to favour election, in analogy with ecclesiastical office. Nor did it attach any special importance to royal blood. The supernatural aspect of kingship lay in the office, not in the king's person. The Law of Succession of 1163/64 is significant as the expression of new ideological principles which were to have great influence in the future, but had no immediate practical importance; no royal succession was ever carried out according to its rules. If it had been practised, however, it would hardly have reduced the importance of dynastic succession; it is difficult to imagine an assembly, even if dominated by the bishops, rejecting the king's eldest son as morally unqualified. The importance of this provision is rather that it would have given the electors, notably the bishops, the opportunity to pose conditions for the election, as actually happened in the neighbouring countries and in Norway in the Later Middle Ages. The clergy could also argue that they gave the king his legitimate power through the ritual of unction and coronation. In fact, the first coronation in 1163/64 strongly expressed the king's subordination and obedience to the Church, as appears from Magnus's coronation oath and privilege to the Church. This, as well as the general ideology, confirm the common opinion among historians that the Church was the main influence behind the law. Nevertheless, the immediate reason for passing the law was the need for the faction which had now gained the upper hand in protecting its new king, Magnus Erlingsson, against rival pretenders by stamping all his opponents as rebels and heretics.

Magnus's enemy and successor Sverre claimed to be the lawful king by virtue of being a king's son and condemned his adversary as a usurper who had no right to the throne because he descended from the dynasty through a king's daughter. Sverre thus opposed the idea of royal blood against the principles behind the law of 1163/64. Sverre's propaganda also dismissed Magnus's coronation as an unsuccessful attempt to compensate for Magnus's lack of royal descent.[86] According to the saga, he also had a more relaxed attitude to divided kingship than Magnus. During a discussion in 1181, Sverre offered to share the country with Magnus, which Magnus rejected, pointing to the responsibility laid upon him at his unction and coronation. Admittedly, Sverre refused to share the kingdom with his alleged brother Eirik, but entirely for pragmatic reasons: he had laboured and suffered so much in order to gain the kingdom that he would not give up any part of it. In denying that his elected and anointed adversary Magnus was a lawful king, Sverre would logically

---

86   For the following, see Bagge, *From Gang Leader*, pp. 61-71.

seem to have rejected the coronation as a necessary ritual for ascending to the throne. Nevertheless, Sverre was eager to receive this dignity himself, as is evident in his dream when he receives unction from the prophet Samuel. After long negotiations and apparently a fair amount of bullying of the bishops, he finally succeeded in being crowned in 1194. How this ritual was performed and what Sverre had to promise in return is unknown, but there are hints in the saga that the coronation became an element in his propaganda.

Thus, Sverre left a somewhat mixed ideological heritage to his grandson Håkon Håkonsson. Like Sverre, Håkon based his claim on his royal blood; he was a king's son, although he was not born out of a lawful marriage. The issue of royal blood is therefore a central element in *Hákonar saga* as well as in *Sverris saga*. On the other hand, the Christian *rex iustus* ideology was more strongly present in royalist circles during Håkon Håkonsson's reign than during the reign of Sverre. The author of *The King's Mirror* argues strongly in favour of individual succession, describing in detail the disastrous consequences of dividing the kingdom between several heirs, which in his opinion was the cause of the previous internal wars. These arguments are directly based on the *rex iustus* ideology, depicting the king as responsible for peace, justice and social order in the country and the division of the kingdom as preventing him from exercising these duties. By contrast, the author is more vague regarding how the succession should take place. He is strongly against ecclesiastical interference in royal elections and indirectly probably an adherent of dynastic succession, but he has no exact solution to the problem of choosing between several legitimate heirs. The same vagueness seems to have been present for a long time in courtly circles. *Hákonar saga* refers to a discussion about the division of the country between the king's two sons in 1255 where Håkon himself wanted to leave the choice to God. Two years later God chose by letting the elder, Håkon, die.[87] In 1260, the king made the final decision, issuing a law about individual succession and primogeniture.

The basic problem for Håkon Håkonsson and his counsellors is that the idea of a "blood line" is in conflict with that of an office, whereas there is a logical connection between the idea of an office and an elective monarchy, as in the case of the clerical office. Regardless of how real the election was – it was in most cases about choosing the one who was regarded as being the nearest of kin to the deceased king – this process corresponds best with the idea of an office into which one is elected, not born. In the case of hereditary kingship, the distinction between office and person tends to be blurred. If the idea of hereditary kingship is derived from an idea of special qualities in the royal blood, it becomes doubtful even if a concept of office exists. The king then becomes king by virtue of inherited personal attributes, not through selection or formal authority. The problem

---

87   *HH* ch. 284; Bagge, *From Gang Leader,* pp. 102 f.

with this concept of kingship is that it contains no criteria for excluding any descendant of the dynasty from succession. To achieve this, an elective element is necessary.

For this purpose, the law of 1163/64 instituted an elective assembly. The law of 1260 did the same, but at the same time made it clear that it was not the duty of that assembly to decide who was to become king, but only to elect the one nearest in the line of succession – the king's eldest son or the nearest heir if the king had no sons. This election was then, in the language of the saga and *The King's Mirror*, defined as God's election. In the words of Håkon's grandson Håkon V: "God elected us to govern the realm after our forefathers".[88] Thus the contemporary dynasty could appropriate the Christian royal ideology in its entirety, which in Magnus Erlingsson's Law of Succession and the privileges to the Church is linked to the idea of election. What becomes most important is no longer the quality of the royal lineage, but God's selection of the nearest within the line of succession, who then becomes another person by virtue of his office. With the laws of 1260 and 1273, both criteria for the institutionalisation of the monarchy are met, the distinction between person and office, and clear rules for accession to the royal office.

The law of 1260 and the ideology at Håkon Håkonsson's court represent a synthesis of the two opposing ideologies of the second half of the twelfth century. The Christian doctrine of the *rex iustus* and kingship as an office had become fully accepted, while the idea of dynastic succession and royal blood had become integrated in this ideology through the idea of God's election. To what extent there was actually a belief in the special qualities of the royal blood in the second half of the thirteenth century is open to discussion; in contrast to *Sverris saga*, *Hákonar saga* portrays its protagonist as a Christian *rex iustus* and legitimate king rather than as a charismatic warrior hero. Moreover, the king's interest in dynastic succession was a sufficient motive for him to support the tradition of hereditary monarchy even without any notion of royal blood.

Håkon was also the one who included unction and coronation in the normal procedure for ascending to the throne, both through his own coronation in 1247 and through that of his son Magnus in 1261. Like his grandfather, Håkon had difficulties in achieving the coronation because of his illegitimate birth; he spent much time and money in getting a papal dispensation and only succeeded after thirty years on the throne. The introduction of coronation serves as further evidence of the acceptance of the *rex iustus* ideology and the idea that the king's power was derived from God. The traditional ritual for the accession to the throne, *konungstekja*, symbolised his instalment by the people: the king was lifted up to an elevated chair by two prominent members of the Thing assembly, so that

---

88 "guð kaus oss til rikis stiornar eftir uart foreldri" (NGL III, p. 45).

he could be seen by everyone.[89] By contrast, at the Christian coronation ritual the king received his insignia from God through the bishop and other clergy and received holy unction which "made him into another man", as stated in the liturgy. The two different rituals look like the perfect illustration of Walter Ullmann's descending and ascending themes respectively.[90] The old ritual continued to exist after the coronation had been introduced, and the acclamation was still regarded as the decisive ritual. This is not a coincidence, despite the fact that the high medieval doctrine of kingship was closer to that of the coronation rituals than that of the *konungstekja*.

The problem was the same as under Magnus Erlingsson and Sverre: the coronation could be interpreted in the sense that the king received his office from the Church. In connection with the coronation in 1247, the saga attributes a proclamation to Håkon in which he rejects the bishops' demand that he swear the same oath as Magnus Erlingsson about obedience to the Church.[91] Here Håkon repeats Sverre's argument about Magnus's need to make concessions to the Church to compensate for his lack of hereditary right and declares that he would rather abstain from the coronation than buy it at such a price. According to the saga, Cardinal William of Sabina, who was the coronator, accepted Håkon's arguments, which seems likely enough, given his master Pope Innocent IV's desperate struggle against the Emperor Frederick II. Still, it was possible to maintain that the one who gave the coronation was higher in rank than the one who received it. This problem is addressed in *The King's Mirror*, in all likelihood written after Håkon's coronation. Here the author argues that the king is the Lord's Anointed (*Christus Domini*) whether he is crowned or not, because in the Old Testament God has used this title for the king, and even for a pagan king, Cyrus. Consequently, the coronation is only a manifestation of the rank the king already holds and does not mean that the Church has the power to add anything to his dignity.[92]

The Courtly Culture

While the sagas and the ancient mythology are largely based on indigenous traditions, another secular element was imported from abroad in the thirteenth century, namely the European, and notably French, courtly culture which served to set the king and his court apart from the rest of the population and thus to enhance the power and prestige of the social elite. From the mid-thirteenth century onwards, a considerable number of chivalrous romances, mainly French, were translated into Norwegian, probably largely at the

---

89 The ritual is described in the Hird Law, ch. 2.
90 Ullmann, *Principles*, pp. 19-26 and *passim*.
91 Bagge, *From Gang Leader*, pp. 102, 105 f.
92 Bagge, *The Political Thought*, pp. 43-49.

initiative of the monarchy.[93] To some extent this literature may be regarded as a kind of "cultural rearmament", directed by the king. Such an aim is explicitly mentioned in some of the prefaces, for example in *Strengleikar*, a translation of the *Lais* of Marie de France. Here the translator points to the importance of reading the stories of the past so as to learn virtues and the fear of God from them, adding that his translation was made on King Håkon's initiative.[94] The moral message of this introduction does not appear entirely convincing, as many of the stories included in the volume deal with illicit love. The fact that these stories had their origin in a courtly and aristocratic culture was probably more important for their use as education than their content.

The corresponding import of the norms and values of the European aristocracy is further testified by the descriptions in *Hákonar saga* of banquets and festivities, of royal embassies to other countries, and above all in quotations from foreign envoys speaking favourably of the manners of the Norwegians and their king.[95] If we compare the sagas dealing with the period until the second half of the twelfth century (*Morkinskinna* and *Heimskringla* and to a lesser extent *Fagrskinna*) with *Hákonar saga* and *The King's Mirror*, we get the impression of a radical change in the king's position in society and the way people had to approach him. In particular, *The King's Mirror* goes very far in underlining the respect for the king and gives detailed rules for how to approach him and how the courtiers should address him and behave in his presence. The author also attaches great importance to such matters, even declaring that the men who behave badly in this respect commit such a serious crime that they deserve to be killed, together with their families – probably an allusion to *crimen laesae maiestatis* in Roman law.[96] In some cases he also directly states that these rules are different from those prevailing in other circles, thus underlining the exclusivity of the court. He also makes a sharp distinction between the members of the court, who live in surroundings which ought to inspire them to true nobility, and all others, who are referred to as "cottars" (*kotkarlar*), whatever their actual wealth and standing.[97]

Admittedly, most of the rules are confined to what in later ages would be regarded as simple rules of polite behaviour: one should not lean over the king's table while addressing him; the king should be addressed in the plural and not in the singular – a rule which forms the subject of a longer explanation – and one should take care to keep the right dis-

---

93 On the chivalric literature and the court milieu in Norway at the time, see Meissner, *Die Strengleikar*; Halvorsen, "Norwegian Court Literature", pp. 17-26; Kalinke, "Norse Romances,"; Kramarz-Bein, *Die Þiðreks saga*, pp. 68-81.
94 *Strengleikar*, p. 4-5. See Fidjestøl, "Romantic Reading", pp. 351-65.
95 Bagge, "The Norwegian Monarchy" and *From Gang Leader*, pp. 105 f.
96 Bagge, *The Political Thought*, pp. 195 f. and 203 f.
97 Ibid., pp. 179-80, and "The Norwegian Monarchy", pp. 168-77.

tance when riding beside the king, so as not to splash water or mud on him or his horse, and so forth. The rules of etiquette in the Hird Law are of a similar kind. Although a respect for the king by virtue of his office on God's behalf is real enough in the normative sources, it did not lead to a corresponding change in courtly etiquette, in contrast to the situation in later centuries, for instance at the courts of Philip II of Spain or Louis XIV of France. Nevertheless, some rules are less innocent than they immediately appear. One rule in particular, namely that one should appear before the king without a cloak, makes the Son (who usually asks the questions in this dialogue between him and his father) comment that a man who did this in ordinary society would be considered ridiculous, which then of course makes the Father embark on a detailed explanation in three points, the most important of which is that appearing without a cloak expresses the willingness to serve. Here another example comes to mind, the confrontation between Håkon and Skule in 1233 during which it was demanded of Skule that he should take off his cloak and kneel for the king in sign of submission (below p. 283).

The difference between the traditional Norwegian culture represented by the sagas and by the ancient poetry and the imported courtly manners and literature has often been emphasised in scholarly literature, in many cases with a strong preference for the former. The romantic ideology of the nineteenth century regarded this literature as popular, an idea that to some extent has lingered on.[98] This literature should probably be classified as aristocratic instead, although the courtly literature and its corresponding manners are more exclusively so and form a step in the formation of a courtly elite more distant from the rest of the population,[99] which corresponds to a shift in the social and political development. Nevertheless, the difference between the two cultures should not be exaggerated; their milieu were largely the same, and contemporary people hardly saw the same opposition between them as did nineteenth-century scholars. Håkon Håkonsson may once more serve as an example. He took the initiative to translate French romances, but was himself the subject of a saga, although in some respects different from the classical tradition. He had Latin legends read to him at his deathbed, but ended by listening to the sagas of his ancestors.[100]

The ideology of the two governing organisations was not confined to doctrine; rituals and iconography also played a prominent part. Here the Church was once more the leader, impressing the population with a wealth of paintings, statues – only a fragment of which has been preserved – and song and rituals in the numerous churches all over the country. On the royal side, the king's portrait appeared on seals and coins, and his officials,

---

98   Kinck, *Storhetstid*, pp. 323-87.
99   Gellner, *Nations*, pp. 8-13.
100 *HH* ch. 329 f.; Bagge, "Nationalism", pp. 9 f.

with fixed districts and relatively well-defined tasks, acted in the king's name and with his authority.[101] The means at the disposal of the monarchy were by contrast more modest and to a considerable extent derived from the arsenal of the Church. The most important example of this is of course the coronation. Similarly, royal weddings and funerals were grand and ceremonious, and the king was, moreover, received by a procession of leading citizens and clergy every time he came to a new city. Public executions during the Middle Ages were probably rarer than in later periods because most crimes could be atoned by fines, and little is actually known about how they took place (see below p. 210). In this regard, both ceremonies and gruesomeness were raised to a higher level in the seventeenth and eighteenth century. Taken together, both religious and political rituals must have contributed to disseminating the truths about the world order, which were expressed in the official literate culture, thus bolstering the authority of the elite.

There has been a widespread understanding that symbolic and ritual communication was replaced by verbal and intellectual communication, in conjunction with the proliferation of writing and the development of a central authority. This may be a correct observation in some cases, even if the issue rarely involves one form displacing the other. Rituals may even increase their importance and complexity in a literate period, as for instance during the Early Modern Period.[102] Medieval Norway seems to be an example of this latter trend. Little is known about rituals and symbols in the Viking Age, but there are indications that verbal communication, both in the forms of skaldic verse and ordinary agitation, played an important role. The sacrifices undoubtedly had their rituals, yet must still have retained the character of social meetings to a larger degree than the strictly ritualized Catholic mass, where the congregation for the most part was reduced to spectators. Concerning the monarchy, older accounts of kings are often detailed when it comes to appearance, clothes, and weapons, while later ones, in the contemporary sagas, say little about this but put greater emphasis on rituals and signs of honour and dignity.[103] The account of Håkon Håkonson's coronation in the saga about him is very detailed, and shows how the entire city (Bergen) was eagerly present on this occasion.

The king's importance as the patron of art and architecture was less than that of the Church, but the castles erected in the thirteenth and early fourteenth centuries not only served military purposes but were also monumental residences for the king, his court and his administration. The castle in Bergen was rebuilt and greatly extended in the thirteenth century. Three halls were used during Magnus Håkonsson's wedding and coronation in

---

101 Sverre Bagge, "Kingship in Medieval Norway", pp. 41-52, and "The Norwegian Monarchy," pp. 159-77.
102 Althoff, *Die Macht der Rituale*, pp. 18-21.
103 Monclair, *Forestillinger om kongen*, pp. 103-7 and *passim*.

1261, two of which, built shortly before, were in stone. The largest of them, now called Håkonshallen after its founder, still exists and was a grand residence in the contemporary European style, resembling and possibly modelled after Westminster Hall in London. Håkon's son Magnus built a wall around the castle, including a tower which could serve as another royal residence which was further extended during the Later Middle Ages (now called Rosenkrantz Tower). Håkon also built a castle in Tønsberg as a combined residence and military stronghold. The castle of Akershus in Oslo was erected under Håkon V and seems to have already been an impressive fortification as well as residence during his reign. Similar buildings were also erected by the bishops. The archbishop's residence in Trondheim is still preserved and resembles the royal residences in size and style. The archbishop also had a residence in Bergen, located precisely in order to face the royal one on the opposite side of Vågen, of which there still remains ruins. The other bishops probably had similar residences, but little remains of them.[104]

Patriotism and Secular Legitimation of Monarchy

The Church was the main producer of explicit ideology in Norway as well as in other countries in the Middle Ages, and the evidence of this production is overwhelming, although its precise effect on the people is difficult to ascertain. Less is known about similar attempts by the monarchy. Recent debates about nationalism have focused on the question of whether this is a specifically modern phenomenon, only to be found in the period after the French Revolution, or whether it goes back to, or at least was anticipated in earlier periods, including the Middle Ages.[105] The answer is largely a matter of definition, but there is at least evidence of patriotic sentiments in the Middle Ages, in Norway as well as in other countries. Despite his strongly religious attitude, even Theodoricus Monachus, writing around 1180, feels some patriotic pride at the exploits of his Viking ancestors who raided all over Europe.[106] One of the most frequently cited examples of such sentiments is to be found in a story of the Battle of Svolder (AD 1000) which appears for the first time in the late twelfth century, where Olav Tryggvason – one of the great heroes of the saga literature – was defeated and probably killed by an overwhelmingly superior force consisting of Danes, Swedes and a Norwegian rival of Olav with his men. Watching the

---

104 Lidén, "Middelalderens steinarkitektur", pp. 104-23.
105 Gellner, *Nations and Nationalism*, Anderson, *Imagined Communities*, and Hobsbawm, *Nations and Nationalism*, regard it as essentially modern, whereas Smith, *Theories of Nationalism* and *National Identity*, assumes a continuity from preindustrial ethnic groups to modern nationalism. On Norway, see Bagge, "Nationalism", and Lunden, "Was there a Norwegian National Identity?"
106 Theodoricus, *Historia*, pp. 3 f.

enemy approaching, Olav states his contempt for the courage and skills of the Danes and the Swedes, while pointing to Eirik Ladejarl and his men as the really dangerous enemies, "for they are Norwegians like us".[107] This story shows a clear awareness of the Norwegian people as opposed to the people of Denmark and Sweden, and a pride in belonging to that people, thus indicating that "Norway" was not solely an artificial creation. However, the story does not meet the crucial criterion in modern definitions of nationalism, the idea that the "national community" should also be expressed in an independent state. On the contrary, it is directly opposed to this idea, containing no objection to the fact that the "good and brave Norwegians" were actually fighting their own king and country.[108] The sagas give several other examples of such behaviour, usually without any negative comments from the authors.[109]

During a conflict with Denmark in the 1160s, Earl Erling Skakke, according to *Heimskringla*, skilfully exploited nationalistic sentiments. At a meeting with the people of Viken in Tønsberg, he declares himself willing to fulfil the treaty he has entered into with Denmark to cede the region to the Danish king if the people prefer "to be subject to the king of Denmark, rather than to the king who has been consecrated and crowned to govern this land".[110] To this leading question he receives the expected answer – the people flatly refusing to serve the Danish king. During the war against the Swedish dukes in 1308-09, King Håkon V in a letter expresses his gratitude to the people of Trøndelag for their brave defence of their region, adding that they will be rewarded for their efforts. Having given instructions for the coming expedition against the enemy, the king ends by expecting that they will defend "the country and their own peace and freedom".[111] In both these examples, there is a close connection between the king and the country. When the king is considered responsible for the welfare of the people as a whole, existing for the sake of the country and its people, the step from loyalty to the king and "nationalism" is not too great. Moreover, there are numerous references in the sagas to the sentiments that Erling Skakke tried to exploit; it seems a commonplace for people to prefer indigenous rulers, thus making it difficult to become ruler of a foreign country. This is not necessarily an indication of nationalistic sentiments in the modern sense, but can be explained by the fact that foreigners lack the social network necessary

---

107 Oddr, *Sága Óláfs*, pp. 210-18; cf. *The Saga of Olaf*, pp.123-26. See also the later version in *HkrOT* ch. 104.
108 Bagge, "Nationalism," p. 6.
109 Bagge, *Society and Politics*, pp. 66-70 and 106.
110 "at þjóna Dana-konungi heldr en þessum konungi, er hér er vígðr ok kórónaðr til landz" (*HkrME* ch. 24). See Bagge, *Society and Politics*, p. 104.
111 "ok þess venttom ver at aller se viliugir til at væria landet ok sialfra sinna frid ok freilsi" (DN I no. 121).

to create loyalty.[112] On the other hand, modern nationalism also has its roots in traditional sentiments of group loyalty.

Furthermore, the thirteenth-century sources show attempts to link the people more closely to the state and to create greater loyalty to its central institutions. The idea of treason against the country (*landráð*) already occurs in the regional laws, which were written down in the early twelfth century, but it is vaguely defined. It appears in a clearer form in the National Law: "If a man acts so as to deprive his king of the country or its inhabitants ...."[113] Apart from a few scattered comments in the earlier sagas, such as *Heimskringla*,[114] the first, though not wholly consistent, attempt to characterise inner strife as a rebellion against the king in the sagas is the description in *Hákonar saga* of the pretender Skule Bårdsson's war against King Håkon Håkonsson in 1239-40.[115] In these sources, and generally in the ideology of the thirteenth century, the main emphasis is on the king, rather than the country. On the other hand, traditional ideas of loyalty to a person might be exploited to create loyalty for an institution. In this way, we should not draw too sharp a line of division between loyalty to the king and loyalty to the nation. *The King's Mirror* seems on occasions to assume a fairly close connection between the two. Commenting on the disasters resulting from the division of the country between several kings, the author states that this division is not only a geographical one, it "divides the people's loyalty".[116] There are also other examples pointing in the same direction.[117]

As these examples are all derived from more or less "official", literary sources, their practical importance may be doubted; Sverrir Jakobsson clearly has a point when regarding them as normative rather than descriptive.[118] The detailed description of the expedition against Scotland in 1263 in *Hákonar saga* may serve as a warning against exaggerating the peasants' enthusiasm for fighting for their king and country. King Håkon had to change his plans several times as the result of his men's unwillingness to do what he wanted, and parts of the fleet left the expedition and went home before Håkon himself withdrew.[119] There were also defections by Håkon V's men to the Swedish dukes and back again during the war in 1308-10. The fact remains, however, that the Norwegian

112 Bagge, *Society and Politics*, pp. 100-5; "Nationalism", p. 7.
113 "ef mann rædr undan konungi sinum lond eða þegna" (L IV 3, NGL II, p. 49).
114 Bagge, *Society and Politics*, pp. 134-35.
115 Bagge, *From Gang Leader*, p. 112-29.
116 "Þviat þeir sma konongar er þa hafa sunndr slitit riki þa slita þeir þægar í iam marga staðe astunndan folksens" (*Kgs.*, p. 52); cf. Bagge, *The Political Thought*, p. 193. The Old Norse term *astundan*, which means attention, desire or aim, must here refer to emotional ties linking the people of a country together, similar to the idea of friendship or the common will as the foundation of a political community in ancient thought.
117 Bagge, *The Political Thought*, pp. 192-94.
118 Jakobsson, "Defining a Nation," 96 f.
119 Bagge, *From Gang Leader*, p. 142.

king did manage to mobilise the peasants for foreign expeditions.[120] I have previously used this fact as an argument to prove that the Norwegian king depended on the peasants for support to a greater extent than most other contemporary kings.[121] There thus seems to be a certain "democratic" basis for some kind of patriotism on the part of the peasant population.

We must therefore conclude that ideas of a national community headed by the king did exist in Norway in the thirteenth century, but that their exact importance is difficult to assess. We know more about the official view in courtly circles than about the common opinion in the country at large, and the number of people who were directly involved in the royal government or even affected by it was very limited compared to modern conditions. Still, to return to the debate between Gellner, Anderson, Smith and others, nationalism is not only the willingness of some idealists to sacrifice everything for an imagined community, but an expression of the fact that every organised government involves a number of people who are interested in its continued existence. A good example of this is the promise made to King Håkon V on his deathbed in May 1319, shortly before Norway entered its first union with Sweden, not to give foreigners military commands or administrative positions in Norway. The king may have believed that native-born men would make better rulers over his subjects than foreigners, but the initiative is more likely to have come from the Norwegian aristocracy which certainly wanted to reserve such positions for its own members.[122] Both the people and the aristocracy repeatedly articulated these demands in the following period of unions with Sweden and Denmark, thus illustrating the concrete interests attached to the existence of an independent Norwegian kingdom.

Conclusion

Whereas the military system and foreign policy show considerable continuity back to the Viking Age, the cultural and religious change is revolutionary. The conversion to Christianity not only introduced a new religion but a new kind of religion, in addition to a wealthy and powerful bureaucratic organisation which was an important factor in the concentration of land in fewer hands as well as in the government of society. The Church

---

120 Lunden, "National Identity", p. 31.
121 Bagge, "Borgerkrig og statsutvikling", pp. 192-94, and "State Building," pp. 138 f.; Moseng et al., *Norsk historie* I, pp. 227-32.
122 DN I no. 156; Lunden, *Norge under Sverreætten*, pp. 457-60; Moseng et al., *Norsk historie*, pp. 168 f. This was a common condition when foreign princes succeeded to the throne; see Bartlett, *The Making of Europe*, p. 232, with reference to John of Luxemburg's election in Bohemia in 1310.

also delivered an ideology that served as a basis for a similar development in secular government, partly as an independent force and partly combined with secular elements of indigenous as well as foreign origin. Traditional ideas of the king as "the best man" to some extent merged with the Christian doctrine of kingship instituted by God, and ancient mythology was used to strengthen the idea of dynastic continuity by making the pagan gods into human beings who had lived in the distant past. All these elements were also used in patriotic appeals and attempts to glorify the Norwegians and their rulers in a way that at least partly resembles the national ideology of later centuries, although the monarchy was clearly inferior to the Church as a producer of ideology. However, both institutions had been able to mobilise in this field in a way that must have contributed to the development of their organisations and their influence in society.

The ideological field is thus an example of the crucial importance of the impulses coming from Western Christendom as the result of the conversion, first and foremost Christianity and the interpretations of society and political power following from contemporary Christian thought on these matters but also the courtly, secular culture. Nevertheless, local traditions were stronger in Norway than in many other "new" countries. The ancient mythology was still used in poetry in the thirteenth century and formed part of the contemporary education, similar to the classical mythology in other parts of Europe, but it also served to link the king and the dynasty to ancient times, in accordance with the official ideology's emphasis on dynastic continuity. Less different from other countries, but still distinctive, is the secular historiography, celebrating the virtues of the competitive pre-state society. Finally, the external impulses were adapted to local conditions, starting with the language: most of the imported literature and ideas were translated into the vernacular. In *A Speech against the Bishops* and to some extent in *The King's Mirror* as well as in some of the royal charters, the European ideology is presented to a lay audience in a rhetoric likely to be derived from traditional public speaking. As far as we can gauge from the limited extant material, a selection was made, favouring practical wisdom rather than theoretical speculations and addressing concrete problems of ethics and rulership. This aspect will be discussed further in the following chapters on justice, administration and the division of power.

Justice, Law and Power

Whereas warfare was mainly under the control of the king and religion under that of the Church, the third main field of public authority, justice, was divided between the two. According to ecclesiastical theory, justice was the king's most important duty. It was also the most important expression of political power in the Middle Ages, and its development, or lack of it, an important criterion of state formation. It was a field where countless local traditions existed but where, from the eleventh and twelfth century onwards, a powerful body of doctrine and practical rules had been developed by the universities and the courts of law of northern Italy under the influence of Roman law, and by the Church through the formation of canon law from Gratian onwards, in the great papal collections and the commentaries by the decretists and decretalists. This influence also reached Norway which, however, had the oldest collections of local written law in Scandinavia and some of the oldest in Christian Europe as a whole. Although the origins of these laws have been the subject of much discussion, their existence allows us, to a greater extent than in most other countries, to study the meeting of international and indigenous legal traditions.

The Regional Laws

Like other Germanic societies – and many others as well – Norway had local assemblies (ON *þing*) to deal with the resolution of conflicts between individuals in society. Such assemblies must have existed long before the unification of the country and continued to exist in the following period. According to the sagas, a regional system was developed soon after the first phase of the unification under Håkon the Good, who is said to have founded the representative assembly for Western Norway, the *Gulating*, which met in Gulen near the entrance to the Sognefjord. The site of the Gulating as well as the districts belonging to it also strongly suggest that the initiative came from the king rather than the people living in the region.[1] This is less certain in the case of the Frostating which covered a homogeneous region with good communication along the Trondheimsfjord and where the people themselves may have organised the assembly. Eastern Norway was divided into two regions, each with its own law and assembly: Eidsivating for the inner area, which met at Eidsvoll, and Borgarting for the land on both sides of the Oslofjord,

---

[1] Taranger, "De norske folkelovbøker (før 1263)"; Helle, *Gulatingslova*, pp. 23-30 with references.

meeting at Borg (now Sarpsborg) on the eastern side of the fjord. The Eidsivating is often believed to have been organised by St Olav, who was apparently active in the region, whereas the Borgarting is usually regarded as younger, possibly the result of the division of the diocese of Oslo into Oslo and Hamar in 1152/53.

The laws of Gulating and Frostating have both been preserved, whereas those from the two eastern *lagting* have been lost, except for the Christian laws, the part that deals with the Church and Christianity. According to the most widespread opinion, the laws were originally written down in the late eleventh or early twelfth century.[2] The Christian law in the Law of Gulating refers to provisions issued by Olav, which clearly means St Olav. Some of the earliest narrative sources also state that St Olav issued written laws.[3] Most modern scholars do not accept this attribution, either identifying this Olav with Olav Kyrre (1066-93) or simply regarding the attribution as an example of the well-known tendency to attribute laws to some great king in the past. Some scholars, most recently Arnved Nedkvitne, nevertheless accept the tradition of St Olav having issued the Christian laws in writing.[4] An argument for this is that writing must have been introduced as early as in the first Church organisation. Although the introduction of literacy in one sense coincided with the introduction of Christianity, as the clergy was literate, there is little evidence of writing in the earliest period; the earliest evidence of texts written in Norway are some liturgical fragments from the end of the eleventh century (below p. 244). Moreover, the ability to write does not necessarily create the need for writing. It is unlikely that a written law would have any authority in the early eleventh century and consequently no particular reason for anyone to write it down. Finally, Nedkvitne fails to discuss what kind of law may have existed at the oral stage and what "writing down the laws" actually means.

Even if the Norwegian laws were not written down until the late eleventh or early twelfth century, they are the oldest laws of Scandinavia and among the oldest in Europe after the barbarian laws in the period of the invasions and the Anglo-Saxon laws. However, the extant versions, in manuscripts from the thirteenth century onwards, are not the original ones but include later revisions. The Law of Gulating refers explicitly to revisions by Magnus Erlingsson and probably also contains later ones, whereas the Law of Frostating was thoroughly revised in the first half of the thirteenth century when the new law, issued at the initiative of Archbishop Øystein Erlendsson (1161-88) was merged with the older, referred to as *Grågås* (Grey Goose) and allegedly going back to Magnus Olavsson, St Olav's son (king 1035-46).[5]

2   Ibid., pp. 20-23 with references.
3   Theodoricus ch. 16; *Passio Olavi*, pp. 70 f.
4   Nedkvitne, *Literacy*, pp. 27 f., 75-83.
5   Hagland and Sandnes, "Om lova", pp. ix-xi, xxx-xxxii.

The character of the regional laws has been subject to much discussion. In contrast to the later National Law, they were not issued by the king, but by the members of the Thing community who refer to themselves as "we". According to the Germanistic school of legal history that dominated in the nineteenth and early twentieth century, the written law was based on a long oral tradition, according to some scholars even a common Germanic law which had been preserved in a purer form in Scandinavia than elsewhere. A related understanding of early medieval law, including the Scandinavian laws, is found in Fritz Kern's view of law as an essential expression of the political community and therefore, in principle, unchangeable: the law can only be "found", not made.[6] Both positions state or imply that the law is essentially oral, and that the writing down of the law means no more than rendering the existing law in a new medium. Neither the Germanistic school nor the idea of law as something that can only be found has a very strong position in contemporary scholarship. The evidence for a common Germanic law is scanty, and the current trend is to place the laws in a concrete social and political context. Kern's position has been criticised within the field of European[7] as well as Scandinavian law. Regarding the latter, the most important objections have been brought forward by Klaus von See, who on the basis of etymology as well as an analysis of concrete texts maintains that the law was actually regarded as "made" in Scandinavian society and that the idea of a law that could only be "found" was of Christian origin and not introduced until the late twelfth century.[8]

Despite widespread acceptance of the criticism of the Germanistic position, there is no general agreement on an alternative one, and many problems remain unsolved, some not even properly discussed. The new orientation implies that the writing of the laws cannot have been a purely passive process, but the relationship between oral and written has only to a limited extent been analysed. Two main positions can be detected. The first is that the written law is based on an already existing oral law or is an attempt to codify existing custom, which in practice, however, may imply a certain amount of new legislation.[9] The second opinion regards the written law as the expression of the interests of the legislator(s) at the time the law was issued, whereas existing customs are irrelevant, either because they are taken for granted and it is thus unnecessary to write them down, or because they

---

6   Kern, *Gottesgnadentum* and *Recht und Verfassung*.
7   Krause, "Dauer und Vergänglichkeit"; Gagnér, *Studien zur Ideengeschichte*; Canning, *A History*, pp. 114-25.
8   von See, *Altnordische Rechtswörter*, pp. 92-102. For a thorough survey of the Scandinavian discussion of these questions until around 1990, see Norseng, "Law Codes". More recent contributions include Lunden, "Rett og realitet", who defends Kern's position, and Helle, "Rettsoppfatninger", who accepts the criticism by von See and others. See also the discussion in Busygin, *The Laws*, pp. 9-15.
9   Helle, *Gulatingslova*, pp. 39-47; Fenger, *Fejde og mandebod*, "Review of Sjöholm" and "Afsluttende bemærkinger".

are deliberately abolished. The most extreme proponent of this view is Elsa Sjöholm who regards the existing Scandinavian laws partly as borrowed from Mosaic or Lombard law and partly as reflecting the interests of political authorities at the time they were written down,[10] but similar conclusions have been drawn by Lars Ivar Hansen, Michael Gelting and Helle Vogt.[11] Gelting and Tore Iversen have also pointed to foreign influence, notably from canon law, and with better arguments than Sjöholm.[12]

What Was Law?

These two positions raise the problem of the relationship between oral and written laws. Is it possible to remember a book of the length of, say, the Law of Gulating over a period of more than a hundred years? The human memory is remarkable, and there are examples of people who are able to recite very lengthy texts word for word. It is therefore not impossible that a substantial body of law could be passed on orally for quite a long time. A more serious problem, however, is how we should understand oral law. Generally, law codes seem to be the product of a literate culture, whereas oral law consisted of implicit rules that were applied to actual situations.[13] Admittedly, the law is often an important expression of identity, even in oral societies, and an expression of a lifestyle and norms,[14] but law in this sense need not imply anything like what we would understand as a law code.

Stronger evidence of this is found in the Icelandic tradition in which one third of the oral law was recited at the Allthing each year, so that the whole law was covered in three years, until it was finally written down in 1117-18.[15] The source for the latter is Ari (d. 1148) who wrote not long after. We may discuss whether the oral law was exactly the same every time it was recited or, like traditional epic poetry, it changed in details from year to year. Furthermore, we may ask what the changes were that, according to Ari, took

---

10   Sjöholm, *Sveriges medeltidslagar*. Whereas Sjöholm's claim that the regional laws reflect the intention of a deliberate legislator is in need of further discussion, her theory of Mosaic and Lombard law is based on superficial similarities and has been almost universally rejected. See Bagge, "Review of Sjöholm" and Norseng, "Law Codes", pp. 156 f. with references.
11   Hansen, "Slektskap, eiendom og sosiale strategier" and "The Concept of Kinship"; Gelting, "Marriage, Peace"; Vogt, *Slægtens funktion*, pp. 85-89.
12   Gelting, "Odelsrett", "Skånske Lov og Jyske Lov" and "Pope Alexander III"; Iversen, "Property and Land Tenancy".
13   Pospisil, *Anthropology of Law*, pp. 1-37 and *passim*; Keesing, *Cultural Anthropology*, pp. 320-28.
14   Bloomfield and Dunn, *The Role of the Poet*, pp. 106-49.
15   Ari, *Íslendingabók* ch. 10, pp. 23 f.; Helle, *Gulatingslova*, p. 15.

place through the transition to writing,[16] as neither this law nor, of course, the oral one preceding it has been preserved. Nor do we know to what extent the situation in Norway was the same as in Iceland. Ari's statement, that the Icelanders in the early tenth century sent a man to Norway to study the Law of Gulating which became the model for the Icelandic law,[17] implies a similar status for this law in the tenth century, but there is no strong reason for trusting this information. Nevertheless, some recent studies claim the existence of an oral law which to some extent must have formed the basis of the extant written ones. The language of the laws seems to have an archaic character. In particular, the alliteration and formulaic expressions point to an oral origin, although such features were also used for stylistic reasons in the literate period.[18] Moreover, there is some legal evidence from the pre-Christian period. Two Swedish runic inscriptions from around 800 contain legal formulae and references to the law, and the treaty between Rus and Byzantium of 911 contains legal provisions that show some but not very great resemblance to those of the later Scandinavian laws.[19] Thus, the strongest evidence for some kind of law code at the oral stage is the Icelandic one, but as so little is known about its contents, it is difficult to decide to what extent it resembled the later written law. The other evidence hardly allows such a conclusion for the rest of Scandinavia, but confirms some continuity in legal practice from the oral to the literate period and probably the existence of some legal formulas.

The problem of what is law is occasionally touched upon in the extant regional laws. The Law of Gulating contains the following paragraph: "Now we have written down our defence organisation and we do not know whether it is correct. But if it is wrong, then we shall have the law about our defence duties that existed before and that Atle explained to the men in Gulen, unless our king will accept anything else from us and we all agree in that".[20] The paragraph clearly distinguishes between the law itself and its written version. A possible interpretation is that the members of the assembly, who were probably all illiterate and consequently did not know what was written in the law, wanted to guard themselves against the possibility of being deceived by the man who wrote. But why would they make this reservation just in this case and not against the whole law? And why would they agree to having the law written down at all, if they felt that they had lost

---

16   Referring to the men who were commissioned to put the law in writing, Ari states that "they should make the changes (*nýmæli*; cf. below p. 184) in the law that they found better than in the earlier law" ("Skyldu þeir gørva nýmæli þau ǫll í lǫgum, es þeim litisk þau betri en en fornu lǫg", ibid.).
17   Ari, *Íslendingabók* ch. 2.
18   Jørgensen, *Studier*, pp. 102 f., 167; Brink, "*Verba volant*", p. 94.
19   Stein-Wilkeshuis, "Legal Prescriptions"; Brink, "*Verba Volant*", pp. 95-97.
20   "Nu hafum vér landvorn vara a skra setta. oc vítum eigi hvárt þat er rett æða ragnt. En þo at ragnt se. þa scolom vér þat logmal hava um utgerðir varar er fyR hever verít. oc atle talde fíri mǫnnum i Gula. nema konongr vár vili oss øðrom iatta. oc verðím vér þat satter aller saman" (G 314).

control? Finally, what was the point in having this statement put down in writing if they did not trust the written text? It is therefore more likely that they were in doubt as to whether the provisions that had been read aloud to them were actually the correct ones, or, possibly, that there was some disagreement among them that could not be solved.

The main point, however, is that the law was different from the written text in front of them, and that the Thing assembly did not feel free just to decide there and then what the law was. The text does not tell what Atle explained in Gulen and where his statement differed from the one that had just been written down. Most probably, Atle's statement was regarded as authoritative, but nobody was absolutely sure what he had said. It would therefore have been possible to appeal to him if there were objections to the rules that were laid down. This reasoning to a certain extent resembles Kern's good old law. The following sentence, however, clearly implies that the law is not unchangeable; the assembly can agree with the king to change the law. The difference from modern or later medieval law is not that the law is unchangeable, but that there are no clear criteria for how and by whom it can be changed.

Two other features in the old laws point in the same direction. The first is the rule about *nymæli* (new paragraphs and revisions of the law), which were valid only for a limited period of time unless they were renewed. On the one hand, they form an argument against Kern's theory of the unchangeable law, on the other, they show the complications inherent in changing the law. The second is the coexistence of paragraphs attributed to Olav (meaning St Olav) and Magnus (meaning Magnus Erlingsson) in the Christian section of the Law of Gulating. Sometimes the two authorities agree, other times they contradict one another. Nevertheless, both are included in the law. We do not know how the contradictions between them were dealt with in practice, but the fact that the two versions coexist clearly confirms the interpretation of G 314 suggested above.

The lack of coexistence between "the law" as such and its text probably also applies to what might have been read aloud in the oral period. The law was not a number of specific paragraphs that could be remembered by old and wise men; such paragraphs might be considered more or less authoritative, but did not form the limits to what could be regarded as law. In a certain sense, this is also the case in modern law. No law code gives a complete account of everything that is regarded as legal or illegal in a certain society; there will always be rights and rules of behaviour that are regarded as self-evident. The distance between explicit and implicit law, however, must have been considerably greater in the early Middle Ages than today. This can also be illustrated by one of the very few concrete cases that may to some extent reflect judicial practice in the Early Middle Ages:

Hrut. Njál is the legal expert who knows the detailed procedure in such cases, whereas the ignorant Gunnar would probably have had his claim rejected on formal grounds if he had tried to present it by himself.[24] Another example from the same saga is the lawspeaker Skafte's reference to a law he thought only he knew about, now that Njál was dead.[25] Although there is no reason to believe that these stories refer to actual events, nor that Icelandic and Norwegian judicial procedures were identical, the story reflects the kinds of procedure used in an oral society without an executive authority.[26] No doubt, this applies to Iceland more than to Norway, but the king's ability to interfere in conflicts between his subjects still seems to have been fairly limited in the eleventh and twelfth century. This is confirmed by several examples in the contemporary sagas from the thirteenth century of violent conflicts between prominent men, in which the king either did not interfere or had difficulties in enforcing his decision,[27] and by the laws themselves which generally implied that conflicts were a matter for the conflicting parties themselves, but tried to lay down some rules for how they were to be solved. Here we can once more turn to the Icelandic example. The Icelanders had a very elaborate and sophisticated law (*Grágás*), but there is little evidence that conflicts were solved according to its provisions.[28] On the contrary, when a case was submitted to the Thing, the decision would normally turn out in favour of the party who could mobilise the larger, stronger and more prominent number of adherents. Moreover, most conflicts were solved by negotiation or arbitration, not by judicial authority, as this was rarely respected, except that it put some pressure on the losing party to yield to some of his opponent's demands.

The same point can be illustrated even more clearly by the detailed account in *Hákonar saga* about the succession to the throne in the years 1217-23. Here the author constantly refers to "the law of St Olav" as Hákon's legitimation, but never specifies the contents of this law. In connection with the assembly in 1223, where the majority of the leading men in the country met to give the final decision about the succession, the saga quotes a series of statements from various *lagmenn* who all conclude that Hákon is the only heir to the throne.[29] They refer to the laws, to St Olav's law, and in one case to the lawbook, but none of them quotes a concrete paragraph laying down the rule for succession as an argument for Hákon's right. It is implied that Hákon, as the son of a king, has the best right and

---

24 *Njáls saga* chs. 21-22.
25 "En þó ætlaða ek, at ek einn munda nú kunna þessa lagarétting, nú er Njáll er dauðr, því at hann einn vissa ek kunna" (ibid., ch. 142, p. 389 f.).
26 Brink, "*Verba volant*", pp. 90 f.
27 See the examples of Håkon Håkonsson acting as a peacemaker in Bagge, *From Gang Leader*, pp. 149 f.
28 Miller, *Bloodtaking*, pp. 221-99 and *passim*; Sigurðsson, *Chieftains and Power*, pp. 17-38, 151-85.
29 Bagge, *From Gang Leader*, pp. 105 f. and *Da boken*, pp. 310-16; cf. *HH* chs. 85-97.

giving law. In addition, it illustrates, more clearly than the laws, the political aspect of judicial decisions. First, the whole case has a background in personal enmity: King Sigurd had no objection to Sigurd Ranesson's management of the Finnferd before Sigurd Ranesson insulted him on account of his behaviour towards Sigurd's sister. When the damage was first done, Sigurd Ranesson became fully aware that no matter how innocent he was, he would not stand a chance unless he could find help from someone who was more powerful than himself, namely King Øystein. When Øystein took on Sigurd Ranesson's case, it may have been partly because of past friendship, and partly because of concern for his own prestige. Even if Øystein had not wished to come into conflict with his brother, it was considered dishonourable for a king or magnate to turn away someone who sought his protection; there would in any case have had to be good reasons to do so. Moreover, if the case involved a powerful and highly respected *lendmann*, married into the royal family and with a distinguished career behind him, as was the case with Sigurd Ranesson, it would have been utterly dishonorable for Øystein to say no – and equally honourable and politically favourable for him to receive Sigurd Ranesson's gratitude, showing other aristocrats that he could protect his friends. The personal aspect of the case is also apparent when both sides tried to place as many armed men at the Thing as possible and declared openly that they viewed an adverse decision as a personal insult and would act accordingly. Justice, culpability and innocence play a part in the story, to be sure, but the emphasis clearly lies on a personal contest between two strong wills.

What on the other hand seems to a certain extent objective is the purely formal aspect of the case. There are evidently rules about procedure, whereas an important question of principle such as the king's right to grant privileges beyond his own lifetime is decided by lots. The significance of formal procedures is evident in the provincial laws, so here the story is most likely authentic. In the present case, Øystein's victory is due to the fact that he has a better command of these formalities than his brother. We also see how such formal procedures can solve problems when two powerful men go head to head. Thus, the story of Sigurd Ranesson gives a vital impression that the tribunals in the old society faced quite different challenges than simply sitting with sole authority, examining the facts before them, and finding the right law paragraphs to apply to them. The division between law and politics was quite thin, and any judge who forgot that risked burning his fingers badly.

In this respect, the story conforms to the impression we get from the numerous lawsuits and conflicts narrated in the sagas of the Icelanders, a category of sources that admittedly is not above suspicion but which, like our present story, fits in with what we would imagine in a society without an executive authority. One example is the famous story in *Njáls saga* about how Njál instructs his friend Gunnar how to bring suit against

cessive times, which, according to the law, means that he has lost it and has no right to raise it any more. The story does not end there; its dramatic continuation is about how the clever Sigurd Ranesson in the end manages to win back King Sigurd's friendship and reconcile the three royal brothers. The actual legal treatment can be said to have ended with this decision.

This story is written long after the event, presumably at the beginning of the thirteenth century, and is not a precise account of what actually happened.[23] As it relates to men on the highest levels of society it is not necessarily representative of normal cases. Still, there is reason to believe that it depicts an event that actually took place and that, to some exent, it may illustrate how cases were tried in contemporary lawsuits, given what we otherwise know about Norwegian society in the eleventh and twelfth century. From a legal point of view, the question put to the *lagmenn* is recognisable in modern terms: Is a king entitled to give away royal revenues for longer than his own lifetime? The question refers to a general legal rule that either makes Sigurd Ranesson innocent or guilty. The answer, however, is ambiguous. It seems to be intended as a compromise and a way for the judges to avoid offending either of the parties. By agreeing to the possibility of the king under certain circumstances giving such grants, they satisfy King Øystein and by the condition of the three Things, they satisfy King Sigurd. Then they can leave the whole matter to the presence or absence of witnesses and their willingness to side with either of the two contending parties. It seems a likely assumption that the rule in question was invented on the spot in order to get the *lagmenn* out of a desperate situation. Stranger from a modern point of view is King Sigurd's demand for a rule that accords with his own opinion on the particular case and even more his final attack against his enemy when the lots have decided in his favour. The Thing is thus both a judging and a legislative assembly, and there seems to be no objection to introducing new rules in the midst of a case. Only King Øystein's formal argument saves Sigurd Ranesson from falling victim to King Sigurd's new legislation. It also saves the *lagmenn* who are once more brought into a situation in which they are bound to become the enemies of one of the two kings.

The case of Sigurd Ranesson confirms our impression of the vagueness of the legislative theory underlying the regional laws and the lack of distinction between finding and

---

23 Storm, "Efterord", dates the text to around 1200 and regards the story as largely trustworthy. Later scholars have taken a more sceptical view. Louis-Jensen, *Kongesagastudier*, pp. 94-108, accepts Storm's date, but is less certain about the relationship between the two main versions. Hødnebø, "Þingasaga", sets the *terminus post quem* to c. 1230, the probable date of *Egils saga*, because of the parallels between Sigurd Ranesson's conflict with King Sigurd and Torolv Kveldulvsson's with King Harald Finehair, pointed out by Bjarni Einarsson, *Litterære forudsætninger*, pp. 148 ff. However, we cannot exclude the possibility that these parallels either reflect actual behaviour or are standard elements in accounts of conflicts between kings and their subordinates.

the conflict between the *lendmann* Sigurd Ranesson and King Sigurd Magnusson in the early twelfth century.[21]

Sigurd Ranesson runs into conflict with King Sigurd because the king has had an affair with his sister. The king strikes right back and accuses Sigurd Ranesson of theft. Sigurd, as a reward for his bravery in war and for services to King Magnus, the father of the current kings, has been given the "Finnferd" (the taxes in furs levied on the Sami people in northern Norway) so that he would only give the king a fixed sum per year and appropriate the rest for himself. This is mentioned in several sources as one of the most lucrative privileges available to the king's friends. The king not only deprives Sigurd of this privilege but even accuses him of having held it illegally. Sigurd understands that he has now fallen in the king's disgrace and finds that his only chance lies in gaining the support of King Sigurd's brother and co-ruler Øystein. King Øystein blames him for his behaviour but is nevertheless willing to help. He first tries to reconcile Sigurd with his brother. Failing at this, he makes use of his legal knowledge which is greater than his brother's to defend Sigurd against him. King Sigurd sues Sigurd Ranesson at three successive Things, but Øystein always manages to prove that the suit has been brought before the wrong Thing and therefore has to be dismissed. Finally, the suit is brought before the Frostating which all agree is the right forum.

The main question here is whether King Magnus was entitled to give away royal revenues for longer than his own lifetime. The *lagmenn*[22] answer this in the affirmative, provided the king has announced his decision on the three *lagting* (Frostating, Gulating, and Eidsivating). No witness, however, can confirm that this was actually done. King Sigurd thus seems to have won, but he wants more; he wants the court to decide that no king can give such gifts for longer than his own lifetime. Øystein is against this, and receives the support of the youngest brother, Olav. The matter is decided by lots. Despite the odds against him, King Sigurd wins. The question whether Sigurd has held the revenues illegally is then put to the court. Both kings threaten the members of the court with their anger if they do not find in their favour. The situation seems deadlocked when King Øystein plays his trump card: calling witnesses from the previous Things where King Sigurd has presented his suit, he shows that he has brought it before the wrong court three suc-

---

21   The text is preserved in several manuscripts as part of two of the large compilations on the Norwegian dynasty, *Morkinskinna* and *Heimskringla*, and edited by Gustav Storm in *Sigurd Ranessøns Proces*. For a more detailed examination of its account of the process, see Bagge, "Law and Justice".

22   The *lagmann* (ON: *lǫgmaðr*) was later, from the late twelfth century onwards, a royal official responsible for interpreting the law, who gradually developed into the real judge (see below p. 199). Earlier sources, like ours here, occasionally refer to *lagmenn* (normally in the plural), most likely as respected members of the local community who were supposed to know the laws and pronounce upon legal questions. These men are commonly thought to have been different from the *lǫgrétta*; see below n. 67.

it is apparently taken for granted that this is the universally recognised criterion. This does not correspond to the law that was still formally valid (the Law of Succession of 1163/64) according to which only legitimate sons had a hereditary right to the throne. Håkon's problem, of course, was his illegitimate birth. Consequently, according to this law, Håkon was not the nearest heir to the throne. The saga must therefore either refer to the law of 1260, which gave illegitimate sons hereditary rights after legitimate ones, or, like the other examples we have considered above, to an implicit law corresponding to what was generally believed – or the author thought was generally believed – to be right. The difference between the two alternatives is not necessarily very great; the argument for regarding the law of 1260 as valid in 1223 must be that it corresponded to some implicit and generally recognised law. In a similar way, Sverre in *Sverris saga* claims to be the right heir despite his illegitimate birth and stamps Magnus Erlingsson's claim as against the law.[30]

This means that the written versions of the regional laws can neither be regarded as authoritative lawbooks, promulgated by a competent legislator or legislative body, nor as purely "private" collections. They were one possible version of the law which could be superseded by others, oral or written, if they were thought to be better. Against this background, let us return to the question about the relationship between oral and written law. Is it possible to draw any conclusions from the laws themselves about this issue? From the examples above, it would seem that the key to the solution is procedure; most probably, procedural rules formed the core of the law at the oral stage. Procedural rules are usually the oldest element in legislation and actually form an important part of the extant laws. Thus, the Law of Gulating, the oldest of the regional laws, gives detailed and largely similar descriptions of how people should go about making contracts or pursuing their claims about debt,[31] buying and selling,[32] contracting a marriage,[33] and *odel*.[34] Specially summoned witnesses were necessary in all these cases. When an accusation was made, the defendant could produce counter-witnesses or he could prove his innocence by oath, alone or with one, five or eleven others, the number increasing with the seriousness of the accusation. In a few cases, the law prescribes proof by ordeal. This applied to some very serious accusations, such as witchcraft or when the evidence against the defendant was

---

30   Bagge, *From Gang Leader*, pp. 61-65; cf. *Ss.* chs. 38, 99.
31   G 35-38.
32   G 40.
33   G 51.
34   I.e. the right for a member of the kindred to buy back land that has been sold out of the kindred, G 87 and 266-70.

strong or he or she lacked co-jurors.[35] The ordeal was probably introduced from Anglo-Saxon England at the time of the conversion,[36] and would thus seem to be a secondary element in the procedure. Some cases in which the ordeal was prescribed also seem to suggest the existence of a public authority, the king or the bishop, as prosecutor.

Admittedly, the detailed description of these rules in many parts of the laws may be an indication that they were new; the more detailed the description, the greater the likehood that the paragraph in question introduces a novelty. Against this it can be argued that the actual procedure described in the regional laws is unlikely to be derived from the most obvious foreign sources: Roman or particularly canon law. Moreover, the procedure is not described as such in a systematic chapter, as later in the National Law, but in the various contexts in which it is supposed to be used. It is also easier for people to remember what they have done than abstract rules; at least the basic procedural rules must have been known to most people who were thus able to control whether or not they were practised correctly, although the previous examples also show that there were experts in the oral as well as the literate period, to the extent that Skafte could believe that he was the only one who knew a certain rule. This of course raises the question of how a legal rule can exist when only one person knows about it. Clearly, because anyone could claim to know such a rule, the ability to convince others about its existence must have been based on personal authority, which thus, as in the case of Sigurd Ranesson, left considerable opportunity for manipulation.

Law and Society

Most importantly, this conclusion corresponds to a picture of society that – although not the only one – is prominent in the regional laws, namely a society that takes a neutral attitude to conflicts between its members, confining itself to laying down some rules for how they should be conducted. To a great extent, the regional laws deal with the relationship between individuals or kindreds, not between a public authority and the individual. There is no distinction between civil and criminal law; transgression of the law is defined as an

---

35   G 24 (Magnus): ordeal as the last resort when the defendant is unable to find oath-helpers; G 32 (Magnus): to refute rumours about homosexuality; G 158: to refute accusation to have killed one's travel mate; G 314: to refute oath from the opposite party. The ordeal is used more often in the more "modern" Law of Frostating: F II.1: a woman shall prove by ordeal her statement that a dead man is the father of her child; F II.45: on procedure by ordeal and generally of ordeal as a resort for the one who lacks oath-helpers; F III.18: ordeal to refute accusation of bestiality; F IV.6, IV.23 and IV.62: ordeal to identify the killer in case of multiple suspects; F IV.35: ordeal to acquit a woman accused of having killed her husband; F V.29: ordeal to refute accusation of witchcraft; F VIII.16: ordeal as proof of being the right heir.
36   Robberstad, *Gulatingslovi*, p. 337; Hagland and Sandnes, *Frostatingslova*, p. 220.

offence against an individual who had to seek compensation for the harm done to him, or in the case of manslaughter, his relatives had to seek compensation for him. The whole system was based on equality or near equality between all concerned, the conflicting parties as well as the judges. There were no experts or authority qualitatively different from the parties, but none were needed because the rules of evidence were simple and formal: the defendant could either muster the necessary co-jurors or he could not. This clearly favoured the well-connected, those with wealth and influence, over the poor and isolated, and the members of the local community over foreigners. Such people, of course, were less likely to be accused, unless there was some substance in the accusation. Finally, in a period of increasing royal and ecclesiastical influence, the procedure protected members of the local community against these higher authorities.

All these features fitted in well with the character of the community that made the laws, a community dominated by a minority of wealthy farmers who acted as patrons to lesser men. The system also favoured social cohesion. Admittedly, there are reasons to doubt the traditional characterisation of the early medieval society as a "society of kindred", but there can be no doubt that networks of relatives, friends, and neighbours were important. These social features become even more important with the fact that the legal procedure prescribed in the laws was only one way of settling conflicts; violence was another. The law did not forbid people to solve their disputes by open fighting; it only tried in some cases to limit the conflicts and lay down rules for how fights were to be conducted. In some cases the law even encouraged people to fight. The Law of Gulating decrees that no man is entitled to fines for dead relatives more than three times, unless he has taken revenge in between.[37]

However, there is a strong sense of the community as a force to which the individual can appeal in order to get his rights. The principle is announced in the introduction to the section of the Law of Gulating dealing with the Thing: "Now everyone shall command over the Thing who seems to need the Thing".[38] Then the paragraph goes on to describe how the Thing is to be summoned and how the summons is to be carried from farm to farm. In a similar way the individual has the right to appeal to the community against stubborn adversaries who have been convicted by ordinary legal means. The most drastic expression of this principle is the paragraph in the Law of Frostating in which a man who has been the victim of an attack by the king, the earl, or the *lendmann* should summon the men from the districts – a larger district for a more prominent adversary – and together

---

37 G 186.
38 "Nu skal hverr þingi raða. er þings þyckizt þurfa" (G 131).

they should expel or kill the culprit.[39] Paragraphs such as the last one quoted here, and the general impression the law gives of being composed in such a way as to protect the interests of the local communities and the people living there, form a strong indication of the popular, which probably also means an oral, origin at least for parts of the law.

By contrast, a late date seems more likely for the casuistic paragraphs, often introduced by "now" or by the sentence: "Then it is well if …but if not …, then …" after which come a series of cases of disrespect for the law. The paragraphs on accidental harm are a case in point. The Law of Gulating contains a series of them, dealing with various examples. A paragraph with the heading "um vaðaverk" (on unintentional harm) deals with the event that two men are cutting a tree and one of them strikes the other with his axe so that he dies.[40] If the victim is still alive when people arrive on the spot, his own statement should decide whether his death should be considered the result of an intentional or accidental action. If he is already dead, his heirs should decide on the matter. After two paragraphs, dealing respectively with the killing of the king's *årmann* and killing on a ship, a series of paragraphs return to the theme of accidental harm, starting with the example of a man harming another by throwing something from a house or a ship.[41] Then a series of other examples follow: when a man is killed by a log when a ship is being launched, by someone colliding with and sinking his boat, by a tree falling down on him during wood-cutting, by being lowered in a rope or by falling from a mountain.[42] In all these cases, full compensation would be paid but with no fine to the king. The reasoning is that no crime has been committed, since the death was an accident, but that the harm to the relatives is the same whether the death was intended or not. The last paragraph has the same heading as paragraph 169 ("On Unintentional Harm") and deals with the same problem, the distinction between intentional and unintentional harm. Two men go together and one of them falls and is killed. If the one who survives reports what has happened and the heir accuses him, he must deny it together with another. If he does not tell, he has to deny together with eleven others, as if he were accused of murder. In the other examples, it is clear that the harm done is unintentional, and the law decrees that compensation should be given to the dead man's heirs but that the king shall have nothing.

---

39   F IV.50-52; cf. Krag, "Motstandsbestemmelsene", pp. 14-23; Bagge, "Kirken, bøndene og motstandsretten", pp. 390 f. Whereas Krag, followed by me, interprets the term *atfǫr* in the sense of execution by force, which is the most frequent meaning in the laws, Sandnes, "Motstandsbestemmelsene", prefers, "attack", which is probably the original sense. I agree with Sandnes that this creates a better understanding.

40   G 169.

41   G 172.

42   G 173, 175, 176, 177.

These paragraphs imply the existence of a public authority deciding on the matter according to general rules, as is evident in the distinction between crimes which are to be punished by a fine to the king and harm for which the heirs should have compensation, a distinction that indicates a relatively late date, possibly contemporary with the writing of the law. A further indication of professional legal thought is the reduction of the compensation by one half in cases where the deceased is partly to blame for his misfortune. If people are sunk while fishing, full compensation should be paid, but only half if they are not fishing, as the event is then apparently defined as a collision in which case both parties are to blame, or, as stated in the law, "then they are half their own killers".[43] The logic is therefore exactly the same as in the previous examples. When someone is harmed accidentally, there is a need for compensation for which the one who committed the act should be responsible, as this is the only way for the deceased's family to receive what it is entitled to. When the deceased has contributed equally to his death, however, as in the case of a collision, the financial loss should be divided equally between the parties. This seems to correspond fairly well to modern rules about compensation for instance in the case of car accidents.[44]

The decisive criterion for whether the king is entitled to a fine is the culprit's intent. The importance of intent is often associated with the Twelfth Century Renaissance and its emphasis on the individual but need not in itself be a novelty. Intent or subjective guilt was not necessarily unknown in earlier periods, but was less relevant in a legal system based on compensation rather than punishment; the loss of life or limbs was equally serious for the victim, whether it had been done intentionally or not. Intent might, however, be relevant in cases of acts that were considered insults rather than bodily harm. In these cases, intent forms the decisive criterion for the distinction between compensation and punishment, although both take the form of financial payment.

Furthermore, these paragraphs point to a difference between a formal rule, namely that the decision is up to the offended party, and objective rules about evidence, such as the conclusion to be drawn from the various ways people are killed. When the law leaves the decision about intentional or accidental harm to the victim, the logic may either be that he is the one to know or that he is the one concerned and therefore the one to prosecute. When the decision is left to his heir in the case that he is already dead when found, it becomes clear that the latter interpretation is the correct one. The rules about evidence are

---

43 "þa ero þeir halver banar sinir" (G 174).
44 Sunde, *Speculum legale*, pp. 141 f., has a different interpretation, regarding the passage as an example of a conflict between two principles, that of balance and that of equity.

thus most probably the result of the introduction of a concept of crime, to be punished by a public authority above the parties, namely the king or the bishop.

It is subject to discussion whether these rules are based on actual cases or whether they are simply invented as examples of a general rule. Although the former hypothesis cannot be completely rejected,[45] the latter is in my opinion the more likely. The rule seems to be the same throughout and can be easily deduced from the examples. Moreover, the examples do not contain more than what is strictly relevant for the legal assessment. Even if some or all of them were based on actual events – after all, the examples mentioned in these paragraphs all refer to situations that were likely to occur in daily life – what is presented in the law is certainly not the "raw materal". This conclusion is further strengthened by the fact that some of the examples are to be found in earlier sources. For example, the case of the man who is killed by an axe that drops out of somebody's hands occurs in the Old Testament and the one of a man being killed by a falling tree in Burckhard of Worms's Decretals.[46]

Whatever the origin of the examples, they were probably intended to illustrate a general rule and might be used to settle cases that were not explicitly mentioned in the law but were legally similar. A case from Sweden supports this hypothesis. The Uppland Law contains a provision about the fine for a man whose servant is killed by falling down from a tree that he has climbed on his master's order. The paragraph was used to settle a case where a maid had been ordered by her mistress to help her move a large kettle of boiling water and then fell into the kettle and was killed. Thus, the general rule implicit in the example in the law is used to decide a parallel case which is not directly dealt with in the law.[47] In a similar way, many paragraphs begin with a general rule about how people should behave and then continue with a series of ways in which they may offend against this rule. Thus, the part of the Law of Gulating dealing with theft has the heading "Here begins the part on theft" and continues by stating "that none of us should steal from another, none of them who want to stay in our king's realm".[48] Then follow the punishments for various kinds of theft: outlawry for stealing the value of more than one *ertog* and running the gauntlet for less, plus procedures when a thief is arrested and various rules about evidence of guilt, most of which seem to point to the existence of a public authority above the parties.

---

45   Sunde, *Speculum legale*, pp. 90-92, argues in favour of this, but some of his own examples point in the opposite direction, see next note.
46   Ibid., pp. 103 f. with reference to G 169, cf. *Deut.* 19, 5; G 175 and F IV.6, cf. Bocardum VI.22.
47   Ståhle, "Medeltidens profana litteratur", p. 51, quoted in Nedkvitne, *The Social Consequences,* pp. 83 f. The example dates from 1490.
48   "at várr scal engi annan stela manna er i landeign konongs várs vilia vera" (G 253).

From the preceding examination of a limited part of the old laws, a neat picture of two stages emerges: one of procedural rules regulating conflicts and competition between individuals and kindreds and one of a public authority introducing substantial rules to preserve the social order and punish those who offend against it. It seems a likely assumption that the former stage is the earlier, and it is tempting to identify this stage with the oral one. The real world is often less neat, and more extensive studies are needed to confirm or reject this picture. Both the king and the bishop emerged as some kind of public authorities before the laws were written down, and there are examples of substantial rules that most probably existed at the oral stage, such as those that Atle explained dealing with the *leidang*. It would nevertheless seem a likely hypothesis that the procedural rules formed the core of the oral law, that this law differed considerably from the later codes and to a great extent consisted of implicit rules that were applied to concrete cases, some identical with a general sense among people of what was right, others invented on the spot by legal experts to escape from difficult situations, as in the case of Sigurd Ranesson, and others again somewhere in between the two extremes.

God's Law: The Rise of Royal and Ecclesiastical Jurisdiction

A major change in the legal system took place as the result of the intervention of the king and the Church. The system was professionalised; new courts of law emerged under the control of the two public authorities; the king and the Church came forward as legislators, and new principles of judging and evaluating evidence were introduced. The first step in this direction can already be traced in the regional laws. The introduction of Christianity meant that a large number of acts were prohibited as sins or crimes – the distinction between the two was vague. All the regional laws contain separate sections on Christianity (*kristinrettar* = Christian laws). There has been considerable discussion about the origin and development of the Christian laws and their relationship to each other. Since Taranger's study of the Anglo-Saxon influence on the Norwegian Church,[49] the most widespread opinion has been that they were influenced by Anglo-Saxon law, but there have been different opinions on whether they have a common or different origins and to what extent they are derived from St Olav's original legislation.[50] Torgeir Landro has, in my opinion, convincingly shown (1) that the common element in the laws, possibly corresponding to St Olav's legislation, forms only a small part, (2) that the Anglo-Saxon

---

49 Taranger, *Den angelsaksiske kirkes*; cf. Myking, *Vart Norge kristna frå England?*, pp. 105-20 and *passim*, with criticism of Taranger.
50 See most recently Rindal, "Liv og død"; Helle, *Gulatingslova*, pp. 177-82, and Landro, *Dei eldste norske kristenrettane*.

influence has been less than usually assumed, (3) that Icelandic law as well as probably Burckhard of Worms's *Decretum* have been important sources of influence, and (4) that the differences between the laws cannot be explained by different adaptations of a common source but go back to the original composition of the laws.

The Christian laws list holidays when it was forbidden to work and compulsory to go to church, ban marriage to relatives within seven degrees, give rules for baptism and burials and for the maintenance of churches, and so forth. Failure to adhere to these rules was in principle not an offence against any individual person but against God, and it was the duty of His servants on earth to prosecute the offenders. In contrast to secular justice, detecting whether a crime had taken place at all might even have been a problem. Admittedly, sudden death might be the result of an accident as well as of murder, and an object that was believed to have been stolen might actually have been mislaid, but these were marginal cases compared to the question of whether somebody had eaten meat during Lent or worked on a holiday. The bishop and his representative were in principle ordinary plaintiffs who had to pursue their claims in the same way as others. The regional laws contain no direct reference to ecclesiastical courts of law; the bishop was supposed to address the Thing in order to secure the conviction of those he prosecuted. As the Thing was normally used as the last resort, however, ecclesiastical courts of law might develop without being mentioned in the regional laws. Formally, this happened through an institution called *sáttmál* (settlement) which is mentioned in the latest of the regional laws, that of Frostating, and in charters and ordinances from the thirteenth century onwards but which is probably older. In the same way as in cases between private persons, an agreement could be made between the parties without involving the Thing. When one of the parties was the bishop or the king or their representative, it was hardly an agreement between equals. The officer might agree to a lower fine than the one decreed in the law in return for a faster and easier decision, and the defendant would normally know that he had little chance of avoiding punishment by appealing to the Thing. Consequently, the *sáttmál* could in practice work as a judgement and the officer administering it as a judge. Both parties had the opportunity to appeal to the Thing, which in practice probably served the interests of the bishop as much or even more as those of the peasants. The Thing would be likely to support the most powerful and might have been useful to have in reserve against the recalcitrant.

In practice, this system gave bishops and their representatives greater liberty than the canonical process that was introduced in the period after Gratian, which set extremely high demands on evidence to secure a conviction.[51] At least two witnesses had to swear

---

51   For the following, see Brundage, *Medieval Canon Law*, pp. 90-96, 141-51.

one deanery are mentioned in the archdiocese in a papal letter from the 1190s, admittedly containing complaints that they were vacant.[53] Jurisdiction was a central task for the archdeacon, and the offices must at least be regarded as an attempt to strengthen this aspect of the ecclesiastical organisation, although the most important officer from this point of view was the provost who eventually replaced the *årmann* as the bishop's local representative regarding jurisdiction. The provost was supposed to be a high-ranking and well-educated cleric who could represent the bishop with greater skill and authority than the *årmann*, although laymen as well as parish priests continued to act as provosts in the Later Middle Ages. An organisation of provosts is therefore an important criterion of the existence of ecclesiastical jurisdiction.

In his great book on ecclesiastical jurisdiction, Jens Arup Seip concludes that this is a late occurrence, from the 1270s, and a reaction to the development of the king's *lagmann* into a real judge.[54] Later scholars have pointed out that the organisation must be older. *Håkonar saga* lists four provosts with regular districts from the Diocese of Oslo (from Oslo, Tønsberg and Konghelle) who were present at the meeting in Bergen in 1223, plus one from Hamar who can be identified as having resided at Gran. This seems to correspond to the ecclesiastical judicial districts of the Diocese of Oslo mentioned in Bishop Øystein's (1388-1407) cadaster of ecclesiastical property, which in turn correspond to the secular districts (*syslur*). A likely hypothesis is that this arrangement goes back to the period of the Crozier Kingdom of Eastern Norway when Bishop Nikolas (bishop 1190-1225) for a long time held a leading position.[55] It is an open question whether the royal or the ecclesiastical organisation is the older, but the fact that there is no trace of a radical reorganisation of the secular law districts in the National Law points in the latter direction. No provost is mentioned from any of the other three dioceses, and later sources show that the judicial organisation was less well developed there, although there is clear evidence of ecclesiastical jurisdiction.[56] Most probably, professional ecclesiastical officers had taken over responsibility for the jurisdiction in the thirteenth century, although the *årmann* is still mentioned in the sources.

It is normal for a developing monarchy to try to interfere in the solution of conflicts between the inhabitants and to punish crimes like manslaughter, murder, robbery or theft. This is likely to strengthen the king's authority and increase his incomes. There is some evidence of the king acting in this way in Norway in the early period. A skaldic poem

---

53   *Lat. dok.* no. 32; Gunnes, "Kirkelig jurisdiksjon", pp. 146 f.; Bagge, "Kirkens jurisdiksjon", p. 144.
54   Seip, *Sættargjerden*, pp. 75-79, 169-71.
55   Gunnes, "Kirkelig jurisdiksjon", pp. 132-34; cf. *HH* ch. 86.
56   Seip, *Sættargjerden*, pp. 77-79.

that they had seen the defendant committing the act he or she was accused of. Moreover, prosecution could only take place as a consequence of a denunciation, where the denouncer was liable to the same punishment as a defendant proved guilty unless he was able to produce the necessary two witnesses. However, the churchmen were aware of these problems resulting from the strict rules of evidence and eventually, beginning in the late twelfth and early thirteenth centuries, developed alternative procedures, first accusations *per notorium*, where a general acknowledgement of the existence of a crime or a criminal allowed prosecution to begin and reduced the evidence needed for conviction, and then the inquisitorial process, where the ecclesiastical judge might start prosecuting on his own initiative and where conviction might follow upon the existence of a sufficient amount of circumstantial evidence. This procedure was developed particularly in connection with accusations of heresy.

Although little is known about how cases under Christian law were settled in practice, there is nothing to suggest that the restrictive rules of canon law were normally used in cases against lay people in Norwegian ecclesiastical courts. However, there were some restrictions in the bishop's possibility to prosecute, namely a procedure resembling the accusation *per notorium* in canon law and possibly influenced by it. In order to prosecute, the bishop's *årmann* had to either produce witnesses or summon the Thing, ask if the assembly had heard about the crime and only if one fourth of them had done so be allowed to prosecute.[52] This differs from normal procedure, according to which a case was brought before the Thing only when there was firm evidence and the defendant refused to comply with it; whereas cases in which there was doubt were settled by a jury (*dom*, ON *dómr*) to which each of the parties appointed half of the members. The reason is clearly that there was an imbalance between the parties in this case which made it necessary to protect the peasants from unjust accusations by the bishop or his representative.

It is not easy to ascertain when the transition of the bishop and his representatives from ordinary plaintiffs to public prosecutors and judges took place, as no court records have been preserved from before the 1270s, when ecclesiastical jurisdiction became an issue between the king and the Church (below pp. 298 ff.). However, some conclusions can be drawn on the basis of institutional changes. The regional laws often refer to the *årmann* as the bishop's representative. He was apparently a layman whose activities were closely connected to the Thing. The same term is used about the king's local representative. More professional officers emerged in the late twelfth century, when three archdeaconries and

---

[52] Seip, *Sættargjerden*, pp. 16-26 with reference to G 9 and 33 and B I.17, II.26 and III.23, and Bagge, "Kirkens jurisdiksjon", pp. 137-41. The provision also occurs in Archbishop Jon's Christian Law (J 47; cf. Riisøy, *Stat og kirke*, p. 47).

praises St Olav for punishing thieves,[57] and the provincial laws give the king the right to fines when one of his subjects is killed, but this does not mean that the king was supposed to punish the act itself. It was up to the deceased's relatives to take revenge or seek compensation; the king's rights depended on their action.[58] As the leader of the country and its military commander, the king might have various reasons to sue or accuse individuals, but there is little evidence of him dispensing justice on behalf of society as a whole in the early period. A clearer idea that this was a central role for the king seems to emerge from the mid-twelfth century, largely under the influence of the Church. This is expressed in Magnus Erlingsson's peace legislation from the 1160s and in a similar statute issued by Sverre and Archbishop Eirik in 1188/89, during the brief period of peace between them. As in the case of the Church, this led to stronger royal interference in the administration of justice.

Royal and ecclesiastical courts of law seem to have developed from about the same time. The crucial criterion in case of the former is the change in the position of the *lagmann*, from a legal expert to be consulted by the Thing when needed to an independent judge, appointed by and subordinated to the king. This change must at least have been well under way in 1223, when a number of *lagmenn* are listed with separate districts on the same occasion as the provosts (p. 198). These men also play an important role in the actual negotiations, as they are told to state what the law says about royal succession. In connection with this, the saga gives voice to one of them who says that he is only used to making legal statements in cases between people of low rank[59] which, if corresponding to the situation around 1220, may at least be taken as an indication that the office was developing into that of a judge. The *lagmann*'s position was further strengthened when Håkon Håkonsson made it compulsory to meet before a *lagmann* if sued by another party, and introduced a fine for those who failed to meet when summoned.[60] The final step was taken in the National Law when the *lagmann* was entitled to set aside the verdicts of the committees appointed by the Things, whereas only the king could change the *lagmann*'s verdict (*orskurd*).[61]

The new position of the *lagmann* also had consequences for the whole judicial organisation of the country. Theoretically, the four *lagtings* are still the basic units in the

---

57 Bagge, "Mellom kildekritikk", p. 199.
58 G 216.
59 *HH* ch. 91.
60 Håkon's New Law ch. 16, NGL I, p. 124 (1260); cf. Sunde, *Speculum legale*, pp. 119 f.
61 L I.11. The term is modelled after the Latin *decisio* (lit. cutting off), i.e. taking out the relevant passage from the law and applying it to the concrete case.

National Law, but were largely becoming obsolete at the time the law was issued.[62] They were replaced by *lagsogn* (legal districts), headed by the *lagmann*, ten altogether within Norway proper. Thus the region of Frostating was divided into two, Hålogaland (Northern Norway) and Trøndelag, the latter with its centre on the site of the Frostating, Frosta. This division probably already existed in practice with a separate Thing in Hålogaland.[63] The third region in this part of the country, Jämtland, was probably never part of the Frostatingslag. Further south, the southern part of the Gulatingslag, Ryfylke and Agder, became a separate *lagsogn* with its centre in Stavanger. Whereas the changes were moderate in the west and north, they were more dramatic in the east, where five new *lagsogn*s, Viken, Skien, Tønsberg, Oslo and Hamar, replaced the two old ones, partly crossing the old division between Eidsivating and Borgarting. It is reasonable to explain this difference as the result of better communication in the coastal areas in the north and west, and possibly also by the greater population density in the east. The *lagmenn* were originally supposed to travel around in their districts but they soon settled in a permanent place, usually a town, where the court met and the parties had to go in order to have their cases settled. The *lagsogn*s were probably not completely new around 1300; the eight *lagmenn* listed by *Hákonar saga* as participants in the meeting of 1223 suggest a similar division earlier.[64] The three from Trøndelag and the two from Gulatingslag may possibly correspond to the later division, whereas the three from Eastern Norway (one from Viken and two from Opplandene) do not; or the difference may simply be due to Eastern Norway being less well represented. The division of the country into eight *patriae* in *Historia Norwegie* (late twelfth century), four along the coast and four inland, has also been regarded as a kind of anticipation.[65] The four coastal *patriae* correspond to the three law districts plus Hålogaland in the north, whereas the four inland ones seem to be a division of the Eidsivatingslag. They do not correspond to the later divisions and may thus equally well have been introduced by the author simply for the sake of symmetry with the coast.[66]

In addition to the *lagmann*, the popular element continued to exist but in a modified form. The *lagrette* (in modern Norwegian a term used in the same sense as the English *jury*) originally consisted of all representatives of the *lagting*s, several hundred men.[67]

---

62 Seip, *Lagmann og lagting*, pp. 8-24.
63 A law of Vågan is mentioned in 1281/82 (see below p. 305 n. 49) but nothing else is known about it.
64 *HH* ch. 86.
65 HN chs. 2-3.
66 Bagge, "Division and Unity", pp. 147-50.
67 There has been some discussion about whether this was a selection of thirty-six men who were to reach the final decision in the case or whether it was identical with the whole assembly. See Seip, *Lagmann og lagting*, pp. 55-59, who argues in favour of the latter view. Cf. also Storm, "Efterskrift", pp. 65-68; Hertzberg, *Grundtrækkene*, pp. 163-65; Andersen, *Samlingen* with references; and Adolfsen, *Maktforholdene*, pp. 42-47.

From the thirteenth century onwards, it was reduced in numbers.[68] It was often up to the *lagmann* how many men he wanted to join him or even whether he wanted to decide alone, but the number of men often corresponded to the seriousness of the case; in particular, the *lagmann* sought to involve others in cases of serious crimes. Eventually, the *lagrette* became a permanent group of men, consisting of mulitiplicates of six, who came to belong to the leading members of local society. In this way, it merged with another old institution, the *dom*, which was appointed by the parties to settle conflicts between them, either to decide about fines or compensation when there was agreement about the legal and factual aspects of the case (*sættardómr*), or to settle the case on the basis of the evidence brought forward (*skiladómr*).[69] The *dom* consisted of six, or multiplicates of six men. There was thus a considerable non-professional element in the courts even after the legal reforms of the second half of the thirteenth century, but this element had to a greater extent been submitted to central control. In addition to the *lagmann*, the *sysselmann* played a prominent part in the jurisdiction, in principle as a prosecutor, but in practice largely also as a judge through the *sáttmál* (above p. 196.). Furthermore, it was the *sysselmann* and not the *lagmann* who in cases of manslaughter examined the witnesses and wrote the report to the king, which formed the basis of the king's decision about pardon and the conditions for obtaining it (below p. 210). Finally, the *lagmann* and the *sysselmann* often acted together in exercising justice.[70]

Royal and Ecclesiastical Legislation: A New Concept of Law

The development of royal and ecclesiastical courts of law has its parallel in royal and ecclesiastical legislation which in turn meant a new understanding of what law is. The introduction of writing played an important part in this. God's word to mankind was inscribed in one book, the Bible, which had been expanded and commented on in a series of other books written by wise and holy men, and which in turn served as a model for the authoritative lawbook. Thus the written law, issued by the king or the bishops, became the authoritative source of law in a different sense from the regional laws. In a similar way, the contents of the laws changed through the introduction of writing. The regional laws already show the influence of "literate thinking" and of canon and Roman law, although both are more prominent in the National Law which contains a greater degree of systematic reasoning and a more explicit formulation of sct rules, partly derived from canon and

---

68   For the following, see Seip, *Lagmann og lagting*, pp. 52-68; Imsen, *Bondekommunalisme* I, pp. 29 f., 103 f., 156, 163, and Sunde, *Speculum legale*, pp. 71 f.
69   For examples of the latter, see Sunde, *Speculum legale*, p. 71 n. 124.
70   Seip, *Lagmann og lagting*, pp. 68-71.

Roman law, although its substantial rules are largely based on the previous national tradition. Generally speaking, objective, unchanging rules are difficult to maintain without written documentation which ensures that the rules are followed in the same way by all royal and ecclesiastical representatives across the country. Furthermore, legal documentation provides stronger guarantees for established rights.

The first step towards a new understanding of legislation was taken by Archbishop Øystein Erlendsson in a letter to the Icelanders of 1179.[71] The Icelanders had introduced his previous commands in the law as "nymæler", temporary resolutions which were to be in force for three years, after which they were to be considered anew. The archbishop points out that his commands concern God's laws, which should be respected by all Christians, so that it is not up to the Icelanders to accept them or not. Thus in practice, the archbishop as the interpreter of this law emerges as the real legislator who may change the existing law to make it conform to that of God. On the other hand, ecclesiastical legislation in Norway was not confined to what the Church managed to have the secular authorities accept as part of the national legislation; canon law, contained in the official collections issued by the pope, was valid in Norway as well as in other Christian countries and was used in ecclesiastical courts. Influence from canon law can already be traced in the regional laws. In the early period, Burckhard of Worms's *Decretum* from the beginning of the eleventh century was apparently an important source, whereas Gratian's *Decretum* must have been known from around 1160 when it became the main source for the collection of rules for the Church of Norway, commonly referred to as *Canones Nidrosienses* and probably dating from 1163/64.[72] Later, the archbishops' correspondence with Pope Alexander III (1159-81) and his successors, parts of which have been preserved, contains important statements on various legal problems. The Christian laws later became a topic of contention between the king and the Church (pp. 297, 310-13). As a consequence of this, in the 1270s Archbishop Jon Raude composed his own Christian law, which, however, was never recognised by the king. In the following period the bishops repeatedly met for provincial councils which resulted in legislation on topics like liturgy, preaching, ecclesiastical discipline and the rights of the Church and the clergy.[73]

---

71 DI I no. 53; cf. Taranger, "De norske folkelovbøker", pp. 200 f., and Bagge, *The Political Thought*, p. 158.
72 *Lat. dok.* no. 11. The collection was discovered in the British Library by Walther Holtzmann and published in 1937. It contains fifteen *canones*, dealing with various matters, including advowson, the clergy and war, lay investiture, elections of bishops and archbishops and clerical marriages and celibacy. There has been considerable discussion about its date; see most recently Bagge, "Den heroiske tid", pp. 55-58 with references, and Landau, "The Importance".
73 Skånland, "Provinsialkonsil".

The development of legislation and the understanding of it in Norway appear most clearly from the royal legislation. Thus, Håkon Håkonson uses a similar reasoning as Archbishop Øystein when issuing his so-called *New Law* of 1260; he claims that he is restoring an old law:

> To begin with it seems to us best that Holy King Olav's Law shall stand, even though it has not been heeded until now due to greed: he who kills an innocent man has forfeited property and the peace for the king as well as the [victim's] kinsmen.[74]

There is nothing to suggest that St Olav introduced such a law, and it is unlikely that a tradition existed in 1260 which claimed that he did.[75] However, the king and those surrounding him had clearly been convinced of the justice of this provision and had either concluded that it corresponded to the law or instead used the reference to St Olav as a pretext to convince the people. This reasoning is expressed in an even more explicit form in *The King's Mirror* where the author warns the king as the highest judge against adhering too much to the letter of the law. Instead, he should judge according to "the holy laws", i.e. God's own laws, as laid down in the Bible and Christian doctrine; the Old Testament holds a particular importance here, as most of the examples set up for the king are taken from this source. Although this work contains no explicit reference to the king as a legislator, its doctrine of the king's duty to do what is just regardless of the existing laws lays the intellectual foundations for royal legislation.[76] According to The National Law, in the final analysis the law is anchored in absolute, objective justice – God's own justice – which supersedes the individual law paragraphs.

This methaphysical view is what Kern interpreted as the Germanic "good, old law", while it actually served as an instrument for the king and the Church to change the existing laws.[77] There were, however, limits to how far it could serve as the legitimation of various solutions to practical problems laid down in the royal or even ecclesiastical law codes. God could hardly be made responsible for the change from two to three months of *leidang* service or changes in the terms of land lease. As in the early period, a certain

---

74 "Lízt os þat lícast til at upphavi. at lög ins helga Ólafs konungs standi eftir því sem hann hafði skipat. þó at þess hafi eigi hertil gœtt verit fyrir fégirndar sakir. At sá er mann drepr saclausan hafi fyrirgört fé oc friði. se útlagr oc úgilldr hvar sem hann verðr staddr bæði konongi oc frændum" (F preface, in NGL I, p. 121).
75 Helle, "Rettsoppfatninger", pp. 57-67.
76 Bagge, *The Political Thought*, pp. 158-61; cf. *Kgs.* 70, 106, 116, 120, 121, 125.
77 von See, *Altnordische Rechtswörter*, pp. 96-102; Bagge, *The Political Thought*, pp. 156-61; Helle, "Rettsoppfatninger", pp. 61-67.

idea of positive law was a necessary element, only that now the question of the authority behind this law was posed more explicitly. When King Magnus issued the National Law, he first presented his plans to the *lagtings* to get permission to carry them out. Having composed the lawbook, he presented it to the *lagtings* once more, one each time, and had it formally promulgated by them in the years 1274-77 (as the *lagtings* met at approximately the same time in different parts of the country, the king could only be present at one of them each year). He was thus very particular about seeking the consent of the people but expresses different attitudes to his legislative authority in the prologue and the epilogue.[78] In the former, he appears like an editor rather than a legislator, stating that the old law sometimes needs to be made more explicit, while in other cases it is too long and can be abbreviated. In the latter, he describes the new law as a synthesis of what is best in the earlier laws, adding that his successors may improve it if they find it necessary. He thus seems to have regarded the acceptance by the Thing as a permanent delegation of authority from the people to the king, in accordance with the doctrine of Roman law that the people had permanently delegated its legislative power to the emperor.[79]

The same idea is expressed even more explicitly when the new law for Iceland was presented at the Allting in 1281 by the Norwegian magnate Lodin Lepp, one of the country's leading men and a member of the regency during King Eirik Magnusson's minority. To Lodin's horror, the Icelanders protested:

> Sir Lodin became very angry that the peasants had the insolence to think they could stipulate the laws of the land, those of which the king ought to be the master. Thereafter, he demanded that everyone accept the law unconditionally. Yet they answered, one by one, that they would not act in a way which would make them lose their country's freedom. Lodin replied against this that they must first accept the law book and then ask the king and his council for mercy regarding the parts they found necessary.[80]

The example clearly shows that the members of the royal government were used to having their legislation accepted by the Norwegian *lagtings*, although Seip explains this and

---

78 L Prol. and X.3; cf. Sunde, *Speculum legale*, p. 123.
79 *Dig.* I.14.1; cf. Pennington, "Law", p. 432.
80 "Herra Loðinn varð við þetta mjök heitr at búkarlar gerðu sik svá digra at þeir hugðu at skipa lögum í landi, þeim sem konungr einn saman átti at raða. Þar næst krafði hann almenning at játa allri bók greinarlaust. Hverir svöruðu fyrir sik at þeir mundu eigi gera at tapa svá frelsi landsins. Loðinn svarar at móti at þeir áttu fyrst at já bókinni ok biðja síðan miskunnar um þá hluti sem nauðsyn þætti til standa, konunginn ok hans ráð" (*Árna saga biskups* ch. 43).

some other statements from the regency of the 1280s as an extreme expression of royalist principles, provoked by the conflict with the Church.[81] However, in accordance with the exalted theory of *The King's Mirror*, the king may well have regarded himself as the supreme legislator, and he certainly regarded himself and the legal experts in his circle as vastly superior in wisdom and knowledge of the laws. A section of the National Law dealing with the situation if the Thing wanted to change the *lagmann*'s decision states that the case should then be brought before the king, "for he is set above (over) the law."[82] This statement alludes to the well-known passages in *Corpus iuris civilis*, according to which the Emperor is not subject to the law and his decisions have the force of law.[83] If "over" ("yfir") means "higher than", then the idea is that the king's authority ranks higher than written law and in the final analysis decides what is right. Yet in the same way as "satt over" in modern Norwegian, "skipaðr yfir" can also mean "placed to protect," and/or "been given responsibility for". There is doubt as to what the law means, in which case the decision must be taken by the one who has the greatest responsibility for interpreting it. The context allows for both interpretations. The paragraph states that the king may change the verdict because he sees that the law code is against it or because he finds, with the consent of wise men, that another solution is more correct.[84] It is not quite clear whether the latter statement means that the king is allowed to decide against the letter of the written law, but this interpretation cannot be excluded given the general statement later in the law that only a fool confines himself to the letter of the law.[85] Thus, even the more moderate interpretation would give the king considerable authority over the law.

The statements about Caesar being above the law were subject to different interpretations in the Middle Ages. They might be used to argue that the ruler was only responsible before God, as in Otto of Freising's prologue to his *Chronica*,[86] or they might be interpreted in a moderate way as stating that he should obey the law voluntarily and not because of fear of punishment.[87] With the increasing distinction between natural and positive law from the twelfth century onwards, the usual interpretation was that the ruler was below the former and above the latter and thus, for most practical purposes, that he was

---

81   Seip, *Sættargjerden*, pp. 156 f., 183, followed by Haug, "Sættargjerden", p. 99.
82   "þvi at hann er ifir login skipaðr" (L I.11).
83   "Princeps legibus solutus est" (*Dig.* I.3.31) and "Quod principi placuit, legis habet vigorem" (*Inst.* I.2.6 = *Dig.* I.4.1).
84   "nema konungr se at logbok uar uatte mote. eða konungr sealfr se annat sannare með vitra manna samðykt" (L I.11).
85   "En eigi eptir þui sua sem margr snapr hefir suarað ... at þeir dœma ecki anat en log" (L IV.17).
86   Otto of Freising, *Chronica* p. 1, referring to "quod principi placuit ..." as well as to Ps. 50.6: "Tibi soli peccavi", i.e. the king's or emperor's sin concerns only God.
87   Thus John of Salisbury, *Policraticus* IV.1-2, 7; cf. Bagge, *The Political Thought*, pp. 167 f. with references.

the one who issued the laws of his country.[88] This would also seem to be the most likely interpretation of the legislative theory of the National Law which thus accords with the more wide-reaching interpretation of the statement about the king being "ifir" the law. It is quite clear in *The King's Mirror* that the king is allowed to change the existing positive law so as to make it conform to God's eternal law – the sacred laws[89] – and, as we have seen, the National Law refers to the fact that the Things had already granted the king the right to revise the law. Thus, Lodin Lepp's statement about the king's legislative authority is no isolated example but conforms to a consistent doctrine about the authority of the monarchy (below pp. 329-45).

The most important example of the king acting as a legislator after the National Law is Håkon V's ordinance (*rettarbot* = improvement of rights) of 2 May 1313 where the king explicitly changes the law on various points regarding family, marriage, inheritance, and other matters. The king refers in the arenga to his duty to improve law and justice according to the task laid upon him since God elected him to govern the realm and to the counsel of wise men – probably a reference to the epilogue of the National Law (above p. 204) – and then proclaims his ordinance on a general assembly in Trondheim, but does not say anything about consent by the people.[90] The fact that the king nevertheless often sought such consent for his revision of the laws did not necessarily imply that he regarded this consent as absolutely necessary, only that he regarded it as an advantage to have the assent of those with whom the law was concerned.[91] Finally, whatever one inferred about the relationship between the king's authority and that of the people, there could be no doubt that the lawbook was now identical with the law.

The Emergence of Public Justice: Intent and Evidence

The new courts of law and the emergence of the king and the Church as legislators in the real sense imply a new understanding of law and justice. Whereas the regional laws aimed at regulating the relationship between individuals or groups of individuals and laid down rules for the inevitable competition between them, an independent power had now emerged above the parties with precise demands for how society should be organised and its members should behave. Although no precise terminology to this effect existed, a distinction between private and public law and between crime and dispute had emerged.

---

88 Gagnér, *Studien*, pp. 208 ff., 228 ff.; Bagge, *The Political Thought*, p. 169; Canning, "Law", p. 455.
89 Bagge, *The Political Thought*, pp. 157-61.
90 NGL III no. 36a. Cf. also the ordinance of 1315 (NGL III.44) about *brefabrot*, i.e. failure to obey the provisions in the king's letters.
91 Post, *Studies*, pp. 108-62.

The clearest and most systematic expression of the new principles of justice is the discussion about judgements in *The King's Mirror* from the mid-thirteenth century.[92] Here the main consideration is objective justice. In accordance with the principles of Roman and canon law as well as the ecclesiastical view of the hierarchy of society as ordered by God, the king should uphold the right balance of society and give every member of it what is due to him. He should punish crimes and violence and is allowed – and even obliged – to use harsh means for this purpose. He can decide over life and death for every subject in his kingdom, so that it is no sin to kill on his orders, whereas, otherwise, it would be a great sin to kill another human being. Also in accordance with contemporary ecclesiastical theory, *The King's Mirror* argues in favour of stricter punishments, first of all the death penalty, and the author makes the whip and the sword a symbol of the king's power.[93] When judging, the king must be free from all interests and social links, and must judge exclusively on the considerations of justice. This doctrine is expressed in the allegory of the four sisters – Truth, Peace, Justice, and Mercy – who sat in judgement together with God after the Fall of Man and who should always agree on the king's judgements. In contrast, the work warns against the "brood of whores" which lead to false judgements, namely fear, greed, friendship or animosity.

Acting as God's representative on earth, the king should judge each case objectively, according to the merits of the parties, and mete out punishment according to the degree of guilt. He should not only consider the act in itself, but the intentions and circumstances, so as to strictly punish those who commit crimes out of arrogance and ill will and mildly punish those who do so out of ignorance or sudden loss of control. The examples the king should follow are taken from God's judgements in the Old Testament. In addition, the work contains frequent references to ecclesiastical doctrine about sin and crime, taken from canon law or from earlier ecclesiastical sources translated into Norwegian, such as the *Old Norse Book of Homilies*.[94] Here the author of *The King's Mirror* conveys the principle of subjective guilt, which was developed particularly in canon law, partly as a logical consequence of the view of crime as an offense against God and society, partly as a result of the greater emphasis on intention and inner life from the twelfth century onwards.

The detailed discussion of these principles and the repeated questions from the Son in this dialogue between the Son and the Father are clear indications of the novelty of

---

92   *Kgs.*, pp. 75-91, 100-15; Bagge, *The Political Thought*, pp. 52-85.
93   Bagge, *The Political Thought*, pp. 114-16. For the attitude of the contemporary Church, despite its prohibitions for ecclesiastical judges against pronouncing sentences of death or mutilation, see Skyum-Nielsen, *Kirkekampen*, p. 63, on Archbishop Jacob Erlandsen's demand that murderers and assaulters be punished against life and limbs.
94   Bagge, *The Political Thought*, pp. 66-71; Vadum, *Dom og straff*, p. 18.

the principles brought forward, at least in a secular context. An argument along the same lines is the reference to ecclesiastical punishment in cases of homicide: Those who have committed this crime must do penance for a long time until they are reconciled with the Church. By contrast, no secular punishment is mentioned.[95] The inconsistency in the application of the principles propagated in the work also indicates this. By stating that God has delegated the power over life and death to the king so that he and his servants may kill without sin, whereas all other killings are sinful, the author implies that killing for revenge is a crime, but still allows it under certain circumstances.

The principles of *The King's Mirror* are largely reflected in the revision of the laws in the second half of the thirteenth century. At this time the peace legislation from the second half of the twelfth century was repeated and extended, particularly in Håkon Håkonsson's New Law of 1260, where – in accordance with the principles of *The King's Mirror* – it was forbidden to take revenge upon others than the killer himself, namely his relatives, as had been customary earlier, and an offer of settlement after a killing had to be accepted.[96] At the same time the extensive and very complicated rules for compensation to the deceased's kindred were abolished; now only the nearest heir was entitled to compensation. Finally, in the National Law of 1274-77 revenge was so severely curtailed as to be virtually banned. The deceased's relatives were only allowed to kill the culprit when he consistently refused to come to terms.[97] The National Law even abolished a man's right to kill his wife's lover if caught in the sexual act. Instead, he was entitled to the financial equivalent of a life, the same fine as the one paid for homicide.[98] On this point, the National Law was more restrictive than the contemporary laws in most other countries, which can be illustrated by the fact that this right was re-introduced in Norway in 1687 from Denmark, where it had not been abolished, and retained until 1842.[99]

In accordance with the doctrine of *The King's Mirror*, Håkon Håkonsson refers in his New Law to St Olav's alleged law about punishment for homicide "which has until now not been practised because of greed",[100] a clear allusion to the fact that the royal officials had their main income from fines. This would seem to be intended as an argument for introducing the death penalty for this crime, in accordance with *The King's Mirror* and with ecclesiastical doctrine and practice in many other countries at the time, but the king confines himself to declaring that from now on homicide will be punished by outlawry

---

95 *Kgs.*, p. 73.
96 NGL I, pp. 121-27.
97 L IV.20.
98 L IV.2; cf. Håkon's New Law, NGL I, p. 122.
99 Sunde, *Speculum legale*, p. 62.
100 "þó at þess hafi eigi hertil gœtt verit fyrir fégirndar sakir" (NGL I, p. 121).

and full confiscation. In practice, he also allows the killer to buy his peace against paying compensation to the victim's nearest relatives and a heavy fine to the king, a practice that was continued in the following period. In such cases, the king issued a letter of pardon[101] which allowed the recipient to remain in peace in the country and actually made it a more serious crime to kill him than to kill any ordinary person. In this way, strong sanctions were enacted against revenge in order to avoid that a single killing would lead to a prolonged feud with a series of other deaths. The king also took action to protect the killer who had offered compensation and paid his fines. Thus, the combination of a stricter rule and the king's mercy was intended to put an end to prolonged feuds. From a financial point of view, this also served the king's interests, as normal fines went partly if not wholly to the *sysselmenn*, whereas the highest ones went directly to the king. Parallel to this, the royal courts of law were intended to serve as an alternative to private conflict, an impartial authority which based its decisions on objective rules which were laid down in writing.

The king's pardon has parallels in other countries. In Norman England, public prosecution had replaced private compensation at a very early stage, but at the cost of obliterating the distinction between intentional and unintentional killing. In contrast to the Anglo-Saxon period which had a very nuanced understanding of these matters, all killings, even unintentional ones, were in principle subject to the death penalty, which might be avoided by appealing to the king's mercy.[102] In France, the king might pardon a crime for a variety of reasons.[103] There was a sharp rise in the number of royal pardons during the fourteenth century, which occasioned considerable debates among the legal experts. Mercy and justice were both virtues, but how should they be reconciled? The king should be merciful but there was also the danger that crime was left unpunished and thus that potential criminals were not sufficiently deterred. A similar awareness underlies the discussion in *The King's Mirror*, and possibly in Håkon's New Law. The intention in the latter seems to be that the normal punishment for homicide should be full outlawry, but that the king may pardon if there are particularly attenuating circumstances. This also seems to be implied in *The King's Mirror*. The cases of *landsvist* form the difficult decisions where the king has to balance carefully between the four sisters and where the young prince discovers the angel with the sword drawn so as to cut him down if he pronounces a false judgement.[104]

---

101 The letter was called the letter of *landsvist* (lit. "residence"), i.e. giving the recipient the right to remain in the country instead of suffering the punishment of outlawry. See Bagge, *The Political Thought*, pp. 75-79.
102 Hurnard, *The King's Pardon*, pp. vii-xiv, 1-30 and *passim*.
103 Gauvard, "*De grace especial*", pp. 907-20; cf. statistics on the number of pardons 1300-1500, p. 65.
104 Bagge, *The Political Thought*, pp. 62, 73-79.

In practice, once the *sysselmann* had examined the case and declared that the killing had taken place *ufyrirsyniu*, i.e. without premeditation,[105] the main problem was apparently to decide the size of the fine, which at least partly depended on the criminal's wealth but possibly also on his degree of guilt. Thus the Norwegian system of pardon, in developing into a routine matter with a relatively fixed procedure and concerning a well-defined category of crimes, became a part of the ordinary judicial system rather than an extraordinary intervention from the king. To what extent the king excercised his right to pardon in other cases as well is not known. Nevertheless, the king insisted on making these decisions in person, so much so that Håkon V in his ordinance for a possible regency only allowed the regents to grant temporary *landsvist* until the king came of age.[106] Not until 1344, twenty-five years after the union with Sweden was entered, was this right temporarily delegated to the chancellor under Håkon VI's minority (below p. 258).

Despite the insistence on stricter punishments, including the death penalty, in *The King's Mirror*, the general impression from the National Law and most other sources from the thirteenth century is that punishments were generally mild and that most crimes could be atoned by fines. However, the National Law does contain references to bodily punishment, including the death penalty, and some other evidence suggests that this must have been more common than usually assumed. Individual cases of executions are known, and we may ask what happened to the criminals who could not pay the often heavy fines prescribed in the laws. They might suffer outlawry, which meant that it was no crime to kill them, but execution, mutilation or flogging may also have been alternatives. The general assumption is that punishments became increasingly more severe after the Reformation, but this development may to some extent have been anticipated in the Middle Ages, particularly towards the end of the period.[107]

Finally, the principle of subjective guilt and the necessity for the judge to use his own discretion when settling the case are made explicit in a separate chapter of the National

---

105 The exact meaning is apparently "rashly", "without foresight". The term does not occur in the laws; it is used for the first time in a legal sense in the first extant letter of *landsvist*, from 23 August 1303 (DN II no. 69), and seems like a translation of a Latin term, for instance *improvide*. Its exact equivalent in modern Norwegian legal terminology is not quite clear. It may resemble "uaktsomt drap" (i.e. manslaughter) but can hardly be synonymous with *váðaverk* which has its own definition in the National Law and in which the king is not involved at all, neither in dealing with the case nor in receiving a fine. The main point seems to be the absence of premeditation and the willingness to come forward and admit one's guilt. Thus, it must include what in modern Norwegian law is called "forsettlig drap", i.e. "intentional killing", but not the third and most serious category, "overlagt drap", i.e. "premeditated killing".
106 NGL III no. 14, p. 50.
107 Riisøy, *Sex, rett og reformasjon*, pp. 79-94. However, the frequent references to the death penalty in *The King's Mirror* can hardly be taken as evidence of practice, as suggested by Riisøy, ibid., p. 93, because these statements have a programmatic function.

Law, strongly influenced by *The King's Mirror*.[108] These principles are also present in the *sysselmenn*'s detailed reports sent to the king with a killer asking for pardon, emphasising the circumstances around the crime and the degree of provocation and whether or not – usually not – there had been any previous conflict between the killer and the victim. Unfortunately, it is impossible to know the importance of this information for the king's decision in the matter, as there are no examples of the *sysselmann*'s report and the king's decision having been preserved for the same case. Intention and individual responsibility are also central in the paragraphs of the National Law dealing with unintended harm. Formally, the law differs from its predecessors in giving a general definition of this concept instead of just listing examples. It also introduces a new distinction, derived from canon law, between necessary and unnecessary actions, with cutting wood as an example of the former and throwing or shooting objects as examples of the latter. In the case of the former, the compensation is reduced to one fourth of the one for an intentional killing and in the latter to one half. In both cases, the perpetrator had to swear with five others that he had not acted intentionally.[109] From the point of view of the family, who lost one of its members, this was of course a change for the worse, but it is a good example of the increasing importance of intent, maybe not only in the circle around the king but also in the general attitudes.

There is a clear connection between these reforms and the emergence of public justice. Intent is of greater importance in a system designed to prevent crime than in one aiming at obtaining compensation for harm suffered. In addition, meting out punishment on the basis of intent and the circumstances behind the crime is more difficult and necessitates professional competence. This in turn accords with the doctrine of *The King's Mirror* which repeatedly underlines the difficulty of judging and the great wisdom and virtue necessary for the judge, while the author expresses his contempt for the amateurs who claim that they only follow the law, a passage that is later quoted in the National Law.[110] The changes in the law can therefore partly be explained by the changes in the organisation of justice, although the rise of public justice is compatible with highly different judicial principles. The explanation must therefore also be sought in a major trend in medieval justice and thought in general: the replacement of collective responsibility with individual responsibility and the trend that is sometimes referred to as "the discovery of the individual".[111]

Whereas the Church has traditionally been regarded as a promoter of individual responsibility and opposed to the influence of the kindred, it has recently been suggested that some of the rules about collective responsibility actually had their origin in the Church, which

---

108 L IV.16-17.
109 L IV.13.
110 Bagge, *The Political Thought*, pp. 72 f.
111 Morris, "The Discovery"; cf. also the objections by Bynum, "Did the Twelfth Century".

wanted to mobilise the kindred in order to keep violent individuals in check.[112] An important argument in favour of this view has been the correspondence between the number of generations constituting the kindred and the ecclesiastical ban against incest. This ban has been explained as the expression of the Church's wish for marriage to create new ties of friendship through extensive exogamy.[113] Furthermore, the units responsible for the collective payment of compensation were first six and then four generations, corresponding to the ban on incest before and after the Fourth Lateran Council of 1215. The same applies to the Norwegian rule about *odel*, the restriction against alienating family property. The length of time for a kindred to have owned a property before this right applied was reduced from six generations to sixty years in the National Law, which corresponds to the reduction of the prohibited degrees.[114] These correspondences are hardly accidental and do suggest ecclesiastical influence on the rules. As the Scandinavian kinship system was bilateral, there were probably no firmly defined kindred groups but rather a sliding transition between friendship and kinship that resulted in flexible divisions.[115] Regarding the kindred as a means of promoting peace by controlling its members, the Church sought to define more clearly the number of generations belonging to one kindred. On the other hand, kindred solidarity was also likely to encourage revenge, which the Church tried to suppress, at least from the twelfth century onwards. Consequently, the Norwegian development in the thirteenth century must be regarded as a victory for the principles of public justice that corresponded best with ecclesiastical and monarchical ideals and interests. Similarly, because the same principles were not introduced at the same time in Denmark and Sweden, the explanation must be greater resistance to these ideals in these countries, most probably by the aristocracy.[116]

The development of royal and ecclesiastical justice also led to changes in the evaluation of evidence. As we have seen, legal evidence had largely been formal in the earlier period, based either on compurgation or ordeal. Admittedly, witnesses also played an important role in the regional laws, as most rights and contracts had to be attested by formally summoned witnesses (*skirskotningsvattar*). In the Law of Gulating, only such witnesses could prevent the defendant from freeing himself by compurgation, whereas the Law of Frostating and the Bjarkøy Law (the older urban law) in some cases let ordinary witnesses who testified to what they had seen or heard play the same role.[117] In addition, some rules

---

112 Gelting, "Marriage, Peace"; Vogt, *Slægtens funktion*, pp. 147-95.
113 d'Avray, "Peter Damian"; Gelting, "Marriage, Peace".
114 Robberstad, "Odelsrett" with references; Hansen, "Slektskap", p. 132; Vogt, *Slægtens funktion*, pp. 253-60.
115 Above, p. 48. There may, however, have been a more stable, smaller group in Norway, consisting of the patrilineal descendants of a common grandfather, or the minimal *ætt* in Vestergaard's terminology (Vestergaard, "The system of kinship", pp. 175-79).
116 Fenger, *Fejde og mandebod*, pp. 434-73; Vogt, *Slægtens funktion*, pp. 190 f.
117 Hamre, "Edgärdsman", col. 498.

were introduced to determine who the guilty party was in certain cases (above pp. 193 f.). An important change occurred in the field of evidence when the Church, in 1215, forbade the clergy from participating in ordeals, which in the course of the thirteenth century led to their disappearance as legal evidence (in Norway from 1247).

The abolishment of the ordeal apparently created greater problems in Danish than in Norwegian law, because of its greater importance there,[118] whereas it occurs rarely in the Norwegian laws. If only compurgation remained when the ordeal was abolished, a well-connected person might get away with almost any crime. The ordeal might thus be difficult to replace. In the case of really serious crimes, those punishable by death or outlawry, the ordeal would have served to take the burden of inflicting such punishments away from the human community by leaving the matter to God. Now the alternatives were either to let the guilty party off too easily or for the members of the court to be responsible for inflicting such punishments themselves. There were two ways to solve the dilemma: either by leaving the matter to the wisdom, legal skill and authority of a professional judge or to involve representatives of the community. The former solution was chosen in most of Continental Europe, inspired by Roman law and the canonical inquisitional process, and the latter in England where the jury gradually came to replace the ordeal. The Norwegian solution was somewhere in the middle between these two.

The National Law is surprisingly silent regarding legal evidence. It eliminated all the references to ordeals found in its sources, the regional laws, but also most of the rules about how to identify the culprit, while still retaining compurgation. However, the question of how to identify the culprit when someone is killed is discussed explicitly. Here the testimony of witnesses is decisive, but the accused has the opportunity to prove his innocence if he can produce twelve men who are willing to swear that they were present with him at a place so far away from the site of the crime that he could not have committed it. Here the compurgators are not only men of good reputation, as in the regional laws, but provide the necessary information to give the accused person an alibi, thus resembling witnesses rather than oath-helpers.[119] In other cases the law also restricts the defendant's opportunity to resort to compurgation when there are witnesses against him as well as his

---

118 Skyum-Nielsen, *Kirkekampen*, pp. 76 f.
119 "Sá skal bane vera er navistar menn bera vitni vm oc þau segia a hendr oc eigi með eiðum vndan fœrazt. nema því at eins at hann hafe sua fiarri verit staddr a því dœgre er vig var vegit at hann matte eigi tuiuegis samdœgris til fara oc fra" (L IV.10). "He shall be the killer against whom those present bring evidence and … should not purge himself by oath unless he has …" The passage is taken from the Law of Frostating where it applies to a man who has killed another in his home, which was aggravating: "En sá er heimsócnarvitni berc á hendr. sá er bane at sannr oc sýnn. oc eigi eiðum undan fœraz. nema því at eins at hann have svá fiarre staddr verit …" (F IV.5); cf. also King Magnus's earlier law for Iceland, *Jarnsiða*, where it occurs in an almost identical form (*Hákonarbók* 24, NGL I, p. 268).

right to select his compurgators.[120] In a general paragraph, inspired by *The King's Mirror*, the law underlines the judge's duty to use his own discretion, not only to follow the letter of the law,[121] which probably indicates the general attitude of King Magnus and the circle of men responsible for the law. This applies particularly to meting out punishment, where the judge should consider the intention and circumstances and not only the act itself, but probably also to the question of evidence, as is directly stated in the paragraph about rape. When a woman declares that she has been raped and the accused deny it and there are no witnesses, a committee of twelve men should decide whose statement is the more likely. This differs from the regional laws as well as from Archbishop Jon's Christian Law which give the man the opportunity to free himself by compurgation, while corresponding to the modern principle of free evaluation of evidence.[122]

By contrast, the ecclesiastical courts went a step further than the royal ones in the provision that the witnesses be examined separately, so that they should not influence one another. Thus, in a marriage case, Bishop Arne of Bergen gives the parish priest detailed instructions about how to proceed, in accordance with the principles of canon law: First, he should make an announcement in the church, demanding witnesses to come forward. Next, he should examine the parties as well as the witnesses separately and thoroughly, and finally he should write down the evidence and send it together with the parties to the bishop. Extant letters of judgement often distinguish between the testimony given by each witness; in some cases, this has even been written down and stored in the archive.[123] Secular courts were less particular about this. In some cases, like the letters regarding evidence in cases of manslaughter, one gets the impression that the *sysselmann*, the witnesses, and the local community together composed the narrative that was written down and sent to the king for the final decision. The ecclesiastical courts also more rarely made use of lay judges, whereas this was normal procedure in the secular courts.

The changes resulting from the professionalisation of justice and the ideas about guilt and punishment and the evaluation of evidence are also reflected in the way the law is composed and formulated. General rules tend to replace concrete cases used as examples, as in the case of unintentional harm, while at the same time these general rules leave room for a certain flexibility, leaving much to the judge's discretion and to considerations about

---

120 Hamre, "Edgärdsman", col. 495-98 with reference to L IV.26, VIII.27 and IX.13.
121 L IV.17.
122 L IV.4.4; cf. Sunde, *Speculum legale*, pp. 130 f.
123 A particularly striking example of this is the episode in the Church of the Apostles, the royal chapel in Bergen, in 1320, when the bishop's representative was attacked during High Mass by one of the canons who prevented him from reading the bishop's letter. The bishop's *Registrum* contains nine testimonies from witnesses to the episode (DN VIII nos. 55-63; Bagge, *Kapellgeistlighet*, pp. 124 f.).

what may be a reasonable solution. On the other hand, the National Law meant no radical change in existing legal rules; it was largely based on the existing regional laws and by selecting what the legislators found most appropriate from each of them with some additions from Roman and canon law. The attitude to these latter sources is respectful but independent. In a later emendation to the Law of Succession, King Håkon V declares: "But some provisions may follow the law of the Emperor or the Church but be very dangerous for the realm …".[124] Like the English, the Norwegian monarchy held on to the traditional laws and customs of the country, with the difference being that these were collected in a code that was defined as the law of the country.

Justice in Practice

The laws thus give clear evidence of extensive judicial reform from the period between around 1160 and 1280, notably during the third quarter of the thirteenth century. What was the practical importance of these reforms? The evidence for this is not overwhelming, but for the first time in Norwegian history we do have documentary evidence of how cases were solved in the courts of law. Steinar Imsen has registered 214 letters from the period 1320-50 dealing with disputes, most of which must have recorded decisions from courts, either presided over by the *lagmann* or members of local elites.[125] The number corresponds fairly exactly to the number of extant letters issued by King Håkon V (below p. 248). This number is of course only a fragment of what once existed. The letters are all preserved by the recipients, not in a public archive, and the likelihood of documents stored in this way surviving until the nineteenth and twentieth century is very small. Against this background, both the number and the fact that large parts of the country are represented suggest that the royal courts of law were used quite frequently, which in turn indicates that they at least partly had been able to replace violence as a means of solving conflicts. The greater amount of evidence of cases being decided in court from the late thirteenth century onwards must of course largely be explained by the fact that writing had now become more common; cases must have been solved by arbitration as well as by courts earlier as well. Nevertheless, the extant evidence of legal decisions from the late thirteenth and early fourteenth century is likely to have resulted from a combination of clearer and more explicit rules laid down in the law and the emergence of royal and ecclesiastical courts of law with greater competence and authority. Moreover, the fact that the

---

124 "en sumt man fylgia lagvm kirkiunnar oc keisarans. en uera skildi rikinu til mykils haska" (NGL III no. 14, p. 45, 1302).
125 Imsen, *Norsk bondekommunalisme*, p. 124.

judgements are preserved in writing is not an accidental feature, but the expression of the same trend that led to increasing involvement by the secular and ecclesiastical authorities in the solution of conflicts.

In addition to explicit letters of judgement, the many official documents of transactions with landed property which have been preserved from the beginning of the fourteenth century onwards (around 600 from the period 1320-50)[126] lead to the same conclusion. They are an expression of the same thinking as in *The King's Mirror* – the idea of the ordered society, with its guarantees of property and other rights. This, of course, did not mean that it was not possible to secure property rights in an oral society. People in local communities must have had a fairly good grasp of who owned what, and the traditional method of proof was through the testimony of the men in the community who were explicitly summoned as witnesses. This was still the practice in the Later Middle Ages. Around 1302, some men testified that they had been present when the *lagmann* settled the suit about the Byrkjo farm at Voss. The judgement had been passed ten years earlier, in March 1292, and the record of it, issued by the *lagmann* himself, is preserved in a transcript from 1306, which means that it must have been extant when the men gave their testimony.[127] Even around 1300, it was considered necessary to supplement written records with oral testimony. In accordance with this, the numerous letters about land transactions that have been preserved from the Later Middle Ages formally appear as testimony of an oral act having taken place, not as the contract itself. Insecurity, and thus the possibility for conflict, were nevertheless greater without documentation. Increased use of documentation is also the result of increased centralisation. Landowners with large holdings had property spread out over large areas, which made documentation necessary, or at least desirable, so that they could oversee their earnings or secure their property rights. Ordinary peasants would then later have followed suit, when it became common to obtain deeds on property transactions.

According to Imsen, most cases were still settled by the local communities themselves without involvement by the royal judge or other authorities.[128] By contrast, in his study of Romerike plus Gudbrandsdalen and Follo, Dørum shows that some local cases were settled by the *lagmann* in Oslo and points to a greater participation of the king's men in this region, which in his opinion supports Seip's earlier conclusion about increasing royal control over local jurisdiction.[129] However, Dørum's criterium for "king's men" is very broad, includ-

---

126 Imsen, *Norsk bondekommunalisme*, p. 41.
127 DN I no. 98 [c. 1303?] and II no. 32 (1292).
128 Imsen, *Norsk bondekommunalisme*, pp. 100-9.
129 Dørum, *Romerike*, pp. 293-388; cf. Seip, *Lagmann*, pp. 68-91.

ing wealthy men, men with coats-of-arms or men with the title "herra" (sir).[130] Of course, such men are more likely to have had a relationship to the king than most others, but they may also have belonged to local elites or they may have had connections to both. We may therefore conclude that the apparent dominance of local men does not exclude some royal influence, but not that the king and his men dominated local jurisdiction. Concerning the authority of the royal courts of law, Dørum gives examples of judgements by the royal judge being set aside by later agreements between the parties, in a similar way as in the sagas (pp. 185-90) and points to the lack of a clear distinction between higher and lower courts of law. As for the former, this may also happen in modern law, either to avoid an appeal from the losing party or for other reasons. In principle it is also still up to the winning party in a civil case to put the court's verdict into effect, although the remedies available in such cases are clearly more efficient than in the Middle Ages. It is therefore likely that the authority of the royal courts of law was less in the Middle Ages than today, but also that it had increased considerably since the conflicts between the three kings in the early twelfth century.

Normally, we do not know more about the solution of the cases brought before the royal courts of law than what is attested in the official charter issued by the court which briefly states its verdict, usually on the basis of testimony from witnesses mentioned by name. The charters normally show good correspondence between the evidence cited and the verdict, but it is of course impossible to know of other evidence that might have led to another conclusion. The National Law is rarely mentioned explicitly in these documents, but the reasons for the judgement are always made clear, by reference to witnesses or in some cases to written evidence.[131] One of the few examples of explicit reference to the law is a letter of judgement by Bishop Kjetil of Stavanger against three monks from Halsnøy and one layman for violence against some peasants, which refers to a paragraph about harm suffered when there are no witnesses.[132] Here the law is only mentioned, although the reference is correct enough.

In some cases, however, the court had to decide about questions not directly dealt with in the law. In 1329, the *lagmann* Bård Petersson acquitted the defendant, Olav, from the plaintiffs' accusation that he had acted negligently when their mother was killed while being carried on horseback across a river.[133] As evidence Bård refers to Olav having successfully denied the accusation by oath, as attested by the sealed letter of six men, listed by name, who must have formed the jury receiving the oath. The verdict is confirmed by nine

---

130 Dørum, *Romerike*, pp. 298 f., and "Aristokratisering". See also the criticism of Dørum by Leistad et al., "Adel, aristokrati og elite", and Dørum, "Fagdebatt eller revirkamp".
131 See e.g. DN II no. 63, 1301; DN I no. 93, 1302; DN III no. 56, 1303; DN IV no. 63, 1306.
132 DN IV no. 90 (1311) with reference to L IV.21.
133 DN III no. 153; Sunde, *Speculum legale*, pp. 153 f.

others who sealed the letter together with Bård. What is new in the verdict is the question of negligence. The National Law distinguishes between necessary and unnecessary actions and demands that the defendant swear with compurgators that he acted without intent. In this case, the action must clearly have been regarded as necessary; Olav must have taken upon himself to conduct the plaintiffs' mother to the place where she wanted to go. However, the plaintiffs did not accuse Olav of having caused her death intentionally, but negligently. The court then lets him swear to his innocence in analogy with what the law prescribes if the accusation had been that he had acted intentionally.

In one of the rare examples of the king passing judgement in person, Håkon V settles a dispute about inheritance. According to the National Law as well as earlier laws, a father, with the consent of the nearest heir, might officially recognise an illegitimate child and give it the right to inherit, which meant including it in the kindred (*ættleida*).[134] The issue on this occasion was whether this recognition meant that the children of the late canon Herjulv were entitled to inherit only from their father or also from his mother who died after him. The *lagmenn* held different opinions on this matter and one of them, Guttorm, had decided in favour of the party who held the more restrictive opinion. By contrast, the king decided in favour of Herjulv's children, pronouncing as a general rule that children who had been included in the kindred had the same right to inherit as legitimate children. As the reason for this decision, the king refers to advice from the wisest men and to "the understanding ... King Magnus, our father, held when he composed the chapter on *ættleiding* in his book of law".[135]

The king here acts as the supreme interpreter of the law, claiming to understand his father's intention, although the National Law contains no explicit statement regarding this. However, the king's interpretation does correspond to the traditional opinion, as stated in the regional laws, whereas the more restrictive interpretation seems to be a novelty in the early fourteenth century, possibly under the influence of the doctrine of adoption in Roman law.[136] It is interesting that the king refers neither to the regional laws nor to normal opinion but only to his own understanding of his father's intention in formulating the paragraph. This shows that the regional laws had now definitively been superseded by the National Law and that the king regarded himself and his counsellors rather than public opinion as the main interpreters of the law. Taken together, both examples serve as practical illustrations of the duty laid upon the judge in the National Law of using his own discretion rather than adhering only to the letter of the law.

---

134 Old Norse *leiða i ætt, ættleiða* – verb, *ættleiðing* – noun.
135 "vndirstadnengh þæim sem uirdulegar herra Magnus konongar fader uar hin keradste hafde þa er han skipade adar nemfnt etleidingar capitolum oc i logbook sina let setia" (NGL III no. 50, 1318).
136 Hamre, "Ættleiing", col. 606.

The practical importance of the law codes promulgated by popes and kings in the thirteenth century and later is a debated issue. The secular and ecclesiastical judges and lawyers were trained in universities and law schools and based their decisions on a long tradition of commentaries, a tradition that was not easily changed by a new code or statute from a political authority. Some of the famous thirteenth-century law codes, such as the *Liber Augustalis* and the *Siete Partidas,* can also be shown to have had limited importance. This does not seem to apply to the National Law. The edition in *Norges gamle Love* lists forty manuscripts, most from the fourteenth century and many containing marginal notes from the fifteenth and sixteenth century, which is an enormous number compared to the preservation of most other Old Norse texts. There can thus be no doubt that the National Law was widely known and used.

To what extent it also formed the basis of actual decisions is more difficult to answer, as the evidence is limited, particularly regarding criminal justice. Although, as we have seen, a large number of settlements of disputes about land have been preserved, these cases were mostly settled on the basis of testimony from witnesses and give little information about legal reasoning. It seems, however, that the Norwegian legal system was quite centralised. The only professional legal personnel were the *lagmenn* who were appointed by the king. The Norwegian towns were too small and poor to support any important group of professional private practitioners of law, in contrast particularly to the Italian towns. On the other hand, there was an important popular element in the practice of law; many cases were settled locally, without the *lagmann,* while the latter also often acted together with popular representatives. Local opinion was thus certainly able to influence the interpretation and practice of law. Moreover, the law itself and the political authorities also showed a flexible attitude towards the letter of the law, as expressed in the National Law itself (above p. 201, cf. 203). This opened up the possibility for considerable changes in the practice of law during the Later Middle Ages, for instance regarding sexual crimes and their punishment, as recently analysed by Anne Irene Riisøy.[137] Nevertheless, the existence of a systematic, written law and professional judges appointed by the king is likely to have made a considerable difference compared to the situation in the early twelfth century when the three kings fought over Sigurd Ranesson's privilege. When Håkon V decided on *ættleiding,* he in principle did the same as a modern judge interpreting an unclear passage in the law, although in practice, his decision was based on tradition and contemporary common sense.

A case from the early fourteenth century gives an impression of the clash between old and new. On 24 June 1322, a conflict about the Aurdal farm was brought before the Thing at Avaldsnes on Karmøy, between Stavanger and Bergen. When Aslak Brattson, represent-

---

[137] Riisøy, *Sex, rett og reformasjon,* pp. 23-116 and *passim.*

ing Gyrid Oddsdatter and her daughter Gunvor, tried to present his witnesses to prove that Gyrid had owned Aurdal in common with her husband according to the law that was valid fifty-five years ago, he was prevented by shouting from a large crowd who declared the opposite party to be the owner of the farm. The *lagmann* forbade this and together with eleven others – the *lagrette?* – appealed to the king and his council to settle the matter.[138] As Peter Andreas Munch points out,[139] this resembles the accounts in the sagas of the Icelanders about similar events, as well as, it may be added, the conflict between the three kings. What is new in this case, however, is the remedy, the appeal to the king. We do not know its result, but it would seem likely that the prompt action by the *lagmann* and other, apparently influential men must have had some effect. Moreover, there seem to be very few parallels in our admittedly limited material. There may in addition be a particular legal reason for the opposite party's behaviour, namely the question of which law applied to the case. Gyrid apparently appealed to the law valid when she got married in 1267, whereas the opposite party may have used the National Law and possibly Håkon V's emendation of 1313.[140] The legal expertise, represented by the *lagmann* and the eleven others, adhered to the principle, familiar to modern lawyers, that a law cannot have retroactive force, thus once more representing a change from the principles followed during the conflict over Sigurd Ranesson's privilege.

A Legal Revolution?

If we compare the account of the conflict between the three co-rulers in the early twelfth century with the system of justice we meet in *The King's Mirror* and the National Law, it appears as if a revolution has taken place. The decisions were now based on clear rules and were made by professional judges; at least the possibility existed of bringing the case before such men. Most importantly, whereas justice in the old society was based on power, now power was based on justice. This of course does not mean that the old society was unjust and the new one just. The royal and clerical elite decided what was just, and were thus able to build their authority on a more solid foundation than that of the old society. We also know more about the system as a norm than in practice.

---

138 DN I no. 168.
139 Munch, NFH *Unionsperioden* I, p. 380.
140 The Law of Gulating (G 53) allows a man and his wife to have their property in common (*félag*) in the way they want, as long as their relatives do not contest it within twenty years after their wedding, whereas the National Law (L V.3) sets definite rules for how to arrange a *félag*, including the provision that the party who contributed most, or his or her heir, also should receive most at the division. Thus, whereas Gyrid claimed the farm as inheritance from her mother who had received it according to the *félag* arrangement with her husband, the opposite party claimed that this arrangement was illegal according to the National Law of 1274-77. My thanks to Jørn Øyrehagen Sunde for clarifying the legal background of the case.

The introduction of public justice is often depicted as a change from chaos to order in earlier scholarship: early medieval society was violent and arbitrary; the strong profited while the weak were suppressed, and feuds might continue almost endlessly.[141] The lack of public justice has been represented as a vacuum which was filled by the new courts of law.[142] Recent studies have modified this picture considerably, concerning Norway as well as the rest of Europe. The mainly clerical sources have exaggerated the chaos and violence of this period. Feuds were often ended by arbitration and negotiations. There was a certain balance of power between the powerful men which kept the violence within limits.[143] There were even courts of law which, without being professional in the same way as the later ones, often came to similar solutions in practice.[144] By contrast, the new system also had its weak sides. *The King's Mirror*'s comment on "broods of whores" suggests the possibility that abuse existed, and a few examples from how law was practised confirm this impression. Connections and friendship still played a role. We may also wonder how a judicial system where the officers' income depended on fines worked in practice. If the *sysselmann* really earned as much from fines as Bjørkvik's calculations suggest (above p. 126), there must either have been a large amount of crime or the *sysselmenn* must have done their best to produce it.

The system of course gave the *sysselmenn* a strong incentive to prosecute crimes,[145] at least when the criminals were able to pay, but it must also have tempted them to prosecute wealthy people without cause, while letting poor ones off lightly. This is exactly what Håkon V accuses the *sysselmenn* of in one of his ordinances.[146] A government judge superior in rank to the parties had greater possibilities for practising objective justice, but also for bending the laws to suit his interests. In the old system the courts were more of an arbitrator between parties. This system tended to favour the strong parties over the weak ones, but it also made it more difficult for the court to advance its own interest at the cost of the parties. The many abuses which the kings, notably Håkon V, complain about in their ordinances may not only be examples of breaking the rules, but may also suggest that the rules were different on the local level and of the survival of the old system according to which legal decisions were the results of negotiations rather that impartiality.[147]

---

141 In the case of Norway, most drastically in Johnsen, *Fra ættesamfunn*, pp. 73-98, 290-322, who describes the emergence of public justice as a transition from chaos to order and regards the civil wars as a series of feuds which were brought to an end by royal and ecclesiastical justice.
142 Helle, *Under kirke og kongemakt*, p. 187.
143 Althoff, *Spielregeln*, pp. 21-56; Geary, "Living with Conflicts"; Kamp, *Friedensstifter*; Miller, *Bloodtaking*, pp. 259-99.
144 Davies and Fouracre, *The Settlement of Disputes*, pp. 1-5, 207-40 and *passim*.
145 Næshagen, "Den kriminelle voldens", pp. 415-18.
146 NGL III no. 18 (1303). On the date, see Hamre, "Håkon V's hirdskipan", pp. 23-27.
147 Orning, "Kongemaktens", p. 678.

It may thus be doubted whether the changes introduced in the thirteenth century were really for the better. It is also uncertain how great their practical importance actually was. The changes seem to have been most dramatic in the field of public justice, or, more correctly, in the introduction of public justice. Dominion over life and death had now passed from the individual to society's representative. The Son's evident surprise at the Father's doctrine in this field may, however, indicate that it was not quite so easy to put the new principles into practice, and there are also examples of violent conflicts between high-ranking men before as well as after the introduction of the new principles.[148] Nor does the terminology distinguish clearly between actions carried out by public authorities and private individuals. The terms for "crime" are generally derived from religious language, so that there was no clear distinction between crime and sin.[149] The close relationship between physical violence and political power can be expressed by the Norse word *vald*, which can mean "violence" as we understand it as well as "lordship" or "authority".[150] A *valdsmaðr* is etymologically the same as modern Norwegian "voldsmann", i.e. "assailant", but actually means "official" or "authority." Correspondingly, there is no word for execute: *drepa* and *drap* is used for killings carried out by the authorities as well as by private individuals.[151] The distinction between revenge and punishment is made very explicit in *The King's Mirror* and other thirteenth-century sources, but a specific term for punishment was slow to develop.[152]

Nevertheless, there was now a clearer and more acceptable alternative to the use of violence than before, and there is at least evidence that the new system was practised, even some indications that killing in revenge declined during the following centuries.[153] It does seem likely that legal settlements largely replaced violence. Nor should the ability of the earlier system to end violence be exaggerated. In contrast to some earlier studies,

---

148 Opsahl, "Feider i Norge" and below pp. 288 f.
149 Bagge, *The Political Thought*, pp. 66 f.
150 Etymologically, *vald* seems to be derived from an Indo-European root meaning "to be strong" (related to Lat. *valere*) but must from early on have been associated with lordship or dominance (von See, *Rechtswörter*, p. 196).
151 F IV.10, F XIV.12, G 262, L IX.2.
152 von See, *Königtum*, pp. 135-51.
153 Wåge, *Drapssakene*, pp. 116-20. Næshagen, "Den kriminelle voldens", maintains, in contrast to most recent scholars, that the Middle Ages were not particularly violent, and that the homicide rate declined from the sixteenth century – the earliest period when we have some kind of statistical evidence – until the late eighteenth, and then rose until the present time, when we are once more back to the level in the sixteenth century. This reasoning is based on the assumption that the registration of homicide was as high as today in the sixteenth century – which had the same judicial system as the Middle Ages – and that the lower death rate today can be explained by better health care, as people in earlier ages died from wounds which could easily be treated nowadays. Neither of these assumptions is above criticism. Admittedly, the fines were an incentive for royal officials to prosecute crimes, but only if the criminal was able to pay. Secondly, the difference between the Middle Ages and today is not only that our health care is better but also that our arms are more destructive; the likelihood of being killed by firearms is far greater than by knives or swords.

it has now been shown that small-scale, "face-to-face" societies of hunters and gatherers could be extremely violent, so much so that the most common cause of death among adult males was being killed by another man.[154] Contemporary European sources often show that feuds and conflicts among great men were solved by compromises and even turned into friendship, but give casual references to massacres of ordinary people and burning of towns or villages during these conflicts.[155] In the case of Norway, there is evidence in the laws as well as in the sagas that revenge was regarded as a more adequate reaction to the killing of a close relative than receiving compensation. Royal justice seems to have presented a real alternative to this by restricting the possibility of revenge and eventually making peaceful settlement more honourable.[156] In this way, its introduction cannot exclusively be explained as the result of pressure from above; it must also have responded to popular needs, as reflected in the numerous examples of people voluntarily bringing their conflicts before the courts of law.

Against this background, the development of Norwegian justice in the thirteenth century is quite impressive in a comparative perspective. Norway was one of the first countries in Europe to have one law for the whole country; only Sicily (the Statutes of Melfi, 1231) and Castile (the *Siete Partidas*, c. 1265, but not accepted as official law until the fourteenth century) were earlier. In addition, from an intellectual point of view, this law was a quite impressive piece of work. Public justice was also more developed than in other countries at the time; in particular the ban on revenge and the king's monopoly of legitimate violence was introduced earlier than in most other countries. England, Sicily under Frederick II and a few other countries were earlier, but Norway was before both of its neighbouring countries. In Denmark, the nobility had the right to conduct armed feuds until 1683, and in France the king made the first attempts to suppress feuds during the Hundred Years War as an emergency measure in a period of crisis. Revenge was largely accepted during the following period, until the king demanded a monopoly of violence from the late fifteenth century.[157] From a practical point of view, the development of jurisdiction gave the king revenues as well as prestige. Since almost all crimes were punished by fines, jurisdiction created an economic surplus which was an important asset for the king as well as his *sysselmenn*. From the point of view of social organisation, ecclesiastical jurisdiction must also be added to the royal one, although here the similarity with other countries is greater.

---

154 Diamond, *Guns, Germs and Steel*, p. 277.
155 E.g. Widukind of Corvey, *Res Gestae Saxonicae* II.6-7, and Thietmar of Merseburg, *Chronicon*, V.12, V.20; cf. Bagge, *Kings, Politics*, pp. 47, 125.
156 Miller, *Bloodtaking*, pp. 237-39, 271-78, 297-99.
157 Gauvard, "*De grace especial*", pp. 753-88.

The royal and ecclesiastical jurisdiction that developed in the High Middle Ages show considerable parallels: the royal *sysselmann* corresponding to the ecclesiastical provost or archdeacon, the *lagmann* to the bishop or his official. The ecclesiastical officers were more specialised than the royal officers, as the *sysselmann* had a number of duties in addition to jurisdiction, but jurisdiction was the main field of the ecclesiastical officers. By contrast, the royal officer was the more specialised on the higher level, as the *lagmann* was mainly a judge, whereas the bishop had a number of other duties. On this higher level, the parallel to the bishop is rather the king, who was the supreme judge in the secular field. The bishop was at the top of the judicial hierarchy of the Church and often presided in person. As there were five bishops and only one king, fewer cases were probably brought before each bishop, while at the same time the distance to his court was shorter. Moreover, the bishops were often experts in the large and complex field of canon law. Finally, jurisdiction probably formed a larger part of the bishop's duties than the king's. The bishop also had his potential rivals in this field in the form of the canons who often demanded participation in judicial decisions. Making judgements in person might therefore form a means for the bishop to uphold his authority.

By contrast, royal jurisdiction was normally exercised by the king's officers. The usual scholarly opinion is that the king rarely or never settled a case in person, in contrast to the description in *The King's Mirror*, depicting him mainly as a judge.[158] This is correct in so far as the system was based on officials and courts of law directly subordinated to the king, but closely supervised by him. The only judicial decision that was routinely left to the king was pardon in cases of homicide, which are probably the cases alluded to in *The King's Mirror*. However, it is likely that the king often served as a court of appeal – as in the case referred to above (p. 218) – or confirmed sentences from the ordinary courts. If more documents had been preserved, we would no doubt have more evidence of the king in this role, but this is a category of documents that is particularly badly preserved (below pp. 254 f.). The author of *The King's Mirror* is therefore correct in presenting the king as essential for the whole judicial system.

The Norwegian practice differs from that of many other countries – we may think of the picture of St Louis judging between his subjects under the oak in Vincennes. The English monarchy forms a certain parallel in this respect, but here the number of cases was far more numerous than in Norway and the law more specialised, so that the king was warned that he could simply not cope on his own.[159] This was hardly the case in Norway, and we even know from some examples (see above p. 218) that the king claimed to have

---

158 Bagge, *The Political Thought*, pp. 52-53, 73-81.
159 Kantorowicz, "Kingship", pp. 155 f.

considerable legal expertise. Whatever the reason for the king to abstain from judging in the first instance, the fact that he could do so indicates that his superior authority was sufficient to make the system run fairly smoothly without his direct intervention. An important factor here must be the absence of rival courts, except for those of the Church whose jurisdiction was also less extensive than in most other countries. The fact that in most cases the king could delegate his power of judging to his subordinates is one of many expressions of strength of the Norwegian monarchy in the judicial field. By contrast, the judicial system in Sweden and Denmark was not directly subjugated to the king in the same way. The fines were also lower, and in contrast to Norway, outlawry applied only to the legal district, not to the country as a whole.[160]

The new judicial system was apparently introduced in a relatively short time. The peace legislation of the second half of the twelfth century may be regarded as an anticipation. Judging from the legal evidence, however, the decisive phase seems to be the period from Håkon Håkonsson's New Law in 1260 to the full development of the royal courts of law under Håkon V, although the limited evidence of the system in practice allows for a shorter or a longer period. Nevertheless, a comparison with the development in Wales may be instructive.[161] Wales resembled the early phase in Norway in that crime and killings were a matter between kindreds until the English conquest in 1282-84, when the English system was imposed on the conquered people, and courts of law, manned by Englishmen, were set up. There may have been some elements of conquest in Norway as well, such as the victory of the Sverre dynasty, but of course the changes were less drastic and far-reaching. The system of royal pardon is a kind of compromise between old and new; bodily punishment, including the death penalty, was still an exception in Norway, and the kindred retained a greater influence in Norway than in England, although less than in Denmark and Sweden. With the Thing assemblies and the regional laws with their influence from canon law, Norway also had a more developed judicial system than Wales before the great reforms of the mid-thirteenth century. The Church, an important driving force in judicial reforms, also seems to have had a more developed organisation from the mid-twelfth century onwards. In this as well as in other respects, Norway represents a "softer" form of state formation. Despite the fact that the new judical system was largely imposed from above, there are reasons to believe that to some extent it fulfilled a need for peaceful conflict resolution.

---

160   Seip, "Problemer og metode", p. 92.
161   Given, *State and Society*, pp. 69-80.

Conclusion

Despite the fact that our knowledge of the earliest period, as usual, is limited, there can hardly be any doubt that considerable changes took place in the field of law and justice. The oldest legal system can be reconstructed from the regional laws, at least in the field of procedure, although the extant laws must largely have been formulated at the time of writing and show influence from the Church and the monarchy. We are dealing with a transition from law and justice regulating issues among equal parties according to formal rules to public justice, exercised by the Church and the monarchy and an impartial judge above the parties, judging according to his own interpretation of written laws. In short, the changes in law and justice are the clearest expression of the application of the ideas about the right order of the world discussed in the previous chapter. This development can be traced from the regional laws via *The King's Mirror* and various royal and ecclesiastical ordinances to the National Law of the 1270s, and its practical consequences can be demonstrated by documentary evidence from the following period. The new position of the professional judge is also confirmed by the introduction of new regional divisions, headed by ecclesiastical or royal judges, the latter of which eventually replaced the old law districts, and by extant letters documenting actual judical decisions. Still, the new courts of law continued to work together with representatives from the people. The exact relationship between the professional and the popular element is difficult to trace and may have varied in different cases and between different parts of the country.

Although we may doubt the degree to which the introduction of royal justice was a change for the better, there can be no doubt that it was a change and clearly in the direction of state formation, actually the most important change that took place in the Middle Ages in this direction. Whereas the military system represents continuity rather than change, and Norway in this field was less advanced than most other European countries, including its neighbours, the country was in the forefront in the field of justice. It had a well-developed and centralised judicial system and courts of law controlled either by the Church or by the king. It had a law for the whole country issued as early as the 1270s, a law that was based on the earlier regional laws but modernised according to the principles of Roman and canon law. Thus, the adaptation of common European law and jurisprudence, which began as early as in the twelfth-century regional laws and was greatly extended in the legislation from the second half of the thirteenth century, had far-reaching consequences. In an international perspective, the Norwegian system may be regarded as a combination of the English and the Continental one. Like in England, the national legal tradition was largely retained, whereas the existence of a law code as well as the influence from Roman and canon law points to continental parallels. The combination of professional judges and popular representatives may also seem to represent a combination of the two traditions, although on this point there are so many different solutions in England as well as on the Continent that it is difficult to make an exact classification. What is clear, however, is that Norway was deeply influenced by the legal revolution, to use Harold Berman's expression,[162] that went on in contemporary Europe. Although the king's greater authority and involvement in legal matters can be explained as a means to extend his power, parallel to what happened in many parts of the world, the particular form this development took as well as the parallel growth of ecclesiastical jurisdiction must be the result of European influence. From this point of view, Norway, as well as the other countries on the northern and eastern periphery, can be said to have had the advantage of being exposed to influence from the centre at a time when new legal and administrative forms were developing there.

---

162 Berman, *Law and Revolution*.

Royal and Ecclesiastical Administration – A Step Towards a Real Bureaucracy?

One of the most important trademarks of a state is an institutional apparatus that functions to exercise power, namely a bureaucracy. As we have seen above, there can be no doubt that the number of bureaucrats, at least in a vague sense of the word, increased from the Viking Age to the thirteenth century, notably through the ecclesiastical organisation. Thus, some amount of bureaucracy was a part of the package imported from Western Europe through Christianisation, an import that increased in size and importance through the development of royal and ecclesiastical bureaucracies in countries like England and France in the twelfth and, above all, the thirteenth century. In Norway, the development of offices like those of *sysselmann* or *lagmann* also suggests a qualitative change, although the extent of this remains open to discussion. The Marxists as well as their empiricist opponents have agreed that the medieval Norwegian state apparatus was well organised, efficient, and logically constructed.[1] The system was erected in a remarkably short period of time, and thereafter quickly deteriorated through "feudal backsliding", which reached maximum in the second half of the fifteenth century.[2] By contrast, the recent "primitivist" opposition has been less convinced about the strength of the state apparatus, pointing to its limited personnel and the distance between the normative sources and the glimpses we get of the system in practice.[3] The following chapter will discuss these questions, starting with the character of the royal and ecclesiastical administrations, continuing with the greatest change in this field in the period – the transition from oral to written administration – and ending with a discussion of royal and ecclesiastical government in practice and the extent of state formation in the period.

The Ecclesiastical Administration

The main example of bureaucratisation is the development of the ecclesiastical organisation. The most important clerical offices, such as bishop and priest, were introduced concurrent with Christianisation. Without them, a Christian cult and congregation would have been unthinkable. Later on, from the end of the eleventh century, permanent

---

1   Holmsen, *Norges historie*, pp. 255-61; Helle, "The Norwegian Kingdom", pp. 379-85.
2   Holmsen, *Norges historie*, p. 368.
3   Orning, *Uforutsigbarhet*, pp. 249-74 and *passim*.

bishoprics were established. They still did not exist when Adam of Bremen wrote his work in the 1070s but must have come into existence shortly afterwards. There were originally three of them: Trondheim, Bergen, and Oslo. The borders between them to some extent corresponded to those of the legal districts which, however, were not districts of government headed by royal officials. This kind of district division was thus introduced by the Church. After the establishment of the archbishopric in 1152/53, there were in total five dioceses, Stavanger having been separated from Bergen in the 1120s and Hamar from Oslo by the erection of the archdiocese, which in addition comprised six dioceses outside Norway, on the islands in the west. The archbishop of Trondheim was himself bishop of Trøndelag, Romsdal, Nordmøre, and Northern Norway. The church province stood directly under the pope.

The social position of the clergy was modest in the beginning. A passage in the Law of Gulating suggests that the priests had previously been disciplined by beating, which means that they were treated like slaves, but were "now", namely in the late eleventh or early twelfth century, respectable members of society.[4] From the mid-twelfth century, coinciding with the Church's intervention in favour of King Magnus Erlingsson, the ecclesiastical elite, bishops, abbots, canons, and other high-ranking clerics belonged to the top aristocracy of the country, and the wealth and importance of the Church continued to grow in the following period. The Norwegian clergy is estimated at around 2000 people around the year 1300, one per 175-225 inhabitants (depending on the size of the population, which is very uncertain), compared to around one per 3700 today.[5] In addition to its landed estates, this class received a tax of one tenth of the agricultural production. Thus, whereas the professionalisation of the military field in Norway was less than in most other countries, religion was as professionalised as elsewhere.

The bishop was the central figure in the system, and in principle the sovereign leader of the diocese. There was a wide gap between the bishops and regular priests. The latter were submitted to the bishop's control, and could be appointed and dismissed by him, while the dismissal of a bishop was a rare occurrence. Opportunities for ordinary priests to become bishops, or even ascend the ladder of advancement, were minimal. The distribution of revenues of land offers a certain perspective on the power relations within the Church (above p. 118), with the archbishop and the other bishops at the very top of the social hierarchy and a number of other ecclesiastics, canons, abbots and abbesses belonging to the upper levels of the aristocracy. The bishops were for the most part recruited from the cathedral chapters, some also from the regular clergy. Most Norwegian bishops seem to have been

---

[4] G 15.
[5] Bull, *Folk og kirke*, pp. 19-24; Bagge, "Kirken og folket", p. 216.

foreigners until the mid-twelfth century; afterwards, they often belonged to prominent magnate families, although such a background seems to have become less usual in the Later Middle Ages. Now the bishops often seem to have been recruited from the laity in the service of the Church and from the canons' own relatives. Thus, there were some tendencies for the Church to become self-recruiting, despite the rule about celibacy.

To become a bishop usually meant the final stage in one's career. There were ideological impediments against moving a bishop to another diocese. His position was compared to a marriage, which was indissoluble. In practice, movements did to a certain extent take place. Above the level of the bishops, the archbishop was more a *primus inter pares*. His authority vis-à-vis the bishops was not clearly defined and generally tended to decline from the thirteenth century onwards, although he seems to have been relatively influential in Norway.[6] Furthermore, the authority of the bishops was partly undermined by exemptions, whereby organisations within the bishopric such as monasteries and religious orders stood directly under the pope. On the other hand, the bishops eventually acquired a considerable apparatus in their service beyond the regular parish organisation. Centrally, the bishop had his own council, the canons of the cathedral chapter, who participated in the management of the bishopric and gradually acquired considerable power. He also had provosts and archdeacons who were attached to the ecclesiastical jurisdiction, partly at the episcopal see, partly placed locally. Many of these officers were also canons.

Moreover, the bishops had a large number of lay servants. According to *Sverris saga*, the archbishop had ninety armed men in his service as early as the late twelfth century. A hundred years later, in the Concordat of 1277, the archbishop received tax exemption for 100 men in his service and the other bishops for forty. Many of these men were apparently administrators rather than soldiers, but the archbishop and bishops at least had the opportunity to have a substantial number of armed men in their service. Not unlike the king's retainers, these men eventually developed into an aristocracy that had various tasks in the service of the archbishop, such as administration, property management, fishing and fish export, and so forth. We hear of them mostly in the 1520s, in connection with a conflict between the archbishop and King Christian II's representatives. At this point in time they were involved in the administration and in the archbishop's extensive fishing interests.[7]

Whereas the division into dioceses was completed by the mid-twelfth century, the parish organisation took longer to develop. It seems that the early parish organisation

---

6   Perron, "Metropolitan Might"; A.M. Hamre, "Visitas", p. 255, points to two examples of the archbishop visiting the diocese of Bergen in the period 1341-52.
7   Daae, "Den throndhjemske Erkestols"; Blom, *St. Olavs by*, pp. 282, 313 f.

resembled the so-called *ecclesiae baptismales*, found in many other countries, including England.[8] They had large districts and a group of priests serving the people there, in some cases with dependent churches, with limited rights, for instance those regarding baptism and burial. This seems to correspond to the system found in the regional laws where the major churches are for the whole *fylke*. In Trøndelag, where the *fylke* was a relatively small unit, these seem to have been intended originally as the only parish churches. In the larger *fylke* of Western Norway, however, there is a complicated hierarchy of churches for various regional divisions from *fylke* and downwards. In Eastern Norway, where the *fylke* organisation was introduced later by the monarchy, there was a similar organisation of churches for larger districts. Moreover, wealthy people all over the country started to build their own churches, called *hægendiskirkjur* ("churches of comfort"), allowing the owner to attend mass within reasonable distance of where he lived. These churches were gradually included in the parish organisation, were used by other people in the surrounding areas and even obtained the right to receive tithes. In this way, they formed the basis of a new parish organisation which from the second half of the twelfth century onwards partly replaced the one of the regional laws. The system does not seem to have been firmly established until the thirteenth century. It appears, however, that the borders between the parishes were less fixed than they became later and that adherence to a parish, at least in part, was based on personal and not only territorial affiliation.[9]

Although far from being a perfect example of bureaucratisation, the ecclesiastical organisation represented a major step in this direction, with its hierarchy and territorial divisions, the professional character of its officials and above all by its extensive control of and interference in people's lives. The Church received the heaviest tax in the country, had its own courts of law and a well-developed legislation which gave its servants wide powers in controlling people's behaviour regarding marriage and sexuality, fasts and holidays, cult and dogma and various rules applying to a wide range of activities. Despite the great distance between ideal and practice, the ecclesiastical organisation consisted of a large number of officers with duties defined by law and bound by loyalty to the hierarchy of the Church. In many ways, the ecclesiastical office became the prototype of the later European bureaucracy.[10] Although it is difficult to trace the influence in detail, the ecclesiastical bureaucracy is also likely to have influenced the development of the royal one.

---

8   For the following, see Hamre, "Sogn"; Smedberg, *Nordens äldsta kyrkor*, pp. 24-63; Brink, *Sockenbildning*, pp. 101-12, 116-22; Skre, "Kirken før sognet"; Brendalsmo, *Kirkebygg*, pp. 138-53; Tryti, "Fra åsatro", pp. 66-68. Most recently, however, Antonsson, "The Minsters", has objected to the theory on the grounds that the minsters had become obsolete in England by the time of the conversion of Norway.
9   Brendalsmo, *Kirker i Trøndelag*, pp. 173-82.
10 Wolter, "The *officium*".

The Royal Administration

The king's local administration was originally based on two representatives, the highborn *lendmann* and the lowborn royal steward (*årmann*, ON *ármaðr*). The former was a "friend," the latter a "servant." According to the most widespread opinion among historians, these two offices merged into that of *sysselmann* who combined the *lendmann*'s high social status with the *årmann*'s subordination to the king. This would suggest that bureaucratisation had taken place, in accordance with the understanding of Norwegian history in the twelfth and thirteenth century as a development towards a state. However, there have also been objections to this understanding. In addition to Orning's general rejection of state formation, Claus Krag has pointed to a considerable continuity in terminology which he interprets as a continuity also in practice, partly because the old system was more bureaucratic than usually believed, partly that the new was less so.[11] Krag's evidence mainly consists of the laws, where similar tasks are attributed both to the *lendmann* and the *årmann*, whereas the sagas make a clear distinction in social status between the two.[12] It would immediately seem likely that the status of the *årmann* rose with the increasing power of the monarchy and thus that there was a sliding transition between the old and the new system. On the other hand, the passages in the laws describing the various tasks of the king's local representatives and their relationship to the local communities do not necessarily tell very much of their recruitment and social status. Nor is the attitude to service and subordination in the sagas likely to be pure fiction, as is illustrated particularly clearly by the story of Sel-Tore in *Heimskringla*. Sel-Tore, a low-born creature serving as a royal *årmann* at Avaldsnes, humiliates Asbjørn, a local chieftain from Northern Norway, and confiscates his cargo, after which Asbjørn kills him in the king's presence. Asbjørn is captured and sentenced to death, but is saved by his uncle, the powerful Erling Skjalgsson of Sola, who forces the king, St Olav, to accept compensation in return for saving his life. The compensation the king demands is that Asbjørn replace Tore as *årmann*, which is clearly regarded as an extreme humiliation.[13] Thus, a free man attaches himself to another by his own free will and on honourable conditions, demanding a reasonable reward for his service.

The conflict between St Olav and Erling Skjalgsson serves as a further illustration of the contrast between the old system and the new. "I serve you best when I serve you voluntarily", says Erling to Olav during a meeting between the two.[14] According to Snorri, Erling had received the government of Western Norway from Olav's namesake and predecessor

---

11   Krag, "Årmannen".
12   Lunden, "Træl og årmann"; Bagge, "Mellom kildekritikk", p. 188.
13   *HkrOH* chs. 117-20; Bagge, *Society and Politics*, pp. 68 f., 133 f.
14   *HkrOH* ch. 60; Bagge, *Society and Politics*, pp. 78 f., and "Kingship", p. 41.

Olav Tryggvason and refused to give it up. Erling apparently had Snorri's sympathy, and the statement can be read as a rejection of any kind of bureaucratic obedience in favour of friendship between equals or near equals, which is further confirmed by Snorri's portraits of the real royal servants, the *ármenn* who are totally dependent on their masters. In a similar way, Snorri's narrative gives a different explanation of Olav's fall from that of his explicit conclusion, that the magnates could not tolerate his objective justice, punishing every man according to his crime, whatever his social status. This is Snorri's concession to the contemporary official ideology, as expressed in *Hákonar saga* and *The King's Mirror*, whereas his narrative shows that Olav made too many enemies at once because he was stubborn and refused compromises even when this would have been the wisest course of action.[15] Snorri generally differs considerably from the official ideology in the latter part of Håkon Håkonsson's reign. Although this may have to do with his background as an Icelandic magnate, similar attitudes probably existed in Norway as well.

In the mid-thirteenth century, *The King's Mirror* launched a frontal attack on this way of thinking, beginning with a question from the Son of why wealthy and prominent men in local society are willing to join the king's service even if they only obtain a low rank. The Father begins his answer by reprimanding the Son for having asked a foolish question, the only time the Father responds in this way in the work and clear evidence of the importance of this issue. He then goes on to refute any idea of a mutual contract between the king and his men: As the king owns the country and all its inhabitants, he can order them to do whatever he likes, whether or not they have specifically entered his service. Consequently, entering the king's service is solely a privilege, giving honour as well as protection.[16] This statement is later developed by a series of biblical examples, addressed to the king's retainers, of the duty of being obedient towards one's superiors, including the example of the slave Joseph, who suffered suppression and injustice without faltering in his loyalty and was finally rewarded by Pharaoh.[17] Thus, the idea of the king's ownership opposes the idea of the subjects' general duty of loyalty and obedience to that of a feudal contract, based on "friendship" with a patron in return for a reward.

The argument seems to be based on similar ideas as the statement in the sagas that Harald Finehair, through his conquests, acquired all the property in the land.[18] A similar argument was used by European lawyers in the twelfth century to justify the king's rights over his vassals, as in the famous example of the Diet in Roncaglia in 1158, where Martinus told Frederick Barbarossa that everything in the realm belonged to the emperor

---

15   Bagge, *Society and Politics*, pp. 66-70.
16   *Kgs.*, p. 42; Bagge, *The Political Thought*, pp. 30 f.
17   Bagge, *The Political Thought*, pp. 29, 177.
18   Bagge, *The Political Thought*, pp. 31-39.

according to the *Codex*.[19] The statement is an obvious misinterpretation, as was pointed out by most Roman lawyers in the Middle Ages. As the clear distinction between public power and private property tended to be blurred in medieval feudal law, however, the idea of the king's or the pope's superior ownership were sometimes used as legitimation for taxation or expropriation.[20] Thus, *The King's Mirror* opposes an idea of bureaucratic subordination to traditional European feudal norms of reciprocity. This idea is further bolstered, in this work as well as others, by norms of personal loyalty, expressed in terms like *trú, trunaðr* etc. which mainly occur from the mid-thirteenth century onwards. These terms do not express traditional ideas of the personal loyalty between a lord and his man, associated with a Germanic ideology of *Gefolgschaft*, but rather new, Christian-monarchic ideals of absolute loyalty to the king, a loyalty not confined to the king's men in the strictest sense, but in principle also including all his subjects.[21] There is thus no opposition between "feudal" ideas of fealty and loyalty and "bureaucratic" ideas of obedience; both are used in a similar way to bolster the king's authority.

The administrative system introduced in the thirteenth century meant that the king's highborn friend and lowborn servant merged in the office of *sysselmann*. The office implied a mental transformation, brought about by the civil wars, the diminishing of the old aristocracy, and by new men being raised to power under Sverre. The extent of this transformation may of course be doubted; people still sought the king's service in order to receive a reward – one which they actually received and without which the king could hardly expect much loyalty and obedience. However, the rhetoric and the rules had changed, and service, obedience and control were not taboo in the same way as earlier. This is expressed in the statement in the Hird Law about how a *sysselmann* was to assume his office. He was to send the king a sealed letter which followed a specific form, and which was quoted in full. Here it is said that on a specific date "my Lord entrusted me this office N. for his kingship's sake, for which God must thank him."[22] In return the *sysselmann* was supposed to swear a number of concrete oaths regarding how he would behave towards the population in his district, and that he would deliver to the king the set revenues of his governance when it was due. He would also report on the size of the revenue at the time he assumed his position.

---

19 "Omnia principis etiam quoad proprietates. ut dixit M. principi apud roncagliam timore vel amore", *Glossa in Codicem*, fol. 222 v. ad *Cod.* VII.37.3, here quoted after McIlwain, *Growth*, p. 190.
20 Mayer, *Das Recht der Expropriation*, p. 87 ; v.d. Heydte, *Geburtstunde*, pp. 320 ff. with references; Brunner, *Land und Herrschaft*, pp. 245 f.; Harriss, *King, Parliament and Public Finance*, pp. 320 ff. with references. See also below p. 319.
21 von See, *Altnordische Rechtswörter*, pp. 204-21, 240 ff.; Bagge, *The Political Thought*, pp. 26-31; Orning, *Uforutsigbarhet*, pp. 47-72, 87-91.
22 "… fek mer min herra þa syslu sina. N. firir sins hærradoms saker sem guð þacke honom" (H 31).

The *sysselmann* is thus the king's local representative and is subservient to him, which in principle makes his position an example of bureaucratic subordination rather than patronage or a feudal relationship. Even though the transition between the old and the new system may have been blurry, it is reasonable to believe that we are dealing with a significant break, which reaches far beyond the purely terminological level. Instead of a local chieftain aristocracy, in which individuals form allegiances with the king, we have a royal servant aristocracy, which functions as the king's permanent representatives in particular districts. Running parallel with the establishment of the dynasty, a distance is established between the king and the aristocracy in which the members of the latter consider themselves the king's servants.

The establishment of permanent, administrative districts is also a new and clear demonstration of official subservience. The division into *sysler* took place gradually from the second half of the twelfth century, presumably beginning in the occupied territories during the civil wars. The system is first presented in its entirety in 1273, in the same paragraph in the Hird Law that deals with the issue of the *sysselmann*'s right and responsibilities. At this time, there were approximately fifty *sysler*. A provision immediately following the *sysselmann*'s oath in the document might indicate that permanent districts were relatively new: If a criminal went to another district, the *sysselmann* there was required to send him back from whence he came as soon as he received a letter from the *sysselmann* in that place. This *sysselmann* should also take care of his case.[23] This is an obvious course of action in an established bureaucratic system but may have been necessary to emphasise when the system was in its infancy. Admittedly, the system must have existed long before the 1270s, when the Hird Law was issued. *Sysler* are mentioned as far back as Sverre's time, and probably existed earlier as well.[24] The importance of the division of the districts during the peace negotiations between the Birchlegs and the Croziers in 1217 also shows that the system must have been fairly well established by the beginning of the thirteenth century. Nevertheless, like in other divisions, exact borders between the districts may have developed gradually, so that the rule in the Hird Law may actually have been a novelty.

This Norwegian local administration corresponds to the local administriations in several countries of Western Europe at the time, with the *sysselmann* as a parallel to the French *balli* or *sénéschal*, the English *sheriff* and the German *Vogt*, all of which were directly subordinated to the king. The difference was that in Norway the whole country was governed by such officials, whereas large areas in other countries were governed by

---

23   H 31, p. 136.
24   Schreiner, "Kong Sverre", pp. 445-47; cf. "Kongemakt og lendmenn", pp. 202 f.

great lords with various degrees of independence from the king. By contrast, the administrative system in the other countries in the northern and eastern periphery which had undergone the military transformation were based on castles whose lords represented the king in the region but could easily develop a power independent of the king. Nevertheless, even there an ideology of service and distance between the king and his men was developed.[25]

There were some other royal officers below as well as above the level of the *sysselmann*. The *lensmann*, mentioned in the sources from the mid-thirteenth century onwards, was the *sysselmann*'s subordinate. He should, according to the king's decree, be elected by and from the local community, not from the king's men, which suggests that this may have happened in practice.[26] In addition, leading men in local society were active in various relationships with the local *sysselmann*. Furthermore, the *sysselmann* had armed men in his service (see above pp. 102 f.). In 1308 a new kind of officer, the treasurer (*fehirde*), was created, who ranked above the *sysselmann*, notably in the judicial field. Earlier only one royal treasurer existed, who belonged to the circle around the king. Now regional treasurers were appointed to Trondheim, Bergen, Tønsberg, and Oslo, and were responsible for tax collection in their respective regions. The regional *fehirde* districts developed in the course of the Later Middle Ages into the large castle districts (*slottslen*), which encompassed a large part of the country and partly replaced the official district divisions.

At the top was the central administration, centred on the king, which partly consisted of court officials and partly of a more informal group of counsellors who for longer or shorter periods resided at the royal court. The court offices have long traditions. The titles show, as they do in the rest of Europe, that they were originally associated with the king's household: *stallare* (constable), *drottsete* (master of ceremonies at official functions, steward), *merkesmann* (standard bearer). To these was added the chancellor, who drew up the king's letters and kept his seal, and who therefore belonged to the era of written administration. The title occurs for the first time in 1208.[27] In the High Middle Ages, these offices most likely functioned as rewards for particularly trusted men, and were also given new functions through the development of the king's administration. For example, the standard bearer (*merkesmann*), presumably in 1303,[28] became the king's deputy in matters of judicial enforcement. Also, the chancellor became one of the king's central counsellors, in addition to being the head of a chancery of scribes who prepared the king's letters.

---

25 Bisgaard, *Tjenesteideal*, pp. 27-36; Bagge, "Ideologies", pp. 471-73.
26 Fladby, "Lensmann"; Imsen, *Norsk bondekommunalisme*, pp. 80 f.
27 Bagge, *Kapellgeistlighet*, p. 66.
28 On the date, see Hamre, "Håkon V's hirdskipan", pp. 23-27.

A New Bureaucracy?

We can point to several changes away from the patron/client system of the Early Middle Ages in the ideological as well as the institutional field. We find a distinction between person and office, both in the clerical and secular arena, and the monarchy had become an institution to a degree it had not been before. In contrast to some other places in Europe at the time, there was a clear distinction between property and public office, which makes the system bureaucratic rather than feudal. This applies to all of Europe regarding clerical offices. Concerning the secular ones, the Norwegian *sysselmann* did not normally hold office in his native district. Nor was the office hereditary, even if Håkon V in 1308 suggested that good and loyal *sysselmenn* would be rewarded by having their sons succeed them. The *sysselmann* was appointed by the king, could be deposed by him or moved to another district, was in principle subject to control by the king and had to account for revenues and expenses and render parts of the former to the royal treasury.

On the other hand, the medieval bureaucracy contrasts significantly with the modern, Weberian one in three ways. First, local offices were normally divided geographically rather than functionally; the *sysselmann* was responsible for all matters pertaining to the king in his district: judicial, financial, military, and administrative. The fifty government districts can be viewed as mini-kingdoms, where the *sysselmann* acted as the king's deputy. Because there was a legal official, the *lagmann*, who functioned as a judge, the *sysselmann*'s office can be compared to that of the police and the public prosecution and the *lagmann* to a judge in our system, but the distinction between the two was in reality less clear. The *lagmann* had a superior position in the legal system which is reflected in the fact that the *lagsogn* normally comprised several *sysler*; there were ten of the former against around fifty of the latter. The bishop stood alone at the top of the hierarchy, while there were separate hierarchies below him; the judicial bureaucracy became at least partly separated from the normal parish system, and moreover the bishops had a large number of lay servants who had no dealings with the parish clerics.

The two main functions subject to bureaucratisation were law and religion. By contrast, the military sector, which may have been the most bureaucratised in the eighteenth century,[29] was not affected to any great extent. Admittedly, Håkon Håkonsson and his successors acted as commanders-in-chief of an organised army to a greater extent than Sverre who depended on his men's voluntary support, but there were no professional officers and no clear command structure. Moreover, war and its rewards were not consistently under state control; war was a means for the individual warrior to enrich himself. Like in the rest of Europe, booty was divided between the participants according to more

---

29 Kroener, "The Modern State and Military Society".

or less formalised rules, and the fate of prisoners was largely decided by those who took them captive.[30] The Hird Law gives detailed rules for the division of booty, and *Sverris saga* tells of a quarrel between Sverre and the *leidang* men when Sverre demanded to buy the men's share of the booty for a price that they found too low.[31] The sagas give several examples of kings attempting to decide, although not always successfully, the fate of captive enemies. Thus, after the Battle of Strindsjøen in 1199, Sverre, contrary to the normal practice the saga attributes to him, forbade his men to grant quarter, but some of his subordinates nevertheless tried to save their friends and relatives who, however, were killed by other of Sverre's men. When the victims' relatives complained to the king, they were advised to take revenge on the killers by killing their relatives, which thus resulted in Sverre's order being carried out.[32]

Secondly, the representatives were not salaried centrally, which thus blurred the distinction between private and public income. This is evident with regard to the office of bishop, who could be viewed more or less as the "owner" of the bishopric during his term of office. According to Kåre Lunden, a bishop had a yearly income which today would correspond to 50 million kr., while an archbishop earned 100 million, which is a little less than £5, or 10 million respectively. In other words, they would earn an amount almost incomprehensibly more than bishops today, or for that matter, the very highest earners in the contemporary Norwegian civil service. Comparisons between contemporary and medieval incomes are always tenuous because the economies are so different, but there can be no doubt that a bishop during the Middle Ages enjoyed a level of power, wealth, and prestige that reached far above that of his contemporary counterpart. However, Lunden compares numbers that are incommensurable, namely the modern bishop's salary with the bishopric's total income in the Middle Ages. If the comparison were relevant, the institution's budget would have to be added to the modern bishop's salary, but this would also be incorrect, because a bishop during the Middle Ages controlled the institution's income in a way which differs significantly from today. With only a few exceptions, he could use the income for whatever he wanted without being held accountable for any expenses. Although there were a number of rules for what the bishop could do as well as restrictions against alienating ecclesiastical property, it was difficult to intervene against a bishop who abused his position. The cathedral chapter eventually limited the bishop's authority and managed to achieve a considerable amount of collective government of the diocese. The

---

30   Contamine, "The Growth of State Control"; cf. also Keegan, *A History of Warfare*, pp. 3-24, on Clausewitz's distinction between "civilised" and "barbaric" warfare.
31   H 33; *Ss.* ch. 136.
32   *Ss.* ch. 159, pp. 168 f. On the attitude to captive enemies in the sagas, see Bagge, *Society and Politics*, pp. 166 f., and "Ideology and Propaganda", pp. 9 f.

sysselmann, on the other hand, was an official to a greater degree. He was to present accounts of his revenue, keep an amount for himself, and deliver the rest to the king. Little is known about how the system worked in practice, but we know of a number of complaints by the king regarding corruption and abuse. Strong and able kings were most likely able to ensure that their *sysselmenn* were loyal to them and performed their duties, while it is more difficult to know how they behaved towards their subordinates.

Thirdly, no clear prerequisites – such as training or other qualifications – existed for appointment to an office, and there was only a limited ladder of promotion on which one could gradually rise according to seniority and qualification. Still, in this regard the clerical bureaucracy was more modern than the secular. A certain amount of academic knowledge was necessary to become a cleric. Clerics had to be able to read and write and know enough Latin to say Mass and preferably to understand at least most of its words. Also required was a degree of insight into the Church's teaching. Little is known about the level of education among Norwegian priests, but judging from conditions elsewhere in Europe, it was probably poor. Training to become a cleric most likely took place at the cathedral chapters, and was probably not very extensive. The sources say little about schooling and training; we have to rely on random references connected with other cases. A few schoolmasters are mentioned, although they do not appear to have been distinguished prelates; normally the schoolmaster was not a canon, although he could advance this far; he might even become a bishop.[33] Higher clerics, on the other hand, were better educated. Most bishops and a good number of canons were educated at foreign universities.[34] The fairly substantial amount of writing in Latin by Norwegian clerics suggests a solid grasp of the language. However, there were no clear requirements for higher clerical positions. Quite often a university education was acquired by people who had already assumed the office of canon; it was only then that they had the necessary means to finance any further studies. Obtaining an education certainly increased the chances of becoming a bishop, but was by no means an absolute prerequisite. The particular requirements involving knowledge which were demanded of the clergy, and especially of the higher clergy, may have contributed to creating a corporate spirit and identification with the institution's purpose, but did not create a clear corporate ladder reminiscent of the ones we find in modern bureaucracies.

For the ecclesiastical reform movement which emerged around the eleventh century, it was of the utmost importance that the clerical offices were occupied by men who

---

[33] On clerical education, see Kolsrud, *Presteutdaningi*. On the schoolmaster elected bishop – Håkon, bishop of Oslo (1248-67, archbishop 1267-68) – see Joys, *Biskop og konge*, p. 218.
[34] Bagge, "Nordic Students", pp. 8 f.

distinguished themselves through learning, piety, and proficiency, and who were independent with regard to family and other worldly interests. Education was one means to promote a corporate identity among the clergy; celibacy was another. Although the main consideration behind the introduction of celibacy was the purity resulting from sexual abstinence, celibacy also aimed to prevent ecclesiastical offices from becoming hereditary. The introduction of celibacy came late in Norway. The *Canones Nidrosienses* from the 1160s emphasised sexual purity among the clergy but only banned marriage for canons; ordinary priests were forbidden to marry widows or women who had been divorced.[35] Formally, celibacy was not introduced until 1237 when the pope complained about the Norwegian practice and banned clerical marriages. During the following period, clerics apparently ceased to marry but continued to keep concubines.[36] In practice, celibacy, in all likelihood, led to greater mobility in the recruitment to clerical office, but family links and friendship continued to play an important role. In Norway, it seems that the higher clergy favoured relatives and other protégés to a large extent. Even as late as in the thirteenth century, there are several examples of bishops' sons being elected bishops.[37] By contrast, after the Church had been fully developed and organised in the thirteenth century, there are fewer indications that kings and aristocrats had any considerable influence (see below pp. 295 f.).

With regard to secular office, the terms of qualifications were even more unclear. A knowledge of the laws was needed to take office as a judge, but there was no formal training in national law. The study of law at the universities consisted solely of Roman and canon law. Traditionally, the assumption has been that most members of the elite were fairly well versed in the law. From the time of the National Law the requirements were most likely tightened, but training must have taken place more on a practical, rather than a formal, academic level. Aside from that, family connections and personal affiliations were probably the most important pre-conditions for employment. *The King's Mirror* discusses at length how one is to apply for admittance into the king's service. The author emphasises the importance of being from a good family and having good manners. An applicant should also contact someone who was already a royal retainer, and through him obtain an audience with the king. Having achieved this, the candidate's ability to make a good personal impression would determine his success or failure.[38]

This does not necessarily mean that the level of education among the king's servants was poor. From the middle of the thirteenth century onwards in particular, many cler-

---

35   *Lat. dok.* no. 7, can. 6-8.
36   Gallén, "Celibat", cols. 546 f.; Gunnes, "Prester og deier".
37   Joys, *Biskop og konge*, pp. 209, 218 f.
38   *Kgs.* pp. 44-47; cf. Bagge, "The Norwegian Monarchy", pp. 168-72.

ics with a solid educational background were recruited into royal service. We also know of secular aristocrats who studied law in Bologna – Europe's foremost centre for such studies – at the end of the thirteenth century.[39] The great law reforms under Magnus Håkonsson and the many decrees from the subsequent period, negotiations with foreign powers, and an increased level of literacy within public administration from the latter half of the thirteenth century and on, undoubtedly required educated people, yet this did not lead to fixed requirements nor any kind of career path. As with the clergy, education was often sought by men who had become members of the bureaucracy, as witnessed by the students in Bologna in the 1290s.

Taken together, these features suggest that the royal and ecclesiastical administration in the period should be regarded as patrimonial rather than bureaucratic, according to Weber's terminology,[40] in a similar way as other medieval administrations. The administrators owed loyalty to a person rather than to an abstract institution and were not governed by general rules nor did they have clearly defined duties. From this point of view, the ecclesiastical administration was more advanced than the royal one, with a clear aim for its work, with canon law governing a substantial part of its duties and with an ideology underlining loyalty to God and the Christian doctrine. On the other hand, the bishop resembled a magnate rather than a bureaucrat, and the rest of the organisation differed in many respects from the classical definition of a bureaucracy. Concerning the royal administration, the patrimonial aspect is evident in one of the reasons *The King's Mirror* adduces for addressing kings and other great men in the plural rather than in the singular. Such men are never alone; they are surrounded by counsellors and a number of men serving them in different ways, who, when their lord dies, seem as if they have lost their father. Thus, to use Kantorowicz's terminology, the king has no immortal body to which his servants' loyalty can be transferred when his mortal body dies.[41] Still, there is no absolute barrier between the patrimonial and the bureaucratic system; in the most advanced royal administration of the period – that of the king of England – the mere size of the organisation and its distance from the king's person must have led to the development of rules and routines and an identification with the government and the administration rather than with the king's person. The modest size and specialisation of the Norwegian royal and ecclesiastical administrations can hardly have had such effects, but the difference from earlier forms of government is nevertheless significant.

---

39   Sällström, *Bologna och Norden*, pp. 177-79; Bagge, "Nordic Students", pp. 5 f.
40   Weber, *Wirtschaft und Gesellschaft*, pp. 739-94.
41   Kantorowicz, *The King's Two Bodies*, pp. 207-32 and *passim*.

The preceding discussion seems to confirm the traditional opinion of Norwegian historians, that Norway was not feudalised in the Middle Ages. Power in local society was based on delegation from the king, whose subordinates were officials rather than vassals. Apart from the Church, there was no jurisdiction independent of the king. In so far as there were tendencies in the direction of feudalism, they were mainly to be found in the Later Middle Ages, when, according to Holmsen and other adherents of the Marxist school, the "firmly built state" of the High Middle Ages broke down, the members of the aristocracy, partly under the influence from the neighbouring countries, started to build up their own power independently of the king and the *leidang* was replaced by professional forces in the service of these magnates. Nevertheless, even then Norwegian society hardly conformed to the classical European model of feudalism. Although the classical model of feudalism has been subject to much discussion in recent years[42] and it is more difficult to define exactly what was feudal and what was not, there is a clear difference between the Norwegian administrative system and the one found in most other countries at the time, which had far greater independence for local lords and private castles and jurisdiction. This was also true of the two other Scandinavian countries, although the aristocracy had a stronger position and greater control over the peasants in Sweden and particularly in Denmark.[43]

From Oral to Written Administration

In discussing the degree of bureaucratisation and "stateness" following from these administrative reforms, let us first turn to the most important routine aspect of bureaucratisation, the introduction of writing, or, more exactly, the routine use of written documents as an element in the administration. Writing itself was known already in the pre-Christian period through the use of the runic alphabet. The runic material preserved today consists of monumental inscriptions on stone, but we cannot exclude the possibility that runes were also used for shorter messages on bark, wax or other perishable material which is of course far less likely to have been preserved.[44] Some hints in the sources may point to

---

42 Poly and Bounazel, *La mutation féodale*; Reynolds, *Fiefs and Vassals*, pp. 1-16 and *passim*.
43 Christensen, *Kongemagt og aristokrati*, 143-78; Paludan, "Tiden 1241-1340", pp. 455-59; Gelting, "Féodalisation".
44 Nedkvitne, *Literacy*, p. 104, argues on the basis of the analogy with Catholic liturgical fragments, which have been preserved in fairly large quantities, that a part of this material would also have been preserved if there had been a widespead use of runes in the pre-Christian period. The analogy is false; the liturgical texts were preserved because they were written on good parchment which could be used for bookbinding and other purposes when the texts themselves became obsolete after the Reformation, whereas no such reason exists for the preservation of runic messages.

this,[45] as may also the fact that runes were apparently widely used for messages in the Christian period. This has been explained by the influence of Latin script but may equally well reflect earlier usage. By contrast, there is little to suggest that runes were used for the composition of longer texts. Thus, they hardly represent more than a small exception to what was essentially an oral society.[46] In any case, the introduction of Christianity must almost immediately have increased the importance of written documents. Liturgical books were necessary for celebrating Mass and must have been brought to Norway by the clergy who were of course also literate. The earliest texts all seem to have been imported, as the first known examples written in Norway date from the end of the eleventh century.[47]

Script must also have been used for correspondence from the Christianisation period onwards, at least with kings and ecclesiastical institutions abroad. A few letters[48] from popes and other foreign ecclesiastics have been preserved, the oldest from around 1065-66.[49] No letters from Norwegian kings or bishops are known to have existed until well into the twelfth century, although kings and bishops must clearly have been able to correspond with their foreign counterparts well before that. *Heimskringla* mentions a correspondence between King Magnus the Good (1035-46) and Edward Confessor, but the letters were probably composed by Snorri himself.[50] A short letter from 1139, quoted in slightly different form in *Morkinskinna* and *Heimskringla*, in which King Inge asks his brother King Sigurd for help against his enemies, is more likely to be authentic.[51] The letter adheres to many of the norms known from later royal letters,[52] and may have been quoted in the sagas because of its rather striking formulation: "It is known to all men what great difficulties we have, as well as our youth, as you are five winters old and I

---

45   Rimbert, *Vita Ansgari* ch. 12, p. 42, contains a reference to a letter sent from the ruler of Birka in Sweden to Louis the Pious written with deformed letters according to their custom ("cum litteris regia manu more ipsorum deformatis"). Cf. Spurkland, "Viking Age Literacy", pp. 143 f.
46   Brink, "Verba volant", pp. 84-86 with references.
47   Karlsen, "Katalogisering"; Ommundsen, *The Beginnings*; Mortensen, "Sanctified Beginnings".
48   For want of a better term, I use "letter" in the following to refer to the various kinds of documents recording deeds as well as serving as communication between individuals or collectivities. Cf. Clanchy, *From Memory*, pp. 60-70.
49   *Lat. dok.* no. 1.
50   Agerholt, *Brevskipnad*, p. 640. This work, from 1929-33, is still the most important study of this aspect of administrative literacy. Vågslid, *Norske skrivarar,* and Hagland, *Riksstyring og språknorm* and *Literacy*, mainly focus on the linguistic aspect, but also give valuable information on scribes and letters. By contrast, Nedkvitne, *Literacy*, pp. 69-75, despite the title, deals only briefly with the subject and brings nothing new.
51   Agerholt, *Brevskipnad*, p. 639.
52   E.g. the *salutatio*: "Ingi konungr ... sendir kveðju ... guðs ok sina" (King Inge ... sends God's and his own greeting ...").

three".[53] The two sagas' source for this particular period is also good, namely Eirik Oddsson's contemporary account which may have contained a quotation of the letter. There are a few more letters from the following period, some of which have been preserved in later transcripts. On the ecclesiastical side, a relatively extensive correspondence between the Norwegian Archbishops Øystein (1161-88) and Eirik (1189-1205) and the curia is preserved in the papal chancery or in collections of decretals, whereas the first letters in Old Norse are from the 1170s and directed to Iceland.[54] The first written versions of the laws probably date from the late eleventh or early twelfth century (above p. 180), but there is little to suggest any extensive use of writing in the royal administration until the beginning of the thirteenth century; the ecclesiastical administration may have been somewhat earlier in this respect, although the direct evidence is scanty.

The reign of Håkon Håkonsson (1217-63) seems to mark a new epoch in this respect. The evidence of this is his saga, composed in 1265, shortly after his death, which contains quotations from or references to ninety-nine letters altogether, thirty to the king, forty-one from the king, and twenty-eight between other persons in the saga.[55] If these are really authentic letters which the author, Sturla Tordarson, found in a royal archive, as Bjørgo believes, it would indicate a fairly advanced level of written administration. The letters are not privileges or donations, which are most likely to be preserved in an archive, but messages of greater or lesser importance between the leading characters in the saga, including orders from the king to his subordinates, all of which would thus seem to have been not only issued, but copied and stored in a royal archive. This was by no means usual practice in the early thirteenth century, although there are examples, even from earlier periods, that it did occur, such as the register of Pope Gregory VII (1073-85) which, however, is not complete, and practice in the English chancery from the end of the twelfth century onwards.[56] If authentic, the ninety-nine letters are of course only a portion of all that existed.

However, we have no firm evidence of the existence of these letters; it is clearly a possibility that at least some of them were composed by the saga writer. Bjørgo discusses this possibility in some detail, but concludes that the letters, at least most of them, are authentic:[57] There are complex links between the letters in the form of reaction and re-

---

53 "Vandreþi okor ero ollom monnom kvNig iþesso … oc sva øsca sv er þv ert .v. vetra gamall. en ec .iii. vetra" (*Msk.* pp. 429 f.; cf. *HkrIngi* ch. 8).
54 See the list of letters earlier than 1280 in Agerholt, *Brevskipnad*, pp. 648-59. The Latin correspondence from the 1160s until 1204, mainly with the pope, is printed in *Lat. Dok.* nos. 11-41.
55 Bjørgo, "Skriftlege kjelder", pp. 197-201.
56 Clanchy, *From Memory*, pp. 48-53.
57 Bjørgo, "Skriftlege kjelder", pp. 201-7.

sponse. The language in Sturla's summaries of letters often corresponds to the language actually used in the extant letters; thus, the king uses the plural to refer to himself when writing but the singular when speaking. Some common formulas, e.g. *poena*, occur in Sturla's rendering of letters. Finally, in some cases there is evidence of the correspondence referred to in the saga in other sources. Against this it may be objected that most letters are rendered extremely briefly in connection with situations when the exchange between the protagonists would likely have taken place in writing, such as in the correspondence between King Håkon and King Erik of Sweden before Håkon's expedition to Värmland to punish the people there for their support of his Norwegian enemies, or the letter sent to Håkon and Skule after the death of the Crozier king Philippus in 1217 to persuade them to use the opportunity to gain control over Eastern Norway, or the correspondence at critical points between Håkon and Skule, who mostly stayed in different parts of the country.[58] Having spent some time at the Norwegian court, Sturla had most probably made himself familiar with some conventions in the chancery, which enabled him to give his references to correspondence an authentic ring, in the same way as he composed the speeches he attributed to his protagonists.

Only two letters are actually quoted in the saga. The first is from Håvard, Bishop elect of Bergen, and the people of the Gulatingslag to the people in Trøndelag concerning the royal election after King Inge's death in 1217.[59] According to the saga, Inge's half-brother Skule had strong support in Trøndelag, and there was a serious risk that he would be preferred to the young Håkon who is of course represented as the lawful candidate. The letter forms a decisive intervention in favour of Håkon by supporting his election in strongly agitative language, to which the messenger carrying it, Dagfinn Bonde, adds an ultimatum: If Håkon is not elected in Trøndelag, he will be brought to Western Norway and elected there. In other words: the Birchlegs will be divided into two factions which will fight one another. The letter thus gives Sturla the same opportunity to excel in dramatic oratory as the speeches in this part of the saga which he has most probably composed himself, while at the same time giving more weight and realism to the intervention from Western Norway. The letter forms far better evidence of substantial support for Håkon than a mere speech from a few representatives of the region in the hostile environment of Trøndelag. Sturla may even have known that a letter was sent on this occasion without knowing its contents. Considering the decisive importance of such a letter, if it did exist, it is not impossible that it was preserved, but as it had no practical importance after it had served its purpose, there was no urgent reason for preserving it.

---

58   See the list in Bjørgo, "Skriftlege kjelder", pp. 197 f.
59   *HH* ch. 17.

The second letter[60] is of the same type. Here Håkon writes to the Earl Skule and Archbishop Peter in 1226, rejecting their attempt to make him share the country with the rebel King Sigurd Ribbung. This is also strongly agitative, more so than one would normally expect in a letter to high-ranking recipients who were not direct enemies. A real letter in such a situation would probably have been couched in more diplomatic terms. The letter also expresses a central idea in the saga: Håkon as God's elect who refuses to share the country with one who has no right to rule it, but who trusts that God will judge between him and Sigurd. As the previous division of the country had resulted in Skule keeping Trøndelag and Håkon the southern part of the country, it would seem more realistic that Håkon expressed these ideas in writing rather than in speech, although in reality, he might well have made his will known through a messenger. If he did compose a letter, there would seem to be no particular reason to preserve a copy of it in a royal archive, unless it was normal practice to store copies of everything that went out.

These two examples also point to the difference between the saga and the typical European chronicle based on written documents, such as monastic chronicles or what Beryl Smalley calls "civil service historiography" where the narrative is broken up by extensive quotations from documents which often serve as evidence of the privileges of the institution in question.[61] The letters quoted in *Hákonar saga* do not have this function. They are normally messages and they rarely break up the narrative. On the contrary, the two letters referred to above add to the drama of the narrative rather than reducing it. Nor is it easy to see that the brief references to letters represent a deterioration of the saga from a literary point of view.[62] Admittedly, *Hákonar saga* is usually regarded as stylistically inferior to earlier works like *Sverris saga* and *Heimskringla*. However, the main reason for this is not the reference to letters but the great amount of factual information presented in a brief and dry form, included because of its importance for the king's dignity and prestige.

The letters most likely to have been copied and preserved, apart from charters concerning privileges or gifts of land, which are not mentioned in the saga, are those addressed to or received from foreign rulers. Thus, correspondence with the pope, the Emperor Frederick II and other rulers is likely to have existed; in some cases there is even direct evidence of correspondence actually having taken place, as Bjørgo points out. The extant treaty with Lübeck was clearly preceded by some negotiations in writing as well as appeals to Frederick II, and the correspondence with the pope in the 1240s actually led to Håkon's coronation in 1247. Such important letters were probably stored, whereas lists

---

60 *HH* ch. 153.
61 Smalley, *Historians*, pp. 113-19.
62 Thus Bjørgo, "Skriftlege kjelder", p. 201, who, however, also admits the dramatic effect of the two quoted letters.

may have been kept of less important ones and of outgoing correspondence. Whatever the origin of the letters in *Hákonar saga*, this saga differs significantly from the earlier sagas which only contain very few letters. Even if Sturla composed most of the letters he quotes or refers to, the saga may still indicate that writing had become a normal means of communication in the thirteenth century. Admittedly, the earlier sagas may have avoided quotations of letters as not "saga-worthy" (*sǫgulikt*), but if so, the change in style from them to *Hákonar saga* must in itself be regarded as evidence of an increased use of writing. In addition to the forty-one letters issued by the king according to the saga, thirty-eight more are known from other sources which, if the ones of the saga are genuine, bring the total number up to seventy-nine, nine of which are preserved in the original, seven in Latin and two in Old Norse.

With the exception of *Magnúss saga*, King Håkon Håkonsson's death in 1263 marks the end of the period of the sagas and their replacement by documentary evidence. Even if the amount of documents produced by the Norwegian chancery is not impressive, it is significantly higher than in the previous period, as is evident from the tables below:

Total number of letters according to *Regesta Norvegica*

1263-1300	1074	29 per year (46 per year 1289-1300)
1301-1319	1156	64 per year
1320-36	1218	76 per year
1337-50	1278	98 per year

Royal letters 1263-1319 according to *Regesta Norvegica*

King	Letters	Letters per year
Håkon Håkonsson 1217-63	79*	1.7
Magnus Håkonsson 1263-80	71	4
Eirik Magnusson 1280-99	157	8
Håkon V Magnusson 1299-1319	213	10.6

* Including references in the saga.

The tables show a gradual rise in the total number of letters as well as in the royal letters during the thirteenth century, a sharp rise from around 1290 with a climax in royal letters during the reign of Håkon V (1299-1319), a total of 213 or a little more than ten per year.

Most interesting in the period after 1320 is the absolute as well as relative decline in the number of letters from the king compared to the reign of Håkon V, mainly because of the union with Sweden and later with Denmark. This perception receives further support from Hagland's comparison between the periods 1310-50 and 1350-90. Whereas the total number of letters is higher in the former period, the number of letters originating in Norwegian local society is higher in the latter.[63] We thus have evidence of the spread of literacy from the royal and ecclesiastical administration to local society.

These numbers are not very impressive compared to other countries. Based on what is extant, the papal chancery was already issuing at least 180 letters per year under Alexander III (1159-81), the king of England issued 115 per year under Henry II (1154-89) and the French king 500 per year under Philip IV (1285-1314), which means that the number issued by all three chanceries by far exceeded the total number of letters known to have been issued in or addressed to Norway in the maximum period from 1337-50. In the thirteenth century there is an explosion of letters in England, which Clanchy indicates by listing the average weekly amount of wax for sealing which increased from 3.63 pounds in 1226-30 to 31.90 pounds in 1265-71.[64] This comparison is not wholly relevant, as both France and England had far greater sources in terms of wealth and population than Norway; England was also by far the "most governed" country of Europe in the Middle Ages and its records have been better preserved than those of any other country except Italy, which was the most literate country of Europe and which had large collections preserved in the papal chancery as well as in some of the cities. Within Scandinavia, Denmark shows a pattern largely similar to that of Norway. *Diplomatarium Danicum* contains 754 letters from the period 1250-74, 1045 from 1275-99 and 1973 from 1300-24, which means around thirty per year in the first period, forty in the second and eighty in the third. The number continues to rise during the rest of the century, reaching 160 per year in the period 1375-99.[65] This is probably the result of an actual rise, although in the case of royal letters we have to take into account that more was preserved after the mid-fourteenth century than before (below p. 250). When comparing with Norway, we also have to take into account that the *Diplomatarium Danicum* only lists extant letters – in original, transcript or summary – whereas *Regesta Norvegica* also includes lost ones that can be reconstructed from others. Swedish statistics of royal letters show a slow rise during the thirteenth century, rising to five per year during a short period towards the end of the century and then a sharp rise from around 1315, with twenty per year in the 1330s.

---

63 Hagland, *Literacy*, pp. 14-17.
64 Clanchy, *From Memory*, p. 43.
65 Poulsen, "Danske bønders", p. 386.

A new drop occurs towards the end of Magnus Eriksson's reign and the beginning of the reign of Albrecht of Mecklenburg in the 1360s, followed by a rise to twenty-five per year in the 1370s.[66]

Writing in the Royal Administration: The Quantitative Evidence

The main problem in comparing Norway to other countries is to what extent the small number of letters known to us means that writing was used relatively seldom in Norway in the Middle Ages or is the result of the great loss of archival material in the Later Middle Ages during the unions with Sweden and particularly Denmark. In Norway, each king seems to have had his own archive which was closed at his death, although his successor might transfer acts that he needed to his own archive, such as treaties with foreign powers and other important documents.[67] Thus, some documents of this kind were moved to Sweden under Magnus Eriksson and to Denmark under Margrete and Erik of Pomerania in the late fourteenth and early fifteenth centuries. In the thirteenth century, the king's archive was probably mostly located in the Church of the Apostles in Bergen, while Håkon V used either Akershus Castle or the Church of St Mary's in Oslo, or both. Whereas Magnus Eriksson and his successor Håkon VI had a Norwegian as well as a Swedish chancery, the union of Kalmar (1397) led to a central chancery in Denmark which dealt with most politically important issues. For Norway, this situation lasted for the rest of the Middle Ages. The provost of St Mary's in Oslo continued to deal with some judicial matters, including letters of pardon in cases of manslaughter, and other local authorities issued various kinds of letters, but no central government remained in Norway except for during shorter periods when the Council of the Realm acted in this capacity. Thus, no strong incentive existed for preserving the remaining archives of the medieval Norwegian kings. Much was lost in the other countries as well, but central archives had earlier developed there. In Denmark, more continuous series of documents are preserved from the reign of Valdemar IV (1340-75), although the place of the archive continued to change until 1582.[68] In Sweden, a central archive of contemporary as well as earlier documents was established under Gustav Vasa (1523-60), against the background of a practice going back to the period after the deposition of Erik of Pomerania in 1439. Only the rise of antiquarianism in the late seventeenth century led to a new interest in the ancient Norwegian archives, at which time much had been lost.

---

66   Larsson, *Svenska medeltidsbrev*, p. 249.
67   For the following, see Schück, *Rikets brev*, pp. 103-52, 560-70.
68   Kroman, "Arkiv".

Consequently, most of the royal letters preserved from the late thirteenth and early fourteenth centuries have been preserved, in the original or in transcript, by the receivers, such as the privileges to the Hanseatic towns, letters of protection or other letters to ecclesiastical institutions, letters to other countries, and, occasionally, letters to individuals preserved on farms in various parts of the country. The best preserved category is emendations of the National Law and royal ordinances which were added to manuscripts of the law and which are often preserved in several copies. An indication of how much has been lost is the fact that a number of central political documents have only been preserved thanks to the chance survival of most of the *Registrum* of the Bishop of Bergen 1305-42. This includes a treaty between Norway and Russia of 1326, the agreement between Swedish and Norwegian representatives about the personal union of 1319, the documents concerning the marriage alliance between Norway-Sweden and Mecklenburg (1321), the decision to depose Duchess Ingebjørg from the regency for her son (1323), a letter from King Robert of Scotland (1321), a treaty between Norway-Sweden and Denmark (1327) and between Duke Knud Porse, Ingebjørg's husband, and the Norwegian magnates (1327), King Håkon Sverresson's letter of reconciliation with the bishops (1202), Magnus Eriksson's ordinance about the foreign merchants in Bergen (1331) and a series of documents concerning Håkon V's alliance with the Swedish dukes and King Erik Menved of Denmark (1307-09) respectively.[69] Fortunately for later historians, the bishops of Bergen, notably Arne (1305-14) and Audfinn (1314-30), were sufficiently involved or interested in the great political events of the day to copy some of the most important documents; otherwise, they would have been entirely lost to us. Nevertheless, there is no reason to suppose that what they copied was anywhere near the total of what existed. A further indication of what once existed is the material registered at Akershus in 1622 from four ecclesiastical institutions, containing brief references to 2375 letters concerning various kinds of land transactions, many of which stem from kings. These letters are not normally dated in the register and only the names of the kings and not their number in the line of rulers are mentioned. Thus "Magnus" may be Magnus Erlingsson (1161-84), Magnus Håkonsson the Law-Mender (1263-80), or Magnus Eriksson (1319-74) and "Håkon" may be Håkon Håkonsson (1217-63), Håkon V Magnusson (1299-1319), or Håkon VI Magnusson (1343-80).

There is somewhat more information on ecclesiastical archives. In the seventeenth century, the learned Icelandic philologist Arni Magnússon asked for information about archives in Norway and got the answer that most of the material from Bergen and Oslo had burnt, but he was able to borrow the material preserved from the cathedral chapters

---

69 The documents mentioned are listed in NGL IV, pp. 620-29.

of Trondheim and Stavanger.[70] A considerable number of documents from these institutions have therefore been preserved, mostly from the prolonged conflicts between the archbishop/bishop and the chapters around 1300. Furthermore, the *Registrum* from the Diocese of Bergen, comprising a total of more than 500 documents, contains the largest amount of documents from any ecclesiastical institution in Norway.[71] This amounts to slightly more per year than the amount known from the royal chancery under Håkon V, thirteen versus 10.6 letters per year. The *Registrum* is preserved in two sets of transcripts by Arni Magnússon; the original was lost in the fire in Copenhagen in 1728. Arni apparently did not copy all the documents of the *Registrum*, nor was this book identical with the diocesan archive. It seems that most of the documents registered there were of particular importance, whereas only a few routine letters were entered to serve as models. Thus, we cannot draw any conclusion from this source about the total number of letters issued and received by the bishop of Bergen. Nor does the *Registrum* contain information about the landed estates of the diocese which were registered in separate cadasters. One such cadaster has been preserved, usually referred to as the Calfskin of Bergen (*Bjorgyniar kalfskinn*), which is the oldest cadaster of Norway.[72] The extant version was probably written around 1360 and registers the revenues of local churches and priests in the diocese and the prebends and altars in the cathedral, plus the tithe, but not the bishops's estates.

We can thus safely assume that a large part of the documents produced in the royal chancery were lost either shortly after they were issued or in the following period. Although it will probably never be possible to estimate how much has been lost, a closer examination of Håkon V's letters may get us a little further.

Preservation of letters from Håkon V. Old Norse[73]

Total Old Norse	110
Law manuscripts	54
Cathedral chapter of Nidaros	11
Cathedral chapter of Stavanger	7

---

70 Agerholt, *Brevskipnad*, p. 399.
71 Berulfsen, *Kulturtradisjon*, pp. 34-46, and "Bergen kopibok".
72 Hødnebø, "Bergens kalvskinn".
73 Listed in Agerholt, *Brevskipnad*, pp. 406-17.

St Mary's in Oslo	10
Munkeliv monastery	2
Registrum of the Bishop of Bergen	6
Jämtland	4
Others	16

Preservation of Letters from Håkon V's Reign. Others (Latin or only mentioned)

Correspondence/treaties with other countries: England, the Vatican or German towns	30
Internordic conflicts: *Registrum*, Huitfeld and archives in Denmark and Sweden	25
Icelandic annals	7
The Akershus register (1622)	4
SUM	66

The two tables above give 176 letters altogether. (The difference between this number and the 213 above is due to the fact that the non-extant documents listed in RN are not included, as it is difficult to say very much about their transmission.) As we see, the largest single category, 54 or nearly one third of the total in this sample, is preserved in law manuscripts, mostly ordinances and amendments of the laws. Many of these exist in more than one copy. All royal justices (*lagmenn*) were supposed to have one copy of the National Law and to add amendments and ordinances when receiving them. These laws were also in use until well after the Reformation and were only finally replaced by Christian V's Code of 1687. Some of them were translated into Danish in the sixteenth or seventeenth century. Thus, the transmission of the legal material is exceptionally good; it may even be that most of what was issued from the late thirteenth century onwards survives. In addition to the legislation concerning the whole country, four letters to Jämtland also mainly contain legislation; they are preserved in Sweden, as Jämtland was ceded to Sweden in 1645.

Letters concerning foreign policy, preserved abroad, form an equally large category: 55 letters altogether. Whereas the archives in England, the Vatican and the German towns are likely to be complete or almost complete, the archives in Denmark and Sweden, the countries with which Håkon was most strongly involved during most of his reign, are very badly preserved. Most of the Danish material is known from extracts and quotations in Arild Huitfeldt's chronicle from around 1600. We can therefore safely assume that the actual number must have been considerably higher than 25. Nevertheless, the preservation of non-legislative documents from Norway is far worse, only 63 of the 176 fall into this category which in all likelihood was the largest by far. Moreover, 36 of these are preserved in collections that happen to have survived relatively well: the archive of the cathedral chapters of Stavanger (7) and Nidaros (11); of Håkon's favourite chapel St Mary's in Oslo (10); of the monastery of Munkeliv in Bergen whose book of letters until 1427 survives (2); and the transcript of the Bishop of Bergen's *Registrum* (6). Most of these letters are gifts or privileges or, in the case of the two cathedral chapters, concern the conflicts between these institutions and the bishop/archbishop. To these can be added seven letters referred to in the Icelandic Annals, mainly concerning Iceland, and four from the Akershus register of 1622. These four donations are the only ones that can be attributed to Håkon V with certainty. As he was probably the greatest donator of the three Håkons, this number can easily be multiplied, although without telling us much more about the administrative use of writing.

Thus, we are left with only sixteen "random" documents, which are the only ones that can tell us about the routine uses of literacy. They are the following:

1. DN VI no. 68, 1 Sept. 1301. Håkon V settles the borders of the farm Skinnenes in Krødsherad. – Transcript in Danske selskabs samling.
2. DN II no. 69. 23 Aug. 1303. Letter of pardon (*landsvistbrev*) for Rolv Kakbretta. – Orig. in Norwegian National Archives (NRA).
3. DN II no. 74. 31 May 1304. Order to two officials to aid the Norwegian and the married foreign shoemakers expelled by the Germans from the king's estate in Oslo. – Orig. in The Arnamagnaean Collection (AM), Copenhagen.
4. DN XIII no. 4. 29 June 1306. Two men are allowed to take up new land in Eggedal. – Copy from the seventeenth century in NRA, from Kopseng in Eggedal, 1883.
5. DN I no. 111. 14 Sept. 1307. Donation for Jon Raud of 1 ½ *øresbol* in Doglo. – Orig. in NRA.
6. DN I no. 121, without date. Vidimation of Håkon V's order of military *leidang* in Trøndelag, 5 April 1309. – Orig. in Danske geheimarkiv.
7. DN VI no. 73. 24 Aug. 1309. Order to transfer legacies to the Franciscans of Oslo. – Orig. in Danske selskabs samling in Oslo.

8. DN II no. 100. 11 Sept. 1309. Order to four men in Valdres to judge in a case about a lake, following complaint from a local man. – Orig. in Danske selskabs samling in Copenhagen.
9. DN II no. 106. 31 Jan. 1311. Confirmation of a judgement between the archpriest of Oslo and a layman. – Orig. in AM, Copenhagen.
10. DN I no. 132. 9 Jan. 1312. Letter about exchange of properties with the king's daughter Agnes. – Orig. in AM, Copenhagen.
11. DN III no. 97. 13 Jan. 1312. Donation for Sir Havtore Jonsson. – Orig. in NRA.
12. DN VI no. 83. 5 March 1314. Order to three men to arrange for the division of the inheritance of Kvåle in Sogndal, according to Sir Sigurd Sveinsson's request. – Orig. in AM, Copenhagen.
13. DN III no. 110. 3 Dec. 1317. Donation for the Royal Chapel St. Michael in Tønsberg. – Orig. in AM, Copenhagen.
14. DN XI no. 8. 26 March 1318. Confirmation of King Håkon's predecessors' donation of a farm. – Copy from the seventeenth century, NRA.
15. DN VI no. 88. [1316]. Confirmation of *ættleiding*. – Fragment of orig., NRA.
16. DN I no. 103 [1304]. Confirmation of an agreement about the farm Byrkjo at Voss. – Orig. in NRA.

As these documents are only a tiny fraction of what once existed, they allow no conclusion concerning the relative importance of the tasks. What they all have in common is that they are reactions from the king to initiatives from others. The king confirms judgements and other decisions made by officials and courts of law. He pardons a man who has committed manslaughter (no. 2). He responds to complaints from local people by ordering his officials to intervene or by setting up a court of law to deal with the matter (nos. 3, 7, 8). Responding to a demand from one of the heirs, he orders a commission to deal with the division of the inheritance to the aristocratic estate of Kvåle in Sogndal (no. 12). The division is carried out, and the commission reports back to the king two and a half months later.[74] He exchanges property with his daughter and donates land to some of his subordinates (nos. 5, 10, 11, 13).

Most of the letters concern people on the higher levels of society – the king's daughter, his son-in-law and his father – or they concern ecclesiastical institutions – other than those with relatively well-preserved archives, the Franciscans of Oslo and the Royal Chapel St Michael in Tønsberg (nos. 7, 13). However, there are also cases concerning

---

74 21 May 1314 (DN VI no. 84).

people somewhat lower down on the social scale, and, not least, there are cases from very different parts of the country (nos. 1, 4, 8). Kvåle in Sogndal was no doubt an aristocratic estate but there is no evidence that its late owner had belonged to the inner circle of the king. Byrkjo at Voss, a farm that had been the object of a prolonged conflict that apparently came to an end through an agreement confirmed by the king, belongs to approximately the same category – an important estate in local society but not one whose owner was close to the king.[75] Finally, there is a very interesting document from the war against the Swedish dukes in 1309, addressed to the community of Trøndelag and thanking the inhabitants for their defence of the region and giving orders for further mobilisation (no. 6). Considering the extreme unlikelihood for documents of this kind to have been preserved for 700 years outside an organised archive, the conclusion from these sixteen letters must be that they are the tiny remains of a quite substantial output from the royal chancery during Håkon V's reign. Various kinds of qualitative evidence point in the same direction.

Writing in the Royal Administration: The Qualitative Evidence

One such source of information is the scribes. Fortunately for the historians, it was the custom in the royal chancery from the late thirteenth century onwards to name the chancellor and the scribe at the bottom of Norwegian letters – as opposed to Latin ones. We know the names of twenty-two scribes from the reign of Håkon V, nine of whom wrote only one letter, two only two, and the rest three or more, including Torgeir Tovesson with thirty.[76] Most of those who wrote only one letter are only mentioned by name, whereas those who wrote more usually have the title *klerkr* or *notarius*. This may suggest a distinction between a core group, employed regularly in the chancery, and people who were used occasionally, although, owing to the small percentage of letters that have been preserved, this distinction does not necessarily coincide with the two groups as presented in the extant material.[77] If we nevertheless deduct the nine with only one letter from those assumed to have been employed regularly, while keeping those with two, we end up with a chancery consisting of thirteen scribes, none of whom, however, can been shown to have been active throughout the reign. Several of them can, moreover, be placed fairly

---

75 No. 16; cf. DN I no. 103, probably from 1304.
76 Bagge, *Kapellgeistlighet*, pp. 135-43, plus a list of scribes at the end of the book, Vågslid, *Norske skrivarar*, pp. 750 f.
77 Thus, the handwriting shows that Bjørn of Marker, who is mentioned as the writer of one letter for Duke Håkon from 24 November 1296, also wrote a Latin letter on the following day (Hagland, *Riksstyring og språknorm*, p. 104).

firmly either in the first or the second half of the reign, such as the most prolific writer on the list, Torgeir Tovesson with thirty, who, with one possible exception, was only active after 1308, and Bård Petersson, second on the list with eight letters, most of which were written in the years 1300-03 – in addition to the ones written during the previous reign, from 1297 – plus two in 1309 and possibly one in 1316. Thus, the core group seems to be reduced to between five and seven. To these can be added the scribes of Latin letters who are not identical to those who wrote the Norwegian ones; we have only three examples before 1350 of scribes who wrote both in Latin and in Norwegian.[78]

The number of scribes that can be deduced from the letters themselves corresponds quite well with the number attached to the government appointed in Håkon V's provision for a regency, with five notaries (two for the chancellor and one for each of the three others) supposed to reside permanently with the king.[79] Still, although only a fraction of the personnel employed by the English chancery, this number would have been sufficient to produce far more than the extant number of letters. If, like Clanchy, we suppose that each scribe produced 1000 letters per year,[80] the total number of letters per year during Håkon V's reign would be 5000-7000 or 500-700 times the number we know today, in addition to the number produced by men outside the core group. From this number we probably have to deduct copies or summaries for the records in the chancery and possibly other copies taken for various purposes. However, we cannot exclude the possibility that such tasks were carried out by more subordinate and consequently anonymous scribes or by personnel belonging to the royal chapels in the towns where most of the letters were issued. In addition to writing letters, the royal scribes were also engaged in other kinds of literary production.

From the following reign, that of Magnus Eriksson, there mostly seem to have been only two scribes at one time. In the first years after Håkon V's death most letters were written by Håkon Ivarsson notarius and Ivar Audunsson klerk, both known from Håkon V's reign, whereas the former was replaced by Pål Styrkårsson in 1325. A Pål klerk also occurs during Håkon's reign, but only in 1303, which makes it unlikely that it is the same person. Pål and Ivar seem to be the only scribes in the following period; Ivar's last letter was written in 1335 and Pål's in 1340. The letters in the following period were written by Halldor Agmundsson and Helge Ivarsson. After 1345, the scribes were no longer named. Thus, Håkon V's reign seems to mark the climax of activity in the royal chancery, whereas that of his successor meant a reduction. On the other hand, the tendency towards increas-

---

78 Vågslid, *Norske skrivarar,* p. 749.
79 NGL III, pp. 49 f., 1302.
80 Clanchy, *From Memory,* p. 42.

ing professionalisation continued; the letters thereafter were always written by permanently employed scribes.

The modest size of the Norwegian chancery is also demonstrated by the fact that it was highly mobile even in the early fourteenth century, whereas the English chancery became permanently settled in Westminster as early as the late twelfth century,[81] as it was too large an organisation to move around with the king. The fact that the king had his own clergy in the three main cities he used to visit – Bergen, Tønsberg and Oslo – plus a number of others along his normal route between them, might make us believe that he used the clergy attached to these churches as scribes when he visited them. It is quite clear from the letters themselves, however, that the scribes followed the king on his journeys.[82] This practice continued under Duchess Ingebjørg, Erling Vidkunsson and the adult Magnus Eriksson until 1343/44, when a new chancellor was appointed who was once more provost of St Mary's in Oslo. Now, for the first time, there seems to have been a separation between the king and the chancery, so that the chancellor issued some letters in the king's name in his absence. Typically, such letters concerned pardon for manslaughter. However, this may have been a temporary arrangement which came to an end when Håkon VI reached majority[83] and was re-introduced when a central chancery had been established in Denmark after the union between the three Nordic countries had been concluded in Kalmar in 1397.

We know a little of the careers of some of the scribes. Bård Petersson, already mentioned as active in the chancery mainly in the period 1297-1303, was a member of a commission of very prominent men, headed by the chancellor, who in 1316 confirmed a confiscation made by the local authorities in Bergen of some German merchants' goods. He became the royal justice (*lagmann*) of Gulating around 1325 and *fehirde* of Trondheim in 1334. Arne Gjavaldsson, who wrote one letter in 1307, is listed before Bård in the letter of 1316 and as *sysselmann* of Jämtland in 1341.[84] Both these examples suggest a slow but steady career in the king's service from young scribes in the chancery to the highest offices in the local administration fairly late in life. Torgeir Tovesson may possibly have

---

81   Clanchy, *From Memory*, pp. 48-53.
82   Bagge, *Kapellgeistlighet*, pp. 135 f.
83   These letters are issued in the king's name and sealed by the chancellor whether the king was present or not, so we need other evidence to know whether he was absent. This was the case in November-December 1359, when Magnus issued a letter of *grid* and one of *landsvist* in Tønsberg in Queen Blanca's presence, while he must have been in Sweden. The same most probably applies to the letters of 1362 and 1363. By contrast, there is no evidence that Håkon was absent when such letters were issued. See the list in Agerholt, *Brevskipnad*, p. 600. The information about the kings' itinerary is based on Erik Opsahl's studies which he has kindly allowed me to use.
84   Bagge, *Kapellgeistlighet*, pp. 137 f.

had a faster career, if he started in the chancery as late as in 1308, as he had received the title of *hirdmann* in 1318.[85] Both he and his colleague Håkon Ivarsson seem to have settled in Bergen as fairly wealthy men. All the men mentioned hitherto are likely to have been laymen. They are never called *sira*, the usual title for clerics, and although they are occasionally called *klerkr*, this does not necessarily indicate clerical status, at least not the higher orders. Moreover, offices like *lagmann* and *sysselmann* were hardly compatible with clerical status, as they might have to pronounce the death sentence which was forbidden to clerics. The same applies to the status of *hirdmann* which would have involved participation in war. Other scribes are more likely to have been clerics, particularly belonging to the royal chapels, but in most cases we have no evidence to support either.[86] The different titles for the scribes, *klerkr* and *notarius*, may suggest a difference of rank. After a certain period of time some scribes seem to have received the latter title which is also only used about men who seem to have belonged to the permanent group. Internationally, *notarius* was used in reference to men with papal or imperial authorisation to guarantee the authenticity of documents, and the royal *notarii* may possibly have had this authorisation.[87]

The subsequent careers of the few scribes about whom we have such information suggest that employment in the royal chancery may have been quite attractive, as does a story from the saga of the Icelandic bishop Laurentius of Holar (bishop 1324-31). Laurentius visited Norway as a young man and composed a letter of proposal in Latin for a Norwegian magnate. The king – Eirik Magnusson – became aware of the letter, was very impressed, and immediately offered Laurentius a position in the chancery.[88] The story reflects the *topos* of the clever Icelander who impresses his Norwegian hosts with his skills, usually in some intellectual field, but also fits in well with the impression we have already received of the small dimensions of the Norwegian chancery, where the scribes must have worked in close contact with the king, who might well then have personally employed some of them.

Nor is the physical distance between the king and his clerks likely to have been very great. Even though various kinds of routine letters eventually developed, there is no evidence of letters having been issued without the king being present. Admittedly, the difference between letters sealed by the chancellor and "in our own presence" ("oss sjǫlfum

---

85 Ibid., pp. 138 f.
86 Ibid., pp. 136-39.
87 Thus Fenger, *Notarius publicus*, pp. 108 f. Nielsen, "Notar", is more in doubt about the authorisation but mentions some Norwegian examples, including Olav Sigvatsson, clearly a Norwegian, who attests to an appeal from Bishop Arne of Bergen and refers to himself as "publicus imperiali auctoritate notarius" (DN VI no. 72, 1309).
88 *Laurentius saga*, pp. 14 f.

hiaverandom") would seem to suggest such a difference, but the latter formula was apparently used when the chancellor was absent.[89] Although we cannot be sure that the king was present in every single case when a letter was issued in his name, there are no examples before 1319 of letters being issued while we know that he was absent. It is impossible to know to what extent he was involved in the actual composition of the letters. We may guess that he dictated the most important ones, for instance the ordinance of 17 June 1308 (below p. 332), while only giving the general outline of others and leaving routine letters entirely to the personnel in the chancery. The different kings may also have differed in this respect – Håkon V is likely to have been closely involved in his correspondence, to the extent that we may detect some personal touches in some of his letters.

Thus, the evidence that has been preserved suggests a moderate size of the royal chancery in the early fourteenth century but nevertheless an increased professionalisation and use of script. A closer examination of the documents themselves, their classification and the development of routines, gives the same impression. Although earlier as well as later royal letters follow standard diplomatic practice in its main outlines, the few extant letters earlier than 1250 are all easily distinguished from the later ones. They are not dated and they show considerable differences in style and the use of formulas. In some of them – Magnus Erlingsson's privilege for the archdiocese (c. 1170), Håkon Sverresson's letter of reconciliation with the Church (1202), and Håkon Håkonsson's renewal of Magnus Erlingsson's privilege for the bishop of Stavanger (c. 1230)[90] – the king speaks in the singular or a mixture of singular and plural, whereas plural is used consistently in the oldest royal letter preserved in the original, a letter of protection from the Crozier king Philippus (1207-17) and in two letters from Håkon Håkonsson from the 1220s. The arenga, which is highly unusual later, occurs both in Magnus Erlingsson's privilege for the archdiocese and in Håkon's privilege for Stavanger. In contrast to later practice, none of these letters mentions the chancellor or scribe or has any corroboration formula. The royal title and salutation formula also show greater divergence in these and other early letters than in the more standardised later ones. The devotion formula *Dei gratia* occurs in Latin as early as in Magnus Erlingsson's privilege, but in Old Norse (*með Guðs miskunn*) only from the end of Håkon Håkonsson's reign.[91] From the late thirteenth century, the king normally refers to himself with the devotion formula and his father's name.

---

89 Bagge, *Kapellgeistlighet*, pp. 180-83.
90 *Lat. dok.* no. 9; NGL I, pp. 444 f.; DN I no. 51.
91 Agerholt, *Brevskipnad*, pp. 759 f. Håkon's privilege for the bishop of Stavanger, probably from around 1230, which is preserved in the original, lacks the formula, whereas an ordinance from 1263, the last year of his reign, has it. This, however, is preserved in a law manuscript from the second half of the fourteenth century, so we cannot be absolutely sure that the formula was there in the original.

Some of the early letters are likely to have been composed by the recipient or beneficiary. The clearest example of this is Håkon Håkonsson's letter of protection for the bishop of Oslo and one or more unnamed monasteries about their exclusive right to the Døvik fisheries in Eiker from around 1225 which is written in the same hand as a contemporary letter issued by the bishop of Oslo.[92] The same most probably applies to Magnus Erlingsson's and Håkon's privileges as well, the former with its elaborate *rex iustus* ideology and the latter in a strongly religious tone and with an arenga about the king's duties towards the Church. The Norwegian custom of naming the chancellor and the scribe was introduced during Magnus Håkonsson's reign; the first certain example is from 1277.[93] The first extant royal letter with an exact date is Håkon Håkonsson's privilege for Lübeck from 6 October 1250, and in the following period, letters in Latin to other countries seem normally to have been dated. The breakthrough regarding letters in Norwegian apparently took place under Håkon's son and successor Magnus, in the beginning with an indication of the year of the king's reign and later with exact dates.[94] Kings and bishops dated their letters according to years AD or their own reign or pontificate or both. The kings mostly used their own reign in letters in Norwegian after 1280. The day was given according to the Roman calendar until around 1250 in the other Scandinavian countries but the lack of material prevents us from determining whether this was also the practice in Norway. In any case, the ecclesiastical calendar was increasingly used in the following period, in the same way as in the other Scandinavian countries, although some bishops continued to use the Roman calendar well into the fourteenth century.[95] The increasing standardisation of the royal letters thus corresponds to the increase in their number during the last decades of the thirteenth century. There is also other, more indirect evidence of the increased use of writing. The author of *The King's Mirror* urges the *hirdmann* to remember the sentences that have been passed; King Magnus Håkonsson orders judgements in major cases to be written down, while King Håkon V in 1308 forbids the *sysselmenn* to ask for the king's letter whenever they bring a suit.[96] Despite the limited size of the chancery and the relative backwardness of Norway in this respect, the use of writing in a legal context changed from an exception to a routine over a period of around fifty years.

---

92 DN II no. 5; cf. RN I no. 534 and DN I no. 7 and note in DN II.
93 NGL II, pp. 483 f. An earlier letter of protection for Munkeliv monastery in Bergen (DN XII no. 3, 1264) is possibly a forgery.
94 See e.g. DN II no. 12 (1265) and NGL II, p. 453 (1267), as examples of the former practice and NGL II, p. 483 (1277), as example of the latter.
95 Nielsen, "Datering", cols. 6-9.
96 Bagge, *The Political Thought*, p. 216 with references.

This routinisation is also revealed in the categories of letters. A passage in Håkon V's ordinance of 1308 on *hird* and administration dealing with fees to the scribes in the chancery for various letters lists several categories: *syslubref* (the *sysselmann*'s letter of appointment), letters of protection (which are divided into the categories of major and minor), letters of *landsvist* (of pardon for homicide), letters of *grið* (giving the killer temporary protection), letters of confirmation (of decisions made in lower instances or by the king's predecessors, and of the decisions made by the royal justices which at this time were routinely issued in writing). There are extant examples of all these categories except the *syslubref*. How many such letters were issued is of course impossible to know. The fees listed in the ordinance are fairly high, so it was clearly not for everyone to procure such a letter, but they may have been well worth the price. Thus, the routine use of writing gave the king and his chancery the possibility of selling extra protection at a high price. A particular fine, *bréfabrot*, is mentioned in the sources from the 1290s onwards for breaking the commands in the king's letters. Full *bréfabrot* was punished by the maximum fine in the law, thirteen marks and eight *ertog*s, which would then clearly come in addition to the normal fine for the offence in question.[97]

The most original feature of Norwegian chancery practice is the extensive use of the vernacular. The royal chancery confined its use of Latin almost exclusively to letters to other countries and in a few cases to the Church, and ecclesiastical institutions also made extensive use of the vernacular, although less than the royal chancery.[98] This differs from Danish and Swedish practice where Latin was in use almost exclusively until the second half of the fourteenth century, and also from that of most other European chanceries. The only parallel – except for Iceland which, of course, had no royal chancery – is Anglo-Saxon England which is likely to have influenced Norwegian practice, as Christianity and thereby writing was introduced to Norway mainly from England. Early Norwegian letters seem to have been modelled on the Anglo-Saxon writ.[99] The Anglo-Saxon tradition in issuing writs in the vernacular continued for some generations after the Norman Conquest, which makes it more likely that it influenced the Norwegian one. A possible objection to this hypothesis may be that we cannot be sure that the earliest letters were actually written in the vernacular. Magnus Erlingsson's privilege to the Church is in Latin, and his lost privilege to the bishop of Stavanger also shows influence from Latin.

---

97   Johnsen, "Bréfabrot".
98   See the list in Agerholt, *Brevskipnad*, pp. 648-57, which includes twenty-five letters from the king in Old Norse before 1280 and four in Latin to Norwegian addressees, all ecclesiastical institutions. Of the letters to Norwegian addressees from the same period issued by bishops eighteen are in Latin and twenty-seven in Old Norse.
99   Agerholt, *Brevskipnad*, p. 646 with reference to Bresslau.

As Håkon Håkonsson's renewal was in Old Norse, it nevertheless seems more likely that the original was also in this language. The absence of the devotion formula (p. 260) points in the same direction. Although the evidence is scanty and we cannot exclude the possibility that Latin was in wider use in the earliest period, it is still possible to point to a link to Anglo-Saxon England. Whereas in England a change to Latin took place gradually in the period after the Conquest, the use of the vernacular continued in Norway where no comparable revolution took place. A further reason for the continued use of the vernacular may be that the less wealthy and exclusive Norwegian aristocrats were not so well equipped with clerical expertise as their European counterparts, and additionally the importance of propaganda during the troubled period in the second half of the twelfth century may have stimulated writing in the vernacular. The extant *Speech against the Bishops* is an example of this, but there may have been others which are now lost. Finally, the existence of written laws in the vernacular may have been of some importance in instigating the issuing of the amendments in the same language of which we have some examples from the twelfth century.

Earlier scholarship has pointed to the importance of the royal chancery for the formation of a standard written language, based on a mixture of several dialects, but the most recent study of the problem, by Jan Ragnar Hagland, finds no strong evidence of this.[100] The tendency towards standardisation, which certainly existed, although it was weaker than for instance in the English chancery, did not extend to the morphology and phonetics of the vernacular. And even if this had been the case, the influence of the royal chancery on writing in general was probably limited and declined in the period after 1319.

Further, somewhat circumstantial evidence for the increased use of writing and bureaucratisation of the administration is the organisation of the royal chapels.[101] There is some evidence of particular royal chapels dating back to the early Christian period, but their great expansion started in the late thirteenth century, when the king had been forced to leave most of the control of the ordinary ecclesiastical organisation to the bishops. In 1308 Håkon V received a papal privilege for a chapel organisation consisting of fourteen churches, four of which were collegiate, led by the provost of the Church of the Apostles in Bergen who reicived the title *magister capellarum regis* and a position within the organisation that resembled, but did not equal, that of a bishop. Most of these churches probably already existed, notably that of the Apostles which had a long tradition as the king's main chapel and was rebuilt in the late thirteenth century (apparently very beauti-

---

[100] Hagland, *Språknorm*, pp. 1-21, on earlier works by Hægstad, Seip, and others and his own conclusions, pp. 192-229. Hagland's material is royal letters in Old Norse from 1220-99 and 1320-30.
[101] For the following, see Bagge, *Kapellgeistlighet*, pp. 89-100, 133-59.

fully in the High Gothic style, although we do not know what it looked like, as it was completely destroyed just before the Reformation). All together, the organisation received nearly half of the king's estates, most of them donated by Håkon V himself.[102] Håkon's favourite church, and in practice the most important within the organisation, was St Mary's Church in Oslo, which he built himself, most probably during his period as duke. Håkon's chancellor, Åke, became its provost, and in 1314 the king decreed that the provost of St Mary's should be royal chancellor permanently. With some exceptions this decree was also respected during most of the following period, although the office of Norwegian chancellor lost much of its importance after around 1400.

This investment in the royal chapels indicates ambitious plans for the expansion of the royal administration, although there is only limited evidence that the royal clergy actually had administrative functions. We know of some of them in prominent positions in the king's service, notably Åke and his successor as provost and chancellor, Ivar Olavsson, but not many others. The king clearly needed clerics in his administration, but continued to use members of the ordinary clergy – abbots, monks, mendicants, in some cases bishops, and, during Håkon V's reign, above all canons. Moreover, as we have seen, some of the scribes were also laymen. Nor was the king's motives for establishing the organisation exclusively administrative; piety, prestige, and ceremony probably also played a considerable role; St Mary's in Oslo was thus intended to be the royal burial church, replacing the Bergen Cathedral which had been the place of most royal burials in the thirteenth century.[103] Nevertheless, we have clear evidence of the importance of the chapels in the royal administration in the form of a letter to the pope from Håkon's successor, Magnus Eriksson, from 1349.[104] Here the king demands that the chapels be exempted from the papal tax levied on ecclesiastical institutions with the argument that the chapels were no ecclesiastical institutions but that their clerics were officers in the royal administration. Admittedly, the aim of this letter might have made the king exaggerate the non-ecclesiastical character of the chapels but his account can hardly have been pure invention. Besides, the few direct examples of links between the chapels and the royal administration may be explained by a lack of sources and the difficulty in identifying the institutional relationship of individual members of the royal administration.

What is the importance of this development? Michael Clanchy, who describes far more drastic changes in the "much governed" country of England, is sceptical about its practical importance: The many documents preserved are more useful to modern historians than to

---

102 Bjørkvik, "Dei kongelege kapella".
103 Roaldset, *Mariakirken*, pp. 28-61 and *passim*.
104 DN VI no. 192; cf. Bagge, *Kapellgeistlighet*, pp. 97 f., 133-35.

contemporary politicians and administrators; the real factors in medieval state formation were castles and armies. In support of this conclusion he points to the difficulty in finding the relevant documents in the enormous archives that were built up in the thirteenth century.[105] Norwegian historians have also been sceptical about the effects of the numerous ordinances issued by Håkon V and his apparent belief in committing his plans and orders to parchment. The distances were long, the communications slow, and the king's chance of controlling whether his orders were actually carried out were limited. Despite the truth of these observations, the conclusion drawn from them may be too pessimistic. The greater awareness of the importance of means of communication in the recent decades is of course no coincidence but clearly determined by the communications revolution we have experienced since the second half of the twentieth century with television, computers, e-mail, and internet. Separating our age from the Middle Ages are not only these and other electronic means of communication, like radio, telephone, and the telegraph, but also the revolutionary effects of the printing press in the fifteenth and sixteenth centuries.[106] The means of communication available to a medieval government were therefore infinitely more primitive than those of the nineteenth and twentieth centuries. Still, we have to ask ourselves what difference it made that writing was adopted by an administration that had previously been predominantly oral.

The medieval commonplace about the value of writing was that it served to preserve the memory of things that had happened. This is the theme of numerous arengas and is also mentioned in prefaces to historical works. Most obviously, kings, prelates or great lords could keep records of their estates and rights and control whether they received what they were entitled to from their subordinates. The concentration of property in few hands over widely different parts of the country is difficult to imagine without written records; at least, such concentrations are likely to have been less stable. The importance of the preservation of memory also applies to the legal field, where the reforms carried out in the thirteenth century would hardly have been possible without writing. Although it might have been difficult to base legal decisions on a broad knowledge of sentences from earlier courts that had dealt with similar cases, precedence might now receive greater importance than before. The same applied to other administrative decisions. Standard procedures and routines became possible to a greater extent than in the oral society, and the decisions of lower instances could be backed up by the king's confirmation. The introduction of writing also served to give the elite greater authority as experts on law, religion and other fields of knowledge which in turn contributed to further centralisation.

105   Clanchy, *From Memory*, pp. 50 f., 145-47.
106   Eisenstein, *The Printing Press*.

Furthermore, there is always some advantage to being in the centre, even in an oral society, in terms of respect and obedience as well as the flow of information. These advantages are enhanced by writing. By means of writing, the royal administration can send its orders and receive information from more people at once faster than with oral communication. Admittedly, as Nedkvitne points out, a letter did not travel faster than a messenger, as it had to be carried, but this was the situation until the telegraph was invented in the nineteenth century. The difference was, first, that a letter could convey the message more exactly and, second, that it could be carried by a person of lower status than what was required of an oral communicator, so that speed could take precedence over dignity. Still there was a close connection between oral and written communication in the Middle Ages; the carrier of the letter was often instructed to give extra information orally.[107] Moreover, there is an aspect of symbolism. In particular, when a royal letter was read to a local assembly, the king was present in a more concrete way than when he had sent a messenger to speak on his behalf. A letter on parchment, with the king's seal attached, was far more than the piece of paper we associate with a letter; it conveyed a similar impression of the royal majesty as the king's presence in person. The way in which particularly early charters were issued was likely to serve this purpose.

As a means of communication, the most important aspect of writing was primarily the opportunity it gave not only to receive and deliver information but to analyse it more systematically by having written reports available from various quarters which could then be compared. In this way, writing gave the central government an advantage that in part compensated for the fact that contemporary military technology tended to favour smaller units over larger ones. This advantage was particularly important in foreign policy and war where information about various potential allies or enemies had to be gathered and analysed before it could be used to make decisions about how to dispose one's own forces and coordinate their movements. Although the traditional *leidang* organisation had its origin in the oral period and local mobilisation took place according to well-established rules about duties and resources, the distribution of these forces between various arenas and their cooperation with allies and elite forces was more complicated and could more effectively be solved by written communication. Moreover, the increasing importance of diplomacy in Norwegian foreign policy also implied an increase in the use of writing. A written instruction for Norwegian envoys for negotiations with the kings of Sweden and Denmark in 1285 has been preserved, giving a glimpse of the use of writing on such an occasion. Here the negotiators are told on what conditions they should agree to a peace treaty and even, if the first offer was rejected, what extra concessions they might agree to

---

107   Nedkvitne, *The Social Consequences*, p. 26; cf. above p. 246 on the letter from 1217.

in order to achieve a settlement.[108] Although this particular instruction might also, and perhaps more safely, have been given orally, as it would have been very dangerous for the content of the instruction to become known to the opposite party, it forms evidence of the widespread use of writing in diplomatic negotiations. It also contains a reference to letters already sent to the opposite party in the negotiations. Thus, in negotiations over alliances as well as peace treaties, the parties worked from written drafts which appear in many cases to have been returned to the government at home for revision before the final treaty was concluded. When a peace had to be worked out on the basis of a normally fairly complex military situation, much depended on the skill of the negotiatiors in expressing the conditions in writing and revising them in the course of the negotiations. The relationship between "hard" factors like armies and castles and softer ones like pen and parchment is therefore closer than what appears from Clanchy's comparison between the two. These observations are confirmed by the situation during the late medieval unions, when the union king had the advantage of a central chancery in Copenhagen – eventually far more developed than the Norwegian one in the early fourteenth century – whereas the potential opposition in Norway and Sweden had difficulties in coordinating its movements and acting together because of their lack of any such institution. No wonder that the constant demands of the council of the realm during negotiations over the kings' election charters was the return of the archive and the seal to Norway.

Predictability and Distance

The introduction of writing was also a step from "unpredictability and presence" to "predictability and distance". Theoretically, writing made it possible for the king or the bishop to say exactly the same thing to people far away as to those in his immediate surroundings – and for the recipient to remind him of what he had said earlier if he changed his mind later.[109] The problem was of course that it took time to transmit the message and receive the answer and, in the case of an order, it was difficult to control whether it had been carried out. Moreover, as every politician and administrator knows, you cannot express your will in writing to everyone. The greater the social distance, the easier simply to transmit

---

108 DN V no. 14.
109 Cf. the criticism of kings in the Later Middle Ages for issuing "letter against letter" ("brev mot brev"), i.e. granting privileges or concessions to one party which were incompatible with those granted to another. Often the king in his election charter had to promise to abstain from this practice which nevertheless continued. The danger of making too firm promises in writing was also clearly perceived by the monarch, as in Queen Margrete's secret instruction for the young King Erik of Pomerania, probably from 1405, in which she warns against making promises in writing, particularly on parchment under the great seal (DN XI no. 110, pp. 100 f., 1405).

the order in writing; the more important the person in question and the more difficult the matter, the more important the personal contact. The change in the king's travel pattern in the thirteenth century serves as an illustration of this truth. In contrast to the bishop, the king had no permanent residence but was almost constantly on the move. However, he confined his travels to a few towns from the thirteenth century onwards, which forms evidence that the number of people who had to be consulted in person was reduced, as does the gradual disappearance of the diets and their replacement by a smaller group of counsellors around the king (below pp. 335 f.). The king usually spent winter, the period from November/December to the beginning of Lent, in one place, where the Christmas celebrations formed the climax of festivities and ceremonials over the year, and spent much of the rest of the year travelling. Håkon Håkonsson spent twenty-three winters in Bergen, eight in Trondheim and five each in Oslo, Tønsberg and Viken (at some place or places in the Oslofjord or Bohuslän area). In contrast to the earlier period, when the king travelled between his farms, he mostly stayed in towns, not only in winter but for longer periods during the rest of the year. Also in contrast to earlier times, it was not necessary for him to switch between winter residences in order to get provisions; when known in advance, it was possible to gather the necessary items in the place the king decided to stay. As is evident from the account of Skule's rebellion, provisions from the east were brought to Bergen to provide for the king there (above p. 82) as well as probably vice versa.

The fact that Bergen was the largest town in the country and had the largest port may nevertheless have contributed to making it the king's favourite winter residence. Additionally, it had the largest and most comfortable royal residence, further developed by Håkon himself, who, however, also extended and improved the royal residences in Trondheim, Tønsberg, Oslo, and Konghelle.[110] Bergen's position as the normal royal residence was even more prominent than appears from the statistics above. Most of the winters Håkon spent in the east have a specific explanation. During the Ribbung Wars in 1220 Tønsberg was Håkon's favourite residence, close enough to the rebels to launch a quick offensive while at the same time sufficiently distant to be safe from sudden attacks. In the late 1240s and early 1250s, the closer relationship to the neighbouring countries led the king to spend more time in the border regions in the east. Finally, six of the eight winter stays in Trondheim belong to the period after Skule's fall. The two others include the stay in 1218-19, when the young Håkon largely travelled together with the older Skule, and 1237-38, when Håkon tried to revive this arrangement, although with Skule in a more subordinate position. In the period 1223-37, when Skule ruled the northern part of the country, Håkon confined his activities to southern Norway, normally the coastal region

---

110 *HH* ch. 333.

between Bergen and the Swedish border. His travels covered most of this area every year, with a few journeys over land between east and west. After Skule's fall, Trøndelag was included in the normal itinerary, whereas there is no evidence that Håkon ever visited Northern Norway. He also conducted most of his foreign policy through intermediaries, although he personally led the expeditions to Denmark and Scotland and several times had meetings with the rulers of the neighbouring countries.

Since there are no extant sagas from after 1263, apart from the fragments of Magnus's saga, the main source for the kings' itineraries are their letters which, after 1280, becomes sufficiently frequent to allow some conclusions to be drawn.[111] In the period 1280-99 the country was in practice divided between King Eirik Magnusson and his brother Duke Håkon, which means that Eirik mostly resided in Bergen, whereas Håkon kept to the eastern and southern part of the country, in the towns of Stavanger, Tønsberg and Oslo. In the autumns of 1282 and 1283, when Håkon was still a minor, the two rulers were together in Bergen and at least in the latter year they most probably spent the winter together there. Eirik is supposed to have reached majority in 1282 and Håkon in 1284, after which he took over his duchy. The two rulers were then together in the east in the summer of 1285, probably in connection with the negotiations with Denmark, Sweden and the German towns that led to the judgement of Kalmar in October (above p. 92). In 1287 they seem to have travelled together from Bergen to the east. In 1289, 1290, 1293 and 1295 they went together on expeditions to Denmark and in the autumn of 1298 they took part in negotiations in Balgö in Halland. In March 1292 they were together in Bergen, which probably means that they had spent the winter there. Later the same year they were together in Tønsberg. They went on a pilgrimage to Trondheim in 1289 and apparently spent the following winter together in Bergen. They thus met frequently, but mainly in connection with war and diplomacy, which confirms the impression that foreign policy was the main field of joint rule between them. In addition, they must have acted together concerning the relationship to the Church, with common negotiations with the archbishop during the pilgrimage in 1289. Both rulers rarely visited Trondheim, apart from the pilgrimage only in 1296 when they negotiated an agreement between the archbishop and his chapter.

As king, Håkon V to some extent continued the pattern from his period as duke, keeping more to the eastern part of the country than his predecessors. Nevertheless, the traditional statement that he moved the capital to Oslo is an exaggeration; Norway had no capital in the real sense of the word, neither under Håkon V nor before. As far as can

---

111 The following is based on Agerholt's list of royal letters, *Gamal brevskipnad* I, pp. 404-17, plus information about Latin letters in *Regesta Norvegica*. For the period 1280-99, see also Helle, *Konge og gode menn*, pp. 337 f. and 608-14.

be deduced from his correspondence, he spent eight to ten winters in Bergen, five in Oslo, three in Tønsberg and one in Trondheim.[112] His residence during the remaining one to three years is unknown, but he is unlikely to have been in any other town than these three. Most of his letters are issued in the same three towns, but some of them in smaller places on the way between them.[113] Håkon's normal travelling pattern, like that of most of his predecessors, was along the coast between Bergen and Oslo. He visited Trondheim only three times (in 1307, 1311 and 1313); every time, he travelled over land from Oslo. He led an expedition abroad in the summer of 1300, which ended without fighting in a renewal of the peace of Hindsgavl. According to the Skálholt Annals, he led a *leidang* expedition into Sweden early in 1310 which ended in a temporary peace and a meeting with Duke Erik in Oslo on 12 March. By contrast, he seems to have been in Bergen in the winter of 1308-09, when Duke Erik attacked Oslo. From there he issued written orders to Trøndelag about a counterattack against Jämtland which had been conquered by the duke's forces[114] and mobilised the *leidang* to move eastwards under his own command. He was present at the betrothal of his daughter to Duke Erik in Solberga in 1302 and at the renewed treaty with King Erik Menved in 1309,[115] but in most cases he concluded his treaties with other rulers through intermediaries. In these respects, Håkon V moved further in the same direction as his grandfather from personal to impersonal government.

Thus, the king's presence was in some cases less important than before. Personal meetings between the king and the people at their local assemblies were apparently rarer in the late thirteenth and early fourteenth centuries than in the period of the civil wars. Still, the king had to be almost constantly on the move to conduct his business in governing the country. It is more difficult to get an impression of what he did during these journeys. *Håkonar saga* mainly deals with foreign policy during the more peaceful periods when the king might have had the opportunity to deal with civilian matters, but occasionally mentions that he was busy with various matters, which may be interpreted as meetings with his officials and other people who wanted to approach him. Later, Håkon V refers to such meetings when travelling around the country. Håkon Håkonsson, and later his son Magnus, also appeared in person at the *lagtings* to have their laws accepted, and Håkon V presented his amendments of the law at an assembly in Trondheim in 1313. Apart from this, he seems mainly to have communicated with the local communities in writing and/or through his officials. Concerning the latter, there seems to have been a combination between writing and personal contact. In his ordinance of 1308, Håkon V wants his

---

112 Helle, *Kongssete og kjøpstad*, p. 555; Nedkvitne og Norseng, *Byen under Eikaberg*, pp. 150 f.
113 Bagge, *Kapellgeistlighet*, p. 141.
114 DN I no. 122.
115 DN IX no. 82, 17 July 1309.

lagmenn and *sysselmenn* to visit him regularly, having the points to be discussed written down on parchment.[116] Even if the king's itinerary was confined to a more limited part of the country than before, the fact that he was so much on the move shows the continued importance of his personal presence. The travels must have been a means to keep in regular contact with the most important people in the country, who probably lived in or near the main towns, and to control his officials. In particular, the long Christmas celebrations were an opportunity to gather the most prominent men in the country around the king. Despite the beginning of bureaucratisation and the increasing use of literacy, the king's presence was still a factor in upholding his authority.

The fact that Håkon's successor Magnus Eriksson was also king of Sweden had obvious consequences for his movements. The union treaty of 1319 specified that the king should spend an equal time in both countries, a provision clearly concerning his minority and not the rest of his reign.[117] Although Magnus spent more time in Sweden than in Norway, he visited Norway every year during his minority (1319-31).[118] In 1320 he spent the whole period from April to September there and in 1324-25 and 1327-28 apparently just the winters. As might be expected, he continued Håkon V's practice of spending more time in the eastern part of the country, but his two winters in Norway were most probably spent in Bergen. He also visited Bergen in 1320 and Trondheim in 1325. Having reached majority in 1331, Magnus continued the same practice of annual visits until 1338, mostly to Eastern Norway. Then there seems to be a gap in the period 1338-44, without any indication in the letters that the king visited Norway. Although it is not impossible that he did, the conflict and negotiations with King Valdemar of Denmark over Scania in 1340-43 may explain his absence in this period. In the following period, 1344-50, after it had been decided that Magnus's son Håkon would succceed his father in Norway when reaching majority, Magnus once more visited Norway regularly, normally Oslo or other places in the east, and normally in the beginning of the year, when he seems to have held meetings with the leading men in the country. From 1350, when the ten-year-old Håkon VI had received his own *hird* and a new regent, Orm Øysteinsson, had been appointed,[119] Magnus's visits once more became more sporadic. The plan was now clearly that Norway should once more have its own king. Norway also became Håkon VI's main residence until his death in 1380. However, the deposition of Magnus in Sweden in 1363 forced Håkon to spend most of his reign fighting to restore Magnus as king of Sweden and thus

---

116   DN XI no. 6, p. 13.
117   DN VIII no. 50.
118   For this and the following, see Grandinsson, *Studier*, pp. 81-115. Thanks to Erik Opsahl for drawing my attention to this information.
119   *Isl. Ann.*, pp. 276, 404 f. (Lögmanns and Flatey Annals).

to save the country for the dynasty. In this war, he had Norway and Western Sweden as his base. Håkon's attempt failed, but the project was taken over by his widow Margrete, daughter of King Valdemar IV of Denmark (1340-75), who succeeded in uniting all three Nordic countries under one king in 1397.

Regarding the king's movements, the decisive change was not the Swedish-Norwegian union of 1319 but the Kalmar Union of 1397 which permanently moved the administrative centre to Denmark, whereas the union king visited Norway only rarely or not at all. By contrast, the pattern during the Swedish-Norwegian union was that of an itinerant king spending most of his time moving between the main centres of his two kingdoms, although admittedly spending more time in Sweden than in Norway. From an internal Norwegian point of view, this pattern meant a continuation of the trend from Håkon V's reign when the king spent more time in the eastern part of the country. There is thus considerable continuity in the king's movements during the whole period from the mid-thirteenth to the end of the fourteenth century, despite the greater distance between him and his subjects resulting from the union with Sweden.

If distance was going to work, it had to be combined with the other element mentioned above, namely predictability. This is most evident in the legal sphere, where the more precise rules laid down in the National Law, combined with a professional judge, made justice more predictable. Additionally, the various categories of routine letters mentioned above (p. 262) are also evidence of greater predictability as well as of the king's authority and his subjects' will to pay for being protected by it. To be sure, although not very detailed, rules for how the king's local officials were to perform their duties were laid down in writing, and the officials had to promise in a sealed letter to adhere to them (above p. 235). The rights and duties of the people towards the king and his officials were also defined more precisely. On the other hand, the fact that the king was almost constantly on the move indicates the limits to predictability and distance and the importance of the king's personal presence.

The Leaders: King and Bishop

How did this, admittedly limited, bureaucratisation affect the tops of the two hierarchies, the bishop and the king? Arne Sigurdsson, bishop of Bergen from 1305-14, had studied abroad, probably in Orléans, and had been a canon for some time, at least since 1292, before he became bishop.[120] He also had experience from serving the king and had been one of the judges appointed by the pope in the conflict between Archbishop Jørund and

---

120   For the following, see Bagge, "Kirken og folket", pp. 226-32.

his chapter. Soon after he had become bishop, he started the *Registrum* (above p. 252) and in the following years entered a considerable number of letters which give an impression of how he governed his diocese. Concerning his relationship to the laity, we mainly learn about his activities as a judge, above all in marriage cases, which mostly concern attempts to annul a marriage or complaints from women about broken marriage vows (below pp. 314 f.). Such cases were brought before the bishop in connection with visitations, or one of both of the parties may have approached their parish priest who then brought the matter before the bishop. Otherwise, the register is mostly concerned with the bishop's relationship to the clergy, including the appointment of priests, the administration of ecclesiastical property, regulations of the borders between parishes and about *cathedraticum*. He also gave rules for the cathedral chapter and decided about some elections of abbots where there had been irregularities on the lower level. The administration of ecclesiastical property was clearly an important task, but here the register gives little information, as there were probably separate cadasters containing this kind of information. A letter to Arne's brother and successor Audfinn, at that time in France, gives information about another important task, the building and maintenance of the cathedral. Arne asks his brother to try to get papal permission for an extraordinary tax on the local churches to finance the repair of the cathedral and to try to engage experts abroad, including a glass painter, to do the job. Cathedrals, in Norway and elsewhere, are still the most visible evidence of the wealth and power of the medieval Church and of the influence of Christianity in medieval society, and their construction was one of the bishop's and the cathedral chapter's most important and prestigious tasks. Bishop Arne was clearly a well-educated man, and his correspondence gives some impression of his canonical learning. We also have information about his library, which consisted of thirty-six books, a relatively large collection by contemporary Norwegian standards. As might be expected, a large part of it consisted of theology and canon law, but there were also some grammatical works and some sagas in the vernacular.[121]

The register also gives information of the bishop's journeys. In the spring and summer of 1308 he was on visitation in Nordfjord, north of Bergen, and in the autumn of 1309 in Hardanger to the south. On the latter occasion, he fulminates against local priests who do not respect the rule about celibacy, expressing his shock when visiting a priest at home who as a matter of course introduced him to his wife.[122] Visitations were an important part of a bishop's duty, in Norway as well as elsewhere, and also gave him part of his income. According to a source from the 1320s, the bishop of Bergen was entitled to a

---

121 Berulfsen, *Kulturtradisjon*, pp. 91-94.
122 DN III no. 84; cf. no. 85.

contribution of 48 barrels of strong beer, 60 pounds (c. nine tons) of ordinary beer, three barrels of wine, twelve pounds (a little less than two tons) of bread and similar quantities of butter and other kinds of food, for twelve days' visitation in Sogn, Sunnfjord and Nordfjord.[123] He must have had a very large entourage to consume all of this, although part of it was probably intended for the bishop's meeting with local people. However, in the fourteenth century, these contributions had developed into a permanent tax which the bishop was entitled to in any case.

In addition to these routine duties, the bishop also acted as the political leader of his diocese and in other political relationships. Bergen was one of the more important dioceses in the country, with the largest town by far and the main royal residence within its boundaries and with a variety of ecclesiastical institutions. Both mendicant orders, the Franciscans and the Dominicans, had houses there, and as usual, there were conflicts between them – in Bergen notably the Dominicans – and the parish priests about pastoral duties and incomes. Five of the fourteen royal chapels, including the residence of the master of the organisation, were situated within the boundaries of the diocese. After the chapel organisation had received its privilege from the pope in 1308, a conflict broke out between the bishop and the master about the extent of the privileges and various other matters in which the king was also involved, although Arne tried to avoid a direct conflict with him.[124] Arne was also engaged in the king's service after having become bishop, participating in a meeting of the king's council in Trondheim in 1307 and in an expedition to Denmark in 1309. This was a normal occurrence; although hardly belonging to the inner circle around the king, the bishops were often summoned to meetings with him and accompanied him on expeditions abroad, not in order to fight, but to take part in negotiations. This was also in accordance with earlier agreements. Bishops were also used as envoys, particularly on more formal and solemn occasions. The bishops' connection to the central government is also evident from the fact that a number important political documents have been preserved thanks to the survival of the *Registrum* of the bishops of Bergen (above p. 251), particularly from the period of Arne's successor Audfinn (1314-30).

The German merchants and artisans who had settled in Bergen at the time also created problems, as they refused to pay tithes, claiming that they were not permanently settled in the town. Arne was involved in a conflict with the German shoemakers over this question which also involved the king who was their protector. Finally, Arne also had to represent his diocese within the church province and the Universal Church. In 1306, he took part in

---

123 DN VII no. 98.
124 Bagge, *Den kongelige kapellgeistlighet*, pp. 101-32.

a provincial council in Oslo, where his legal learning may have been useful, and in 1311-12 he participated in the Council in Vienne. In 1308, he was engaged in a conflict with the archbishop about the episcopal election on the Faroe Islands. By contrast, there is no evidence of any conflict between Arne and his cathedral chapter, unlike the situation with the archbishop of Trondheim and the bishop of Stavanger at about the same time. The same applies to his two nearest successors, Audfinn and Håkon. The explanation may be the many other rival organisations and the bishops' willingness to defend the interests of the chapter against them.

The sources do not tell much of Bishop Arne's personality, nor of that of other bishops, many of whom are merely names to us. The numerous Icelandic bishops' sagas are somewhat more enlightening. Some of them, such as the one about Bishop Jon of Holar (d. 1121), are close to hagiography and written so long after their protagonists' death that they are unlikely to give much accurate information about them. From this point of view the most valuable accounts are those of Arne of Skálholt (bishop 1268-98) and Laurentius Kalvsson of Holar (bishop 1324-31), both of which must have been based on fairly extensive and reliable information and composed not long after the two bishops' death.[125] Both portraits are idealised but give a similar impression as that of the documentary sources the bishops' role. The bishops are pious but not otherworldly ascetics. They are depicted as chieftains who have at least some features in common with their lay counterparts.[126] They act as patrons for their subordinates; they are friendly and hospitable and make great efforts in procuring good food and drink for their guests and household, despite the fact that the Icelandic sees were poor, much more so than the Norwegian ones. The description of their activities focuses on law and administration rather than preaching and pastoral work. This applies particularly to Bishop Arne who spent most of his long pontificate fighting for the rights of the Church against secular lords. The subject of this conflict was the control of local churches which were still largely in the hands of lay patrons who appropriated most of their incomes and appointed the priests. The struggle ended with Archbishop Jørund's judgement in 1297, which largely supported Arne's point of view. Thus, the saga depicts Arne as the conscientious ecclesiastical bureaucrat who fought for the introduction of canon law in his diocese and was willing to suffer hardship and resistance from the laity without faltering from his purpose. At the same time, he was also a diplomat who managed to maintain a good personal relationship with his main adversary, the royal representative Hrafn Oddsson, and an intellectual, whose

---

125 *Árna saga; Laurentius saga.*
126 On the courtly ideal in the portraits of Icelandic bishops, see Bandlien, *Man or Monster?*, pp. 217-29.

Christian law for Iceland has been considered the masterpiece of Old Norse legislation.[127] Altogether, he emerges from the pages of the saga as an impressive personality.

The only real exception from this picture is Bishop Gudmund Arason of Holar (bishop 1203-37) who also fought against the lay chieftains, but whose struggle was apparently to a far greater extent based on his own interpretation of Christian doctrine and ethics. According to Edvard Bull, he was the only person in medieval Old Norse culture who was really inspired by the Gospel.[128] Although Bull's understanding of the Gospel depends too much on twentieth-century Protestant ideals of personal religion to be very helpful in interpreting the Middle Ages, he is probably correct in describing Bishop Gudmund as an exception. Gudmund is portrayed in the sources not only as a saint and ascetic but also as something like a social revolutionary who spends ecclesiastical wealth on the poor and is accused by the lay patrons of squandering the property of the Church. However, Gudmund's real character is not easy to grasp. His *vita* exists in several versions which have undergone considerable changes in the period after his death.[129]

Despite considerable differences between medieval bishops and modern bureaucrats regarding role expectations, control from above, incomes and so forth, the sources suggest a fairly clear framework for the bishop's role. The ideal bishop was depicted in numerous *vitae* and in theological and legal sources concerned with how he should administer his office. Canon law had undergone an enormous development since the early twelfth century and laid down detailed rules for the rights and duties of clerics and how the Church should be ruled. Parallel with this development, the pope had emerged as the real leader of the Church who, despite long distances and slow communications, interfered in numerous cases even in distant countries like Norway and Iceland. And finally, on the local level a newly elected bishop took over a well-developed administration which he was only able to change to a limited extent. In addition, most bishops were elected at an advanced age and normally did not hold their office for very long, usually for considerably shorter periods than kings. There were good and bad bishops; there might be considerable differences between ideal and practice, and there were great differences between the size and wealth of various dioceses and the complexity of their organisations, but a bishop's office was nevertheless fairly well defined all over Western Christendom.

The Norwegian dioceses were probably well below the average in absolute terms of wealth, at least if we confine ourselves to Europe north of the Alps where the dioceses

---

127 Seip, "Ennu en kristenrett", p. 602; Beistad, *Kirkens frihet*.
128 Bull, *Folk og kirke*, pp. 53 f.
129 Skorzewska, *Constructing a Cultus*, pp. 142-76, 226-28 and *passim*, points out that the picture of Gudmund as "the father of the poor" and in strong opposition to almost all the chieftains is mainly to be found in the later tradition, particularly in his last and longest *Vita* by the Benedictine monk Arngrímr from around 1350.

were considerably larger and richer than those of the south, particularly Italy. In relative terms, however, the five bishops belonged to the very top of Norwegian society. The archbishop was next to the king, and few if any lay magnates surpassed any of the others. In contrast to bishops in many other countries, notably Germany, the Norwegian bishops had little or no real secular power. According to a privilege from Magnus Erlingsson, renewed by Håkon Håkonsson,[130] the bishop of Stavanger ruled the town of Stavanger which had hardly more than a few hundred inhabitants. Occasionally, individual bishops also became *sysselmenn* on the king's behalf. Archbishop Jørund was even appointed the king's earl under Eirik Magnusson's reign, but Håkon V abolished this title in 1310, after Jørund's death.

As we have seen, an idea of the royal office also existed, but it was more vaguely defined than that of the bishop. The king's duties were not defined by law, and although the Church had developed a relatively detailed picture of the ideal king, there were also more secular ideals and considerable room for an individual king to define his office. In accordance with his exalted view of the king as God's representative on earth, the author of *The King's Mirror* depicts the king as mainly occupied with dispensing justice and urges him to devote most of his spare time to prayer and meditation. Neither statement should be regarded as an exact description of reality. The king may have acted as a judge more often than on the few occasions we have actual evidence of, and more often in the period before around 1280 than later, but this can hardly have been his main preoccupation (above pp. 224 f.). Engaging in prayer and meditation is also more likely to be an ideal than a reality, although many of the kings of the Sverre dynasty seem to have been pious men, in particular Magnus Håkonsson.

Confronted with the Father's august vision of the king, the Son in *The King's Mirror* – who is not depicted as being without knowledge of the world – takes courage to ask if this is really all there is to say about him: Should he not be allowed to amuse himself, for instance by hunting, as most kings actually seem to do? The Father's answer steers a middle way between the strict condemnation of hunting found in clerical moralists, and the enthusiasm for this sport in aristocratic circles: hunting gives the king necessary physical excercise and should be allowed as long as it does not interfere with more important duties; but the king should live for his kingdom and his office, not in order to amuse himself.[131]

---

130 DN no. 51, 1226-45; see Helle, *Stavanger*, pp. 80-85, 126-30.
131 *Kgs.*, p. 97; L, p. 297 f.; Bagge, *The Political Thought*, pp. 107 f. On the clerical condemnation of hunting, see e.g. John of Salisbury, *Policraticus* I.1, I.3-4. It may thus be significant that there is no evidence of St Louis hunting (Le Goff, *Saint Louis*, pp. 411, 691-93).

How much paperwork did the Norwegian king have to perform? In some of his letters, King Håkon V (1299-1319) refers to his sleepless nights, when he is absorbed in thoughts and worries on behalf of his kingdom – an allusion to *The King's Mirror*?[132] – and to the fact that he has been so busy with his many important tasks that he has not had the time for settling some particular business.[133] This is most probably an exaggeration, as the emphasis on the king's duties in *The King's Mirror* also seems to imply. The author cannot imagine any other duty than settling cases between people, and he implies that the king has ample time for prayer and meditation – if he is only willing.[134] Thus, the thirteenth-century Norwegian king was hardly a hard-working bureaucrat, although we should not go as far as one modern historian who suggests that the king's administrative duties were not more than he could manage easily, even if – as was likely – he spent most of his days with a hangover from the previous night's drinking.[135] Contemporary kings spent a large part of their time and resources hunting, when they were not at war, and the same was the case with the Norwegian kings, although the sources say very little about it. According to *Hákonar saga*, Håkon Håkonsson's son, Håkon the Younger, was spending much time hunting on horseback with hawks and dogs when he caught the illness that killed him.[136] There is evidence that this aristocratic sport was practised in Norway from the Viking Age onwards,[137] although there may have been considerable variation between individual kings. Most kings of the Sverre dynasty seem to have been well educated and had intellectual interests, in accordance with the saying "Rex illiteratus est quasi asinus coronatus".[138] Håkon Håkonsson went to school as a child, admittedly at a time when he was hardly considered as a candidate for the throne. His son and successor Magnus is said to have listened to theological lectures from the Franciscans in Bergen[139] and was probably personally engaged in the revision of the laws. Of Magnus's two sons, we know least of the elder, Eirik, who suffered from bad health from his youth, whereas the younger, Håkon, according to *Laurentius saga*, made a speech in Latin at a meeting to solve the conflict between the archbishop and his canons.[140] His commission of the very ambitious translation of Genesis and Exodus to be read at court in Lent is also evidence of intel-

---

132 *Kgs.*, p. 92, on the king's nightly meditation.
133 NGL III, pp. 117 and 121 (1316).
134 Bagge, *The Political Thought*, pp. 90-92, 189-92.
135 Lunden, *Sverrættens kongedømme*, p. 428.
136 *HH* ch. 288.
137 Scheel, "Falke og høgejagt".
138 John of Salisbury, *Policraticus* IV.6.
139 Munch, *NFH* IV.1, p. 674 with reference to the *Chronicon de Lanercost*.
140 *Laurentius saga*, pp. 14 f.

lectual interests.[141] It is therefore hardly a coincidence that his reign is the one from which we have most documents, which in turn strengthens the likelihood that he was personally involved in issuing them.

Even if the king spent a large part of his time on various forms of entertainment, this does not necessarily mean that he neglected the government of his realm. The picture of the drinking, hunting and womanizing king who had no serious business to undertake requires a modern view of such activities, including the distinction between working hours and leisure hours. The king was king all the time, and his company in hunting and drinking parties consisted of the great men of the realm, whose assistance he needed and whom he had to cultivate in order to carry out his political goals. He had to develop a good relationship with them, settle conflicts between them, and strike the right balance between generosity and friendliness on the one hand, and strictness and authority on the other, all of which demanded a considerable amount of diplomatic skill. In 1256, Tord Kakale, Snorre's nephew, and Gissur Torvaldson, who were bitter enemies, stayed at Håkon's court. Tord urged the king to send Gissur away, and said that it was likely that conflicts would arise if they both were in the same city. The king answered: "How can you expect me to send away my friend Gissur based on what you have said; would you rather not be in Heaven if Gissur was there?" "I would gladly be there, my Lord!" replied Tord, "but we would have to be far apart."[142]

The conflicts between the Norwegian aristocrats were probably not as serious as those between the Icelandic chieftains, whom Håkon often invited to Norway in order to gain control over Iceland. Yet they were present, and it required a good bit of political handiwork from the king to deal with them. In the saga we often encounter Håkon as a "fire extinguisher" when conflicts break out between aristocrats or between their followers. From the king's point of view, the problem had been to have the best possible relationship with these men, and to use his resources in such a way as to get as much as possible out of their service. Not only were diplomatic skills and favours and concessions needed, however; the king also had to possess the personal qualities that made him respected. To take an English example: in addition to several matters of conflict between King Henry III and his brother-in-law Simon de Montfort, who eventually rebelled against him, an episode from the war in France in 1242 caused a heavy strain on the relationship between the two men. Simon was ordered by the king to come to his aid, which he did, without

---

141 *Stjórn*, pp. 1-299; covering Genesis and Exodus 1-18, with extensive theological commentaries; cf. Astås, *Biblical Compilation* and above p. 158.

142 "Konungr svarar: 'hver ván er þér þess, at ek reka Gizur, frænda minn, frá mér fyrir þessi ummæli þín; eða mundir þú eigi vilja vera í himinríki, er Gizur væri þar fyrir?' 'Vera gjarna, herra!' segir Þórðr, 'ok væri þó langt í milli okkar'" (*Sturl.* II, p. 300).

being able to save him from a humiliating defeat, after which Simon lost his temper and told the king that he should have been locked up.[143] Part of Henry's troubles during his reign may have been due to performances like this, as is even more evident in the case of his grandson Edward II who was eventually deposed.

The idea of the royal office was strong enough in the thirteenth century to give its holder a considerable amount of protection against criticism and deposition, but to be an efficient ruler he had to make himself respected with qualities like courage, skill, prudence, eloquence, and the ability to deal with various kinds of people. From this point of view, the kings' sagas can be read as a series of mirrors of princes, of secular and pragmatic rather than religious character, with a continuous presentation and discussion of royal qualities and royal behaviour. The king has to show his intelligence, wit, eloquence and various skills in competition or interaction with other men, and the results of these encounters largely determine his success or failure. Although respect for high status and the royal office usually results in some positive comments, there are also examples of kings who fail to make themselves respected and have to suffer the consequences:[144] the cruel and greedy Eirikssons who are killed one after the other, the stingy Øystein Haraldsson who is told by some of his men before they leave him to use his gold chests to defend his kingdom, and the foolish and arrogant Magnus Sigurdsson who is taken captive by his enemy and blinded, castrated, and mutilated. The positive contrast to these examples is represented by great and heroic kings like Olav Tryggvason, St Olav, and Magnus Barelegs, great sportsmen and warriors, with sharp and piercing eyes, and great leaders of men; or the more peaceful type, like Øystein Magnusson; or a mixture of the two, like Håkon the Good and Magnus the Good, and finally, closer to the time of writing, King Sverre, who was mainly a warrior king but of a new kind, a tactician and strategist rather than a hero, and with a marvellous ability to lead and inspire his men.[145]

Clearly, the royal ideal had undergone a considerable change from the heroic-charismatic warrior in the skaldic poetry to the Christian *rex iustus* of *The King's Mirror*, a change that has a parallel in increasing bureaucratisation and the king acting more through intermediaries. A change from hero to strategist had already taken place under Sverre, who directed the operations rather than fighting in person, as had been the practice earlier, and who even joked about his lack of personal courage.[146] His grandson Håkon Håkonsson continued the practice, apparently keeping even more distant from the actual fighting,

---

143 Maddicott, *Simon de Montfort*, pp. 31 f.
144 For the following examples, see Bagge, *Society and Politics*, pp. 147-53, 156-58.
145 Bagge, *From Gang Leader*, pp. 21-51.
146 Ibid., p. 28.

while being involved in war to a lesser extent.¹⁴⁷ In the peaceful period after Håkon's death, his successors became more like administrators than warriors, leading most of the relatively few larger expeditions that took place during their reign but mainly dealing with other matters. As we have no narrative source dealing with these rulers, we cannot measure how much the ideal changed, although the portrait of Håkon Håkonsson in his saga may give some indication. Most modern scholars have found this portrait somewhat pale, which they have explained partly as the result of the deficiency of the author, Sturla, in describing character and partly as an expression of Håkon's actual dullness and mediocrity.¹⁴⁸ The most likely explanation, however, is the greater importance of the royal office and the Christian *rex iustus* ideology in the saga which must have prevented Sturla from giving the personal glimpses that make the earlier sagas so fascinating. It would be contrary to the new ideas of the royal office to show the king in competition with other men in order to prove his superiority. In the final portrait at the end of the saga, civilian matters are also more prominent than in earlier portraits, including the one of Sverre in his saga. Sturla lists Håkon's building activities and legal reforms and points to his kindness to the poor, a typical *rex iustus* feature which is absent in earlier descriptions in the secular sagas. In the narrative, Sturla is also more concerned with Håkon's justice and defence of the principles of Christian monarchy than with his cleverness and heroic qualities. Despite these limitations, *Hákonar saga* is in many ways a remarkable piece of literature and a renewal of the saga genre.¹⁴⁹

Nevertheless, there is also a certain amount of continuity. Qualities like intelligence and eloquence are highly regarded in the sagas, and the ability to achieve one's aims is considered more important than heroic behaviour. Given this, we are dealing with the same qualities applied to other circumstances in *Hákonar saga*. Sturla gives many examples of Håkon acting as a strong and resolute king who on a number of occasions reaches the right decisions, with or against the advice of his counsellors, a picture that must at least to some extent correspond to reality. Håkon would hardly have achieved what he did without considerable ability. The need for the king to be able to deal with people and impress them must also have been largely similar to that in the earlier period. As far as we can judge from the limited sources available, most of kings in the period 1217-1319 must have been quite successful in this respect.

---

147 Ibid., pp. 143-46.
148 Koht, "Skule jarl", p. 429; Paasche, "Norges og Islands litteratur", p. 404; Helle, "Innleiing", pp. 12 f.; Bjørgo, "Skriftlege kjelder", pp. 227-29; Pálsson, "Hákonar saga", pp. 53 f.; Magerøy, "Innleiing", pp. 8-14.
149 Bagge, *From Gang Leader*, pp. 91-93, 114-19, 147-55, 157 f.

Did Norway Become a State? Government, Obedience and Clientelism

The previous discussion has given the impression of a considerable social change through the development of the royal and ecclesiastical bureaucracy, the increased use of writing, public justice and legislation, the formation of a royal and ecclesiastical hierarchy, a clearer concept of public office, and patronage and personal links which to some extent were replaced with bureaucratic structures. The problem with this conclusion is that it is mostly based on official evidence, which, as already pointed out, may give an exaggerated impression of bureaucratisation.[150] There is little evidence to confirm and correct this picture, but we get some glimpses in the later sagas, notably *Hákonar saga*, and in royal ordinances complaining about various kinds of abuse from the royal officials.

Hákonar saga presents a clear contrast to *Sverris saga* regarding the relationship between the king, the magnates and royal officials and the people. Whereas *Sverris saga* contains numerous examples of magnates being disloyal to the king, *Hákonar saga* has only two examples within Norway itself, Bishop Nikolas Arnesson and Skule.[151] Neither of these two are examples of men directly subordinated to the king who fail to obey him. Although bishops had some duties towards the king and owed him loyalty in the sense that they should not support his enemies within or outside the country, their loyalty was divided between the king and the Church, and they were not the king's servants in any direct sense. Moreover, Bishop Nikolas, who according to the saga and most probably also in actuality was repeatedly intriguing against Sverre as well as Håkon during the long period he held office as bishop of Oslo (1190-1225), was also one of the greatest magnates in the country, linked with family ties to Magnus's faction. His office as bishop made it difficult to punish his disloyalty, particularly as the Birchlegs' position in Eastern Norway was weak until after Nikolas's death. Thus, the case of Nikolas does not tell us more than we might have expected in advance, namely that it took time for Håkon to get a firm grasp on the whole country.

The example of Skule may serve as an example of a new relationship between the king and his men; the conflict between the two seems mainly to have been the result of Håkon's systematic attempt to weaken Skule's position.[152] The relationship between Håkon and Skule seems originally to have been very close to a co-rulership, not only in

---

150 As underlined particularly by Orning, *Uforutsigbarhet*.
151 Orning, *Uforutsigbarhet*, pp. 86 ff., 150-63, claims that the different representation of the two reigns in the sagas are an expression of ideology rather than reality, but there is much to suggest that the reality was also different. See Bagge, Review of Orning, *Uforutsigbarhet*, pp. 644-47.
152 Lunden, *Norge under Sverreætten*, pp. 198-208; Bagge, *From Gang Leader*, pp. 113 f. There has been a number of different interpretations of the conflict; see Bagge, *From Gang Leader*, pp. 107-19 with references. Orning, "Håkon Håkonsson" and *Uforutsigbarhet*, pp. 125-27, 134 f., regards the conflict as the result of accidental clashes.

the sense that Skule actually held nearly one half of the country but also because he was nearly Håkon's equal in rank, with only the royal title as a distinction between them.[153] After Håkon's election in 1217, he refused to swear an oath to him until the relationship between the two had been settled, and the oath he finally swore was conditional on Håkon keeping the settlement. Moreover, the retainers swore oaths to both Håkon and Skule.[154] A reduction of Skule's power was clearly Håkon's aim at the meeting in 1223 (below pp. 336-39). Here he partially succeeded, although without any clear subordination on Skule's part. Thereafter, the saga only gives a few examples of rivalries between the two rulers, until 1233, when a dramatic confrontation took place, clearly staged by Håkon.[155] The saga mentions accusations from Håkon and particularly from his men against Skule, against which Skule defends himself with great eloquence. This, however, leads to the final challenge from one of Håkon's men: To show his obedience towards the king, Skule should take off his overcoat and kneel for the king, leaving the whole matter to his power and mercy. The king then demands all who will serve him to follow him into the church – with the meeting taking place outside Bergen Cathedral. Skule remains outside, but the archbishop finally manages to reconcile him to Håkon to the latter's satisfaction, and the earl gives his hand to the agreement. Sturla ends the passage by remarking that things went better between the two than before but that, according to people who knew them, there was no longer full trust between them.

Although the saga gives no details about the background of this confrontation, it seems pretty clear that we are dealing with a challenge from Håkon against Skule's whole position, with the intention of changing it from that of a co-ruler to that of a subject. The act of submission demanded of Skule resembles a *deditio*, where a rebel or an enemy receives the king's grace by humiliating himself.[156] The ritual seems to have been unusual in Norway and reserved for people who were in great need of forgiveness, such as Torstein Kugad, a man of far lower rank than Skule who had twice surrendered to Sverre's enemies and joined them,[157] and the earl of Orkneys, Harald, who had given support to rebels against Sverre.[158] The Son's surprise at being told by the Father in *The King's Mirror* that a man approaching the king should take off his cloak (above p. 172) points in the same direction. Skule has clearly never done anything similar before and resists. The interpretation of the

---

153   Although there is no direct evidence about Skule's degree of independence within his territory, it was probably considerable. See the discussion by Blom, *Samkongedømme*, pp. 20-27.
154   *HH* chs. 17, 24.
155   *HH* ch. 177; Bagge, "Changing the Rules".
156   Althoff, *Spielregeln*, pp. 99-125.
157   *Ss.* ch. 153. *Ss.* chs. 108, 137, 152-53; Orning, *Uforutsigbarhet*, p. 127.
158   *Ss.* ch. 125.

conflict as the result of an offensive from Håkon is further confirmed by the brief remark in the saga shortly before about the friendship between Skule and Knut Håkonsson being broken. Knut had been the leader of the Ribbungs during the final phase of the rebellion but had surrendered on honorable terms and received a small fief (*lén*).[159] He had also married Skule's daughter Ingrid. The saga explains the end of the friendship between the two men with her death in 1232, which seems reasonable enough, as there was no longer any tie of loyalty between them.[160] Moreover, the saga points to Knut's discontent with the size of his fief which, understandably enough, he turned against Skule rather than Håkon, as Skule's position was in some sense parallel to his own – he also had a share in the king's power without being king himself, and governed nearly half the country. Knut's complaint was shared by several of the *lendmenn* who may have had similar ambitions.[161] Combined with the fact that Håkon now had the time to consolidate his grip on the country after the end of the Ribbung rebellion in 1227, these reactions presented a good opportunity to move against Skule.

The saga's account of the result of this confrontation is vague. It is not quite clear whether the statement that Skule gave his hand to Håkon refers to the normal shaking of hands between equal parties to seal an agreement[162] or to a greater amount of submission, as suggested by the skaldic stanza,[163] but he hardly performed the ritual initially demanded of him. The reference to the mediation of the archbishop and the bishops suggests some kind of compromise, which is confirmed by a papal letter from 11 October 1234, taking Skule under papal protection and confirming the recent agreement between him and Håkon.[164] The letter refers to a recent conflict which was solved by the mediation of good men and demands that this agreement be respected. The agreement in question must either be the one from 1233, which must then have been more satisfactory to Skule than the saga implies, or a later one not mentioned in the saga, in that case from the summer of 1234, when the two were together and according to the saga things were going

---

159 According to the saga (*HH* ch. 174), he had half of Sogn and half of Rygjafylke which probably amounted to two normal districts (*sýslur*).
160 On the importance of the ties of loyalty formed through women and dissolved through their death, see Hermanson, *Släkt, vänner och makt*, pp. 99-102, 108-11 and *passim*.
161 Lunden, *Norge under Sverreætten*, pp. 199-203.
162 Hamre, "Handarband".
163 The skaldic stanza is rendered somewhat differently in the various manuscripts. Finnur Jónsson reconstructs its second half in the following way: "alt lagði þá fromuðr frægða, / fekk sætt af því stillir rekka, / snildar skýrs ok seldi vára / sitt mál í kné lituðs stála" ("he who performed famous deeds submitted his whole cause to the eloquent warrior's decision and gave sworn promises; the prince of men received a settlement in this way") (*Skjalded.* B II, p. 105; cf. A II, p. 93).
164 DN I no. 15.

well between them.[165] The former interpretation is the more likely,[166] which in turn means that the meeting in 1233 ended in a compromise and not in a victory for Håkon, as the saga and particularly Olav's stanza seem to imply. This also confirms that Håkon was the aggressive party, that he wanted to reduce Skule's territory, and that Skule was the more eager to uphold the compromise entered into in 1233.

The saga's account of the following years consists of a series of negotiations between the two rivals in which attempts are made to solve various issues between them. These issues are rarely specified; mostly, anonymous slanderers are blamed for them, whereas the relationship between Håkon and Skule is usually said to have been good as long as they were together. The reason for Sturla's reticence is clearly the respect due to Skule as the dowager queen's father – she was still living when the saga was composed – and the grandfather of the ruling king, Magnus. Thus, Sturla tries to harmonise two conflicting aims: the distinction between the lawful king and the rebel on the one hand, and the wish to blame Skule as little as possible on the other. It is therefore hardly possible to distinguish between neutral narrative and ideological interpretation in the saga's account, as is Orning's argument for regarding the conflict as a series of accidental clashes (above p. 282). Most probably, Sturla only repeats the official interpretation from Håkon's own time, as the main elements of this presentation are already present in his brother Olav Kvitaskald's poem, probably composed shortly after Skule's death.[167] Only one concrete issue is mentioned in the saga, namely Skule's attempt to have his son Peter succeed him, which Håkon refused.[168] Håkon was married to Skule's daughter and would therefore have been the alternative successor, whereas Skule's grandson through his daughter would in turn have succeeded Håkon. This issue is also closely connected to the main conflict between the two. If Skule was a co-ruler, his demand might be regarded as reasonable, although there was no rule about an earl's right to pass his part of the country on to his sons. By contrast, he could hardly claim any right as a subject; the best he could hope for was a special privilege from the king, which might even be contested by the king's suc-

---

165 *HH* ch. 179.
166 The arguments for this are, first, that a settlement is actually mentioned in the saga in the autumn of 1233 but not in the summer of 1234, and, second, that the papal letter is issued together with two others, defending the bishop of Hamar against Håkon's attempt to reclaim Helgøya, DN I no. 13 (5 Oct.) and no. 14 (11 Oct.). The saga informs that this conflict broke out in the spring of 1234 and caused Bishop Pål to go to Rome to appeal to the pope. As he received support from Skule in this conflict (see below), he most probably returned the favour by aiding Skule in obtaining the pope's protection.
167 *Skjalded.* B II, pp. 105-8, see above n. 163.
168 *HH* ch. 187. Peter was Skule's son by a woman who only admitted that Skule was the father after her husband's disappearance around 1229-30 (*HH* ch. 164).

cessors (see p. 300). In addition, the saga hints that Skule supported Bishop Pål of Hamar against Håkon in the conflict over Helgøya in Mjøsa.[169]

It seems a likely hypothesis that the various issues mentioned in the saga all relate to the essential question brought up at the confrontation in 1233: the relationship between the two rulers. Håkon wanted Skule to submit to him more directly than he had before 1233, and probably also to reduce his territory. He had only partially succeeded in this in 1233 and probably continued his pressure against Skule during the following years. Nevertheless, he hardly aimed at deposing Skule and he probably did not want a war; if so, he would have used the opportunity in 1235-36, when, according to the saga, he saved the situation by a compromise, allowing Skule to dispose of one third of the administrative districts (*sýslur*) in Eastern Norway over the winter 1235-36.[170] This led to a new arrangement between the two; Skule now received his third of the country in the form of one third of all the districts throughout the country instead of as one block. In addition, he received a higher rank by being appointed duke, the first in Norwegian history. This change has usually been interpreted as a deterioration of Skule's position, despite the advancement. However, it also meant an opportunity for Skule to increase his influence in other parts of the country, notably in Eastern Norway,[171] whereas he might have calculated that his influence in Trøndelag would in any case have been considerable. From Håkon's point of view, the new arrangement seems to be intended to get Skule under stricter control, perhaps combined with an effort to appease him by involving him more in the central government. In any case, it is clear that Håkon and Skule spent considerably more time together in the period 1237-39 than previously. Quite possibly, Håkon had now achieved what he wanted and could afford to wait for Skule' death to take over his part of the country; Skule turned fifty in 1239, when Håkon was only thirty-five. Thus, Skule's rebellion can neither be understood as deliberately provoked by Håkon nor as the result of accidental clashes between the two. The most likely explanation is that it was the result of a systematic attempt from Håkon to change the relationship between the two from one of co-rulers of nearly the same rank to that of a king and his mightiest subject; he probably also hoped to reduce Skule's territory, a change Skule resisted.

Håkon's twenty-three years as sole ruler of the country should therefore be regarded as the beginning of a new epoch in Norwegian state formation, in accordance with common scholarly opinion. Håkon's consistent attempts to define Skule's position as that of a subject coincides with the clearer distinction between rulers and subjects expressed in

---

169   *HH* ch. 188; see also the papal intervention in the issue, DN I no. 13-14. The island had been given to the see by a Crozier king whom Håkon did not recognise.
170   *HH* chs. 185-87.
171   Blom, *Samkongedømme*, pp. 26 f.

The King's Mirror, the National Law, the Hird Law and the oaths demanded of the king's officials in the latter. In particular, it anticipates the statement in the Hird Law that it will be best if there were no earl at all[172] and Håkon V marking as traitors those who made the young king promote others than members of the dynasty to princely rank (below p. 327). Skule's fall marked a new relationship between the king and the aristocracy and was largely the result of the king's deliberate attempt to introduce such a change. From now on, positions like Skule's would be reserved for the king's direct descendants. Skule held his rank as the result of the unclear rules of succession which had now been replaced by the Law of Succession of 1260, combined with the fact that he was the king's father-in-law. Since the eleventh century, it had been unusual for kings to marry daughters of Norwegian magnates (above p. 48), and Håkon was the last Norwegian king in the Middle Ages to do so. The opposite relationship, that of magnates marrying women of the royal house, which was more common earlier, also came to an end during Håkon's reign. Only the king's illegitimate daughters could contract such marriages, such as when Håkon V's daughter Agnes married Havtore Jonsson, a marriage that greatly increased the prestige of Havtore and his descendants. Although, as is evident from the examples of Denmark and Sweden, the introduction of individual succession was no guarantee against rivalry between the king's sons, the number of potential rivals of the ruling king had been significantly reduced during the twelfth and thirteenth centuries. Moreover, it was far safer to be king at that time than before, which was not only important for the king himself, but a good indication of social change. The last Norwegian king recognised as the ruler of the whole country to suffer a violent death was Magnus Erlingsson in 1184. Before that time, a violent death had been the rule and a peaceful one the exception. As far as we know, only six kings before that time died peacefully in their beds: Harald Finehair, Magnus the Good, Magnus Haraldsson, and the three sons of Magnus Barelegs.

Turning to the king's officials, it is clear that the *sysselmenn* and their subordinates were neither perfect bureaucrats nor objective attorneys or judges. On the one hand, they were greedy and tried to promote their own interests; on the other, they were no representatives of an almighty administrative power but had to adapt to local conditions and establish a working relationship with powerful local groups.[173] Håkon V frequently complained about the corruption and abuse among his local officials: they summoned people without turning up themselves, they failed to settle cases while still taking the fines, they accused

---

172 H 9.
173 Orning, "Kongemaktens lokale maktgrunnlag", p. 680 n. 18 with references, including NGL III no. 18 (1303) on threats against royal officials from the relatives of criminals who had been arrested or punished by them. The king commands that such men should be fined and imprisoned until they find men to guarantee for their good behaviour.

wealthy people wrongly in order to profit from the fines and neglected to punish crimes committed by those who could not pay, they favoured their friends and relatives in lawsuits or accepted bribes from the parties.[174] As Orning points out, these abuses should not simply be understood as wrongdoings but also as evidence that norms in local society differed from the legal and bureaucratic ones of the official sources; the ideal of objective justice counted for less in local society, whereas the traditional ideals of friendship and patronage lingered on. Still, the existence of the royal officials increased the king's control of local society. He could appoint and depose them, they were his subordinates and under some control by him, and although their relationship to their subordinates as well as to the king may be regarded as clientelistic rather than bureaucratic, this relationship might also be exploited by the king who had now become the patron of most of the powerful men in the country in a more direct sense than before.

In some cases the saga shows the king as a negotiator and peacemaker when conflicts are about to break out between his and Skule's men.[175] In one case, Håkon acts according to the principle laid down in the New Law of 1260, forbidding revenge on an innocent kinsman of the killer. By contrast, an example in *Sturlunga saga* shows Håkon intervening in a conflict in the 1250s between the Icelandic chieftain Torgils Skardi and Earl Knut, the former Ribbung leader. Håkon supports Torgils because of his friendship with him, despite the fact that Torgils had protected a man who had committed a crime by wounding one of the earl's men. Thus, Håkon acts as a patron protecting his friend, not as an objective judge.[176] An incident reported in *Hákonar saga* supports this. After the settlement between the Birchlegs and the Croziers in 1217, Ragnvald Hallkjellsson, a former *sysselmann* for the Croziers in Romerike, was transferred to Follo near Oslo. He had a bad reputation for being harsh and greedy, and at his first meeting with his new subordinates, they killed him. Learning of this, Håkon declares that he will not seek revenge for him because Ragnvald and his kinsmen have always been enemies of Håkon's kindred. Since the people of the region killed him without cause, however, he will allow Skule to take revenge.[177] This is a remarkable statement from a king at the killing of one of his officials and shows the limitation of the state and *rex iustus* perspective in the saga. Although it may not be surprising that the fourteen-year-old Håkon Håkonsson reacted in such a manner in 1218, it is more difficult to understand why none of his counsellors had any

---

174 Orning, "Kongemaktens lokale maktgrunnlag", pp. 678-80 with references. See also above p. 221 and Holmsen, *Nye studier*, pp. 175-79.
175 Bagge, *From Gang Leader*, pp. 149 f.
176 Orning, *Uforutsigbarhet*, pp. 269 f.
177 *HH* chs. 32, 70. Håkon's words are rendered somewhat differently in the various manuscripts, but the wording given above makes the best sense. See Bagge, *From Gang Leader*, pp. 150 f.

objections. Above all, the fact that the incident was recorded, without further comment, nearly fifty years later in the official biography of Håkon is an indication of the limitation of the bureaucratic mindset in Norway in the thirteenth century.

Nevertheless, the king would probably have reacted differently to the killing of his local representative towards the end of the thirteenth century, partly for "bureaucratic" reasons, but at least because it would have been difficult to imagine a local representative at this time who was not the king's friend. All men in the country owed loyalty to the king, although they may have been more or less actively engaged in his service, and there was no alternative patron to turn to, unless they went abroad. *The King's Mirror* adduces as an argument for entering the king's service that higher fines were to be paid for killing the king's men than other men,[178] which may be interpreted as an argument based on a patron/client relationship rather than on bureaucratic rules: Being more powerful than other men, the king was able to punish those more severely who killed or harmed his clients. The effect of this reasoning might nevertheless be the same as that of the bureaucratic one.

The episodes referred to above might be considered as a modification of the saga's usual description of Håkon as a *rex iustus* above the parties. However, the sagas, including *Hákonar saga*, do not deal with the routine aspects of the royal administration, including justice; the episodes referred to here are all included because they gave rise to dangerous situations and concerned the relationship between Håkon and Skule. We may conclude from them that the king had to play other roles than that of the impartial judge, but not that the judicial system remained unchanged in the thirteenth century. Of course, kings acted as patrons and protected their friends throughout the *ancien régime*. The difference compared to the early period is, first, the greater social distance between the king and his friends and clients, and, second, the existence of a bureaucratic or quasi-bureaucratic system in addition to the friendship. Whereas earlier, the king formed alliances with magnates, giving them incomes from land in return for political and military support that was not very specified, he now gave them clearly defined districts to govern as well as duties that were to some extent specified, as stated in the *sysselmann*'s oath (above p. 235).

In discussing the bureaucratisation of society it is also necessary to focus on the Church and not only the monarchy. The addition of the Church means a doubling of the amount of bureaucratisation, with another hierarchy and organisation, covering the whole country and controlling important aspects of people's lives and another judicial system. The sources contain very little evidence of royal and ecclesiastical government in practice on the local level before the fourteenth century. Magne Njåstad's recent study gives a very

---

178 *Kgs.* p. 40.

different picture of two local regions during the Later Middle Ages – Østfold and Jämtland – with strong central control in the former and a weaker one in the latter.[179] However, as Jämtland was a very distant inland region, belonging to the Swedish rather than to the Norwegian church province, it seems a likely hypothesis that Østfold was the more representative of the two, which is further confirmed by Dørum's examination of Romerike.[180] The highland regions in the inner part of the country may have resembled Jämtland, but the lowlands in the east and the coastal regions in Western Norway and Trøndelag, where most of the people lived, are more likely to have resembled Østfold.

In analysing the degree of bureaucratisation in thirteenth- and fourteenth-century Norway, we have to be aware that a loyal and incorrupt civil servant who obeys the rules regardless of the personal presence of his master is probably rare before the nineteenth century, when it can be illustrated by the famous anecdote of the government minister Niels Vogt (1817-94) who kept two ink-pots on his desk, one for official letters, paid for by the state, and one for private ones, paid for by himself. To the question of whether he really wrote private letters while working in his office, Vogt replied that of course he did not, but it happened that he remained there after the official working hours in order to write some private letters. This is the rational and essentially modern bureaucracy theorised by Max Weber which is not to be found in fully developed form until the end of the eighteenth century.[181] By contrast, the *ancien régime* of the Middle Ages and the Early Modern Period was characterised by widespread corruption and an extensive use of patronage. Patronage was essential to advancement in the royal or ecclesiastical bureaucracy. Making a good impression on the king was the key to any advancement in his service, in *The King's Mirror* as well as at the court of Louis XIV or Frederik IV of Denmark-Norway (1699-1730).[182] The same of course applied to the ranks below the king. Not only friendship and patronage but also family was essential. All Louis XIV's ministers belonged to two families which were in turn related; the top of his bureaucracy was a family network.[183] Thus medieval and early modern bureaucratisation did not mean that patronage was replaced with objective standards and impersonal connections, but that the king – or, in the Church, the pope – became the supreme patron with no rival.

The bureaucracy of the *ancien régime* might in many respects be inefficient as well as harmful to the people but it did make a substantial number of men identify their interests with those of the government and thus add to the wealth, power, and prestige of the

---

179 Njåstad, *Grenser*, pp. 219-26 and *passim*.
180 Dørum, *Romerike*, pp. 293-422.
181 Reinhard, "Introduction", p. 13.
182 Lind, "Clientelism", pp. 144 f. and *passim*.
183 Reinhard, "Introduction", p. 9.

ruler. Moreover, the "objectivity" of the bureaucracy in modern society implies a distinction between the administrative and political sphere that did not exist in the Middle Ages. Law and administration should be predictable and governed by rules, but this does not apply to politics, which concerns conflicting interests and necessitates flexibility and compromises in concrete situations. Medieval politics was often conducted in a legal and religious language which concealed the interest aspect, but we cannot conclude from this that law and bureaucracy generally was an illusion. From this point of view, what seems to have happened according to sources like *Hákonar saga* and above all *The King's Mirror* was "the end of politics". Whereas in the earlier sagas, notably *Heimskringla*, it is easy to follow "a game of politics" familiar to modern observers, where the actors try to achieve their aims by forming alliances, outwitting their opponents or by direct use of violence, politics in these later sources is clouded in a language of objective justice. It is easy to agree with Orning that this is ideology rather than a description of reality; no king would survive if he only behaved in accordance with this ideology. The king continued to favour his friends and punish his enemies, but this does not mean that the new principles were an illusion. Although neither the judicial system nor the royal and ecclesiastical bureaucracies functioned in perfect accordance with them, they served as a legal basis for an organisation of society that differed significantly from the earlier one.

Conclusion

We can thus conclude that the development of a bureaucracy and a bureaucratic mentality forms another argument in favour of state formation in the period 900-1350. Admittedly, the earliest period lies in the dark, in this as in other fields, and we may easily exaggerate its primitive character because of the lack of written sources. We should not underestimate the power and resources available to the Viking chieftains who ruled Norway or parts of it in the tenth and first half of the eleventh centuries, but it is nevertheless difficult to believe in a very developed bureaucratic system. The king depended on his wealth, personal ability and charisma, and the magnates he enlisted in his service were "friends" rather than subordinates in a bureaucratic system. The introduction of the ecclesiastical organisation and its full development from around the time of the establishment of the archbishopric in 1152/53 and the introduction of royal justice and transformation of the royal administration during and after the civil wars changed this. A bureaucratic or quasi-bureaucratic system took shape, with formal appointments, fixed districts and at least some definitions of rights and duties. The system differed significantly from the Weberian model of a bureaucracy and may also be considered rudimentary compared to later bureaucratic organisations during the old regime, but nevertheless marks a significant change compared to the previous period. The increased use of script in the administration and the greater standardisation of the documents underline this change, although Norway was behind the more advanced contemporary administrations. At the top of the royal and ecclesiastical organisation, the positions of the leaders, the king and the bishops, had become more clearly defined and their authority less dependent on their personal ability, although it was still important. Whereas bureaucratisation in Norway may thus in many respects seem modest compared to that of countries like England at the same time, it was in one respect more advanced. On the secular side, there was no exemption from the king's authority, no hereditary fiefs and no private jurisdiction. On the ecclesiastical side, the difference between Norway and other countries was less, but the Norwegian Church seems to have been less dependent on lay patronage and more united under the leadership of the archbishop and bishops than the Church in many other countries.

This bureaucratisation forms another element in the package introduced to Norway from Western Christendom as the result of the conversion. This is most obvious in the case of the Church which was clearly introduced from abroad and which had an organisation that was basically similar to most other countries, although with some local adaptation. The royal administration, based on *sysselmenn*, also shows some basic similarity to the local administration in other countries at that time, although external influence is not necessary to explain such a simple organisation. For the royal as well as the ecclesiastical organisation, the most obvious change that took place during the period was the introduction of writing as a standard element, another consequence of the integration into Western Christendom. An original feature in Norway, compared to most other countries, including the neighbouring ones, was the extensive use of the vernacular. This is often taken as evidence of greater spread of literacy, from a few experts to wider layers of the population.[184] It is still uncertain to what extent this was the case in Norway; the extant amount of administrative documents does not point in this direction, but we have to take into account that only a fragment of what once existed has been preserved.

Altogether, the conclusion from the previous chapter suggests an intermediate position between the two opposite views: a greater distance from the modern state than envisaged by the most eager adherents of the notion of "Norway becomes a state", but a greater change from the early medieval society based on friendship, patronage and competition between powerful magnates than has been maintained by their critics.

---

184 Pollock, "The Transformation", pp. 255-59.

The Division of Power and its Social Foundation

As we have seen, the main trend in the development of Norwegian society from the tenth to the thirteenth century is centralisation. A greater amount of wealth and power was vested in the king and his court and in bishops and prelates. The military forces were increasingly controlled by the king and the royal government; the new religion and the development of public justice worked in the same direction, as did bureaucratisation and the introduction of script in the administration. The same development is expressed in the changes in the central political institutions. The reality behind this arrangement has been the subject of much discussion, a discussion that has usually centred on the relationship between four main groups: the king, the Church, the secular aristocracy, and the peasants.[1] Schematically, most nineteenth-century scholars can be said to have assumed an alliance between the king and the peasants against the Church and the aristocracy, while the Marxist historians from the beginning of the twentieth century operated with a basic affiliation between the king, the Church and the aristocracy in their capacity as landowning upper class against the peasants, who had to carry the burdens of the tightly organised society of the High Middle Ages. From the middle of the twentieth century, there has been a certain tendency towards the older view. The discussion in this context has centred specifically on the power of the monarchy. While the Marxist school claims that the king was an instrument of the landowning upper class, and had little real power (the theory of the "instrument monarchy"), current research claims that the king's personal position was on the contrary very strong. This view has primarily been combined with the view that the king was relatively free in relation to the other groups, and could for example acquire an independent platform in relationship to the landowning aristocracy through "a functional relationship to peasant society." However, the most recent version of the "instrument monarchy", brought forward by Kåre Lunden, accepts the idea of a strong personal monarchy, but argues that from a social point of view this monarchy nevertheless acted as an instrument of the landed aristocracy.[2] The following discussion will deal with these interpretations, the purely constitutional aspect, how the formal power was divided, as well as the social basis of this division. In connection to

---

1   For the following, see Helle, "Tendenser", pp. 349 ff., and "Norway in the High Middle Ages", pp. 176 ff.; Bagge, "The Middle Ages", pp. 118-24.
2   Lunden, "Det norske kongedømet".

this, the reception of contemporary constitutional theories will be discussed, as well as the political consequences of the changes in social structure discussed above.

The King and the Church: From the Foundation of the Church Province to the Death of Håkon Håkonsson

The most explicit constitutional discussion in medieval Norway was conducted between the monarchy and the Church. Both parties in principle accepted a kind of division between the spiritual and the secular sphere, but the borderline between the two was not easy to draw in practice. Moreover, theories involving the superiority of one party over the other were developed on both sides. The importance of the Church and Christianity for the king's power is evident from its doctrine of the king ruling on God's behalf, expressed particularly clearly in the unction and coronation, as well as its contribution to the change in justice and legislation. However, the Church's demand for liberty from lay interference (*libertas ecclesiae*) and even a certain amount of superiority over the secular power, based on its greater insight in doctrine and Christian ethics, was also a challenge to the monarchy. A royal privilege from the foundation of the archdiocese in 1152/53, now lost, apparently went very far in granting the Church freedom from royal interference on the elections of bishops and priests. This privilege was confirmed and extended by Erling Skakke and Magnus Erlingsson. The *Canones Nidrosienses*, which most probably dates from 1163/64, contains a chapter on church patronage taken directly from Gratian's *Decretum* which allows the founder of the church the right of presentation of the priest to the bishop and supervision of the funds of the church, but forbids economic exploitation or regarding the church as his own property.[3] By contrast, the earlier arrangement meant that the owner, in addition to appointing the priest, also received an income from the church, in accordance with the system of proprietary churches, known from other parts of Europe in the Early Middle Ages when the local churches were largely outside the bishops' control.

Having defeated Magnus, Sverre tried to abolish these reforms. He demanded the right to influence episcopal elections, although without any great success, and he defended lay control over local churches. The archbishop accused Sverre of claiming ownership over the *fylke* churches, whereas Sverre accused the bishops of urging laymen to build churches without giving them any control of them. Most probably, Sverre could have gained popularity among wealthy laymen, particularly in Trøndelag, by defending their right to control churches. This conflict ended in a vague compromise in 1202, shortly after Sverre's death, but the tradition from Sverre lingered on in royalist circles in the following period.

---

3   Can. 1, *Lat. dok.* p. 42; Skånland, *Provinsialstatutt*, pp. 67-84.

Hákonar saga reports several controversies with leading churchmen about classical themes like episcopal elections and ecclesiastical privilege.[4] Håkon Håkonsson also repeatedly tried to influence episcopal elections and complained when he had not been heard. In 1224-25, during the rivalry between Håkon and Skule, Håkon managed to get the pope to reject the postulation of Sigurd, Abbot of Tautra, as archbishop and replace him with Peter of Husastad, on the grounds that Sigurd had been suspended from his abbacy because of irregularities, which actually seems to have been the case.[5] After a series of archbishops with connections to the Erling-Magnus faction in the second half of the twelfth and beginning of the thirteenth centuries – Øystein (1161-88), Eirik (1189-1205) and Tore (1205-14) – the archbishops in the following period mostly seem to have had a Birchleg affiliation. This applies to Guttorm (1215-24), Peter of Husastad (1225-26), Sigurd Eindridesson (1231-52) and Einar Smjorbak (1255-63).[6] In the election in Hamar in 1260, King Håkon opposed his own candidate to the one elected by the chapter and won in the end; the chapter had to admit that it was difficult to elect a bishop who was not the king's friend.[7] There is also other evidence that the chapter tried to avoid the election of candidates not wanted by the king, as in the prolonged and difficult election of the archbishop after Jon Raude's death in 1282. We have examples of royal servants being elected, such as Åskjell (one of Håkon Håkonssons clerics, who became bishop of Stavanger in 1226), and Askatin (former royal chancellor and envoy, who became bishop of Bergen in 1270). In the first half of the fourteenth century, two royal chancellors became bishops: Pål Bårdsson, archbishop 1333-46; and Arne Aslaksson, who was elected bishop of Stavanger in 1350 but died before he had received papal confirmation. His predecessor was Guttorm, former Master of the Royal Chapels and royal treasurer. However, it is open to discussion whether Pål should really be regarded as a royal servant, as his appointment to chancellor was probably a concession to the Church (below pp. 312, 359). Arne, Bishop of Bergen from 1305-14, also had a background in the king's service. We may also suspect royal influence in the case of another bishop of Bergen, who had been a Dominican, Narve (1278-1303), as the relationship between the cathedral chapter and

---

4 Bagge, *From Gang Leader*, pp. 102, 119-21.
5 Johnsen, "Fra den eldste tid", p. 205 with references.
6 Guttorm was the son of a Birchleg mentioned in *Sverris saga* and probably a relative of Skule (Bagge, "Den heroiske tid", p. 75). Peter descended from *lendmenn* on both sides, of somewhat different political colour, on his mother's side from Peter Byrdesvein, who was Archbishop Øystein's second cousin, but belonged to the opposite faction. Archbishop Peter's own affiliation was probably to the Birchlegs. He was originally close to Håkon and in opposition to Skule, but later became closer to Skule (Johnsen, "Fra den eldste tid", pp. 206 f.). Sigurd was the son of a Birchleg hero in a battle in 1198, Eindride Peine (ibid., p. 210). Einar Smjorbak was also the son of a Birchleg.
7 *HH* ch. 299, 302; Joys, "Tidsrommet 1253-1280", pp. 276 f.

the Dominicans was bad.[8] The king also managed to retain some formal influence in the Concordat of 1277, in contrast to the Concordat of 1273. Whereas both versions state that the whole decision should be made by the lawful electors ("ipsi ad quos electio pertinet"), namely the cathedral chapter, the Concordat of 1277 contains an addition about the king's right to be informed before the confirmation.[9] Thus, despite the fact that the chapter's formal right was respected, the king had similar possibilities to those in other countries to influence the election. He seems mostly to have been able to avoid unwanted candidates and to have had some possibility for rewarding faithful clerical servants by promoting them to a bishopric, but as far as we can conclude from the limited evidence, there is little to suggest that royal favourites were imposed on the Church or that elections were generally decided by the king. Håkon V's great investment in a clergy in the king's service, attached to the royal chapels, may therefore be regarded as a compensation for his limited possibilites to control and use the ordinary clergy, although canons and other clerics did not disappear from the king's service in the following period.

Less is known about the control of the local churches after the conflict under Sverre. Jan Brendalsmo, who has carried out a thorough examination of churches and ecclesiastical organisation in Trøndelag, concludes that the archbishop had to fight until the fourteenth or fifteenth century to gain full control of the churches which had earlier been in the hands of local church owners.[10] Although the evidence is scarce, an objection to this conclusion may be that if so, it is strange that we do not hear more about the local churches in Norway during the conflict between the Church and the regency for Eirik Magnusson in the 1280s, or in connection with Bishop Arne's struggle with the Icelandic magnates over this issue in the 1280s and 90s. The barons supported the church owners against the bishops in Iceland, but had only modest demands regarding this matter in Norway. They decreed that there should still be church wardens, which accords with canon law, and that founders of private chapels and their descendants should not be obliged to uphold them if the bishop would not appoint a priest there.[11] The fact that the strongly anti-clerical government did not demand more from the bishops than this must be taken as evidence that the situation in Norway was different from that in Iceland and that the bishops had by this time won the conflict over the local churches, at least against the lay patrons.

Whereas the great breakthrough of the Church in the twelfth century has received much attention, less has been done to trace its further development in the thirteenth and early fourteenth centuries. The relatively numerous sources from this period, mostly of

---

8   For these and other examples, see Joys, *Biskop og konge,* pp. 198-247.
9   "De nunciantes ante confirmationem electionem factam domino regi" (NGL II, p. 464).
10 Brendalsmo, "Kirker og sogn", pp. 238-40.
11 NGL III no. 1 § 2, p. 5, and NGL III no. 26, p. 84.

secular origin, give an impression of a kind of containment on the part of the monarchy; the anti-clerical tradition from Sverre continued in a more moderate form under his successors until 1319. Despite the truth of this observation, there is likely to have been a gradual growth in the wealth and complexity of the ecclesiastical organisation of which the sources only give limited evidence. The cathedral chapters increased their size and importance, as is evident from their conflicts with the archbishop and the bishop of Stavanger, as well as from the importance of the cathedral chapter of Bergen in the bishop's *Registrum* (above p. 252). New religious orders were introduced, notably the mendicants, and new monasteries were founded and older ones expanded. Evidence of building activities, in existing churches as well as in ruins, and references in written sources add to the picture. This includes the Gothic Trondheim Cathedral, finished in 1320, most of which must have been built in the thirteenth century; the choir of Stavanger Cathedral from the late thirteenth century; the Franciscan church in Bergen, now the cathedral, finished in 1301; the monastery of Utstein from the second half of the thirteenth century; the royal chapels in Oslo and Bergen, and a number of large local churches in stone all over the country. A closer examination of the admittedly limited source material may possibly give a more precise picture of this development.

The Conflict about Jurisdiction and the Concordat of Tønsberg

Thus, by the second half of the thirteenth century, the Church largely seems to have carried out the programme from the reform movement of the 1160s, in addition to strengthening its organisation and increasing its wealth. Nevertheless, a new struggle between the monarchy and the Church occurred in the 1280s, preceded by long and hard negotiations between Archbishop Jon Raude (1268-82) and King Magnus Håkonsson (1263-80). A central issue in these conflicts, in contrast to the previous period, was legislation and jurisdiction. King Håkon had begun and King Magnus continued a thorough revision of the laws which made the Christian laws an issue of contention between the two parties. In the late 1260s, King Magnus sought the approval of the *lagtings* to revise the laws. He managed to revise the laws of Borgarting, Eidsivating and Gulating[12] but was blocked at Frostating regarding the Christian laws by the newly elected Archbishop Jon Raude. While Magnus revised the secular laws, negotiations were conducted about the privileges of the Church, particularly in the field of jurisdiction. The result was the Concordat of

---

12 These laws are extant and edited in NGL II, pp. 291-338. See below pp. 310, 312 f. on the discussion about the Christian laws.

Bergen in 1273 which was made conditional on papal approval.[13] When the pope demanded an extra concession from the king – probably on the archbishop's advice – the king cancelled the concordat. New negotiations started somewhat later and resulted in a final concordat, entered in Tønsberg in 1277 and not subject to papal approval, with largely the same content as the original one of 1273, although without the extra concession.[14] In an appendix to the concordat, the two parties agreed to extend the payment of tithes from the surplus of agriculture and fisheries to various other incomes, including trade, crafts, and above all land rents. Finally, the king extended the archbishop's and bishops' privileges in a separate charter, issued shortly after the concordat.[15]

The concordats of 1273 and 1277 were clearly a victory for the Church; how great a victory has been the subject of much discussion. To most nineteenth-century historians it was the breakthrough for independent ecclesiastical jurisdiction. This was opposed in the early twentieth century, notably by Halvdan Koht, who regarded it mainly as a confirmation and extension of earlier practice.[16] Jens Arup Seip returned to the older view, claiming that the concordat introduced independent ecclesiastical jurisdiction for the first time, admittedly against the background of a practice that gave the Church considerable influence over legal matters.[17] Although Seip's work remains the fundamental study of the subject, most later scholars have found it difficult to accept this conclusion.[18] One of Seip's arguments for the lack of independent ecclesiastical jurisdiction in the previous period is that it is so rarely mentioned in the regional laws, according to which the normal procedure, as we have seen, was that the bishop or his representative acted as the prosecutor in the same way as anyone else who regarded himself as wronged, and brought the defendant before the Thing if the latter refused to come to terms. However, this is also the procedure described in Archbishop Jon's Christian law, issued at a time when the Church demanded fully independent jurisdiction. The law also contains a similar list of cases to be decided by ecclesiastical courts as the concordat, but nevertheless frequently refers to the Thing and makes extensive use of compurgation.[19] The reason for this must be that there were obvious advantages for the Church in having the support of the people when

---

13   NGL II, pp. 455-62.
14   NGL II, pp. 462-67.
15   NGL II, no. 4, pp. 481-83.
16   Koht, *Innhogg og utsyn*, pp. 259-72.
17   Seip, *Sættargjerden*, pp. 26-66.
18   Schreiner, "Konge og kirke"; Gunnes, "Kirkelig jurisdiksjon"; Helle, *Norge blir en stat*, pp. 138-41 with reference to earlier scholarship; Bagge, "Kirkens jurisdiksjon"; Sandvik, "Sættargjerda"; Sunde, *Speculum legale*, pp. 127-35, and Bagge, "Salvo semper regio iure".
19   Bagge, "Kirkens jurisdiksjon", pp. 141 f. with reference to J 20 and J 47. See also J 49 and 60-62. For a comparison between the two lists, see below n. 27.

proceeding against the recalcitrant; the Thing presented no danger, in contrast to the royal courts which might have taken a different attitude to that of the Church. Moreover, the Norwegian Christian laws did not represent the entire ecclesiastical law in the country. Like other local churches, the Norwegian Church was bound by universal canon law, and the specifically Norwegian Christian law only contained one selection of particular relevance for the laity. The background to the conflict over the jurisdiction can therefore hardly have been that the Church in the 1270s raised new and revolutionary claims, but rather that the monarchy during the previous decades had tried to expand its jurisdiction at the cost of the Church, a development that was now checked.[20] King Magnus's laws actually give evidence of this, by insisting that both the king and the bishop shall prosecute in cases under Christian law, whereas the earlier laws only mention the bishop.[21]

Both versions of the concordat open with an almost identical account of its background. The archbishop had found that some cases that belonged to the ecclesiastical forum were dealt with by secular judges and that some ecclesiastical privileges issued by Magnus Erlingsson had not been respected, notably the sacrifice of the late king's crown to the cathedral of Nidaros and the Law of Succession which gave the bishops a decisive influence on royal elections. The king denied that the Church had any of these rights, but after long discussions, the two parties agreed on a compromise, set down in the following treaty. The archbishop renounced the right he might have had to the sacrifice of the crown and the participation in royal elections, except in the case that there was no heir to the throne – this was then codified in the revised Law of Succession of 1274. The king in the same way renounced his possible rights regarding ecclesiastical jurisdiction. Both parties agreed to this on behalf of themselves as well as their successors forever. The following paragraphs, seventeen altogether, contain various privileges for the Church, most of them renewals of earlier ones, but some new, and all of them without any mention of their duration.

In Norwegian scholarship the two treaties are usually referred to as the concordat of 1273 and *sættargjerden* of 1277 respectively, the latter term having been used in the contemporary sources.[22] The documents themselves and other Latin sources use the term *compositio*. According to the form as well as the contents of the documents, concordat seems to be the appropriate modern term, although technically concordats are a post-medieval

---

20 Bagge, "Kirkens jurisdiksjon", pp. 151-58; cf. Schreiner, "Konge og kirke", pp. 588-93.
21 NG 3, as compared to e.g. G 28; Bagge, "Kirkens jurisdiksjon", pp. 152 f.
22 Old Norse *sættargerð* means "the making of an agreement". It is not used exclusively about this particular agreement, but the more usual term is simply *sætt*.

phenomenon.[23] The introduction and the first two paragraphs define the document as a treaty between two equal parties, similar to the treaties the Norwegian king entered into with the kings of other countries and to those between the monarchy and the Church in other countries at that time. Conversely, treaties with non-royal partners, such as the Hanseatic cities, took the form of one-sided privileges from the king, even if they were actually the results of negotiations between two independent parties. The concordats thus form a remarkable example of the king formally negotiating on equal terms with another power within the nation's boundaries. This is not radically new in a European context, but it is the first time in Norway. Both previous and subsequent concessions from the king to the Church came in the form of royal privileges. When in 1290 a kind of reconciliation followed the conflicts of the 1280s, it was announced in the form of a decree from the king with a reference to an agreement with the archbishop and bishops.

Against a Norwegian background, the form would therefore signal a gain for the Church, which was now regarded as an equal partner to the king, in contrast to the secular aristocracy. This is also in accordance with King Magnus's doctrine of equality, most clearly formulated in the chapter on the king and the bishop in the National Law. From a pragmatic point of view, this form meant a certain guarantee that the concordat would last. Whereas privileges, according to what was most probably the contemporary legal understanding, were only valid during the reign of the king who issued them, treaties were mutually binding and meant to oblige the king's successors as well, as was explicitly stated in the concordats. This would thus also seem to favour the Church. However, the clergy usually denied the limited validity of privileges to the Church, arguing that the Church was also a public institution and that its rights could only increase, not diminish.

A comparison between the first two paragraphs might also suggest that the Church in reality was the winner, gaining an extension of its jurisdictional rights in return for renouncing a more than one-hundred-year-old privilege which had never been practised and which the king had consistently refused to respect. The reason for the king's attitude towards this privilege is also stated in the *narratio* introducing the treaty: the Sverre dynasty did not recognise Magnus Erlingsson as a lawful king. This is expressed in the formulation: "privilegio Magni cuiusdam ut dicebatur regis Norvegie", which must be understood as a neutral way of referring to him. According to Jon, he was a lawful king, according to King Magnus, he was not. Admittedly, King Magnus's father, Håkon Håkons-

---

23 Various agreements were entered between the Church and secular powers in the Middle Ages, beginning with the Concordat of Worms in 1122, but a technical terminology and a legal theory of concordats did not develop until the Early Modern Period, with some anticipation in the fifteenth century (Swanson, "Concordat"). On the treaties of 1273 and 1277 as concordats, see Hamre, "Sættargjerda", pp. 386 f., 389 f., and "Traktat", and Haug, "Konkordat", p. 89 with references.

son, had not been consistent in this. He recognised Magnus Erlingsson in his privilege for the bishop of Stavanger (above p. 277), but refused to recognise most of his privileges to the Church on the grounds that they had been conceded in return for a coronation to which he was not entitled.[24] The fact that in the *narratio* to the concordat Magnus calls himself Magnus IV forms further evidence of this conclusion. According to modern reckoning, he is Magnus VI. He must therefore have omitted Magnus Haraldsson, who reigned a few years together with Olav Kyrre (1066-69), and Magnus Erlingson.[25]

Thus, from a royal point of view, not only had King Magnus Erlingsson's privilege never been practised, but the ruling King Magnus and his counsellors were apparently convinced that they had good reasons for rejecting its validity. Nevertheless, the asymmetry in the concordat is not as great as it may immediately appear. It was not easy to make the Church agree in formally renouncing a privilege. The Church had a long horizon; it could wait through bad times and raise its demands again and again. God's rights could only increase, not decrease. The Church might have used a disputed royal election or a situation of rivalry among the leading men to have its privileges recognised. Magnus might have considered the example of Denmark, where his wife's cousin and his predecessors had been engaged in a prolonged conflict with the archbishop. A solemn renunciation of the former King Magnus's privilege was therefore an obvious gain which was clearly also the view of Magnus's successors. Nor was it easy for the archbishop to renounce the privilege, as is evident from the pope's condition for confirming the concordat (above p. 298), namely that the archbishop's renunciation should be withdrawn if the king broke the concordat, a condition the king refused to accept and eventually managed to exclude from the final version of 1277.

Moreover, a comparison between the two versions of the concordat shows a considerable change in the king's favour in 1277. Between them was the National Law. By omitting the Christian part of the law, Magnus was respecting the archbishop's protest against the secular power legislating in matters pertaining to the Church. On the other hand, he introduced a number of paragraphs concerning matters on the borderline between the two spheres and aimed at defending royal jurisdiction against ecclesiastical encroachments.[26] In 1277 he also managed to set a formal limit to the ecclesiastical jurisdiction by qualifying his concessions with a reference to the rights of the king. After the list of cases pertaining to the ecclesiastical forum,[27] the concordat continues:

---

24   Bagge, *The Political Thought*, pp. 149 f. with references.
25   Hamre, "Sættargjerda", pp. 393 f., rejects this interpretation but fails to explain the reason for this unique reference to a king's predecessor.
26   Sandvik, "Sættargjerda", pp. 569-76; Sunde, *Speculum legale*, pp. 129-33.
27   The list represents a compromise; some cases included in Archbishop Jon's Christian Law are not listed (Seip, *Sættargjerden*, pp. 113-15).

and other similar ones which belong to the Church according to its own law, with the king's rights reserved in all cases where fines should be paid according to established custom or the laws of the country.[28]

Having first extended the list almost infinitely by mentioning "all other cases which belong to the Church according to its own law",[29] the text next brings in the boundary, the king's rights according to established custom and the laws of the country. If interpreted narrowly, this only refers to the king's right to fines, but as the text introduces a general reservation based on the king's rights (*regium ius*), it may also be understood as the king's rights to participate in the decision or to deal with the secular aspect of these cases, which actually amounts to most cases, with some differences between the different parts of the country.

The concordat was thus not a complete surrender on the part of the monarchy. Nor can the conflict in the 1270s be understood in light of Seip's picture of the heavy, resolute and ever demanding archbishop and the weak, yielding, conscience-ridden king.[30] Despite his concessions to the Church, Magnus was a staunch defender of the rights of the monarchy and apparently an able politician and negotiatior.[31] He had retained control over a number of important cases in the National Law and set a limit to ecclesiastical encroachments by referring to the king's rights as a criterion for the interpretation of the Concordat of 1277. In addition, the question of who had the right to issue the Christian laws was still unsolved, and the king consistently refused to submit to ecclesiastical superiority in the sphere he regarded as his own. The principle proclaimed in the National Law, of two equal powers, the spiritual and the secular, each being responsible in its own field, remained intact in the concordat.

---

28 "et alie consimiles que ad ecclesiam spectant mero iure saluo semper regio iure in hijs causis ubicumque debetur ex consuetudine approbata uel legibus regni mulcta pene pecuniaria persoluenda" (NGL II, p. 464); cf. the version of 1273, NGL II, pp. 458 f., which is more accommodating to the Church.

29 "mero iure" (NGL II, p. 464) must refer to the Church's own law, i.e. canon law. The corresponding passage in the Concordat of 1273, "de iure communi", has often been understood as a more explicit reference to canon law (e.g. by Seip, *Sættargjerden*, p. 115), but is actually the opposite. *Ius commune* probably refers to the law common to both parties, which thus gives the king a similar but less firm guarantee than the one in 1277 (Sandvik, "Sættargjerda", pp. 578 f.; cf. also Bagge, "Sættargjerden", cols. 327 f.).

30 Seip, *Sættargjerden*, pp. 140 f. Admittedly, there is evidence for Magnus's tender conscience. The saga of Bishop Arne relates a story about him, talking to his men and complaining about the difficulties in governing a large kingdom. "But the greatest difficulty seems to me to decide between clerics and laymen without erring" (þá lítz mér sá hæstr at tempra dómagreinir á milli lærdómsins ok leikmanna svá at eigi verði stór missmíði á", *Arna saga* ch. 66).

31 For this revision of Seip's picture, see particularly Sandvik, "Sættargjerda".

The Conflict in the 1280s

Nevertheless, Magnus's concessions were not respected by his successors. Very soon after his death on 9 May 1280 and the coronation of his son and successor Eirik on 2 July, a violent conflict broke out. The regency government for Eirik, who was twelve years old at the time, issued a general ordinance, evidently intended as an amendment to the National Law (*rettarbót*), which did not primarily deal with the Church, but contained some paragraphs on ecclesiastical matters.[32] The archbishop retorted promptly with a statute threatening all those who infringed upon the privileges of the Church with excommunication.[33] Some negotiations seem to have taken place in the summer and autumn. As early as the autumn of 1280 the archbishop issued formal warnings to the barons about their injustice to the Church.[34] As a compromise he suggested that the government postpone the legislation until the king reached majority or that the matter be brought before the pope. However, neither protests nor attempts at compromise seem to have had any effect. The ordinance of 1280 was followed up by two others, apparently from 1281-82. The most detailed of them, probably the older, gives the most complete account of the barons' programme at the height of the conflict.[35] The barons also appeared at the local assemblies to put their programme into effect; we have evidence of one such meeting when Bjarne Erlingsson appeared at the assembly of Vågan in Northern Norway in the summer of 1281.[36] At about the same time, the barons revoked the archbishop's mint privilege and the rest of King Magnus's concessions in addition to the concordat,[37] after which Bjarne and some of the other barons were excommunicated. The barons answered by outlawing the archbishop and the clerics who supported him. The archbishop and two of the other bishops left the country, his residence was taken over by the regents and one of them slept with his wife in the archbishop's bed. When one of the members of the regency government, Andres Plytt, died excommunicate, his fellow regents had the church

---

32   NGL III no. 1, 2-29 July 1280.
33   NGL III, pp. 229-41. Much of the statute is of a general character, including the ban against selling arms, ships or iron to the Saracens, but some passages are direct reactions against the barons' policy. The list of fourteen acts leading to excommunication was possibly inspired by or derived from a similar list, read in the Lateran Church on Maundy Thursday (Haug, "Konkordat", pp. 84, 99 with references).
34   DN III nos. 20-21, 5 Oct. 1280 and 17 March 1281.
35   NGL III no. 26, there dated to 1308-09 and said to be issued by Håkon V. As the majority of the manuscripts do not give the king's name, Munch, NFH IV.2, p. 172 n. 2, dates it to the beginning of Eirik's reign in accordance with internal evidence. This has been followed by most later scholars.
36   DN III no. 30, 9 March 1291, testimony of various clerics about Bjarne's actions against the Church.
37   The privilege extended the right granted in the concordat to the archbishop and bishops to receive fines from their men if they fought one another, whereas the ordinance of 1281/82 restricted even the rights conceded in the concordat.

tower broken up in order to ring the bells during his funeral.[38] The bishops received little aid from the pope, and Archbishop Jon died in exile in Skara in Sweden late in 1282. The situation was gradually normalised in the following years. The bishops started to return, a new archbishop, Jørund, was elected in 1287, after several years' vacancy, and the king – who had now personally taken over the government – issued a proclamation of peace in 1290, although without renewing the concordat. The new archbishop tried to summon the former regents to answer for their actions and registered the evidence about their attacks on the Church (see note 45), but soon had to give up because of the conflict that broke out between him and his chapter.

To Seip, this conflict was mainly about jurisdiction and an attempt by the regency government to wipe out all that had been conceded to the Church in 1277, which in turn forms evidence that the concordat was a revolutionary gain for the Church and contrary to all earlier practices.[39] A closer examination of the actual issues during the conflict raises some doubt about this conclusion; financial issues might have been equally important if not more so. The crucial issue was the taxation of ecclesiastical property. The ordinance of 1280 decrees that clerics' and bishops' men should pay *utfareleidang* (see above p. 79) and *skipafé*[40] like others. Although neither of these taxes is mentioned in the concordat, this demand seems difficult to reconcile with the privileges given therein. The first ordinance of 1281-82 pursues this by stating that all should pay *leidang* according to how much land and cattle they owned, as stated in the law. It was clearly not the barons' intention to abolish the traditional tax privileges of the clergy, which were well established in the laws to which the ordinance refers. The context was that the *leidang* tax was being changed from a tax on persons to a tax on land. Whereas tenants had earlier paid the personal tax, the government now demanded the same tax from them, but in proportion to the amount of land their farms comprised. As the Church was technically the owner of the land cultivated by its tenants, it now saw the opportunity to claim that this land belonged to the Church and should not be taxed. This claim had been brought forward earlier but had been rejected by the king.[41] As the Church was by far the greatest landowner in the country, possibly with up to forty percent of the landed income (above p. 111), this would have meant a dramatic reduction in the king's

---

38   *Árna saga* chs. 73, 91.
39   For the following, see Seip, *Sættargjerden*, pp. 143-71 with references.
40   The tax to be paid when the *leidang* ship had to be repaired or rebuilt.
41   According to *Hákonar saga*, the bishops asked Cardinal William to suggest to the king that he should give a part of the *leidang* to the Church but the Cardinal refused (*HH* ch. 255, Sk. p. 601). This must imply an arrangement similar to what the bishops demanded in the 1270s and 1280s, that the Church kept the *leidang* tax its tenants had earlier been paid to the king.

revenues. King Magnus had left the matter pending,[42] but the regency government took prompt action and started registration of the Church's lands, an action which was met with staunch resistance. Furthermore, the barons rejected the new and extended rules for the tithe issued as an attachment to the concordat. This matter is not very prominent in the ordinances directed to Norway,[43] but is well documented in those directed to Iceland[44] as well as in the later complaints from the bishops. Thus, several witnesses testify to Bjarne Erlingsson having banned the new tithes and fined those who had paid it and the clerics who had received it.[45] The revocation of the archbishop's mint privilege and trading rights in Iceland, plus the clergy's rights to sell the tithe received in kind where they wanted and the ban against selling silver to the clergy,[46] also belong in this category, although these steps may possibly have been intended to put pressure on the bishops to make them come to terms.[47]

Concerning jurisdiction, the barons proclaimed that the old Christian law should still be valid.[48] This was a clear rejection of Archbishop Jon's Christian law, probably issued in 1273,[49] as well as, indirectly, of the concordat. At least it meant that its paragraph on jurisdiction should be interpreted in a restrictive sense, in accordance with the rules of the old laws. The old Christian Law was also used to argue for the barons' solution to concrete issues. What exactly did the barons mean by the old Christian law? According to the testimonies of 1291, Bjarne Erlingsson defined it as the one in force at the time of King Håkon and Archbishop Sigurd (1231-52) which has usually been interpreted as the old regional laws.[50] This seems to be confirmed by Håkon V's ordinance of 1316, which orders the *lagmenn* and the clergy to recognise "the Christian law that has been with you here of old and neither the one that Magnus our father let be composed, nor the one Archbishop

---

42 DN III no. 20; cf. Seip, *Sættargjerden*, pp. 147-49.
43 The ordinance of 1280 states that the old Christian law should be valid regarding the tithe for renting cows. This is probably a later addition (Seip, *Sættargjerden*, p. 150 n. 27). The ordinance of 1281/82 only mentions that the tithe to the poor should be paid as before, i.e. that it should belong to the people and not to the clergy.
44 Seip, *Sættargjerden*, pp. 150 f. with references.
45 DN III no. 30.
46 This was occasioned by the papal tax imposed on the clergy which had to be paid in silver. This ban was the pope's main cause of complaint about the regency's anticlerical measures.
47 Seip, *Sættargjerden*, pp. 152 f. with references.
48 NGL III no. § 27; NGL III no. 26 § 1.
49 On the date, see Seip, "Ennu en kristenrett", pp. 584-88, 607 f.; *Sættargjerden*, pp. 137 f. Bjarne Erlingsson is also said to have banned the reading of the lawbook of Vågan at the assembly there, which probably means that this law – now lost – was more favourable to the Church than the old Christian laws.
50 "oc at kristinn rettr saa forne æinn skilldi ganga er var vm dag Sigurdar ærchibiskups oc Hakonar konungs" (DN III no. 30, p. 30); cf. Seip, "Ennu en kristenrett", p. 617, and *Sættargjerden*, pp. 158-60.

Jon let be composed, but the one that was before".[51] Recently, however, Riisøy and Spørck have revived the older interpretation, by Hertzberg, that Håkon and Sigurd actually issued a Christian Law which can be identified with the extant laws attributed to Magnus in the manuscripts.[52] As evidence of this, they point to the reference by the regency for Magnus Erikson in 1327 to the Christian law issued by King Håkon and Archbishop Sigurd, claiming that the regents must have known that this law existed. As the earlier sources simply refer to the old law without any mention of who issued it, however, this may well have been just a slip of the pen.[53] On the other hand, it seems strange that the government from the 1280s onwards should have preferred the old regional laws to King Magnus's revisions. Did they regard the latter as too accommodating to the Church? Or, on the contrary, were these laws even less acceptable to the bishops than the old ones, as the paragraph about the king's and the bishop's common responsibility for suing in cases under Christian law may suggest? If so, it can explain Håkon V's attitude but hardly that of the barons. A more thorough examination of the entire Christian legislation will be necessary to decide the issue.

Concerning the actual decisions under Christian law, the only evidence for the barons' intention to abolish ecclesiastical jurisdiction completely is the testimony of one witness, Sira Audun, canon of Nidaros, who accused Bjarne Erlingsson of having said that there should be no provosts and that the king's *lagmann* should judge in Christian cases.[54] However, Audun is the only one of the witnesses present at the meeting whose testimony includes these accusations, which means that they cannot serve as evidence for the government's consistent policy. Moreover, as we shall see, they probably have to be interpreted in the light of their specific context. Apart from this statement, the barons' initiatives in this field concerned specific issues. They decreed that cases about property should be brought before the *lagmann* who should decide on them, whether the plaintiff was a cleric or a layman.[55] This was clearly an attempt to restrict ecclesiastical jurisdiction, although technically it was not against the concordat, which only states that such cases should be brought before an ecclesiastical court if the *defendant* were a cleric. Further-

---

51 "þann kristinsdoms retth sem veirit heifver at forno her med ydr. oc þo hvarke þan sem Maghnus fader var lett saman seitia oc ei þan er Jon erkibiskup lett saman seitia. en þan sem adr var" (NGL III no. 46, 28 July 1316).
52 Riisøy and Spørck, "Dateringen", pp. 65-67; cf. Hertzberg, "Endu et Kristenretsudkast", pp. 201 f.
53 Hertzberg, "Endu et Kristenretsudkast", p. 202 n. 2, supported by Riisøy and Spørck, "Dateringen", p. 66, claims that the expression "var vm daga" in itself means that the persons in question had issued the law. However, the example to which Hertzberg refers as evidence of this contains a verb meaning "issued" or "settled": "A dögum ... Gizurar byskyps ... var þessi tiundar gerd almenniliga lögtekin" (NGL V, p. 32 n. 17).
54 DN III no. 30, p. 30.
55 NGL III no.1 § 23.

more, the ordinance of 1280 forbids priests who have parishes and hear secret confessions to serve as provosts.[56] This was obviously in the interest of the laity who might otherwise risk being prosecuted for sins they had confessed under the secrecy of confession. It would also seem to be a reasonable provision from the point of view of the bishops, except that they might object that it was not for laymen to decide on this matter. The barons also issued rules about laymen as church wardens and about testaments, intended to protect the heirs against excessive generosity to the Church, and decreed, contrary to the rules introduced by the bishops, that sails and other *leidang* equipment should continue to be stored in the churches.[57]

Even more important and controversial were the provisions regarding marriage. The ordinance of 1280 decreed that a marriage should only be considered legal when the banns had been published three times in church and furthermore that no man should be forced to swear to marry the woman who had been his concubine if he went to bed with her after having gone to confession and done penance.[58] These provisions were followed up by Bjarne Erlingsson during his meeting in Vågan. Two witnesses testified that Bjarne fined Canon Audun and forced him to pay back the fines he had received for adultery.[59] This may be understood as evidence that the regents demanded jurisdiction as well as the right to fines in such cases, as suggested by Riisøy.[60] However, the text does not say that Bjarne claimed the fines for himself, but rather that he forced Audun to pay them back. If the statement is to be taken literally, the fines must therefore have been returned to those who paid them. Although we cannot be sure that this was exactly what the witness said or intended, this interpretation makes sense in the context. According to Audun's own testimony, Bjarne expressed himself as follows: "… and that there should be no provosts. Also that the king's *lagmann* should judge about Christian law as about the National law and that secret betrothals should not be regarded as valid".[61] The last statement in the list may explain why Bjarne forced Audun to pay back the fines he had received. The person or persons (no names are given) who had been fined by Audun must have refused to respect the marriage wows he – it was in all likelihood a man – had given in secret and was now

---

56 NGL III no.1 § 1.
57 NGL III no. 1 § 2 and 11; NGL III no. 26, p. 82.
58 NGL III no. 1 §§ 6-7.
59 The testimony of Arne, monk of Nidaroholm runs as follows: "jtem dœmde hann oc fear pinu upp a Audunn a Þrondar nese. oc baud honom aftr at grœida sæctir þær sem hann hafde tækit firir hordom. oc sua vart gort" (DN III no. 30, pp. 30 f.). Audun's colleague, the canon Erlend, only states that Audun was fined (ibid., p. 30).
60 Riisøy, *Stat og kirke*, p. 130.
61 "… oc at prouastar skilldu ængi vera. Jtem at konongs logmadr skilldi sua dœma jvir kristnum rette sem jvir adrum landzlagum oc at i klefa fæstinng skilldi ængi halldazt" (ibid.).

living with another woman which made him an adulterer in the eyes of the Church, or he or she may have married someone who, according to the Church's definition but not the secular one, was already married. Bjarne had then intervened on behalf of these people, ordered the *lagmann* to deal with the matter according to the National Law which did not share the Church's definition of what constituted a legal marriage and ordered Sira Audun to return the fine. As Audun was also the only witness to have accused Bjarne of totally rejecting ecclesiastical jurisdiction, it would seem reasonable to interpret Bjarne's words as related to this specific issue. Bjarne rejected the ecclesiastical definition of marriage in favour of the secular one and as a consequence must have demanded that secular courts should decide whether or not a marriage was legitimate. This was against canon law as well as, most probably, the concordat, but need not necessarily imply a total rejection of ecclesiastical justice.

Moreover, in attacking Audun, Bjarne may have had in mind the earlier ban against parish priests serving as provosts. Audun was already one of the most prominent members of the cathedral chapter of Nidaros at this time.[62] He was one of the witnesses to the concordat and for a long time held the wealthy and important parish of Trondenes in Northern Norway. He later became one of the leaders of the chapter in its conflict with Archbishop Jørund and ended his life as bishop of Holar in Iceland (1313-22). Bjarne's action against him implies that he must have acted as provost. As he is referred to as Audun of Trondenes, he must have combined this position with that of a parish priest, thus breaking the rule laid down by the barons in 1280 which may in turn have occasioned an outburst against provosts like the one recorded in the testimony of 1291. We will of course never know what Bjarne actually said, but it seems likely that the definition of a lawful marriage was at least one of the issues between him and Sira Audun.

The importance of this issue is further attested by the legislation from the previous period. In the older laws, marriage was primarily a contract between families, and the father or another male relative decided about a woman's marriage. By contrast, canon law from the pontificate of Alexander III (1159-81) defined legal marriage as the result of the free consent of the two partners, a doctrine that gradually came to influence the regional laws.[63] The paragraph about marriage in Magnus Håkonsson's Christian laws is introduced by a reference to God's institution of marriage in Paradise, giving a precise formula for what a man should say if he engages a woman to marry him and prescribes that she should give her consent in the presence of witnesses.[64] By contrast, the National

---

62   Bull, "Audun Torbergsson Raude".
63   Sandvik, "Ægteskab. Norge", col. 494; Berman, *Law and Revolution*, pp. 226-30; Brundage, *Law, Sex and Christian Society*, pp. 268 f., 331-37; Christensen-Nugues, "Och de skall vara", pp. 9-17, 158-65, 209-46.
64   NB I.15; NG II.23; cf. also NB II.19.

Law states that the father or a male guardian should decide over a woman's marriage but admits the possibility that she may contract a legal marriage on her own, in which case, however, she would lose her right to an inheritance, unless the reason for the denial is that the guardian has prevented her from contracting a marriage with an equal partner.[65] This paragraph occurs in the part of the law dealing with inheritance, whereas the National Law lacks a separate Christian Law because of the archbishop's resistance. The paragraph in the National Law should therefore not be understood as a rejection of King Magnus's earlier legislation but as dealing with the social consequences of marriage rather than its legal definition. The secular authorities could not neglect the Church's doctrine of legal marriage, but they could force a woman to pay a high price for opposing her guardian.

However, Archbishop Jon's Christian law[66] takes one step further than the earlier royal laws. Jon follows King Magnus's laws in referring to God's institution of marriage and describing the procedure for when a man seeks a wife, including the reference to witnesses and banns in the church, but emphasises the consent in a more radical way, in accordance with Pope Alexander III's definition of marriage. The essential act is the mutual consent between the partners, according to a formula quoted in the law, which may take place even before the banns.[67] This act is defined in the law as betrothal (*festarmál*) which is equally binding as a marriage, so that even if the woman is betrothed in the same way to another man and they celebrate their marriage and live together, she still belongs to the first one. In his statute of 1280, Jon sets one year and three months after the betrothal as the deadline for a man to celebrate his wedding. Failing to do this, he would fall under interdict until he fulfilled his obligation.[68] This provision must have been intended as a sanction against men who fail to take seriously the consequences of the vows they have given to a woman. Later statutes also dealt with this issue.[69]

Before Jon, wealthy parents had a double guarantee against disobedient daughters, the threat of loss of inheritance and the demand that a betrothal take place in public. Now the latter had been removed. The former guarantee might suffice in many, perhaps most, cases, but parental control had been reduced. Moreover, there was another danger which was

---

65   L V.2.
66   J 40.
67   "En ef þæim synnzt braðare at raða. oc frammare att at gera. fyr en lyst er. þa er lofat at handsælia ef vill, a þessa lund. at þar felst undir handsale okkro. at mit sculum hiunskap saman tængia at guðs logum. oc hæilaghra fæðra setning. oc ef sua er gort. þa ero þetta rethleg fæstar mall." ("And if they want to decide more quickly and sooner, before the banns, then they are allowed to take each others' hands if they want, in this way: 'We hold our hands together so that we shall join in marriage according to God's laws and the holy fathers' commandment. And if this is done, then it is a lawful betrothal") (J 40, NGL II, p. 368).
68   NGL III, p. 231.
69   Tryti, *Bergen bispedømme*, pp. 188, on Eiliv's third statute, NGL III, pp. 252 f., 274, 276 f.; cf. also 279 on the consolidation of ecclesiastical jurisdiction through the introduction of sworn clerks.

probably the barons' main concern, namely that the validity of secret betrothals might force a man to marry a mistress or concubine against his will. This was in practice the main issue in the cases about the validity of a marriage brought before the ecclesiastical courts (below pp. 314 f.). Normally the plaintiff in such cases was a woman who claimed that a man had married her in secret. The court in such cases had to make their judgement based on very subtle nuances. What exactly had the man said? The matter might be decided on the basis of the difference between the present and the future tense. Canon law did not demand any particular formula, but distinguished between an act and a promise, *verba de presenti* versus *verba de futuro*. If the man had said: "I marry you", they were legally married. If he had said: "I shall marry you", they were not. Then he had just given a promise, which might be broken. As we have seen, this was applied to the betrothal in Jon's Christian law and Norwegian ecclesiastical practice, as the betrothal was the decisive act, but the canonistic terminology occurs in Norwegian sources as well (see below p. 314). These consequences were probably largely intended by the contemporary clergy. Whereas the Church had earlier tolerated concubinage as long as it was kept distinct from marriage – there is no prohibition of it in the old Christian laws – it now aimed at making marriage the only lawful sexual relationship and, particularly in the fourteenth century, introduced stricter rules against concubinage, which the monarchy, at least partly, supported.[70] Jon's revision of the law might be a means to this end, by making it more difficult to keep a long-term relationship with a woman without marriage. For what might not a man say in a passionate moment? Even more, as appears from the barons' ordinance, the Church had a direct means to achieve such a result; it might force a man who had confessed a sexual relationship to a woman who was not his wife to swear either to be chaste or to marry.[71] It was here the barons reacted, forbade such promises and directly challenged the Church's definition of a legal marriage by demanding banns as a precondition for a legal marriage and by forbidding secret betrothals.

Rather than a full-scale attack on ecclesiastical jurisdiction, the barons' anticlerical policy should be seen as an attempt to check the progress made by the Church in the previous period and to defend the interests of the laity on some concrete but crucial points. Given the relatively modest incomes of the monarchy, they must have regarded the loss of the *leidang* of up to forty percent of the land in the country as a disaster. In a similar way, they insisted on keeping the ancient Christian laws which still gave the king and his representatives authority and incomes from a wider field of cases than allowed by Archbishop Jon's new Christian law. They also refused to accept the extension of the tithe

---

70 Holtan, *Ekteskap*, pp. 84-88; Riisøy, *Sex, rett og reformasjon*, pp. 23-44.
71 The technical term is "sub pena nubendi", i.e. that a relapse into the confessed sin would automatically lead to marriage. See Christensen-Nugues, *De skall vara*, pp. 225-39, with examples from practice in Normandy in the fourteenth century.

to include rent incomes, which would further increase the wealth of the Church, while at the same time hitting the wealthier part of the laity who received most of these incomes. Finally, they protested against the ecclesiastical doctrine of marriage which threatened fathers' control over their families' future as well as constituted a severe risk for men that they would have to pay dearly for their amorous adventures. These issues were in addition well suited to mobilising large parts of the laity for the policy of the barons, who also seem to have been successful in finding the rhetorical means to gain this support, as emerges particularly clearly from their final, general proclamation (below p. 317). The complete elimination of ecclesiastical jurisdiction may well be regarded as the logical consequence of their programme, and the ideological foundation of such a claim is also to be found in *The King's Mirror*. However, when the barons did not explicitly make such a claim even at the height of the conflict, we cannot assume that it was part of their policy to the extent that they intended to carry it out in practice. What politicians might dream of doing in an ideal situation is of little interest when examining their aims. What matters are the aims they regard as realistic and take concrete steps to fulfil.

From a legal point of view, the barons seem to have taken a different attitude to the Church's privileges and the concordat. Whereas they had no qualms about explicitly revoking the former, they were more cautious regarding the latter, although they directly or indirectly rejected some of its provisions. This confirms the impression from the text of the concordat itself. It would seem that the barons made a distinction between the first two paragraphs, which were explicitly said to have permanent force, and the rest, which did not, a distinction that may actually have been intended by King Magnus. According to this interpretation, the barons saw no problem in revoking the mint privilege and reducing the bishops' right to fines from their men, despite the fact that both were included in the concordat, while they made no general statements regarding jurisdiction. They must have found their legal argument for restricting ecclesiastical jurisdiction on specific points in a wide interpretation of the restriction clause ("salvo semper regio iure") in the Concordat of 1277 (above p. 302), an interpretation approaching the theory of the sovereign state in later ages: they regarded the concordat as a special concession from the king, which meant that it had to be interpreted by him, in the sense that its provisions were only valid in so far as they did not infringe on the king's normal judical prerogatives according to the law and monarchical doctrine. Such an interpretation would fit well in with the general doctrine expressed by the regency government. Although its merits are of course open to discussion, it does serve to explain the regents' different attitudes to the different parts of the concordat. In the case of the marriage legislation, they might have pointed to the National Law, which deals with this question in some detail and its importance from a secular point of view. They might also have pointed to the parallel to England, where there were different rules regarding legitimate birth in secular and ecclesiastical law.[72] As we have seen, a wide range of cases in Christian law had secular ramifications. Although it is an open-ended question how much the regency government cared about formally offending against points in the concordat, it is significant that they never explicitly revoked it, nor did the succeeding kings.[73]

The Results of the Struggle – Monarchy and Church in the Fourteenth Century and Later

The conflict ended in defeat for the Church, at least if we measure the result against Archbishop Jon's high ambitions and what he had achieved by the end of the 1270s. The extent of the defeat is difficult to assess. The most controversial part of King Magnus's concessions, the increase of the tithe, was clearly abolished, even with the bishops' consent,[74] as were also, although without such consent, the mint privilege and King Magnus's other extra concessions in addition to the concordat; there is no evidence of the archbishop issuing mint until the end of the fifteenth century.[75] The kings in the following period continued the restrictive policy towards the Church initiated by the barons; both Håkon V and Magnus Eriksson renewed their anticlerical ordinances and demanded that the old Christian law be valid, until the king and the bishops found time to issue a new one, as Håkon V expressed it.[76] An attempt from the Church in 1327 – during another regency – to renew the claims of Archbishop Jon led to a quick retreat, in return for the appointment of a prominent cleric as chancellor (below p. 359). The principle of the old Christian law continued to be official royal policy under King Eirik as well as his successor Håkon V. In practice, a variety of Christian laws were in use, those of the old regional laws, King Magnus's revisions, and Archbishop Jon's law, as well as various combinations of these

---

72 Helmholz, *The Oxford History*, p. 558.
73 Herman Schück's observation regarding the later fate of the document containing the concordat gives an additional argument for this conclusion (Schück, *Rikets brev*, pp. 144 f.). Schück argues that this document is the king's copy which was joined with a papal indulgence privilege from 1331. These documents belonged to King Magnus's *capella* and were carried around in his entourage. After his death, near Bergen, in 1374, the documents were acquired by Bergen Cathedral and later by the Danish Rosenkrantz family. If Schück's hypothesis is correct, it is difficult to imagine that Magnus took such good care of a document that was regarded as obsolete.
74 NGL III no. 3, 14 May 1290.
75 Seip, *Sættargjerden*, p. 153.
76 "at ver oc erkibiskupinn oc biskuparnar hafva ei lidughir til vordhet kristindomsbolken sva saman at seitia sem oss likar" (NGL III no. 46, 1316).

sources.[77] It is disputed whether a new Christian law was ever issued. Seip claims that this happened around 1370 and regards the new law as more favourable to the Church than Magnus Håkonsson's earlier revisions, while Riisøy and Dahle Spørck have recently identified this text with one of Magnus's laws from the 1260s.[78]

The situation seems to have been equally unclear regarding jurisdiction in practice. According to Seip, the government continued the line from the 1280s and managed to limit ecclesiastical jurisdiction until around 1350, but the decline of state power caused by the Black Death and its consequences led to a revival of ecclesiastical jurisdiction which reached a climax in the second half of the fifteenth century.[79] At least formally, the renewal of the concordat in 1458 was an important victory for the Church,[80] and some royal ordinances point in the same direction. However, a recent study by Anne Irene Riisøy of jurisdiction in practice draws a different conclusion, agreeing with Seip on the period until 1350 but finding little evidence for the revival of the following period.[81] It must be admitted that the evidence for conclusions in this field is meagre; only 107 documents concerning decisions in cases under Christian law have been preserved from the whole period 1280-1537, in addition to some evidence from cadasters and registers of fines, mostly from the end of the period.[82] Examining this material, Riisøy finds no consistent tendency towards ecclesiastical monopoly on jurisdiction in cases under Christian law, nor does she find a significant professionalisation of the ecclesiastical judicial administration. Lay provosts were still present in the Later Middle Ages, and parish priests continued to serve in legal capacities in some dioceses.[83] Thus, there is no reference to provosts in the *Registrum* from the Diocese of Bergen; here the bishop orders the parish priests to summon the parties and the witnesses and provide the necessary information for the bishop to settle the matter. As Riisøy has examined the sources more closely than Seip, paying particular attention to the various categories of cases, her conclusion seems preferable, even more so because it receives support from recent studies of the Later Mid-

---

77 Seip, *Sættargjerden*, pp. 188 f., showing the distribution of manuscripts of the various laws and the combinations of them.
78 Seip, "Ennu en kristenrett", pp. 573-627, and Riisøy and Spørck, "Dateringen", pp. 57-74. The law is usually referred to as Nyere Borgartings kristenrett II (=NB II) and was earlier thought to be another version of Magnus Håkonsson's revision of this law from the 1260s. Its text is preserved in three manuscripts, the only complete one from the mid-sixteenth century with a strange mixture of Old Norse and Danish. It is printed in NGL IV, pp. 160-82.
79 Seip, *Sættargjerden*, pp. 183-226.
80 Seip, *Sættargjerden*, pp. 200-2.
81 Riisøy, *Stat og kirke*, pp. 91-139.
82 Ibid., p. 92; cf. pp. 12 f. and 114-33.
83 Riisøy, *Stat og kirke*, pp. 84-89.

dle Ages which suggest that government and administration did not decline as much as maintained by earlier historians.

Concerning the period of greatest interest in the present connection, 1280-1350, Riisøy rejects Erik Gunnes's conclusion that the Church was in a stronger position than assumed by Seip, pointing to the fact that the chance survival of the *Registrum* of the bishops of Bergen gives an exaggerated picture of the number of cases decided by ecclesiastical courts.[84] Most of the cases listed in the *Registrum* concern marriage and its validity. Riisøy regards these cases as relatively uncontroversial, but the previous account of the conflict in the 1280s shows that this can hardly have been the case. The *Registrum* of the bishop of Bergen contains eight sentences on such cases from the period 1308-28.[85] Admittedly, this is not much, but the *Registrum* is far from complete (above p. 252). Since two such cases were brought before Bishop Arne during a visitation to the tiny rural community of Naustdal north of Bergen (either in Sunnfjord or in Nordfjord), there are reasons to believe that they must have been quite frequent. Most of these cases concern secret betrothals, on which the bishop pronounced his sentence in accordance with canon law and Jon's Christian Law.[86] In some cases, only the decision, ordering a certain man to accept a certain woman as his wife, is preserved,[87] whereas in others, the circumstances or reasons for the sentence are recorded. In 1309 Bishop Arne ordered a woman to return to her first husband, despite having lived for a long time with another man,[88] and in 1328 Bishop Audfinn decided in favour of the plaintiff, Magnhild, that Ivar Salvesson had married her "per verba de presenti".[89] The most detailed and colourful of these sentences serves as a perfect illustration of the dangers the barons saw in the ecclesiastical marriage doctrine. Here Bishop Audfinn decided in favour of the plaintiff Domhild against the defendant Eirik that the two were legally married, although expressing some doubt regarding the evidence. The betrothal had taken place in a tavern, where Eirik had wanted to go to bed with Domhild, who, however, had set marriage as a condition for agreeing. As this had been confirmed by a witness who had been listening at the door and there was evidence for the intercourse as well as for Eirik having stayed in Domhild's house for

---

[84] Ibid., pp. 94-97; cf. Gunnes, "Kirkens jurisdiksjon", p. 155.
[85] Cf. also Tryti, *Bergen bispedømme*, pp. 184-86, with reference to DN VII no. 30 (1305), IV no. 62 (1306) and VIII no. 17 (1306).
[86] An exception is DN IV no. 166a-b (Latin and Old Norse), 23 February 1325, where Bishop Audfinn decided on a case about legitimate birth, in which the plaintiff had to admit that he had been present in church during the couple's wedding.
[87] DN X nos. 7-8, 14 May 1308, and III no. 82, 25 September 1309.
[88] DN III no. 83, 2 October 1309.
[89] DN IV no. 173, 12 February 1328.

four nights, the bishop found sufficient grounds to pronounce the marriage valid.[90] We cannot exclude the possibility that some such cases were brought before secular courts which came to a different conclusion, but it seems at least clear that the barons' attempt to stop secret marriages had failed.[91]

In addition to the marriage cases, there are also examples of ecclesiastical jurisdiction on adultery, fornication, sacrilege, tithes and sorcery and of secular jurisdiction on sacrilege and tithes.[92] Riisøy points in particular to the apparent absence of ecclesiastical jurisdiction in cases involving fines which then becomes her main argument for agreeing with Seip. Nevertheless, despite the pertinence of her observation regarding the *Registrum*, a total number of five cases decided by secular courts against twenty-one by ecclesiastical courts seems too little evidence to draw any clear conclusions about the relationship between the two powers. Furthermore, it is curious that four of these five cases concern tithes which would seem to be an example *par excellence* of a category pertaining to the ecclesiastical forum and of little interest to secular courts, except in cases of the Church applying the rejected rules of 1277. In fact, the secular court in all these cases acted at the initiative of an ecclesiastical institution which had failed to make the defendant pay and now turned to the secular power. There are also other examples of clerics and ecclesiastical institutions appealing to secular courts. Thus, the provost of St Mary's in Oslo, Ivar Olavsson, who was also royal chancellor, sued the monks of Hovedøy before the *lagmann* in a suit over some timber.[93] As a high-ranking royal servant, he probably found his interests best served by bringing his case before a secular court. An example of cooperation between clergy and laity is the bishop of Stavanger appointing a mixed court of clerics and laymen, including some prominent royal officials, to pass sentence on the friars of Halsnøy who had assaulted some lay adversaries during their conflict over the fishing rights in Fakstad in Ryfylke in 1311. These examples show that a completely independent ecclesiastical jurisdiction, according to Jon Raude's model, might be a mixed blessing for the Church; it needed the secular arm against the recalcitrant, as even Jon himself had recognised by retaining the sentence by the Thing in his Christian law. Rather than regarding the period 1280-1350 as a period of victory for the secular power over the Church, we may therefore regard it as marked by unclear borders between the two jurisdictions and a fair amount of pragmatism on both sides. This seems also to be expressed in the compromise of 1337, when a local conflict over the jurisdiction in cases concerning fines under Christian law

---

90   DN V no. 72, 16 March 1325.
91   Seip, *Sættargjerden*, p. 221, also believes that the Church had won in this field, although without being aware of the controversy over this issue.
92   Riisøy, *Stat og kirke*, pp. 64, 94.
93   Seip, *Sættargjerden*, p. 209 with references.

in Trondheim was solved by the parties agreeing that the bishop's official and the king's *lagmann* should judge one day each and act together in greater and more complicated cases. The settlement was to last until the king and the archbishop had managed to agree on a permanent solution.[94]

The Ideological Aspect: A Brain Trust in the Service of the Monarchy

As the representatives of Latin and European book learning and experts on theology and canon law, the prelates would seem to have the upper hand ideologically in the struggle with the secular power. It is therefore surprising to see how well equipped the monarchy was in the ideological field. *The Speech against the Bishops* and *The King's Mirror* contain an elaborate defence of the royal position, based respectively on Gratian and the Old Testament, and *Hákonar saga*, laws and charters contain similar arguments. *A Speech against the Bishops* goes very far in subordinating the Church under the king, concluding from the specific example of laymen having patronage over individual churches that God had made the king responsible for the welfare of the Church and thus given him supreme government over it.[95] *The King's Mirror* modifies this claim, basing its arguments partly on royal superiority, partly on the idea of equality between the two parties, in a way that is not entirely consistent. However, even the arguments based on equality in practice favour the king. The author states that both the king and the bishop carry a sword and that they should support each other, but adds that the bishop's sword only harms when it is used correctly, which probably means that the ecclesiastical jurisdiction is confined to confession and penitence. Thus, the borderline between the royal and the ecclesiastical sphere is drawn in such a way as to severely curtail the power of the Church in the field of jurisdiction.[96] The National Law expresses a consistent principle of equality: God has given the king secular power and the bishop spiritual power, and the two should work together in harmony. The same principle is expressed in the Concordats of 1273 and 1277. The king's insistence on equality has its background in the theory of ecclesiastical superiority that was developed by the papacy in the thirteenth century in connection with the theory of the two swords: The pope has received both the spiritual and the secular sword but delegated the latter to the king. This in practice does not mean that the pope sought secular power for himself – except within the *Patrimonium Petri* – but that he claimed the power to define the borderline between the two powers. *The King's Mirror* already seems

---

94   NGL III no. 73, 30 August 1337; cf. Seip, *Sættargjerden*, p. 197.
95   *En tale*, p. 7 and *passim*; see Gunnes, *Kongens ære*, and Bagge, *The Political Thought*, pp. 143-45.
96   Bagge, *The Political Thought*, pp. 113-54.

to argue against this theory, in particular by insisting that the division of power between the king and the high priest in the Old Testament is still valid,[97] and the declaration in the National Law must be understood in the same way.

In all the sources mentioned above, the king argues from strictly religious principles. By contrast, the documents from the struggle in the 1280s mainly confine themselves to concrete provisions intended to limit the power of the prelates. One of them, however, an undated ordinance, issued by King Eirik and Duke Håkon and addressed to all *sysselmenn*,[98] has far-reaching ideological implications. The two rulers start by thanking all good men who have been obedient and loyal to the monarchy (*konongdomen*) during the reigns of their father and grandfather and since God elected themselves, though unworthy, to the kingdom, and express their confidence that this will continue. Now, however, they have heard what they find difficult to believe, that some clerics and even laymen want to deny them their due obedience and loyalty by failing to pay fines and contribute to the defence of the country. If this proves true, there will once more be petty kings (*neskongar*) in the country. The text then goes on: "and we and the good men who act as our counsellors find that if we will uphold the king's name and the honour of the crown, we will only let those people remain and live in the country who will act as our loyal subjects and obey our commands. And those who will shrink from this, let them go where they need to belong to nobody but themselves, nor have any power, whatever kind of people they are".[99] The two rulers conclude by declaring that they will grant both clerics and laymen the same freedom (*frialsi*) as in the reigns of their predecessors, despite the unprecedented threats that are now facing them.

The ordinance is composed with considerable rhetorical skill. Thanking the subjects for their loyalty and obedience serves as a *captatio benevolentiae* as well as a contrast to the following description of the clergy, while the pretended disbelief underlines the enormity of the clerics' behaviour and prepares for the final climax in which the clerics exclude themselves from human society. Furthermore, the regents allude to several important arguments for the power and independence of the monarchy. The terms "monarchy" (*konongdom*) and even more "honour of the crown" (*sæmd koronannar*) had for a long time played an important part in the defence of the monarchy and show a clear awareness of its

---

97 Bagge, *The Political Thought*, pp. 135-41.
98 NGL III no. 9, probably dating from 1281/82.
99 "oc þvi finz oss sua i oc þæim godom monnum er rad gera med oss ef ver uilium halda konongs namfneno oc sæmd koronannar at ver munum þæim verda at byggia landet oc hafa i rikinu er i vare þengskyldu uilia vera. oc varo iuirbode lita. en hinir sem vundan þui skiliaz þa fare þengat sem þæir þurfa eingom til at hœyra uttan sialfom ser oc ecki ifirbod at hafa huat manna sem þeir ero" (NGL III p. 33).

character as an institution.[100] The mention of the king's name may possibly be a reference to *The King's Mirror*, according to which the king bears God's name.[101] The greatest novelty, however, is the final line of the quote: By their disobedience, the clerics act against nature, they cannot live in society but have to go where there is no community, no ruler and no ruled, in other words, wilderness and anarchy.

This is an echo of the Aristotelian doctrine of man as a social animal, which in contemporary political thought was used as an argument for society and thus for royal government. According to Aristotle, human beings could only live a good life in a larger community which to him was identical with the city state. Aristotle's *Politics* was translated into Latin by William of Moerbeke in the 1260s and was shortly afterwards used by Albertus Magnus and Thomas Aquinas.[102] In his treatise on royal power from 1271-73,[103] Thomas points both to biological and social needs for a community. Animals have claws and teeth that they can use to get food, whereas human beings must depend on their reason and have to act together to safisfy their needs. Moreover, reason and speech are social qualities, which then leads Aristotle to his conclusion about society being necessary for the good life. From this, Thomas deduces the necessity of government: All that exists has a purpose; government is necessary to achieve this purpose, in the same way as a ship cannot get where it is heading without a captain. Although this government may also be a collective group, Thomas, in contrast to Aristotle, arrives quite quickly at the conclusion that government by a king is the best way of organising a society. Thomas's theory was adapted by a series of other theorists and was used directly to defend the king against the Church in the conflict between King Philip IV of France and Pope Boniface VIII, in a similar way to how the text quoted above was used.[104]

Aristotle's political doctrine was thus a new discovery in the 1280s, but several of the regents seem to have been well acquainted with the legal and philosophical learning at the universities. Moreover, the brief reference does not necessitate any deeper study of Aristotle and may even have been picked up without any direct knowledge of his work. Nevertheless, despite the brevity of their reference, the regents made much out of the doctrine by iden-

---

100 Dunbabin, "Government", pp. 498-501.
101 Bagge, *The Political Thought*, pp. 22-25.
102 According to Flüeler, *Rezeption*, pp. 28 f., who refers to F. Bossier, the first, incomplete translation was finished around 1260 and the later, complete one during the first half of 1265. Thomas refers to the Politics for the first time in 1262-64, Albertus a little earlier, between 1250 and 1261.
103 Thomas Aquinas, *De regimine principum* I.1 – also, and probably more correctly – called *De regno*. This work was earlier dated to c. 1265/66, but closer studies of Thomas's use of William of Moerbeke's translation have shown that it must be later, and that Thomas first used the *Politics* in his theological works (Flüeler, *Rezeption*, pp. 23-29).
104 Aegidius Romanus, *De regimine principum* III.1-5 (c. 1277) ; Scholz, *Publizistik*, 324-27, on John of Paris.

tifying loyalty and obedience to the ruler so closely with society and the social order itself. In this, they may also have been influenced by contemporary interpretations of Roman law which laid the foundation for the later doctrine of the sovereignty of the state, and by the contemporary trend, notably in France, to emphasise the king's prerogatives; here Aegidius Romanus' work, composed for Philip IV as a young prince, is a famous example.[105] These arguments may also suggest a different general ideology than that of King Magnus, replacing the equality between the monarchy and the Church by a "statist" doctrine of all power being derived from the king, also in accordance with the more advanced secular theory based on Roman law and Aristotle, a doctrine that also underlies the barons' interpretation of the reservation clause in the concordat. Generally, the terminology indicates a considerable development of political theory from the 1270s and 1280s onwards. Whereas the term *lands nauðsynjar* (the necessities/needs of the realm), despite its obvious derivation from the Latin *necessitas regni*, has a vague and untechnical meaning in *The King's Mirror*,[106] it becomes more technical in the ordinances from 1280 onwards.[107] It was even used directly to legitimate new burdens on the population, as when the Icelandic Bishop Arne used it to support the royal demand for *leidang* from Iceland in 1286.[108] Although *sæmd*, together with *tign*, is used in *A Speech against the Bishops* and *The King's Mirror* at least partly about the king's rights and prerogatives in the same sense as *honor*, another important term, *kóróna/krúna* (Lat. *corona*), is not.[109] *Sæmd kórónanar* in the ordinance of 1281/82 is therefore a novelty, while most other examples are from the early fourteenth century. Thus, despite the lack of a systematic treatise like *The King's Mirror*, there are many indications that the brain trust in the regency of the 1280s was familiar with the political thought of European courts and universities and had a clear theory of royal prerogatives and the power of the state. This ideology might have radical consequences but was in practice used with greater moderation to defend the king's and the laity's interests against those of the Church and to reject most of the provisions of the concordat without formally revoking it.

Regnum *and* Sacerdotium *in Norway*

The negotiations and conflicts in the 1270s and 1280s, like the ones in the twelfth century, show a relationship between the monarchy and the Church similar to that found in

---

105 Dunbabin, "Government", pp. 482-98.
106 Bagge, *The Political Thought*, pp. 189-93; cf. also Berges, *Fürstenspiegel*, p. 183, who regards it as a technical term, resembling the later concept of reason of state.
107 NGL III p. 6 (1280), p. 32 (1280-99) and p. 46 (1302).
108 *Árna saga* ch. 110; cf. Bagge, *The Political Thought*, pp. 36 f.
109 Bagge, *The Political Thought*, pp. 195 f.

most other countries in Europe. Within Scandinavia the Norwegian conflict in the 1270s and 1280s has a parallel in the contemporary conflicts between the Danish king and the Church, notably under the Archbishops Jacob Erlandsen (1252-74), Jens Grand (1289-1302) and Esger Juul (1310-25). The Danish conflict was more prolonged and bitter as well as more complex. Danish historians have also held widely different opinions on the relationship between legal and ideological issues and political interests during these struggles.[110] Jurisdiction and legal arguments played an important role there as well, and the legal position of both parties can be examined through detailed petitions brought before the papal court. Nor was the question of jurisdiction confined to that of the division between the competence of the two powers. The conflict between the king and Archbishop Jacob Erlandsen started as a conflict between the archbishop and the inhabitants of his diocese, in which the archbishop demanded more severe punishment for violence, murder and homicide, whereas the people resisted any change in the law, demanding a return to the old law from the late twelfth century. There was also a conflict over appointments to clerical offices, like in Norway. The most important difference, however, was the feudal aspect of the conflict which concerned the archbishop as one of the king's main vassals with extensive secular power within his diocese, above all in connection with the *leding*. The king complained that the archbishop did not perform his duties in this field, whereas the archbishop demanded greater independence than the king was willing to allow him.[111] The struggle between the king and the archbishop also tended to merge with the other conflicts at the time, whereas in Norway the secular aristocracy was the main enemy of the Church, as is well illustrated by the aggressive policy of the regency government. This was particularly the case under Jens Grand who was related to some of the magnates convicted of the murder of Erik Klipping. Although the Danish aristocracy did not have equally strong motives as the Norwegian one to oppose the Church, however, its majority usually sided with the king. Finally, the ecclesiastical party in the Danish conflicts was confined to the archbishop and a small minority of the other bishops, which serves to explain the Church's defeat. The archbishop's influence outside his own diocese also seems to have been more limited than that of his Norwegian counterpart. Although the Norwegian bishops were hardly united behind Jon Raude in the 1280s, the conflict seems to have affected a larger part of the Church in this country. The Church in Norway also managed fairly well compared to its Danish counterpart, where the archbishops were

---

110 For brief surveys of the conflicts, see Paludan, "Tiden 1241-1340", pp. 484-89, and Skovgaard-Petersen, "The Danish Kingdom", pp. 363-66. The most detailed account is Skyum-Nielsen, *Kirkekampen i Danmark*.
111 Skyum-Nielsen, *Kirkekampen*, pp. 63-88, 103-6 and *passim*.

repeatedly defeated, and, despite the dramatic episodes in the beginning of the 1280s, the antagonism between the parties was less than in Denmark.

There were also conflicts between the monarchy and the Church in Sweden.[112] After King Magnus Ladulås (1275-90) had favoured the Church considerably, the regency for his son Birger, led by the magnate Torgils Knutsson, reversed this policy, which led to a conflict between the two powers. The conflict ended in 1305, when King Birger had reached majority and the conflict had begun between him and his brothers. In this conflict, King Birger seems, at least initially, to have returned to his father's policy, whereas his brothers continued that of Torgils Knutsson, but the lines of division were not consistent, nor was the Church united during the struggles. Whereas the archbishop supported the king, the bishops of Linköping and Skara – the two richest sees in the country – were on the side of the dukes. After 1319, the Church seems to have improved its position, both during the regency and after King Magnus reached majority. Thus, we find the same tendency as in Norway towards rivalry between the Church and the lay aristocracy, whereas the king might use the Church to counterbalance the latter which was stronger in Sweden than in Norway. The relative wealth and power of the two churches is more difficult to assess. The ecclesiastical organisation was slow to develop in Sweden but had reached an advanced stage around 1300, and the Swedish Church played an important political role during the Later Middle Ages.

Concerning the general status of the Norwegian Church, it may immediately seem that its privileges were modest. Its tax privileges were clearly less extensive than normal, and the rights of jurisdiction it fought for in the 1270s and 1280s were well established in most other countries. From this point of view, Seip's picture of Jon Raude as an extremist who always demanded more than the other party was able to give is wrong. On the other hand, these privileges must be considered against the background of those of the lay aristocracy which were also far more restricted in Norway. By the thirteenth century, the bishops largely seem to have controlled the local churches; there is little evidence of lay patronage at this time, although, like in other countries, monasteries and cathedral chapters controlled local churches. With regard to the election of bishops, the king was probably the only layman powerful enough to have any influence which he also managed to exert, although hardly to the extent that the cathedral chapters' rights were seriously diminished. It would thus seem that Archbishop Jon must take a considerable part of the responsibility for the bitterness of the conflict, and that things calmed down fairly quickly after his death. Most of the other bishops and archbishops seem to have been more pragmatic and intent on having a good working relationship with the secular power

---

112 For the following, see Brilioth, *Svenska kyrkans historia* II, pp. 22-90.

– something they achieved with the exception of the early 1280s and a new conflict under the next regency government in the 1320s (below p. 359).

From the king's point of view, the Church certainly represented a limit to his power, but in the High Middle Ages was not to any great extent directly involved in running the royal government – although this changed in the Later Middle Ages. In so far as the higher clergy was involved in the royal government, it was on an individual basis where the prelates would act in a similar way as members of the secular aristocracy. Nor would the Church necessarily stand united during conflicts with the monarchy. Usually the king, in Norway as elsewhere, could mobilise support from some clerics in such conflicts. Moreover, the Church was a highly complex organisation with considerable tension between its various institutions. Thus, one of the reasons why the Church failed to continue the struggle against the monarchy after the 1280s was the conflict that broke out between the cathedral chapter of Trondheim and the new archbishop Jørund, elected in 1287.

As already mentioned, the monarchy and the Church together formed the equivalent to the state of later ages. In several respects, the Church may be said to be more state-like than the organisation headed by the king, having more salaried officials of a more professional character, a more fine-meshed administration, and a more direct contact with the majority of the population. The Church was also wealthier than the monarchy. Not only were its incomes from landed estates far superior to those of the king, but it also had similar incomes to those of the king from public administration, namely taxes in the form of the tithe, which was actually the heaviest tax in the country, and fines. It was also to some extent able to get free labour services from the people, notably in building and maintaining the churches, but was apparently inferior to the king in this respect. Moreover, the Church lacked the king's opportunity to impose extra taxes.[113] When measuring the sigificance of this wealth, we of course have to take into account that it had to be divided between a significantly larger number of people than those of the king, around 2000 clerics, according to Bull's calculation, plus a number of laymen in the service of the Church.

Economically as well as administratively, the Church was thus a much centralised institution. Nevertheless, compared to the monarchy, it had its greatest strength on the local level; it was in most respects weaker on the central level. Admittedly, the Church was a universal power, with the pope as the leader of the whole of Western Christendom, and he had no secular parallel – the universal Empire was never more than a dream of some intellectuals serving or admiring the German emperor, like Dante. By contrast, the pope's leadership of the ecclesiastical organisation was a reality, although he was never strong enough to defeat secular rulers alone; he always needed aid from other secular

---

113 Bjørkvik, *Folketap*, pp. 63 f.

rulers. Thus, the Norwegian bishops could appeal to the pope during struggles with the king and receive support in the form of letters and spiritual sanctions whose importance largely depended on other factors. To Sverre, who already had to fight repeated rebellions, the Church was a dangerous enemy, and the Norwegian archbishop and bishops also received the pope's support in the form of excommunication and interdict. The regency government in the 1280s, however, had nothing to fear from an internal opposition and could use harsh measures against the clergy without any immediate fear of punishment. The pope's support for the bishops on this occasion was lukewarm.

The pope's control of the Church under more normal circumstances is open to discussion. It was no doubt less in practice than in theory; the numerous proclamations from the popes about their universal, God-given power to rule the Church, and the enormous output of documents from the papal chancery from the thirteenth century onwards give an exaggerated impression. Nevertheless, considering the distances, the slowness of communication and the limited means the popes had to enforce their authority, their ability to rule the Church at all is quite impressive. Despite the fact that Norway was one of the most distant countries of Western Christendom, there is no doubt that the pope's authority was felt even there. Although there is little evidence of contact with the curia until around 1150, the ties were strengthened after the foundation of the church province. A regular correspondence started under Archbishop Øystein and was continued under his successor Eirik, in which the archbishop sought advice on various matters regarding theology, liturgy and canon law.[114] The archbishops also normally went to the curia to receive their pallium and at least partially fulfilled their obligation of *ad limina* visits, normally by proxy. The pope was also involved in episcopal elections in case of irregularities, and there is ample evidence in our limited source material of contested issues among Norwegian ecclesiastical institutions being appealed to the pope. From the point of view of the local clergy, the pope's leadership might be an asset as well as a liability. It contributed to the wealth, power and prestige of the local churches, whereas papal interference in local matters was often detested, and the possibility of appeals might have led to endless conflicts and suits before the curia.

Despite the strength resulting from the pope's leadership, the Church lacked a leadership as strong as the monarchy's on the national level. The archbishop was only a *primus inter pares*, although apparently more involved in governing the Norwegian Church than his counterparts in Denmark and Sweden. Still, his options for interfering in the other dioceses were limited. He had little influence over episcopal elections and no regular control over the other bishops, at least not over the Norwegian ones – although he seems to

---

[114] *Lat. dok.* nos. 11-41; cf. Bagge, "Den heroiske tid", pp. 59-62.

have been in a stronger position in relationship to the bishops in the less developed dioceses outside Norway, notably Iceland. His only real possibility to rule the whole Church province was through the provincial councils which, as we shall see (p. 336), were infrequent occurrences and probably required the consent of the other bishops. Moreover, the wealth and complexity of the ecclesiastical organisation was not only an asset but also a liability. The bishops' sovereignty over their dioceses was limited by other ecclesiastical bodies: monasteries, religious orders (notably the mendicants) and during the thirteenth century increasingly by the cathedral chapters.

In addition, there is the issue of physical versus ideological power. The king of Norway's physical power was clearly superior to that of the bishops and serves to explain what happened in the 1280s. On the other hand, physical power depends on loyalty which can be undermined by ideological power. Would the Norwegian monarchy have been able to withstand a prolonged resistance from a united Church, for instance in the form of an interdict against the country in which the whole clergy took part? The drastic action against the Church in the early 1280s shows the superiority of the monarchy's physical power in the short run, probably also of its ideological power, as it seems to have chosen the right issues to mobilise the population against the demands of the Church. Nevertheless, the general ideological strength of the Church in religious and cultic matters set limits for how far the monarchy could go by means of its greater physical power. Nor should we focus exclusively on the conflicts between the monarchy and the Church in discussing the relationship between them. Conflicts like the ones in the 1190s and the 1280s were after all rare. Despite occasional rivalries and disagreements in other periods as well, there was a great amount of cooperation and considerable common interests. Both powers wanted to strengthen public justice; the king saw it as his duty to strengthen the Christian religion and needed the bishops' and the clergy's help in governing the country, whereas the Church needed the king to keep peace in the country and to provide the necessary physical power to protect the clergy and the interests of the Church. The king's conquest of the Church, its organisation and estates, which took place at the Reformation was still unthinkable in the late thirteenth and early fourteenth centuries. In this period, the governmental power was divided between two organisations, largely in cooperation, occasionally in conflict, while the king was exterting a kind of superiority over the largely independent and well-developed ecclesiastical organisation.

The Secular Aristocracy

There has been a strong tradition in Norwegian historiography of understanding the secular aristocracy as a class or an estate. The struggle between the monarchy and the aristocracy was a central theme in nineteenth-century historiography,[115] until it was replaced by the idea of a solidarity between the two in the Marxist tradition from the early twentieth century onwards. At the same time, the earlier idea of the defeat of the aristocracy by the Sverre dynasty was changed to that of a victory, so that from the early thirteenth century the king became an instrument of the aristocracy, together with the Church. Although this particular interpretation was modified by the empiricist tradition of the post-war period, the idea of a relatively well-defined aristocracy which played an important political role in Norway has remained.[116]

Norway in the period between 1240-1350 was no doubt an aristocratic society by modern, if not so much by contemporary standards, in a period when the wealth and importance of the great landowners was greater than in any other period before or after. As we have seen, it is also a likely hypothesis that the lay aristocracy was relatively wealthier than in Bjørkvik's calculation. However, the political consequences of this observation are more difficult to draw. There is no evidence of an aristocratic consolidation as a cause of the civil wars; such a consolidation may rather be regarded as a result of the wars, in the sense that it took place because a large number of prominent men were included in the victorious Birchleg faction. The king was also clearly interested in joining as many of the wealthy and influential men to his service as possible, as emerges quite clearly from *The King's Mirror*. As this consolidation had its origin in the king, his service became the definition for aristocratic rank. From a political point of view, the core of the aristocracy were the men in the king's direct service, the *sysselmenn* and highest officers in the central administration, to whom were added a wider circle of men (*handgengnir menn*) who had pledged themselves to particular loyalty to the king through a special ceremony, the *handganga*.[117] The organisational framework for these men was the king's *hird*. The *hird* originally denoted elite forces in the king's or other great men's service but in the more peaceful period after the end of the civil wars developed into an organisation of the aristocracy, whether its members were permanently in the king's household or not. The *hird* is described in detail in the Hird Law.[118] It consisted of three classes: from the top downwards the *hirdmenn*, the "guests" and the housecarls. Above the *hirdmenn* were the leaders of the hird, the *hirdstjorar*, first the *lendmenn* and then the *skutilsveinar*. The law

---

115 Dahl, *Norsk historieforskning*, pp. 60-64, 165-78; Bagge, "The Middle Ages", pp. 112-16. An exception is Hertzberg, *Det norske aristokratis*, pp. 106-10, 119 f., 124, who points out that the aristocracy did not form a coherent class or estate with common interests.
116 Holmsen, *Norges historie*, pp. 251-78; Benedictow, "Norge", pp. 9-29; Helle, *Norge blir en stat*, pp. 30-32 with references.
117 I.e. men who had touched the king's hands as a sign of loyalty. See Hamre, "Handgengnir menn" and below p. 331 on the ceremony.
118 Hamre, "Hird"; Bagge, "Hird".

emphasises the loyalty and obedience its members owed to the king as well as the solidarity between them, the latter in a manner resembling a guild.

From this startingpoint, the *hird* might have developed into an aristocratic estate and there were actually tendencies in this direction. First, membership became more exclusive after 1240. The opportunity for proletarians to ascend to the highest positions in society was an episode from Sverre's early years and may even have been exaggerated in the saga, but social mobility was certainly decreasing during the thirteenth century, even from *The King's Mirror* in the 1250s to the Hird Law in the 1270s. *The King's Mirror* points out that low-born men were more loyal, because they only had the king to look to for support,[119] but also underlines the importance of attaching the aristocracy to the king's service. The Hird Law seems to take for granted that the members of the *hird* come from the upper levels of society which largely corresponded to the reality at that time; many members also descended from other members. Admittedly, there are a few examples, also in later years, of men who had advanced from scribe in the chancery to *sysselmann* or judge (above pp. 258 f.). Since we do not know the social background of the scribes, it is difficult to determine the significance of these examples; nor do we know how representative they are. No form of established promotional ladder existed, and genuine aristocrats are not likely to have spent any significant time in a subservient position before they became *sysselmenn*. On the other hand, there is no evidence of positions in the king's service being hereditary, despite some examples of several generations of the same family acting as royal office-holders.

Second, an aristocratic ethos and norm system was introduced in the mid-thirteenth century onwards under the influence from the neighbouring countries and European chivalrous literature.[120] Institutionally, this influence was expressed in the introduction of knighthood, aristocratic privileges and European aristocratic titles. The first step in this direction was taken by King Magnus Håkonsson who in 1277 replaced the titles of *lendmann* and *skutilsvein* by baron – probably intended as an equivalent to the English crown vassals – and knight respectively.[121] Under Håkon V, "squire" (*sveinn*) was used as a title for ordinary *hirdmenn*. Further, Håkon abolished the title of baron or *lendmann* in 1308 (below p. 327). Finally, the introduction of seals and coats of arms as well as honorary titles and addresses (Herr = Sir and Fru = Lady, honourable, etc.) may be understood

---

119 Bagge, *The Political Thought*, pp. 178 f.
120 Löfqvist, *Riddarväsen*, pp. 112-52.
121 The change of titles is only mentioned in the Icelandic Annals, and it was hardly consistent. When Håkon V in 1300 gave the clerics of the royal chapel of St Mary's aristocratic rank, he used the old titles (DN I no. 92). On the other hand, Löfqvist, *Riddarväsen*, pp. 113-17, points to some anticipation of the new titles in Latin documents before 1277, but the significance of this is doubtful, as the change of language necessitated an adaptation to European terminology.

as steps towards the formation of an aristocratic estate.[122] Karl-Erik Löfqvist, who traces this development in considerable detail, concludes that it led to the dissolution of the *hird* shortly after 1319, but that it was otherwise of limited importance.[123] The Norwegian aristocracy appropriated titles and other elements from its European counterparts but without any fundamental change in its character. By contrast, Ole Jørgen Benedictow concludes from the same evidence that a fundamental change took place when the *hird* and its complex ranking system was replaced by an aristocratic estate divided into two levels, those of knight and squire.[124] The titles were still conferred by the king but they did not imply an organisation headed by him, nor a particular service function; they simply served to denote aristocratic rank.

However, the importance of these changes is less obvious than Benedictow assumes. As pointed out by Löfqvist, the new names may simply be an adaptation of the traditional ranks to the European style. Nor are the ranks of knight and squire incompatible with more finely graded systems. As they coexisted with various aristocratic ranks – like duke, marquis, earl and baron – in almost all countries of Europe, there is no reason why they should not do so in Norway as well. A more likely explanation for the suppression of the rank of baron/*lendmann* is the administrative changes in the previous period (below pp. 347-49). Nor is there much evidence that the *hird* was becoming obsolete in the period before 1319 and even less that the kings at the time intended to abolish it. It is strongly present in Håkon V's ordinance of 1308 in which he abolishes the title of *lendmann*.[125] In this ordinance a new deputy leader is appointed, while at the same time the king insists on his own personal leadership of the organisation. Provisions are made for a hospital for old and diseased *hirdmenn* and for recruitment to the *hird*, and membership of the *hird* is still the defining criterion for aristocratic status and thus a necessary mark of distinction. Finally, we should not attribute too much importance to the *hird* members' physical absence from the king. The king was not confined to an apartment in the palace, surrounded by a limited number of top bureaucrats; he was almost constantly on the move between the main towns of his kingdom, and he was surrounded by his court, probably consisting of a considerable number of people. We know very little about the Norwegian court in the thirteenth and early fourteenth centuries, but get some glimpses from the sources. As we have seen, *The King's Mirror* suggests a fairly simple and straightforward ceremonial, but nevertheless customs that are clearly distinct from those prevailing outside the court and which serve

---

122 Benedictow, "Norge", pp. 22 f.
123 Löfqvist, *Riddarväsen*, pp. 141 f., 148 f.; Benedictow, "Konge, Hird", pp. 260-73, and Opsahl, *Herresvein-institusjonen*, pp. 67-70, also maintain that the *hird* disappeared.
124 Ibid.
125 DN XI no. 6, see below.

to underline the respect for the king. The author's insistence on the right manners and his severe criticism of the *hirdmenn* may suggest the introduction of a number of novelties in life at court, in line with the import of courtly romance. Finally, *Hákonar saga* gives some descriptions of festivities at court, in addition to the annual Christmas celebrations, notably coronations and weddings, where a large number of people were gathered. *Erikskrönikan* gives a glimpse of the festivities for Christmas 1302, when Duke Erik charmed his future mother-in-law.[126] Most telling, however, is the story of Håkon Håkonsson breaking up and selling his silver plate during Christmas 1239-40 to be able to entertain his men despite the lack of provisions resulting from the war with Skule (above p. 82).

Thus, with the exception of the suppression of the rank of *lendmann*, the change of titles was of limited importance for the development of the aristocracy and can hardly be understood as a development in the direction of the suppression of the *hird*. Nor is the fact that the *hird* had disappeared in the neighbouring countries a good argument for concluding that it was bound to disappear in Norway as well. The reason why it had become superfluous in Denmark and Sweden was that both these countries had developed an aristocratic estate based on specialised military service in return for privileges. Both the elite forces and the privileges in Norway were too modest for this to happen there, although there were tendencies towards this, the most important of which were elite forces and sub-infeudation.[127] Despite some chivalrous ethos, the Norwegian aristocracy was an administrative more than a military class. Less than two years of land warfare during the whole period 1240-1319 is unlikely to have contributed to the formation of a truly military aristocracy. For a young man wanting to enter the king's service it might have been an equally good or even better investment to go to the University of Orléans or Bologna and return with some volumes of Justinian's *Corpus iuris civilis*[128] than to enter the service of some foreign king and return with horse and armour. Thus, in the early fourteenth century, membership of the *hird* was still the only distinction between aristocrats and commoners. Although this membership did not in itself entail very substantial privileges, it did distinguish a man from others of the same wealth and standing and it was an important instrument for the king to gain the loyalty and service of the prominent men in the country. In the case of the *sysselmenn*, who were bound to the king with strong ties of loyalty, the *hird* may be regarded as superfluous, but the king also depended on many other prominent men, living throughout the country, who served him in various capaci-

---

126 *Erikskrönikan*, pp. 89-93.
127 See pp. 102 f. and Opsahl, *Herresvein-institusjonen*, pp. 10-12, 161-76.
128 The example is not invented. Bjarne Audunsson, a prominent member of Håkon V's council, was in Bologna in the 1290s and owned a copy of the *Corpus iuris civilis* (Helle, *Konge og gode menn*, pp. 599 f.) – although according to his testament (DN XVI no. 2), he also owned various arms.

ties, apparently in return for a relatively small compensation. In the case of these men, the *hird* and the ceremony of *handganga* formed an important link to the king.

The *hird* is also mentioned after 1319; the title *hirdmann* for individual members lingered on, occurring as late as the late fifteenth century.[129] Between 1319 and 1350, the *hird* occurs in 1323 when Queen Ingebjørg was deposed as a regent and replaced by Erling Vidkunsson at a meeting referred to as a *hirðstefna*. The *hirðstefna* also met in 1328 in Bergen in connection with the conflict between the regency and the bishop of Bergen.[130] Finally, the Icelandic Annals state that King Magnus in 1350 placed his two sons on the throne and gave them *hird*.[131] Erik Opsahl concludes that neither of the two meetings conform to a *hirðstefna* as described in the Hird Law and that the reference in the Icelandic Annals is an archaism.[132] However, there is little or no evidence of the Hird Law's *hirðstefna* in practice even before 1319, and quite likely many of the provisions in the law had little practical importance. Thus, the examples referred to above do not in themselves indicate that the *hird* had become obsolete. On the other hand, both the unions and the development of a more exclusive aristocracy, partly based on birth, with the Council of the Realm as its political forum, eventually led to the decline of the *hird*, although this process is not easy to follow in detail.

The *hird* therefore still had a function in Norwegian society in the early fourteenth century, and at least formally the aristocracy was not very different in 1319 from what it had been in 1240. Its relationship to the king was thus fundamentally different from that of the ecclesiastical aristocracy. Whereas the Church was an independent institution on which the king's influence was confined to the opportunity to exert some pressure on episcopal elections and the awareness on the part of the cathedral chapters that it would not be acceptable to appoint the king's enemies, the whole secular aristocracy was defined by its relationship to the king. Formally, it is therefore more difficult to discuss the king's relationship to the aristocracy than to the Church, although in reality particular aristocratic interests may well have existed, partly coinciding and partly conflicting with those of the king.

The King and the Aristocracy: Ideology

The thirteenth century was a period of constitutional struggles in many countries of Europe. Earlier constitutional theories had been vague, based on a general consensus that the king should rule with the advice of the leading men in the country but without any duty

---

129 Hamre, "Hird", col. 576; Opsahl, *Herresvein-institusjonen*, pp. 70-77.
130 DN IX no. 100; Helle, *Kongssete og kjøpstad*, p. 605; Opsahl, *Herresveininstitusjonen*, pp. 71 f.
131 *Isl. Ann.*, pp. 276, 404 (*Lögmanns* and *Flatey* annals).
132 Opsahl, *Herresveininstitusjonen*, pp. 74-77.

to consult them on specific issues as long as he was able "to live from his own", meaning his own estates and other regular incomes. Now, however, conflicts occurred in many countries, and the opposition between two kinds of government, *dominium regale* and *regimen politicum*, were formulated under the influence of Aristotle's political thought.[133] Although the exact importance of these explicit theories in Scandinavia is not quite clear,[134] there is evidence of similar constitutional conflicts in Denmark and Sweden in the late thirteenth and early fourteenth centuries. By contrast, the relationship between the king and the aristocracy in Norway seems to have been harmonious and the statements about this relationship are less numerous and vaguer than those concerning the Church. The most explicit theory is found in the *The King's Mirror* which shows no influence from Aristotle but which has a general ideology that clearly conforms to *dominium regale*. This is similar to the ideology expressed in the National Law and the regency's propaganda against the Church, the latter of which is based on Aristotelian ideas combined with a strong emphasis on the king as responsible for the social order (although with the possible reservation implied in the reference to his consultations with "good" or "wise" men). There can thus be no doubt about the *dominium regale* as a general ideology for the king's relationship to the people. On the other hand, the reference to the king's council plus the fact that the clearest expression of the monarchical ideology comes from the aristocratic council ruling the country in the early 1280s may suggest a different relationship between the king and the secular aristocracy.

The main ideological evidence for this relationship comes from the Hird Law and from various royal ordinances from the late thirteenth and early fourteenth centuries. Regarding the former, there has been some discussion as to whether it is based on a contract between the king and his men or on the king as the sovereign authority over his retainers.[135] The Hird Law is vague regarding constitutional principles, but a number of specific statements seem to point to the former conclusion, whereas its general ideology points in the direction of the latter.[136] When a new king takes over, the *hirdmenn* should

---

133 Dunbabin, "Government", pp. 482-88.
134 The main contribution to the discussion of these theories in Scandinavia is Lönnroth, *Kalmarunionen*, pp. 17-40, and Christensen, *Kongemagt og aristokrati*, pp. 195-238, based particularly on medieval theorists like Marsilius of Padua and William Occam and modern scholars like the Carlyles and McIlwain who most probably exaggerate the importance of the idea of *regimen politicum*, in particular its influence on practical politics. See also Linton, "Regimen regale et politicum".
135 Benedictow, "Konge, hird", pp. 233-54 with references.
136 Concerning the general ideology, Benedictow, "Konge, hird", p. 253, points to a passage allegedly stating that the king is *jafnskyldugr maðr* = "a man with equal obligations", as the *hirdmenn* (H 51, p. 176). However, the word in the text is *jafnskyldr* = "equally related to" and does not refer to the king at all, but to the case when a man in a battle gives quarter (*grið*) to his relative and the king or the *hirdmenn* do not want the latter to remain in the *hird*, in which case he shall have *grið* in escaping, "because he had been given it by his relative."

swear an oath of loyalty to him; which probably implies that he was normally supposed to take over his predecessor's *hird*.[137] The king is obligated to consult the *hirdmenn* when admitting new members[138] and the *hirdmenn* have to pass judgement together with the king when a member commits a serious crime.[139] Apart from these provisions, there are very few contractual elements in the Hird Law, not only because of the general royalist ideology, but also because so few passages actually deal with specific rights and duties. The law gives clear descriptions of how the king was to appoint the members of the *hird* and retainers of various ranks but does not specify the number of such men to be appointed, nor prescribes that the king was obliged to appoint them. In the case of the earl, it even states that it is best to have no earl at all.[140] Contrary to Benedictow's interpretation, the *handganga* ceremony contains no element of mutual contract: The candidate kneels before the king on both knees, touches the hilt of the coronation sword and kisses the king's hand. Then he gets up and swears an oath of fealty. Then he kneels once more and, joining his hands together, he reaches out to the king who folds his own hands around the candidate's hands. Finally, he kisses the king.[141] The reception of the sword, the kisses[142] and the king holding the *hirdmann*'s hands in his own all express subordination and loyalty on the part of the latter, and the oath, sworn only by the *hirdmann*, is solely about his duties towards the king. He swears loyalty and trust, to follow the king wherever he wants and not part from him without permission, and to keep the king's oaths to the people. Numerous allusions to this ceremony or parts of it in the sagas form evidence that it must have existed in a similar form well before the Hird Law, although the strong emphasis on obedience may well have been a novelty from the thirteenth century.

The general ideology of the Hird Law is clearly expressed in the agreements the king made with his retainers, *sysselmenn*, and other servants in 1273-74 concerning the elite force they were to provide in case of war. For the most part, the responsibilities dominate these negotiations. What kind of negotiations took place, and what the king's men were given in return for the mostly military burdens they took on, is unknown. What the king genuinely achieved through his servants is in other words uncertain, but the formal sub-

---

137 H 6.
138 H 25.
139 H 35.
140 H 9.
141 H 26. Cf. Benedictow, "Konge, Hird", p. 252: "Forholdet mellom kongen og hans håndgangne menn har vært et gjensidig forpliktende vassalitetsforhold."
142 In both cases, the *hirdmann* kisses the king, not vice versa, as Benedictow claims regarding the kiss after the oath (Benedictow, "Konge, Hird", p. 249). Even this possible evidence of mutuality is thus absent. By contrast, the lord kissing the vassal in the European ritual is interpreted by Guilaume Durand as an expression of mutual trust (Le Goff, 'Le rituel symbolique de la vassalité", p. 335).

servience to the king is clear: "And then the cases which follow were perfectly resolved through the faithfulness which they [the king's men] owed God and him [the king]."[143] Here the spirit of *The King's Mirror*, which also occurs in other passages in the Hird Law, is manifest, with the king as "owner" of the inhabitants of the realm and as someone who can impose whatever task he chooses, and the obedient king's servant as Joseph who is promoted by Pharaoh! By appealing to faithfulness, the king is able to carry out his wishes; when the king's men give assent it is not because they have the right of refusal, but because the king is to be completely certain that they will obey him. In contrast to the Icelanders, the king's Norwegian servants would not make themselves "so grand" that they were given to questioning the king's commands. This was in sharp contrast to the contemporary agreements with the Church as an equal counterpart.

The same ideology is expressed in Håkon V's ordinance of 17 June 1308, where the king proclaims his intention of personally taking over the government of his kingdom and gives a number of detailed provisions about various political and administrative matters.[144] Both the interpretation and the status of this ordinance, including its validity, have been subject to discussion. As for the latter, Andreas Holmsen has suggested that it was not really intended as an ordinance to be put into practice but as a kind of political testament, whereas Ole Jørgen Benedictow maintains that the king here took decisions that needed the consent of his retainers and consequently was breaking the law.[145] An argument for both these conclusions is that the ordinance, contrary to normal practice, has only been included in a few lawbooks. According to Holmsen this means that it was not intended to have any long-term effects, whereas Benedictow explains this anomaly with the hypothesis that it was withdrawn because it was contrary to the law and replaced by an ordinance issued in the proper way with the consent of the retainers, an ordinance of which no trace remains in the sources.

It appears quite clearly from the text of the ordinance that the king did in fact believe that he was entitled to legislate on these matters without asking his retainers. His proclamation about taking his whole patrimony (*fǫðurleifð*) under him can be read as a direct answer to Benedictow's objection.[146] Håkon V alludes to the statement in *The King's Mirror* about the king as the owner of the country and its inhabitants, to the saga tradition of Harald Finehair's appropriation of all property in the country, and to contemporary

---

143 "ok stauððuzt þa fulkomlega þæir lutir sem her fylgia. vpp. a þa tru sum þæir ero guði skylðugir oc honom" (H 31, p. 132).
144 DN XI no 6.
145 Holmsen, "Retterboten av 1308"; Benedictow, "Konge, hird". Cf. also the critical comments to Holmsen's article by Lunden, "Om Håkon V's skipan".
146 "Þa takum ver oss til forraða fadur læifð vaara allt Noregs konungs riki" (DN XI no. 6, p. 11).

feudal ideas about the vassals' possession of land being derived from the king's superior ownership.[147] Not only the initial proclamation but also many of the provisions suggest that Håkon V believed that he had the right to issue provisions for his retainers and representatives in the central and local administration without any formal consent on their part. In this respect, he adhered to the usual understanding of the king's prerogatives in the previous century, as was clearly stated in King Louis IX's judgement in the conflict between Henry III of England and his barons in Amiens in 1264.[148] Normal theory gave the king considerable freedom in governing his realm and appointing and deposing officials. The limits to the king's power did not relate to the duty to seek the consent of his subjects, apart from a general idea that he should seek the advice of vassals and magnates, but rather to the duty to respect individual rights and privileges. Håkon would probably have been met with resistance if he had tried to deprive the existing *lendmenn* of their rights and privileges, but any legal objection against his ban on future appointments could hardly be raised. In principle, no individual could claim the right to be appointed *lendmann*. The same, of course, applies even more to the rest of the provisions, notably those concerning the *sysselmenn*. Whereas the Hird Law probably put some restrictions on the king's ability to exclude members of the *hird*, a membership that was largely honorary, this certainly did not apply to the *sysselmenn*. Although the *sysselmenn* must have been members of the *hird*, they are not listed as a separate rank, but are referred to in other sources as the king's servants, to be appointed or deposed by him.

There is therefore little to suggest that Håkon's ordinance of 17 June 1308 was not in accordance with the law as expressed in the Hird Law and other documents. There can hardly be any doubt that the king believed that he was entitled to issue the provisions contained in the document. Nor is it likely that his men openly expressed a different view and why should they? The provision allowed existing *lendmenn* to retain their rank; thus, no one was directly offended. Those who hoped eventually to become *lendmenn* might of course not have been very happy with the provision, but it would not have served them very well to protest. Even if their protest had been successful, it was up to the king himself to make the appointment, and he would not be particularly likely to promote those who had refused to obey his provision, especially as there might be enough rivals who would curry favour from the king by declining to join the opposition.

Furthermore, regarding the fact that the document is only preserved in a few copies, it is more significant that it exists at all. Nor does the fact that it exclusively concerns the king's men make it difficult to explain its limited transmission; the ordinances included

---

147 Bagge, *The Political Thought*, pp. 31-38 with references.
148 *Documents* 37A-C, pp. 252-91.

in manuscripts of the National Law are usually aimed at the people as a whole. It must also be pointed out that the majority of the provisions in the ordinance had their roots in the situation in 1308 and were hardly very relevant in the following decades. Admittedly, the suppression of the office of *lendmann* was most probably intended to have permanent validity, but as long as no one really thought of appointing any, the paragraph was of limited importance.[149] Finally, it hardly makes sense from a methodological point of view to conclude from the limited transmission of the document that it was considered illegal while at the same time claiming that it was replaced by another, lawful and constitutional document that has not been preserved at all. Empirically, it must also be added that documents of this kind are better preserved than those in any other category of letters issued by Håkon V's chancery (above p. 253). As for Holmsen's interpretation, his main argument is the lack of correspondence between Håkon's appointments and what actually seems to have happened in the following period. However, the fact that Håkon changed his decisions later is no argument against his intentions to put them into practice at the time.

The preceding discussion has shown that the current ideology in thirteenth-century Norway was closer to *dominium regale* than *regimen politicum* and consequently that *The King's Mirror* was not too far removed from the main line of contemporary thought. There were few exact limits to what the king could do on his own. Later kings seem to have regarded King Magnus's mandate from the people to revise the laws as permanent and to have acted accordingly when issuing emendations and improvements to the National Law. Whether this also applied to the Hird Law is less certain. On the one hand, there is no explicit statement to the effect that the king had received a permanent mandate to emend it; on the other, its general ideology is very concerned with loyalty and obedience towards the king. Nor did the fact that the king sought consent necessarily mean that he regarded the consenting parties as having decisive power. The idea of consent is in many cases combined with the idea of the duty of consenting, as for instance in the episode with Lodin Lepp at the Icelandic Allthing, which may also be compared to Edward I of England's and other kings' insistence on representatives to their parliaments having *plena potestas*, not in order to increase their power but in order to be able to force the bodies they were representing to accept what the king had made them agree to.[150] Moreover, not only did the king himself proclaim this ideology, but some of the strongest expressions of it came from the lay aristocracy itself, directed to the Church as well as to the people. Thus, the aristocracy, or at least those of its members who formulated these ideas, must

---

149 Hamre, "Håkon V's hirdskipan", p. 34 with reference to Gravelsæter's conclusion from her examination of the manuscripts that the ordinance must have been transcribed at least three times by the time it was issued or shortly afterwards but not often after that (Gravelsæter, "Håkon V Magnusson sin skipan", p. 87).
150 Post, *Studies*, pp. 108-62.

either have accepted the king's sovereign power or shared this power. In the case of the latter alternative, this must have happened at various kinds of meetings, from local or central assemblies to smaller circles in the king's surroundings.

From Assemblies of the Best Men to the King's Council

Until the mid-twelfth century, the only way for the king to influence legislation and communicate with the people was through negotiations at the *lagtings*.[151] Thereafter, assemblies for the whole country developed as an alternative forum for the king as well as the Church. These were held at irregular intervals and had different functions in each case, but clearly took over some of the functions of the *lagtings*, eventually even royal elections. Our estimate of the frequency of these meetings is largely a matter of definition. Knut Helle has listed seventy-two larger political meetings in the period 1130-1319, in addition to forty-one assemblies in the form of meetings with other kings or princes or mobilisations of the *leidang* for warfare or negotiations.[152] He regards twenty-five of these meetings as diets in the real sense, namely assemblies that were representative of the whole country and dealt with matters of national interest. The distinction between the two categories is not always clear, both because of the sources and because of the fact that the diet was not a clearly defined institution with fixed membership and competence and regular meetings. The king needed to discuss matters with or get support for his decisions from the people but had a flexible attitude regarding how many and whom he had to consult on such occasions. The only assemblies with a fixed competence and clearly defined representatives were the assemblies electing the king, consisting of the bishops and abbots, the *hird*, twelve representatives from each diocese, and according to the law of 1260, also the *lagmenn*. Although this was already decreed in the Law of Succession of 1163/64, no such assembly met until after the Law of 1260.

The meetings that can be said to have functioned as diets were thus both infrequent and irregular, twenty-five in 169 years makes only one per seven years. However, if we add all the others, which also formed occasions for the king to consult with important people, we arrive at nearly one per year. Furthermore, the meetings were not evenly distributed over the period. Twenty-two of the twenty-five "official" meetings took place in the period 1188-1281, or one every four years, and the last of them in 1302. This is hardly a coincidence. The first decades after 1150 were still dominated by regional meetings, whereas after 1281 increasing centralisation led to the assemblies' replacement by the king's coun-

---

151   For this and the following, see Helle, *Konge og gode menn*, pp. 103-310.
152   Helle, *Konge og gode menn*, pp. 185 f.; cf. also the list of the assemblies on pp. 111-84.

cil. The higher clergy was normally well represented at the meetings which in some cases even coincided with the provincial councils. This applies to the first recorded meeting, in connection with the foundation of the church province in 1152/53, as well as to the meetings in 1189/90, 1247 and 1280, and most likely the one in 1163/64.[153] As far as we know, however, provincial councils were relatively rare in the period when the secular meetings were most frequent. Most provincial councils for which we have information took place in the period 1280-1351, when statutes were preserved from ten councils, or one every seven years, which is nevertheless considerably less than the prescribed frequency of one per year. After 1351 statutes were only preserved from the council of 1436, but several others took place in the intermediate period.[154]

The best documented national meeting is the one in Bergen in 1223 which finally recognised Håkon Håkonsson as king and which is described in great detail in *Hákonar saga*.[155] Sixty-six participants are mentioned by name, in addition to "the best commoners from each *fylke*". The meeting lasted for around one month, from 29 July (St Olav's Day) until the end of August. According to the saga, most of the time was spent on meetings in smaller groups, either between the "chieftains" (probably mainly the two pretenders, Håkon and Skule) or between them and their adherents and counsellors. The saga regards the session of 20 August as the climax of the meeting. Here the *lagmenn* were asked to express their opinion on who was the rightful heir to the throne, and the archbishop declared Håkon to be the legitimate king based on their verdicts. This meeting was, according to the saga, attended by the leading men but not by the popular representatives who may, however, have given their formal acclamation at a later meeting.[156] Thus, the important decisions were clearly taken by the leading men. In the speeches attributed to them, even the *lagmenn* were reluctant to express their opinion in this august assembly, much like their counterparts in the story of Sigurd Ranesson (above p. 187). Most probably, however, they had less to fear, as the formal declarations at the meeting were likely to have been the result of the various informal meetings during the previous weeks.

However, it seems strange that the meeting was actually convoked to deal with the problem of succession.[157] Håkon had already been elected in 1217 and had proved his royal descent through his mother's ordeal in 1218. His position as king is well attested in the period 1217-23, not only in the saga but also in a few documents. Did Skule really attempt either to replace Håkon as king or, more likely, to achieve a full division of the

---

153 Helle, *Konge og gode menn*, pp. 216-20.
154 Skånland, "Provinsialkonsil", cols. 527-29; Haug, *Provincia Nidrosiensis*, pp. 347-51.
155 *HH* chs. 85-98.
156 Helle, *Konge og gode menn*, p. 137.
157 For the following, see Bagge, *From Gang Leader*, pp. 98-100 with references.

kingdom with himself as king beside Håkon? An argument for this would be that Skule now seemed to be in a strong position, having just defeated the Ribbungs in Eastern Norway and taken Sigurd Ribbung captive. However, a full division of the kingdom between two or more kings had not been practised since the mid-twelfth century, when it had resulted in open conflict between the co-rulers. Normal practice, on the Birchleg as well as the Crozier side, was to solve the problem of rival claimants to the throne by making one of them king and the other earl, which was also the arrangement agreed upon in 1217-18. It would seem that the real issue was the relationship between the two leaders rather than the succession itself. This was also, according to the saga, the subject of intense and complicated negotiations between Skule and Håkon after the meeting of 20 August, in which Skule demanded more land, while Håkon's counsellors and eventually Håkon himself wanted to reduce his part of the country. The discussion ended in a compromise to the effect that Skule, who had until then governed Eastern Norway, should move to Trøndelag. Afterwards new negotiations began about the border between the two territories which apparently ended in a compromise suggested by the archbishop.

If the real issue was the division of land between Håkon and Skule, the initiative for the meeting most probably came from Håkon. Admittedly, Skule might have used his victory to try to get more, as is hinted at in the saga, but the negotiations actually ended in victory for Håkon who was also the one who had the most to complain about before the meeting. A further argument to support this is the letter referred to in the saga from Håkon to Skule in 1222, pointing out that he had far more than a third of the country and threatening with war if he did not accept to reduce his part.[158] The fact that the meeting took place in Bergen also indicates that the initiative came from Håkon, as Western Norway was the region where he had the greatest support. Not only was the size of Skule's territory probably reduced, but moving him to Trøndelag also diminished his influence. Trøndelag was Skule's home region and natural stronghold, and his influence in this region would in any case be considerable. Having defeated the Ribbungs, he was now in a position to consolidate the Birchlegs' hold on Eastern Norway, which might make him Håkon's equal. Now Håkon would have this opportunity and be able to add this region to his own core region, Western Norway. There is also other evidence to show that Skule had to submit to Håkon to a greater extent after 1223 than before; he no longer acted as the co-ruler of the country together with Håkon. It was therefore hardly a coincidence that Sigurd Ribbung escaped from captivity soon afterwards, so that Håkon would have to spend several years fighting the Ribbungs.[159]

158 *HH* ch. 80.
159 *HH* ch. 103.

Thus, the meeting in 1223 had a more ad hoc and tactical character than immediately appears; the session of 20 August was not its climax but a mobilisation from Håkon before the difficult negotiations with Skule about the division of the country which was the real issue. This in turn means that the essential part of the great meeting was the direct negotiations between Skule and Håkon where both parties tried to mobilise as many men as possible to their side and where the archbishop and other prominent men intervened in order to reach a compromise. If the description in the saga of the assembly of 1223 is representative, it would seem that the assemblies in medieval Norway differed considerably from such institutions in more recent periods. On the one hand, they bear some resemblance to the *Hoftage* in medieval Germany and similar meetings between the king and the great men in other countries in medieval Europe where the social aspect (including eating and drinking together) was important, where there was no clear borderline between official sessions and more informal meetings and where the most important decisions were made in the latter.[160] In this latter respect, they probably also bore some resemblance to the Things as described in the Icelandic family sagas where negotiations and lobbying outside the formal sessions were also crucial in determining the outcome. We have no equally detailed description from the Norwegian *lagting*s but may imagine similar conditions there. It would also seem likely that the elite had a dominating influence there as well, although the fact that these were regional assemblies may have meant relatively greater influence for ordinary people or at least for the local leaders. The sagas contain several descriptions of negotiations at the *lagting* and other local Things over important matters, notably in connection with the introduction of Christianity. Here the king often addresses the whole assembly and either receives a response from one of its members, usually a local leader, or is met with expressions of either acceptance or rejection from the assembly as a whole in the form of acclamation or silence respectively.[161] In accordance with this, the sagas attribute great importance to the king's eloquence; a good leader had to possess the ability to address a large assembly in such a way that he obtained acceptance for his proposals.[162] The description of Sverre in *Sverris saga* can be generalised as follows: The winner is the one who is able to mobilise the people to follow him, whether he addresses his army before a battle or a Thing assembly, demanding to be elected or to obtain support for a law, an amendment or even a new religion.

It would seem from the description of the assembly of 1223 that this form of eloquence had become less important at the great assemblies compared to winning the support of a

160 Althoff, *Spielregeln*, pp. 157-84.
161 Bagge, *Society and Politics*, pp. 105-10 and 137-39 with references.
162 Bagge, *Society and Politics*, p. 149, and *From Gang Leader*, pp. 25-33. For examples in the sagas when kings negotiate at the Things about conversion to Christianity, see e.g. Oddr, pp. 94-96, 103-6, 114.

few leading men. There may therefore have been a change from *colloquium publicum* to *colloquium secretum* in Gerd Althoff's terminology.[163] In the following period, communication with the people took place in writing to a greater extent, although it was still necessary to address the Thing assemblies on special occasions, notably in connection with royal elections.[164] The elitist character of the central assemblies anticipated the emergence of a new governmental institution, the royal council, which from the reign of Håkon V (1299-1319) onwards replaced the assemblies. The royal council was in principle nothing new – the king had a circle of trusted men around him from early on – but before the thirteenth century, this circle consisted of individual men around the king, namely his friends. *Hákonar saga* contains more detailed references to the king's counsellors than earlier sagas; during the early years of Håkon's reign, the saga even regularly lists the names of a group of men who may have formed a kind of council.[165] This, however, must be an arrangement made because of the king's youth – he was only thirteen years old when he was elected – which was ended when he got older. In the following period, reference to the king's council only occurs in connection with periods of minority, after 1280, when Eirik Magnusson succeeded to the throne at the age of twelve, and in Håkon V's provisions for a future regency. It is clear from the sources, however, that both Eirik and Håkon were surrounded by a circle of trusted counsellors who, during Håkon's reign, replaced the larger assemblies. The main explanation for this development must clearly be political; the number of people important enough to need to be consulted diminished and power was concentrated in fewer hands. In a similar way, charters, laws, and other documents issued by the king or the ecclesiastical leaders tend to regard "peasants, merchants, and common people" as an undistinguished mass at the bottom of society (above p. 114). While aware of this development, Knut Helle also suggests geography as an explanation; the distances and long winters made it more difficult to organise such meetings in Norway than in many other countries.[166] However, this is unlikely to have been a factor, as sea communication made it easier to travel in Norway than in most other countries at the time. Surprisingly enough, from this point of view Sweden, which had the greatest difficulty in communication of all the Scandinavian countries, was also the country where the medieval meetings developed into a permanent institution. A Swedish Diet, consisting of four estates, eventually emerged towards the end of the Middle Ages and, as one of the few such institutions in Europe, survived until 1866 when it was replaced by a modern parliament with two chambers.

163 Althoff, *Spielregeln*, pp. 157-84.
164 Bagge, *Da boken*, pp. 416-29.
165 Helle, *Konge og gode menn*, p. 317.
166 Helle, *Konge og gode menn*, p. 310; cf. p. 304.

Who Were "The Best Men"?

Thus, around 1300 the most important political and governmental functions were, at least apparently, vested in the king and a small group of men, the king's counsellors and local representatives plus the bishops and the members of the higher clergy, not totalling much more than one hundred. Thus, from a political point of view, the development towards a more homogenous and exclusive aristocracy was crossed by another one, the change from the larger assemblies to the king's council and the emergence of the latter as the main forum for decision-making. Who were these men and how did they influence the king's decisions? Concerning the recruitment to the council and the offices in the central administration, Knut Helle distinguishes between three categories of men in the king's service: prelates, lay aristocrats, and what he calls the "service element", men selected because of their professional skills.[167] Helle concludes that there was a major shift from a regime dominated by the secular aristocracy under Eirik Magnusson to one based on the "service element" under Håkon V.[168] Only one member of the great *lendmenn* kindreds held a prominent position during Håkon's reign, namely Baron Bjarne Erlingsson of Bjarkøy. Two of Eirik's leading men fell into disgrace during Håkon's reign. Baron Audun Hugleiksson was hanged in 1302,[169] and another leading member of the former regency, Bjarne Lodinsson, was put in prison in 1302 but released somewhat later, at least before May 1304. When the war broke out between King Håkon and Duke Erik, Bjarne joined the latter. He died in 1311. Others continued in Håkon's service but were used less frequently. In addition, a number of new men of unknown background entered the royal service, according to Helle because of their skill and loyalty. Thus the aristocratic dominance was confined to Eirik Magnusson's reign; the more vaguely defined council before 1280 can hardly have been dominated by the aristocracy in the same way.

The problem with this view is that it is impossible to distinguish between men belonging to the aristocracy and to the "service element" in the king's council. Apart from a few men, such as Bjarne Erlingsson who belonged to one of the wealthiest families in the country, we know nothing of the wealth and family background of most of the counsel-

---

167 Helle, *Konge og gode menn*, pp. 393-414; cf. also 591-603.
168 Helle, *Konge og gode menn*, pp. 402-14.
169 Nothing is known about the circumstances and reason for this other than some brief notes in the Icelandic Annals stating that he was arrested in 1299 and hanged in 1302. Additionally, there is a ballad and some popular tales about his fate, although of doubtful value. Partly on the basis of them, various theories have been suggested by Munch, NFH IV.2 pp. 325, 348-52; Storm, "Audun Hestakorn", and Munthe, "Audun Hugleiksson" II , pp. 47-69. Helle, *Konge og gode menn*, p. 581, rejects these theories as guesswork but finds a reaction from Håkon against Audun's independent position in financial and foreign policy the most likely explanation. Brynildsrud arrives at a similar conclusion after a detailed discussion of the various ballads and tales. See most recently Nedrebø, *Audun Hugleiksson*, pp. 174-77.

lors, but as the criteria for aristocratic status were notoriously vague in the period, this does not necessarily indicate low status. Nor are high education and administrative skills characteristic of the service element in contrast to the aristocracy. Two of the best educated laymen in the period, Audun Hugleiksson and Bjarne Lodinsson, who were both prominent under Eirik Magnusson and fell into disgrace under Håkon V, belonged to the top aristocracy.[170] There was clearly a shift in personnel in the council and top administration when Håkon took power in 1299, although it is not easy to ascertain how extensive it was. We do not know how many disappeared because of death or old age and how many because they were replaced by others. It is therefore difficult to explain this as a change in the recruitment basis of the king's administration and even less as the expression of an anti-aristocratic attitude. There is evidence that Håkon reacted against some political measures taken under the previous regime and punished some individuals he regarded as responsible for this. However, the main explanation for the changes in personnel from Eirik's reign to Håkon's is that Håkon brought with him men from southern and eastern Norway whom he had secured in his service during his period as duke of this part of the country.[171]

All or most of the men in prominent positions in the king's service must probably be defined as aristocrats according to the economic criterion above (p. 120), and it is in practice very difficult to distinguish between the ones whose employment was more or less unavoidable because of their wealth and rank and the "service element". It does not follow from this, however, that the king was under the domination of the aristocracy and had little opportunity to choose his own counsellors and officials. The king's administration was very small, its upper levels consisting of around fifty *sysselmenn* plus a few high-ranking officials in the central administration, whereas the aristocracy as a whole is believed to have consisted of around 600 families (above p. 120).

170   For condensed biographies of the two, see Helle, *Konge og gode menn*, pp. 578-81 and 591 f. Bjarne Erlingsson has been mentioned as a third possible example of the combination of education and aristocratic status because of a reference to a "dominus Bernerus" in Bologna (Helle, *Konge og gode menn*, p. 577) but here Bjarne Audunsson (cf. Helle, *Konge og gode menn*, pp. 599 f.) is a more likely alternative (Bagge, "Nordic Students", p. 10).

171   This includes: Jon Ivarsson Raud and his son Havtore who married King Håkon's illegitimate daughter Agnes (Helle, *Konge og gode menn*, pp. 585 and 587) and who belonged to the Sørum family, one of the three richest in the country; Ogmund Sigurdsson of Hesby in Ryfylke, whose descendants belonged to the top aristocracy in the fourteenth century and who is already mentioned as knight in 1295 (ibid., p. 595); Snare Aslaksson, most probably from southwestern Norway (ibid., pp. 596 f.); and possibly Bjarne Audunsson, who seems to come from southeastern Norway but who is not mentioned in connection with the king until 1305. As Bjarne donated ninety *markebol* to the Church, i.e. six times the amount of land a *lendmann* held of the king (p. 348) and the largest known donation from a contemporary aristocrat, he must have been very wealthy. Thanks to my former student Are Gustavsson for this information. Håkon's chancellor as duke, Åke, also took over as royal chancellor after 1299 (ibid., pp. 594 f.).

The king therefore had plenty of men from whom he could choose. If Bjørkvik's calculation about the various categories within the aristocracy is correct, the king would actually seem to be in an ideal position. Even if he was more or less forced to appoint one member of each of the most prominent families as *sysselmann* – which is not very likely – this would only have taken up a maximum of twenty districts, while he could still pick those he wanted from the nearly 600 remaining for the rest, which was around thirty. Admittedly, the members of the aristocracy hardly faced the king directly as individuals; like most other aristocracies, there were probably links of patronage between a small elite and the rest. Nevertheless, there is little to suggest that the king was bound to appoint certain men to positions in his central or local administration. The fact that members of the top aristocracy occasionally sought higher education abroad may form evidence that even at this level of the social hierarchy personal qualifications were necessary in order to enter the king's service. It may be objected that the king's poverty was a weakness in this as well as other respects. Poverty, however, is a relative concept. If we accept Bjørkvik's calculations (above p. 111), the king's seven percent of the land would make him immensely wealthy compared to most members of the aristocracy.

According to R. I. Moore, one of the characteristic features of "the first European revolution" (975-1215) was the rise of a class of professional bureaucrats in the king's service, recruited from outside the aristocracy proper, from the gentry, bourgeoisie, or from younger sons of aristocratic families in a system of primogeniture.[172] Although it can be doubted how specifically European this pattern is,[173] such a class did develop in countries like England and particularly France and to some extent formed a counterweight to the top aristocracy. This happened to a lesser extent in Germany and East Central Europe, where the aristocracy, at least from the thirteenth century onwards, was strong enough to prevent such encroachments. Scandinavia in this respect conforms to the Eastern rather than the Western pattern. At least in the case of Norway, however, this was not the result of the strength of the aristocracy but of the king, which made it less necessary for him to recruit men from lower layers of society as a counterweight to the aristocracy.

The Decision-Making Process

We must therefore conclude that the impression we receive from the official sources of Norway as a *dominium regale* has not been seriously weakened by this examination of political practice. The king had considerable freedom in selecting his counsellors, which

---

172 Moore, *Revolution*, pp. 132-34, 193 f.
173 Bagge, "Transformation", pp. 157-60.

probably also implies that he was central in the decision-making. According to Knut Helle, who has carried out the most complete study of this, the governing circle around the king was so vaguely defined and so elusive that it is very difficult to imagine that it can have formed an effective barrier against the king's ability to make the day-to-day decisions he wanted. This conclusion seems to have won general acceptance.[174] Unfortunately, however, the documentary sources from the late thirteenth and early fourteenth centuries give no explicit information about how the decisions were made. Adult kings as well as aristocratic councils during periods of minority referred in the same way to the king and his good men or council as authorities, and the royal letters sometimes include names of individual counsellors who were present when they were issued but give no clue to any discussions or meetings that may have preceded the decisions. The somewhat earlier sagas often contain such references, however, even if they are often sketchy and suspected of literary embellishment.

One of the classical examples of counselling is the account of King Magnus Sigurdsson's deliberations in the winter of 1134-35 after his adversary, Harald Gille, had returned to Norway with a large army.[175] After Magnus's victory over Harald in the summer of 1134, he dismissed his army, contrary to the advice of the wisest of his men, and went to Bergen to stay there over the winter. Learning of Harald's conquests in the east and his approach, Magnus asks his men what to do. Sigurd Sigurdsson, apparently his most trusted man, suggests that he should send an embassy to Harald and offer to share the country with him. Magnus rejects the advice and asks for another suggestion, stating that this would mean that his recent victory had been in vain. Sigurd's next advice is to kill the *lendmenn* who had failed to join him, give their estates to poorer men who had been faithful and in so doing gather an army to fight Harald. Magnus rejects this as well, adding that it will not serve him well to kill magnates and promote those of low rank. Concluding that Magnus is unwilling both to seek peace and to fight, Sigurd next suggests that they should move to the more populous region of Trøndelag, gathering all the people they can on their way. When Magnus rejects this as well, Sigurd concludes with the plan he knows that Magnus will follow, to remain in Bergen and wait for Harald, which will result in death or shame. He then leaves Magnus. Sigurd's prophecy proves true, Harald arrives in Bergen with a greatly superior force, defeats Magnus and takes him captive and has him maimed, blinded, and castrated. In the description of the two rivals, Magnus's foolishness and stubbornness is contrasted to Harald's popularity and willingness to listen

---

[174] Helle, *Konge og gode menn*, pp. 562-73; cf. Lunden, "Stat".

[175] *HkrMB* ch. 5; cf. *Fsk.* ch. 79, pp. 337 f. The sequence of the suggestions given by Sigurd differs in the two sagas, see below n. 185.

to advice.[176] This example, as well as several others in the sagas, might suggest some kind of "constitutional" attitude, demanding that the king rule with the advice and consent of the leading men in the country.

On the other hand, the best king is not necessarily the one who lets his counsellors decide. Most saga authors seem to regard Harald as a better king than Magnus, but he hardly belongs to the great heroes of the saga literature.[177] *Sverris saga* contains a number of deliberation scenes with Sverre himself as the main decision-maker.[178] He asks his men what to do but brings forward his own suggestions which are usually followed. When they are not, the result is failure, as in the few battles Sverre loses and in the election of Nikolas Arnesson as bishop, in which Sverre lets himself be persuaded by his wife and some other counsellors who guarantee his loyalty but where Sverre's suspicion proves well founded.[179] In a similar way, Håkon Håkonsson sometimes rejects his men's advice and follows his own head. He is warned against trusting the people in Eastern Norway during the war against the Ribbungs but does not heed the warning and is proved right.[180] During the war against the Ribbungs as well as that against Skule, he is advised to seek reconciliation, but refuses, pointing to his divine vocation.[181] When the question of how to arrange matters between Håkon's two sons is brought up at the archbishop's initiative, Håkon refuses to take a decision, leaving the matter to God. Thus, while the archbishop thinks in secular and practical terms, the king is the one who trusts in God's providence and is proved right, as God solves the problem by letting the elder of the two sons die two years later.[182] By contrast, Skule's problem is not that he does not listen to advice but that he listens to the wrong one. He declares himself king because he has listened to bad arguments from bad counsellors.[183] In the final deliberation scene before his fall, he also takes the wrong decision, returning to Trøndelag rather than fighting in Eastern Norway (above p. 84), although Sturla may have thought that his situation would be hopeless in any case.

Likewise, *The King's Mirror* points to the importance of counsel as well as to the king's personal responsibility and independent power of decision. It is a disaster for the realm

---

176 See the comparative characteristic in *HkrMB* ch. 1.
177 On the evaluation of Harald, see Bagge, *Society and Politics*, p. 157, and more recently Arstad, "Harald Gilles ættermæle", who is probably right that modern historians have attributed too negative a picture of Harald to the saga writers.
178 Bagge, *From Gang Leader*, pp. 25-33.
179 Bagge, *From Gang Leader*, p. 75; Orning, *Uforutsigbarhet*, pp. 154 f.
180 *HH* ch. 148; Bagge, *From Gang Leader*, pp. 132 f.
181 *HH* chs. 134, 143 and 222; Bagge, *From Gang Leader*, pp. 102, 136.
182 *HH* ch. 284; cf. ch. 288 and Bagge, *From Gang Leader*, pp. 102 f.
183 *HH* ch. 198; Bagge, *From Gang Leader*, p. 112.

when one of the king's leading, aristocratic counsellors dies and his estates are divided. The king should be addressed in plural because he is not on his own in governing the realm but surrounded by counsellors and *hirdmenn*. In the prayer prescribed for the king, a number of people governing the kingdom with him are mentioned, including the queen. On the other hand, the king's sole responsibility is emphasised in the depiction of his nightly meditation on God's wisdom and judgements and above all in the story of the king's son who for one day replaces his father in the seat of judgement and discovers the terrible responsibility laid upon him: an angel stands over him with a drawn sword, ready to cut him down as soon as he pronounces a false judgement.[184]

From a constitutional point of view, the king's position may seem to resemble that of a modern military commander who is obliged to listen to advice but not to follow it. The main objective in these examples is to reach the right decision, from a moral or a pragmatic point of view or both. Thus, the objection to King Magnus's behaviour is not that he rejects the advice given to him but that he chooses a plan that is bound to fail. This is pointed out particularly clearly in *Heimskringla*'s version where Sigurd concludes that Magnus is neither willing to negotiate nor to prepare for battle.[185] Magnus is unwilling to face the fact that the situation has changed since his victory over Harald and has to pay the price. The counsellors' function is to help the king reach the right decisions. The European mirrors of princes normally pay great attention to the king's choice of counsellors, and the sagas and *The King's Mirror* imply the same, although the question of how the king should select them is not discussed explicitly in the latter (above p. 242). But the king should also be able to suggest a brilliant solution to a problem himself and thus to impress his surroundings, as Sverre repeatedly does according to his saga.[186] Nor is there apparently any rule about who needs to be consulted and under what circumstances, as also seems evident from the documentary sources. On the other hand, no king would gain

---

184 Bagge, *The Political Thought*, pp. 161 f.
185 *Heimskringla* here resembles some other famous examples of counselling, such as Livy's account of the Samnites' discussion of what to do with the captive Roman army (Livy, *Ab urbe condita libri* IX.3). Here the two sensible courses of action are also radically different; either to release the soldiers without harm, thus winning the Romans' friendship, or to kill the whole army, thus weakening the Romans' strength, whereas the course of action taken, humiliating the Romans and then setting them free, serves neither purpose. In a similar way, Sigurd in *Heimskringla* suggests either a very mild alternative – sharing the kingdom with Harald – or a very tough, full mobilisation against Harald including extermination of all who had proved disloyal. Snorre here seems deliberately – for rhetorical effect? – to have changed the account of his source which is likely to have corresponded to *Fagrskinna*'s version, in which the sequence between the options is peace, withdrawal to Trøndelag, and killing the disloyal, a sequence that seems more logical.
186 Cf. also Althoff's example of Einhard's account of Charlemagne listening to various suggestions from his counsellors about how to deal with his daughter and her illicit lover and than finally settling on an entirely different solution: to hide the shame in the best possible way by allowing the couple to marry (Althoff, *Spielregeln*, pp. 160 f.).

respect if he did not surround himself with wise and influential men and consult them regularly.

Most of the kings' sagas were composed in the first half of the thirteenth century and are likely in many ways to reflect practice and ideals from a period before the great expansion of the royal administration from the second half of the thirteenth century. In their accounts of decision-making, however, they differ little from the latest saga, *Hákonar saga*, and from *The King's Mirror* and may therefore also give some impression of the ideals of the following period, although hardly about the practice of individual kings. The greatest difference between the earlier and the later works would seem to be in the respect due to the king from his men and the distance between the two parties, which in turn is the result of the king's power monopoly in this period in contrast to the previous one. It was no longer possible to leave a king and turn to his rival or to another magnate within the country. Admittedly, it was possible to go abroad, which some aristocrats also did, but this was hardly a very attractive option. Now the king could, at least in principle, order his men to do what he wanted, whereas in the earlier period, the point of counselling was partly to persuade the magnates and retainers to follow the king. The friendship between the king and a *lendmann* obliged both parties to use their clients and resources to aid the other, but both had to ask for consent. By contrast, the *sysselmenn* could be ordered to use the resources they disposed over on the king's behalf to support him. Admittedly, the difference was not as clear-cut in practice as in theory, but the relationship between the individual *sysselmann*'s private resources and those he had from the king was nevertheless such that his options for refusing to come to the king's aid were limited; only a collective action by the *sysselmenn* might lead to this result. Although the earlier sagas contain a number of passages about the king's anger and the men's fear of approaching him, there are examples of quite direct discussions and open challenges which gave the king honour if he managed to meet them and shame if he did not.[187] The ideology of *The King's Mirror* may possibly have resulted in a somewhat different style, but this is difficult to know because of the lack of narrative sources. The change from larger assemblies to a more closed circle around the king plus the shifting composition of this circle clearly indicates the predominance of *consilium secretum* rather than *consilium publicum*.

Whereas the documentary sources give little information about the way in which the decisions were made, they have more to tell about the decisions themselves which may give us some information about the policies actually conducted and the interests behind them. The period 1263-1350 ought to give us some indications regarding these matters,

---

[187] E.g. the story of St Olav and Torarin Nefjolfsson, discussing Torarin's ugly feet (*HkrOH* ch. 85; cf. Bagge, "Norwegian Monarchy", pp. 164-66).

as it contains the reigns of four different kings plus two periods of regency, dominated by the king's counsellors. We then have to conclude that the whole period shows considerable continuity regarding domestic policy and legislation. The king as well as the regency governments tried to prevent various wrongs by royal officials and to protect the people against them and secure royal control over the local administration. Nor does it seem that the aristocratic regency government exploited the situation to grant privileges to the aristocracy. Quite the contrary; some of the most explicit expressions of the royalist ideology stem from the regency government of the 1280s, such as Lodin Lepp's insistence on the king's sole responsibility for legislation and the criticism of the clergy for disobeying lawful government (above pp. 204, 317). Thus, the aristocratic circle dominating the government during Eirik Magnusson's reign can hardly be blamed for representing a "feudal" opposition to the royal government, although its individual members may well have used their position to gain personal advantages.

Generally, there also seems to be considerable continuity between the internal policy of the regency and that of Håkon V who renewed some of their ordinances and probably regarded others as still valid.[188] However, it has also been suggested that Håkon pursued an anti-aristocratic policy that was radically different from that of his predecessor. The discussion about this has mainly circled around the great ordinance of 17 June 1308 (above pp. 332 f.). As we have seen, there can be no doubt about its monarchical ideology. On the other hand, a similar ideology was also expressed by the regents in the 1280s, although with reference to the king's council, whether this should be explained by the king's minority or by a doctrine of the council ruling together with the king. We therefore have to examine its concrete provisions, most of which deal with the duties of the king's retainers, notably the *sysselmenn* who are the subject of various complaints and mandates. In many cases it is not clear whether these mandates are new or only repeat older provisions. On the other hand, the king also shows his clemency in introducing provisions in favour of his men, for instance a preference for sons of good and trustworthy *sysselmenn* to succeed their fathers and various provisions in favour of the *hird*, including care for old and diseased *hirdmenn*. In addition, the king appoints some new officials. He ends his ordinance with a strong appeal to his men's loyalty.

Apparently the most important of the provisions politically and those that have been subject to most discussion by modern scholars are the abolition of the offices of earl and *lendmann* and the revocation of all *sysler*. The former is followed by a strong admonition

---

188 This includes the ordinance from 1281/82 (NGL III no. 26) which is attributed to Håkon in some of the manuscripts, and the great ordinance from 1280 (NGL III no. 1) which is preserved in a large number of manuscripts from the early fourteenth century.

to a possible future regency: "And we call those real traitors who from now on give a young king the advice that there should be more chieftains with secular power in the king of Norway's realm than those who are descended from the right kindred."[189] From an administrative point of view, the *lendmann* had become superfluous through the introduction of the office of *sysselmann*; the title had now become purely honorary. Honorary titles might of course also have their function, not least in a society so concerned with honour as the medieval one, but they might also be replaced by others. Håkon created several new offices and generally expanded the royal administration. The standard-bearer (ON *merkismaðr*), an old office, was redefined as the king's vicar in the legal sphere. To the treasurer (ON *fehirði*) in the central administration were added four regional treasurers – new in 1308? – an office that later developed into the leadership of the main administrative areas in the country. Thus, the king needed men in his service and was not afraid of rewarding them, but he preferred offices with specific functions to old style magnates with men in their own service.

It may be objected that if the title was incompatible with that of *sysselmann*, why was it not abolished long before, as the office of *sysselmann* was firmly established by the early thirteenth century? The answer is that Sverre was apparently very reluctant to appoint *lendmenn*, that there were probably fewer *lendmenn* in the thirteenth century than before and thus that the office had lost much of its importance. Nor was the financial remuneration very substantial; fifteen markebol equalled the rent from a very large farm, which was of course a good income, but far less than that of a *sysselmann*. The most important of the *lendmann*'s privileges was probably the right to have armed men in his own service – up to forty, a force with which he was obliged to serve the king but which might also be used for his own purposes. Depending on the extent to which this was really a novelty, however, the organisation of the elite forces commanded by the *sysselmenn* in 1273-74 might make the king regard the *lendmenn*'s forces as both superfluous and dangerous. Why allow a limited number of men such liberties, when the *sysselmann*'s forces could serve the same purpose better? Such a reasoning might fit in well with what we know about Håkon V. Similar warnings against the office of earl occur as early as in the Hird Law. Thus, rather than a step in the direction of the consolidation of the aristocracy, as suggested by Benedictow (above p. 327), the suppression of the *lendmann* was the suppression of a relict from a period of independent magnates who were the king's friends rather than his subordinates and who were allowed to keep a *hird*. It is thus a measure of the same kind as Håkon Håkonsson's offensive against Skule in the 1230s. Such a measure would not have

---

189 "En hina kallum ver sanna landraada menn sem þat raaða heðan af. vngum konungj. at fleire (se) hofðingiar verallegs velldis j Norges konungs riki en af rætto ætterne ero komnir" (DN XI no. 6, p. 12).

been taken by King Eirik and of course not by the regency of the early 1280s either. So far, the ordinance must be understood as directed at least against a part of the aristocracy. On the other hand, neither its actual nor its intended consequences were very drastic, as the existing *lendmenn* – some of whom had been appointed by Håkon himself – were allowed to retain their rank. As these were few in number, between ten and fifteen, the ordinance was hardly directed against the aristocracy as such. Finally, the rank of *lendmann* was most probably replaced by other possibilities for a career in the king's service, as the royal administration expanded under Håkon.

The provision concerning the *sysler* has normally been interpreted as directed against the *sysselmenn* and a wish from the king to redistribute the *sysler* or to renew the appointments to them on new and probably stricter conditions. Further, the passage immediately follows upon the king's ideological proclamation, in which he takes control over his "patrimony", the whole realm of the king of Norway.[190] This may be a reference to Duke Erik who held Elvesysle in the southeast as a fief from King Håkon, having been engaged to his daughter since 1302.[191] The ordinance was issued at a time when Håkon had either joined King Erik Menved of Denmark against the duke or was planning to do so. However, there is evidence to suggest that the provision was also aimed against the ordinary *sysselmenn*. The king revokes all charters issued "in maiori forma", which includes letters of appointment for *sysselmenn*, and the ordinance contains several apparently new and stricter demands on them. Thus, the passage should be regarded as a continuation of the initial proclamation about the king's patrimony and as giving the legal foundation for the following provisions about the *sysselmann*'s duties.[192] However, the revocation of the charters may also be understood as a fiscal measure, possibly in connection with the preparations for the war against the Swedish dukes.

Insistence on the *sysselmenn*'s duties towards the king and his subjects was nothing new under Håkon V; it occurs already in the additions to the Hird Law resulting from Magnus Håkonsson's meetings in 1273-74, as well as in some passages in the regency's ordinance of 1280. However, Håkon V was far more specific in his attempts to control the *sysselmenn*,

---

190 Þa takum ver … alt Norges kongungs riki. allar syslur vm alt landit se vndir oss kallaðar með þerso vaaro brefue" (DN XI no. 6, p. 11).
191 Hamre, "Håkon V's hirdskipan", p. 21.
192 According to Hamre, "Håkon V's hirdskipan", p. 22, the normal term for revoking is *kalla aptr*, which means that the formulation here, *kalla undir*, has a vaguer meaning, an expression of the king's will to take over the government of the whole country in accordance with the initial formulation. The dictionary in NGL V regards the two terms as synonymous and lists an example of *kalla undir* to mean confiscating a property (NGL III no. 105, 1373, on Petersgården in Bergen which had been deserted and therefore fell under the king). Hamre's terminological distinction therefore seems doubtful, but the connection to the initial proclamation nevertheless suggests that the king's aim was to increase his control over the country, not to replace the *sysselmenn*.

and his explicit criticism of them, in the ordinance of 1308 as well as in other documents, is unprecedented. Although this criticism is directed against various kinds of abuse and is balanced by rewards to those who behave well, it does express a more restrictive attitude towards the people who were the core element in the aristocracy. At least some of the abuses Håkon criticised must have been very widespread and possibly implicitly accepted by his predecessors (above p. 288). Håkon's successor, Magnus Eriksson, seems to have followed in his grandfather's footsteps, particularly in the period 1331-44.[193] Thus, there are differences in the measures taken towards the aristocracy between the various rulers in the period, but not so much so that we are dealing with radically different attitudes. Generally, the monarchy's relationship to the aristocracy must be characterised as harmonious compared to that to the Church and to the situation in the two other Nordic countries.

The economic policy, in so far as this can be said to have existed in the Middle Ages, also shows considerable continuity. Radical interference in the normal, agricultural economy was not usual in the Middle Ages, neither in Norway nor elsewhere. Concerning agriculture, the laws gave some rules about manuring and fallow fields, and Håkon Håkonsson issued an ordinance forbidding potential workers from moving to the towns because of complaints from the landowners about the lack of people to work the land,[194] thus clearly acting according to the interests of the landowners. The National Law also gave more detailed provisions about the lease of land than the regional laws. An analysis of the interest aspect of these provisions would necessitate a detailed examination of them plus a good knowledge of the actual conditions which is not easy to come by, but we can nevertheless assume that the actual provisions were not directly against the interests of the landowners. On the other hand, there is little evidence of drastic new measures in the interest of the landowners and against those of the tenants. The National Law also takes some steps to protect the poor, notably in the provision that those who stole because of extreme need should not be punished.[195]

The main area of royal interference in the economy was trade, notably because of the increasing influence of the merchants from Northern German towns, which eventually

---

[193] Ordinance of 18 Dec. 1332 (NGL III no. 71); Blom, *Norge i union*, pp. 114 f. In addition, most of Håkon V's ordinances directed at the *sysselmenn* and the clergy or insisting on people's obedience towards the king are preserved in several copies from the reign of Magnus Eriksson and Håkon VI. This applies to NGL III no. 18 on the relatives of criminals threatening royal officials (1303); no. 23 on the payment of fines (1307); no. 26 on the clergy and the Christian law, issued by Eirik Magnusson and renewed by Håkon V and Magnus Eriksson (1308/09, see above p. 303 n. 35); no. 27 on the *sysselmenn*'s and *lagmenn*'s abuses (1309); no. 28 on royal and ecclesiastical officials' presence on the *lagting* (1310); no. 41 on outlaws present in inhabited areas (1315) and no. 44 on *brefabrot* (1315).
[194] NGL I p. 125, 1260. A similar ordinance was issued in 1384 (DN V no. 331).
[195] L IX.1.

(from 1358) became organised in the Hanseatic League. They are mentioned in Bergen already in the twelfth century, but did not become really important until the second half of the thirteenth century. In 1250, King Håkon Håkonsson issued the first letter of protection for the German merchants (above p. 261); in 1284-85, the German towns were able to force the Norwegian government to concessions through a trade blockade (above p. 92), and by the early fourteenth century, there was a fairly large colony of German merchants and artisans in Bergen, some as well in other Norwegian towns. Traditionally, Norwegian historians have held a negative attitude to the German merchants, blaming them for destroying Norwegian trade and contributing to the decline of the country in the Later Middle Ages.[196] Recent interpretations have been more moderate: because of their extensive trade network, the Germans were necessary intermediaries between the Norwegian exporters of fish, butter and other commodities and the markets in Western Europe; Norwegian merchants would not have been able to do this alone.[197] In the long run, however, it was a detriment that the surplus from this exchange went to the Germans instead of to Norwegian merchants. Specifically, it probably contributed to the decline of Norway that Norwegian merchants were much slower in infiltrating and taking over the German networks than merchants in other countries. Whereas the Hanseatic trade organisation was clearly in decline by the mid-fifteenth century, it retained a dominating position in Norway for a further hundred years.[198]

It has usually been assumed that considerations like this determined the Norwegian government's attitude to the German merchants.[199] Normally, however, the trade policy conducted by governments in the High Middle Ages was determined by consumer rather than producer interests. King Sverre's famous speech against drink, according to the saga held in Bergen in 1186, is an example of this attitude.[200] In addition to depicting the disastrous consequences of drink – occasioned by the German import of cheap wine – Sverre blames the German merchants for exporting butter and fish from the country in return for wine, whereas he praises the English ones who bring useful commodities, like honey, wheat, fine flour, and cloth in return for their export. Thus, as was often done in the Middle Ages, he distinguishes between useful and useless commodities, clearly from the point of view of the consumers who also clearly belonged to the upper levels of society, as is evident from the commodities mentioned.

---

196   Schreiner, *Hanseatene*; Blom, "Norge".
197   Helle, *Kongssete*, pp. 378-90; Nedkvitne, *Utenrikshandelen*, pp. 230-45.
198   Nedkvitne, *Utenrikshandelen*, pp. 310-35; Bagge, *Norge i dansketiden*, pp. 47-54.
199   Helle, *Kongssete*, pp. 387 f., 412-22, who consistently refers to the Norwegian government's policy towards the German merchants as "the national trade policy".
200   *Ss.* ch. 104; Bagge, *From Gang Leader*, pp. 71-74.

Sverre's reasoning is probably representative of the normal attitude at the time. In most countries professional merchants were politically a marginal group from the perspective of kings and great lords; only city states, ruled by a merchant aristocracy, conducted policies in accordance with such interests.[201] By contrast, the Norwegian king himself, the prelates, and the aristocracy gathered vast quantities of fish, butter, meat, hides and other commodities which they wanted to exchange for luxury articles – cloth, wine, strong beer, and commodities that could not be procured in sufficient quantities in Norway, such as grain.[202] Conflicts with the Germans concerned the price of these commodities and in some cases what was to be given in return for what was exported. Thus, in 1282 and again in 1316 the Norwegian government forbade export of Norwegian food unless food was imported in return; at least in the latter case probably because of the famine affecting Northern Europe at the time. Additionally, there was a political reason for the conflict, namely that the Norwegian government forbade the Germans to settle in Norwegian towns unless they became normal Norwegian burghers and took upon them the same duties as the Norwegians. This expresses the same attitude as the policy towards the Church, the wish to prevent the emergence of privileged groups within the country. In practice, however, the Germans formed a separate community in Bergen in the Later Middle Ages, probably numbering around one thousand men (they were all men), which represents between one fifth and one tenth of the population.

Most of the actual provisions issued by the Norwegian government are compatible with this interpretation. The most important ones seem to have been intended to protect consumer interests, probably mainly those of the elite, although the common people, the town population as well as the fishermen in Northern Norway would also have been interested in them. By contrast, there is no certain example of a provision aiming at protecting Norwegian foreign trade, although some may be intended to protect domestic trade. This applies to Håkon V's ordinance of 1299 that merchants must sell their merchandise in the towns,[203] which means that peasants who wanted to buy commodities imported by the foreigners would have to do so through Norwegian retailers, which of course increased the price. An ordinance from the beginning of the fourteenth century forbade the foreigners to sell Norwegian goods in retail, a ban that in 1316 was extended to include their own imported goods.[204] Thus, in these cases the government protected retail traders at the cost of the consumers, although the great consumers were hardly affected; they were able to buy in large quantities. Moreover, concentration of the trade in towns was

---

201 Miller, "The Economic Policies", pp. 281-90, 302-16.
202 For this and the following, see Nedkvitne, *Utenrikshandelen*, pp. 198-230.
203 NGL III no. 12.
204 NGL III no. 53, 1302-13; cf. also NGL III no. 47.

probably to the advantage of the great landowners, as they gathered the surplus from their estates there and could buy in large quantities from the foreigners and probably obtain better prices. It was also to their advantage that the foreign merchants were obliged to sell all their merchandise in town if they had already unloaded parts of it. Finally, the king secured his own interests by claiming the right of pre-emption during a certain period after a foreign merchant had entered a town.

Thus, the economic policy shows a community of interests between the king and the aristocracy, clerical as well as secular, and considerable continuity between the regency periods and those of adult kings. When changes of policy nevertheless occurred, it was the result of the relative strength of Norway compared to that of the Hanseatic towns and with the connection between the Hanseatic policy and other aspects of foreign policy. The measures taken against the Germans in the ordinance of 1282 were repeated and even sharpened under Håkon V, without any similar reactions by the Germans. The reason is that the Northern German towns were in a very difficult situation during the first two decades of the fourteenth century because of the Danish king Erik Menved's policy of conquest in the area. Håkon himself might possibly have been somewhat more reluctant to challenge the Germans when he was involved in conflicts with Denmark. The modifications of the strict measures of 1316 in 1318 might thus be explained by his engagement in favour of the Swedish opposition against King Birger and his ally Erik Menved, although at least some of the measures of 1316 were intended to be temporary as the result of the famine in 1316 which had ended by 1318.

There are clearer differences between the periods of regency and those of adult kings in two other fields. The first is the relationship to the Church, where there is a connection between regency, meaning aristocratic government, and anti-clericalism. Whereas King Magnus after prolonged negotiations agreed to a concordat favourable to the Church, the regency for his son launched an offensive against the Church. This policy was somewhat softened when Eirik came of age and under his brother and successor Håkon, but neither of them returned to their father's pro-ecclesiastical policy. The new regency in the 1320s also ran into conflict with the Church, although it was not as serious as the one in the 1280s. Such a connection also makes sense in light of the fact that the lay aristocrats, particularly in their capacity as *sysselmenn*, received a substantial part of their incomes from the royal administration and consequently resisted any attempt to weaken the monarchy's financial basis, whether in the field of jurisdiction or taxation. Even though the king had the same interests personally, he would be less affected by concessions to the Church in the field of jurisdiction and might in addition receive benefits from the prelates' services. He might even use the Church to balance the lay aristocracy. It must be admitted, however, first that the regency's policy in the 1280s was more in accordance with the normal policy of the Sverre dynasty than that of Magnus Håkonsson, and, second, that even the latter was less accommodating to the Church than has often been thought.

The second field is foreign policy, where the two regency periods stand in marked contrast to each other. The regency of the 1280s broke with King Magnus's peaceful policy and launched an offensive against Denmark that was continued during the following period, whereas the regency of the 1320s reacted against Duchess Ingebjørg's continuation of Håkon V's anti-Danish policy, deposed her from the regency and replaced her with the greatest of the magnates, Erling Vidkunsson. As we have seen, Håkon V accused the regency on behalf of himself and his brother of conducting a policy that caused the realm great harm, a statement that has given rise to some discussion among scholars. There is little to suggest that Håkon reacted against either the regency's anti-clerical or anti-Danish policy. Admittedly, in the case of the latter he states that the conflict was begun in his childhood, thus indicating that he could not be made responsible for it. The statement occurs in a proclamation in connection with his alliance with the Swedish dukes against Denmark and should most probably be understood as an attempt to proclaim his innocence and blame his enemies for the outbreak of the war.[205] The most likely interpretation is that his criticism of the regency refers to specific events, notably Alv Erlingsson's rebellion in 1287 in which Håkon's local representative was killed. Furthermore, even if he had identified with the regency's anti-Danish aims, he may with some justice have regarded their means to pursue them as inadequate, and he clearly reacted to Alv Erlingsson's attacks on German ships in 1285 (below p. 357). This interpretation receives support from Håkon's actual policy during the conflicts in the first decade of his reign which was cautious rather than bold, aiming at preserving the peace of Hindsgavl and securing a favourable marriage for his daughter.

In contrast to Håkon, and as a matter of fact to all adult kings in the period, the regents conducted a policy that eventually brought them into conflict with Denmark and the German towns at the same time. The regency's foreign policy in the 1280s can hardly be regarded as the expression of specifically aristocratic interests. Its initiator is most probably to be found in Eirik and Håkon's mother, the Dowager Queen Ingeborg who descended from a sideline of the ruling Danish dynasty and who fought to gain her inheritance. This has been suggested by several scholars, and although there is no hard evidence in favour of it, it is the most likely explanation. The same applies to the old hypothesis of a special relationship between the queen and Alv Erlingsson who rebelled

---

205 DN VI no. 69, 2 May 1307.

against Håkon in 1287 after the queen's death, which seems to have led to a deterioration of his position.[206]

Although the sources are meagre as usual, we know a little of Ingeborg as a person. She was originally supposed to enter a convent so as not to give birth to an heir that might compromise her cousin Erik Klipping's hold on the throne and thus showed some personal initiative in accepting Håkon's offer to marry his son and leaving the convent to join the Norwegian envoys.[207] According to *Hákonar saga*, Håkon was very impressed by her when he met her.[208] This may of course have been conventional flattery on Sturla's part, but was probably more than that, as it actually was because of her that Sturla was accepted at court and possibly also received the commission to write Håkon's saga. When Sturla arrived in Norway in the king's disgrace and was allowed to travel on King Magnus's ship, he had tried to improve his position by telling stories to the *hirdmenn*. The queen started to listen, offered him her friendship, and finally reconciled him with her husband.[209] These small glimpses of an individual in an age when so little is known about people's personality, in particular that of women, are entirely compatible with the picture of a queen who, when the opportunity rose, had the ambition to play a political role and the ability to persuade other people to follow her. She also seems to have been actively engaged in the barons' anti-clerical policy.[210] The fact that the anti-German and anti-Danish policy was ultimately unsuccessful may be attributed to greater ambition than experience, or perhaps to a lesser degree of coordination in a situation when there was no one with the firm authority of an adult king. From this point of view, there is a certain parallel to the situation under Ingeborg's granddaughter and namesake in the 1320s who had similar ambitions but who was able to get support for her policy only for a short period.

In this way, the difference between the foreign policy of the two regencies becomes less than it would immediately appear. The king's dynastic policy probably did not correspond to the interests of the aristocracy. Individual aristocrats conducted their own dynastic policies, trying to gain land and positions for themselves and their descendants through favourable marriages and a good relationship to the king. They had much to gain by joining the king's service as *sysselmenn* but were likely to prefer a secure income from administrative work to

---

206 The hypothesis was put forward by Munch, NFH IV.2, pp. 95 f., 119 ff., 126 f., 136 f.; Helle, *Konge og gode menn*, pp. 354 f., and "Opptakten", pp. 16 f., rejects it, pointing to the lack of evidence, but Alv's fall from grace shortly after the Queen's death is an argument in its favour.
207 *HH* ch. 306.
208 *HH* ch. 308.
209 *Sturlunga saga*, pp. 324-27.
210 *Árna saga* ch. 73, p. 109, says that the queen and the leading men in the country had become deaf to the Christian liturgy, i.e. probably that they were excommunicated, and refers to a letter from the king and the queen about ecclesiastical conditions in Iceland.

risky foreign enterprises which might not turn out to be very profitable even if successful. A conquest of a wealthy region like Halland might imply some lucrative administrative posts in the area for Norwegian aristocrats, but from the king's point of view, this would probably have to be balanced by the need to have a good relationship with the local Danish aristocracy. The actual gain of Scania in 1332 hardly offered any opportunities for Norwegian aristocrats, as the region became attached to Sweden and not Norway. Whereas a dynastic union corresponded to the wishes of the king and other members of the dynasty, it was hardly in the interest of the aristocracy. It might in principle open up new opportunities abroad, but as the aristocracies in both the neighbouring countries were stronger and more numerous, the likelihood was greater that foreigners received positions in Norway. After 1323 the regency for Magnus Eriksson managed to keep the links to Sweden to a minimum, which happened to correspond to the interests of the Swedish regency as well.

Thus, the initiative for the active foreign policy and the dynastic alliances is likely to have come from the king rather than from the aristocracy. It therefore becomes a paradox that Eirik Magnusson, the weakest ruler during the period 1240-1319, conducted the most risky and aggressive foreign policy. The main explanation must be that the regents and counsellors dominating the government during this period identified their interests with those of the king rather than the aristocracy as a whole. The contrast between Magnus's and Eirik's reigns must then be explained partly by the former's peaceful and cautious character and partly by the fact that the situation after 1286 offered exceptional opportunities for a successful interference in Denmark, while the situation in the British Isles seemed to offer similar opportunities in the 1290s. The main line in the period, represented by Håkon Håkonsson and Håkon V, was somewhere in between: an active dynastic policy and attempts to exploit weaknesses in the neighbouring countries, but with a reluctance to engage in war.

The Problem of Regencies

From this point of view, the periods of regency show another contrast with those of adult kings. Although it is very difficult to draw conclusions about consistency or the lack of it on the basis of the available evidence, the periods of regency show greater vacillation which in turn indicates that the absence of a firm authority gave room for a greater variety of interests. In the early period, the years 1284-85 form the best example of this. Admittedly, this was technically not a period when the king was a minor, but King Eirik was only sixteen or seventeen years old and had just suffered the fall from his horse that incapacitated him for the rest of his life, whereas his more capable brother was only fourteen or fifteen years old. To what extent the restrictive policy against the German merchants of 1282 was coordinated with the pressure against Denmark remains an open question, but it is likely that Alv Erlingsson's attacks against German ships in 1284 happened of his own intent and against the will of the government, as stated in Duke Håkon's letter where he declares himself not responsible for the deed.[211] It is also difficult to know whether the queen was responsible. On the one hand, a good relationship with the Germans would seem to be in her interests, as it would have increased her chances to gain her inheritance; on the other, she still seems to have protected Alv.

The next minority gives a similar impression. There is no evidence that the council appointed by Håkon V ever functioned according to his ordinance. Instead, his daughter, Duchess Ingebjørg, became the central person in the regency until she was deposed at a meeting of most of the leading men in Oslo in February 1323, where Erling Vidkunsson, the wealthiest man in the country, was elected as *drottsete*. The proclamation from the meeting[212] directs strong accusations against the duchess, although without naming her: the revenues of the king and the realm have been squandered; loans have been taken up against future revenues, without any explanation of how the money is to be used; the peace with Denmark has been broken, so that a war is now going on, not for the realm but for the sake of Knud Porse – Ingebjørg's fiancé – and his followers; and the royal seal has been misused, among other things to hire mercenaries. The accusations have been accepted by most modern historians, and Ingebjørg has commonly had a bad reputation, although Grethe Blom has attempted a rehabilitation.[213] She maintains that Ingebjørg's position can hardly have been against Håkon's will and that she cannot have acted without support from the leading circles. She also doubts the common interpretation, that the chancellor Ivar Olavsson, provost of St Mary's in Oslo, was deposed shortly after Håkon's death.

The proclamation of 1323 is rhetorically a very skilful document, the purpose of which was to give legitimacy to the drastic steps to be taken, and clearly has to be read as such. The assembled men claim to act on behalf of the realm and its people and to restore the good order from King Håkon's reign. However, the new ruler did not belong to Håkon's inner circle; at the age of around thirty, he was apparently a new man in the political elite, although his uncle, Bjarne Erlingsson (d. 1313), had held a prominent position during Eirik's as well as Håkon's reign. Are we dealing with an aristocratic reaction, and is Ingebjørg actually representing the continuity from Håkon's reign? Although it seems reasonable to suppose, with Blom,[214] that Håkon did not intend his daughter to be completely without political influence, this is exactly what the ordinance of 1302 for the

---

211   DN V no. 15.
212   DN VII no. 100.
213   Blom, "Ingebjørg" and "Forhandlingene på Båhus".
214   Blom, "Ingebjørg", p. 428.

regency suggests. Neither the dowager queen nor the king's daughter is mentioned in any polical context, whereas the latter's future husband was meant to play a central part. Admittedly, Ingebjørg was only one year old in 1302 when this ordinance was issued, and the passage about her future husband was clearly part of the deal between Håkon and Duke Erik. From this point of view, the ordinance would seem to need a revision before it was put into practice seventeen years later. Nevertheless, there is no indication of this in the oath sworn on Håkon's deathbed, where the eight counsellors promised to keep all its provisions.[215] Although it is possible that Ingebjørg's influence may have been taken for granted or that there were oral arrangements to this effect or documents that are now lost, it is not impossible that Håkon really intended her to be without influence. He may have doubted her political acumen, and, above all, he may have been thinking of his own mother's influence and her relationship to Alv Erlingsson. He explicitly states in the ordinance of 1302 that its purpose was to avoid the disasters occurring during his own and his brother's minority and, as we have seen (p. 354), this is most probably a reference to his mother's protégé Alv Erlingsson. Håkon may have suspected that his daughter would let her political decisions be influenced by a protégé with other interests than those of Håkon and the circle around him, and that is what actually happened.

On the other hand, it was probably difficult to exclude the king's daughter from political influence when she herself wanted it. With the clearer distinction between the dynasty and the rest of the aristocracy since the mid-thirteenth century, women within the royal house had a stronger position than the concubines who were the mothers of kings in earlier ages. By April 1320 at the latest, Ingebjørg seems to have controlled the royal seal and must thus have moved to the political centre.[216] The chancellor, Ivar Olavsson, was probably deposed, or at least in practice, removed from his office around the same time and thus seems to have lost the position Håkon V had intended for him as the leader of the regency.[217] We do not know for sure why this happened, but we may suspect that Ivar's position and Håkon's generosity to the Church of St Mary's caused jealousy among the lay aristocrats, among whom Ingebjørg must have found allies. Blom is therefore right that Ingebjørg did not act completely without support from Håkon's counsellors; some of the men who condemned her in 1323 had actually participated in the decisions they criticised.

---

215 DN I no. 156.
216 Thus, the fact that six letters from the period 9 April-5 September 1320 are sealed "oss sjolfum hjáverandom" (Agerholt, *Gamal brevskipnad*, pp. 417 f.) can hardly mean anything other than that Ingebjørg had the seal and used it on behalf of her son. Blom, "Ingebjørg", p. 432, correctly points out that Håkon V also used this formula quite often but does not take into account the difference between its use by an adult king and a four year old boy. It is difficult to imagine anyone other than the king's mother authenticating his acts in this way.
217 Bagge, "Kanslerembetet", pp. 144-48.

From a formal perspective, the opposition in 1323 may have been right in labelling the previous regime as against Håkon's intentions and the promises made to him at his deathbed, although Ingebjørg alone can hardly be blamed for this. The main issue, however, was clearly the foreign policy. On this point, Ingebjørg can be said to have followed in her father's footsteps. Admittedly, Håkon was a cautious player and did not conduct the aggressive policy against Denmark that he has been accused of, but he was facing the formidable Erik Menved, whereas Denmark was in deep crisis during the reign of Erik's successor Christoffer II. The events in the years 1319-23 thus serve as an illustration of the king's and the aristocracy's different attitudes to foreign policy and confirm the impression that the usually cautious foreign policy of the previous period may at least partly have been the result of a compromise between the king and the aristocracy. It is nevertheless likely that Håkon would have received greater support for an aggressive policy against Denmark than his daughter, partly because of his position as an adult king and partly because of the suspicion that Ingebjørg's policy was actually in the interst of Knud Porse rather than Norway and the Norwegian dynasty.

After 1323, Erling Vidkunsson ruled together with the council of the realm (*ríkis ráð*, see below p. 362), which did not correspond to the council of Håkon's ordinance, but seems to have been a vaguely defined circle of men, similar to the practice during Håkon's reign. A peace treaty between Erling and his adherents, including the deposed duchess, and another aristocratic faction, led by Finn Ogmundsson, entered on Christmas Eve 1326, suggests opposition against Erling within the aristocracy.[218] Likewise, Håkon V's death was an opportunity to raise claims that he had rejected. Thus, the conflict between the bishop of Bergen and the master of the royal chapels from 1309-11 was revived in 1319, shortly after the king's death. Although the issue about the master's competence had been decided by the pope in 1311, largely in the bishop's favour, this decision had not been respected by the king. The new conflict ended in a compromise in 1320-21 which improved the situation from the bishop's point of view, although it did not fulfil the conditions in the pope's verdict.[219] In the following period, Erling Vidkunsson's government was less successful in its anti-clerical policy than its counterpart in the 1280s. A united front from the Church at the province council of 1327 apparently brought the government to a compromise in appointing one of the leading prelates, the king's chancellor and provost of St Mary's in Oslo, in return for a withdrawal of the ban against laymen judging in Christian cases.[220]

---

[218] DN VI no. 128; Munch, NFH.*Un.per.* II, pp. 86-88; Bagge, "Kanslerembedet", p. 151, and Opsahl, "Feider i Norge", p. 143. The treaty is only preserved in a fragment, which makes it difficult to know what the conflict was about. See Blom, *Norge i union*, pp. 92-94, who regards it as a normal judicial settlement.
[219] Bagge, *Kapellgeistlighet,* pp. 101-32.
[220] Bagge, "Kanslerembedet", pp. 149-51; Riisøy, *Stat og kirke,* pp. 92 f.

Shortly afterwards, a violent conflict broke out in Bergen about the payment of tithes. The vice treasurer in the town was forced to pay tithe from the rent of houses by threat of excommunication and was outlawed by the government when he gave in to the Church.[221] The relationship to the Church seems to have improved towards the end of the regency, as the bishops are mentioned as active participants in the council in 1331.[222]

Monarchy, Aristocracy and Union during the Reign of Magnus Eriksson

When Magnus Eriksson took over the government in 1331 at the age of fifteen, the situation returned to normal with an adult ruler, although with the important exception that Norway was now governed by a king who mainly resided in another country. After the king came of age, two rebellions against him took place, in 1333 and 1338-39. Whereas the earlier rebellion seems to have been the result of discontent from a few magnates, with the former *drottsete* Erling Vidkunsson as the most important, the rebellion of 1338-39 had a broader base and apparently met with some success, but it is clear from the extant documents that it was confined to a portion of the Norwegian aristocracy, and the king seems in the following years to have had good contact with leading men in Norway, clerics as well as laymen.[223] In 1343-44 a decision was made to end the union with Sweden by making King Magnus's younger son Håkon, then three years old, king of Norway. Håkon was first acclaimed king by a group of counsellors in 1343 and then by popular representatives the year after.[224] However, the latter acclamation only gave him a part of the country, apparently mainly the western and northern part, whereas Magnus was still supposed to rule the rest. He also seems to have acted as regent over Håkon's portion until 1350, when Håkon was formally installed as king with Orm Øysteinsson as *drottsete* – the same title as Erling Vidkunsson had used. Finally, Håkon took over his portion as adult king in 1355. After Magnus's deposition in Sweden in 1363, Norway became the main residence of the dynasty until Håkon's death in 1380.

---

221 Helle, *Kongssete*, pp. 605 f. The conflict is also mentioned by Blom, *Norge i union* I, pp. 88, 196 f., who attaches little importance to it.
222 Schreiner, "Formynderstyret", pp. 396-400, and "Høvdingmøte og riksråd", pp. 416, 427, 488-91, 521, 558, regards this as a dramatic constitutional change, as the bishops in his opinion had been excluded from the council since the 1260s. To this may be objected, firstly, that Schreiner's view implies that the council was a more clearly defined institution than was actually the case, and, secondly, that there is evidence from most of this period that bishops were consulted by the king and performed services for him, although they still did not belong to his inner circle (Helle, *Konge og gode menn*, pp. 366-89).
223 Blom, *Norge i union*, pp. 126-32.
224 NGL IV, pp. 370-74.

The rebellions and the relationship between them and the dissolution of the union have been the subject of different interpretations. Whereas Norwegian historians have usually seen a clear connection, Swedish historians have been more inclined to explain the election of Håkon as part of King Magnus's dynastic policy.[225] The correspondence between nationality and attitudes towards this issue is hardly a coincidence; modern Norwegian historiography came into being in a period of forced union with Sweden (1814-1905) and nationalistic attitudes were also widespread among Swedish historians. However, some historians have joined the opposite camp, including the Swedish historian Sven Axelson and the Norwegian Grethe Authén Blom. In her detailed study of Magnus Eriksson's reign, Blom supports the dynastic interpretation,[226] claiming that Norwegian historians have exaggerated the importance of the conflicts in the 1330s, whereas a closer examination of the documents from the dissolution of the union in 1343-44 shows that the whole process was the result of the king's initiative. Erik Lönnroth's interpretation of the later conflicts about the Nordic unions as conflicts between monarchy and aristocracy has only been applied to the period 1331-44 to a limited extent, although several historians have pointed to the interests of the Norwegian aristocracy.[227]

The sources for the political history of this period are scanty, so most conclusions rest on shaky foundations. Nevertheless, whereas King Magnus clearly wished to give his two sons a kingdom each,[228] it is more difficult to explain the decision to make the younger of them king at the age of three, while the elder was supposed to wait until Magnus's death.[229] Carlsson and Blom's explanation, that the reason was to avoid the complica-

---

225 Munch, *NFH. Un.per.* pp. 151-63, 222-45, 289-302, writing in the 1850s, under the influence of the Norwegian struggle for equality during the union with Sweden, was the founder of the Norwegian interpretation. On the Swedish side, Carlsson, "Den svensk-norska unionen", presents a detailed criticism of Munch's arguments, whereas Schreiner, "Formynderstyret" and "Norge og unionskongedømmet", largely defends Munch's interpretation.
226 Blom, *Norge i union* I, pp. 105-50.
227 Lönnroth, *Sverige och Kalmarunionen*. See also the presentation of the different interpretations in Moseng et al., *Norsk historie* I, pp. 170-76, and Holmsen, *Norges historie*, pp. 317-23; Imsen, *Avfolkning og union*, pp. 26-57; Albrectsen, *Fællesskabet bliver til*, pp. 50-53. The relationship between monarchy and aristocracy is also a central theme in Blom's analysis of the period (*Norge i union*, pp. 105-82), but she regards the aristocratic policy during Magnus's majority as less successful than earlier historians, notably Holmsen.
228 This is explicitly stated in the document from the counsellors who also mention that Håkon was being brought up in Norway. The names might also be interpreted in this direction, as Håkon was a typically Norwegian name with no tradition in the Swedish dynasty. A more likely explanation, however, is that the elder son was named after his paternal grandfather and the younger after his maternal. It was by no means unusual to introduce new names into a dynasty by naming children after their maternal grandparents. Thus, the name Valdemar (after the Russian Vladimir) was introduced in the Danish dynasty in this way, and the Norwegian King Eirik was named after his maternal grandfather Erik Plovpenning.
229 Moseng et al., *Norsk historie* I, pp. 163 f.

tion that Erik as the elder was entitled to Norway according to Norwegian law,[230] is not convincing. On the contrary, Håkon's succession in Norway might easily have made Erik jealous and demand the same in Sweden, which actually seems to have happened, as he rebelled against his father in 1356. Furthermore, even if Blom may be right that the two rebellions are not necessarily evidence of widespread discontent with the union or Magnus's regime, they nevertheless represent a contrast to the preceding period back to 1240. There would also appear to be reasons for such discontent in addition to the grievances of individual aristocrats, such as the former regent Erling Vidkunsson, for not having received the offices they wanted. The main problem was apparently Magnus's foreign policy which was even less in the aristocracy's interest than that of his Norwegian predecessors.[231] Magnus Eriksson's great project was to gain Scania from Denmark which at the time was in full dissolution. He succeeded in this in 1332, but only with an enormous sum of money which he had to borrow. The Norwegian aristocracy was not likely to have been very interested in this acquisition – similar attempts in the same direction had resulted in Duchess Ingebjørg's deposition from the government in 1323 – and certainly not in paying for it. They may not have been against the union as such but, in accordance with the agreement with the Swedish aristocracy in 1319, they wanted a limited union and opposed extra burdens following from the king's policy in his capacity as king of Sweden. Thus, the reign of Magnus Eriksson confirms the conclusion from the examination of the previous reigns about the aristocracy's reluctance to engage in a risky and costly foreign policy and the importance of the individual king for the policy conducted.

Were the conflicts in the 1330s and the dissolution of the union also the result of a conflict of interest between the monarchy and the aristocracy? Magnus was a king who insisted on the royal prerogative and sought to limit the influence of the aristocracy, a policy that led him into great difficulties in Sweden, ending with his deposition in 1363. As the monarchy had traditionally been stronger in Norway, a similar reaction was less likely there. However, there is some evidence of an aristocratic consolidation in the period after 1319 that may have led to greater reactions against a monarchical policy. One aspect of this consolidation is the emergence of the council of the realm. The term is mentioned for the first time in the union treaty of 1319, which is also said to have been sealed with the council's seal.[232] It may have increased its importance during the regency in the 1320s, although there is no direct evidence of a more clearly organised council then than under Håkon V. Such evidence becomes stronger after Magnus took over the government.[233]

230 Carlsson, "Den svensk-norska unionen", pp. 276 f.; Blom, *Norge i union* I, p. 137.
231 Fladby, "Oppløsningen", pp. 96-100.
232 DN VIII no. 50, p. 76.
233 DN VIII no. 108; Blom, *Norge i union*, pp. 108-13.

There is a brief reference to formal membership of the council, and the role it played in 1343 seems to form a first step towards its role in royal elections in the following period. Although the judgement between King Magnus and the Havtoresons in 1347 (below p. 366) was not formally passed by the council of the realm, the majority of the court members were counsellors, thus anticipating the later function of the council as the supreme court of the realm. There is also evidence of a clearer distinction between an aristocratic elite and the rest of the population which increased in the course of the fourteenth century,[234] most clearly exemplified in the more widespread use and greater importance of armed retainers in the service of the aristocrats. In the period 1319-50, this probably coincided with the maximum wealth for the landowning aristocracy. The political climax came somewhat later, after 1363, when Magnus and his son Håkon VI depended on the Norwegian aristocracy and their retainers in their attempt to regain Sweden and ruled in close cooperation with the council of the realm. By this time, however, the economic base of the Norwegian lay aristocracy had been seriously weakened, which in the long run prevented it from playing a similar role during the following unions with stronger partners, except for shorter periods.

Returning to the situation in the 1330s, we may ask whether the two rebellions that took place were the result of a consolidation of the aristocracy and an increasing rivalry between monarchy and aristocracy. Had the solidarity between the monarchy and the aristocracy resulting from the civil wars been replaced by the re-emergence of a potential aristocratic opposition as new generations took over their ancestors' positions and formed an elite that had been used to offices and privileges? Despite the long-term trends towards a consolidation of the aristocracy, it seems that the problems created by the union were of greater importance for the rebellions in the 1330s and the subsequent dissolution of the union, although with the aristocratic consolidation as a contributory factor. Additionally, a likely reason for aristocratic discontent may have been the frequent absence of the king. Although King Magnus cannot be accused of governing Norway from Sweden or imposing Swedish favourites on the Norwegians, he had to divide his attention between the two countries and clearly spent more time in Sweden than in Norway. His visits to Norway were also mostly confined to the southeastern part of the country, mainly Oslo and Tønsberg.[235] This meant a radical change from the situation before 1319, with serious consequences for the government of the country. It seems that the local administration and jurisdiction continued largely in the same way as before; in fact, the best evidence we

---

234 Benedictow, "Norge", pp. 19-29, and above p. 326.
235 See also Blom, *Norge i union*, p. 112, on the dominance of men from the southeast in the council, which, however, may have to do with the greater chance of such men being mentioned in connection with the king's visits.

have about activities in this area stems from the period 1320-50. The central government, however, must have reduced its activities, as is evident from the more modest amount of royal correspondence, carried out by only two scribes.

In principle there might have been several ways of compensating for the king's absence. He could make his will known in writing, and actually did, notably in the period 1339-44, when there is no evidence of any visit to Norway and when the conflicts and negotiations with King Valdemar of Denmark over Scania (1340-43) took much of his time and interest. Nevertheless, this can hardly have happened to any great extent, as the royal correspondence diminished rather than increased. The reason for this reduction is partly because Magnus conducted most of his foreign policy in his capacity as Swedish king, which means that a main area of interest for his predecessors became less important, and partly because there were limits to his chances of being obeyed unless he had consulted with the leading men in the country. He could summon Norwegian counsellors to meetings in Sweden, as he occasionally did, but this was a costly and cumbersome procedure, and one usually resented by the counsellors. And finally, he could delegate more power to the Norwegian council, which he was not often willing to do, as it was contrary to his ideas about the king's sovereign power, as well as the tradition established by his predecessors. After 1343/44, however, he did take some steps in this direction, by delegating his pardoning power to the chancellor, perhaps even making the chancery at St Mary's a kind of administrative centre in his absence. However, this delegation of power was balanced by more frequent visits to Norway and regular meetings with the council in the beginning of each year.[236] From 1350 onwards, the situation largely returned to the normal pattern from before 1319, with the king residing permanently in the country, first as a minor, then, from 1355, with full royal powers. In addition to the governmental problems caused by the king's absence, we may also point to the personal aspect – the importance of close contacts between the king and the members of the aristocracy. Frequent contacts with the leading men on various social occasions, notably the great Christmas celebrations, and skill in handling problems and conflicts within this group and between him and them must have been an important factor in Håkon Håkonsson's and his successors' good relationship with the aristocracy and ability to uphold the peace in the country. Physical absence may explain why Magnus had greater difficulties. An additional factor may have been personal inadequacy, as has often been pointed out against the background of the disasters Magnus experienced in Sweden from 1356 onwards, but his Norwegian policy from 1331-44 gives no clear evidence of this.

---

[236] Blom, *Norge i union*, pp. 151-82, who convincingly rejects Holmsen's hypothesis of a government of the council of the realm during these years.

In this way, the period 1331-44 serves to illustrate some of the essential features of the whole period 1240-1350: the importance of the king's personal presence, despite institutionalisation and an increasing use of writing, the necessity for him to have a good relationship with at least a large part of the leading men in the country, despite the strictly monarchical ideology, and last but not least, the importance of this latter tradition for the relative success of a king whose main base was in another country and who started his reign at the age of fifteen.

A Strong Monarchy

The conclusion to be drawn from the previous discussion is that it confirms Seip and Helle's view regarding the king's liberty as a decision-maker, but without pointing to any fundamental conflicts of interest between the king and the aristocracy. Although Magnus Håkonsson's Church policy was clearly against the interests of the lay aristocracy, it had the support of the ecclesiastical sector. Moreover, the difference between Magnus and his predecessor and successors is less than often assumed in earlier scholarship. Nor is there any strong evidence that Håkon V conducted an anti-aristocratic policy, as some scholars have maintained. No doubt, Håkon was a stronger king than his brother and insisted on the royal prerogative to a greater extent than he did. He intervened against individual aristocrats, but the changes in the leading circles during his reign were more likely the result of his wish to promote the men who had served him during his period as duke of Southern and Eastern Norway than of a general anti-aristocratic attitude. The clearest evidence of the king's personal importance is not the examples of the king acting against the interests of the aristocracy, but the contrast between the periods of adult and capable kings with a firm authority to conduct their policy and the periods of regency which show less consistency and more conflicts of interests.

Although the adherents of the "instrument" theory may be right in stating that it would have been difficult for the king to conduct a policy diametrically opposed to the interests of the great landowners, this is not the same as claiming that the kind of monarchy that existed in Norway in the period 1240-1350 was established by the landowning aristocracy and existed to serve their interests, as maintained by the young Holmsen and later by Kåre Lunden. The problem in these theories is the concrete link between the governing class and their instrument. How did the landowning aristocracy make the king their instrument, and how did they manage to control him? Holmsen avoids the problem by stating that the individual members of the aristocracy who served the king did so without being aware that it served their own interests, thereby running into the common objection against functionalist theories that they fail to explain how a certain number of people can act to fulfil a purpose of which they are not aware.[237] Empirically, both Holmsen and Lunden pay considerable attention to what they regard as the consolidation of the landed aristocracy in the period 1202-40. As we have seen, however, what happened in this period should rather be understood as a consolidation of an "in faction" around the king, and our examination of the following period has given little evidence of any opportunity for the landowning aristocracy as a whole to control the king.

Two examples may confirm this reasoning. First, although the Church tried to exploit the change in the tax system to gain tax exemption for its lands, there is no evidence of any similar attempt by the secular aristocracy, despite the fact that the greatest secular landowners acted as regents for the king. Their policy was to preserve the royal revenues as well as possible, for the benefit of the king and the men who served him, including themselves. As we have seen, this was probably a wise policy from the point of view of the members of the landed aristocracy who held royal office, who nevertheless formed a small minority among the landowners. Thus, the majority might have profited from the alternative policy, but as the minority included the leading men in the country, they had no say.

The second example is the judgement passed on 12 January 1347 by members of the council of the realm plus two *lagmenn* in the case between King Magnus Eriksson on the one side and Jon and Sigurd Havtoreson on the other. The two brothers had presented a charter from King Håkon V, appointing them governors of Borgarsysle, apparently for life, which the king refused to respect. The court found in favour of the king, declaring that King Håkon could not give away such a large part of his realm for longer than his own lifetime: "For according to the laws, lordship and command over subjects and people, together with the government of the country, belong to and devolve to the one who has come to the king of Norway's realm through rightful inheritance".[238] As we see, the problem here is the same as was the object of the conflict between Kings Sigurd and Øystein in the early twelfth century (pp. 185 ff.). If we disregard the purely legal aspect of the issue, which may have been dubious, and focus on the interest aspect, we see that the members of the top aristocracy come down on the same side as the king. A more consolidated aristocracy with greater opportunities for using the king as their instrument might have arrived at the opposite conclusion, regarding the judgement in favour of the two brothers as a precedent that might benefit them equally. As members of the top aristocracy, they would probably have been the nearest to profit from such a precedent, if they had been able to control the king. As this was clearly not the case, they found their interests best served by supporting

---

237 Dahl, "Noen teoretiske problemer", p. 192; Elster, *Ulysses and the Sirens*, pp. 87-103.
238 "þui at herra dœmi ok ifuir bod ifuir þægnna ok almuga a ok æfter laghum æignazst med allre annara Rikis stiorn j Norege þan sem aat Rettre ærfd er till Norges konongs Rikis komen" (DN I no. 303).

the king, which would have kept a maximum of positions open to competition among the members of the aristocracy. Thus, in both these cases the secular aristocracy supported the king. Although the members of the group who made these decisions did so in their own interest, they did not act as representatives of the aristocracy as a whole, and the decisions they made left the king with a considerable amount of independent power.

An important explanation for this strong position of the monarchy is the fact that the king inherited his office while the members of the aristocracy did not. A comparison between the internal conditions within the ecclesiastical and secular organisation demonstrates the significance of hereditary kingship. Both popes and bishops had their councils – the pope his college of cardinals, the bishop his cathedral chapter – both of which at this time brought about a considerable division of power. In Norway, a protracted and bitter conflict raged between the bishop and archbishop and the cathedral chapters in Stavanger and Trondheim around 1300. And in both places – as in the other Norwegian cathedral chapters – the result was the same. There were specific rules governing the cathedral chapter's right to participate in the bishop's decision-making, and for individual canons' rights in relation to the bishop. Outwardly, both sides could stand together in defending the bishopric's power and authority. However, a cathedral chapter consisted of a clearly defined group of persons, with fixed incomes and offices from which they could not be removed – at least not if they were not convicted of serious offences – and who moreover elected the bishop. The cathedral chapter could thus set conditions before an election. In addition, it was a corporation which "never died," while bishops were appointed and died on a regular basis. They were often elderly men who did not remain very long in office. Thus the development moved in the direction of the cathedral chapter continually extending its power and becoming a "government" which governed alongside the bishop.

By contrast, the king had considerable freedom to choose to whom he wanted to grant power and influence, while his own position was inherited. The growth of a more permanently organised council of the realm from the fourteenth century onwards resulted in a development similar to that within the Church, but was slower and achieved less, expressly because the council of the realm was not an elective body to the same extent. The nearest parallel is France, where the monarchy gradually became hereditary, largely because of the Capetians' success in passing the kingdom over from father to son. In France, however, this was combined with a considerable degree of decentralisation, expressed in a number of princes and aristocrats with hereditary rights to their principalities or fiefs. Norway, where only the royal office was hereditary, thus becomes a quite striking example of a *dominium regale*. By contrast, Denmark and Sweden developed into elective monarchies and were formally defined as such in the early fourteenth century. Largely as a consequence of the union with the neighbouring countries, Norway also became an elective monarchy over the course of the later Middle Ages – this was formally established in 1450 – and the council of the realm's position was thus bolstered. However, the monarchy was never subjected to free elections in the same way as the bishoprics. The king's eldest son was usually the only candidate. What the elections did involve were the conditions for how he should govern.

In a comparative perspective, it is surprising that the Norwegian king managed to introduce the rules of hereditary succession in the law of 1260, which completely eliminated any elective element. By contrast, the two neighbouring countries developed in a different direction from the same startingpoint: from the beginning of the fourteenth century both Sweden and Denmark were defined as elective monarchies. Denmark is particularly interesting from this point of view. The Danish dynasty is probably older than the Norw[egian] one, going back to the mid-tenth century and continuing without any break until the [late] Middle Ages. Like Norway, Denmark had its internal struggles in the twelfth ce[ntury] – the critical period was the years 1134-57 – but the crisis was overcome more qu[ickly]. During the following century, 1157-1241, three successive kings combined with stre[ngth] and stability seemed on the way to consolidate the tradition of hereditary kingship. [Un]fortunately, however, the death of King Valdemar the Victorious in 1241 led to a pe[riod] of internal unrest, dynastic struggles between Valdemar's three sons and their descend[ants] and conflicts between the king, the Church and an aristocratic opposition, lasting until 1340, which resulted in the monarchy being defined as elective. In 1320, the new King Christoffer II had to issue an election charter ("håndfæstning") with precise promises to the aristocratic council about how he would govern the country. In Denmark as in most other elective monarchies – with the partial exception of Germany – dynastic continuity was usually the same as in hereditary monarchies, but the electors had the possibility to set conditions for the election and might even depose the elected monarch.

In comparison with Denmark as well as France, the development in Norway becomes a paradox. Here hereditary monarchy was not introduced after a long period of stable and uncontested dynastic succession but, on the contrary, after a series of violent struggles for the throne. Even the succession of the king who introduced the law of hereditary succession, Håkon Håkonsson, had been contested, and he had faced a rebellion as late as in 1240, twenty years before the law was passed. Nevertheless, there is little to suggest that the law of 1260 met with opposition. Admittedly, somewhat later the Church tried to revive Magnus Erlingsson's law of 1163/64 which gave more room for election, but there seems to have been no opposition from the lay aristocracy. The reservations about the law came from the king himself who was reluctant to discriminate between his sons.

The usual explanation of this paradox is the relative weakness of the Norwegian aristocracy whose individual members were less wealthy than their Danish and Swedish counterparts and whose wealth consisted in scattered farms and parts of farms which formed no

solid basis for territorial power. Both factors made the aristocrats more dependent on the king's service and more likely to support the king, to the extent that they might even swallow hereditary monarchy. This explanation gives at least a substantial part of the answer. However, the law of 1163/64 did give election a more prominent place than the one of 1260, and the Norwegian aristocrats were not always the obedient royal servants they became after the mid-thirteenth century. The explanation must therefore also be sought in the special conditions prevailing in the period before the law was passed. An important factor in this context is the faction around Sverre's dynasty which was less dominated by the top aristocracy than the opposite one, or, for that matter, than most previous factions during the internal struggles. On the one hand, this contributed to greater discipline and internal coherence and on the other resulted in a considerable renewal of the aristocracy. A large part of the old aristocracy was killed in the prolonged struggles in the late twelfth century and replaced by new men from Sverre's faction who identified their interests with those of the dynasty. Moreover, the conflict between Sverre and the Church left its mark on the adherents of the dynasty; there is still some anti-clericalism in sources like *The King's Mirror* and *Hákonar saga*, although in a more moderate form. This means that the king might easily obtain support from the lay aristocracy to reject the law of 1163/64 which favoured the Church. These conditions would clearly not last forever; the identification with the dynasty and the faction around it must have faded during the thirteenth century while a clearer identification with the aristocracy as an estate gradually emerged. However, their effects lasted long enough to secure support for the law of 1260. Once the principle of hereditary succession was established, it was more difficult to change. Thus, the king apparently secured support quite easily for the revisions of the laws of 1274 and 1302 which upheld the hereditary principle but made some changes in the priority between the various heirs. Despite the importance of long-term factors, hereditary monarchy was hardly an inevitable result of the structural conditions in medieval Norway. If the Erling-Magnus faction had remained in power, the elective element might easily have become more important.

The king's position was further strengthened by the fact that he was not faced by a united landowning aristocracy. The ecclesiastical and secular aristocracy had different interests and were often opposed to one another. Moreover, neither of the two was united internally. Ecclesiastical institutions were often in conflict with one another, and the individual members of the aristocracy were competing for offices in the king's service, in addition to the fact that there were often conflicts between aristocratic families. The disproportion between the high number of aristocratic families and the small number of offices in the king's service was from one point of view an advantage for the king, but it might also be a danger, leading to discontent within the aristocracy which in turn might lead to rebellion. How great this risk was is difficult to tell, but it may at least partly have been the explanation for the many conflicts in Sweden in the Later Middle Ages. Concerning Norway, we know neither how many of the 600 families really aspired to positions in the king's service, nor what alternatives they had for gaining wealth and honour. It is unlikely that we are dealing with a close-knit aristocracy with a constitutional ideology in opposition to the king. The members of the aristocracy largely related to the king as individuals rather than as an estate, probably often even as rivals, as the Icelandic magnates mentioned above (p. 279).

This also means that the frequent references to the king acting together with "wise men" or "good men", which should probably be understood as his council, cannot be taken as evidence of aristocratic dominance. No doubt, these men were aristocrats, not only in the sense that they were appointed by the king to the highest positions in the realm, but also in the sense that they were great landowners. Nevertheless, there is no evidence that they regarded themselves as the representatives of the aristocracy as an estate. They were appointed by the king to govern the realm together with him, and probably identified themselves with the central government, defending the interests of the monarchy against the Church and external powers and attempting to control the king's local representatives in the same way as the king himself had. Politically as well as economically, there was a vast difference between the majority of the aristocrats (mostly moderate landowners with mainly local influence), and the circle around the king in Norway as in most other countries, and there is no reason to assume any fundamental solidary between the two groups. Internal division is even more characteristic of the lay aristocracy than of the Church.

Even if a great alliance of the aristocracy against the king was an unlikely event, there were men sufficiently wealthy and influential to create trouble for the royal government. When this did not happen in the period 1240-1319, the explanation can at least partly be found through informal channels and close personal relations with the king. The royal counsellors and officials were not so numerous for the king not to have known them personally, even if they did not reside at his court. And the court was of course not just a bureaucratic centre, but a place where kings, aristocrats and courtiers ate and drank, listened to music and readings, went on hunting expeditions, exchanged gossip, and plotted against one another. Still, much could be achieved and solved through personal contacts. As long as the king did not initiate drastic measures, aimed at the aristocracy as a whole, one could readily adapt to inherited kingship and *dominium regale*. On the other hand, it was part of the king's political acumen to be able to accommodate with, and manoeuvre between, the kingdom's aristocrats in a way such that most of them remained his friends and supporters. Most of the kings of the Sverre dynasty seem to have grasped this. Although there is evidence of a gradual consolidation of an aristocratic elite from the early fourteenth century onwards with a greater will and ability to defend its own interests, the main reason for the problems occurring during Magnus Eriksson's reign therefore seems to be the greater distance between the king and the Norwegian magnates because of the union, as well as the king's youth and lack of experience.

The King and the People

The hereditary monarchy, the absence of institutions to control the king, rivalry between the ecclesiastical and the secular aristocracy, the latter's dependence on the king's service and its competition for public office and the shifts in policy from reign to reign examined above all imply a strong personal monarchy, in accordance with the views of Seip and Helle. Does this also imply some kind of alliance between the king and the peasantry? In discussing this issue, the High Middle Ages in Norway should not be compared with an imagined ideal, where there was no state authority over and beyond what served the people's interests, but with more realistic alternatives, such as earlier periods, or other countries, preferably the Nordic neighbouring countries at the time. Arguments supporting the state authority's functional relationship to the peasant communities are expressed first of all by the monarchy itself, firstly by Håkon V's attentiveness to the peasants' complaints and criticism of the officials' abuse of power. Secondly, it was in the monarchy's interest to have a strong peasant class, since the peasants made up the majority of the country's military power. Thirdly, it has been claimed that the development of the monarchy's system of law enforcement could only be understood as based on the needs of the general population.

None of these arguments is absolutely binding. Regarding the first, there is no reason to doubt the monarchy's noble intentions; on the other hand, one can question how much practical significance they had, and how far the monarchy was willing to challenge the aristocracy in the interests of the peasants. Kåre Lunden in particular draws very negative conclusions on this point. The king's control of his officials was almost non-existent, and he admitted himself that there were a number of abuses.[239] Secondly, one can debate how much power membership in the *leidang* organisation gave the peasants. In the contemporary sagas, especially *Sverris saga*, the peasants emerge as inferior to the king's retainers. And even though the peasants were a formidable force when united, we may ask whether they were capable of functioning together, or if peasants from one part of the country could be used to suppress uprisings elsewhere. Here examples from more recent times may be adduced, such as eighteenth-century Prussia where the soldiers were recruited from unfree peasants without any improvement of the conditions of this class. It must be added, however, that the peasants' military importance probably gave them more influence in the Middle Ages than in the Early Modern Period, because the gap in military efficiency between a peasant

---

[239] Lunden, *Sverreættens kongedømme*, pp. 426-29; cf. Holmsen, *Nye studier*, pp. 169-79.

conscript and a trained and professional soldier was narrower, and because "peasant soldiers" at that time were not taken from their local communities and subjected to military exercise and discipline to the same extent. An alternative to this use of peasants can be found in Denmark and parts of Sweden where the peasants were replaced by the magnates' elite forces, which in turn were financed through the higher burdens imposed on them.

With regard to law enforcement, recent international research, which has distanced itself from the Maitland tradition's "functional" view of state authority, has often argued against this view, pointing partly to conflict-resolving mechanisms in pre-state society, partly to corruption within public law enforcement, and partly to the new public authorities – the Church and the state – which, particularly the former, introduced new crimes. The same arguments can be applied to the Norwegian situation. Still, there are indications that public law enforcement at least somewhat met the needs of the people. The fact that it came earlier and was better developed in Norway than in the neighbouring countries and contributed to a greater share of the monarchy's revenues suggests, firstly, that the functional aspect was a more important part of the king's power base in Norway, and, secondly, a connection to the peasants' military contributions. The king secured peace, order, and conflict resolution domestically, while the peasants, partly in their own interests, partly in the king's, contributed to asserting the country's interests against other countries. The Later Middle Ages, when the elite's resources were drastically reduced, put the question regarding the state authority's functional aspect to the test. For a long time state authority was believed to have broken down almost completely as a result of the agrarian crisis. Recent studies, carried out by Grethe Authén Blom and by Steinar Imsen,[240] suggest that this was not the case, but that state authority to a considerable degree continued to function more or less as it always had. Its loss of revenues was also less than the decline in land rent. One possible explanation for this could be precisely because conditions had been brought down to the "bedrock" of state functions, and that the peasants gave only minimal support to the state, namely inasmuch as it served their interests. It is characteristic of the local administration that it continued to function in the Later Middle Ages largely in the same way as in the previous period.

The fact that the king directly referred to complaints about abuses from his officials can also be interpreted as supporting the opposite conclusion of Lunden's. An important argument in favour of this point of view is the fact that local government, despite increasing professionalisation and bureaucratisation, was characterised by an extensive use of non-professionals. This applies to the military as well as the judicial sector. Local government was largely in the hands of a group of prominent farmers or burghers who frequently appear in the charters as witnesses, judges, or juries, with or without the king's local repre-

---

240 Blom, *Norge i union*, vol. II, pp. 543-711; Imsen, *Bondekommunalisme*, pp. 139 ff.

sentative. They are less prominent in ecclesiastical government, but do occur there as well, in Norway as well as in other countries. The king and the central government's control over these people was probably stronger in the thirteenth and early fourteenth centuries than both earlier and later, but there can hardly be any doubt that these local elites had considerable influence. Certainly, the aristocracy became increasingly affiliated with the king and the central government as *sysselmenn* who acted as royal representatives rather than local leaders, but this did not mean that local society was "drained" of leaders. If the top aristocracy ever lost touch with local society, and it is by no means certain that they had, there was a sufficient number of men of second rank to take their place. Apart from some scattered evidence in the sagas and other sources of prominent commoners speaking against the king on behalf of their communities, *The King's Mirror* gives clear evidence of this. Answering the question from the Son about why prominent men in local society agree to join the king's *hird* with such a low rank as housecarls, the Father blames him for not asking wisely – the only such blame in the work – and explains the far greater honour in being at the king's *hird* than remaining in local society. He spends so much energy in convincing the Son of the glory and prestige in serving the king that we can be fairly certain that common opinion outside the royal circles was closer to that of the Son than of the Father.[241] There was clearly an increasing tendency for men of wealth and standing to join the king's service as well as for members of the aristocracy to identify their interests with those of the central government, but there were enough left in local society to serve as its leaders. These were the men who formed the elite of the *leidang* forces, who might join *sysselmenn* and bishops as retainers and who served in local courts of law. They were not necessarily in opposition to the king but derived a substantial part of their status from their position in local society and were able, if necessary, to defend its interests.

The people's influence is also demonstrated in a number of other ways. They managed to get their candidates elected in the royal elections in 1204 (the Croziers) and 1207 (the Birchlegs), rejecting those from the warriors who wanted to continue the war.[242] The curious paragraph in the Law of Frostating about the people's right to kill or expel the king or his representatives for illegal use of violence against individual members of the local community remained in force until the National Law of the 1270s, despite several revisions of the law. This can hardly be explained in any other way than by the people's wish to keep it.[243] There are also several examples of resistance in practice, including the killing of Ragnvald Hallkjellsson (above p. 288), for which Earl Skule did take a bloody revenge

---

241 *Kgs.* p. 42; cf. Bagge, *The Political Thought*, p. 183, and "Motstandsretten", pp. 407 f.
242 *Bogl.* pp. 28 f., 81-87 (both versions).
243 F IV.50-52; Bagge, "Motstandsretten", pp. 399-410.

but which King Håkon refused to punish. A rebellion in Trøndelag in 1213 is described in detail in *Boglunga sogur*.[244] Bad harvests which made the people refuse to pay their taxes led to this event. During a meeting to discuss the matter, at which the king was also present, the *sysselmann* dealt a man a blow. The man reacted by cutting off the *sysselmann*'s leg at the thigh. The king then asked his men to withdraw but the people went after them and killed several of them. The year after, the king gathered an army, invaded Trøndelag and forced the people to pay their tax for this and the preceding years, but the saga does not mention any other punishment. In a similar way, a rebellion in the regions north of Oslo against a new tax introduced by Duke Håkon in the 1290s was only punished by forcing the people to pay the tax. The contrast to the massacres following peasant revolts in many other countries, such as the *jacquerie* in France in the 1350s or the suppression of the peasant rebellion in Hungary in 1514,[245] is striking, showing that the peasants were a force to be reckoned with. Generally, Norwegian peasants for the most part seem to have been able to defend their interests without resorting to open rebellion.[246] From their point of view, a stable state authority after 1240 became a lesser evil than the period of turmoil which preceded it. To what extent this meant that the peasants were actively interested in the royal government and to what extent the king derived his power from a good relationship with the peasants can certainly be subject to discussion. It seems fairly clear, however, that the peasants were not helpless objects of suppression by the aristocracy.

Despite their greater subservience to the king in the second half of the thirteenth century, expressed in Lodin Lepp's harangue against the Icelanders (above p. 204), the peasants were still able to protect their most vital interests, as appears from The National Law's statement about their economic contributions:

> In the name of the same Jesus Christ, our rightful Norwegian king, His servant, shall decide over commands and bans and our expeditions and rule by law and not against law, for God's praise and honour, for his own benefit, and for our needs. We shall not deny him *leidang* or mobilisation if he decrees according to the rules which here follow.[247]

---

244 *Bogl.* pp. 125-27. The passage occurs only in a version which is in all likelihood the later one but cannot be much later than the early 1220s.
245 Freedman, "Rural Society", pp. 95-101; Engel, *The Realm of St Stephen*, pp. 363 f.
246 Imsen and Vogler, "Communal Autonomy", pp. 18-27.
247 "I þess hins sama Jhesu Krist nafne skal uar logligr Noregs konungr hans þionn raða boðe oc banne oc vtforum uarum. oc raðe at lagum en eigi at olaugum guði til lofs oc dyrðar ser til gangns oc oss til þarfenda. Eigi skolum ver honum leiðangrs ne vttboða synia ef hann byðr vtt með þuilikri skilorðe sem her fylgir" (L III.1); cf. Holmsen, *Nye studier*, pp. 163 f.

Then a series of detailed rules follow which determine how much tax the king could levy during peacetime, and how long and in what way the peasants were obliged to follow him into war. Here it is not the sovereign king who speaks, but the peasants, through "we." It is clear that negotiations had taken place, and the result was a compromise. The king received his fixed taxes, but the amount was meticulously established. This amount was also very modest compared with that paid in Sweden and Denmark, as well as with the land rent and the tithe to the Church in Norway. At the same time, the peasants were obliged to perform military service. Yet even here there were clear limitations; their duty only extends to the defence of the country and the colonies. There is a suggestion that the peasants may contribute to the king more than what they were strictly obliged to, if "such an emergency struck him, the people will give him more out of love to him ... if they are met with mercy and good will from his side."[248] It is thus a matter of negotiation if the peasants expected compensation for their "good will."

We may therefore conclude that despite the fact that the behaviour of contemporary royal officials differed considerably from that of Weberian bureaucrats, the power relationship between them and the people they governed was not such that they could get away with any kind of behaviour. On the positive side, it must also be pointed out that the peasants' military service formed an important part of the king's power; without it, he would have been considerably worse off in his relationship with other countries. Likewise, the participation of the upper levels of local society in legal decisions was essential for the royal government to work, while at the same time giving these people power and prestige. Thus at least the upper levels of the peasants were likely to support the royal government, while at the same time their relative strength compared to that of the aristocracy made the latter less inclined to challenge the king.

Conclusion

The conclusion to the preceding discussion must be that there was a strong personal monarchy in Norway during the High Middle Ages. The formal barriers to the king's power were few and poorly defined, a picture which becomes even clearer if we compare it to the Church and the neighbouring countries. The most important limitation to the king's power concerned his relationship to the Church which had its own organisation, largely independent of the king, and consisting of both a clerical and secular aristocracy. The social basis of the king's power is more difficult to assess. Generally, there is little

---

248 "... einhuer þorf falle til með honum at menn uilia frammar gort hafa firir astsemdar saker uið hann með goðra manna samðykt ef þeir kenna af honum miskunn oc goðuilia" (ibid.).

evidence of political measures against the secular aristocracy, more of similar measures against the Church, but no evidence of measures against the interests of the landowners in general. Overall, the monarchy can therefore be said to have conducted a policy in accordance with the interests of the landowning aristocracy. This, however, hardly makes it an "instrument" of this class. First, the landowning class can only to some degree be said to have common interests. There was rivalry between the lay and the ecclesiastical aristocracy, between various ecclesiastical institutions and between individual aristocrats. Second, the practical means for the great landowners to control the king were limited. Third, the king was clearly interested in protecting the peasants who played an important part in the armed forces as well as in the administration and who also may have been able to protect their interests to some extent. Finally, the monarchy as such may have been able to act as an institution with its own interests. This is expressed particularly clearly in the area of foreign policy which was largely determined by dynastic interests and where the king could usually count on the support of the aristocratic elite in his service. Nor should we underestimate the advantage of being an institution at the centre of the decision-making process, even with the limited degree of bureaucratisation in medieval Norway.[249] A strong sense of dynastic continuity, a series of able kings succeeding one another by virtue of the law of hereditary succession and an ideology largely identifying the social order with the monarchic government strengthened the king's authority. Moreover, he had now emerged as the main patron in the country and could join men to his service who identified their interests with those of the monarchy. From this point of view, the existence of an "in faction" around the king may have been equally important as whatever existed within the landed aristocracy.

Admittedly, the king's personal power is not necessarily evidence of a strong state. The king may have the liberty to make the decisions he wants and he may arbitrarily kill or punish his officials and retainers but his decisions may have no consequences outside his immediate surroundings. By contrast, a well-developed bureaucracy may increase the importance and efficiency of the government while at the same time reducing the influence of the monarch. In a similar way, the introduction of more precise rules for the division of power between the king and the "people" – in practice usually the aristocracy – may be an expression of the strength of the monarchy, while the lack of such provisions may be understood as evidence of a monarchy that is too weak to be a challenge to other powers of society. England, the strongest state of medieval Europe, is a good illustration of this point. Here the monarchy was wealthier, the bureaucracy more developed and the government interfered in local society to a greater extent than anywhere else, while at the same

---

[249] Mann, *The Sources of Social Power*, pp. 6 f.

time the king had to share his power with the aristocracy. By contrast, the king's personal power was stronger in France, while the monarchy's institutional power was weaker.

From this point of view, the Norwegian monarchy was of course far weaker than the English one, and it is debatable whether it was stronger or weaker than the Danish and Swedish ones. In some respects, however, it was not only personally but also institutionally strong. Public justice was well developed, there was a law for the whole country and the king was recognised as the supreme legislator. It was able to mobilise the population for services with little or no payment, which is demonstrated in the mobilisation of the *leidang* during the conflicts in the late thirteenth and early fourteenth centuries and in the participation of the leading layers of local society in various kinds of judicial contexts. Despite the considerable independence of the Church, secular society was largely subservient to the king's authority, and the king represented the top of a hierarchy which stretched from the ordinary peasant up to the government milieu around the king. The king's formal authority over this hierarchy was also recognised by members of the secular aristocracy. Thus, whereas the relationship between the king and the Church conforms to what was common in the rest of Europe, the position of the secular aristocracy was weaker than in most other countries, including Denmark and Sweden. Despite the expansion of the secular aristocracy in the first half of the fourteenth century, there were still no hereditary fiefs, no private castles (or few if any) and no aristocratic rank except by appointment to the king's service. In sum, there were few exact limits to the king's power other than those posed by his financial capacity and his relatively simple bureaucratic apparatus. It is unlikely that the lay or ecclesiastical aristocracy was able to force the king to act according to their interests, but more uncertain to what extent the king was able to make the aristocrats in his service an effective instrument of his will.

In explaining these features of the division of power in medieval Norway, geography and social structure are of course important factors, which in turn were strengthened by the concentration of power and the reshuffling of the lay aristocracy during the prolonged civil wars. In addition, the monarchy made good use of the hierarchical doctrine introduced at the time of the Christianisation in its relationship to the Church as well as the aristocracy and from the second half of the thirteenth century managed to join the latter in a common ideology of the royal prerogative based on Roman law and Aristotle's philosophy.

How, Why, When and How Much?
The Extent and Character of Norwegian State Formation in the Middle Ages

The conclusion from the previous discussion is that there was indeed state formation in Norway in the Middle Ages, although not quite to the extent claimed by the most eager adherents of "Norway becomes a state". More importantly, we have been able to distinguish more clearly between the different aspects of this process. The first stage of the formation of the Norwegian kingdom was mainly achieved by military means. Norway was united through conquest, and its exact borders were determined by the fact that the main military force in the early period was sea-based. The internal wars from 1130-1240 were also crucial for political centralisation, the strength of the monarchy and the development of the local administration. By contrast, there is little to suggest that the military element was of any great importance for the further development of the state after the end of the civil wars. Although the king of Norway conducted an active foreign policy during this period, he rarely resorted to the use of force, and the changes he introduced in the military system to support his foreign policy were limited. He favoured diplomacy, often supplemented by the use of the fleet for power demonstrations, and he sought to extend his power and territory by marriage alliances rather than by armed force. Nor did Norway undergo the same military transformation as the other new kingdoms in the northern and eastern periphery of Western Christendom, but instead retained a system based on the popular levy, supplemented with a limited number of elite forces, on foot rather than mounted, and a few castles. Although the relative importance of elite forces increased during the fourteenth century, this happened too late to influence the pattern of landownership and was also of limited importance for state formation.

Despite the contrast between the warlike Viking Age and the peaceful High Middle Ages, the military technology and organisation thus seems to show considerable continuity between the Viking Age and the early fourteenth century, although the changes are greater in other areas. The introduction of Christianity was a revolutionary event. The Church introduced an organised bureaucracy, contributed to the centralisation of landed wealth and brought considerable aspects of daily life under the control of a central authority. The Church must also have served as a model for the monarchy to a great extent, not least in the field of justice, which provides the clearest example of state formation in medieval Norway. Although our limited source material for the High Middle Ages, and even more for the earlier period, makes it difficult to decide exactly what is new and what is not, the law as well as documentary sources point to a considerable expansion of public justice and a greater involvement on the part of the authorities in settling conflicts between people, as does the import of canon and Roman law. Admittedly, we should not underestimate the conflict-solving mechanisms in the old society, nor the popular element in the courts of law in the thirteenth century and later. The legal system also largely formed the basis of the administrative one. Whereas the bureaucracy may seem rudimentary from a modern point of view, it was centralised by contemporary standards and directly subject to leaders who represented a higher authority than their personal ability and charisma, the king on the one hand and the bishops on the other. Further, whereas the degree of state formation may seem modest if we focus only on the king, it appears quite impressive if we also consider the Church.

In the long run, civilian means were therefore more important than military ones for Norwegian state formation. Whereas Norway may be considered backwards from a military point of view, its legal system was advanced. In a comparative perspective, the main characteristics of the Norwegian state in the period 1240-1350 are the following: (1) a king with a strong personal and to some extent institutional power, combined with a relatively small economic surplus; (2) a Church with great wealth, a well-developed administrative apparatus, and extensive control over considerable aspects of the people's life and behaviour which over a relatively short period of time had managed to gain considerable independence and form the main limits to the royal power; (3) a relatively weak secular aristocracy, largely dependent on the king; (4) a peasantry more clearly subordinated to the king than previously, but still relatively strong. Together, these features point in the direction of fairly advanced, but "soft" state formation. From this conclusion, we can turn upside-down Lunden's interpretation of the civil wars: Although they did result in stronger royal power, increased incomes and a more centralised administration, they also led to a greater mobilisation of the common people who increased their influence in the royal elections in the early thirteenth century and contributed to the end result. The final victory was not won by professional warriors under the leadership of Sverre or Skule Bårdsson but by the popular levy led by Håkon Håkonsson, which confirms the conclusion above about the role of the people in state formation.

From the point of view of this "soft" interpretation of Norwegian state formation it seems a paradox that Norway was the Scandinavian Viking kingdom par excellence, almost exclusively founded by Viking warriors. Holmsen hints at this paradox when stating that the kingdom of Norway was founded by force but eventually came to be governed by law.[1]

---

1   Holmsen, *Nye studier*, pp. 180-85.

Both parts of the paradox may be explained by Norway's geography, the long, protected coast that gave such excellent lines of communication, and its scattered population. Norway was easy to conquer and easy to hold, once a strong power had managed to establish itself. It could be kept without too much violence but gave relatively little surplus, which in turn meant that the most profitable way to govern it was with some degree of consent from the population and by making use of its services.

When the landowners nevertheless appropriated a substantial part of the agricultural surplus towards the end of the High Middle Ages, the explanation, as Holmsen suggests, must be sought in demographic-economic conditions rather than in military specialisation. Population growth had led to a shortage of agricultural land which in turn led to an increase in the land rent. However, Holmsen fails to explain why the Church rather than the secular aristocracy profited from this shortage. Nor does this explanation really confront the historical development and the various aspects of royal and ecclesiastical government, or, in so far as it does (as in the case of the civil wars), it is hardly able to explain them. Even if the material conditions can demonstrate a certain degree of centralisation, it might in practice have assumed different forms under different cultural conditions. The Church's income from land rent – which may have been up to forty percent – and other vast sources of income, as well as its generally strong status, point firmly in the direction of a religious explanation. One might object, in the spirit of Holmsen, that the primary explanation still lies in the demographic-economic area, that the Church's power was a result of the coincidence that Christianity was introduced around the same time as the shortage of land began to make its mark, and that the king, the secular aristocracy, or someone else would have cashed in on the same prize if the Church had not been there, so that the outcome would largely have been the same. Yet if the Church's wealth came mostly from gifts, would any other cause have unleashed a corresponding level of generosity? And would it have been possible to bureaucratise any other social function as much as religion? It has been noted, probably correctly, that the Church's strong position was a weakness for Norway in the Later Middle Ages, because it involved a weakening of the country's military class, the secular aristocracy. Although the Church had its military resources, they amounted to far less than what its economic power would suggest. If these resources had not belonged to the Church, who would they have belonged to? The peasants and the secular aristocracy seem the most likely suggestion, but this would probably have led to more inner conflict, perhaps as in Sweden in the Later Middle Ages, although it might have saved the country in 1537.

The argument regarding bureaucratisation should be extended to the monarchy as well. Rather than regarding the economic-demographic conditions as cause and state formation as effect as Holmsen and the agrarian school suggest, we should consider the interaction between the factors. Economic-demographic conditions serve to explain the high land rent by the end of the High Middle Ages and may also partly explain the greater concentration of landed wealth. However, the two great organisations, the monarchy and the Church, and their bureaucracy contributed to this result, partly by offering benefits that the population was willing to pay for, such as conflict solution and protection against evil in this life and the next, and partly by imposing the payment of taxes, tithes and fines.

Finally, we arrive at the contingent factors. It is easy for the historian to regard what actually happened as inevitable and look for deep-rooted structural explanations for phenomena of fairly limited scope. How much is needed to explain Norway's hundred years of greatness in 1240-1350? We tend to seek for a structural explanation for the difference between the well-organised state and the harmonious relationship between the king, the aristocracy and the people of Norway in this period and the frequent conflicts in Denmark and Sweden. However, the latter conflicts were largely the result of disputes over the succession, between the sons of Valdemar II after 1241, and later between Erik Menved (1286-1319) and his brother Christoffer in Denmark and between King Birger (1290-1319) and his two brothers Erik and Valdemar in Sweden. What would have happened in Norway if Håkon Håkonsson had left more than one son? Or if the relationship between King Eirik and his brother Håkon had been bad? Or if King Eirik had lived longer and been succeeded by a son, while his brother Duke Håkon also had sons? Would Norway have been permanently divided? Would similar conflicts have broken out as in the neighbouring countries? We cannot exclude these possibilities and consequently have to include some amount of dynastic luck in our explanation of the Norwegian success in the period. On the other hand, Norway is from a topographical and economic point of view less easily divided than Denmark and Sweden. No single part of the country could be easily defended against the rest and – at least before the fourteenth century – the small number of castles made this even more difficult. Territorial division actually lasted only for a short time. After the Croziers had been confined to Eastern Norway by the end of Sverre's reign, it took less than twenty years before their kingdom succumbed to the Birchlegs, and Skule's rebellion based in Trøndelag was crushed after only half a year.

While these contrafactual speculations must sooner or later end in guesswork, some structural explanations can be improved with the addition of contingent factors. This applies to the relationship between the king and the aristocracy. Much can be said in favour of Holmsen's reasons for the aristocrats' need for employment in the king's service and the relationship between supply and demand which brought the king in a favourable position. However, a crucial factor is also the hereditary monarchy which prevented the aristocracy from forcing the king to the same concessions as their Danish and Swedish counterparts and as the cathedral chapters could demand from the future bishop. An important factor in introducing this rule must have been the tradition from the Birchleg faction which had fought for a particular dynasty as well as for the principle of agnatic succession. In addition came the understanding of the disastrous consequences of inner strife, which actually served as an argument for individual, hereditary succession in *The King's Mirror*, probably composed shortly before the law was passed. As we have seen, the factional divisions do not correspond entirely to those of Denmark which were dominated more by the top aristocracy and family connections. If not exactly a social revolution, the victory of the Birchlegs led to a considerable renewal of the upper level of society, while at the same time the faction maintained a strong internal cohesiveness and a great loyalty to its leader, which at least partly serve to explain Håkon's success in introducing hereditary succession.

Of course, the duration of this effect was limited; it can hardly have lasted longer than the reign of Håkon Håkonsson, but by then it had resulted in some changes with lasting effect, notably the Law of Succession of 1260. We may therefore ask how long the relationship between the king and the aristocracy would have remained harmonious if Norway had continued as an independent kingdom throughout the Middle Ages. There were already problems under Håkon V's grandson and successor Magnus Eriksson. Were these problems the result of the union or of a young and inexperienced king ascending to the throne, or of the greater physical distance between the king and the Norwegian aristocracy? Or may we compare the situation in the 1330s and 1340s with the possible resource crisis that served to prolong and embitter the civil wars in the twelfth century? Was the old solidarity created by the Birchleg kings and their faction waning and the rivalry between numerous aristocrats over a small number of offices in the royal administration increasing? If so, what would then have happened if the Black Death in 1349-50 and the following years had not created a deep economic crisis that weakened the aristocracy so much that its only remaining option was to seek the king's favour, thus increasing the loyalty and obedience to the king from the previous period of greatness? It must be admitted that the limited conflicts in the 1330s can hardly be considered evidence of such a wide-reaching conclusion, but it may at least prevent us from regarding the harmonious relationship between monarchy and aristocracy as inevitable in 1240-1319 and largely also in the following period.

Why then did Norway finally succumb to the Danish power? This is not strictly the theme of the present book and should be discussed against the background of a thorough examination of the whole period from 1319-1537. Nevertheless, some remarks on the question may prove fruitful here, mainly as a contribution to the discussion of the structural conditions underlying Norwegian state formation. Was Norway doomed eventually to submit to the power of one of the neighbouring countries, so that the successful state formation dealt with in the previous pages was only a passing episode, or was the loss of independence rather the result of unfortunate circumstances in the early sixteenth century? Two main lines of explanation have been applied to the problem of the decline of Norway, one political and one economical.[2] The former has mainly focused on the strong monarchy in the High Middle Ages which allegedly led to the decline of the secular aristocracy, thus depriving the country of the military power necessary to resist foreign encroachments. The latter has partly pointed to the general poverty of the country and partly to the disastrous consequences of the Black Death. Most historians in the twentieth century have supported the economic explanation, notably the agrarian school which, by quantifying the desertion and fall of land rent in the Later Middle Ages, has concluded that the crisis in Norway was considerably more serious than in the neighbouring countries. Ole Jørgen Benedictow goes to the greatest length in pessimism. Comparing the population and resources of Norway with those of the neighbouring countries, notably Denmark, he concludes that the difference was so enormous that the question should rather be why the Norwegian state existed at all than why it collapsed in the Later Middle Ages. He finds the explanation in the fact that Denmark had other interests than conquering Norway, above all in Northern Germany which was a far wealthier region.[3]

The previous examination does not support this conclusion. Neither political nor economic facts point to the same Norwegian weakness compared to the neighbouring countries before 1350 as after. Regarding the period after 1350, it is possible to explain that the agrarian crisis must have been more serious for the Norwegian elite than for its counterpart in the other Nordic countries, even without assuming that more people died from the plague, with the observation that the Norwegian elite lacked the means to compensate for the loss of their labour force that were available elsewhere (above p. 121). Moreover, it seems that the period when Norway lost its independence corresponds to the period of the greatest economic difference between it and the neighbouring countries. While Denmark and Sweden were on their way to overcoming the crisis from around 1450, it lasted nearly a hundred more years in Norway.[4] In the following period, however, Norway experienced rapid growth, demographically, agriculturally and through the export of new commodities like timber and metals.

Thus, Norway was more vulnerable in the period 1450-1550 than it was before and after. Nevertheless, this vulnerability did not necessarily lead to a loss of independence. Many of the petty principalities in Germany were weaker than Norway but continued to exist until the early nineteenth century, some even to the unification of Germany in 1870.

---

2   See most recently Imsen, *Norges nedgang* with references, and for the demographic and economic decline of Scandinavia after 1350, Vahtola, "Population".
3   Benedictow, *Fra rike til provins*, pp. 445-58.
4   Albrectsen, *Fællesskabet bliver til*, pp. 229-35.

We therefore need to look at the political factors as well, one of which is dynastic policy. Although the first union of 1319 was partly caused by chance events, the kings' dynastic policy would probably have led to this result sooner or later anyway.[5] The kings' aim was not to preserve Norwegian independence but to extend the power and influence of their dynasty. On the other hand, the permanent Danish-Norwegian union that eventually led to the loss of independence in 1537 was not directly the result of dynastic succession but of the more or less voluntary election of the Danish kings at various stages. Moreover, a union did not necessarily mean loss of independence; there is a vast difference between the personal union with Sweden in the fourteenth century, when the king ruled two independent countries with different institutions and visited Norway regularly, and the union with Denmark during most of the fifteenth and early sixteenth centuries when the country was mostly governed by an absentee king and a central administration in Denmark, despite formal equality. A more decisive factor is therefore the Reformation. Formally, the loss of independence consisted in the suppression of the council of the realm which was dominated by the Catholic bishops, with the archbishop as chairman. This, as well as the fact that the archbishop had worked against the new Lutheran king during the previous civil war in Denmark (1534-36), was given as the reason for suppressing the institution, and it was probably also an important motive. More fundamentally, the suppression of the Catholic hierarchy meant that a substantial part of the lower nobility and upper level of the peasants lost their patron and were replaced in administrative positions by imported Danes in the service of the Danish noblemen who then took over the administration of the country.[6]

Furthermore, despite the drastic consequences of the Danish takeover, it was carried out with a surprisingly little amount of violence. Most castles in the country were already in the hands of the Danish king; only the residences of the two most stubborn prelates, Archbishop Olav Engelbrektsson and Bishop Mogens of Hamar, had to be conquered. This underlines the traditional political explanation: a strong Norwegian monarchy to which the king of Denmark had become the legitimate successor because of the union. It must be added, however, that the Norwegian elite had become even more dependent on the king's service in the Later Middle Ages than before because of their loss of other incomes as a consequence of the crisis. Finally, we can point to a strategic reason, the same that serves to explain the ease with which the country was unified. During the Later Middle Ages, Denmark had once more become the leading sea power in Scandinavia and

---

5   Lunden, *Norge under Sverreætten*, pp. 456 f.
6   Rian, *Maktens historie*, pp. 22-25.

could therefore easily control Norway from the coast.[7] Once the Danes had gained the few important castles which were all in reach of the coast, they had full control. When attempting to conquer Sweden – which was of course also a stronger country than Norway – they usually managed to gain bridgeheads along the coast, notably Stockholm and Kalmar, but this was insufficient for control of the whole country. Conquering the inland regions was considerably more difficult and was only achieved for shorter periods of time and with the aid of Swedish allies. Thus, we have come back full circle: the same factor that explains the rise of the kingdom of Norway also serves to explain its decline. While a Danish conquest of Norway in the Viking Age would have meant a piecemeal struggle against various power holders along the coast, in the sixteenth century, the Norwegian dynasty had already unified the country and the Danish king could take it over as their successor.

In conclusion, the decline of Norway in the sixteenth century must be considered neither inevitable nor unlikely. Its main explanation must be sought in the particular conditions of the Later Middle Ages, notably the period 1450-1550, not in inevitable weaknesses. The state building carried out by the monarchy and the Church from the Viking Age to the fourteenth century had created conditions that might be exploited by a stronger country in a union. This, however, does not mean that the Norwegian kingdom, the development of which we have followed in the previous pages, was doomed to submit to one of the neighbouring countries.

In a comparative perspective, the previous account has mainly focused on the difference between Norway and the rest of Europe's northern and eastern periphery, notably regarding the absence of a military revolution and generally the relatively soft state formation which can be explained partly by the ecology and topography of the country and partly by its distance from the centres of power in Western Christendom. Although the civilian contingency was stronger in Norwegian state formation than in other countries at the time, it points to a characteristic feature of the Middle Ages. The military factor was less important than in the Early Modern Period, not because the Middle Ages were particularly peaceful, but because medieval military technology did not favour large units in the same way as did the following period. This applies particularly to the combination of castles and heavy cavalry present in most other countries at the time, to some extent also in the Norwegian system, based on broad mobilisation of the peasant population, mainly for naval warfare. By contrast, the costly and complicated military machinery of the Early Modern Period, with artillery, elaborate fortifications, trained and organised professional

7   Mortensen, "Naval Artillery".

soldiers, and large and expensive warships, led to an increased bureaucratisation of society, while at the same time favouring larger political units at the cost of smaller ones.

In so far as centralisation did take place in the Middle Ages, "civilian" means were probably more important than military ones. This includes justice and legislation which were important factors in strengthening the monarchy and building up a bureaucratic organisation, and, above all, the Church and the Christian religion. In a general way, the Christianisation of Europe's northern and eastern periphery meant the export of forms of government present in Western Christendom. It also contributed to stabilising the combination of cultural unity and multiple and relatively stable political units that had characterised Europe until the development of the European Union in the second half of the twentieth century. The unification of the Scandinavian kingdoms or, more correctly, the division of Scandinavia into three relatively stable kingdoms is one example of this process: centralisation, a greater concentration of economic resources in the hands of the elite, bureaucratisation, and a considerable amount of correspondence between national borders and church provinces. The fall of the Catholic Church meant the fall of the independent kingdom of Norway, while the reformed ecclesiastical organisation was taken over by the king and contributed to the further development of the Danish-Norwegian state. There is thus a close connection between Christianity and state formation; and the previous account of Norway may serve as an example of a more general development. How close the connection is should be discussed further by comparing Western Christendom to other religious traditions, such as Eastern Christendom and Islam, and not least a main "test case" – pagan Lithuania – which did not convert to Christianity until 1386, but apparently had a well-developed political organisation since the early thirteenth century, which, however, in part may have been modelled on the Christian kingdoms.[8] There are also many examples of failed state formation in Christian Europe and of the prelates, together with the lay aristocracy, fighting for their privileges to such an extent that it threatened the survival of the states in question, like in Germany, Hungary and Poland and even in Denmark and Sweden in periods. Christianity was no universal recipe for smooth state formation, but it was probably more successful in this respect than other religions.

---

8   Rowell, "Baltic Europe", pp. 705-12.

The Kings of Norway, c. 900-1380

The early chronology, before the year 1000, is very uncertain. Most of the pretenders during the civil wars are not included.

Harald Finehair, late ninth century-c. 931/32
Eirik Haraldsson Bloodaxe, c. 931/32-c. 933/34
Håkon Haraldsson the Good, c. 933/34-c. 960
Harald Eiriksson Greycloak, c. 960-c. 970
Håkon Sigurdsson Ladejarl, c. 970-95
Olav Tryggvason, 995-1000
Eirik Håkonsson and Svein Håkonsson Ladejarls, 1000-1015/16
Olav Haraldsson, 1015-1030
Cnut the Great, 1028-35
Magnus Olavsson the Good, 1035-47
Harald Sigurdsson Hardrada, 1046-66
Magnus Haraldsson, 1066-69
Olav Haraldsson Kyrre, 1066-93
Håkon Magnusson, 1093-94
Magnus Olavsson Barelegs, 1093-1103
Øystein Magnusson, 1103-23
Sigurd Magnusson, 1103-30
Olav Magnusson, 1103-15
Magnus Sigurdsson the Blind, 1130-35, 1136-39
Harald Magnusson Gille, 1130-36
Inge Haraldsson, 1136-61
Sigurd Haraldsson, 1136-55
Øystein Haraldsson, 1142-57
Håkon Sigurdsson the Broadshouldered, 1157-62
Magnus Erlingsson, 1161-84
Sverre Sigurdsson, 1177-1202
Inge Magnusson, 1196-1202 (Crozier king)
Håkon Sverresson, 1202-04
Guttorm Sigurdsson, 1204
Inge Bårdsson, 1204-17

Erling Magnusson Stonewall, 1204-07 (Crozier king)
Filippus Simonsson, 1207-17 (Crozier king)
Håkon Håkonsson, 1217-63
Magnus Håkonsson the Law-Mender, 1263-80
Eirik Magnusson, 1280-99
Håkon V Magnusson, 1299-1319
Magnus Eriksson, 1319-55/74, king of Sweden 1319-64
Håkon VI Magnusson, 1355-80, king of Sweden 1362-64

Literature, Sources and Abbreviations

Adam Bremensis. *Gesta Hamaburgensis ecclesiae pontificum, Monumenta Germaniae Historica. Scriptores in usum scholarum 2* (=*Gesta*), ed. Bernhard Schmeidler (Hannover and Leipzig 1917).

Adolfsen, Erik. *Maktforholdene på tingene i Norge ca. 900-ca. 1200* (Master's thesis, University of Bergen, 2000).

Aegidius Romanus. *De regimine principum* (Venice 1498).

Agerholt, Johan. *Gamal brevskipnad. Etterrøkjingar og utgreidingar i norsk diplomatikk*, I-II (Oslo 1929-32).

Ágrip af Nóregskonungasǫgum, ed. and trans. Matthew Driscoll, *Viking Society for Northern Research* (London 1995).

Albrectsen, Esben. Review of Niels Lund, *Lid, leding og landeværn*, *Historisk Tidsskrift* [Danish] 98 (1998), pp. 395-401.

Albrectsen, Esben. "Svar til Niels Lund", *Historisk Tidsskrift* [Danish] 99 (1999), pp. 208-10.

Althoff, Gerd. *Freunde, Verwandte und Getreue. Zum politischen Stellenwert der Gruppenbindungen im früheren Mittelalter* (Darmstadt 1990).

Althoff, Gerd. "Die Beurteilung der mittelalterlichen Ostpolitik als Paradigma für zeitgebundene Geschichtsbewertung", in Gerd Althoff (ed.), *Die deutschen und ihr Mittelalter* (Darmstadt 1992), pp. 147-64.

Althoff, Gerd. *Kaiser Otto III* (Darmstadt 1996).

Althoff, Gerd. *Spielregeln der Politik im Mittelalter* (Darmstadt 1997).

Althoff, Gerd. *Die Macht der Rituale. Symbolik und Herrschaft im Mittelalter* (Darmstadt 2003).

Althoff, Gerd. *Heinrich IV* (Darmstadt 2006).

Andersen, Per Sveaas. *Samlingen av Norge og kristningen av landet 800-1130, Handbok i Norges historie* II (Oslo 1977).

Anderson, Benedict. *Imagined Communities. Reflections on the Origins and Spread of Nationalism* (London 1989).

Andersson, Hans. "Urbanisation", in Knut Helle (ed.), *The Cambridge History of Scandinavia* I. *Prehistory to 1520* (Cambridge 2003), pp. 312-42.

Andersson, Ingvor M. *Erik Menved och Venden. Studier i dansk utrikespolitik 1300-1319* (Lund 1954).

Andersson, Theodore M. "The Conversion of Norway According to Oddr Snorrason and Snorri Sturluson", *Medieval Scandinavia* 10 (1977), pp. 83-95.

Andersson, Theodore M. "Kings' Sagas", in Carol Clover and John Lindow (eds.), *Old Norse-Icelandic Literature. A Critical Guide, Islandica* 45 (Ithaca 1985), pp. 197-238.

Andrzejewski, Stanislaw. *Military Organization and Society* (London 1954).

Antonsson, Haki. "Some Observations on Martyrdom in Post-Conversion Scandinavia", *Saga-Book of the Viking Society for Northern Research* 28 (2004), pp. 70-94.

Antonsson, Haki. "The Minsters. A Brief Review of the 'Minster Hypothesis' in England and Some General Observations on its Relevance to Scandinavia and Iceland", in Helgi Þorlaksson (ed.), *Church Centres in Iceland from the 11th to the 13th Century and their Parallels in other Countries* (Reykholt 2005), pp. 175-86.

Antonsson, Haki. *St Magnus of Orkney. A Scandinavian Martyr-Cult in Context, The Northern World* 29 (Leiden 2007).

Ari fróði, *Íslendingabók*, ed. Jakob Benediktsson, *Íslenzk fornrit* I (Reykjavík 1986), pp. 3-28.

Arna saga biskups, ed. Guðrun Ása Grímsdóttir, *Biskupa sögur* III, pp. 1-212, *Íslenzk fornrít* XVII (Reykjavík 1998).

Arstad, Knut. *Kongsemner og maktkonstellasjoner i innbyrdesstridenes Norge* (Master's thesis, Oslo 1994).

Arstad, Knut. "Ribbungopprør, riksenhet og enekongedømme", *Collegium medievale* 8 (1995), pp. 63-90.

Arstad, Knut. "'... han var svag av Character og uden ringeste Herskergaver, hvilket også fremgår av hele hans Historie.' En undersøkelse av Harald Gilles ettermæle", *Historisk tidsskrift* 78 (1999), pp. 435-60.

Arstad, Knut. "'... underlig forjaget og planløs ...?' Strategi og feltherregenskaper i Norge i første halvdel av 1200-tallet", in Knut Arstad (ed.), *Krigføring i middelalderen. Strategi, ideologi og organisasjon c. 1100-1400, Rapport fra Clio og Mars-seminaret på Forsvarsmuseet 6-7. nov. 2002* (Oslo 2003), pp. 27-61.

Arstad, Knut. "Castle Warfare in Norway in the 12th and 13th Centuries", in Knut Arstad (ed.), *Krigføring i middelalderen. Strategi, ideologi og organisasjon ca. 1100-1400, Rapport fra Clio og Mars-seminaret på Forsvarsmuseet 6-7. nov. 2002* (Oslo 2003), pp. 163-73.

Arvidsson, Rolf and Hans Aarsleff. *Kritiska undersökningar i Weibull-mytens historia* (Lund 2000).

Astås, Reidar. *An Old Norse Biblical Compilation. Studies in Stjórn, American University Studies*, Ser. VII, vol. 109 (New York 1991).

Autrand, Françoise. "The Peacemakers and the State: Pontifical Diplomacy and the Anglo-French Conflict in the Fourteenth Century", in Philippe Contamine (ed.), *War and Competition between States: The Origins of the Modern State in Europe* (Oxford 2000), pp. 249-77.

Axelson, Sven. *Sverige i utländsk annalistik 900-1400 med särskild hänsyn til de isländska annalerna* (Stockholm 1955).

Axelson, Sven. "Om orsakerna til den svensk-norska unionens upplösning", *Historisk tidsskrift* 43 (1964), pp. 274-80.

Baetge, Walter. "Yngvi und die Ynglingar. Eine Quellenkritische Untersuchung über das nordische 'Sakralkönigtum'", *Sitzungsberichte der sächsischen Akademie der Wissenschaften zu Leipzig. Phil-hist. Kl.* 109.3 (Berlin 1964).

Bagge, Sverre. "Kanslerembedet og Mariakirken i Oslo", in Fridtjov Birkeli et al. (eds.), *Oslo bispedømme 900 år* (Oslo 1975), pp. 143-61.

Bagge, Sverre. "Samkongedømme og enekongedømme", *Historisk tidsskrift* 54 (1975), pp. 239-74.

Bagge, Sverre. *Den kongelige kapellgeistlighet 1150-1319* (Bergen 1976).

Bagge, Sverre. "Sættargjerden i Tønsberg", *Kulturhistorisk leksikon for nordisk middelalder* XXI (Oslo 1977), cols. 492-99.

Bagge, Sverre. "Kirken og folket", *Norges kulturhistorie* II (Oslo 1979), pp. 211-48.

Bagge, Sverre. "Kirkens jurisdiksjon i kristenrettssaker før 1277", *Historisk tidsskrift* 60 (1981), pp. 133-59.

Bagge, Sverre. "Nordic Students at Foreign Universities", *Scandinavian Journal of History*, 9 (1984), pp. 1-29.

Bagge, Sverre. "Herrens Salvede. Kroning og salving i Norge 1163-1247", Martin Blindheim et al. (eds.), *Kongens makt og ære* (Oslo 1985), pp. 29-34.

Bagge, Sverre. "Borgerkrig og statsutvikling i Norge i middelalderen", *Historisk tidsskrift* 65 (1986), pp. 145-97.

Bagge, Sverre. *The Political Thought of The King's Mirror, Medieval Scandinavia. Supplements* III (Odense 1987).

Bagge, Sverre and Knut Mykland. *Norge i dansketiden* (Oslo 1987).

Bagge, Sverre. Review of Elsa Sjöholm, *Sveriges medeltidslagar*, *Historisk tidsskrift* 68 (1989), pp. 500-7.

Bagge, Sverre. *Society and Politics in Snorri Sturluson's Heimskringla* (Berkeley 1991).

Bagge, Sverre. "Kingship in Medieval Norway. Ideal and Reality", in H. Duchhardt et al. (eds.), *European Monarchy. Its Evolution and Practice from Roman Antiquity to Modern Times* (Stuttgart 1992), pp. 41-52.

Bagge, Sverre. "Oratio contra clerum Norvegiae", in Ph. Pulsiano (ed.), *Medieval Scandinavia. An Encyclopedia* (New York 1993), p. 455.

Bagge, Sverre. "Hirð", in Ph. Pulsiano (ed.), *Medieval Scandinavia. An Encyclopedia* (New York 1993), p. 284.

Bagge, Sverre. "The Norwegian Monarchy in the Thirteenth Century", in Anne Duggan (ed.), *Kings and Kingship in Medieval Europe* (Exeter 1993), pp. 159-78.

Bagge, Sverre. "Ideology and Propaganda in *Sverris saga*", *Arkiv för nordisk filologi* 108 (1993), pp. 1-18.

Bagge, Sverre. "Samfunnsbeskrivelsen i *Heimskringla*. Svar til Birgit Sawyer", *Historisk tidsskrift* 73 (1994), pp. 205-15.

Bagge, Sverre. "Nature and Society in *The King's Mirror*", *Arkiv för nordisk filologi* 109 (1994), pp. 5-42.

Bagge, Sverre. "Nationalism in Norway in the Middle Ages", *Scandinavian Journal of History* 20 (1995), pp. 1-18.

Bagge, Sverre. "The Middle Ages", in W.H. Hubbard et al. (ed.), *Making a Historical Culture. Historiography in Norway* (Oslo 1995), pp. 111-31.

Bagge, Sverre. *From Gang Leader to the Lord's Anointed. Kingship in Sverris saga and Hákonar saga Hákonarsonar*, The Viking Collection (Odense 1996).

Bagge, Sverre. "Udsigt og innhogg. 150 års forskning om eldre norsk historie", *Historisk tidsskrift* 75 (1996), pp. 37-77.

Bagge, Sverre. "Ideas and Narrative in Otto of Freising's *Gesta Frederici*", *Journal of Medieval History* 22 (1996), pp. 345-77.

Bagge, Sverre. "The Structure of Political Factions in the Internal Struggles of the Scandinavian Countries during the High Middle Ages", *Scandinavian Journal of History* 24 (1999), pp. 299-320.

Bagge, Sverre. "The Scandinavian Kingdoms", in David Abulafia (ed.), *The New Cambridge Medieval History* V (Cambridge 1999), pp. 720-42.

Bagge, Sverre. "Old Norse Theories of Society. From *Rígspula* to *Konungs skuggsiá*", in Jens Eike Schnall and Rudolf Simek (eds.), *Speculum regale. Der altnorwegische Königsspiegel (Konungs skuggsiá) in der europäischen Tradition* (Vienna 2000), pp. 7-45.

Bagge, Sverre. "Kristendom og kongemakt", in Niels Lund (ed.), *Viking og hvidekrist. Norden og Europa in den sene vikingetid og tidligste middelalder* (Copenhagen 2000), pp. 9-29.

Bagge, Sverre. "Law and Justice in Norway in the Middle Ages: A Case Study", in Lars Bisgaard et al. (eds.), *Medieval Spirituality in Scandinavia and Europe. A Collection of Essays in Honour of Tore Nyberg* (Odense 2001), pp. 73-85.

Bagge, Sverre. *Da boken kom til Norge 1000-1537*, Trond Berg Eriksen and Øystein Sørensen (eds.), *Norsk idéhistorie* I (Oslo 2001).
Bagge, Sverre. "Mellom kildekritikk og historisk antropologi. Olav den hellige, aristokratiet og rikssamlingen", *Historisk tidsskrift* 81 (2002), pp. 173-212.
Bagge, Sverre. *Kings, Politics, and the Right Order of the World in German Historiography c. 950-1150. Studies in the History of Christian Thought 103* (Leiden 2002).
Bagge, Sverre. "Eleventh Century Norway: The Formation of a Kingdom", in Przemyslaw Urbaczyk (ed.), *The Neighbours of Poland in the 11th Century* (Warsaw 2002), pp. 29-47.
Bagge, Sverre. "*Sårt biter sulten lus*", in Knut Arstad (ed.), *Krigføring i middelalderen. Strategi, ideologi og organisasjon c. 1100-1400, Rapport fra Clio og Mars-seminaret på Forsvarsmuseet 6-7. nov. 2002* (Oslo 2003), pp. 10-26.
Bagge, Sverre. "Ideologies and Mentalities", in Knut Helle (ed.), *The Cambridge History of Scandinavia* I. *Prehistory to 1520* (Cambridge 2003), pp. 465-86.
Bagge, Sverre. "Den heroiske tid – kirkereform og kirkekamp 1153-1214", in Steinar Imsen (ed.), *Ecclesia Nidrosiensis 1153-1537. Søkelys på Nidaroskirkens og Nidaroprovinsens historie, Senter for middelalderstudier, NTNU. Skrifter* no. 5 (Trondheim 2003), pp. 47-80.
Bagge, Sverre. "A Hero between Paganism and Christianity. Håkon the Good in Memory and History", in Karin Hoff et al. (eds.), *Poetik und Gedächtnis. Festschrift für Heiko Uecker zum 65. Geburtstag* (Frankfurt 2004), pp. 185-210.
Bagge, Sverre. "The Transformation of Europe: the Role of Scandinavia", in Johann P. Arnason and Björn Wittrock (eds.), *Eurasian Transformations, Tenth to Thirteenth Centuries. Crystallizations, Divergences, Renaissances* (Leiden 2004), pp. 131-65.
Bagge, Sverre. "On the Far Edge of the Dry Land: Scandinavian and European Culture in the Middle Ages", in J. Adams and K. Holman (eds.), *Scandinavia and Europe 800-1350. Contact, Conflict, and Coexistence* (Tournout 2004), pp. 355-69.
Bagge, Sverre. "Christianization and State Formation in Early Medieval Norway", *Scandinavian Journal of History* 30 (2005), pp. 107-34.
Bagge, Sverre. "Norsk kirkehistorie – tradisjoner og utfordringer", in Steinar Imsen (ed.), *Den kirkehistoriske utfordring* (Trondheim 2005), pp. 13-26.
Bagge, Sverre. "Kirken, bøndene og motstandsretten i Norge i middelalderen", *Historisk tidsskrift* 84 (2005), pp. 385-410.
Bagge, Sverre. Review of Hans Jacob Orning, *Uforutsigbarhet og nærvær. En analyse av norske kongers maktutøvelse i høymiddelalderen*, *Historisk tidsskrift* 84 (2005), pp. 641-48.

Bagge, Sverre. "The Making of a Missionary King – the Medieval Accounts of Olaf Tryggvason and the Conversion of Norway", *Journal of English and Germanic Philology* 105 (2006), pp. 473-513.

Bagge, Sverre. "Aims and Means in the Inter-Nordic Conflicts 1302-1319", *Scandinavian Journal of History* 32 (2007), pp. 5-38.

Bagge, Sverre. "'Gang leader' eller 'the Lord's anointed' i *Sverris saga*? Svar til Fredrik Ljungqvist og Lars Lönnroth", *Scripta Islandica* 58 (2008), pp. 101-19.

Bagge, Sverre. "Salvo semper regio iure. Kampen om sættargjerden 1277-1290", *Historisk tidsskrift* 87 (2008), pp. 201-224.

Bagge, Sverre. "Division and Unity in the Kingdom of Norway in the Middle Ages", in Patrick Geary, Ildar Garipzanov and Przemyslaw Urbancyk (eds.), *Franks, Northmen and Slavs: Identities and State Formation in Early Medieval Europe* (Tournhout 2008), pp. 145-68.

Bagge, Sverre. "Du savoir-vivre pratique aux vices et vertus. La doctrine éthique en Norvège au Moyen Âge", in *Itinéraires du savoir de l'Italie à la Scandinavie (Xe-XVIe siècle). Etudes offertes à Elisabeth Mornet* (Paris 2009), pp. 115-36.

Bagge, Sverre. "Die Spielregeln ändern. Norwegische Politik im 12. und 13. Jahrhundert", Claudia Garnier and Hermann Kamp (eds.), *Spielregeln der Mächtigen. Mittelalterliche Politik zwischen Gewohnheit und Konvention* (Darmstadt 2010), pp. 133-64.

Bagge, Sverre and Sæbjørg Walaker Nordeide. "The Kingdom of Norway", in Nora Berend (ed.), *Christianization and the Rise of Christian Monarchy. Scandinavia, Central Europe and Rus' c. 900-1200* (Cambridge 2007), pp. 121-66.

Bandlien, Bjørn. *Strategies of Passion. Love and Marriage in Old Norse Society* (Turnhout 2005).

Bandlien, Bjørn. *Man or Monster? Negotiations of Masculinity in Old Norse Society* (Oslo 2005).

Barraclough, Geoffrey. *The Origins of Modern Germany* (Oxford 1972).

Barth, Fredrik. "Segmentary Opposition and the Theory of Games: A Study of Pathan Organization", *Features of Person and Society in Swat. Collected Essays on the Pathans. Selected Essays of Fredrik Barth* II (London 1981), pp. 55-82.

Bartlett, Robert. *The Making of Europe. Conquest, Colonization and Cultural Change 950-1350* (London 1993).

Bartlett, Robert. *England under the Norman and Angevin Kings 1075-1225*, The New Oxford History of England (Oxford 2000).

Beistad, Heidi Annett Øvergård. *Kirkens frihet. Biskop Arne Torlaksson som Islands reformator* (Master's thesis, Trondheim 2008).

Benedictow, Ole Jørgen. "Norge", *Den nordiske adel i senmiddelalderen. Struktur, funktioner og internordiske relationer, Det nordiske historikermøde i København. Rapporter* (Copenhagen 1971), pp. 9-44.

Benedictow, Ole Jørgen. "Konge, hird og retterboten av 17. juni 1308", *Historisk tidsskrift* 51 (1972), pp. 233-84.

Benedictow, Ole Jørgen. *Fra rike til provins, Norges historie* V, ed. Knut Mykland (Oslo 1977).

Benham, J.E.M. "Philip Augustus and the Angevin Empire. The Scandinavian Connection", *Mediaeval Scandinavia* 14 (2006), pp. 37-50.

Berges, Wilhelm. *Die Fürstenspiegel des hohen und späten Mittelalters*, MGH Schriften II (Leipzig 1938).

Berglund, Åsa. "Upplösningen av den svensk-norska unionen 1343", *Historisk tidsskrift* 34 (1946-48), pp. 365-81.

Berman, Harold J. *Law and Revolution. The Formation of the Western Legal Tradition* (Cambridge, Mass. 1983).

Bernheim, Ernst. *Mittelalterliche Zeitanschauungen in ihrem Einfluss auf Politik und Geschichtsschreibung* (Aalen 1964 [orig. 1918]).

Berulfsen, Bjarne. *Kulturtradisjon fra en storhetstid. En kulturhistorisk studie på grunnlag av den private brevlitteratur i første halvdel av det 14. hundreår* (Oslo 1948).

Bill, Jan. "Castles at Sea. The Warship of the High Middle Ages", in Anne Nørgård Jørgensen et al. (eds.), *Maritime Warfare in Northern Europe. Technology, Organization, Logistics and Administration 500 BC-1500 AD, Papers from an International Research Seminar at the Danish National Museum, Copenhagen, 3-5 May 2000* (Copenhagen 2002), pp. 47-56.

Bjørgo, Narve. "Skipstypar i norrøne samtidssoger", *Sjøfartshistorisk årbok* (1965), pp. 7-20.

Bjørgo, Narve. "Om skriftlege kjelder for Hákonar saga", *Historisk tidsskrift* 46 (1967), pp. 185-229.

Bjørgo, Narve. "Samkongedøme og einekongedøme", *Historisk tidsskrift* 49 (1970), pp. 1-33.

Bjørgo, Narve. "800-1536. Makt – og avmakt", in N. Bjørgo, Ø. Rian and A. Kaartvedt, *Selvstendighet og union. Fra middelalderen til 1905, Norsk utenrikspolitikks historie*, vol. I (Oslo 1995), pp. 19-132.

Bjørgo, Narve. "Langs diplomatiets frontlinjer. Norske strategiar og posisjonar i den fransk-engelske konflikten i 1290-åra", in *Med Clio til Kringsjå. Festskrift til riksarkivar John Herstad* (Oslo 2002), pp. 27-43.

Bjørkvik, Halvard. *Jordeige og jordleige i Ryfylke i eldre tid. Fordelinga av jordeigedomen på Vestlandet og Agdesida i 1661 og i seinkatolsk tid* (Stavanger 1958).

Bjørkvik, Halvard. "Leidang", *Kulturhistorisk leksikon for nordisk middelalder* X (Oslo 1965), cols. 432-42.

Bjørkvik, Halvard. "Eit kyrkjeleg godskompleks i mellomalderen. Munkeliv klosters jordegods", *Heimen* 14 (1967), pp. 51-70.

Bjørkvik, Halvard. "Dei kongelige kapella. Framvokster og økonomisk grunnlag", *Bergens historiske forenings skrifter* 69/70 (1970), pp. 45-82.

Bjørkvik, Halvard. "Nyare forskning i norsk seinmellomalder", *Norsk lektorlags faglig-pedagogiske skrifter. Nytt fra norsk middelalder* II (Oslo 1970), pp. 70-105.

Bjørkvik, Halvard. *Folketap og sammenbrudd 1350-1520, Aschehougs Norges historie*, IV (Oslo 1996).

Bjørkvik, Halvard. "Grenselandproblem", *Historisk tidsskrift* 86 (2007), pp. 85-91.

Bjørsvik, Elisabeth. *Ideologi og tendens i Baglersagaen* (Masters thesis, Bergen, 1994).

Blix, Einar. "Hadde Norge et riksarkiv i middelalderen?", *Historisk tidsskrift* 43 (1964), pp. 165-80.

Blom, Grethe Authén. "Norge", *Det nordiske syn på forbindelsen mellom Hansestæderne og Norden, Det nordiske historikermøde i Århus 7-9. august 1957* (Aarhus 1957), pp. 1-54.

Blom, Grethe Authén. *Samkongedømme – Enekongedømme – Håkon Magnussons Hertugdømme, Kgl. Norske Videnskabers Selskab. Skrifter* 18 (Oslo 1972).

Blom, Grethe Authén. "Ingebjørg med Guds miskunn kong Håkons datter, hertuginne i Svearike. Bruddstykker av et politisk kvinneportrett", *Historisk tidsskrift* 60 (1981), pp. 432-54.

Blom, Grethe Authén. "Forhandlingene på Båhus omkring 24. juli 1321. Dokumenter, diplomater og skrivere", in Steinar Imsen and Gudmund Sandvik (eds.), *Hamarspor. Eit festskrift til Lars Hamre* (Oslo 1982), pp. 61-81.

Blom, Grethe Authén. *Norge i union på 1300-tallet* I-II (Trondheim 1992).

Blom, Grethe Authén. *St. Olavs by. Middelalder til 1537*, in Jørn Sandnes et al. (eds.), *Trondheims historie 997-1997* (Oslo 1997).

Blomkvist, Nils. *The Discovery of the Baltic. The Reception of the Catholic World System in the European North (AD 1075-1225)* (Leiden 2005).

Blomkvist, Nils, Stefan Brink and Thomas Lindkvist. "The Kingdom of Sweden", in Nora Berend (ed.), *Christianization and the Rise of Christian Monarchy. Scandinavia, Central Europe and Rus' c. 900-1200* (Cambridge 2007), pp. 167-213.

Bloomfield, Morton W. and Charles W. Dunn. *The Role of the Poet in Early Societies* (Cambridge 1989).

Bolin, Sture. "Muhammed, Karl den store och Rurik", *Scandia* 12 (1939), pp. 181-222.

Bregnsbo, Michael and Kurt Villads Jensen, *Det danske imperium. Storhed og fald* (Copenhagen 2004).
Brendalsmo, Jan. "Kirker og sogn på den trøndske landsbygda ca. 1000-1600", in Steinar Imsen (ed.), *Ecclesia Nidrosiensis 1153-1537. Søkelys på Nidaroskirkens og Nidarosprovinsens historie, Senter for middelalderstudier, NTNU. Skrifter* no. 5 (Trondheim 2003), pp. 223-53.
Brendalsmo, Jan. *Kirkebygg og kirkebyggere. Byggherrer i Trøndelag ca. 1000-1600* (Tromsø 2003).
Bresslau, Harry. *Handbuch der Urkundenlehre für Deutschland und Italien* I-II, 4th ed. (Berlin 1969).
Brilioth, Yngve. *Svenska kyrkans historia*, II, *Den senare medeltiden 1274-1521* (Stockholm 1941).
Brink, Stefan. *Sockenbildning og sockennamn. Studier i äldre territoriell indelning i Norden* (Uppsala 1990).
Brink, Stefan. "Mytologiska rum och eskatologiska föreställningar i det vikingtida Norden", in Anders Andrén et al., *Ordning mot kaos. Studier i förkristen kosmologi* (Lund 2004), pp. 291-316.
Brink, Stefan. "*Verba volant, scripta manent?* Aspects of Early Scandinavian Oral Society", in Pernille Hermann (ed.), *Literacy in Medieval and Early Modern Scandinavian Culture* (Odense 2005), pp. 77-135.
Brink, Stefan. "Skiringssal, Kaupang, Tjølling – the Toponymic Evidence", in Dagfinn Skre (ed.), *Kaupang in Skiringssal. Kaupang Excavation Project. Publication Series* I (Aarhus 2007), pp. 53-64.
Brown, Peter. *The Rise of Western Christendom* (Malden, Mass. 1997).
Brundage, James. *Law, Sex and Christian Society in Medieval Europe* (Chicago 1987).
Brundage, James. *Medieval Canon Law* (New York 1995).
Brunner, Otto. *Land und Herrschaft: Grundfragen der territorialen Verfassungsgeschichte Österreichs im Mittelalter* (Darmstadt 1984 [repr. after 5th ed., 1965]).
Brynildsrud, Lars Petter. *Audun Hugleiksson av Hegranes. Hans karriere og fall* (Master's thesis, Oslo 1970).
Bulhosa, Patricia. *Icelanders and the Kings of Norway. Medieval Sagas and Legal Texts* (Leiden 2005).
Bull, Edvard. *Folk og kirke i middelalderen* (Kristiania 1912).
Bull, Edvard. [opposition to] Fredrik Paasche, *Kristendom og kvad, Rikssamling og kristendom. Norske historikere i utvalg* I (Oslo 1967 [orig. 1914]), pp. 422-26.
Bull, Edvard. "Borgerkrigene og Haakon Haakonssons kongstanke", *Historisk tidsskrift* 5 rk. IV (1917), pp. 177-94.

Bull, Edvard. *Leding. Militær- og finansforvaltning i Norge i ældre tid* (Kristiania 1920).
Bull, Edvard. "Audun Torbergsson Raude", *Norsk biografisk leksikon* I (Kristiania 1923), pp. 322 f.
Bull, Edvard. *Fra omkring 1000 til 1280. Det norske folks liv og historie* II (Oslo 1931).
Busygin, Alexander. *The Laws of the Saint King. Aspects of Political and Legal Culture in Norway from the Eleventh Century to the End of Hákon Hákonarson's Reign* (Master's thesis, University of Oslo, 2003).
Bynum, Carolyne. "Did the Twelfth Century Discover the Individual?" *Journal of Ecclesiastical History* 31 (1980), pp. 1-17.
Canning, J.P. *A History of Medieval Political Thought* (London and New York 1996).
Canning, J.P. "Law, Sovereignty and Corporation Theory 1300-1450", in J-H. Burns (ed.), *The Cambridge History of Medieval Political Thought* (Cambridge 1988), pp. 454-76.
Cantor, Norman F. *Inventing the Middle Ages* (New York 1991).
Carlsson, Gottfried. "Den svensk-norska unionen under Magnus Eriksson", *Kgl. Humanistiska vetenskapssamfundet i Lund. Årsberättelse 1927-28* (Lund 1928), pp. 225-82.
Carpenter, David. "The Plantagenet Kings", *The New Cambridge Medieval History* V (Cambridge 1999), pp. 314-57.
Christensen, Aksel E. *Kongemagt og aristokrati. Epoker i middelalderlig dansk statsopfattelse* (Copenhagen 1968 [orig. 1945]).
Christensen-Nugues, Charlotte. *Och de skall vara ett hjärta. Konsensusdoktrinen i medeltida kanonisk rätt* (Lund 2003).
Claessen, Henri J. M. and Peter Skalník (eds.). *The Early State, New Babylon studies in the social sciences* 32 (The Hague 1978).
Claessen, Henri J. M. and Peter Skalník. "*Ubi sumus?* The Study of the State conference in retrospect", in Henri J.M. Claessen and Peter Skalník (eds.), *The Study of the State* (The Hague 1981), pp. 469-510.
Clanchy, Michael. *From Memory to Written Record: England 1066-1307*, 2nd ed. (Oxford 1993).
Clover, Carol. "Regardless of Sex. Men, Women, and Power in Early Northern Europe", *Speculum* 68 (1993), pp. 363-87.
Clunies Ross, Margaret. *Prolonged Echoes. Old Norse Myths in Medieval Northern Society*, I, *The Myths, The Viking Collection* 7 (Odense 1994).
Contamine, Philippe (ed.). *War and Competition between States, The Origins of the Modern State in Europe* (Oxford 2000).
Contamine, Philippe. "The Growth of State Control. Practices of War, 1300-1800: Ransom and Booty", in Philippe Contamine (ed.), *War and Competition between States* (Oxford 2000), pp. 163-93.

Corpus iuris civilis, I-II, ed. P. Krüger and Th. Mommsen (Berlin 1895).

Daae, Ludvig. "Den throndhjemske Erkestols Sædesvende og Frimænd", *Historisk tidsskrift* 3 Rk. I (1890), pp. 1-27.

Dahl, Ottar. *Norsk historieforskning i 19. og 20. århundre* (Oslo 1959).

Dahl, Ottar. "Noen teoretiske problemer i sosialhistorien", *Historisk tidsskrift* 37 (1955), pp. 185-203.

Dahlerup, Troels. "Tiend. Danmark", *Kulturhistorisk leksikon for nordisk middelalder* XVIII (Copenhagen 1961), cols. 291-95.

Davies, Rees. "The Medieval State: The Tyranny of a Concept?", *Journal of Historical Sociology* 16.2 (2003), pp. 280-300.

Davies, Wendy and Paul Fouracre (eds.). *The Settlement of Disputes in the Early Middle Ages* (Cambridge 1986).

D'Avray, David L. "Peter Damian, Consanguinity and Church Property", in Lesley Smith and Benedicta Ward (eds.), *Intellectual Life in the Middle Ages: Essays Presented to Margaret Gibson* (London 1992), pp. 71-80.

De Vries, Jan. *Altgermanische Religionsgeschichte* I-II (Berlin 1956-57).

Diamond, Jared. *Guns, Germs and Steel. A Short History of Everybody for the Last 13.000 Years* (London 2005).

Diplomatarium Norvegicum I-, ed. C.C.A. Lange and C.R. Unger (Christiania 1849-).

DN = *Diplomatarium Norvegicum*.

Documents of the Baronial Movement of Reform and Rebellion, ed. R.F. Treharne and I.J. Sanders (Oxford 1973).

Douglas, Mary. *Purity and Danger* (London 1978 [orig.1966]).

Douglas, Mary. *Natural Symbols*, 2nd ed. (London 1973).

Duby, Georges. *Les trois ordres ou l'imaginaire du féodalisme* (Paris 1978).

Duby, Georges. *Guerriers et paysans* (Paris 1973).

Dunbabin, Jean. "Government", in J-H. Burns (ed.), *The Cambridge History of Medieval Political Thought* (Cambridge 1988), pp. 477-519.

Düwel, Klaus. *Das Opferfest von Lade, Wiener Arbeiten zur germanischen Altertumskunde und Philologie* (Vienna 1985).

Dybdahl, Audun. "Bjarne Erlingssons testamente og Giskeættens jordegods", *Historisk tidsskrift* 77 (1998), pp. 403-36.

Dybdahl, Audun. "Nidaros erkesetes økonomi", in *Ecclesia Nidrosiensis 1153-1537. Søkelys på Nidaroskirkens og Nidarosprovinsens historie*, ed. Steinar Imsen, *Senter for middelalderstudier, NTNU. Skrifter* no. 5 (Trondheim 2003), pp. 279-319.

Dyer, Christopher. *Making a Living in the Middle Ages: The People of Britain 850-1520: The New Economic History of Britain* (New Haven 2002).

Dyrvik, Ståle. "1536-1814", in Rolf Danielsen et al., *Norway: A History from the Vikings to Our Own Times* (Oslo 1995), pp. 123-214.

Dyrvik, Ståle. *Truede tvillingriker 1648-1720, Danmark-Norge 1380-1814* III (Oslo 1998).

Dørum, Knut. *Romerike og riksintegreringen. Integreringen av Romerike i det norske rikskongedømmet i perioden ca. 1000-1350, Acta humaniora* 183 (Oslo 2004).

Dørum, Knut. "Materiell basis og den antropologiske vendingen", *Historisk tidsskrift* 85 (2006), pp. 87-105.

Dørum, Knut. "Aristokratisering av stat og samfunn i Norge ca. 1250-1350", *Heimen* 44 (2007), pp. 277-92.

Dørum, Knut. "Fagdebatt eller revirkamp. Tilsvar til Geirr Leistad, Magne Njåstad, Erik Opsahl og Jo Rune Ugulen", *Heimen* 45 (2009), pp. 241-44.

Edda. Die Lieder des Codex Regius, ed. Gustav Neckel and Hans Kuhn, 4th ed. (Heidelberg 1962).

Egils saga Skalla-Grímssonar, ed. Sigurður Nordal, *Íslenzk fornrít* II (Reykjavík 1933).

Eide, Ole Egil. "Om Utsteinklosterets bygningshistorie", *Collegium Medievale* 19 (2006), pp. 164-76.

Einarsdóttir, Óláfía. *Studier i kronologisk metode i tidlig islandsk historieskrivning, Bibliotheca historica Lundensis* 13 (Lund 1965).

Einarsson, Bjarni. *Litterære forudsætninger for Egils saga* (Reykjavík 1975).

Eisenstein, Elizabeth. *The Printing Revolution in Early Modern Europe* (Cambridge 1983).

Ejerfeld, Lennart. "Magi", *Kulturhistorisk leksikon for nordisk middelalder* XI (Oslo 1966), cols. 214-18.

Ellehøj, Svend. "Olaf Tryggvasons fald og venderne", *Historisk tidsskrift* [Danish] 11 Rk. IV (1953), pp. 1-55.

Elster, Jon. *Ulysses and the Sirens. Studies in Rationality and Irrationality* (Cambridge 1984).

Elucidarius, ed. Gunnar Harðarson, *Þrjár Þýðingar lærðar frá miðöldum* (Reykjavík 1989), pp. 43-120.

Emmanuelsson, Anders. *Kyrkojorden och dess ursprung. Oslo biskopsdöme perioden ca 1000-ca 1400* (Gothenburg 2005).

En tale mot biskopene, ed. Anne Holtsmark, *Skrifter utgitt av Det Norske Videnskapsakademi i Oslo. Hist.-fil. Klasse* 1930 no. 9 (Oslo 1931).

Engel, Pál. *The Realm of St Stephen: a history of medieval Hungary, 895-1526*, International library of historical studies vol. 19 (London 2001).

Erikskrönikan, ed. with an introduction and commentary by Sven-Bertil Jansson (Stockholm 2003).
Ersland, Geir Atle. "Kongshird og leidangsbonde", in G.A. Ersland and Terje Holm (eds.), *Norsk forsvarshistorie* I (Oslo 2000), pp. 11-154.
Erslev, Kristian. *Valdemarernes storhedstid. Studier og omrids* (Copenhagen 1898).
F = The Law of Frostating.
Fagerland, Tor Einar. *Krigføring og politisk kultur i nordisk middelalder. De mellomnordiske konfliktene 1286-1319 i et europeisk perspektiv* (Doctoral thesis, Trondheim 2005).
Fagrskinna. Nóregs kononga tal, ed. Finnur Jónsson (Copenhagen 1902-03).
Fenger, Ole. *Fejde og mandebod. Studier over slægtsansvaret i germansk og gammeldansk ret* (Aarhus 1971).
Fenger, Ole. Review of Elsa Sjöholm, *Sveriges medeltidslagar, Historisk tidsskrift* [Danish] 79 (1979), pp. 112-24.
Fenger, Ole. "Afsluttende bemærkninger", *Historisk tidsskrift* [Danish] 81 (1981), pp. 219-22.
Fenger, Ole. *Notarius publicus. Notaren i latinsk middelalder* (Aarhus 2000).
Fidjestøl, Bjarne. Review of Claus Krag, *Ynglingatal og ynglingesaga. En studie i historiske kilder, Maal og minne* (1994), pp. 191-99.
Fidjestøl, Bjarne. "Romantic Reading at the Court of Hákon Hákonarson," in *Selected Papers* (Odense 1997), pp. 351-65.
Fidjestøl, Bjarne. "'Have you heard a Poem worth more? Economic Aspects of Skaldic Poetry'", in *Selected Papers* (Odense 1997), pp. 117-32.
Fidjestøl, Bjarne. *The Dating of Eddic Poetry, Bibliotheca Arnamagnæana* XLI (Copenhagen 1999).
Finer, Samuel E. "State- and Nation-Building in Europe: The Role of the Military", in Charles Tilly (ed.), *The Formation of National States in Western Europe* (Princeton 1975), pp. 84-163.
Fladby, Rolf. "Oppløsningen av den svensk-norske unionen i 1343", *Historisk tidsskrift* 43 (1964), pp. 85-102.
Fladby, Rolf. "Lensmann", *Kulturhistorisk leksikon for nordisk middelalder* II (Oslo 1965), cols. 505 f.
Flüeler, Christoph. *Rezeption und Interpretation der Aristotelischen Politica im späten Mittelalter, Bochumer Studien zur Philosophie* 19 (Amsterdam 1992).
Freedman, Paul. "Rural society", in Michael Jones (ed.), *The New Cambridge Medieval History* VI (Cambridge 2000), pp. 82-101.
Fried, Johannes. "Der karolingische Herrschaftsverband im 9. Jh. zwischen 'Kirche' und 'Königshaus'", *Historische Zeitschrift* 235 (1982), pp. 1-43.

Fried, Johannes. "*Gens* und *regnum*. Wahrnehmungs- und Deutungskategorien politischen Wandels im früheren Mittelalter: Bemerkungen zur doppelten Theoriebindung des Historikers", in Jürgen Mietke and Klaus Schreiner (eds.), *Socialer Wandel im Mittelalter: Wahrnehmungsformen, Erklärungsmuster, Regelungsmechanismen* (Sigmaringen 1994), pp. 92-104.

Frostatingslova, translated by Jan Ragnar Hagland and Jørn Sandnes (Oslo 1994).

Frøjmark, Anders. *Mirakler och helgonkult: Linköpings biskopsdöme under senmedeltiden* (Uppsala 1992).

Fsk. = *Fagrskinna*.

G = The Law of Gulating.

Gagnér, Sten. *Studien zur Ideengeschichte der Gesetzgebung*, Acta Universitatis Upsaliensis: Studia Iuridica Upsaliensia 1 (Stockholm 1960).

Gallén, Jarl. "Celibat", *Kulturhistorisk leksikon for nordisk middelalder* II (Oslo 1957), cols. 545-48.

Gamal norsk homiliebok: Cod. AM 619 4:to, ed. Gustav Indrebø (Oslo 1931).

Garipzanov, Ildar. "Ships, Collective Identities, and State Formation in Scandinavia" (forthcoming).

Garipzanov, Ildar. "Frontier Identities: Carolingian Frontier and *Gens Danorum*", in Patrick Geary, Ildar Garipzanov and Przemyslaw Urbancyk (eds.), *Franks, Northmen and Slavs: Identities and State Formation in Early Medieval Europe* (Tournhout 2008), pp. 113-43.

Gaunt, David. *Familjeliv i Norden* (Malmö 1983).

Gauvard, Claude. "De grace especial". *Crime, état et société en France à la fin du Moyen Âge* (Paris 1991).

Geary, Patrick. "Living with Conflicts in Stateless France: A Typology of Conflict Management Mechanisms, 1050-1200", in Patrick Geary, *Living with the Dead in the Middle Ages* (Ithaca 1994), pp. 125-160.

Gellner, Ernest. *Nations and Nationalism* (Oxford 1983).

Gelting, Michael. "Marriage, Peace and the Canonical Incest Prohibitions: Making Sense of an Absurdity?", in Mia Korpiola (ed.), *Nordic Perspectives on Medieval Canon Law* (Helsingfors 1999), pp. 93-124.

Gelting, Michael. "Det komparative perspektiv i dansk højmiddelalderforskning", *Historisk Tidsskrift* [Danish] 99 (1999), pp. 169-81.

Gelting, Michael. "Odelsrett – lovbydelse – bördsrätt – retrait lignager. Kindred and Land in the Nordic Countries in the Twelfth and Thirteenth Centuries", in Lars Ivar Hansen (ed.), *Family, Marriage and Property Devolution in the Twelfth and Thirteenth Centuries* (Tromsø 2000), pp. 133-65.

Gelting, Michael. "Féodalisation sans féodalité dans le Danemark médiéval: une question mal posée?", in Natalie Fryde, Pierre Monnet and Otto Gerhard Oexle, *Die Gegenwart des Feudalismus* (Göttingen 2002), pp. 137-51.

Gelting, Michael. "Skånske Lov og Jyske Lov. Danmarks første kommissionsbetænkning og Danmarks første retsplejelov", in H. Dam et al., *Jura & Historie. Festskrift til Inger Dübeck som forsker* (Copenhagen 2003), pp. 43-80.

Gelting, Michael. "Pope Alexander III and Danish Laws of Inheritance", in Ditlev Tamm and Helle Vogt (eds.). *How Nordic Are the Nordic Medieval Laws?* (Copenhagen 2005), pp. 86-115.

Gelting, Michael. "The Kingdom of Denmark", in Nora Berend (ed.), *Christianization and the Rise of Christian Monarchy. Scandinavia, Central Europe and Rus' c. 900-1200* (Cambridge 2007), pp. 73-120.

Gillingham, John. "Conquering the Barbarians. War and Chivalry in Twelfth-Century Britain", *The Haskins Society Journal* 4 (1992), pp. 67-84.

Gillingham, John. "1066 and the introduction of chivalry into England", in George Garnett and John Hudson (eds.), *Law and government in medieval England. Essays in honour of Sir James Holt* (Cambridge 1994), pp. 31-55.

Gissel, Svend et al. *Desertion and Land Colonization in the Nordic Countries c. 1300-1600: Comparative Report from the Scandinavian Research Project on Deserted Farms and Villages* (Stockholm 1981).

Given, James. *State and Society in Medieval Europe. Gwynedd and Languedoc under Outside Rule* (Ithaca 1990).

Gjerløw, Jens A.R. "Utskylden. Funksjon, opprinnelse, avvikling", *Historisk tidsskrift* 67 (1988), pp. 361-98.

Gluckman, Max. *Politics, Law and Ritual in Tribal Society* (Oxford 1965).

Goetz, Hans Werner. "*Regnum:* Zum politischen Denken der Karolingerzeit", *Zeitschrift der Savigny-Stiftung für Rechtsgeschichte. Germanistische Abteilung* 104 (1987), pp. 110-89.

Goldstone, Jack. *Revolution and Rebellion in the Early Modern World* (Berkeley 1991).

Goldstone, Jack. "Efflorescence and Economic Growth in World History: Rethinking the 'Rise of the West' and the Industrial Revolution", *Journal of World History* 13 (2002), pp. 323-89.

Grandinsson, Karl Gustaf. *Studier i hanseatisk-svensk historia II. Åren 1332-1365* (Stockholm 1885).

Gullbekk, Svein. *Pengevesenets fremvekst og fall i Norge i middelalderen* (Oslo 2003).

Gullbekk, Svein. "Lite eller mye mynt i Norge i middelalderen?", *Historisk tidsskrift* 84 (2005), pp. 551-72.

Gunawardana, R.A.L.H. "Social function and political power: a case study of state formation in irrigation society", in Henri J.M. Claessen and Peter Skalník (eds.), *The Study of the State* (The Hague 1981), pp. 133-54.

Gunnes, Erik. *Kongens ære. Kongemakt og kirke i "En tale mot biskopene"* (Oslo 1971).

Gunnes, Erik. "Kirkelig jurisdiksjon i Norge 1153-1277", *Historisk tidsskrift* 49 (1979), pp. 121-60.

Gunnes, Erik. "Prester og deier – sølibatet i norsk middelalder", in Steinar Imsen and Gudmund Sandvik (eds.), *Hamarspor. Et festskrift til Lars Hamre* (Oslo 1982), pp. 20-44.

Gunnes, Erik. *Erkebiskop Øystein. Statsmann og kirkebygger* (Oslo 1996).

Gustafsson, Harald. *Gamla riken, nya stater. Statsbildning, politisk kultur och identiteter under Kalmarunionens upplösningsskede 1512-1541* (Stockholm 2000).

Gåvobrevet 1085. Föredrag och diskussioner vid Symposium kring Knut den heliges gåvobrev och den tidiga medeltidens nordiska samhälle, ed. Sten Skansjö and Hans Sundström (Lund 1988).

H = the Hird Law.

Hagland, Jan Ragnar. *Riksstyring og språknorm. Spørsmålet om kongskanselliets rolle i norsk språkhistorie på 1200- og første halvdel av 1300-tallet* (Oslo 1986).

Hagland, Jan Ragnar and Jørn Sandnes. "Om lova og lagdømmet", *Frostatingslova*, translated by Jan Ragnar Hagland and Jørn Sandnes (Oslo 1994), pp. ix-li.

Hagland, Jan Ragnar. *Literacy i norsk seinmellomalder* (Oslo 2005).

Hákonar saga, ed. Guðbrandur Vigfusson, *Rerum Britannicarum medii ævi scriptores* 88.1-2 (London 1857).

Halvorsen, Eyvind Fjeld. "Norwegian Court Literature in the Middle Ages," *Orkney Miscellany* 5 (1973), pp. 17-26.

Halvorsen, Eyvind Fjeld. "Trolldom", *Kulturhistorisk leksikon for nordisk middelalder* XVIII (Oslo 1974), cols. 657-61.

Hamre, Anne-Marit. "Visitasen", in Steinar Imsen (ed.), *Ecclesia Nidrosiensis 1153-1537. Søkelys på Nidaroskirkens og Nidarosprovinsens historie*, Senter for middelalderstudier, NTNU. Skrifter no. 5 (Trondheim 2003), pp. 215-30.

Hamre, Lars. "Edgärdman. Norge", *Kulturhistorisk leksikon for nordisk middelalder* III (Oslo 1958), cols. 492-99.

Hamre, Lars. "Handarband", *Kulturhistorisk leksikon for nordisk middelalder* VI (Oslo 1961), cols. 110-13.

Hamre, Lars. "Hangengnir menn", *Kulturhistorisk leksikon for nordisk middelalder* VI (Oslo 1961), cols. 190-92.

Hamre, Lars. "Hird. Norge", *Kulturhistorisk leksikon for nordisk middelalder* VI (Oslo 1961), cols. 571-77.

Hamre, Lars. "Sogn. Norge", *Kulturhistorisk leksikon for nordisk middelalder* XVI (Oslo 1971), cols. 377-80.

Hamre, Lars. "Tiend. Norge", *Kulturhistorisk leksikon for nordisk middelalder* XVIII (Oslo 1974), cols. 280-87.

Hamre, Lars. "Traktat", *Kulturhistorisk leksikon for nordisk middelalder* XVIII (Oslo 1974), cols. 541-47.

Hamre, Lars. "Litt om og omkring Håkon V's hirdskipan 17. juni 1308", *Historisk tidsskrift* 72 (1993), pp. 6-36.

Hamre, Lars. "Ein diplomatarisk og rettshistorisk analyse av Sættargjerda i Tunsberg", *Historisk tidsskrift* 82 (2003), pp. 381-431.

Hamre, Lars. "Striden mellom erkebiskop Jørund og domkapitlet i Nidaros", in Steinar Imsen (ed.), *Ecclesia Nidrosiensis 1153-1537. Søkelys på Nidaroskirkens og Nidarosprovinsens historie, Senter for middelalderstudier, NTNU. Skrifter* no. 5 (Trondheim 2003), pp. 187-213.

Hansen, Gitte. *Bergen c. 800-1170. The Emergence of a Town, The Bryggen Papers. Main Series* no. 6 (Bergen 2005).

Hansen, Lars Ivar. "Slektskap, eiendom og sosiale strategier i nordisk middelalder", *Collegium Medievale* 7 (1994), pp. 103-54.

Hansen, Lars Ivar. "The Concept of Kinship According to the West Nordic Medieval Laws", in Ditlev Tamm and Helle Vogt (eds.), *How Nordic Are the Nordic Medieval Laws?* (Copenhagen 2005), pp. 170-201.

Hansen, Lars Ivar and Bjørnar Olsen. *Samenes historie fram til 1750* (Oslo 2004).

Harriss, G.L. *King, Parliament and Public Finance in Medieval England* (Oxford 1975).

Haug, Eldbjørg. *Provincia Nidrosiensis i dronning Margretes unions- og maktpolitikk* (Trondheim 1996).

Haug, Eldbjørg. "Konkordat-konflikt-privilegium. Sættargjerden som indikator på forholdet stat-kirke fra Magnus Lagabøter til Christian I (1277-1458)", in Steinar Imsen (ed.), *Ecclesia Nidrosiensis 1153-1537. Søkelys på Nidaroskirkens og Nidarosprovinsens historie, Senter for middelalderstudier, NTNU. Skrifter* no. 5 (Trondheim 2003), pp. 83-119.

Haug, Eldbjørg. "Klosteret på Utstein", in Eldbjørg Haug (ed.), *Utstein kloster – og Klosterøyas historie* (Utstein 2005), pp. 103-213.

Heimskringla, ed. Finnur Jónsson (Copenhagen 1893-1900), I-IV.

Heimskringla: History of the Kings of Norway, translated with introduction by L.M. Hollander (Austin 1967).

Helle, Knut. "Tendenser i norsk høymiddelalderforskning", *Historisk tidsskrift* 40 (1961), pp. 337-70.

Helle, Knut, "Innleiing", *Soga om Håkon Håkonsson* (Oslo 1963).
Helle, Knut. *Konge og gode menn i norsk riksstyring ca. 1150-1319* (Bergen 1972).
Helle, Knut. *Norge blir en stat, 1130-1319. Handbok i Norges historie* III (Bergen 1974).
Helle, Knut. *Stavanger fra våg til by* (Stavanger 1975).
Helle, Knut. "Norway in the High Middle Ages. Recent Views on the Structure of Society", *Scandinavian Journal of History* 6 (1981), pp. 161-89.
Helle. Knut. *Kongssete og kjøpstad: fra opphavet til 1536, Bergen bys historie* I (Bergen 1982).
Helle, Knut. *Under kirke og kongemakt, Aschehougs Norgeshistorie* III (Oslo 1995).
Helle, Knut. "Down to 1500", in Rolf Danielsen et al., *Norway: A History from the Vikings to Our Own Times* (Oslo 1995), pp. 3-119.
Helle, Knut. "Rettsoppfatninger og rettsendringer. Europa og Norge i middelalderen", *Festskrift til Historisk institutts 40-års jubileum 1997, Historisk institutt, Universitetet i Bergen, Skrifter* 2 (Bergen 1997), pp. 41-70.
Helle, Knut. *Gulatingslova* (Leikanger 2001).
Helle, Knut. "Opptakten til de nordiske unioner i senmiddelalderen", *Forum mediaevale*, New Series no. 4 (2002), pp. 3-31.
Helle, Knut (ed.). *The Cambridge History of Scandinavia*, I, *Prehistory to 1520* (Cambridge 2003).
Helle, Knut. "Growing inter-Scandinavian entanglement", in Knut Helle (ed.), *The Cambridge History of Scandinavia*, I, *Prehistory to 1520* (Cambridge 2003), pp. 411-20.
Helle, Knut. "Fra opphavet til omkring 1500", in K. Helle et al., *Norsk byhistorie. Urbanisering gjennom 1300 år* (Oslo 2006), pp. 23-142.
Helle, Knut. "Den opphavlige vestlandsregionen", in K. Helle et al., *Vestlandets historie* II (Bergen 2006), pp. 8-59.
Helle, Knut. "Stavanger by og Utstein kloster", *Historisk tidsskrift* 97 (2008), pp. 577-605.
Helle, Knut and Arnved Nedkvitne. *Forskningsrapport om de norske middelalderbyene til det nordiske historikermøtet i Trondheim* (Trondheim 1977).
Helmholz, R.H. *The Oxford History of the Laws of England*, I, *The Canon Law and Ecclesiastical Jurisdiction from 597 to the 1640s* (Oxford 2004).
Hermanson, Lars. *Släkt, vänner och makt. En studie av elitens politiska kultur i 1100-talets Danmark, Avhandlingar från Historiska institutionen, Göteborgs universitet* (Gothenburg 2000).
Hertzberg, Ebbe. *Grundtrækkene i den ældste norske Proces* (Christiania 1874).
Hertzberg, Ebbe. "Endnu et Kristenretsudkast fra det 13de Aarhundrede", *Sproglig-historiske Studier tilegnede Professor C.R. Unger* (Kristiania 1896), pp. 189-204.

Heydte, F.A. v.d. *Die Geburtstunde des souveränen Staates* (Regensburg 1952).

HH = *Hákonar saga.*

[Hird Law] *Hirdloven til Norges konges menn*, ed. Steinar Imsen (Oslo 2000).

Historia Norwegie, ed. Inger Ekrem and Lars Boje Mortensen, trans. by Peter Fischer (Copenhagen 2003).

HkrHG = *Heimskringla*, The Saga of Håkon the Good, in *Heimskringla* I, pp. 165-222.

HkrHH = *Heimskringla*, The Saga of Harald Finehair, in *Heimskringla* I, pp. 98-164.

HkrHHard = *Heimskringla*, The Saga of Harald Hardrada, in *Heimskringla* III, pp. 74-224.

HkrIngi = *Heimskringla*, The Saga of Ingi and his brothers, in *Heimskringla* III, pp. 348-97.

HkrMB = *Heimskringla*, The Saga of Magnus the Blind, in *Heimskringla* III, pp. 314-47.

HkrME = *Heimskringla*, The Saga of Magnus Erlingsson, in *Heimskringla* III, pp. 432-92.

HkrOH = Heimskringla, The Saga of St Olav, in *Heimskringla* II.

HkrOT = *Heimskringla*, The Saga of Olav Tryggvason, in *Heimskringla* I, pp. 255-459.

Hobsbawm, Eric. *Nations and Nationalism since 1780* (Cambridge 1991).

Hoffmann, Erich. *Die heiligen Könige bei den Angelsachsen und den skandinavischen Völkern. Königsheiliger und Königshaus, Quellen und Forschungen zu Geschichte Schleswig-Holsteins* 69 (Neumünster 1975).

Holmsen, Andreas. "Var 'Retterboten av 1308' en retterbot?", *Historisk tidsskrift* 49 (1970), pp. 34-57.

Holmsen, Andreas. *Nye studier i gammel historie* (Oslo 1976).

Holmsen, Andreas. *Norges historie. Fra de eldste tider til 1660*, 4th ed. (Oslo 1977 [orig. 1939]).

Holmsen, Andreas. "Integreringen av innlandsdistriktene i det gammelnorske riket", in Steinar Imsen and Gudmund Sandvik (eds.), *Hamarspor. Eit festskrift til Lars Hamre* (Oslo 1982), pp. 9-19.

Holt, Richard. "What if the Sea Were Different? Urbanization in Medieval Norway", in Christopher Dyer, Peter Coss and Chris Wickham (eds.), *Rodney Hilton's Middle Ages. An Exploration of Historical Themes, Past & Present Supplement* 2 (Oxford 2007), pp. 132-47.

Holtan, Inger. *Ekteskap, frillelevnad og hor i norsk middelalder* (Oslo 1996).

Housley, Norman. "*Pro deo et patria mori*: Sanctified Patriotism in Europe, 1400-1600", in Philippe Contamine (ed.), *War and Competition between States* (Oxford 2000), pp. 221-48.

Hubbard, William H. et al. *Making a Historical Culture. Historiography in Norway* (Oslo 1995).

Hultgård, Anders. "Altskandinavische Opferrituale und das Problem der Quellen", in Tore Ahlbäck (ed.), *The Problem of Ritual* (Åbo 1993), pp. 221-59.

Hultgård, Anders. "*Ár* – '*gutes Jahr und Ernteglück*' – ein Motivkomplex in der altnordischen Literatur und sein religionsgeschichtlicher Hintergrund", in Wilhelm Heizmann et al. (eds.), *Runica – Germanica – Mediaevalia, Ergänzungsbände zum Reallexikon der Germanischen Altertumskunde* 37 (Berlin 2003), pp. 282-308.

Hultgård, Anders. "The Askr and Embla Myth in a comparative perspective", in Anders Andrén et al. (eds.), *Old Norse religion in long-term perspectives. Origins, changes, and interactions* (Lund 2006), pp. 58-62.

Hurnard, Naomi D. *The King's Pardon for Homicide before AD 1307* (Oxford 1969).

Hybel, Nils and Bjørn Poulsen. *The Danish Resources c. 1000-1550, The Northern World* 34 (Leiden 2007).

Hødnebø, Finn. "Þingasaga", *Kulturhistorisk leksikon for nordisk middelalder* XX (Oslo 1976), cols. 377-79.

Hørby, Kai. *Status regni Dacie. Studier i Christofferliniens ægteskabs- og alliancepolitik 1252-1319* (Copenhagen 1977).

Imsen, Steinar and Jørn Sandnes. *Avfolkning og union. Norges historie* IV, ed. Knut Mykland (Oslo 1977).

Imsen, Steinar. *Norsk bondekommunalisme fra Magnus Lagabøte til Kristian Kvart. Del I. Middelalderen* (Trondheim 1990).

Imsen, Steinar and Günter Vogler. "Communal Autonomy and Peasant Resistance in Northern and Central Europe", in Peter Blickle (ed.), *Resistance, Representation and Community: The Origins of the Modern State in Europe* (Oxford 1997), pp. 5-43.

Imsen, Steinar. "Earldom and Kingdom. Orkney in the Realm of Norway 1195-1379", *Historisk tidsskift* 79 (2000), pp. 163-80.

Imsen, Steinar. *Norges nedgang* (Oslo 2002).

Isl. Ann. = *Islandske Annaler.*

Islandske Annaler indtil 1578, ed. Gustav Storm (Christiania 1888).

Iversen, Frode. *Eiendom, makt og statsdannelse: kongsgårder og gods i Hordaland i yngre jernalder og middelalder* (Doctoral thesis, University of Bergen, 2004).

Iversen, Tore. *Trelldommen. Norsk slaveri i middelalderen, Historisk institutt i Bergen Skrifter* no. I (Bergen 1997).

Iversen, Tore. "Property and Land Tenancy – Norwegian Medieval Laws and the European Learned Law", in Ditlev Tamm and Helle Vogt (eds.), *How Nordic Are the Nordic Medieval Laws?* (Copenhagen 2005), pp. 128-68.

Jakobsson, Sverrir. "Defining a Nation", *Scandinavian Journal of History* 24 (1999), pp. 91-101.
Jakobsson, Sverrir. "'Erindringen om en mægtig Personlighed.' Den norsk-islandske historiske tradisjon om Harald Hårfagre i et kildekritisk perspektiv", *Historisk tidsskrift* 81 (2002), pp. 213-30.
Janson, Henrik. *Templum nobilissimum. Adam av Bremen, Uppsalatempelet och konfliktlinjerna i Europa kring år 1075, Avhandlingar från historiska institutionen i Göteborg* 21 (Gothenburg 1998).
[John of Salisbury] Johannes Sarisberiensis *Policraticus sive De nugis curialium et vestigiis philosophorum*, ed. C.C.I. Webb, I-II (Oxford 1909).
Johnsen, Arne Odd. *Studier vedrørende cardinal Nicolaus Brekespears legasjon til Norden* (Oslo 1945), pp. 379-82.
Johnsen, Arne Odd. *Fra ættesamfunn til statssamfunn* (Oslo 1948).
Johnsen, Arne Odd. "Svar til Jens Arup Seip", *Historisk tidsskrift* 35 (1949-51), pp. 499-512.
Johnsen, Arne Odd. "Fra den eldste tid til 1252", *Nidaros erkebispestol og bispesete 1153-1953* (Oslo 1955), pp. 3-269.
Johnsen, Arne Odd. "Audun Hugleiksson til Hegranes", in Albert Joleik (ed.), *Soga um Jølst* (Bergen 1967), pp. 751-65.
Johnsen, John Birger. "Bréfabrot", *Kulturhistorisk leksikon for nordisk middelalder* II (Oslo 1957), cols. 213 f.
Joys, Charles. *Biskop og konge. Bispevalg i Norge 1000-1350* (Oslo 1948).
Joys, Charles. "Tidsrommet 1253-1280", *Nidaros erkebispestol og bispesete 1153-1953* (Oslo 1955), pp. 273-324.
Joys, Charles. "Tidsrommet 1280-1450", *Nidaros erkebispestol og bispesete 1153-1953* (Oslo 1955), pp. 327-448.
Jørgensen, Nils. *Studier över syntax och textstruktur i nordiska medeltidslagar, Skrifter utgivna av svenska fornskriftssällskapet*, no. 256 (Uppsala 1987).
Kalinke, Marianne. "Norse Romances", in Carol Clover and John Lindow (eds.), *Old Norse-Icelandic Literature. A Critical Guide, Islandica* 45 (Ithaca 1985), pp. 316-63.
Kamp, Hermann. *Friedensstifter und Vermittler im Mittelalter* (Darmstadt 2001).
Kantorowicz, Ernst H. "Deus per naturam, Deus per gratiam", *Harvard Theological Review* 45 (1952), pp. 253-77.
Kantorowicz, Ernst H. *The King's Two Bodies. A Study in Medieval Political Theology* (Princeton 1957).
Kantorowicz, Ernst H. "Kingship under the Impact of Scientific Jurisprudence", in Ernst H. Kantorowicz *Selected Studies* (New York 1965), pp. 151-66.

Karlsen, Espen. "Katalogisering av latinske membranfragmenter som forskningsprosjekt. Del 2", *Arkivverkets forskningsseminar, Gardermoen 2003* (Oslo 2003), pp. 58-88.

Keegan, John. *A History of Warfare* (London 1994).

Keesing, Roger M. *Cultural Anthropology. A Contemporary Perspective* (New York 1981).

Keller, Hagen. *Zwischen regionaler Begrenzung und universalem Horizont. Deutschland im Imperium der Salier und Staufer 1024 bis 1250* (Frankfurt 1990).

Kern, Fritz. *Gottesgnadentum und Widerstandsrecht im früheren Mittelalter* (Münster/Cologne 1954 [orig. 1914]).

Kern, Fritz. *Recht und Verfassung im Mittelalter* (Darmstadt 1992 [orig. 1919]).

Kinck, Hans E. *Storhetstid: om vort aansliv og den literære kultur i det trettende aarhundrede* (Kristiania 1922).

[The King's Mirror] *Konungs skuggsiá*, ed. Ludvig Holm-Olsen (Oslo 1945).

Klaniczay, Gábor. *Holy Rulers and Blessed Princesses. Dynastic Cults in Medieval Central Europe* (Cambridge 2002).

Kleivane, Kjell-Jørund. *Høvding, jordegodseier og kongelig ombudsmann. En studie i lendmannsinstitusjonen fra slutten av 1000-tallet til Magnus Lagabøters død* (Master's thesis, University of Oslo, 1981).

Klingenberg, Heinz. *Heidnisches Altertum und nordisches Mittelalter. Strukturbildende Perspektive des Snorri Sturluson* (Freiburg 1999).

Koht, Halvdan. *Innhogg og utsyn* (Kristiania 1921).

Koht, Halvdan. *Det gamle norske riksarkive og restane frå det*, Skrifter utgitt av Det Norske Videnskaps-Akademi i Oslo II, Hist.-fil. Klasse 1927 no. 1 (Oslo 1927).

Koht, Halvdan. *Kong Sverre* (Oslo 1952).

Koht, Halvdan. "Skule jarl", *Historisk tidsskrift* 5 rk. V (1924), pp. 428-52.

Koht, Halvdan. "Norsk historie i lys frå ættehistoria", *Norsk slektshistorisk tidsskrift* 5 (1936), pp. 89-104.

Kolsrud, Oluf. "Kirke og folk", *Norsk theologisk Tidsskrift* 14 (1913), pp. 35-59, 131-56.

Kolsrud, Oluf. *Norges kyrkjesoga* I. *Millomalderen* (Oslo 1958).

Kolsrud, Oluf. *Presteutdaningi i Norge* (Oslo 1962).

Korpiola, Mia. "On Ecclesiastical Jurisdiction and the Reception of Canon Law in the Swedish Provincial Laws", in Ditlev Tamm and Helle Vogt (eds.), *How Nordic Are the Nordic Medieval Laws?* (Copenhagen 2005), pp. 202-31.

Koziol, Geoffrey. *Begging Pardon and Favor. Ritual and Political Order in Early Medieval France* (Ithaca 1992).

Krag, Claus. "Årmannen", *Historisk tidsskrift* 61 (1982), pp. 105-27.

Krag, Claus. "Norge som odel i Harald Hårfagres ætt", *Historisk tidsskrift* 68 (1989), pp. 288-302.

Krag, Claus. *Ynglingatal og ynglingesaga. En studie i historiske kilder* (Oslo 1991).
Krag, Claus. *Vikingtid og rikssamling 800-1130, Aschehougs Norgeshistorie* II (Oslo 1995).
Krag, Claus. "Motstandsbestemmelsene i Frostatingsloven", *Forum Mediaevale* 1-2 (1999), pp. 2-42.
Krag, Claus. "Perspektiver på den norske rikssamlingen – et forsøk på en revisjon", in Olav Skevik (ed.), *Kongemøte på Stiklestad. Rapport fra seminar om kongedømmet i vikingtid og tidlig middelalder* (Stiklestad 1999), pp. 11-28.
Krag, Claus. "The Early Unification of Norway", in Knut Helle (ed.), *The Cambridge History of Scandinavia*, I, *Prehistory to 1520* (Cambridge 2003), pp. 411-20.
Krag, Claus. "Lauritz Weibull", in Rosemarie Müller et al. (eds.) *Reallexikon der Germanischen Altertumskunde*, vol. 33 (Berlin 2004), cols. 347-56.
Krag, Claus. *Sverre – Norge største middelalderkonge* (Oslo 2005).
Kramarz-Bein, Susanne. *Die Þiðreks saga im Kontext der altnorwegischen Literatur* (Tübingen 2002).
Krause, Hermann. "Dauer und Vergänglichkeit im mittelalterlichen Recht", *Zeitschrift der Savigny-Stiftung für Rechtsgeschichte. Germanistische Abteilung* 75 (1958), pp. 208-71.
Kroener, Bernhard R. "The Modern State and Military Society in the Eighteenth Century", in Philippe Contamine (ed.), *War and Competition between States: The Origins of the Modern State in Europe* (Oxford 2000), pp. 195-220.
Kroman, Erik. "Arkiv. Danmark", *Kulturhistorisk leksikon for nordisk middelalder* I (Oslo 1956), cols. 232-35.
L = *Landsloven*.
Landau, Peter. "The Importance of Classical Canon Law in Scandinavia in the 12th and 13th Centuries", in Ditlev Tamm and Helle Vogt (eds.), *How Nordic Are the Nordic Medieval Laws?* (Copenhagen 2005), pp. 24-39.
Landro, Torgeir. *Dei eldste norske kristenrettane. Innhald og opphav* (Master's thesis, University of Bergen, 2005).
Landsloven, NGL II, pp. 1-178.
Lange, Guðrun. *Die Anfänge der isländisch-norwegischen Geschichtsschreibung, Studia Islandica* 47 (Reykjavík 1989).
Larsson, Gunilla. *Ships and Society. Maritime Ideology in Late Iron Age Sweden* (Doctoral thesis, Uppsala 2007).
Larsson, Inger. *Svenska medeltidsbrev* (Stockholm 2001).
Laurentius saga biskups, ed. Árni Björnsson, *Rit Handritastofnunar Íslands* 3 (Reykjavík 1969).
[The Law of Frostating] "Den ældre Frostathings-Lov", NGL I, pp. 119-258.

[The Law of Gulating] *Den eldre Gulatingslova*, ed. Bjørn Eithun, Magnus Rindal and Tor Ulset, *Norrøne tekster* no. 6 (Oslo 1994).

Leach, Edmund. "Talking about Talking about Feudalism", in Edmund Leach, S.N. Mukherjee and John Ward (eds.), *Feudalism: Comparative Studies, Sydney Studies in Society and Culture* no. 2 (Sydney 1985), pp. 6-24.

Le Goff, Jacques. *Saint Louis* (Paris 1996).

Le Goff, Jacques. "Le rituel symbolique de la vassalité", in Jacques Le Goff, *Un autre Moyen Âge* (Paris 1999), pp. 333-93.

Leistad, Geirr, Magne Njåstad, Erik Opsahl and Jo Rune Ugulen. "Adel, aristokrati og elite: Nokre kommentarar til Knut Dørums artikkel i *Heimen* 4/2007", *Heimen* 45 (2009), pp. 167-71.

Lewis, Herbert S. "Warfare and the origin of the state: another formulation", in Henri J.M. Claessen and Peter Skalník (eds.), *The Study of the State* (The Hague 1981), pp. 201-21.

Lidén, Hans-Emil. "Middelalderens steinarkitektur i Norge", *Norges kunsthistorie*, II, *Høymiddelalder og Hansa-tid* (Oslo 1981), pp. 7-125.

Lind, Gunner. "Great Friends and Small Friends: Clientelism and the Power Elite", in Wolfgang Reinhard (ed.), *Power Elites and State Building: The Origins of the Modern State in Europe* (Oxford 1996), pp. 123-47.

Lindkvist, Thomas. *Landborna i Norden under äldre medeltid*, Studia historica Upsaliensia 110 (Stockholm 1979).

Lindkvist, Thomas. *Plundring, skatter och den feodala statens framväxt. Organisatoriska tendensar i Sverige under övergången från vikingatid til tidig medeltid*, Opuscula Historica Upsaliensia 1 (Uppsala 1988).

Lindkvist, Thomas. "Kings and Provinces in Sweden", in Knut Helle (ed.), *The Cambridge History of Scandinavia*, I, *Prehistory to 1520* (Cambridge 2003), pp. 221-34.

Linton, Michael. "Regimen regale et politicum", *Kulturhistorisk leksikon for nordisk middelalder* XIII (Oslo 1968), cols. 377-79.

Livius, Titus. *Ab urbe condita libri* II (VI-X), ed. Charles F. Walters and Robert S. Conway (Oxford 1919).

Ljungqvist, Fredrik Charpentier. "Kristen kungaideologi i *Sverris saga*", *Scripta Islandica* 57 (2006), pp. 79-95.

Lönnroth, Lars. "Sverrir's Dreams", *Scripta Islandica* 57 (2006), pp. 97-110.

Louis-Jensen, Jonna, *Kongesagastudier. Kompilasjonen Hulda-Hrokkinskinna*, Bibliotheca Arnamagnæana 32 (Copenhagen 1977).

Lund, Niels. "Scandinavia c. 700-1066", in Rosamond McKitterick (ed.), *The New Cambridge Medieval History* II (Cambridge 1995), pp. 202-27.

Lund, Niels. *Lid, leding og landeværn. Hær og samfund i Danmark i ældre middelalder* (Roskilde 1996).

Lund, Niels. "Is leidang a Nordic or European phenomenon?", in Anne Nørgård Jørgensen and Birthe L. Clausen (eds.), *Military Aspects of Scandinavian Society in a European Perspective, AD 1-1300, Publications from The National Museum. Studies in Archaeology & History*, Vol. 2 (Copenhagen 1997), pp. 195-99.

Lund, Niels. "Leding, bønder og inerti", *Historisk Tidsskrift* [Danish] 99 (1999), pp. 189-207.

Lund, Niels. "Leding, skjaldekvad og bønder", *Historisk Tidsskrift* [Danish] 106 (2006), pp. 243-52.

Lunden, Kåre. *Økonomi og samfunn. Synspunkt på økonomisk historie* (Oslo 1972).

Lunden, Kåre. "Om Håkon V's skipan av 17/6 1308", *Historisk tidsskrift* 50 (1971), pp. 18-57.

Lunden, Kåre. *Sverreættens kongedømme, Norges historie* III, ed. Knut Mykland (Oslo 1976).

Lunden, Kåre. "Det norske kongedømet i høgmellomalderen (ca. 1150-1319) – Funksjon, makt, legitimitet", in Jon Elster and Henning Poulsen (eds.), *Magt, normer og sanktioner, Studier i historisk metode* 13 (Oslo 1978), pp. 124-40.

Lunden, Kåre. "Træl og årmann. Replikk til Claus Krag", *Historisk tidsskrift* 62 (1983), pp. 449-54.

Lunden, Kåre. "Was there a Norwegian National Identity in the Middle Ages?", *Scandinavian Journal of History* 20 (1995), pp. 19-33.

Lunden, Kåre. "Rett og realitet. Rettsreglane i norsk mellomalder, på ein kulturell og sosial bakgrunn", *Forum mediaevale* 1 (1998), pp. 1-51.

Lunden, Kåre. "Money Economy in Medieval Norway", *Scandinavian Journal of History* 24 (1999), pp. 245-65.

Lunden, Kåre. "Mynt, andre pengar og politisk-økonomisk system i mellomalderen", *Historisk tidsskrift* 86 (2007), pp. 7-34.

Löfqvist, Karl-Erik. *Om riddarväsen och frälse i nordisk medeltid* (Lund 1935).

Lönnroth, Erik. *Sverige och Kalmarunionen 1397-1457* (Gothenburg 1934).

Lönnroth, Erik. *Statsmakt och statsfinans* (Gothenburg 1940).

McIlwain, Charles H. *The Growth of Political Thought in the West* (New York 1932).

McNeill, William H. *The Pursuit of Power. Technology, Armed Force, and Society since AD 1000* (Oxford 1983).

Maddicott, J.R. *Simon de Montfort* (Cambridge 1994).

Magerøy, Hallvard. "Føreord", *Soga om Håkon Håkonsson, Noregs kongesoger*, vol. 4 (Oslo 1979), pp. 7-17.

Magnúsdóttir, Auður. *Frillor och fruar. Politikk och samlevnad på Island 1120-1400* (Gothenburg 2001).

Malmros, Rikke. "Kongemagt og leding i Norge og Danmark omkring 1100", *Historisk Tidsskrift* [Danish] 105 (2005), pp. 321-80.

Malmros, Rikke. "Fyrstedigtningens kildeværdi" *Historisk Tidsskrift* [Danish] 105 (2005), pp. 253-63.

Mann, Michael. *The Sources of Social Power*, I, *A History of Power from the Beginning to AD 1760* (Cambridge 1986).

Mayer, Georg. *Das Recht der Expropriation* (Leipzig 1868).

Mayer, Theodor. "Die Ausbildung der Grundlagen des modernen deutschen Staates im hohen Mittelalter", *Historische Zeitschrift* 159 (1939), pp. 457-87.

Meissner, Rudolf. *Die Strengleikar* (Halle 1902).

Meulengracht Sørensen, Preben. *Saga og samfund* (Copenhagen 1977).

Meulengracht Sørensen, Preben. *Fortælling og ære* (Aarhus 1993).

Meulengracht Sørensen, Preben. *At fortælle historien. Telling History. Studier i den gamle nordiske litteratur. Studies in Old Norse Literature* (Trieste 2001).

Miller, Edward. "The Economic Policies of Governments. Introduction" and "France and England", in M. M. Postan and H. J. Habakkuk (eds.), *The Cambridge Economic History of Europe* (Cambridge 1963), pp. 281-340.

Miller, William Ian. *Bloodtaking and Peacemaking. Feud, Law, and Society in Saga Iceland* (Chicago 1990).

Molaug, Petter B. "Oslo blir by – fra 1000 til 1200", in Hans Andersson, Gitte Hansen and Ingvild Øye (eds.), *De første 200 årene – nytt blikk på 27 skandinaviske byer* (Bergen 2008), pp. 73-92.

Monclair, Hanne. *Forestillinger om kongen i norsk middelalder gjennom ritualene og symbolene rundt ham* (Oslo 1995).

Monclair, Hanne. *Lederskapsideologi på Island i det trettende århundree. En analyse av gavegivning, gjestebud og lederfremstilling i islandsk sagamateriale* (Oslo 2003).

Moore, R.I. *The First European Revolution* (Oxford 2001).

Moore, R.I. "The Transformation of Europe", in Johann P. Arnason and Björn Wittrock (eds.), *Eurasian Transformations, Tenth to Thirteenth Centuries. Crystallizations, Divergences, Renaissances* (Leiden 2004), pp. 77-98.

Morkinskinna, ed. Finnur Jónsson (Copenhagen 1932).

Morris, Colin. *The Discovery of the Individual* (London 1972).

Mortensen, Lars Boje. "Sanctified Beginnings and Mythopoietic Moments. The First Wave of Writing on the Past in Norway, Denmark and Hungary", in L.B. Mortensen (ed.), *The Making of Christian Myths in the Periphery of Latin Christendom (c. 1000-1300)* (Copenhagen 2006), pp. 247-73.

Mortensen, Michael. "Early Danish Naval Artillery c. 1500-1523 – The Beginning of a New Era", in Anne Nørgård Jørgensen et al. (eds.), *Maritime Warfare in Northern Europe. Technology, Organization, Logistics and Administration 500 BC-1500 AD, Papers from an International Research Seminar at the Danish National Museum, Copenhagen, 3-5 May 2000* (Copenhagen 2002), pp. 83-104.

Moseng, Ole, Erik Opsahl, Gunnar Pettersen and Erling Sandmo. *Norsk historie,* I, *750-1537,* 2nd ed. (Oslo 2007).

Msk. = *Morkinskinna.*

Munch, Peter Andreas. *Historisk-geografisk Beskrivelse over Kongeriget Norge i Middelalderen* (Moss 1849).

Munch, Peter Andreas. *Det norske Folks Historie* (= NFH) I-IV.2 (Christiania 1852-59).

Munch, Peter Andreas. *Det norske Folks Historie. Unionsperioden* (= NFH. Unionsperioden) I-II (Christiania 1862).

Mundal, Else. "The perception of the Samis and their religion in Old Norse sources", in Juha Pentikäinen (ed.), *Shamanism and Northern Ecology* (Berlin 1996), pp. 97-116.

Mundal, Else. "Skaping og undergang i Vǫluspá", in Ásdís Egilsdóttir and Rudolf Simek (eds.), *Sagnaheimur. Studies in Honour of Hermann Pálsson on his 80th Birthday, 26th May 2001, Studia Medievalia Septentrionalia* 6 (Vienna 2001), pp. 195-207.

Mundal, Else. "Austr sat in aldna. Giantesses and female powers in Vǫluspá", in Rudolf Simek and Wilhelm Heizmann (eds.), *Mythological Women. Studies in Memory of Lotte Motz (1922-1997), Studia Medievalia Septentrionalia* 7 (Vienna 2002), pp. 185-95.

Munthe, C.O. "Hr Audun Hugleiksson Hestakorn til Hegranes og hans herre, kong Eirik Magnusson", I-II, *Bergens historiske forenings skrifter* 38 (1932), pp. 107-226 and 39 (1933), pp. 13-84.

Myhre, Bjørn. "Boathouses and naval organization", Anne Nørgård Jørgensen and Birthe L. Clausen (eds.), *Military Aspects of Scandinavian Society in a European Perspective, AD 1-1300, Publications from The National Museum. Studies in Archaeology & History* II (Copenhagen 1997), pp. 169-83.

Myhre, Bjørn. "The Iron Age", in Knut Helle (ed.), *The Cambridge History of Scandinavia,* I, *Prehistory to 1520* (Cambridge 2003), pp. 60-93.

Myking, Marit. *Vart Noreg kristna frå England? Ein gjennomgang av norsk forsking med utgangspunkt i Absalon Tarangers avhandling Den angelsaksiske kirkes indflydelse paa den norske (1890)* (Oslo 2001).

The National Law, see *Landsloven.*

Nedkvitne, Arnved. *Utenrikshandelen fra det vestafjelske Norge 1100-1600* (Doctoral thesis, Bergen 1983).
Nedkvitne, Arnved. *The Social Consequences of Literacy in Medieval Scandinavia* (Tournhout 2004).
Nedkvitne, Arnved and Per Norseng. *Byen under Eikaberg, Oslo bys historie* I (Oslo 1991).
Nedrebø, Yngve et al. *Audun Hugleiksson: frå kongens råd til galgen* (Førde 2002).
Nenseter, Olav. *Å lære andre gjennom ord og eksempel. Augustinerklostrene på Vestlandets religiøse funksjoner* (Master's thesis, Oslo 2002).
NGL = *Norges gamle Love*.
Nielsen, Herluf. "Datering", *Kulturhistorisk leksikon for nordisk middelalder* III (Oslo 1958), cols. 2-15.
Nielsen, Herluf. "Notar", *Kulturhistorisk leksikon for nordisk middelalder* XII (Oslo 1967), cols. 363-65.
[*Njáls saga*] *Brennu-Njáls saga*, ed. Einar Óláfur Sveinsson, *Íslenzk fornrít* XII (Reykjavík 1954).
Njåstad, Magne. *Grenser for makt. Konflikter og konfliktløsning mellom lokalsamfunn og øvrighet ca. 1300-1540, Skriftserie fra Institutt for historie og klassiske fag* (Trondheim 2003).
Nordeide, Sæbjørg Walaker. *The Viking Age as a Period of Religious Transformation: The Christianization of Norway from AD 560 – 1150/1200* (forthcoming).
Norges gamle Love, I-V, ed. Rudolf Keyser, P. A. Munch et al. (Christiania 1846-95).
Norseng, Per. "Law Codes as a Source for Nordic History in the Early Middle Ages", *Scandinavian Journal of History* 16 (1991), pp. 137-66.
Næshagen, Ferdinand. *Fra selvtekt til demokratisk politi. En komparativ studie av rettshåndhevelsens historie i Vesten* (Oslo 1999).
Næshagen, Ferdinand. "Medieval Norwegian Religiosity: Historical Sources and Modern Social Science", *Scandinavian Journal of History* 25 (2000), pp. 297-316.
Næshagen, Ferdinand. "Den kriminelle voldens U-kurve fra 1500-tallet til nåtid", *Historisk tidsskrift* 84 (2005), pp. 411-27.
Oddr Snorrason munkr. *Sága Óláfs Tryggvasonar*, ed. F. Jónsson (Copenhagen 1932): pp. 210-18.
Oddr Snorrason munkr. *The Saga of Óláfr Tryggvason*, trans. Theodore M. Andersson (Ithaca 2003).
Odén, Birgitta. *Lauritz Weibull och forskarsamhället* (Lund 1975).
Olsen, Olaf. *Hørg, hov og kirke: historiske og arkæologiske vikingetidsstudier, Aarbøger for nordisk oldkyndighed og historie* (Copenhagen 1965).

Ommundsen, Åslaug (ed.). *The Beginnings of Nordic Scribal Culture, ca. 1050-1300. Report from a Workshop on Parchment Fragments, Bergen 28-30 October 2005* (Bergen 2006).
Opsahl, Erik. "Bastard Feudalism or Sub-vassality in Medieval Norway?", *Collegium Medievale* 4 (1991), pp. 177-214.
Opsahl, Erik. *Framveksten av herresvein-institusjonen og dens betydning for militærvesen, maktforhold og sosial eliteutvikling i Norge ca. 1270-1390* (Master's thesis, University of Oslo, 1991).
Opsahl, Erik. *I kongenes tid. Del I. 900-1537*, ed. Knut Kjeldstadli, *Norsk innvandringshistorie* I (Oslo 2003), pp. 1-223.
Opsahl, Erik. "Feider i Norge", in Erik Opsahl (ed.), *Feider og fred i nordisk middelalder* (Oslo 2007), pp. 135-51.
Ormrod, W.M. "The West European Monarchies in the Later Middle Ages", in Richard Bonney (ed.), *Economic Systems and State Finance* (Oxford 1995), pp. 123-60.
Orning, Hans Jacob. "Håkon Håkonsson, Skule Bårdsson og norsk statsdannelse i første halvdel av 1200-tallet", *Historisk tidsskrift* 76 (1997), pp. 2-19.
Orning, Hans Jacob. *Uforutsigbarhet og nærvær. En analyse av norske kongers maktutøvelse i høymiddelalderen* (Oslo 2004).
Orning, Hans Jacob. "Den materielle basis for den norske kongemaktens maktutøvelse i høymiddelalderen", *Historisk tidsskrift* 84 (2005), pp. 455-69.
Orning, Hans Jacob. "Kongemaktens lokale maktgrunnlag i middelalderen. Svar til Knut Dørum", *Historisk tidsskrift* 85 (2006), pp. 675-84.
Orrman, Eljas. "Church and Society", in Knut Helle (ed.), *The Cambridge History of Scandinavia*, I, *Prehistory to 1520* (Cambridge 2003), pp. 421-62.
Orrman, Eljas. "The Condition of the Rural Population", in Knut Helle (ed.), *The Cambridge History of Scandinaviu*, I, *Prehistory to 1520* (Cambridge 2003), pp. 581-610.
[Otto of Freising] *Ottonis episcopi Frisingiensis Chronica sive Historia de duabus civitatibus*, ed. Adolf Hofmeister, *Monumenta Germaniae historica Scriptores rerum Germanicarum in usum scholarum* vol. 45 (Hannover 1912).
[Otto of Freising] *Ottonis et Rahewini Gesta Frederici I Imperatoris*, ed. G. Waitz and B. von Simson, *MGH Scriptores rerum Germanicarum in usum scholarum* (Hannover 1912).
Paasche, Fredrik. "Norges og Islands litteratur inntil utgangen av middelalderen", *Norsk litteraturhistorie* I (Oslo 1924).
Paasche, Fredrik. *Kristendom og kvad*, in Fredrik Paasche, *Verker i utvalg* I (Oslo 1948 [orig. 1914]), pp. 25-218.
Pálsson, Hermann. "Hakonar Saga – Portrait of a King", *Orkney Miscellany* 5 (1973), pp. 49-56.

Paludan, Helge. "Tiden 1241-1340", in Inge Skovgaard-Petersen, Aksel E. Christensen and Helge Paludan, *Danmarks historie, I, Tiden indtil 1340* (Copenhagen 1977), pp. 401-511.

Pennington, Kenneth. "Law, legislation and government 1150-1300", in J-H. Burns (ed.), *The Cambridge History of Medieval Political Thought* (Cambridge 1988), pp. 424-53.

Perron, Anthony. "Metropolitan Might and Papal Power on the Latin-Christian Frontier: Transforming the Danish Church around the Time of the Fourth Lateran Council", *The Catholic Historical Review* 89 (2003), pp. 182-212.

Pollock, Sheldon. "The Transformation of Culture-Power in Indo-Europe, 1000-1300", in Johann P. Arnason and Björn Wittrock (eds.), *Eurasian Transformations, Tenth to Thirteenth Centuries. Crystallizations, Divergences, Renaissances* (Leiden 2004), pp. 247-78.

Poly, Jean-Pierre and Eric Bounazel. *La mutation féodale – Xe-XII siècles* (Paris 1980).

Pospisil, Leopold. *Anthropology of Law. A Comparative Theory*, 2nd ed. (New Haven 1974).

Post, Gaines. *Studies in Medieval Legal Thought. Public Law and the State, 1100-1322* (Princeton 1964).

Postan, M.M. and Edward Miller. *The Cambridge Economic History*, II, *Trade and Industry in the Middle Ages*, 2nd ed. (Cambridge 1987).

Poulsen, Bjørn. "Kingdoms on the Periphery of Europe: The Case of Medieval and Early Modern Scandinavia", in Richard Bonney (ed.), *Economic Systems and State Finance* (Oxford 1995), pp. 101-22.

Poulsen, Bjørn. "Danske bønders brug af skrift i senmiddelalderen", in Agnes S. Arnorsdóttir, Per Ingesman and Bjørn Poulsen, *Konge, kirke og samfund. De to øvrighedsmagter i dansk senmiddelalder* (Aarhus 2007), pp. 381-414.

Powicke, Maurice. *The Thirteenth Century. 1216-1307, The Oxford History of England* III, ed. George Clark (Oxford 1962).

Prestwich, Michael. *Edward I*, 2nd ed. (New Haven 1997).

Rasmussen, Kirsten J. "Kong Eriks døtre", *Individ, slægt og magt i dansk middelalder, Den jyske historiker* 42 (1987), pp. 47-67.

Regesta Norvegica I-VIII (822-1404), ed. Erik Gunnes et al. (Oslo 1978-2006).

Reinhard, Wolfgang (ed.). *Power Elites and State Building, The Origins of the Modern State in Europe* (Oxford 1996).

Reinhard, Wolfgang. "Introduction: Power Elites, State Servants, Ruling Classes, and the Growth of the State", in Wolfgang Reinhard (ed.), *Power Elites and State Building* (Oxford 1996), pp. 1-18.

Retsø, Dag. *Länsförvaltningen i Sverige 1434-1520* (Stockholm 2008).

Reuter, Timothy. *Germany in the Early Middle Ages c. 800-1056* (London 1991).
Reynolds, Susan. *Kingdoms and Communities in Western Europe* (Oxford 1984).
Reynolds, Susan. *Fiefs and Vassals. The Medieval Evidence Reinterpreted* (Oxford 1994).
Reynolds, Susan. "The Historiography of the Medieval State", in Michael Bentley (ed.), *Companion to Historiography* (London 1997), pp. 117-38.
Reynolds, Susan. "There Were States in Medieval Europe: A Response to Rees Davies", *Journal of Historical Sociology* 16.4 (2003), pp. 550-55.
Rian, Øystein. *Maktens historie i dansketiden, Makt- og demokratiutredningen 1998-2003, Rapportserien* no. 68 (Oslo 2003).
Riisøy, Anne Irene. *Stat og kirke. Rettsutøvelsen i kristenrettssaker mellom Sættargjerden og reformasjonen* (Oslo 2004).
Riisøy, Anne Irene. *Sex, rett og reformasjon* (Oslo 2006).
Riisøy, Anne Irene and Bjørg Dale Spørck. "Dateringen av nyere Borgartings kristenretter", *Collegium Medievale* 12 (1999), pp. 57-74.
Rimbert. *Vita Ansgari*, ed. Werner Trillmilch, *Quellen des 9. und 11. Jahrhunderts zur Geschichte der hamburgischen Kirche und des Reiches, Ausgewählte Quellen zur deutschen Geschichte des Mittelalters* vol. XI, 7th ed. (Darmstadt 2000), pp. 16-133.
Rindal, Magnus. "Liv og død i kyrkjas lover", in M. Rindal (ed.), *Fra hedendom til kristendom* (Oslo 1996), pp. 141-49.
RN = *Regesta Norvegica*.
Roaldset, Hege. *Mariakirken i Oslo. De religiøse funksjonene* (Master's thesis, University of Oslo, 1996).
Robberstad, Knut. "Odelsrett: Norge, Vesterhavsøyane", *Kulturhistorisk leksikon for nordisk middelalder* XII (Oslo 1967), cols. 493-99.
Rosén, Jerker. *Striden mellan Birger Magnusson och hans bröder* (Lund 1939).
Rosén, Jerker. *Svensk historia I. Tiden före 1718*, 2nd ed. (Stockholm 1964).
Rowell, S.C. "The Central European Kingdoms", in David Abulafia (ed.), *The New Cambridge Medieval History* V (Cambridge 1999), pp. 754-78.
Rowell, S.C. "Baltic Europe", in Michael Jones (ed.), *The New Cambridge Medieval History* VI (Cambridge 2000), pp. 705-12.
Sahlins, Marshall. "Poor Man, Rich Man, Big Man, Chief", *Comparative Studies in Society and History* 5 (1963), pp. 285-303.
"Sakralkönigtum", *Reallexikon der Germanischen Altertumskunde*, ed. Rosemarie Müller et al. (Berlin 2004), pp. 179-320.
Salvesen, Helge. "Landskyldutviklingen", in Jørn Sandnes and Helge Salvesen, *Ødegårdstid i Norge* (Oslo 1978), pp. 109-41.

Salvesen, Helge. "The Strength of Tradition: A Historiographical Analysis of Research into Norwegian Agrarian History during the Later Middle Ages", *Scandinavian Journal of History* 7 (1982), pp. 75-113.

Sandaaker, Odd. "Magnus Erlingssons kroning. Ein 'politiserande' sagatradisjon", *Historisk tidsskrift* 77 (1998), pp. 181-96.

Sandnes, Jørn. "Kronologi og årsaker", in Jørn Sandnes and Helge Salvesen, *Ødegårdstid i Norge* (Oslo 1978), pp. 154-70.

Sandnes, Jørn. "Totalhistorie og mentalitetshistorie", *Heimen* 18 (1981), pp. 561-70.

Sandnes, Jørn. Review of Claus Krag, *Ynglingatal og ynglingesaga. En studie i historiske kilder*, *Historisk tidsskrift* 73 (1994), pp. 229-31.

Sandnes, Jørn. Review of Niels Lund, *Lid, leding og landeværn. Hær og samfund i Danmark i ældre middelalder*, *Historisk tidsskift* 76 (1997), pp. 408-12.

Sandnes, Jørn. "Engi maðr skal atfǫr at ǫðrum gera. Noen merknader til motstandsbestemmelsene i Frostatingsloven", *Historisk tidsskrift* 85 (2006), pp. 289-98.

Sandvik, Gudmund. "Ægteskab. Norge", *Kulturhistorisk leksikon for nordisk middelalder* XX (Oslo 1976), cols. 493-95.

Sandvik, Gudmund. "Sættargjerda i Tunsberg og kongens jurisdiksjon", *Samfunn, rett, rettferdighet – festskrift til Torstein Eckhoffs 70-årsdag* (Oslo 1986), pp. 563-85.

Sars, J.E. *Udsigt over den norske Historie* II. 2nd ed. (Christiania 1893).

Sawyer, Birgit. "Samhällsbeskrivningen i Heimskringla", *Historisk tidsskrift* 72 (1993), pp. 223-37.

Sawyer, Birgit. "The 'Civil Wars' revisited", *Historisk tidsskrift* 82 (2003), pp. 43-73.

Sawyer, Birgit and Peter Sawyer. *Medieval Scandinavia: from conversion to Reformation, circa 800-1500* (Minneapolis 1993).

Sawyer, Peter. "Harald Fairhair and the British Isles", in Regis Boyer (ed.), *Les Vikings et leur civilisation. Problèmes actuels* (Paris 1976), pp. 105-9.

Sawyer, Peter. *Kings and Vikings* (London 1982).

Sawyer, Peter. *Da Danmark blev Danmark. Fra ca. år 700 til ca. 1050, Gyldendals og Politikens Danmarkshistorie* III, ed. Olaf Olsen (Copenhagen 1988).

Sawyer, Peter. *När Sverige blev Sverige* (Alingsås 1991).

Sawyer, Peter. "The Viking Expansion", in Knut Helle, *The Cambridge History of Scandinavia*, I, *Prehistory to 1520* (Cambridge 2003), pp. 105-120.

Saxo Grammaticus. *Gesta Danorum*, ed. Karsten Friis-Jensen with Danish translation by Peter Zeeberg, I-II (Copenhagen 2005).

Scheel, Henning. "Falke og høgejagt", *Kulturhistorisk leksikon for nordisk middelalder* IV (Oslo 1959), cols. 154-56.

Scholz, Richard. *Die Publizistik zur Zeit Philipps des Schönen und Bonifax VIII* (Stuttgart 1903).

Schramm, Percy Ernst. "Die Krönung in Deutschland bis zum Beginn des Salischen Hauses (1028)", *Zeitschrift der Savigny-Stiftung für Rechtsgeschichte. Kanonistische Abteilung* 55 (1935), pp. 184-332.

Schramm, Percy Ernst. *Der König von Frankreich* I-II (Darmstadt 1960 [orig. 1939]).

Schramm, Percy Ernst. *Geschichte des englischen Königtums im Lichte der Krönung* (Darmstadt 1970 [orig. 1937]).

Schreiner, Johan. *Hanseatene og Norges nedgang* (Oslo 1935).

Schreiner, Johan. "Norge og unionskongedømmet i det 14. århundre", *Historisk tidsskrift* 30 (1934-36), pp. 374-99.

Schreiner, Johan. "Kongemakt og lendmenn i Norge i det 12. århundre", *Scandia* 9 (1936), pp. 161-203.

Schreiner, Johan. "Konge og kirke i Norge 1247-77", *Historisk tidsskrift* 33 (1943-46), pp. 573-93.

Schreiner, Johan. "Formynderstyret i Norge for Magnus Eriksson", *Historisk tidsskrift* 34 (1946-48), pp. 382-400.

Schreiner, Johan. "Høvdingmøte og riksråd i Norge", *Historisk tidsskrift* 35 (1949-51), pp. 157-72, 405-28, 484-93, 521-59.

Schreiner, Johan. "Hærmakt og riksstyre", *Historisk tidsskrift* 36 (1952-53), pp. 99-139.

Schreiner, Johan. Review of Halvdan Koht, *Kong Sverre*, *Historisk tidsskrift* 36 (1952-53), pp. 439-48.

Schück, Herman. "Tiend. Sverige", *Kulturhistorisk leksikon for nordisk middelalder* XVIII (Oslo 1961), cols. 295-99.

Schück, Herman. *Rikets brev och register. Arkivbildande, kansliväsen och tradition inom den medeltida svenska statsmakten* (Stockholm 1976).

See, Klaus von. "Studien zum Haraldskvæði", *Arkiv för nordisk filologi* 76 (1961), pp. 96-111. Reprinted in Klaus von See, *Edda, Saga, Skaldendichtung. Aufsätze zur skandinavischen Literatur des Mittelalters* (Heidelberg 1981), pp. 295-310.

See, Klaus von. *Altnordische Rechtswörter. Philologische Studien zur Rechtsauffassung und Rechtsgesinnung der Germanen* (Tübingen 1964).

See, Klaus von. *Königtum und Staat im skandinavischen Mittelalter* (Heidelberg 2002 [orig. 1953]).

Segev, Dror. *Medieval Magic and Magicians – in Norway and Elsewhere: Based upon 12th-15th Centuries Manuscripts and Runic Evidence* (Oslo 2001).

Seip, Jens Arup. *Lagmann og lagting i senmiddelalderen og det 16de århundre, Skrifter utgitt av Det norske Videnskaps-Akademi i Oslo* II. Hist-fil. Kl. no. 3 (Oslo 1934).

Seip, Jens Arup. "Ennu en kristenrett fra gammelnorsk tid", *Historisk tidsskrift* 31 (1937-40), pp. 573-627.

Seip, Jens Arup. "Problemer og metode i norsk Middelalderforskning", *Historisk tidsskrift* 32 (1940-42), pp. 49-131.

Seip, Jens Arup. *Sættargjerden i Tunsberg og kirkens jurisdiksjon* (Oslo 1942).

Seip, Jens Arup. Review of Arne Odd Johnsen, *Fra ættesamfunn til statssamfunn, Historisk tidsskrift* 35 (1949-51), pp. 197-202.

Seip, Jens Arup. "Svar til Arne Odd Johnsen", *Historisk tidsskrift* 35 (1949-51), pp. 512-14.

Sigurd Ranessøns Proces, ed. Gustav Storm (Kristiania 1877).

Sigurðsson, Jon Vidar. *Chieftains and Power in the Icelandic Commonwealth* (Odense 1999).

Sjöholm, Elsa. "Replikk til Ole Fenger", *Historisk tidsskrift* [Danish] 81 (1981-82), pp. 219-22.

Sjöholm, Elsa. *Sveriges medeltidslagar* (Stockholm 1988).

Skansjö, Sten and Hans Sundström (eds.). *Gåvobrevet 1085* (Lund 1988).

Skinner, Quentin. *The Foundations of Modern Political Thought* I-II (Cambridge 1977).

Skjalded. = *Den norsk-islandske Skjaldedigtning*, ed. Finnur Jónsson A1-B2 (Copenhagen 1908-14).

Sk. = *Skálholtsbók yngsta*, eds. A. Kjær and L. Holm-Olsen (Oslo 1947).

Skórzewska, Joanna Agnieszka. *Constructing a* Cultus. The *Life and Veneration of Guðmundr Arason (1161-1237)* (Oslo 2007).

Skovgaard-Petersen, Inge. "The Making of the Danish Kingdom", in Knut Helle (ed.), *The Cambridge History of Scandinavia*, I. *Prehistory to 1520* (Cambridge 2003), pp. 168-83.

Skovgaard-Petersen, Inge. "The Danish Kingdom: Consolidation and Disintegration", in Knut Helle (ed.), *The Cambridge History of Scandinavia*, I, *Prehistory to 1520* (Cambridge 2003), pp. 353-68.

Skre, Dagfinn. "Kirken før sognet. Den tidligste kirkeordningen i Norge", in Hans-Emil Lidén (ed.), *Møtet mellom hedendom og kristendom i Norge* (Oslo 1995), pp. 170-233.

Skre, Dagfinn. "Missionary Activity in Early Medieval Norway. Strategy, Organization and the Course of Events", *Scandinavian Journal of History* 23 (1998), pp. 1-19.

Skre, Dagfinn. *Herredømmet. Bosetning og besittelse på Romerike 200-1350 e. Kr., Acta Humaniora* 32 (Oslo 1998).

Skre, Dagfinn. "The Dating of *Ynglingatal*", in Dagfinn Skre (ed.), *Kaupang in Skiringssal. Kaupang Excavation Project. Publication Series* I (Aarhus 2007), pp. 407-29.

Skre, Dagfinn. "The Emergence of a Central Place: Skiringssal in the 8th Century", in Dagfinn Skre (ed.), *Kaupang in Skiringssal. Kaupang Excavation Project. Publication Series* I (Aarhus 2007), pp. 431-43.

Skre, Dagfinn. "Towns and Markets, Kings and Central Places in South-western Scandinavia c. AD 800-950", in Dagfinn Skre (ed.), *Kaupang in Skiringssal. Kaupang Excavation Project. Publication Series* I (Aarhus 2007), pp. 445-69.

Skyum-Nielsen, Niels. *Kirkekampen i Danmark 1241-1290* (Copenhagen 1963).

Skånland, Vegard. "Provinsialkonsil", *Kulturhistorisk leksikon for nordisk middelalder* XIII (Oslo 1968), cols. 527-29.

Skånland, Vegard. *Det eldste norske provinsialstatutt* (Oslo 1969).

Smalley, Beryl. *Historians in the Middle Ages* (London 1974).

Smedberg, Gunnar. *Nordens första kyrkor. En kyrkorättslig studie* (Lund 1973).

Smith, A.D. *Theories of Nationalism* (London 1971).

Smith, A.D. *National Identity* (London 1991).

Snorri Sturluson, see *Heimskringla*.

Spurkland, Terje. "Viking Age Literacy in Runes – a Contradiction in Terms?", in Pernille Hermann (ed.), *Literacy in Medieval and Early Modern Scandinavian Culture* (Odense 2005), pp. 136-50.

Ss. = *Sverris saga*.

"Staat und Souveränität", in Otto Brunner, Werner Conze and Reinhart Koselleck (eds.), *Geschichtliche Grundbegriffe. Historisches Lexicon zur politisch-sozialen Sprache in Deutschland* VI (Stuttgart 1997), pp. 1-154.

Steinnes, Asgaut. *Gamal skatteskipnad* I (Oslo 1930).

Steinsland, Gro. *Det hellige bryllup og norrøn kongeideologi: en analyse av hierogami-myten i Skírnismál, Ynglingatal, Háleygjatal og Hyndluljóð* (Oslo 1991).

Steinsland. Gro. *Den hellige kongen. Om religion og herskermakt fra vikingtid til middelalderen* (Oslo 2001).

Steinsland, Gro. *Norrøn religion: myter, riter, samfunn* (Oslo 2005).

Stein-Wilkeshuis, Martina. "Legal Prescriptions on Manslaughter and Injury in a Viking Age Treaty Between Constantinople and Northern Merchants, *Scandinavian Journal of History* 19 (1994), pp. 1-16.

Stjórn. Gammelnorsk bibelhistorie, ed. Richard Unger (Christiania 1862).

Storm, Gustav. "Om Lendermandsklassens Tallrighed i det 12. og 13. Århundede", *Historisk Tidsskrift*, 2. Rk. IV (1884), pp. 129-88.

Storm, Gustav. "Audun Hestakorn og St. Margrete på Nordnæs", *Historisk Tidsskrift*, 2. Rk. IV (1884), pp. 209-52.

Storm, Gustav. "Forord", in *Isl. Ann.*, pp. xv-xviii, xxv-xxxii.

Storm, Gustav. "Efterskrift", *Sigurd Ranessøns Proces*, pp. 65-68.
Storm, Gustav. "De kongelige Byanlæg i Norge i Middelalderen", *Historisk Tidsskrift*, 3. Rk. V (1899), pp. 433-38.
Strayer, Joseph. *The Medieval Origins of the Modern State* (Princeton 1970).
Strayer, Joseph. *The Reign of Philip the Fair* (Princeton 1980).
Strengleikar: An Old Norse translation of Twenty-One Old French lais, edited from the manuscript Uppsala De la Gardie 4-7, AM 666 b, 4:to by Robert Cook and Mattias Tveitane (Oslo 1979).
Strzelzcyk, Jerzy. "Bohemia and Poland: Two Examples of Successful Western Slavonic State-formation", in Timothy Reuter (ed.), *The New Cambridge Medieval History*, III, *c. 900-1024* (Cambridge 1999), pp. 514-35.
Strzelzcyk, Jerzy. "The Church and Christianity about the Year 1000 (the missionary aspect)", in P. Urbanzyk (ed.), *Europe around the Year 1000* (Warsaw 2001), pp. 41-67.
Sturlunga saga, ed. Kr. Kålund, I-II (Copenhagen 1906-11).
Stylegar, Frans Arne. "Hovedgårder, stormenn og landnåm", in Marit Synnøve Vea and Helge Rolf Naley (eds.), *Fiender og forbundsfeller. Regional kontakt gjennom historien, Karmøyseminaret 1999* (Karmøy 2001), pp. 37-64.
Stylegar, Frans-Arne and Oliver Grimm. "Boathouses in Northern Europe and the North Atlantic", *The International Journal of Nautical Archaeology* 34 (2005), pp. 253-68.
Ståhle, Carl Ivar. "Medeltidens profana litteratur", in *Ny illustrerad svensk litteraturhistoria* (Stockholm 1955), pp. 35-121.
Sunde, Jørn Øyrehagen. *Speculum legale – rettspegelen. Ein introduksjon til den norske rettskulturen si historie i eit europeisk perspektiv* (Bergen 2005).
Sundqvist, Olof. *Freyr's offspring. Rulers and religion in ancient Svea society* (Uppsala 2002).
Sundqvist, Olof. "Aspects of Rulership Ideology in Early Scandinavia – with Particular References to the Skaldic Poem Ynglingatal", in Franz-Reiner Erkens (ed.), *Das Frühmittelalterliche Königtum, Ergänzungsbände zum Reallexikon der Germanischen Altertumskunde* 49 (Berlin 2003), pp. 87-124.
Sundqvist, Olof. "Sakralkönigtum. Skandinavische Quellen", *Reallexikon der Germanischen Altertumskunde*, ed. Rosemarie Müller et al. (Berlin 2004), pp. 279-93.
Sundqvist, Olof. "Uppsala och Asgård. Makt, offer och kosmos i fortida Skandinavien", *Ordning mot kaos. Studier i förkristen kosmologi* (Lund 2004), pp. 145-79.
Sverris saga, ed. Gustav Indrebø (Kristiania 1920). – This is the text used.
Sverris saga, ed. Þorleifur Hauksson (Reykjavík 2007).
Swanson, Robert N. "Concordat", *Dictionary of the Middle Ages* III (New York 1983), pp. 525-27.

Taranger, Absalon. *Den angelsaksiske kirkes indflydelse paa den norske* (Kristiania 1890).

Taranger, Absalon. *Tidsrummet 1319-1442, Norges historie fremstillet for Det norske folk* III.1 (Kristiania 1915).

Taranger, Absalon. "De norske folkelovbøker (før 1263)", *Tidsskrift for Retsvidenskap* (1926), pp. 183-211 and (1928), pp. 1-68.

Taranger, Absalon. "Om kongevalg i Norge i sagatiden", *Historisk tidsskrift* 5 rk. IX =30 (1934-36), pp. 110-66, 273-308.

Tellenbach, Gerd. *Libertas: Kirche und Weltordnung im Zeitalter des Investiturstreites. Forschungen zur Kirchen- und Geistesgeschichte* VII (Stuttgart 1936).

Theodoricus Monachus. *Historia de antiquitate regum Norwagiensium, Monumenta Historica Norvegiae*, ed. Gustav Storm (Christiania 1880).

Thomas Aquinas. *De regimine principum ad regem Cypri, Opuscula philosophica*, ed. M. Spiazzi (Rome 1954), pp. 257-358.

Tilly, Charles. "Reflections on the History of European State Making", in Charles Tilly (ed.), *The Formation of National States in Western Europe* (Princeton 1975), pp. 3-83.

Tilly, Charles. *Coercion, Capital, and European States, AD 990-1990* (Cambridge, Mass. 1990).

Tjersland, Leif. "Studier i saga-ætter", *Historisk tidsskrift* 31 (1937-40), pp. 103-38.

Tobiassen, Torfinn. "Tronfølgelov og privilegiebrev. En studie i kongedømmets ideologi under Magnus Erlingsson", *Historisk tidsskrift* 43 (1964), pp. 181-273.

Torsteinsson, Björn. *Island* (Copenhagen 1985).

Torstendal, Rolf. *Källkritik och vetenskapssyn i svensk historisk forskning 1820-1920, Studia historica Upsaliensia* 15 (Uppsala 1964).

Třeštik, Dušan. "Von Svatopluk zu Boleslaw Chrobry. Die Entstehung Mitteleuropas aus der Kraft des Tatsächlichen und aus einer Idee", in P. Urbanzyk (ed.), *The Neighbours of Poland in the 10th Century* (Warsaw 2000), pp. 111-45.

Tryti, Anna Elisa. "Fra åsatro til reformasjon", in Knut Helle et al. (eds.), *Vestlandets historie* III (Bergen 2006), pp. 54-103.

Tøtlandsmo, Ole Steinar. *Før Norge ble Norge. Politiske forhold på Sørvestlandet i vikingtid* (Sola 1996).

Ugulen, Jo Rune. *"alle the knaber ther inde och sædescwenne..." Ei undersøking i den sosiale samansetninga av den jordeigande eliten på Vestlandet i mellomalderen* (Doctoral thesis, Bergen 2007).

Ullmann, Walter. *Principles of Government and Politics in the Middle Ages* (London 1966).

Ulriksen, Eli. "Tønsberg – bebyggelse og beboere fra 1000-tall til 1200-tall", in Hans Andersson, Gitte Hansen and Ingvild Øye (eds.), *De første 200 årene – nytt blikk på 27 skandinaviske byer* (Bergen 2008), pp. 93-108.

Ulsig, Erik. "Landboer og bryder, skat og landgilde. De danske fæstebønder og deres afgifter i det 12. og 13. århundrede", *Middelalder, metode og medier. Festskrift til Niels Skyum-Nielsen på 60-årsdagen den 17. oktober 1981* (Copenhagen 1981), pp. 137-65.

Vadum, Kristoffer. *Dom og straff i Kongespeilet. En analyse av verkets rettslære i forhold til en norsk og europeisk bakgrunn, Centre for Viking and Medieval Studies. Occasional Papers* vol. 7 (Oslo 2004).

Vahtola, Jouko. "Population and Settlement", in Knut Helle (ed.), *The Cambridge History of Scandinavia*, I, *Prehistory to 1520* (Cambridge 2003), pp. 559-80.

Varenius, Bjørn. "Maritime Warfare as an organizing Principle in Scandinavian Society", in Anne Nørgård Jørgensen et al. (eds.), *Maritime Warfare in Northern Europe. Technology, Organization, Logistics and Administration 500 BC-1500 AD, Papers from an International Research Seminar at the Danish National Museum, Copenhagen, 3-5 May 2000* (Copenhagen 2002), pp. 249-56.

Vauchez, André. *La Sainteté en Occident aux derniers siècles du Moyen Age d'après le proces de canonisation et les documents hagiographiques* (Rome 1980).

Verbruggen, J.F. *The art of warfare in Western Europe during the Middle Ages* (Amsterdam 1977).

Vestergaard, Torben. "The System of Kinship in Early Norwegian Law," *Medieval Scandinavia* 12 (1988), pp. 160-193.

Vogt, Helle. *Slægtens funktion i nordisk højmiddelalderret – kanonisk retsideologi og fredsskabende lovgivning* (Ph.d. thesis, Copenhagen 2005).

Vågslid, Eivind. *Norske skrivarar i mellomalderen* (Oslo 1989).

Wamers, Egon. "The 9th Century Danish-Norwegian Conflict", in Anne Nørgård Jørgensen et al. (eds.), *Maritime Warfare in Northern Europe. Technology, Organization, Logistics and Administration 500 BC-1500 AD, Papers from an International Research Seminar at the Danish National Museum, Copenhagen, 3-5 May 2000* (Copenhagen 2002), pp. 237-48.

Weber, Max. *Wirtschaft und Gesellschaft. Grundriss der Verstehenden Soziologie* (Cologne 1964).

Weibull, Lauritz. *Kritiska undersökningar i Nordens historia omkring år 1000* (Lund 1911).

Weidling, Tor. "Kven åtte jorda? En vurdering av resultater og metode i studiet over jordeiendomsforhold i middelalder og tidlig nytid", *Historisk tidsskrift* 82 (2003), pp. 349-79.

Wellendorf, Jonas. *Kristelig visionslitteratur i norrøn tradition* (Doctoral thesis, University of Bergen, 2007).

Wickham, Chris. "Rural Society in Carolingian Europe", in Rosamond McKitterick (ed.), *The New Cambridge Medieval History* II (Cambridge 1995), pp. 510-37.
Williams, Gareth. "Hákon *Aðalsteinsfóstri:* Aspects of Anglo-Saxon Kingship in Tenth-Century Norway", in Thomas R. Liszka and Lorna E.M. Walker (eds.), *The North Sea World in the Middle Ages. Studies in the Cultural History of North-Western Europe* (Dublin 2001), pp. 108-26.
Wittfogel, Karl A. *Oriental despotism: a comparative study of total power* (New Haven, Conn. 1957).
Wolter, Udo. "The *officium* in Medieval Ecclesiastical Law as a Prototype of Modern Administration", in Antonio Padoa Schioppa (ed.), *Legislation and Justice: The Origins of the Modern State in Europe* (Oxford 1997), pp. 17-36.
Wærdahl, Randi Bjørshol. *"Norges konges rike og hans skattland" Kongemakt og statsutvikling i den norrøne verden i middelalderen* (Doctoral thesis, NTNU, Trondheim, 2006).
Wåge, Hilde. *Drapssakene i norsk seinmiddelalder: prosedyre, straff, frekvens, motiv og miljø* (Master's thesis, University of Bergen, 1991).
Þorlaksson, Helgi. Review of Patricia Bulhosa, *Icelanders and the Kings of Norway*, *Historisk tidsskrift* 86 (2007), pp. 142-47.

Index

A
abbesses 230
abbots 118, 156, 230, 264, 273, 335
Abel, king of Denmark 90
Adam and Eve 149, 163
Adam of Bremen 29, 147, 230
ad limina visits 323
adultery 307, 315
Aegidius Romanus 319
Agder 22, 200
Agnes, daughter of King Håkon V 255, 287, 341
Agnes, queen of Denmark 92
agrarian crisis 115, 372, 384
Akershus 104, 105, 174, 250-51, 253-54
Albertus Magnus 318
Albrecht of Mecklenburg, king of Sweden 250
Alcuin 149, 153
Alexander II, king of Scotland 86
Alexander III, king of Scotland 86-87, 92-93
Alexander III, pope 47, 182, 202, 249, 308-9
alibi 213
Alsnö stadga 71
Althoff, Gerd 339, 345
Alv Erlingsson, earl 92, 132, 354, 357-58
ancien régime 289-90
Anderson, Benedict 177
Andres Plytt, baron 303
Anglo-Saxon England 22, 34, 74, 165, 180, 190, 195, 209, 262-63
Annales School 14-15
Apostles' Church In Bergen 214, 250, 263
archaeology 22, 37, 73, 79, 113, 124, 146
archbishop, office of 61, 88, 118, 132, 159, 174, 202, 231, 239-40, 252, 254, 269, 277, 284, 292, 294, 296-304, 312, 316, 320-21, 323, 337-38, 344, 367, 385
archbishopric 230, 291
archive 214-15, 245, 247, 250, 252, 254, 256, 267
aristocratic status, definition of 119-20, 255-56, 326-29, 340-41
Aristotle 318-19, 330, 377
Ari the Wise 25
Arne, monk of Nidarholm 307
Arne Aslaksson, chancellor, bishop of Stavanger 295
Arne Gjavaldsson, scribe, *sysselmann* 258

Arne Sigurdsson, bishop of Bergen 214, 251, 259, 272-75, 295, 314
Arne Torlaksson, bishop of Skálholt 275, 296, 319
Arup, Erik 73-74
Asbjørn Fitjaskalle 31
Asbjørn Selsbane 30, 147, 233
Askatin, chancellor, bishop 295
assemblies (local or regional, cf. Thing) 40, 59, 119, 150, 152, 166, 169, 179, 188, 225, 270, 303, 335-36, 338-40, 346
Athalstan, English king 25-26
Atle 9, 183-84, 195
Audfinn, bishop of Bergen 251, 273-75, 314
Audun Hugleiksson, baron 94, 96, 340-41
Audun Raude, canon, bishop 306-8
Aurdal farm 219
Avaldsnes 219, 233

B
Balder, god 142-43
Baltic Sea 15, 38-39, 85
Bannockburn, Battle of 97
banns 307, 309-10
barons 87, 296, 303-8, 310-12, 314-15, 319, 333, 355
Bédier, Joseph 18
beer 274, 352
Benedictow, Ole Jørgen 327, 331-32, 348, 384
Bergen 27, 42-44, 80-81, 104, 116, 118, 122, 124-25, 173-74, 198, 214, 219, 230-31, 237, 246, 250-54, 258-59, 261, 263-64, 268-74, 278, 283, 295, 297-98, 309, 312-14, 329, 336-37, 343, 349, 351-52, 359-60
betrothals 307, 310, 314
Bible 151, 158, 201, 203, 279
Birchlegs 45-46, 49-50, 52-54, 57-58, 63-64, 80, 82, 236, 246, 282, 288, 295, 337, 373, 382-83
Birger Magnusson, king of Sweden 97-99, 321, 353, 382
Birger, Swedish earl 39, 65, 89-90
Birgittine movement 154
bishoprics 117, 230, 368
bishops 88, 117-18, 120, 122-23, 125, 132, 152, 155, 166-68, 170, 174, 196, 201-2, 224, 230-31, 238-41, 244, 251-52, 261-64, 274-77, 282, 284, 292-96, 298-300, 303-7, 311-12, 314, 320-21, 323-24, 335, 340, 360, 367, 373, 380, 385

Bjarkøy 119-20, 123, 212, 340
Bjarkøy Law 123, 212
Bjarne Audunsson, baron 328, 341
Bjarne Erlingsson, baron 303, 305-7, 340-41, 357
Bjarne Lodinsson, baron 340-41
Bjørgo, Narve 41, 94, 245, 247, 295
Blindheim 42, 59
Black Death, the 67, 121, 313, 383-84
Blom, Grethe Authén 357-58, 361-62, 372
blót 146
Bohemia 16, 23, 24, 154, 177
Bohuslän (Norway, now Sweden) 42, 268
Bolin, Sture 34
Bologna 242, 328, 341
Boniface VIII, pope 318
Book of Homilies 149, 207
books 149-51, 201, 244, 273
Borgarting 179-80, 200, 297
Borgarting, Law of 297
Brandenburg 16
Brendalsmo, Jan 232, 296
British Isles 35, 42, 69, 85-87, 100, 356
Brunner, Otto 13
Bull, Edvard 152-53, 276
Burckhard of Worms 194, 196, 202
bureaucracy 12, 14, 155-56, 160, 177, 229, 232-36, 238, 240, 242, 282, 288-91, 370, 376, 379-80, 382, 387
butter 118, 126, 131, 274, 351-52
Byrkjo farm 216
Byzantium 32, 34, 126, 183
Bård Petersson, scribe, *lagmann* 217, 257-58

C

cadaster 116, 128, 198, 252
Calfskin of Bergen 252
Canones Nidrosienses 202, 241, 294
canon law 179, 182, 190, 197, 202, 207, 211, 214-15, 224-26, 241-42, 273, 275, 296, 299, 302, 308, 314, 316, 323
canons 118, 156, 214, 224, 230-31, 240, 241, 264, 278, 296, 367
Capetians 367
Carlsson, Gottfried 361
Castile 89, 109, 223
castles 57, 66, 69, 71-72, 76, 80-81, 100-1, 103-4, 109, 110, 130-33, 173, 237, 243, 265, 267, 377, 379, 382, 385-86
cathedral chapter 73, 231, 239, 273, 275, 295, 296, 297, 308, 322, 367
cathedraticum 273

chancellor 210, 237, 256, 257-61, 264, 295, 312, 315, 341, 357-59, 364
chancery 161, 237, 245, 246, 248-50, 252, 256-63, 267, 323, 326, 334, 364
chapels 296
chapels, royal 115, 118, 257, 259, 263-64, 274, 296-97, 359
charters 19, 119, 153, 178, 196, 217, 247, 266, 267, 316, 339, 349, 372
chiefdoms 22-23, 28-29, 34-36, 85, 88, 114, 116, 149, 275-76, 279, 291, 336, 348
China 16, 22
Christian laws 180, 195-96, 202, 297, 299, 302, 305, 308, 310, 312
Christianisation, *see* conversion
Christmas celebrations 82, 268, 271, 328, 364
Christoffer I, king of Denmark 90
Christoffer II, king of Denmark 100, 359, 368
Church Province 294
Clanchy, Michael 249, 257, 264
clergy 110, 150-56, 167, 170, 173, 180, 202, 213, 230, 238, 240-42, 244, 258-59, 264, 273, 295-96, 300, 302-5, 310, 315, 317, 322-24, 326, 336, 340, 347, 350, 360
cloth 87, 351-52
Clunies Ross, Margaret 139
Cnut, *see also* Knud
Cnut the Great, king of Denmark, England and Norway 25, 29, 31, 32, 34, 70, 86,
Cnut Svensen, St, king of Denmark 73
coats-of-arms 217
Codex, see *Corpus iuris civilis*
coinage 126-28, 303, 305, 311-12
colloquium publicum 339
colloquium secretum 339
compurgation 190-91, 212-14, 298
concordat 197-98, 205, 298, 301-2, 304-5, 312-13, 315-16
concubinage 43, 144, 194, 307, 310
confiscation 52, 121, 209, 258
constitution, theories of 14, 293-94, 329, 330, 334, 344-45, 360, 370
conversion 16, 23-24, 28-29, 36-37, 39, 115, 137, 146, 149, 155, 177-78, 190, 229, 232, 244, 292, 338, 377, 387
Copenhagen 252, 254-55, 267
coronation 24, 59-62, 158, 160, 163, 167-70, 173, 175, 247, 294, 301, 303, 331
coronation oath 167
Corpus iuris civilis 205, 235, 328
corruption 240, 287, 290, 372
council, ecclesiastical 47, 156, 212, 275

council of the realm 250, 267, 329, 359-60, 362-64, 366-68, 370, 385
council, provincial 275, 324, 336, 359
council, royal 204, 220, 274, 328, 330, 339-41, 343, 347, 357, 360, 364, 370
counter-witnesses 189
court of law 119, 179, 185, 195-97, 199-200, 217-18, 221, 223-26, 232, 255, 265, 298-99, 306, 308, 310, 314-15, 320, 363, 366, 373, 380
court of law, ecclesiastical 196-97, 199, 201-2, 214-15, 298, 310, 314-15
court, royal 34, 53, 114, 120, 158, 162, 164-65, 168-70, 172-73, 177, 237, 246, 278-79, 290, 293, 319, 327-28, 355, 363, 370
courtly culture 170-72, 178, 275, 328
Courtrai, Battle of 106
creation 138-40, 142-43, 145, 148-49
crime 102, 171, 192, 194, 196-97, 206-11, 213, 221-22, 225, 234, 288, 331
crown 60, 104, 115, 299, 317, 326
crown, honour of the 317, 319
cult, Christian 36, 155-56, 165, 229, 232, 324
cult, pagan 30, 37, 137, 147, 153, 155

D

Dagfinn Bonde 246
Dannevirke 24
David 62, 158, 160, 163
Davies, Rees 12
decretalists 179
decretists 179
deditio 283
Denmark 16, 18, 22-27, 29, 31-33, 36-39, 42, 47-50, 54, 64-67, 70-73, 78-79, 85-86, 89-93, 96-101, 107, 109-11, 114, 124, 127, 129-30, 132-33, 147, 154, 175, 177, 208, 212, 223, 225, 243, 249-51, 253, 258, 266, 269, 271 72, 274, 287, 290, 301, 321, 323, 328, 330, 349, 353-54, 356-57, 359, 362, 364, 367-68, 372, 375, 377, 382-85, 387
diets 268, 335; *see also* assemblies
dioceses 59, 111, 118, 125, 198, 230, 231, 274, 276, 313, 323, 324
diplomacy 24, 47, 91, 109, 110, 134, 171, 266, 269, 274, 279, 355, 379
dom (dómr) 207
Dominicans 274, 296
dominium regale 330, 334, 342, 367, 370
donations 115-17, 120, 153, 155, 245, 254
Douglas, Mary 143
drottsete 237, 357, 360

dynasty 22, 26-29, 38, 45-46, 60, 65, 90-92, 99, 101, 108-9, 134, 141, 147, 159, 165-67, 169, 178, 185, 225, 236, 272, 277-78, 287, 300, 325, 354-56, 358-61, 368-70, 376, 383, 385-86
Dørum, Knut 112, 116-17, 128, 130, 216-17, 290

E

Eastern Norway 30, 32, 41, 46, 54, 58-59, 78, 81-82, 84, 124, 131, 179, 198, 200, 232, 246, 271, 282, 286, 337, 344, 365, 382
ecclesiae baptismales 232
ecclesiastical organisation 36, 52, 198, 229, 232, 263, 291-92, 296-97, 321-22, 324, 387
economic policy 350, 353
education 147, 151, 171, 178, 198, 240-42, 273, 278, 341-42
Edward I, king of England 92-93, 95-96, 110, 334
Edward II, king of England 93, 280
Edward Confessor, king of England 86, 244
Eidsivating 179, 180, 185, 200
Eidsivating, Law of 297
Eidsvoll 82, 179
Eirik, defendant 314
Eirik Haraldsson Bloodaxe, king of Norway 26
Eirik Håkonsson, earl of Lade 29, 175
Eirik Ivarsson, archbishop 49, 61-62, 199, 245, 323
Eirik Magnusson, king of Norway 90, 92-96, 98, 100, 108-9, 204, 248, 259, 269, 277-78, 296, 303, 312, 317, 339-41, 347, 349-50, 353-54, 356-57, 361, 382
Eirik Oddsson 44, 245, 275
Eirik Sigurdsson, earl (Sverre's alleged brother) 167
Eirikssons, kings 26-28, 31, 35, 148, 280
elections, episcopal 178, 273, 275, 294-96, 321, 323, 329, 344, 367-69, 385
elections, royal 40-41, 58-60, 63, 166-69, 177, 246-47, 283, 299, 301, 335, 339, 361, 363, 368, 373, 380
elite force 71, 73, 80, 101-2, 104, 108, 132-33, 331
eloquence 78, 144, 150-51, 162, 280-81, 283, 338
Emmanuelsson, Anders 115, 117
England 13-14, 18, 22, 24-27, 29, 31-32, 50, 65, 70, 73-74, 79, 86-87, 92-96, 100, 125, 128, 130-31, 190, 195, 209, 213, 223, 225-27, 229, 232, 242, 249, 253, 262-64, 292, 312, 333-34, 342, 376
Erik Abelsen, Danish duke 90
Erik dynasty (Sweden) 50, 65
Erik Emune, king of Denmark 48-49
Erik Eriksson, king of Sweden 246
Erik Klipping, king of Denmark 90, 92, 97, 320, 355
Erik Magnusson, Swedish duke 97-99, 104-6, 107-10, 175-76, 251, 252, 270, 328, 340, 349, 354, 358, 382

Erik Menved, king of Denmark 71, 97-100, 107-10, 130, 251, 270, 349, 353, 359, 382
Erik of Pomerania, king of Denmark, Norway and Sweden 250, 267
Erik Plovpenning, king of Denmark 90, 361
Erikskrönikan 105-6, 328
Erling Ormsson Skakke, earl 45-51, 54-56, 59-60, 117, 163-64, 175, 269, 294-95
Erling Magnusson Stonewall, pretender 83
Erling Skjalgsson, magnate 28-31, 80, 147, 233-34
Erling Vidkunsson, *drottsete* 108, 120, 258, 329, 354, 357, 359-60, 362
Esger Juul, archbishop of Lund 320
estates, doctrine of 159, 339
Ethelred, English king 27, 29
Eufemia of Arnstein, queen of Norway 97
Exodus 158, 278-79
exogamy 212

F
Fall of Man 158, 207
Färlev, Battle of 42
Faroe Islands 275
fehirde, see treasurer
feudalism 14, 35, 69, 125, 132, 229, 234-36, 238, 243, 320, 333, 347
fief 49, 94, 109, 116, 284, 349
fine 92, 118, 192-94, 196, 199, 208-10, 262, 308, 322, 351
Finn Arnesson, magnate 32, 80
Finn tax 89, 127, 185, 187
fishing rights 315
Fitjar 27, 74
Fjolne, mythic king 147
fleet 33, 57-58, 66, 76, 78, 81, 83-84, 86, 94, 102, 104-5, 107, 130, 134, 176, 379
Follo 288
forbidden degrees 196
foreign policy 66-67, 69, 85, 89, 91, 96, 97, 100, 104, 108-10, 126, 130, 134, 177, 253, 266, 269-70, 340, 353-56, 359, 362, 364, 376, 379
formulas 183, 246, 260
Four sisters 158, 207, 209
France 22, 79, 93-96, 100, 127, 130, 171-72, 209, 223, 229, 249, 273, 279, 318-19, 342, 367, 368, 374, 377
Franciscans 254-55, 274, 278
Frederick I Barbarossa, German emperor 47, 234
Frederick II, German emperor 65, 87, 170, 223, 247
Frederik IV, king of Denmark and Norway 290
Fried, Johannes 12

friendship 26, 31-32, 47-49, 87, 93, 160, 162, 176, 186-87, 207, 212, 221, 223, 233, 234-35, 241, 279, 284, 288-90, 292, 295, 345-46, 355
Frostating 179, 185, 200, 297
Frostating, Law of 72, 75-76, 114, 180, 190-91, 196, 212-13, 373
Frøy, god 141, 147
Frøya, goddess 141, 143
fylke 232, 336
fylke churches 294
fyrd 74

G
Gascony 94-95, 110
Gefolgschaft 235
Geirstein, magnate 43
Gellner, Ernest 172, 174, 177
Gelting, Michael 182
genealogy 147
generosity 31, 35, 42, 52, 82, 145, 279, 307, 358, 381
Genesis 138, 148, 158, 278, 279
Germanic law 181
Germanistic school, of legal history 147, 181
Germans 24, 92, 254, 351-53, 357
German towns 92-93, 101, 105, 109-10, 253, 269, 350-54
Germany 13-14, 16, 23-24, 29, 35, 38-39, 65, 69, 79, 85, 100, 109, 164, 277, 338, 342, 368, 384, 387
giants 139-44
gifts 31, 35, 153, 156, 162, 185, 247, 254, 381
Gimsøy, nunnery 117
Giske 119-20
Gissur Torvaldsson, Icelandic magnate 279
Gjerde 59
Goetz, Hans-Werner 12
Gothic style 264
Gottskalk Annals 106
Grágás (Icelandic law) 188
Gran 198
Gratian 61, 179, 196, 202, 294, 316
Greenland 87, 100, 134
Gregorius Dagsson, magnate 43-45, 47, 80, 117
Gregory VII, pope 245
Grenland 30
Gudmund Arason, bishop of Holar 276
"guests" 103, 325
Gulating 76, 179, 185, 258
Gulating, Law of 72, 75-76, 180-84, 189, 191-92, 194, 212, 220, 230, 297
Gulatingslag 28, 76, 77, 200, 246

Gulen 179, 183, 184
Gullbekk, Svein 126, 127
Gunnes, Erik 59-61, 198, 241, 298, 314, 316
Gustav Vasa, king of Sweden 250
Guttorm, archbishop of Nidaros 162
Guttorm, master of the royal chapels, bishop of Stavanger 295
Göta Älv 39, 90, 104
Götaland (Sweden) 39
Grágás (Norwegian law) 180

H

Hafrsfjord 25, 124
hagiography 154, 162, 172, 275
Hagland, Jan Ragnar 249, 263
Haithabu 24, 34
Hákonar saga 63, 109, 162, 164, 168-69, 171, 176, 188, 198, 200, 234, 247-48, 278, 281-82, 288-89, 291, 295, 304, 316, 328, 336, 339, 346, 355, 369
Halland, Denmark (now Sweden) 89, 91, 98-99, 269, 356
Halsnøy, Augustinian house 117-18, 217, 315
Hamar 125, 180, 198, 200, 230, 285-86, 295, 385
handganga, ceremony of 325, 329, 331
Hanseatic League 351
Hansen, Gitte 124
Hansen, Lars Ivar 182
Harald Bluetooth, king of Denmark 24, 26, 74
Harald Eiriksson Greycloak 26
Harald Halvdansson Finehair, king of Norway 25-28, 36-37, 38, 72, 85, 116, 147, 165, 186, 234, 287, 332
Harald Maddadson, earl of the Orkneys 86, 283
Harald Magnusson Gille, king of Norway 42-46, 48-49, 163, 343-45
Harald Sigurdsson Hardrada, king of Norway 25, 35, 51-52, 86, 116, 124, 126, 165
Haraldskvæði 25
Hávamál 145, 149, 153
Havtore Jonsson, magnate 255, 287, 341
Havtoresons 363; *see* Jon and Sigurd
Hebrides 79, 86-87, 91, 95, 100, 134
Heimskringla 36, 43-44, 53, 56, 124, 146, 162, 164, 171, 175-76, 185, 233, 244, 247, 291, 345
Helge Ivarsson, scribe 257
Helgeland 88
Helle, Knut 15, 112, 340, 343, 365, 371
Henry II, king of England 45, 65, 249
Henry III, king of England 87, 279, 333
Henry I, king of Germany 35
hereditary succession 163, 167-69, 368-69, 376, 383

heretics 167
Hindsgavl, Peace of 79, 93, 96-98, 270, 354
hird 101, 103, 108, 170, 172, 235-36, 239, 259, 261, 287, 325-27, 329, 330-34, 348-49
Hird Law 101, 103, 108, 170, 172, 235-36, 239, 287, 325-26, 329-34, 348-49
hirðstefna 329
hirdstjorar 325
holidays 156, 196, 232
Holmsen, Andreas 41, 51, 55, 63, 111-14, 121, 131, 243, 332, 334, 361, 364-66, 381-82
homicide 208, 209, 222, 224, 262, 320
honour 91, 145, 147, 160, 173, 234, 346, 348, 370, 373, 374
Horda-Kåre, magnate 26-28
Hordaland 22, 74-75
Hovedøy, Cisterciencian monastery 118, 315
Hrafn Oddsson, royal representative in Iceland 275
Hrut 188
Hungary 16, 23-24, 35, 51, 127, 131, 374, 387
hunting 87, 102, 277-79, 370
Huseby 22
hypergamy 141, 144; *see also* marriage
Hälsingborg, Treaty of 99
hægendiskirkjur 232
Høne, god 140
Håkon, bishop of Bergen 275
Håkon, bishop of Oslo 209
Håkon Eiriksson, earl of Lade 29, 35
Håkon Haraldsson the Good, king of Norway 25-28, 35, 72, 74-75, 148, 179, 280
Håkon Håkonsson, king of Norway 46, 59, 62, 64, 78-79, 81-84, 86-91, 102-5, 108-9, 134, 164, 168-74, 176, 188-89, 199, 203, 208, 209, 225, 234, 238, 245-48, 251, 260-61, 263, 268-70, 277-89, 294-95, 297, 300, 305, 328, 336-39, 344, 348, 350-51, 355-56, 364, 368, 374, 380, 382-83, 390
Håkon Håkonsson the Younger, king of Norway 83, 168, 278
Håkon Ivarsson, magnate 32
Håkon Ivarsson, *notarius* 257, 259
Håkon V Magnusson, duke, king of Norway 67, 88, 92-93, 96-104, 107-10, 115, 169, 174-77, 206, 210, 215, 218-21, 237-38, 248-57, 262-65, 269-72, 277-78, 287, 296, 303, 305-6, 312, 317, 326-28, 332-34, 339-41, 347-50, 352-55, 357-59, 362, 365-66, 371, 374, 382-83
Håkon VI Magnusson, king of Norway 108, 210, 251, 258, 272, 350, 360-63
Håkon Sigurdsson, the Broadshouldered, king of Norway 47, 54

INDEX

Håkon Sigurdsson, earl of Lade 26-29, 35, 148
Håkon Sverresson, king of Norway 251, 260
Håkonshallen 174
Håleygjatal 147

I

Iceland 85, 87-88, 100, 134, 145, 151, 154, 183, 187-88, 202, 204, 213, 220, 245, 254, 262, 276, 279, 296, 305, 308, 319, 324, 332, 355, 374
Icelandic annals 253
Icelandic law 183, 196
Imsen, Steinar 86, 126, 201, 215-16, 237, 361, 372, 374, 384
incomes 70, 120, 126-31, 133, 135, 150, 185-86, 208, 221, 223, 235, 238-39, 252, 273, 294, 304, 305, 348, 355, 357, 366, 372, 381
Inge Bårdsson, king of Norway 46, 59, 117, 176, 295, 380
Inge Haraldsson, king of Norway 42-49, 60, 244
Ingebjørg Håkonsdatter, duchess 91, 97-100, 105, 109, 251, 258, 329, 354, 357-59, 362
Ingeborg, queen of Denmark 97
Ingeborg, queen of Norway 90, 109, 354-55
Ingrid Ragnvaldsdatter, queen of Norway 49
Innocent IV, pope 170
intent 98, 193, 211, 218, 321, 357
Investiture Contest 65, 157
Islamic world 16
Italy 18, 23-24, 179, 249, 277
itinerary, royal 28, 125, 258, 269, 271-72
Ivar Audunsson, scribe 257
Ivar Olavsson, chancellor and provost 264, 315, 357-58
Iversen, Tore 182

J

jacquerie 374
Jakobsson, Sverrir 176
Jelling stone 24
Jens Grand, archbishop of Lund 320
Jerusalem 150
John Balliol, king of Scotland 93, 96
John, king of England 50, 128
Jon Havtoreson, *sysselmann* 366
Jon Ivarsson Raud, magnate 341
Joseph 13, 18, 234, 332
judge 158, 160, 185, 187, 196-99, 201, 203, 207, 210-11, 213-14, 216-19, 221, 224, 226, 238, 241, 247, 255, 272-73, 277, 281, 288-89, 306-7, 316, 326
judgements 207, 216-17, 224, 255, 261, 345

jurisdiction 12, 73, 119, 126, 158, 197, 198, 201, 216, 217, 223-25, 227, 231, 243, 292, 297-99, 301, 304-11, 313, 315-16, 320-21, 353, 363
jurisdiction, ecclesiastical 126, 158, 195, 197-98, 223-24, 227, 231, 298-99, 301, 306, 308-11, 313, 315-16
Jämtland 200, 253, 258, 270, 290
Jølster 132
Jørund, archbishop of Nidaros 272, 275, 277, 304, 308, 322

K

Kalmar 67, 92, 250, 269, 386
Kalmar, union of 67, 250, 258, 272
Kalv Arnesson, magnate 32
Kantorowicz, Ernst 242
Kern, Fritz 181, 184, 203
King's Mirror, The 114, 150, 153-54, 158-62, 164, 168-71, 176, 178, 203, 205, 206-11, 214, 216, 220-22, 224, 226, 234-35, 241-42, 261, 277-78, 280, 283, 287, 289-91, 311, 316, 318-19, 325-27, 330, 332, 334, 344-46, 369, 373, 383
kinship 47-50, 138, 148, 212
Kjetil, bishop of Stavanger 217
klerkr 256, 259
Knud, *see also* Cnut
Knud Lavard, Danish duke 48-49
Knud Porse, Danish duke 251, 357, 359
Knut Håkonsson, Norwegian pretender and earl 50, 82, 284
Koht, Halvdan 18-19, 85, 156, 298
Kola Peninsula 34, 85
Konghelle 124, 198, 268
konungstekja 169, 170
kotkarlar 114, 171
Krag, Claus 19, 147, 192, 233
Kristin, King Magnus Erlingsson's mother 45
Kvåle farm 255-56

L

Lade 25-26, 29, 146, 147
lagmenn 185-86, 188, 199-200, 218-19, 253, 271, 305, 335-36, 350, 366
lagrette 200-1, 220
lagsogn 200, 238
lagting 180, 185, 200-1, 338, 350
landownership 111-12, 115, 118-19, 121, 129, 131, 304, 379
land rent 111-12, 114-15, 121, 123, 125-26, 128-30, 372, 375, 381-82, 384
Landro, Torgeir 195

lands nauðsynjar (= *necessitas regni*) 319
landsvist 209-10, 258, 262
Lateran Council (1215) 156, 212
Latin 11, 148, 150-52, 161, 172, 199, 210, 240, 244-45, 248, 253, 256-57, 259-63, 269, 278, 299, 314, 316, 318-19, 326
laupar, *see* pails
Laurentius Kalvsson, bishop of Holar 275
Laurentius saga 259, 275, 278
law code 182-84, 205, 226
Laws of Succession 41, 63, 119, 158, 166-67, 169, 189, 208, 215, 220, 287, 299, 335, 368-69, 383
law, oral 73, 181-83, 195
law, written 179-81, 183, 189, 201, 205, 219
lawspeaker 188
legislation 158, 181, 186, 189, 195, 199, 201-4, 206, 208, 225-26, 232, 253-54, 276, 282, 294, 297, 303, 306, 308-9, 311, 335, 347, 387
legislator 181-82, 189, 202-6, 377
leidang 57, 72-81, 83, 85-86, 90-91, 94, 101, 103-5, 107-8, 120, 130, 132-33, 195, 203, 239, 243, 254, 266, 270, 304, 307, 310, 319, 335, 371, 373-74, 377
leding 72-74, 79, 128, 320
ledung 72
legends, *see* hagiography
lendmenn 53, 80, 82, 102, 185, 187, 191, 233, 326-28, 333-34, 341, 346-49
Lent 156, 196, 268, 278
letters 161, 206, 214-16, 226, 237, 244-63, 267, 269-273, 278, 290, 323, 334, 343, 349, 358
letters, categories of 262
Lewes, Battle of 87
Liber Augustalis 219, 223
libertas ecclesiae 42, 60, 294
library 273
literacy 180, 242, 244, 249, 254, 271, 292
Lithuania 387
liturgy 149, 151, 170, 180, 202, 243, 323, 355
Lodin Lepp, magnate 151, 204, 206, 334, 347, 374
Lodur, god 140
Lofoten 22, 88, 147
Loke 142-43
lordship 11, 14, 22, 28-29, 34-36, 91, 158, 222, 366
Louis IX, king of France and saint 14, 224, 277, 333
Louis XIV, king of France 172, 290
luck 29, 83, 146, 148, 163, 382
Lübeck 247, 261
Lund, Niels 9, 24, 27, 73-74, 79
Lunden, Kåre 112, 121, 239, 293, 365-66, 371-72, 380, 385

Löfqvist, Karl-Erik 327
Lönnroth, Erik 131, 163, 330, 361
Låka, Battle of 82

M

magister capellarum regis 263
Magnus Birgersson, Swedish prince 98-99
Magnus Birgersson Ladulås, king of Sweden 92, 99, 321
Magnus Eriksson, king of Norway and Sweden 67, 97, 100, 107-8, 132, 250-51, 257-58, 271, 306, 312, 321, 329, 350, 356, 360-64, 366, 370, 383
Magnus Erlingsson, king of Norway 41, 45-46, 49-50, 53-57, 60-63, 76-79, 120, 158-61, 163-64, 167, 169, 170, 180, 184, 189, 199, 230, 251, 260-62, 277, 282, 287, 294-95, 299-301, 368-69
Magnus Haraldsson, king of Norway 287, 301
Magnus Håkonsson the Law-Mender, king of Norway 79, 87, 90-92, 104, 109, 115, 169, 173-74, 204, 213-14, 218, 242, 248, 261, 270, 277, 278, 285, 297, 299-303, 305-6, 308-9, 311-13, 319, 326, 334, 349, 353-56, 365
Magnus Nielsen, Danish prince 48-49
Magnus Olavsson Barelegs, king of Norway 42, 86, 185, 280, 287
Magnus Olavsson the Good, king of Norway 32, 180, 244, 280
Magnus Sigurdsson the Blind, king of Norway 42-44, 48-49, 280, 343-45
Magnúss saga 248, 269
markebol (= land worth one mark) 341, 348
marks 15, 70, 92, 94-96, 100, 103, 126-28, 131, 248, 262, 291
Marxism 19, 41, 56, 152, 229, 243, 293, 325
Mass 214, 240, 244
mendicant orders 274
merkesmann (standard-bearer) 237, 348
Merovingian period 21
Midgard 141, 143, 150
military technology 16, 66, 69-71, 101, 105, 107, 109-10, 131, 134, 137, 266, 379, 386
mint privilege, the archbishop's 303, 305, 311-12
mirrors of princes 280, 345
Mogens, bishop of Hamar 385
monarchy, *see* office, royal
monastery 42-43, 115-17, 253, 254, 261, 297
Moore, R. I. 14, 342
Munch, Peter Andreas 122, 303, 361
mythology 137-40, 142-43, 147, 170, 178

N

Narve, bishop of Bergen 295, 397
nationalism 174-77
National Law 77, 94, 103, 111, 114, 159, 176, 181, 190, 198-201, 203-6, 208, 210, 211-13, 215, 217-20, 226, 241, 251, 253, 272, 287, 300-3, 308-9, 311, 316-17, 330, 334, 350, 373-74
necessitas regni, see *lands nauðsynjar*
Nedkvitne, Arnved 162, 244, 266
New Law (of Håkon Håkonsson) 199, 203, 208-9, 225, 288
Nicholas Brekespeare, cardinal 47
Nikolas Arnesson, bishop of Oslo 61, 198, 282, 344
Njåstad, Magne 15, 154, 289-90
Nordeide, Sæbjørg 37
Northern Norway 22, 25, 29-31, 33-34, 88-89, 134, 147, 200, 230, 233, 269, 303, 308, 352
North Sea 25, 27, 66, 85, 134
notarius 256, 257, 259
Novgorod 89
nunnery 117
Nyköping 97
Næshagen, Ferdinand 153

O

oath 42, 107-8, 132, 167, 170, 189-90, 213, 217, 235-36, 283, 287, 289, 331, 358
obedience 149, 158, 160, 167, 170, 234-35, 266, 283, 317, 319, 326, 331, 334, 350, 383
odel 26, 189, 212
Odin, god 139-43, 147, 150
office 53, 57, 154, 156, 199, 235, 238, 240-41, 264, 282, 326, 334, 348, 358, 371
office, ecclesiastical 159, 167-68, 232, 238-41, 276, 282, 367
office, royal 158-60, 164-70, 172, 238, 277, 280-81, 366-67
Olav 217-18
Olav Engelbrektsson, archbishop of Nidaros 385
Olav Haraldsson, king of Norway and saint 29-32, 34-35, 37, 51, 80, 85-86, 89, 116, 124, 154, 162, 163, 165, 166, 180, 184, 188, 195, 199, 203, 208, 233, 280, 336, 346
Olav Haraldsson Kyrre, king of Norway 124-25, 180, 301
Olav Sigurdsson, king of Norway 185
Olav Sigvatsson, *notarius* 259
Olav Tordsson Kvitaskald 285
Olav Tryggvason, king of Norway 27-31, 34, 37-38, 85, 123, 174-75, 233-34, 280

Olav Ugjæva, pretender 54, 62
Old Testament 138, 170, 194, 203, 207, 316-17
Opsahl, Erik 103, 258, 271, 329
orality 73, 137, 148-49, 152, 180-84, 188-90, 192, 195, 216, 229, 244, 265-67, 358
ordeal 42, 189, 190, 212-13, 336
ordinance, royal 79, 103, 107-8, 206, 210, 251, 260, 262, 270, 303-5, 307, 310, 317, 319, 327, 332-34, 347, 349-50, 352-53, 357-59
original sin 149
Orkneys 53, 85-87, 91, 93, 283
Orléans 272, 328
Orm Øysteinsson, *drottsete* 271, 360
Orning, Hans Jacob 127-28, 233, 285, 288, 291
Orosius 34
Oslo 61, 78, 82-84, 104-6, 116-18, 124-25, 174, 180, 198, 200, 216, 230, 237, 240, 250-51, 253-55, 258, 261, 264, 268-71, 275, 282, 288, 297, 315, 357, 359, 363, 374
Otto I, German emperor 24, 35
Otto II, German emperor 24
Otto of Freising 131, 205
Otto Morena 47
Ottonians 16, 24, 69
outlaws, Danish 92-93, 98, 108-9
outlawry 166, 194, 208-10, 213, 225, 350
ownership, the king's, of the country 114, 119-21, 160, 234-35, 294, 333

P

paganism 27, 29-30, 36-37, 116, 137-38, 146-49, 153, 155, 157, 159, 161, 166, 170, 178, 387
pails 118, 120, 126, 130-31
parishes 232, 273, 307
patriae 200
patrimony 332, 349
patronage 30, 44, 125, 160, 163-64, 234, 236, 238, 282, 288-90, 292, 294, 316, 321, 342, 376, 385
peasants 41, 55, 70, 73, 75-77, 80, 102-3, 106-7, 110-14, 116-17, 119-21, 128-32, 152, 176-77, 196-97, 204, 216-17, 243, 293, 339, 352, 371-72, 374-76, 381, 385
per notorium 197
Perth, Treaty of 79, 100
Peter Byrdesvein, magnate 295
Peter of Husastad, archbishop of Nidaros 295
Peter, son of Duke Skule 285
petty kings 24, 30, 317
Pharaoh 163, 234, 332
Philip IV, king of France 94, 127, 249, 318-19
Philippus, Crozier king 246, 260

plena potestas 334
poetry 18, 35, 74, 79, 138, 143, 145, 147-48, 152, 172, 178, 182, 280
pope 47, 202, 230-31, 235, 241, 245, 247, 264, 272, 274, 276, 285, 290, 295, 298, 301, 303-5, 316, 322, 323, 359, 367
population, size of 18, 21-23, 40-41, 89, 112-14, 121-23, 125-29, 131, 149, 200, 230, 235, 249, 352, 381, 386
provincial laws, *see* regional laws
Pål, bishop of Hamar 285-86
Pål Bårdsson, chancellor, later archbishop of Nidaros 295
Pål Styrkårsson, scribe 257

Q
quarter 215, 239, 330

R
Ragnvald Hallkjellsson, *sysselmann* 288, 373
rebellion 27, 30, 50, 54, 58, 60, 71, 73, 81-84, 86, 95, 98, 108, 149, 167, 176, 268, 283, 284, 286, 354, 360, 368-69, 374, 382
Reformation 18, 115, 123, 125-26, 154, 210, 243, 253, 264, 324, 385
regency 67, 79, 90, 92-93, 100, 108, 120, 204-5, 210, 251, 257, 271, 296, 303-7, 311-12, 317-23, 329-30, 339-40, 347-49, 353-54, 356-58, 360, 362, 365-66
Regesta Norvegica 248-49, 269
regimen politicum 330, 334
regional laws 74, 103, 111, 113-14, 144, 179, 181-83, 186, 189-90, 195-97, 201-202, 206, 212-15, 218, 225-26, 232, 298, 305-6, 308, 312, 350
Registrum, of the bishops of Bergen 214, 251, 252 54, 273-74, 297, 313-15
regium ius 302
retainers 58, 72, 102-3, 107-8, 119, 132, 231, 234, 283, 330-33, 346-47, 363, 371, 373, 376; *see also* hird; hirdmenn
rettarbot, *see* ordinance
revenues, *see* incomes
rex iustus 63, 162-64, 167-69, 261, 280-81, 288-89
rhetoric 106, 161, 178, 235, 311, 317, 345
Rigstula 114, 144-45, 147, 150, 159
Riisøy, Anne Irene 197, 210, 219, 306-7, 310, 313-15, 359
Rikitza, daughter of Earl Birger of Sweden 89
rituals 13, 17, 137, 155, 170, 172-73
Robert Bruce, Scottish magnate 93
Robert Bruce, Scottish magnate and later king 96
romances 170, 172

Roman law 171, 179, 201-2, 204, 213, 218, 319, 377, 380
Rome 157, 285
Romerike 22, 75, 101-2, 112, 116-17, 126, 161, 216-17, 288, 290
Roncaglia 234
Rosén, Jerker 71, 98
Rosenkrantz Tower 174
runes 150, 183, 243-44
Rus 183, 396, 398

S
sacred kingship 147-48, 165-66
saints 146-47, 153-55, 165-66
Samis 88-89, 144, 185
Sarpsborg 124, 180
Sars, Ernst 56
sáttmál 196, 201
Saxony 24
Scania 38-39, 73, 79, 98, 100, 271, 356, 362, 364
Schramm, Percy Ernst 13
Scotland 86-87, 91-97, 100-2, 105, 107, 109, 125, 176, 251, 269
scribes 237, 244, 256-59, 262, 264, 326, 364
script, *see* writing
seals 172, 326
See, Klaus von 181
Seip, Jens Arup 11, 17, 198, 204, 298, 304, 313-15, 365, 371
Selja 125
Sel-Tore, *årmann* 233
Shetland 87, 91
ships, types of 38, 50, 57-58, 64, 69, 74-76, 78, 82, 84, 86, 88-89, 92, 94, 105, 303, 354, 357
Sicily 223
Siete Partidas 219, 223
Sigurd, Abbot of Tautra 295
Sigurd Agnhatt, magnate 62
Sigurd, earl of Lade 26
Sigurd Eindridesson, archbishop of Nidaros 295, 305-6
Sigurd Haraldsson, king of Norway 42-48, 53-54
Sigurd Havtoreson, *sysselmann* 366
Sigurd Magnusson, king of Norway 42, 45-46, 48, 124, 185-87, 366
Sigurd Ranesson, magnate 185-87, 190, 195, 219, 220, 336
Sigurd Ribbung, pretender 50, 82-83, 247, 268, 284, 288, 337
Sigurd of Røyr, magnate 45
Sigurd Sigurdsson, magnate 343, 345

Sigurd Slembe, pretender 42-43
Simon de Montfort 87, 279-80
Simon Skalp, magnate 44
Sjöholm, Elsa 182
skaldic poetry 35, 74, 79, 138, 145, 147-48, 280
Skálholt 106, 270, 275
Skálholt Annals 270
skipafe 304
skipreide 75, 103
Skiringssal 22, 122-23
Skre, Dagfinn 116-17
Skule Bårdsson, earl, duke and pretender 46, 59, 64, 82-84, 86, 88, 103, 117, 162, 172, 176, 246, 247, 268, 269, 282-89, 295, 328, 336-38, 344, 348, 373, 380, 382
skutilsveinar 325; *see also* barons
slaves 70, 113, 144-45, 230
Slavs 35
slottslen 237
Snare Aslaksson, baron 341
Snorri Sturluson 25, 28, 30-31, 50, 56, 80, 137, 139-40, 143, 146-47, 162, 233-34, 244
social structure 21, 51-52, 69, 111, 119, 294, 377
sorcery 143-44, 315
Speech against the Bishops, A 61-62, 114, 159-61, 164, 178, 263, 316, 319
speeches 55, 61, 163, 246, 278, 336, 351
Spørck, Bjørg Dale 306, 313
squire 326-27
stallare 237
Standard-bearer, see *merkesmann*
status rei publicae 11
Statutes of Melfi, see *Liber Augustalis* 223
Stavanger 25, 27, 75, 115-16, 125, 200, 217, 219, 230, 252, 254, 260, 262, 269, 275, 277, 295, 297, 301, 315, 367
Steinnes, Asgaut 70, 126-27, 130
Stiklestad, Battle of 29
St Mary's in Oslo, royal chapel 250, 253-54, 258, 264, 315, 357, 359
St Michael in Tønsberg, royal chapel 255
stockfish 127
Stockholm 125, 386
Storm, Gustav 119, 122, 186
Strayer, Joseph 13
Strengleikar 171
Strindsjøen, Battle of 104, 239
Sturlunga saga 288, 355
Ståreim 59
succession to the throne 40-41, 57, 61-63, 65-66, 83, 90, 93, 96, 100, 119, 158, 166, 167-69, 188-89, 199, 215, 287, 299, 335-37, 362, 368-69, 376, 382, 383, 385

Sunniva, St 125
Sunnmøre 27, 42
Sven Estridsen, king of Denmark 32
Sven Forkbeard, king of Denmark 24, 27, 29
Sweden 18, 23, 29, 34, 36-39, 50, 58, 65-67, 70-72, 85, 89, 92, 97-101, 107-9, 129-34, 147, 154, 175, 177, 194, 210, 212, 225, 243-44, 246, 249-51, 253, 258, 266-67, 269, 270-72, 287, 304, 321, 323, 328, 330, 339, 356, 360-64, 367-68, 370, 372, 375, 377, 381-82, 384-87, 390
Swedish dukes, *see* Erik Magnusson; Valdemar Magnusson
sysselmenn 53, 63, 101-3, 108, 130-32, 201, 209, 210-11, 214, 221, 223-24, 229, 238, 240, 258-59, 261-62, 271, 277, 287, 288-89, 292, 317, 325-26, 328, 331, 333, 341, 346-50, 353, 355, 373-74
sættargjerden, *see* concordat
sæmd kórónanar, *see* crown, honour of the
Sørum 120, 341

T

Taranger, Absalon 166, 179, 195, 202
Telemark 30, 47
tenants 22, 111, 113, 116-17, 119-20, 304, 350
testimony 153, 213-14, 216-17, 219, 303, 306-8
theology 138, 154, 273, 316, 323
Thing (cf. assembly) 169, 181, 184, 185-88, 191, 196-97, 199-200, 204-5, 219, 225, 298-99, 315, 338-39
Thomas Aquinas 318
Tilly, Charles 13, 69
tithes 118, 155, 232, 274, 298, 305, 315, 360, 382
titles 119, 204, 217, 237, 259, 326-28, 348, 259
Tor, god 141-43
Torberg Arnesson, magnate 32
Tord Kakale, Icelandic magnate 279
Tore, archbishop of Nidaros 295
Tore Hund, magnate 31, 80, 147
Torgeir Tovesson, scribe 256-58
Torgils Knutsson, Swedish regent 321
Torgils Skardi, Icelandic magnate 288
Torstein Kugad 283
towns 57, 80, 92-93, 101, 105-6, 109-11, 116, 121-23, 125-26, 130, 135, 219, 223, 251, 253, 257, 268-71, 327, 350-54
trade 23, 34, 70, 88, 92-93, 122-26, 135, 150, 298, 350-53
treason 176
treasurer 60, 237, 258, 295, 348, 360
Trondenes 308
Tryggve Olavsson, petty king 27, 180, 264, 315, 357-58, 389

INDEX

Trøndelag 22, 25-31, 41, 58-59, 61, 76-78, 81-82, 84, 103, 116-17, 123, 175, 200, 230, 232, 246, 247, 254, 256, 269-70, 286, 290, 294, 296, 337, 343-45, 374, 382
Two swords, doctrine of 316
Tønsberg 64, 104, 124, 174-75, 198, 200, 237, 255, 258, 268-70, 297-98, 363

U

ufyrirsyniu 210
unintentional harm 192, 214
union of Kalmar 67, 250, 258, 267, 272
unions 11, 67, 88, 97, 98, 108-9, 134, 177, 210, 249-51, 267, 271-72, 329, 356, 360-63, 367, 383, 385, 386
universities 179, 219, 240-41, 318-19
utfareleidang 79, 304
Utgard 141

V

vaðaverk, see unintentional harm
vadmål 87
Valdemar, duke of Southern Jutland 79
Valdemar I, king of Denmark 47, 49, 65
Valdemar IV, king of Denmark 250, 271-72, 364
Valdemar II, the Victorous, king of Denmark 89, 128, 268, 382
Valdemar Birgersson, king of Sweden 90, 92
Valdemar Magnusson, Swedish duke 97-99, 105, 107-10, 251, 256, 349, 354, 382
Vaner, gods 140-41
Vardøhus 104
Vauchez, André 154
veizla 40
verba de futuro 310
verba de presenti 310, 314
vernacular 152, 154, 178, 262-63, 273, 292
Victor IV, anti-pope 47
Viken 27-28, 39, 41, 45, 47, 49, 64, 75, 82, 175, 200, 268
Viking Age 21, 35, 37, 51, 69-70, 72, 111, 113-14, 120-21, 123, 134-35, 165, 173, 177, 229, 244, 278, 379, 386
Vikings 22-24, 33-37, 40, 48, 51, 69-70, 72, 79, 85-86, 91, 113, 114
Vogt, Helle 182, 212
Vogt, Niels 290
Vågan 200, 303, 305, 307
Vǫluspá 138-40, 148

W

Wales 225
Weber, Max 156, 238, 290-91, 375
Weibull, Curt 19
Weibull, Lauritz 18-19
Wessex 34
Western Christendom 15-16, 23, 35, 39-40, 134, 137, 144, 153, 178, 276, 292, 322-23, 379, 386-87
Western Norway 22, 25-30, 33, 41, 45, 47, 57-59, 75, 78, 103, 124-25, 132, 179, 232-33, 246, 290, 337
Westminster 174, 258
William of Moerbeke 318
Winchester, Treaty of 92
wine 274, 351-52
witchcraft 189-90
witnesses 185-86, 189, 196-97, 201, 212-14, 216-17, 219-20, 305-9, 313, 372
Witzlaw, prince of Rügen 97
writing 149-51, 158, 173, 180-84, 193, 201, 209, 215-16, 226, 240, 243-48, 250, 254, 257, 260-63, 265-68, 270, 272, 280, 282, 292, 293, 339, 361, 364, 365

Y

Yme, giant 139, 142
Ynglingatal 19, 22, 147, 165

Æ

æser, male gods 140-41
ættleiding 218-19, 255

Ø

Øresund 29, 38
Øreting 40, 83, 166
Østfold 290
Øystein Aslaksson, bishop of Oslo 116, 198
Øystein Erlendsson, archbishop of Nidaros 60-61, 180, 202, 245, 295, 323
Øystein Haraldsson, king of Norway 43-47, 54, 280
Øystein Magnusson, king of Norway 54, 185-87, 280, 366

Å

Åke, chancellor and provost 264, 341
årmann 30, 192, 197-98, 233
Åsgard 141
Åskjell, bishop of Stavanger 295
åsynjer, female gods 140-41

Þ

Þrymskviða 141